Programming Logic and Design

with elements of Linux Shell Script Progr

Joyce Farrell / Todd Meadors

CENGAGE
Learning™

Australia • Brazil • Japan • Korea • Mexico • Singapore • Spain • United Kingdom • United States

CENGAGE
Learning™

**Programming Logic and Design
with elements of Linux Shell Script
Programming**

Joyce Farrell / Todd Meadors

Executive Editors:
 Michele Baird

 Maureen Staudt

 Michael Stranz

Project Development Manager:
 Linda deStefano

Senior Marketing Coordinators:
 Sara Mercurio

 Lindsay Shapiro

Senior Production / Manufacturing Manager:
 Donna M. Brown

PreMedia Services Supervisor:
 Rebecca A. Walker

Rights & Permissions Specialist:
 Kalina Hintz

Cover Image:
 Getty Images*

For product information and technology assistance, contact us at
Cengage Learning Customer & Sales Support, 1-800-354-9706

For permission to use material from this text or product,
submit all requests online at **cengage.com/permissions**
Further permissions questions can be emailed to
permissionrequest@cengage.com

ISBN-13: 978-1-4188-4850-7

ISBN-10: 1-4188-4850-6

Cengage Learning
5191 Natorp Boulevard
Mason, Ohio 45040
USA

Cengage Learning is a leading provider of customized learning solutions with
office locations around the globe, including Singapore, the United Kingdom,
Australia, Mexico, Brazil, and Japan. Locate your local office at:
international.cengage.com/region

Cengage Learning products are represented in Canada by
Nelson Education, Ltd.

For your lifelong learning solutions, visit **custom.cengage.com**

Visit our corporate website at **cengage.com**

Printed in the United States of America

BRIEF CONTENTS

PROGRAMMING
LOGIC AND DESIGN
COMPREHENSIVE

THIRD EDITION

Joyce Farrell
William Rainey Harper College

1

AN OVERVIEW OF COMPUTERS AND LOGIC

After studying Chapter 1, you should be able to:

- ☐ Understand computer components and operations
- ☐ Describe the steps involved in the programming process
- ☐ Describe the data hierarchy
- ☐ Understand how to use flowchart symbols and pseudocode statements
- ☐ Use and name variables
- ☐ Use a sentinel, or dummy value, to end a program
- ☐ Use a connector symbol
- ☐ Assign values to variables
- ☐ Recognize the proper format of assignment statements
- ☐ Describe data types
- ☐ Understand the evolution of programming techniques

1

UNDERSTANDING COMPUTER COMPONENTS AND OPERATIONS

The two major components of any computer system are its hardware and its software. **Hardware** is the equipment, or the devices, associated with a computer. For a computer to be useful, however, it needs more than equipment; a computer needs to be given instructions. The instructions that tell the computer what to do are called **software**, or programs, and are written by programmers. This book focuses on the process of writing these instructions.

TIP □ □ □ □ | Software can be classified as application software or system software. Application software comprises all the programs you apply to a task—word-processing programs, spreadsheets, payroll and inventory programs, and even games. System software comprises the programs that you use to manage your computer—operating systems, such as Windows or Unix. This book focuses on the logic used to write application software programs, although many of the concepts apply to both types of software.

Together, computer hardware and software accomplish four major operations:

1. Input
2. Processing
3. Output
4. Storage

Hardware devices that perform **input** include keyboards and mice. Through these devices, **data**, or facts, enter the computer system. **Processing** data items may involve organizing them, checking them for accuracy, or performing mathematical operations on them. The piece of hardware that performs these sorts of tasks is the **central processing unit**, or **CPU**. After data items have been processed, the resulting information is sent to a printer, monitor, or some other **output** device so people can view, interpret, and use the results. Often, you also want to store the output information on storage hardware, such as magnetic disks, tapes, or compact discs. Computer software consists of all the instructions that control how and when the data are input, how they are processed, and the form in which they are output or stored.

Computer hardware by itself is useless without a programmer's instructions or software, just as your stereo equipment doesn't do much until you provide music on a CD or tape. You can buy prewritten software that is stored on a disk, or you can write your own software instructions. You can enter instructions into a computer system through any of the hardware devices you use for data; most often, you type your instructions using a keyboard and store them on a device such as a disk or CD.

You write computer instructions in a computer **programming language**, such as Visual Basic, Pascal, COBOL, RPG, C#, C++, Java, or Fortran. Just as some people speak English and others speak Japanese, programmers also write programs in different languages. Some programmers work exclusively in one language, whereas others know several and use the one that seems most appropriate for the task at hand.

No matter which programming language a computer programmer uses, the language has rules governing its word usage and punctuation. These rules are called the language's **syntax**. If you ask, "How the get to store do I?" in English, most people can figure out what you probably mean, even though you have not used proper English syntax. However, computers are not nearly as smart as most people; with a computer, you might as well have asked, "Xpu mxv ot dodnm cadf B?" Unless the syntax is perfect, the computer cannot interpret the programming language instruction at all.

Every computer operates on circuitry that consists of millions of on-off switches. Each programming language uses a piece of software to translate the specific programming language into the computer's on-off circuitry language, or **machine language**. The language translation software is called a **compiler** or **interpreter**, and it tells you if you have used a programming language incorrectly. Therefore, syntax errors are relatively easy to locate and correct—the compiler or interpreter you use highlights every syntax error. If you write a computer program using a language such as C++, but spell one of its words incorrectly or reverse the proper order of two words, the translator lets you know it found a mistake by displaying an error message as soon as you try to run the program.

TIP ◻ ◻ ◻ ◻ | Although there are differences in how compilers and interpreters work, their basic function is the same—to translate your programming statements into code the computer can use. When you use a compiler, an entire program is translated before it can execute; when you use an interpreter, each instruction is translated just prior to execution. You do not choose which type of translation to use—it depends on the programming language.

For a program to work properly, you must give the instructions to the computer in a specific sequence, you must not leave any instructions out, and you must not add extraneous instructions. By doing this, you are developing the **logic** of the computer program. Suppose you instruct someone to make a cake as follows:

```
Stir
Add two eggs
Add a gallon of gasoline
Bake at 350 degrees for 45 minutes
Add three cups of flour
```

Even though you have used the English language syntax correctly, the instructions are out of sequence, some instructions are missing, and some instructions belong to procedures other than baking a cake. If you follow these instructions, you are not going to end up with an edible cake, and you may end up with a disaster. Logical errors are much more difficult to locate than syntax errors; it is easier for you to determine whether "eggs" is spelled incorrectly in a recipe than it is for you to tell if there are too many eggs or if they are added too soon.

Just as baking directions can be given correctly in French, German, or Spanish, the same logic of a program can be expressed in any number of programming languages. This book is almost exclusively concerned with the logic development process. Because this book is not concerned with any specific language, the programming examples could have been written in Japanese, C++, or Java. The logic is the same in any language. For convenience, the book uses English!

Once instructions have been input to the computer and translated into machine language, a program can be **run**, or **executed**. You can write a program that takes a number (an input step), doubles it (processing), and tells you the answer (output) in a programming language such as Java or C++, but if you were to write it using English-like statements, it would look like this:

```
Get inputNumber.
Compute calculatedAnswer as inputNumber times 2.
Print calculatedAnswer.
```

TIP ▫ ▫ ▫ ▫ You will learn about the odd elimination of the space between words like "input" and "Number" and "calculated" and "Answer" in the next few pages.

The instruction to `Get inputNumber` is an example of an input operation. When the computer interprets this instruction, it knows to look to an input device to obtain a number. Computers often have several input devices, perhaps a keyboard, a mouse, a CD drive, and two or more disk drives. When you learn a specific programming language, you learn how to tell the computer which of those input devices to access for input. Logically, however, it doesn't really matter which hardware device is used, as long as the computer knows to look for a number. The logic of the input operation— that the computer must obtain a number for input, and that the computer must obtain it before multiplying it by two— remains the same regardless of any specific input hardware device. The same is true in your daily life—if you follow the instruction "Get eggs from store," it does not really matter if you are following a handwritten instruction from a list or a voice mail instruction left on your cell phone—the process of getting the eggs, and the result of doing so, are the same.

TIP ▫ ▫ ▫ ▫ Many computer professionals categorize disk drives and CD drives as storage devices rather than input devices. Such devices actually can be used for input, storage, and output.

Processing is the step that occurs when the mathematics is performed to double the `inputNumber`; the statement `Compute calculatedAnswer as inputNumber times 2` represents processing. Mathematical operations are not the only kind of processing, but they are very typical. After you write a program, the program can be used on computers of different brand names, sizes, and speeds. Whether you use an IBM, Macintosh, Linux, or Unix operating system, and whether you use a personal computer that sits on your desk or a mainframe that costs hundreds of thousands of dollars and resides in a special building in a university, multiplying by 2 is the same process. The hardware is not important; the processing will be the same.

In the number-doubling program, the `Print calculatedAnswer` statement represents output. Within a particular program, this statement could cause the output to appear on the monitor (which might be a flat panel screen or a cathode-ray tube), or the output could go to a printer (which could be laser or inkjet), or the output could be written to a disk or CD. The logic of the process called "Print" is the same no matter what hardware device you use.

Besides input, processing, and output, the fourth operation in any computer system is storage. Storage comes in two broad categories. All computers have **internal storage**, probably referred to more often as **memory**, **main memory**, or **primary memory**. This storage is inside the machine and is the type of storage most often discussed in this book. Computers also have **external storage**, which is permanent storage outside the main memory of the machine, on a device such as a floppy disk, hard disk, or magnetic tape. In other words, external storage is outside of the main memory, not necessarily outside the computer. Both programs and data sometimes are stored on each of these kinds of media.

To use computer programs, you must first load them into memory. You might type a program into memory from the keyboard, or you might use a program that has already been written and stored on a disk. Either way, a copy of the instructions must be placed in memory before the program can be run.

A computer system needs both internal memory and external storage. Internal memory is needed to run the programs, but internal memory is **volatile**—that is, its contents are lost every time the computer loses power. Therefore, if you are going to use a program more than once, you must store it, or **save** it, on some nonvolatile medium. Otherwise, the program in main memory is lost forever when the computer is turned off. External storage (usually disks or tape) provides a nonvolatile medium.

> **TIP** ☐ ☐ ☐ ☐ Even though a hard disk drive is located inside your computer, the hard disk is not main, internal memory. Internal memory is temporary and volatile; a hard drive is permanent, nonvolatile storage. After one or two "tragedies" of losing several pages of a typed computer program due to a power failure or other hardware problem, most programmers learn to periodically save the programs they are in the process of writing, using a nonvolatile medium, such as a disk.

Once you have a copy of a program in main memory, you want to execute or run the program. To do so, you must also place any data that the program requires into memory. For example, after you place the following program into memory and start to run it, you need to provide an actual `inputNumber`—for example, 8—that you also place in main memory.

```
Get inputNumber.
Compute calculatedAnswer as inputNumber times 2.
Print calculatedAnswer.
```

The `inputNumber` is placed in memory in a specific memory location that the program will call `inputNumber`. Then, and only then, can the `calculatedAnswer`, in this case 16, be calculated and printed.

> **TIP** ☐ ☐ ☐ ☐ Computer memory consists of millions of numbered locations where data can be stored. The memory location of `inputNumber` has a specific numeric address, for example, 48604. Your program associates `inputNumber` with that address. Every time you refer to `inputNumber` within a program, the computer retrieves the value at the associated memory location. When you write programs, you seldom need to be concerned with the value of the memory address; instead, you simply use the easy-to-remember name you created.

> **TIP** ☐ ☐ ☐ ☐ Computer programmers often refer to memory addresses using hexadecimal notation, or base 16. Using this system, they might use a value like 42FF01A to refer to a memory address. Despite the use of letters, such an address is still a number. When you use the hexadecimal numbering system, the letters A through F stand for the values 10 through 15.

UNDERSTANDING THE PROGRAMMING PROCESS

A programmer's job involves writing instructions (such as the three instructions in the doubling program in the preceding section), but a professional programmer usually does not just sit down at a computer keyboard and start typing. The programmer's job can be broken down into six programming steps:

1. Understand the problem.
2. Plan the logic.
3. Code the program.
4. Translate the program into machine language.

5. Test the program.
6. Put the program into production.

UNDERSTAND THE PROBLEM

Professional computer programmers write programs to satisfy the needs of others. For example: the Human Resources Department that needs a printed list of all employees, the Billing Department that wants a list of clients who are 30 or more days overdue in their payments, and the office manager who wants to be notified when specific supplies reach the reorder point. Because programmers are providing a service to these users, programmers must first understand what it is the users want.

Suppose the director of human resources says to a programmer, "Our department needs a list of all employees who have been here over five years, because we want to invite them to a special thank-you dinner." On the surface, this seems like a simple enough request. An experienced programmer, however, will know that he or she may not yet understand the whole problem. Does the director want a list of full-time employees only, or a list of full- and part-time employees together? Does she want people who have worked for the company on a month-to-month contractual basis over the past five years, or only regular, permanent employees? Do the listed employees need to have worked for the organization for five years as of today, as of the date of the dinner, or as of some other cutoff date? What about an employee who worked three years, took a two-year leave of absence, and has been back for three years? Does he or she qualify? The programmer cannot make any of these decisions; the user is the one who must address these questions.

More decisions still might be required. For example, what does the user want the report of five-year employees to look like? Should it contain both first and last names? Social Security numbers? Phone numbers? Addresses? Is all this data available? Several pieces of documentation are often provided to help the programmer understand the problem. This documentation includes print layout charts and file specifications, which you will learn about in Chapter 3.

Really understanding the problem may be one of the most difficult aspects of programming. On any job, the description of what the user needs may be vague—worse yet, the user may not even really know what he or she wants, and users who think they know what they want frequently change their minds after seeing sample output. A good programmer is often part counselor, part detective!

PLAN THE LOGIC

The heart of the programming process lies in planning the program's logic. During this phase of the programming process, the programmer plans the steps to the program, deciding what steps to include and how to order them. You can plan the solution to a problem in many ways. The two most common tools are flowcharts and pseudocode. Both tools involve writing the steps of the program in English, much as you would plan a trip on paper before getting into the car, or plan a party theme before going shopping for food and favors.

TIP ▢ ▢ ▢ ▢   You may hear programmers refer to planning a program as "developing an algorithm." An **algorithm** is the sequence of steps necessary to solve any problem. You will learn more about flowcharts and pseudocode later in this chapter.

The programmer doesn't worry about the syntax of any particular language at this point, just about figuring out what sequence of events will lead from the available input to the desired output. You will learn more about planning the logic later; in fact, this book focuses on this crucial step almost exclusively.

CODE THE PROGRAM

Once the programmer has developed the logic of a program, only then can he or she write the program in one of more than 400 programming languages. Programmers choose a particular language because some languages have built-in capabilities that make them more efficient than others at handling certain types of operations. Despite their differences, programming languages are quite alike—each can handle input operations, arithmetic processing, output operations, and other standard functions. The logic developed to solve a programming problem can be executed using any number of languages. It is only after a language is chosen that the programmer must worry about each command being spelled correctly and all of the punctuation getting into the right spots—in other words, using the correct *syntax*.

Some very experienced programmers can successfully combine the logic planning and the actual instruction writing, or **coding** of the program, in one step. This may work for planning and writing a very simple program, just as you can plan and write a postcard to a friend using one step. A good term paper or a Hollywood screenplay, however, needs planning before writing, and so do most programs.

Which step is harder, planning the logic or coding the program? Right now, it may seem to you that writing in a programming language is a very difficult task, considering all the spelling and grammar rules you must learn. However, the planning step is actually more difficult. Which is more difficult: thinking up the twists and turns to the plot of a best-selling mystery novel, or writing a translation of an already written novel from English to Spanish? And who do you think gets paid more, the writer who creates the plot or the translator? (Try asking friends to name any famous translator!)

TRANSLATE THE PROGRAM INTO MACHINE LANGUAGE

Even though there are many programming languages, each computer knows only one language, its machine language, which consists of many 1s and 0s. Computers understand machine language because computers themselves are made up of thousands of tiny electrical switches, each of which can be set in either the on or off state, which is represented by a 1 or 0, respectively.

Languages like Java or Visual Basic are available for programmers to use because someone has written a translator program (a compiler or interpreter) that changes the English-like **high-level programming language** in which the programmer writes into the **low-level machine language** that the computer understands. If you write a programming language statement incorrectly (for example, by misspelling a word, using a word that doesn't exist in the language, or using "illegal" grammar), the translator program doesn't know what to do and issues an error message identifying a **syntax error**, or misuse of a language's grammar rules. You receive the same response when you speak nonsense to a human language translator. Imagine trying to look up a list of words in a Spanish-English dictionary if some of the listed words are misspelled—you can't complete the task until the words are spelled correctly. Although making errors is never desirable, syntax errors are not a major concern to programmers, because the compiler or interpreter catches every syntax error, and the computer will not execute a program that contains them.

A computer program must be free of syntax errors before you can execute it. Typically, a programmer develops a program's logic, writes the code, and then compiles the program, receiving a list of syntax errors. The programmer then corrects the syntax errors, and compiles the program again. Correcting the first set of errors frequently reveals a new set of errors that originally were not apparent to the compiler. For example, if you could use an English compiler and submit the sentence `The grl go to school`, the compiler at first would point out only one syntax error to you. The second word, `grl`, is illegal because it is not part of the English language. Only after you corrected the word `girl` would the compiler find another syntax error on the third word, `go`, because it is the wrong verb form for the subject `girl`. This doesn't mean `go` is necessarily the wrong word. Maybe `girl` is wrong; perhaps the subject should be `girls`, in which case `go` is right. Compilers don't always know exactly what you mean, nor do they know what the proper correction should be, but they do know when something is wrong with your syntax.

When writing a program, a programmer might need to recompile the code several times. An executable program is created only when the code is free of syntax errors. When you run an executable program, it typically also might require input data. Figure 1-1 shows a diagram of this entire process.

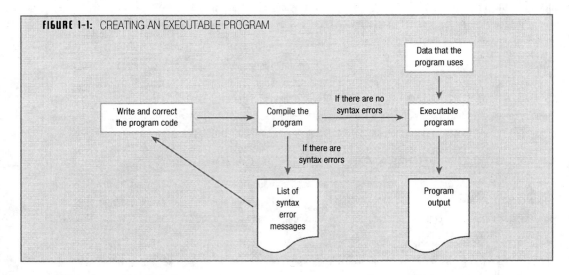

FIGURE 1-1: CREATING AN EXECUTABLE PROGRAM

TEST THE PROGRAM

A program that is free of syntax errors is not necessarily free of **logical errors**. For example, the sentence `The girl goes to school`, although syntactically perfect, is not logically correct if the girl is a baby or a dropout.

Once a program is free from syntax errors, the programmer can test it—that is, execute it with some sample data to see whether the results are logically correct. Recall the number-doubling program:

```
Get inputNumber.
Compute calculatedAnswer as inputNumber times 2.
Print calculatedAnswer.
```

If you provide the value 2 as input to the program and the answer 4 prints out, you have executed one successful test run of the program.

However, if the answer 40 prints out, maybe it's because the program contains a logical error. Maybe the second line of code was mistyped with an extra zero, so that the program reads:

```
Get inputNumber.
Compute calculatedAnswer as inputNumber times 20.
Print calculatedAnswer.
```

The error of placing 20 instead of 2 in the multiplication statement caused a logical error. Notice that nothing is syntactically wrong with this second program—it is just as reasonable to multiply a number by 20 as by 2—but if the programmer intends only to double the `inputNumber`, then a logical error has occurred.

Programs should be tested with many sets of data. For example, if you write the program to double a number and enter 2 and get an output value of 4, that doesn't necessarily mean you have a correct program. Perhaps you have typed this program by mistake:

```
Get inputNumber.
Compute calculatedAnswer as inputNumber plus 2.
Print calculatedAnswer.
```

An input of 2 results in an answer of 4, but that doesn't mean your program doubles numbers—it actually only adds 2 to them. If you test your program with additional data and get the wrong answer—for example, if you use a 3 and get an answer of 5—you know there is a problem with your code.

Selecting test data is somewhat of an art in itself, and it should be done carefully. If the Human Resources Department wants a list of the names of five-year employees, it would be a mistake to test the program with a small sample file of only long-term employees. If no newer employees are part of the data being used for testing, you don't really know if the program would have eliminated them from the five-year list. Many companies don't know that their software has a problem until an unusual circumstance occurs—for example, the first time an employee has more than nine dependents, the first time a customer orders more than 999 items at a time, or when (in an example that was well-documented in the popular press) a new century begins.

PUT THE PROGRAM INTO PRODUCTION

Once the program is tested adequately, it is ready for the organization to use. Putting the program into production might mean simply running the program once, if it was written to satisfy a user's request for a special list. However, the process might take months if the program will be run on a regular basis, or if it is one of a large system of programs being developed. Perhaps data entry people must be trained to prepare the input for the new program, users must be trained to understand the output, or existing data in the company must be changed to an entirely new format to accommodate this program. **Conversion**, the entire set of actions an organization must take to switch over to using a new program or set of programs, can sometimes take months or years to accomplish.

TIP □ □ □ □ | You might consider maintaining programs as a seventh step in the programming process. After programs are put into production, making required changes is called maintenance. Maintenance is necessary for many reasons: for example, new tax rates are legislated, the format of an input file is altered, or the end user requires additional information not included in the original output specifications. You might consider retiring the program as the eighth and final step in the programming process. A program is retired when it is no longer needed by an organization—usually when a new program is in the process of being put into production.

UNDERSTANDING THE DATA HIERARCHY

Some very simple programs require very simple data. For example, the number-doubling program requires just one value as input. Most business programs, however, use much more data—inventory files list thousands of items, personnel and customer files list thousands of people. When data are stored for use on computer systems, they are often stored in what is known as a **data hierarchy**, where the smallest usable unit of data is the character. **Characters** are letters, numbers, and special symbols, such as "A", "7", and "$". Anything you can type from the keyboard in one keystroke (including a space or a tab) is a character. Characters are made up of smaller elements called bits, but just as most human beings can use a pencil without caring whether atoms are flying around inside it, most computer users can store characters without caring about these bits.

TIP □ □ □ □ | Computers also recognize characters you cannot enter from the keyboard, such as foreign alphabet characters like φ or Σ.

Characters are grouped together to form a field. A **field** is a single data item, such as `lastName`, `streetAddress`, or `annualSalary`. For most of us, an "S", an "m", an "i", a "t", and an "h" don't have much meaning individually, but if the combination of characters makes up your last name, "Smith", then as a group, the characters have useful meaning.

Related fields are often grouped together to form a record. **Records** are groups of fields that go together for some logical reason. A random name, address, and salary aren't very useful, but if they're your name, your address, and your salary, then that's your record. An inventory record might contain fields for item number, color, size, and price; a student record might contain ID number, grade point average, and major.

Related records, in turn, are grouped together to form a file. **Files** are groups of records that go together for some logical reason. The individual records of each student in your class might go together in a file called CLASS. Records of each person at your company might be in a file called PERSONNEL. Items you sell might be in an INVENTORY file.

Some files can have just a few records; others, such as the file of credit card holders for a major department store chain or policyholders of an insurance company, can contain thousands or even millions of records.

Finally, many organizations use database software to organize many files. A **database** holds a group of files, often called **tables**, that together serve the information needs of an organization. Database software establishes and maintains relationships between fields in these tables, so that users can write questions called **queries**. Queries pull related data items together in a format that allows businesspeople to make managerial decisions efficiently. Chapter 16 of the Comprehensive version of this text covers database creation.

In summary, you can picture the data hierarchy, as shown in Figure 1-2.

FIGURE 1-2: THE DATA HIERARCHY

```
Database
    File
        Record
            Field
                Character
```

A database contains many files. A file contains many records. Each record in a file has the same fields. Each record's fields contain different data items that consist of one or more stored characters in each field.

As an example, you can picture a file as a set of index cards, as shown in Figure 1-3. The stack of cards is the EMPLOYEE file, in which each card represents one employee record. On each card, each line holds one field—name, address, or salary. Almost all the program examples in this book use files that are organized in this way.

FIGURE 1-3: EMPLOYEE FILE REPRESENTED AS A STACK OF INDEX CARDS

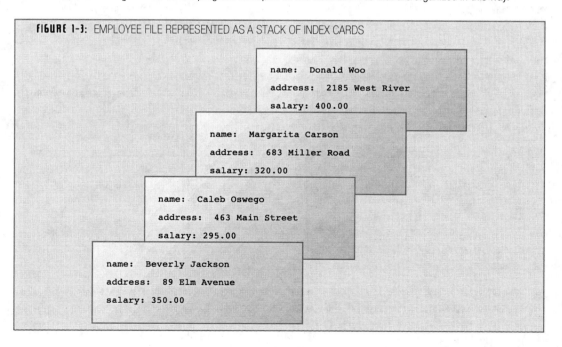

```
name:   Donald Woo
address:   2185 West River
salary: 400.00
```

```
name:   Margarita Carson
address:   683 Miller Road
salary: 320.00
```

```
name:   Caleb Oswego
address:   463 Main Street
salary: 295.00
```

```
name:   Beverly Jackson
address:   89 Elm Avenue
salary: 350.00
```

USING FLOWCHART SYMBOLS AND PSEUDOCODE STATEMENTS

When programmers plan the logic for a solution to a programming problem, they often use one of two tools, **flowcharts** or **pseudocode** (pronounced "sue-doe-code"). A flowchart is a pictorial representation of the logical steps it takes to solve a problem. Pseudocode is an English-like representation of the same thing. *Pseudo* is a prefix that means "false," and to *code* a program means to put it in a programming language; therefore, *pseudocode* simply means "false code," or sentences that appear to have been written in a computer programming language but don't necessarily follow all the syntax rules of any specific language.

You have already seen examples of statements that represent pseudocode earlier in this chapter, and there is nothing mysterious about them. The following five statements constitute a pseudocode representation of a number-doubling problem:

```
start
   get inputNumber
   compute calculatedAnswer as inputNumber times 2
   print calculatedAnswer
stop
```

Using pseudocode involves writing down all the steps you will use in a program. Usually, programmers preface their pseudocode statements with a beginning statement like "start" and end them with a terminating statement like "stop". The statements between "start" and "stop" look like English and are indented slightly so that "start" and "stop" stand out. Most programmers do not bother with punctuation such as periods at the end of pseudocode statements, although it would not be wrong to use them if you prefer that style. Similarly, there is no need to capitalize the first word in a sentence, although you might choose to do so. This book follows the conventions of using lowercase letters for verbs that begin pseudocode statements and omitting periods at the end of statements.

Some professional programmers prefer writing pseudocode to drawing flowcharts, because using pseudocode is more similar to writing the final statements in the programming language. Others prefer drawing flowcharts to represent the logical flow, because flowcharts allow programmers to visualize more easily how the program statements will connect. Especially for beginning programmers, flowcharts are an excellent tool to help visualize how the statements in a program are interrelated.

Almost every program involves the steps of input, processing, and output. Therefore, most flowcharts need some graphical way to separate these three steps. When you create a flowchart, you draw geometric shapes around the individual statements and connect them with arrows.

When you draw a flowchart, you use a parallelogram to represent an **input symbol**, which indicates an input operation. You write an input statement, in English, inside the parallelogram, as shown in Figure 1-4.

FIGURE 1-4: INPUT SYMBOL

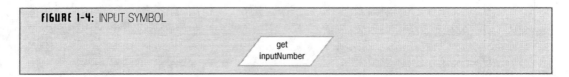

TIP □ □ □ □ When you want to represent entering two or more values in a program, you can use one or multiple flowchart symbols or pseudocode statements—whichever seems more reasonable and clear to you. For example, the pseudocode to input a user's name and address might be written as:

```
get inputName
get inputAddress
```

or as:

```
get inputName,inputAddress
```

The first version implies two separate input operations, whereas the second implies a single input operation retrieving two data items. The end result is the same in both cases—after the statements have executed, inputName and inputAddress will have received values from an input device.

Arithmetic operation statements are examples of processing. In a flowchart, you use a rectangle as the **processing symbol** that contains a processing statement, as shown in Figure 1-5.

FIGURE 1-5: PROCESSING SYMBOL

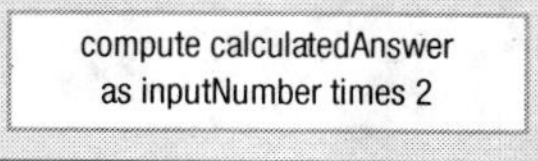

compute calculatedAnswer
as inputNumber times 2

To represent an output statement, you use the same symbol as for input statements—the **output symbol** is a parallelogram, as shown in Figure 1-6.

FIGURE 1-6: OUTPUT SYMBOL

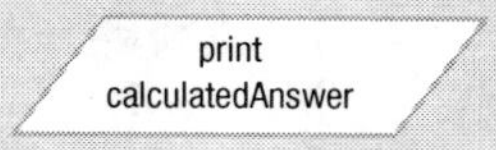

print
calculatedAnswer

TIP □ □ □ □ As with input, output statements can be organized in whatever way seems most reasonable. A program that prints the length and width of a room might use the statement:

```
print length
print width
```

or:

```
print length, width
```

In some programming languages, using two print statements places the output values on two separate lines on the monitor or printer, whereas using a single print statement places the values next to each other on the same line. This book follows the convention of using one print statement per line of output.

To show the correct sequence of these statements, you use arrows, or **flowlines**, to connect the steps. Whenever possible, most of a flowchart should read from top to bottom or from left to right on a page. That's the way we read English, so when flowcharts follow this convention, they are easier for us to understand.

To be complete, a flowchart should include two more elements: a **terminal symbol**, or start/stop symbol, at each end. Often, you place a word like "start" or "begin" in the first terminal symbol and a word like "end" or "stop" in the other. The standard terminal symbol is shaped like a racetrack; many programmers refer to this shape as a **lozenge**, because it resembles the shape of a medicated candy lozenge you might use to soothe a sore throat. Figure 1-7 shows a complete flowchart for the program that doubles a number, and the pseudocode for the same problem.

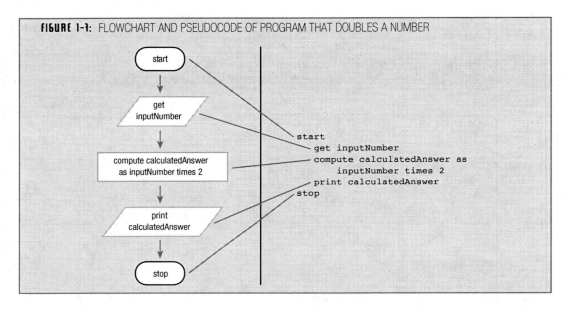

FIGURE 1-7: FLOWCHART AND PSEUDOCODE OF PROGRAM THAT DOUBLES A NUMBER

```
start
    get inputNumber
    compute calculatedAnswer as
            inputNumber times 2
    print calculatedAnswer
stop
```

TIP □ □ □ □ | Programmers seldom create both pseudocode and a flowchart for the same problem. You usually use one or the other.

The logic for the program represented by the flowchart and pseudocode in Figure 1-7 is correct no matter what programming language the programmer eventually uses to write the corresponding code. Just as the same statements could be translated into Italian or Chinese without losing their meaning, they also can be coded in C#, Java, or any other programming language.

After the flowchart or pseudocode has been developed, the programmer only needs to: (1) buy a computer, (2) buy a language compiler, (3) learn a programming language, (4) code the program, (5) attempt to compile it, (6) fix the syntax errors, (7) compile it again, (8) test it with several sets of data, and (9) put it into production.

"Whoa!" you are probably saying to yourself. "This is simply not worth it! All that work to create a flowchart or pseudocode, and *then* all those other steps? For five dollars, I can buy a pocket calculator that will double any number for me instantly!" You are absolutely right. If this were a real computer program, and all it did was double the value of a number, it simply would not be worth all the effort. Writing a computer program would be worth the effort only if you had many—let's say 10,000—numbers to double in a limited amount of time—let's say the next two minutes. Then, it would be worth your while to create a computer program.

Unfortunately, the number-doubling program represented in Figure 1-7 does not double 10,000 numbers; it doubles only one. You could execute the program 10,000 times, of course, but that would require you to sit at the computer telling it to run the program over and over again. You would be better off with a program that could process 10,000 numbers, one after the other.

One solution is to write the program as shown in Figure 1-8 and execute the same steps 10,000 times. Of course, writing this program would be very time-consuming; you might as well buy the calculator.

FIGURE 1-8: INEFFICIENT PSEUDOCODE FOR PROGRAM THAT DOUBLES 10,000 NUMBERS

```
start
     get inputNumber
     compute calculatedAnswer as inputNumber times 2
     print calculatedAnswer
     get inputNumber
     compute calculatedAnswer as inputNumber times 2
     print calculatedAnswer
     get inputNumber
     compute calculatedAnswer as inputNumber times 2
     print calculatedAnswer
     . . . and so on
```

A better solution is to have the computer execute the same set of three instructions over and over again, as shown in Figure 1-9. With this approach, the computer gets a number, doubles it, prints out the answer, and then starts over again with the first instruction. The same spot in memory, called `inputNumber`, is reused for the second number and for any subsequent numbers. The spot in memory named `calculatedAnswer` is reused each time to store the result of the multiplication operation. The logic illustrated in the flowchart shown in Figure 1-9 contains a major problem—the sequence of instructions never ends. You will learn to handle this problem later in this chapter.

FIGURE 1-9: FLOWCHART OF INFINITE NUMBER-DOUBLING PROGRAM

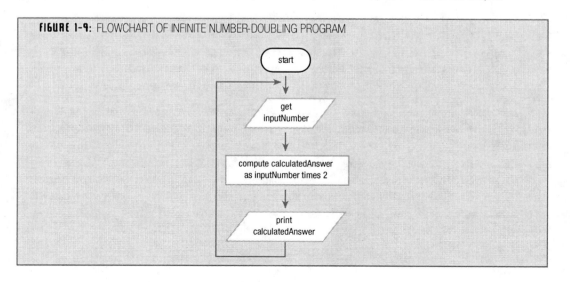

USING AND NAMING VARIABLES

Programmers commonly refer to the locations in memory called `inputNumber` and `calculatedAnswer` as variables. **Variables** are memory locations, whose contents can vary or differ over time. Sometimes, `inputNumber` can hold a 2 and `calculatedAnswer` will hold a 4; at other times, `inputNumber` can hold a 6 and `calculatedAnswer` will hold a 12. It is the ability of memory variables to change in value that makes computers and programming worthwhile. Because one memory location can be used over and over again with different values, you can write program instructions once and then use them for thousands of separate calculations. *One* set of payroll instructions at your company produces each individual's paycheck, and *one* set of instructions at your electric company produces each household's bill.

The number-doubling example requires two variables, `inputNumber` and `calculatedAnswer`. These can just as well be named `userEntry` and `programSolution`, or `inputValue` and `twiceTheValue`. As a programmer, you choose reasonable names for your variables. The language interpreter then associates the names you choose with specific memory addresses.

A variable name is also called an **identifier**. Every computer programming language has its own set of rules for naming identifiers. Most languages allow both letters and digits within variable names. Some languages allow hyphens in variable names, for example `hourly-wage`. Others allow underscores, as in `hourly_wage`. Still others allow neither. Some languages allow dollar signs or other special characters in variable names, for example `hourly$`; others allow foreign alphabet characters, such as π or Ω.

> **TIP** ▫ ▫ ▫ ▫ You also can refer to a variable name as a **mnemonic**. In everyday language, a mnemonic is a memory device, like the sentence "Every good boy does fine," which makes it easier to remember the notes on the musical scale. In programming, a variable name is a device that makes it easier to reference a memory address.

Different languages put different limits on the length of variable names, although in general, newer languages allow longer names. For example, in some very old versions of BASIC, a variable name could consist of only one or two letters and one or two digits. You could have some cryptic variable names like `hw` or `a3` or `re02`. In other languages, variable names can be very long. COBOL, for example, allows up to 30 characters in its variable names, so names like `AMOUNT-OF-SALE` and `TOTAL-FOR-JANUARY` are common. In addition, COBOL allows hyphens in its variable names for better readability.

Many modern languages, such as C++, C#, and Java, allow more than two hundred characters in a variable name. Variable names in these languages usually consist of lowercase letters, don't allow hyphens, but do allow underscores, so you can use a name like `price_of_item`. These languages are case sensitive, so `HOURLYWAGE`, `hourlywage`, and `hourlyWage` are considered three separate variable names, although the last example, in which the new word begins with an uppercase letter, is easiest to read. Most programmers who use the more modern languages employ the format in which multiple-word variable names are run together, and each new word within the variable name begins with an uppercase letter. This format is called **camel casing**, because such variable names, like `hourlyWage`, have a "hump" in the middle. The variable names in this text are shown using camel casing.

Even though every language has its own rules for naming variables, when designing the logic of a computer program, you should not concern yourself with the specific syntax of any particular computer language. The logic, after all, works with any language. The variable names used throughout this book follow only two rules:

1. *Variable names must be one word.* The name can contain letters, digits, hyphens, underscores, or any other characters you choose, with the exception of *spaces*. Therefore, `r` is a legal variable name, as is `rate`, as is `interestRate`. The variable name `interest rate` is not allowed because of the space. No programming language allows spaces within a variable name. If you see a name such as `interest rate` in a flowchart or pseudocode, you should assume that the programmer is discussing two variables, `interest` and `rate`, each of which individually would be a fine variable name.

TIP □ □ □ □ | As a convention, this book begins variable names with a lowercase letter.

TIP □ □ □ □ | When you write a program, your compiler may show variable names in a different color from the rest of the program. This visual aid helps your variable names stand out from words that are part of the programming language.

2. *Variable names should have some appropriate meaning.* This is not a rule of any programming language. When computing an interest rate in a program, the computer does not care if you call the variable `g`, `u84`, or `fred`. As long as the correct numeric result is placed in the variable, its actual name doesn't really matter. However, it's much easier to follow the logic of a program with a statement in it like `compute finalBalance as equal to initialInvestment times interestRate` than one with a statement in it like `compute someBanana as equal to j89 times myFriendLinda`. You might think you will remember how you intended to use a cryptic variable name within a program, but several months or years later when a program requires changes, you, and other programmers working with you, will appreciate clear, descriptive variable names.

Notice that the flowchart in Figure 1-9 follows these two rules for variables: both variable names, `inputNumber` and `calculatedAnswer`, are one word, and they have appropriate meanings. Some programmers have fun with their variable names by naming them after friends or creating puns with them, but such behavior is unprofessional and marks those programmers as amateurs. Table 1-1 lists some possible variable names that might be used to hold an employee's last name and provides a rationale for the appropriateness of each one.

TIP □ □ □ □ | Another general rule in all programming languages is that variable names may not begin with a digit, although usually they may contain digits. Thus, in most languages budget2013 is a legal variable name, but 2013Budget is not.

TABLE 1-1: VALID AND INVALID VARIABLE NAMES FOR AN EMPLOYEE'S LAST NAME

Suggested variable names for employee's last name	Comments
employeeLastName	Good
employeeLast	Good—most people would interpret Last as meaning Last Name
empLast	Good—emp is short for employee
emlstnam	Legal—but cryptic
lastNameOfTheEmployeeInQuestion	Legal—but awkward
last name	Not legal—embedded space
employeelastname	Legal—but hard to read without camel casing

ENDING A PROGRAM BY USING SENTINEL VALUES

Recall that the logic in the flowchart for doubling numbers, shown in Figure 1-9, has a major flaw—the program never ends. This programming situation is known as an **infinite loop**—a repeating flow of logic with no end. If, for example, the input numbers are being entered at the keyboard, the program will keep accepting numbers and printing out doubles forever. Of course, the user could refuse to type in any more numbers. But the computer is very patient, and if you refuse to give it any more numbers, it will sit and wait forever. When you finally type in a number, the program will double it, print the result, and wait for another. The program cannot progress any further while it is waiting for input; meanwhile, the program is occupying computer memory and tying up operating system resources. Refusing to enter any more numbers is not a practical solution. Another way to end the program is simply to turn the computer off! But again, that's neither the best nor an elegant way to bring the program to an end.

A superior way to end the program is to set a predetermined value for `inputNumber` that means "Stop the program!" For example, the programmer and the user could agree that the user will never need to know the double of 0 (zero), so the user could enter a 0 when he or she wants to stop. The program could then test any incoming value for `inputNumber` and, if it is a 0, stop the program. Testing a value is also called making a **decision**.

You represent a decision in a flowchart by drawing a **decision symbol**, which is shaped like a diamond. The diamond usually contains a question, the answer to which is one of two mutually exclusive options—often yes or no. All good computer questions have only two mutually exclusive answers, such as yes and no, true and false, or less than and not less than. For example, "What day of the year is your birthday?" is not a good computer question because there are 366 possible answers. But "Is your birthday June 24?" *is* a good computer question because, for everyone in the world, the answer is either yes or no.

TIP ▫ ▫ ▫ ▫ | A yes-or-no decision is called a **binary decision**, because there are two possible outcomes.

The question to stop the doubling program should be "Is the `inputNumber` just entered equal to 0?" or "`inputNumber = 0`?" for short. The complete flowchart will now look like the one shown in Figure 1-10.

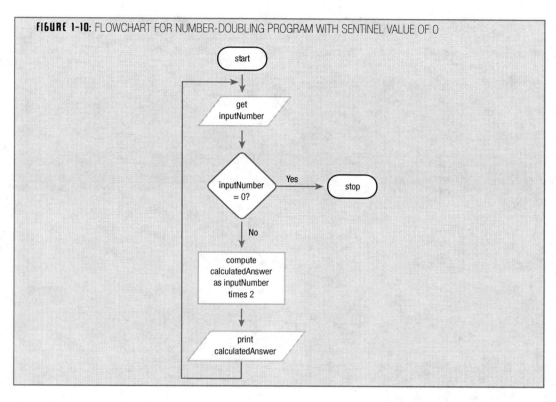

FIGURE 1-10: FLOWCHART FOR NUMBER-DOUBLING PROGRAM WITH SENTINEL VALUE OF 0

One drawback to using 0 to stop a program, of course, is that it won't work if the user *does* need to find the double of 0. In that case, some other data entry value that the user never will need, such as 999 or –1, could be selected to signal that the program should end. A preselected value that stops the execution of a program is often called a **dummy value** because it does not represent real data, but just a signal to stop. Sometimes, such a value is called a **sentinel value** because it represents an entry or exit point, like a sentinel who guards a fortress.

Not all programs rely on user data entry from a keyboard; many read data from an input device, such as a disk or tape drive. When organizations store data on a disk or tape, they do not commonly use a dummy value to signal the end of the file. For one thing, an input record might have hundreds of fields, and if you store a dummy record in every file, you are wasting a large quantity of storage on "non-data." Additionally, it is often difficult to choose sentinel values for fields in a company's data files. Any `balanceDue`, even a zero or a negative number, can be a legitimate value, and any `customerName`, even "ZZ" could be someone's name. Fortunately, programming languages can recognize the end of data in a file automatically, through a code that is stored at the end of the data. Many programming languages use the term **eof** (for "end of file") to talk about this marker that automatically acts as a sentinel. This book, therefore, uses `eof` to indicate the end of data, regardless of whether the code is a special disk marker or a dummy value such as 0 that comes from the keyboard. Therefore, the flowchart and pseudocode can look like the examples shown in Figure 1-11.

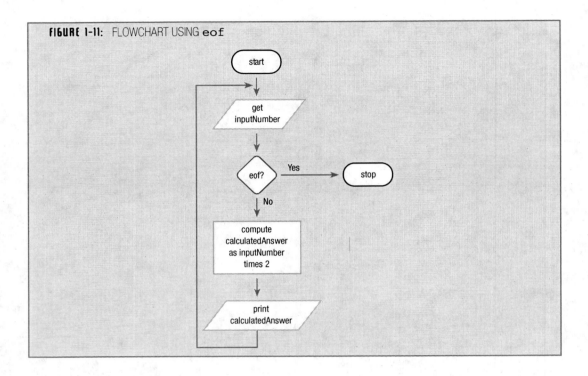

FIGURE 1-11: FLOWCHART USING `eof`

USING THE CONNECTOR

By using just the input, processing, output, decision, and terminal symbols, you can represent the flowcharting logic for many diverse applications. When drawing a flowchart segment, you might use only one other symbol, the **connector**. You can use a connector when limited page size forces you to continue a flowchart in an unconnected location or on another page. If a flowchart has six processing steps and a page provides room for only three, you might represent the logic as shown in Figure 1-12.

By convention, programmers use a circle as an on-page connector symbol, and a symbol that looks like a square with a pointed bottom as an off-page connector symbol. The on-page connector at the bottom of the left column in Figure 1-10 tells someone reading the flowchart that there is more to the flowchart. The circle should contain a number or letter that can then be matched to another number or letter somewhere else, in this case on the right. If a large flowchart needed more connectors, new numbers or letters would be assigned in sequence (1, 2, 3... or A, B, C...) to each successive pair of connectors. The off-page connector at the bottom of the right column in Figure 1-10 tells a reader that there is more to the flowchart on another page.

When you are creating your own flowcharts, you should avoid using any connectors, if at all possible; flowcharts are more difficult to follow when their segments do not fit together on a page. Many programmers would even say that if a flowchart must connect to another page, it is a sign of poor design. Your instructor or future programming supervisor may require that long flowcharts be redrawn so you don't need to use the connector symbol. However, when continuing on a new location or page is unavoidable, the connector provides the means.

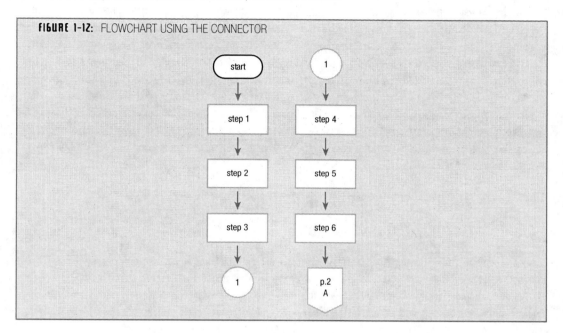

FIGURE 1-12: FLOWCHART USING THE CONNECTOR

ASSIGNING VALUES TO VARIABLES

When you create a flowchart or pseudocode for a program that doubles numbers, you can include the statement `compute calculatedAnswer as inputNumber times 2`. This statement incorporates two actions. First, the computer computes the arithmetic value of `inputNumber` times 2. Second, the computed value is stored in the `calculatedAnswer` memory location. Most programming languages allow a shorthand expression for **assignment statements** such as `compute calculatedAnswer as inputNumber times 2`. The shorthand takes the form `calculatedAnswer = inputNumber * 2`. The equal sign is the **assignment operator**; it always requires the name of a memory location on its left side—the name of the location where the result will be stored.

TIP □ □ □ □ | In Pascal, the same expression is calculatedAnswer := inputNumber * 2. You type a colon followed by an equal sign to create the assignment symbol. Java, C++, C#, Visual Basic, and many other languages all use the equal sign for assignment.

TIP □ □ □ □ | Most programmers use the asterisk (*) to represent multiplication. When you write pseudocode, you can use an X or a dot for multiplication (as most mathematicians do), but you will be using an unconventional format. This book will always use an asterisk to represent multiplication.

According to the rules of algebra, a statement like `calculatedAnswer = inputNumber * 2` should be exactly equivalent to the statement `inputNumber * 2 = calculatedAnswer`. That's because in algebra, the equal sign always represents equivalency. To most programmers, however, the equal sign represents assignment, and `calculatedAnswer = inputNumber * 2` means "multiply `inputNumber` by 2 and store the result in the variable called `calculatedAnswer`." Whatever operation is performed to the right of the equal sign results in a value that is placed in the memory location to the left of the equal sign. Therefore, the incorrect statement `inputNumber * 2 = calculatedAnswer` means to attempt to take the value of `calculatedAnswer` and store it in a location called `inputNumber * 2,` but there can't be a location called `inputNumber * 2`. For one thing, `inputNumber * 2` can't be a variable because it has spaces in it. For another, a location can't be multiplied. Its contents can be multiplied, but the location itself cannot be. The backwards statement `inputNumber * 2 = calculatedAnswer` contains a syntax error, no matter what programming language you use; a program with such a statement will not execute.

> **TIP** ☐ ☐ ☐ ☐ When you create an assignment statement, it may help to imagine the word "let" in front of the statement. Thus, you can read the statement calculatedAnswer = inputNumber * 2 as "Let calculatedAnswer equal inputNumber times two." The BASIC programming language allows you to use the word "let" in such statements.

Computer memory is made up of millions of distinct locations, each of which has an address. Fifty or sixty years ago, programmers had to deal with these addresses and had to remember, for instance, that they had stored a salary in location 6428 of their computer. Today, we are very fortunate that high-level computer languages allow us to pick a reasonable "English" name for a memory address and let the computer keep track of where it is. Just as it is easier for you to remember that the president lives in the White House than at 1600 Pennsylvania Avenue, Washington, D.C., it is also easier for you to remember that your salary is in a variable called `mySalary` than at memory location 6428104.

Similarly, it does not usually make sense to perform mathematical operations on names given to memory addresses, but it does make sense to perform mathematical operations on the *contents* of memory addresses. If you live in `blueSplitLevelOnTheCorner`, adding 1 to that would be meaningless, but you certainly can add 1 person to the number of people already in that house. For our purposes, then, the statement `calculatedAnswer = inputNumber * 2` means exactly the same thing as the statement `calculate inputNumber * 2 and store the result in the memory location named calculatedAnswer`.

> **TIP** ☐ ☐ ☐ ☐ Many programming languages allow you to create named constants. A named constant is a named memory location, similar to a variable, except its value never changes during the execution of a program. If you are working with a programming language that allows it, you might create a constant for a value like pi = 3.14 or countySalesTaxRate = .06.

UNDERSTANDING DATA TYPES

Computers deal with two basic types of data—character and numeric. When you use a specific numeric value, such as 43, within a program, you write it using the digits and no quotation marks. A specific numeric value is often called a

numeric constant, because it does not change—a 43 always has the value 43. When you use a specific character value, or **string** of characters, such as "Chris", you enclose the string, or **character constant**, within quotation marks.

TIP ▢ ▢ ▢ ▢ | Some languages require single quotation marks surrounding character constants, whereas others require double quotation marks. Many languages, including C++, C#, Java, and Pascal, reserve single quotes for a single character such as 'C', and double quotes for a character string such as "Chris".

Similarly, most computer languages allow at least two distinct types of variables. One type of variable can hold a number, and is often called a **numeric variable**. In the statement `calculatedAnswer = inputNumber * 2`, both `calculatedAnswer` and `inputNumber` are numeric variables; that is, their intended contents are numeric values, such as 6 and 3, 150 and 75, or −18 and −9.

Most programming languages have a separate type of variable that can hold letters of the alphabet and other special characters such as punctuation marks. Depending on the language, these variables are called **character**, **text**, or **string variables**. If a working program contains the statement `lastName = "Lincoln"`, then `lastName` is a character or string variable.

Programmers must distinguish between numeric and character variables, because computers handle the two types of data differently. Therefore, means are provided within the syntax rules of computer programming languages to tell the computer which type of data to expect. How this is done is different in every language; some languages have different rules for naming the variables, but with others you must include a simple statement (called a **declaration**) telling the computer which type of data to expect.

Some languages allow for several types of numeric data. Languages such as Pascal, C++, C#, and Java distinguish between **integer** (whole number) numeric variables and **floating-point** (fractional) numeric variables that contain a decimal point. Thus, in some languages, the numbers 4 and 4.3 would have to be stored in different types of variables.

Some programming languages allow even more specific variable types, but the character versus numeric distinction is universal. For the programs you develop in this book, assume that each variable is one of the two broad types. If a variable called `taxRate` is supposed to hold a value of 2.5, assume that it is a numeric variable. If a variable called `inventoryItem` is supposed to hold a value of "monitor," assume that it is a character variable.

TIP ▢ ▢ ▢ ▢ | Values such as "monitor" and 2.5 are called constants or literal constants because they never change. A variable value *can* change. Thus, inventoryItem can hold "monitor" at one moment during the execution of a program, and later you can change its value to "modem".

By convention, this book encloses character data like "monitor" within quotation marks to distinguish the characters from yet another variable name. Also, by convention, numeric data values are not enclosed within quotation marks. According to these conventions, then, `taxRate = 2.5` and `inventoryItem = "monitor"` are both valid statements. The statement `inventoryItem = monitor` is a valid statement only if `monitor` is also a character variable. In other words, if `monitor ="color"`, and subsequently `inventoryItem = monitor`, then the end result is that the memory address named `inventoryItem` contains the string of characters "color".

Every computer handles text or character data differently from the way it handles numeric data. You may have experienced these differences if you have used application software such as spreadsheets or database programs. For example, in a spreadsheet, you cannot sum a column of words. Similarly, every programming language requires that you distinguish variables as to their correct type, and that you use each type of variable appropriately. Identifying your variables correctly as numeric or character is one of the first steps you have to take when writing programs in any programming language. Table 1-2 provides you with a few examples of legal and illegal variable assignment statements.

TIP □ □ □ □ | The process of naming program variables and assigning a type to them is called **making declarations**, or **declaring variables**. You will learn how to declare variables in Chapter 4.

TABLE 1-2: SOME EXAMPLES OF LEGAL AND ILLEGAL ASSIGNMENTS

Assume lastName and firstName are character variables.

Assume quizScore and homeworkScore are numeric variables.

Examples of valid assignments	Examples of invalid assignments
lastName = "Parker"	lastName = Parker
firstName = "Laura"	"Parker" = lastName
lastName = firstName	lastName = quizScore
quizScore = 86	homeworkScore = firstName
homeworkScore = quizScore	homeworkScore = "92"
homeworkScore = 92	quizScore = "zero"
quizScore = homeworkScore + 25	firstName = 23
homeworkScore = 3 * 10	100 = homeworkScore

UNDERSTANDING THE EVOLUTION OF PROGRAMMING TECHNIQUES

People have been writing computer programs since the 1940s. The oldest programming languages required programmers to work with memory addresses and to memorize awkward codes associated with machine languages. Newer programming languages look much more like natural language and are easier for programmers to use. Part of the reason it is easier to use newer programming languages is that they allow programmers to name variables instead of using awkward memory addresses. Another reason is that newer programming languages provide programmers with the means to create self-contained modules or program segments that can be pieced together in a variety of ways. The oldest computer programs were written in one piece, from start to finish; modern programs are rarely written that way—they are created by teams of programmers, each developing his or her own reusable and connectable program procedures. Writing several small modules is easier than writing one large program, and most large tasks are easier when you break the work into units and get other workers to help with some of the units.

TIP ☐ ☐ ☐ ☐ You will learn to create program modules in Chapter 3.

Currently, there are two major techniques used to develop programs and their procedures. One technique, called **procedural programming**, focuses on the procedures that programmers create. That is, procedural programmers focus on the actions that are carried out—for example, getting input data for an employee and writing the calculations needed to produce a paycheck from the data. Procedural programmers would approach the job of producing a paycheck by breaking down the paycheck-producing process into manageable subtasks.

The other popular programming technique, called **object-oriented programming**, focuses on objects, or "things," and describes their features, or attributes, and their behaviors. For example, object-oriented programmers might design a payroll application by thinking about employees and paychecks, and describing their attributes (such as last name or check amount) and behaviors (such as the calculations that result in the check amount).

With either approach, procedural or object-oriented, you can produce a correct paycheck, and both techniques employ reusable program modules. The major difference lies in the focus the programmer takes during the earliest planning stages of a project. Object-oriented programming employs a large vocabulary; you can learn this terminology in Chapter 13 of the Comprehensive version of this book. For now, this book focuses on procedural programming techniques. The skills you gain in programming procedurally—declaring variables, accepting input, making decisions, producing output, and so on—will serve you well whether you eventually write programs in a procedural or object-oriented fashion, or in both.

CHAPTER SUMMARY

☐ Together, computer hardware (equipment) and software (instructions) accomplish four major operations: input, processing, output, and storage. You write computer instructions in a computer programming language that requires specific syntax; the instructions are translated into machine language by a compiler or interpreter. When both the syntax and logic of a program are correct, you can run, or execute, the program to produce the desired results.

☐ A programmer's job involves understanding the problem, planning the logic, coding the program, translating the program into machine language, testing the program, and putting the program into production.

☐ When data are stored for use on computer systems, they are stored in a data hierarchy of character, field, record, file, and database.

☐ When programmers plan the logic for a solution to a programming problem, they often use flowcharts or pseudocode. When you draw a flowchart, you use parallelograms to represent input and output operations, and rectangles to represent processing.

☐ Variables are named memory locations, the contents of which can vary. As a programmer, you choose reasonable names for your variables. Every computer programming language has its own set of rules for naming variables; however, all variable names must be written as one word without embedded spaces, and should have appropriate meaning.

☐ Testing a value involves making a decision. You represent a decision in a flowchart by drawing a diamond-shaped decision symbol containing a question, the answer to which is either yes or no. You can stop a program's execution by using a decision to test for a sentinel value.

☐ A connector symbol is used to continue a flowchart that does not fit together on a page, or must continue on an additional page.

☐ Most programming languages use the equal sign to assign values to variables. Assignment always takes place from right to left.

☐ Programmers must distinguish between numeric and character variables, because computers handle the two types of data differently. A variable declaration tells the computer which type of data to expect. By convention, character data values are included within quotation marks.

☐ Procedural and object-oriented programmers approach program problems differently. Procedural programmers concentrate on the actions performed with data. Object-oriented programmers focus on objects and their behaviors and attributes.

KEY TERMS

Hardware is the equipment of a computer system.

Software, or programs, are written by programmers and tell the computer what to do.

Input devices include keyboards and mice; through these devices, data enter the computer system. Data can also enter a system from storage devices such as magnetic disks and CDs.

Data are facts.

Processing data items may involve organizing them, checking them for accuracy, or performing mathematical operations on them.

The central processing unit, or CPU, is the piece of hardware that processes data.

Information is sent to a printer, monitor, or some other output device so people can view, interpret, and work with the results.

Programming languages, such as Visual Basic, Pascal, COBOL, RPG, C#, C++, Java, or Fortran, are used to write programs.

The syntax of a language consists of its rules.

Machine language is a computer's on-off circuitry language.

A compiler or interpreter translates a high-level language into machine language and tells you if you have used a programming language incorrectly.

You develop the logic of the computer program when you give instructions to the computer in a specific sequence, without leaving any instructions out or adding extraneous instructions.

The running, or executing, of a program occurs when the computer actually uses the written and compiled program.

Internal storage is called memory, main memory, or primary memory.

External storage is permanent storage outside the main memory of the machine, on a device such as a floppy disk, hard disk, or magnetic tape.

Internal memory is volatile—that is, its contents are lost every time the computer loses power.

You save a program on some nonvolatile medium.

An algorithm is the sequence of steps necessary to solve any problem.

Coding a program means writing the statements in a programming language.

High-level programming languages are English-like.

Machine language is the low-level language made up of 1s and 0s that the computer understands.

A syntax error is an error in language or grammar.

Logical errors occur when incorrect instructions are performed, or when instructions are performed in the wrong order.

Conversion is the entire set of actions an organization must take to switch over to using a new program or set of programs.

The data hierarchy represents the relationship of databases, files, records, fields, and characters.

Characters are letters, numbers, and special symbols such as "A", "7", and "$".

A field is a single data item, such as `lastName`, `streetAddress`, or `annualSalary`.

Records are groups of fields that go together for some logical reason.

Files are groups of records that go together for some logical reason.

A database holds a group of files, often called tables, that together serve the information needs of an organization.

Queries are questions that pull related data items together from a database in a format that enhances efficient management decision making.

A flowchart is a pictorial representation of the logical steps it takes to solve a problem.

Pseudocode is an English-like representation of the logical steps it takes to solve a problem.

Input symbols are represented as parallelograms in flowcharts.

Processing symbols are represented as rectangles in flowcharts.

Output symbols are represented as parallelograms in flowcharts.

Flowlines, or arrows, connect the steps in a flowchart.

A terminal symbol, or start/stop symbol, is used at each end of a flowchart. Its shape is a lozenge.

Variables are memory locations, whose contents can vary, or differ, over time.

A variable name is also called an identifier.

A mnemonic is a memory device; variable identifiers act as mnemonics for hard-to-remember memory addresses.

Camel casing is the format for naming variables in which multiple-word variable names are run together, and each new word within the variable name begins with an uppercase letter.

An infinite loop is a repeating flow of logic without an ending.

Testing a value is also called making a decision.

You represent a decision in a flowchart by drawing a decision symbol, which is shaped like a diamond.

A yes-or-no decision is called a binary decision, because there are two possible outcomes.

A dummy value is a preselected value that stops the execution of a program. Such a value is sometimes called a sentinel value because it represents an entry or exit point, like a sentinel who guards a fortress.

Many programming languages use the term eof (for "end of file") to talk about an end-of-data file marker.

A connector is a flowchart symbol used when limited page size forces you to continue the flowchart on the same or following page.

An assignment statement stores the result of any calculation performed on its right side to the named location on its left side.

The equal sign is the assignment operator; it always requires the name of a memory location on its left side.

A numeric constant is a specific numeric value.

A string constant, or character constant, is enclosed within quotation marks.

Numeric variables hold numeric values.

Character, text, or string variables hold character values. If a working program contains the statement `lastName = "Lincoln"`, then `lastName` is a character or string variable.

A declaration is a statement that names a variable and tells the computer which type of data to expect.

Integer values are whole number, numeric variables.

Floating-point values are fractional, numeric variables that contain a decimal point.

The process of naming program variables and assigning a type to them is called making declarations, or declaring variables.

The technique known as procedural programming focuses on the procedures that programmers create.

The technique known as object-oriented programming focuses on objects, or "things," and describes their features, or attributes, and their behaviors.

REVIEW QUESTIONS

1. **The two major components of any computer system are its _____.**

    a. input and output
    b. data and programs
    c. hardware and software
    d. memory and disk drives

2. **The major computer operations include _____.**

    a. hardware and software
    b. input, processing, output, and storage
    c. sequence and looping
    d. spreadsheets, word processing, and data communications

3. **Another term meaning "computer instructions" is _____.**

    a. hardware
    b. software
    c. queries
    d. data

4. **Visual Basic, C++, and Java are all examples of computer _____.**

    a. operating systems
    b. hardware
    c. machine languages
    d. programming languages

5. **A programming language's rules are its _____.**

    a. syntax
    b. logic
    c. format
    d. options

6. **The most important task of a compiler or interpreter is to _____.**

    a. create the rules for a programming language
    b. translate English statements into a language such as Java
    c. translate programming language statements into machine language
    d. execute machine language programs to perform useful tasks

7. **Which of the following is a typical input instruction?**

    a. `get accountNumber`

    b. `calculate balanceDue`

    c. `print customerIdentificationNumber`

    d. `total = janPurchase + febPurchase`

8. **Which of the following is a typical processing instruction?**

    a. `print answer`

    b. `get userName`

    c. `pctCorrect = rightAnswers / allAnswers`

    d. `print calculatedPercentage`

9. **Which of the following is not associated with internal storage?**

    a. main memory

    b. hard disk

    c. primary memory

    d. volatile

10. **Which of the following pairs of steps in the programming process is in the correct order?**

    a. code the program, plan the logic

    b. test the program, translate it into machine language

    c. put the program into production, understand the problem

    d. code the program, translate it into machine language

11. **The two most commonly used tools for planning a program's logic are _____.**

    a. flowcharts and pseudocode

    b. ASCII and EBCDIC

    c. Java and Visual Basic

    d. word processors and spreadsheets

12. **The most important thing a programmer must do before planning the logic to a program is _____.**

    a. decide which programming language to use

    b. code the problem

    c. train the users of the program

    d. understand the problem

13. **Writing a program in a language such as C++ or Java is known as _____ the program.**

    a. translating

    b. coding

    c. interpreting

    d. compiling

14. **A compiler would find all of the following programming errors except** _____.

   a. the misspelled word "prrint" in a language that includes the word "print"

   b. the use of an "X" for multiplication in a language that requires an asterisk

   c. a `newBalanceDue` calculated by adding a `customerPayment` to an `oldBalanceDue` instead of subtracting it

   d. an arithmetic statement written as `regularSales + discountedSales = totalSales`

15. **Which of the following is true regarding the data hierarchy?**

   a. files contain records

   b. characters contain fields

   c. fields contain files

   d. fields contain records

16. **The parallelogram is the flowcharting symbol representing** _____.

   a. input

   b. output

   c. both a and b

   d. none of the above

17. **Which of the following is not a legal variable name in any programming language?**

   a. `semester grade`

   b. `fall2005_grade`

   c. `GradeInCIS100`

   d. `MY_GRADE`

18. **In flowcharts, the decision symbol is a** _____.

   a. parallelogram

   b. rectangle

   c. lozenge

   d. diamond

19. **The term "eof" represents** _____.

   a. a standard input device

   b. a generic sentinel value

   c. a condition in which no more memory is available for storage

   d. the logical flow in a program

20. **The two most broad types of data are** _____.

   a. internal and external

   b. volatile and constant

   c. character and numeric

   d. permanent and temporary

EXERCISES

1. **Match the definition with the appropriate term.**

   1. Computer system equipment   a. compiler
   2. Another word for programs   b. syntax
   3. Language rules   c. logic
   4. Order of instructions   d. hardware
   5. Language translator   e. software

2. **In your own words, describe the steps to writing a computer program.**

3. **Consider a student file that contains the following data:**

LAST NAME	FIRST NAME	MAJOR	GRADE POINT AVERAGE
Andrews	David	Psychology	3.4
Broederdorf	Melissa	Computer Science	4.0
Brogan	Lindsey	Biology	3.8
Carson	Joshua	Computer Science	2.8
Eisfelder	Katie	Mathematics	3.5
Faris	Natalie	Biology	2.8
Fredricks	Zachary	Psychology	2.0
Gonzales	Eduardo	Biology	3.1

   Would this set of data be suitable and sufficient to use to test each of the following programs? Explain why or why not.

   a. a program that prints a list of Psychology majors
   b. a program that prints a list of Art majors
   c. a program that prints a list of students on academic probation—those with a grade point average under 2.0
   d. a program that prints a list of students on the dean's list
   e. a program that prints a list of students from Wisconsin
   f. a program that prints a list of female students

4. **Suggest a good set of test data to use for a program that gives an employee a $50 bonus check if the employee has produced more than 1,000 items in a week.**

5. **Suggest a good set of test data for a program that computes gross paychecks (that is, before any taxes or other deductions) based on hours worked and rate of pay. The program computes gross as hours times rate, unless hours are over 40. Then, the program computes gross as regular rate of pay for 40 hours, plus one and a half times the rate of pay for the hours over 40.**

6. **Suggest a good set of test data for a program that is intended to output a student's grade point average based on letter grades (A, B, C, D, or F) in five courses.**

7. **Suggest a good set of test data for a program for an automobile insurance company that wants to increase its premiums by $50 per month for every ticket a driver receives in a three-year period.**

8. **Assume that a grocery store keeps a file for inventory, where each grocery item has its own record. Two fields within each record are the name of the manufacturer and the weight of the item. Name**

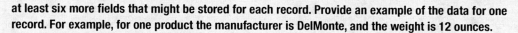

at least six more fields that might be stored for each record. Provide an example of the data for one record. For example, for one product the manufacturer is DelMonte, and the weight is 12 ounces.

9. Assume that a library keeps a file with data about its collection, one record for each item the library lends out. Name at least eight fields that might be stored for each record. Provide an example of the data for one record.

10. Match the term with the appropriate shape.

1. Input   A.

2. Processing   B.

3. Decision   C.

4. Terminal   D.

5. Connector   E.

11. Which of the following names seem like good variable names to you? If a name doesn't seem like a good variable name, explain why not.

    a. c
    b. cost
    c. costAmount
    d. cost amount
    e. cstofdngbsns
    f. costOfDoingBusinessThisFiscalYear
    g. cost2004

12. **If myAge and yourRate are numeric variables, and departmentCode is a character variable, which of the following statements are valid assignments? If a statement is not valid, explain why not.**

    a. myAge = 23
    b. myAge = yourRate
    c. myAge = departmentCode
    d. myAge = "departmentCode"
    e. 42 = myAge
    f. yourRate = 3.5
    g. yourRate = myAge
    h. yourRate = departmentCode
    i. 6.91 = yourRate
    j. departmentCode = Personnel
    k. departmentCode = "Personnel"
    l. departmentCode = 413
    m. departmentCode = "413"
    n. departmentCode = myAge
    o. departmentCode = yourRate
    p. 413 = departmentCode
    q. "413" = departmentCode

13. **Complete the following tasks:**

    a. Draw a flowchart to represent the logic of a program that allows the user to enter a value. The program multiplies the value by 10 and prints out the result.
    b. Write pseudocode for the same problem.

14. **Complete the following tasks:**

    a. Draw a flowchart to represent the logic of a program that allows the user to enter a value that represents the radius of a circle. The program calculates the diameter (by multiplying the radius by 2), and then calculates the circumference (by multiplying the diameter by 3.14). The program prints both the diameter and the circumference.
    b. Write pseudocode for the same problem.

15. **Complete the following tasks:**

    a. Draw a flowchart to represent the logic of a program that allows the user to enter two values. The program prints the sum of the two values.
    b. Write pseudocode for the same problem.

16. **Complete the following tasks:**

    a. Draw a flowchart to represent the logic of a program that allows the user to enter three values. The first value represents hourly pay rate, the second represents the number of hours worked this pay period, and the third represents the percentage of gross salary that is withheld. The program multiplies the hourly pay rate by the number of hours worked, giving the gross pay; then, it multiplies the gross pay by the withholding percentage, giving the withholding amount. Finally, it subtracts the withholding amount from the gross pay, giving the net pay after taxes. The program prints the net pay.
    b. Write pseudocode for the same problem.

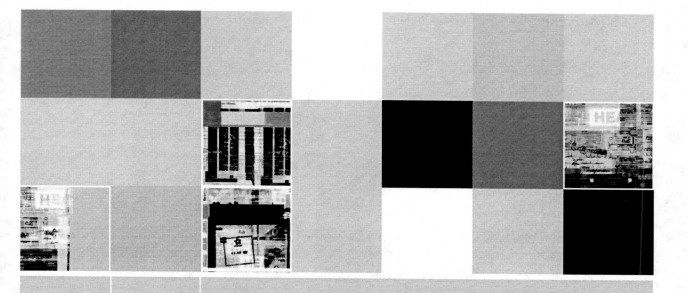

2

UNDERSTANDING STRUCTURE

After studying Chapter 2, you should be able to:

☐ Describe the features of unstructured spaghetti code

☐ Describe the three basic structures of sequence, selection, and loop

☐ Use a priming read

☐ Appreciate the need for structure

☐ Recognize structure

☐ Describe two special structures—case and do until

UNDERSTANDING UNSTRUCTURED SPAGHETTI CODE

Professional computer programs usually get far more complicated than the number-doubling program from Chapter 1, shown in Figure 2-1.

FIGURE 2-1: NUMBER-DOUBLING PROGRAM

```
get inputNumber
calculatedAnswer = inputNumber * 2
print calculatedAnswer
```

Imagine the number of instructions in the computer program that NASA uses to calculate the launch angle of a space shuttle, or in the program the IRS uses to audit your income tax return. Even the program that produces a paycheck for you on your job contains many, many instructions. Designing the logic for such a program can be a time-consuming task. When you add several thousand instructions to a program, including several hundred decisions, it is easy to create a complicated mess. The popular name for snarled program statements is **spaghetti code**. The reason for the name should be obvious—the code is as confusing to read as following one noodle through a plate of spaghetti.

For example, suppose you are in charge of admissions at a college, and you've decided you will admit prospective students based on the following criteria:

- You will admit students who score 90 or better on the admissions test your college gives, as long as they are in the upper 75 percent of their high-school graduating class. (These are smart students who score well on the admissions test. Maybe they didn't do so well in high school because it was a tough school, or maybe they have matured.)

- You will admit students who score at least 80 on the admissions test if they are in the upper 50 percent of their high-school graduating class. (These students score fairly well on the test, and do fairly well in school.)

- You will admit students who score as low as 70 on your test if they are in the top 25 percent of their class. (Maybe these students don't take tests well, but obviously they are achievers.)

Table 2-1 summarizes the admission requirements.

TABLE 2-1: ADMISSION REQUIREMENTS

Test score	High-school rank (%)
90–100	25–100
80–89	50–100
70–79	75–100

The flowchart for this program could look like the one in Figure 2-2. This kind of flowchart is an example of spaghetti code. Many computer programs (especially older computer programs) bear a striking resemblance to the flowchart in

Figure 2-2. Such programs might "work"—that is, they might produce correct results—but they are very difficult to read and maintain, and their logic is difficult to follow.

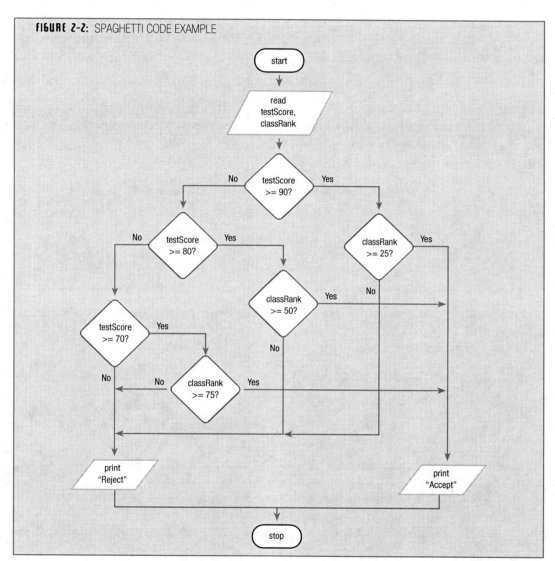

FIGURE 2-2: SPAGHETTI CODE EXAMPLE

UNDERSTANDING THE THREE BASIC STRUCTURES

In the mid-1960s, mathematicians proved that any program, no matter how complicated, can be constructed using only three sets of flowcharting shapes or structures. A **structure** is a basic unit of programming logic; each structure is a sequence, selection, or loop. With these three structures alone, you can diagram any event, from doubling a number to performing brain surgery.

The first of these structures is a sequence, as shown in Figure 2-3. With a **sequence structure**, you perform an action or event, and then you perform the next action, in order. A sequence can contain any number of events, but there is no chance to branch off and skip any of the events. Once you start a series of events in a sequence, you must continue step-by-step until the sequence ends.

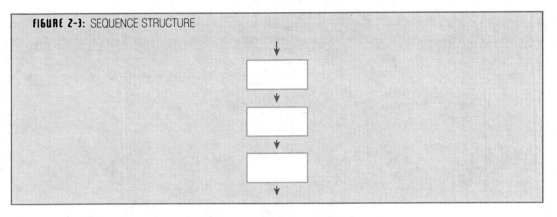

FIGURE 2-3: SEQUENCE STRUCTURE

The second structure is called a **selection structure** or **decision structure**, as shown in Figure 2-4. With this structure, you ask a question, and, depending on the answer, you take one of two courses of action. Then, no matter which path you follow, you continue with the next event.

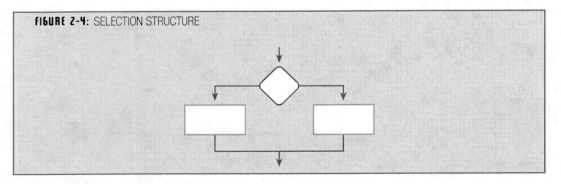

FIGURE 2-4: SELECTION STRUCTURE

Some people call the selection structure an **if-then-else** because it fits the following statement:

```
if someCondition is true then
   do oneProcess
else
   do theOtherProcess
```

For example, while cooking you may decide the following:

```
if we have brownSugar then
    use brownSugar
else
    use whiteSugar
```

Similarly, a payroll program might include a statement such as:

```
if hoursWorked is more than 40 then
    calculate overtimePay
else
    calculate regularPay
```

The previous examples can also be called **dual-alternative ifs**, because they contain two alternatives—the action taken when the tested condition is true and the action taken when it is false. Note that it is perfectly correct for one branch of the selection to be a "do nothing" branch. For example:

```
if it is raining then
    take anUmbrella
or
if employee belongs to dentalPlan then
    deduct $40 from employeeGrossPay
```

The previous examples are **single-alternative ifs**, and a diagram of their structure is shown in Figure 2-5. In these cases, you don't take any special action if it is not raining or if the employee does not belong to the dental plan. The case where nothing is done is often called the **null case**.

FIGURE 2-5: SINGLE-ALTERNATIVE DECISION STRUCTURE

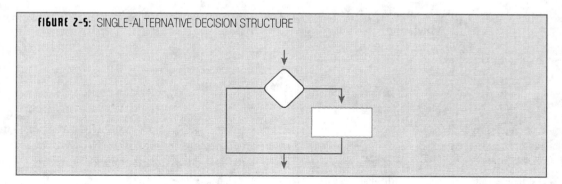

The third structure, shown in Figure 2-6, is a loop. In a **loop structure**, you ask a question; if the answer requires an action, you perform the action and ask the original question again. If the answer requires that the action be taken again, you take the action and then ask the original question again. This continues until the answer to the question is such that the action is no longer required; then you exit the structure. You may hear programmers refer to looping as **repetition** or **iteration**.

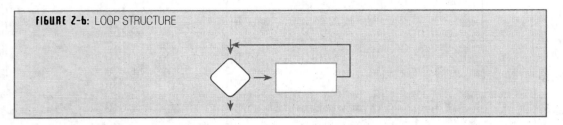

FIGURE 2-6: LOOP STRUCTURE

Some programmers call this structure a **do while** because it fits the following statement:

```
while testCondition continues to be true,
    do someProcess
```

You encounter examples of looping every day, as in:

```
while you continue to beHungry
    take anotherBiteOfFood
```

or

```
while unreadPages remain in the readingAssignment
    read another unreadPage
```

In a business program, you might write:

```
while quantityInInventory remains low
    continue to orderItems
```

or

```
while there are more retailPrices to be discounted
    compute a discount
```

All logic problems can be solved using only these three structures—sequence, selection, and looping. The three structures, of course, can be combined in an infinite number of ways. For example, you can have a sequence of steps followed by a selection, or a loop followed by a sequence. Attaching structures end-to-end is called **stacking** structures. For example, Figure 2-7 shows a structured flowchart achieved by stacking structures, and also shows pseudocode that might follow that flowchart logic.

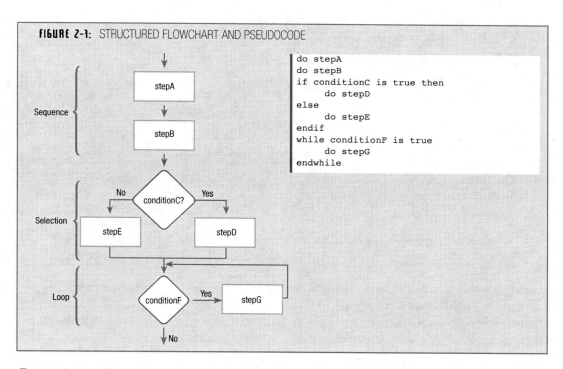

FIGURE 2-7: STRUCTURED FLOWCHART AND PSEUDOCODE

The pseudocode in Figure 2-7 shows two end-structure statements—endif and endwhile. You can use an endif statement to clearly show where the actions that depend on a decision end. The instruction that follows if occurs when its tested condition is true, the instruction that follows else occurs when the tested condition is false, and the instruction that follows the endif occurs in either case—it is not dependent on the if statement at all. In other words, statements beyond the endif statement are "outside" the decision structure. Similarly, you use an endwhile statement to show where a loop structure ends. In Figure 2-7, while conditionF continues to be true, stepG continues to execute. If any statements followed the endwhile statement, they would be outside of, and not a part of, the loop.

Besides stacking structures, you can replace any individual steps in a structured flowchart diagram or pseudocode segment with additional structures. In other words, any sequence, selection, or loop can contain other sequences, selections, or loops. For example, you can have a sequence of three steps on one side of a selection, as shown in Figure 2-8. Placing a structure within another structure is called **nesting** the structures.

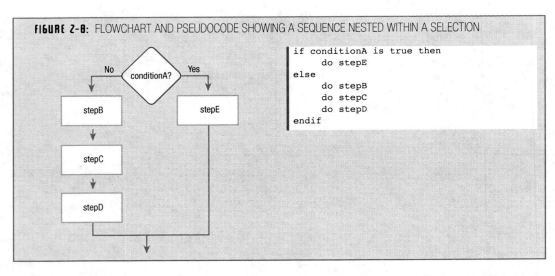

FIGURE 2-8: FLOWCHART AND PSEUDOCODE SHOWING A SEQUENCE NESTED WITHIN A SELECTION

```
if conditionA is true then
      do stepE
else
      do stepB
      do stepC
      do stepD
endif
```

When you write the pseudocode for the logic shown in Figure 2-8, the convention is to indent all statements that depend on one branch of the decision, as shown in the pseudocode. The indentation and the `endif` statement both show that all three statements (`do stepB`, `stepC`, and `stepD`) must execute if `conditionA` is not true. The three statements constitute a **block**, or group of statements that executes as a single unit.

In place of one of the steps in the sequence in Figure 2-8, you can insert a selection. In Figure 2-9, the process named `stepC` has been replaced with a selection structure that begins with a test of the condition named `conditionF`.

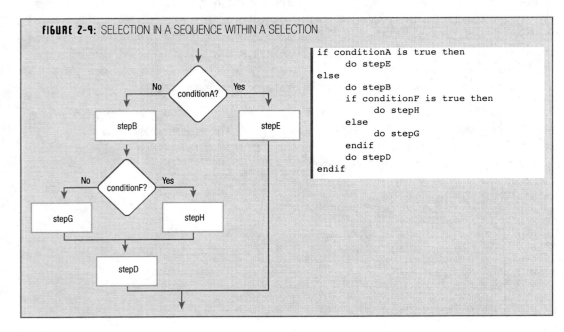

FIGURE 2-9: SELECTION IN A SEQUENCE WITHIN A SELECTION

```
if conditionA is true then
      do stepE
else
      do stepB
      if conditionF is true then
            do stepH
      else
            do stepG
      endif
      do stepD
endif
```

In the pseudocode shown in Figure 2-9, notice that `do stepB`, `if conditionF is true then`, `else`, and `do stepD` all align vertically with each other. This shows that they are all "on the same level." If you look at the same problem flowcharted in Figure 2-9, you see that you could draw a vertical line through the symbols containing `stepB`, `conditionF`, and `stepD`. The flowchart and the pseudocode represent exactly the same logic. The `stepH` and `stepG` processes, on the other hand, are one level "down"; they are dependent on the answer to the `conditionF` question. Therefore, the `do stepH` and `do stepG` statements are indented one additional level in the pseudocode.

Also notice that the pseudocode in Figure 2-9 has two `endif` statements. Each is aligned to correspond to an `if`. An `endif` always partners with the most recent `if` that does not already have an `endif` partner, and an `endif` should always align vertically with its `if` partner.

In place of `do stepH` on one side of the new selection in Figure 2-9, you can insert a loop. This loop, based on `conditionI`, appears inside the selection that is within the sequence that constitutes the "No" side of the original `conditionA` selection. In the pseudocode in Figure 2-10, notice that the `while` aligns with the `endwhile`, and that the entire `while` structure is indented within the true half of the `if` structure that begins with the decision based on `conditionF`. The indentation used in the pseudocode reflects the logic you can see laid out graphically in the flowchart.

FIGURE 2-10: FLOWCHART AND PSEUDOCODE FOR LOOP WITHIN SELECTION WITHIN SEQUENCE WITHIN SELECTION

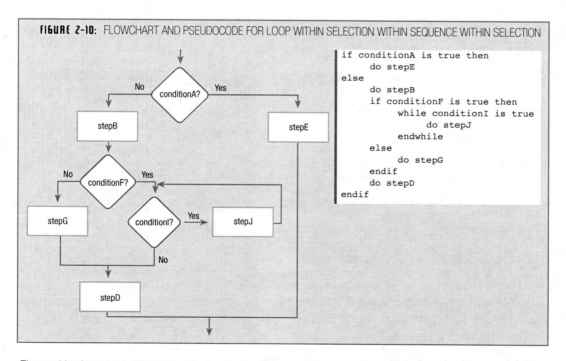

```
if conditionA is true then
    do stepE
else
    do stepB
    if conditionF is true then
        while conditionI is true
            do stepJ
        endwhile
    else
        do stepG
    endif
    do stepD
endif
```

The combinations are endless, but each of a structured program's segments is a sequence, a selection, or a loop. The three structures are shown together in Figure 2-11. Notice that each structure has one entry and one exit point. One structure can attach to another only at one of these entry or exit points.

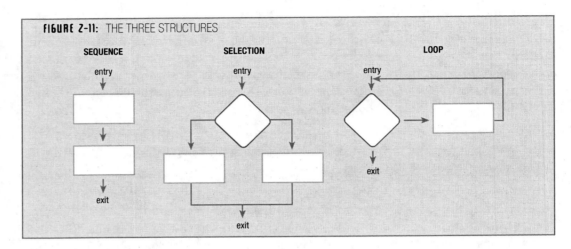

FIGURE 2-11: THE THREE STRUCTURES

In summary, a structured program has the following characteristics:

- A structured program includes only combinations of the three structures—sequence, selection, and loop.
- Structures can be stacked or connected to one another only at their entrance or exit points.
- Any structure can be nested within another structure.

USING THE PRIMING READ

For a program to be structured and also work the way you want it to, sometimes you need to add extra steps. The priming read is one kind of added step. A **priming read** or **priming input** is the first read or data input statement in a program. If a program will read 100 data records, you read the first data record in a statement that is separate from the other 99. You must do this to keep the program structured.

At the end of Chapter 1, you read about a program like the one in Figure 2-12. The program gets a number and checks for end of file. If it is not end of file, then the number is doubled, the answer is printed, and the next number is input.

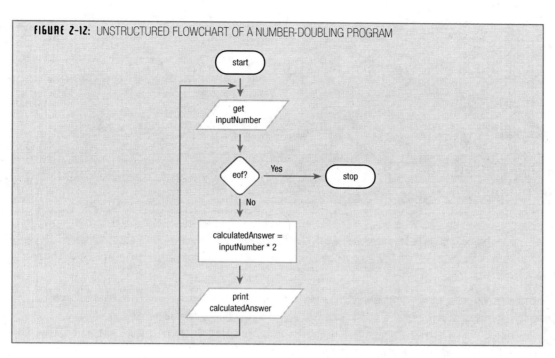

FIGURE 2-12: UNSTRUCTURED FLOWCHART OF A NUMBER-DOUBLING PROGRAM

Is the program represented by Figure 2-12 structured? At first, it might be hard to tell. The three allowed structures were illustrated in Figure 2-11.

The flowchart in Figure 2-12 does not look exactly like any of the three shapes shown in Figure 2-11. However, because you may stack and nest structures while retaining overall structure, it might be difficult to determine whether a flowchart as a whole is structured. It's easiest to analyze the flowchart in Figure 2-12 one step at a time. The beginning of the flowchart looks like Figure 2-13.

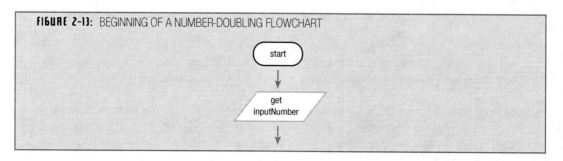

FIGURE 2-13: BEGINNING OF A NUMBER-DOUBLING FLOWCHART

Is this portion of the flowchart structured? Yes, it's a sequence. Adding the next step of the flowchart looks like Figure 2-14.

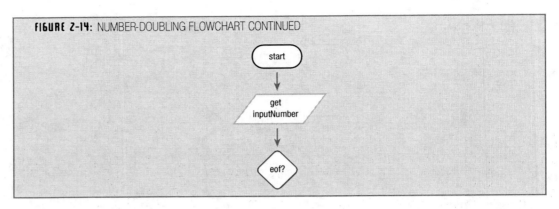

FIGURE 2-14: NUMBER-DOUBLING FLOWCHART CONTINUED

The sequence is finished; either a selection or a loop is starting. You might not know which one, but you do know the sequence is not continuing, because sequences can't contain questions. With a sequence, each step must follow without any opportunity to branch off. Therefore, which type of structure starts with the question in Figure 2-14? Is it a selection or a loop?

With a selection structure, the logic goes in one of two directions after the question, and then the flow comes back together; the question is not asked a second time. However, in a loop, if the answer to the question results in the loop being entered and the loop statements executing, then the logic returns to the question that started the loop; when the body of a loop executes, the question that controls the loop is always asked again.

In the doubling problem in the original Figure 2-12, if it is not `eof` (that is, if the end-of-file condition is not met), some math is done, an answer is printed, a new number is obtained, and the `eof` question is asked again. In other words, while the answer to the `eof` question continues to be *no*, eventually the logic will return to the `eof` question. (Another way to phrase this is that while it continues to be true that `eof` has not yet been reached, the logic keeps returning to the same question.) Therefore, the doubling problem contains a structure beginning with the `eof` question that is more like the beginning of a loop than it is like a selection.

The doubling problem *does* contain a loop, but it's not a structured loop. In a structured loop, the rules are:

1. You ask a question.
2. If the answer indicates you should perform a procedure, you do so.
3. If you perform the procedure, then you must go right back to repeat the question.

The flowchart in Figure 2-12 asks a question; if the answer is *no* (that is, while it is true that the `eof` condition has not been met), the program performs two tasks: it does the arithmetic and it prints the results. Doing two things is acceptable because two steps constitute a sequence, and it is fine to nest a structure within another structure. However, when the sequence ends, the logic doesn't flow right back to the question. Instead, it goes *above* the question to get another number. For the loop in Figure 2-12 to be a structured loop, the logic must return to the `eof` question when the sequence ends.

The flowchart in Figure 2-15 shows the flow of logic returning to the `eof` immediately after the sequence. Figure 2-15 shows a structured flowchart, but the flowchart has one major flaw—it doesn't do the job of continuously doubling numbers.

FIGURE 2-15: STRUCTURED, BUT NONFUNCTIONAL, FLOWCHART OF NUMBER-DOUBLING PROBLEM

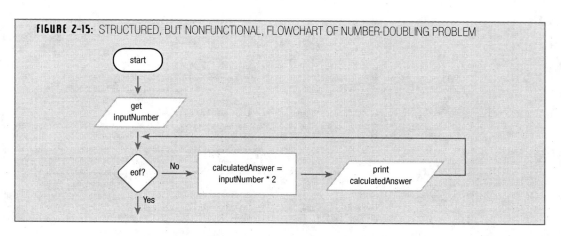

Follow the flowchart in Figure 2-15 through a typical program run. Suppose when the program starts, the user enters a 9 for the value of `inputNumber`. That's not `eof`, so the number doubles, and 18 prints out as the `calculatedAnswer`. Then the question `eof?` is asked again. It can't be `eof` because a new value representing the sentinel (ending) value can't be entered. The logic never returns to the `get inputNumber` step, so the value of `inputNumber` never changes. Therefore, 9 doubles again and the answer 18 prints again. It's still not `eof`, so the same steps are repeated. This goes on *forever*, with the answer 18 printing repeatedly. The program logic shown in Figure 2-15 is structured, but it doesn't work; the program in Figure 2-16 works, but it isn't structured!

TIP ☐ ☐ ☐ ☐   The loop in Figure 2-16 is not structured because in a structured loop, after the steps that execute within the loop, the flow of logic must return directly to the loop-controlling question. In Figure 2-16, the logic does not return to the loop-controlling question; instead it goes "too high" outside the loop to repeat the `get inputNumber` step.

FIGURE 2-16: FUNCTIONAL BUT NONSTRUCTURED FLOWCHART

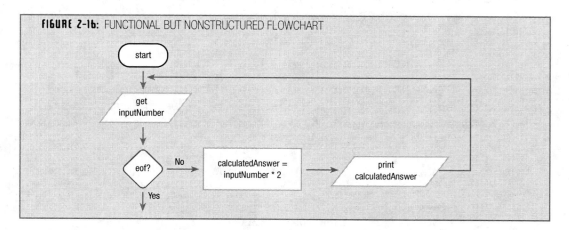

How can the number-doubling problem be both structured and work? Often, for a program to be structured, you must add something extra. In this case, it's an extra `get inputNumber` step. Consider the solution in Figure 2-17; it's structured, *and* it does what it's supposed to do! The program logic illustrated in Figure 2-17 contains a sequence and a loop. The loop contains another sequence.

FIGURE 2-17: FUNCTIONAL, STRUCTURED FLOWCHART AND PSEUDOCODE FOR THE NUMBER-DOUBLING PROBLEM

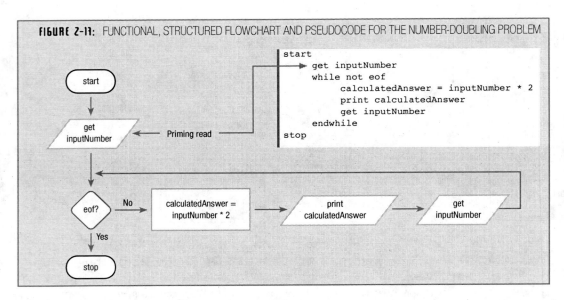

The additional `get inputNumber` step is typical in structured programs. The first of the two input steps is the priming input, or priming read. The term *priming* comes from the fact that the read is first, or *primary* (what gets the process going, as in "priming the pump"). The purpose of the priming read step is to control the upcoming loop that begins with the `eof` question. The last element within the structured loop gets the next, and all subsequent, input values. This is also typical in structured loops—the last step executed within the loop alters the condition tested in the question that begins the loop, which in this case is the `eof` question.

As an additional way to determine whether a flowchart segment is structured, you can try to write pseudocode for it. Examine the unstructured flowchart in Figure 2-12 again. To write pseudocode for it, you would begin with the following:

```
start
     get inputNumber
```

When you encounter the `eof` question in the flowchart, you know that either a selection or looping structure should begin. Because you return to a location higher in the flowchart when the answer to the `eof` question is *no* (that is, while the `not eof` condition continues to be *true*), you know that a loop is beginning. So you continue to write the pseudocode as follows:

```
start
     get inputNumber
     while not eof
          calculatedAnswer = inputNumber * 2
          print calculatedAnswer
```

Continuing, the step after `print calculatedAnswer` is `get inputNumber`. This ends the `while` loop that began with the `eof` question. So the pseudocode becomes:

```
start
    get inputNumber
    while not eof
        calculatedAnswer = inputNumber * 2
        print calculatedAnswer
        get inputNumber
    endwhile
stop
```

This pseudocode is identical to the pseudocode in Figure 2-17, and now matches the flowchart in the same figure. Creating the pseudocode requires you to repeat the `get inputNumber` statement. The structured pseudocode makes use of a priming read and forces the logic to become structured—a sequence followed by a loop that contains a sequence of three statements.

TIP □ □ □ □ | Years ago, programmers could avoid using structure by inserting a "go to" statement into their pseudocode. A "go to" statement would say something like "after print answer, go to the first get number box", and would be the equivalent of drawing an arrow starting after "print answer" and pointing directly to the first "get number" box in the flowchart. Because "go to" statements cause spaghetti code, they are not allowed in structured programming.

Figure 2-18 shows another way you might attempt to draw the logic for the number-doubling program. At first glance, the figure might seem to show an acceptable solution to the problem—it is structured, containing a single loop with a sequence of three steps within it, and it appears to eliminate the need for the priming input statement. When the program starts, the question `eof?` is asked. The answer is *no*, so the program gets an input number, doubles, and prints it. Then, if it is still not `eof`, the program gets another number, doubles it, and prints it. The program continues until `eof` is encountered when getting input. The last time the `get inputNumber` statement executes, it encounters `eof`, but the program does not stop—instead it calculates and prints one last time. This last output is extraneous—the `eof` value should not be doubled and printed. As a general rule, an `eof` question should always come immediately after an input statement. Therefore, the best solution to the number-doubling problem remains the one shown in Figure 2-17—the solution containing the priming input statement.

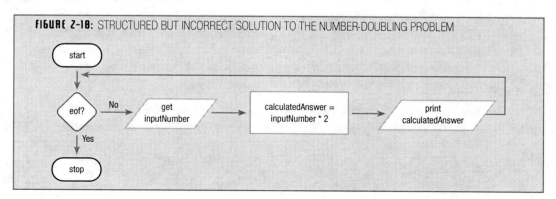

FIGURE 2-18: STRUCTURED BUT INCORRECT SOLUTION TO THE NUMBER-DOUBLING PROBLEM

TIP ▫ ▫ ▫ ▫ A few languages do not require the priming read. For example, programs written using the Visual Basic programming language can "look ahead" to determine if the end of file will be reached on the next input record. However, most programming languages cannot predict the end of file until an actual read operation is performed, and they require a priming read to properly handle file data.

UNDERSTANDING THE REASONS FOR STRUCTURE

At this point, you may very well be saying, "I liked the original doubling program just fine. I could follow it. Also, the first program had one less step in it, so it was less work. Who cares if a program is structured?"

Until you have some programming experience, it is difficult to appreciate the reasons for using only the three structures—sequence, selection, and loop. However, staying with these three structures is better for the following reasons:

- *Clarity*—The doubling program is a small program. As programs get bigger, they get more confusing if they're not structured.
- *Professionalism*—All other programmers (and programming teachers you might encounter) expect your programs to be structured. It's the way things are done professionally.
- *Efficiency*—Most newer computer languages are structured languages with syntax that lets you deal efficiently with sequence, selection, and looping. Older languages, such as assembly languages, COBOL, and RPG, were developed before the principles of structured programming were discovered. However, even programs that use those older languages can be written in a structured form, and structured programming is expected on the job today. Newer languages such as C#, C++, and Java enforce structure by their syntax.
- *Maintenance*—You, as well as other programmers, will find it easier to modify and maintain structured programs as changes are required in the future.
- *Modularity*—Structured programs can be easily broken into routines that can be assigned to any number of programmers. The routines are then pieced back together like modular furniture at each routine's single entry or exit point. Additionally, often a module can be used in multiple programs, saving development time in the new project.

Most programs that you purchase are huge, consisting of thousands or millions of statements. If you've worked with a word-processing program or spreadsheet, think of the number of menu options and keystroke combinations available to the user. Such programs are not the work of one programmer. The modular nature of structured programs means that work can be divided among many programmers; then the modules can be connected, and a large program can be developed much more quickly. Money is often a motivating factor—the more quickly you write a program and make it available for use, the sooner it begins making money for the developer.

Consider the college admissions program from the beginning of the chapter. It has been rewritten in structured form in Figure 2-19, and is easier to follow now. Figure 2-19 also shows structured pseudocode for the same problem.

TIP ▫ ▫ ▫ ▫ Don't be alarmed if it is difficult for you to follow the many nested ifs within the pseudocode in Figure 2-19. After you study the selection process in more detail, reading this type of pseudocode will become much easier for you.

FIGURE 2-19: FLOWCHART AND PSEUDOCODE OF STRUCTURED COLLEGE ADMISSION PROGRAM

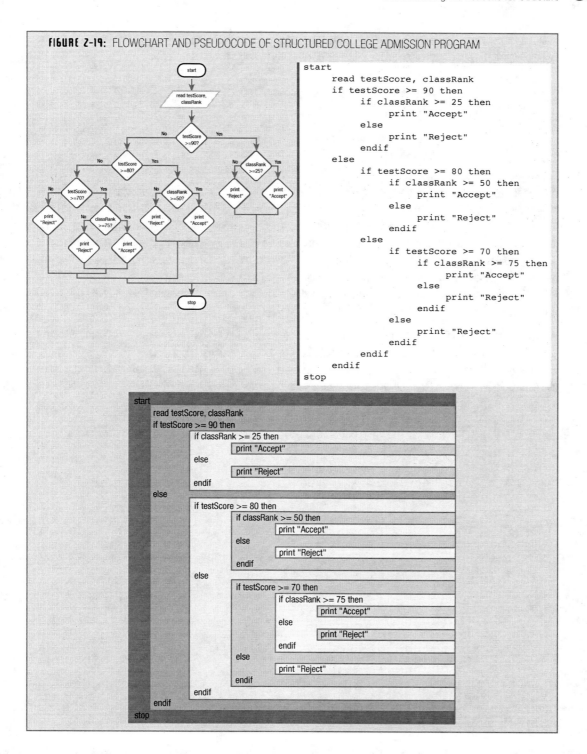

```
start
    read testScore, classRank
    if testScore >= 90 then
        if classRank >= 25 then
            print "Accept"
        else
            print "Reject"
        endif
    else
        if testScore >= 80 then
            if classRank >= 50 then
                print "Accept"
            else
                print "Reject"
            endif
        else
            if testScore >= 70 then
                if classRank >= 75 then
                    print "Accept"
                else
                    print "Reject"
                endif
            else
                print "Reject"
            endif
        endif
    endif
stop
```

In the lower portion of Figure 2-19, the pseudocode is repeated using colored backgrounds to help you identify the indentations that match, distinguishing the different levels of the nested structures.

TIP □ □ □ □ | As you examine Figure 2-19, notice that the bottoms of the three `testScore` decision structures join at the bottom of the diagram. These three joinings correspond to the last three `endif` statements in the pseudocode.

RECOGNIZING STRUCTURE

Any set of instructions can be expressed in a structured format. If you can teach someone how to perform any ordinary activity, then you can express it in a structured way. For example, suppose you wanted to teach a child how to play Rock, Paper, Scissors. In this game, two players simultaneously show each other one hand, in one of three positions—clenched in a fist, representing a rock; flat, representing a piece of paper; or with two fingers extended in a V, representing scissors. The goal is to guess which hand your opponent might show, so that you can show the hand that beats it. The rules are that a flat hand beats a fist (because a piece of paper can cover a rock), a fist beats a hand with two extended fingers (because a rock can smash a pair of scissors), and a hand with two extended fingers beats a flat hand (because scissors can cut paper). Figure 2-20 shows the pseudocode for the game.

Figure 2-20 shows a fairly complicated set of statements. Its purpose is not to teach you how to play a game (although you could learn how to play by following the logic), but rather to convince you that any task to which you can apply rules can be expressed logically using only combinations of sequence, selection, and looping. In this example, a game continues while a friend agrees to play, and within that loop, several decisions must be made in order to determine the winner.

FIGURE 2-20: PSEUDOCODE FOR THE ROCK, PAPER, SCISSORS GAME

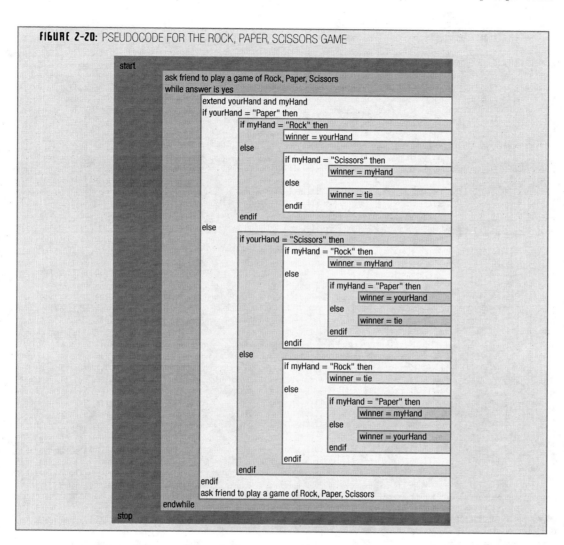

When you are just learning about structured program design, it is difficult to detect whether a flowchart of a program's logic is structured. For example, is the flowchart segment in Figure 2-21 structured?

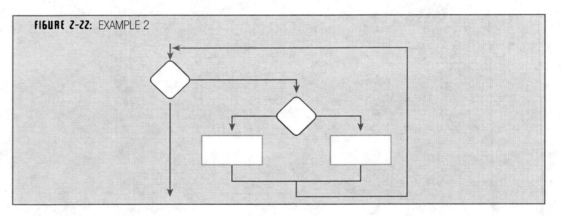

FIGURE 2-21: EXAMPLE 1

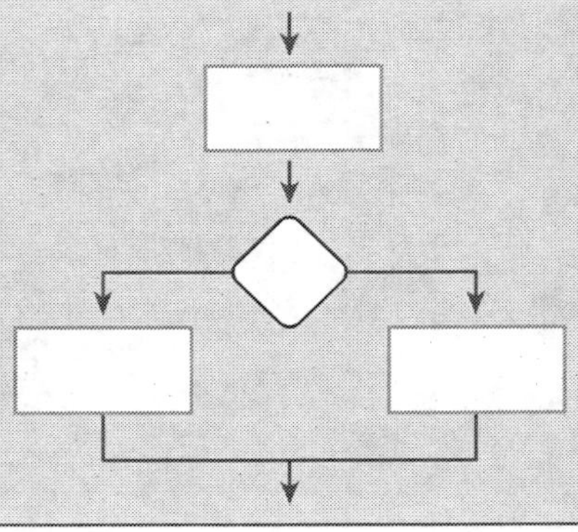

Yes, it is. It has a sequence and a selection structure.

Is the flowchart segment in Figure 2-22 structured?

FIGURE 2-22: EXAMPLE 2

Yes, it is. It has a loop, and within the loop is a selection.

Is the flowchart segment in Figure 2-23 structured? (The symbols are lettered so you can better follow the discussion.)

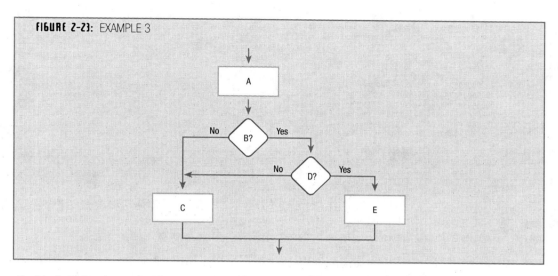

FIGURE 2-23: EXAMPLE 3

No, it isn't; it is not constructed from the three basic structures. One way to straighten out a flowchart segment that isn't structured is to use what you can call the "spaghetti bowl" method; that is, picture the flowchart as a bowl of spaghetti that you must untangle. Imagine you can grab one piece of pasta at the top of the bowl, and start pulling. As you "pull" each symbol out of the tangled mess, you can untangle the separate paths until the entire segment is structured. For example, with the diagram in Figure 2-23, if you start pulling at the top, you encounter a procedure box, labeled A. (See Figure 2-24.)

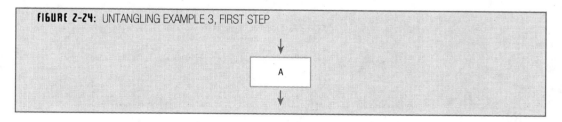

FIGURE 2-24: UNTANGLING EXAMPLE 3, FIRST STEP

A single process like A is part of an acceptable structure—it constitutes at least the beginning of a sequence structure. Imagine you continue pulling symbols from the tangled segment. The next item in the flowchart is a question that tests a condition labeled B, as you can see in Figure 2-25.

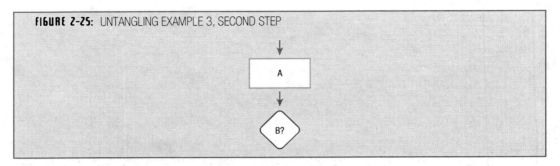

FIGURE 2-25: UNTANGLING EXAMPLE 3, SECOND STEP

At this point, you know the sequence that started with A has ended. Sequences never have decisions in them, so the sequence is finished; either a selection or a loop is beginning. A loop must return to the question at some later point. You can see from the original logic in Figure 2-23 that whether the answer to B is yes or no, the logic never returns to B. Therefore, B begins a selection structure, not a loop structure.

To continue detangling the logic, you pull up on the flowline that emerges from the left side (the "No" side) of Question B. You encounter C, as shown in Figure 2-26. When you continue beyond C, you reach the end of the flowchart.

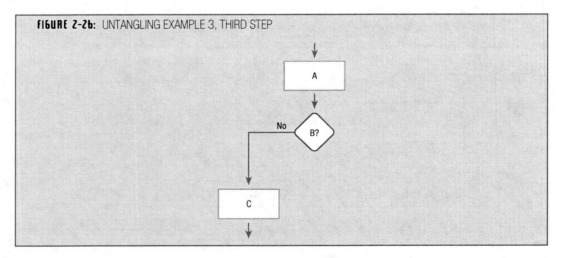

FIGURE 2-26: UNTANGLING EXAMPLE 3, THIRD STEP

Now you can turn your attention to the "Yes" side (the right side) of the condition tested in B. When you pull up on the right side, you encounter Question D. (See Figure 2-27.)

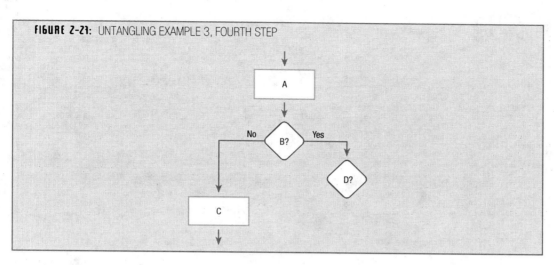

FIGURE 2-27: UNTANGLING EXAMPLE 3, FOURTH STEP

Follow the line on the left side of Question D. If the line is attached somewhere else, as it is (to Step C) in Figure 2-23, just untangle it by repeating the step that is tangled. (In this example, you repeat Step C to untangle it from the other usage of C.) Continue pulling on the flowline that emerges from Step C, and you reach the end of the program segment, as shown in Figure 2-28.

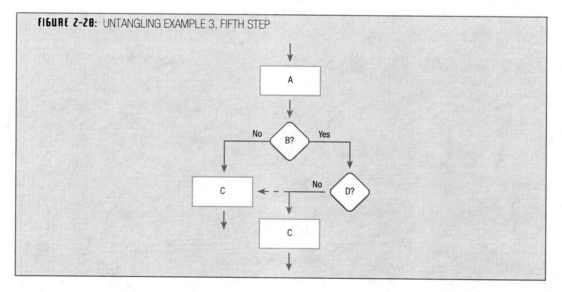

FIGURE 2-28: UNTANGLING EXAMPLE 3, FIFTH STEP

Now pull on the right side of Question D. Process E pops up, as shown in Figure 2-29; then you reach the end.

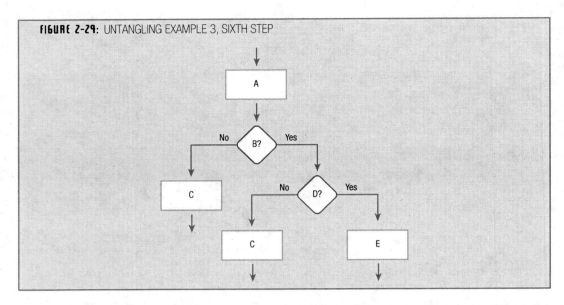

FIGURE 2-29: UNTANGLING EXAMPLE 3, SIXTH STEP

At this point, the untangled flowchart has three loose ends. The loose ends of Question D can be brought together to form a selection structure, then the loose ends of Question B can be brought together to form another selection structure. The result is the flowchart shown in Figure 2-30. The entire flowchart segment is structured—it has a sequence (A) followed by a selection inside a selection.

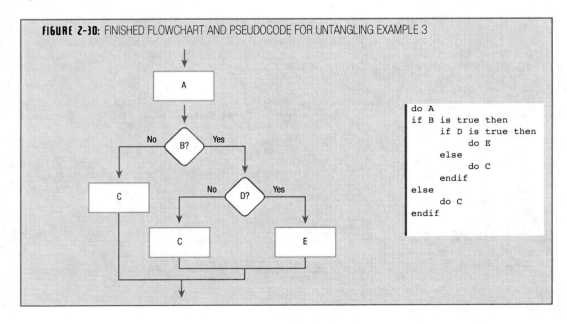

FIGURE 2-30: FINISHED FLOWCHART AND PSEUDOCODE FOR UNTANGLING EXAMPLE 3

```
do A
if B is true then
      if D is true then
            do E
      else
            do C
      endif
else
      do C
endif
```

TIP ☐ ☐ ☐ ☐   If you want to try structuring a very difficult example of an unstructured program, see Appendix A.

TWO SPECIAL STRUCTURES—CASE AND DO UNTIL

TIP ☐ ☐ ☐ ☐   You can skip this section for now without any loss in continuity. Your instructor may prefer to discuss the case structure with the Decision chapter, and the do until loop with the Looping chapter.

You can solve any logic problem you might encounter using only the three structures: sequence, selection, and loop. However, many programming languages allow two more structures: the case structure and the do until loop. These structures are never *needed* to solve any problem—you can always use a series of selections instead of the case structure, and you can always use a sequence plus a do while loop in place of the do until loop. However, sometimes these two additional structures—the case and the do until—are convenient. Programmers consider them both to be acceptable, legal structures.

THE CASE STRUCTURE

You can use the **case structure** when there are several distinct possible values for a single variable you are testing, and each value requires a different course of action. Suppose you administer a school at which tuition is $75, $50, $30, or $10 per credit hour, depending on whether a student is a freshman, sophomore, junior, or senior. The structured flowchart in Figure 2-31 shows a series of decisions that assigns the correct tuition to a student.

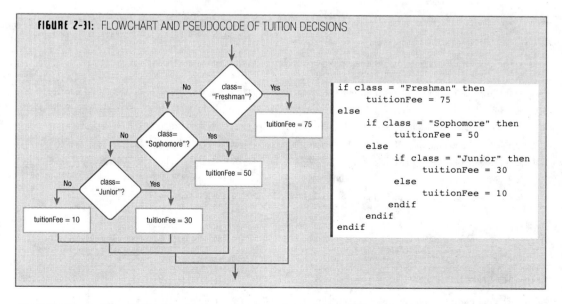

FIGURE 2-31: FLOWCHART AND PSEUDOCODE OF TUITION DECISIONS

```
if class = "Freshman" then
    tuitionFee = 75
else
    if class = "Sophomore" then
        tuitionFee = 50
    else
        if class = "Junior" then
            tuitionFee = 30
        else
            tuitionFee = 10
        endif
    endif
endif
```

The logic shown in Figure 2-31 is absolutely correct and completely structured. The `class="Junior"` selection structure is contained within the `class="Sophomore"` structure, which is contained within the `class="Freshman"` structure. Note that there is no need to ask if a student is a senior, because if a student is not a freshman, sophomore, or junior, it is assumed the student is a senior.

Even though the program segments in Figure 2-31 are correct and structured, many programming languages permit using a case structure, as shown in Figure 2-32. When using the case structure, you test a variable against a series of values, taking appropriate action based on the variable's value. To many, such programs seem easier to read, and the case structure is allowed because the same results *could* be achieved with a series of structured selections (thus making the program structured). That is, if the first program is structured and the second one reflects the first one point by point, then the second one must be structured also.

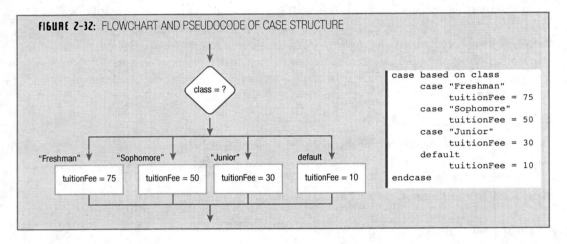

FIGURE 2-32: FLOWCHART AND PSEUDOCODE OF CASE STRUCTURE

```
case based on class
    case "Freshman"
        tuitionFee = 75
    case "Sophomore"
        tuitionFee = 50
    case "Junior"
        tuitionFee = 30
    default
        tuitionFee = 10
endcase
```

TIP □ □ □ □ | The term "default" used in Figure 2-32 means "if none of the other cases were true." Each programming language you learn may use a different syntax for the default case.

Even though a programming language permits you to use the case structure, you should understand that the case structure is just a convenience that might make a flowchart, pseudocode, or actual program code easier to understand at first glance. When you write a series of decisions using the case structure, the computer still makes a series of individual decisions, just as though you had used many if-then-else combinations. In other words, you might prefer looking at the diagram in Figure 2-32 to understand the tuition fees charged by a school, but a computer actually makes the decisions as shown in Figure 2-31—one at a time. When you write your own programs, it is always acceptable to express a complicated decision-making process as a series of individual selections.

TIP □ □ □ □ | You usually use the case structure only when a series of decisions is based on different values stored in a single variable. If multiple variables are tested, then most programmers use a series of decisions.

THE DO UNTIL LOOP

Recall that a structured loop (often called a do while) looks like Figure 2-33. A special case loop called a do until loop looks like Figure 2-34.

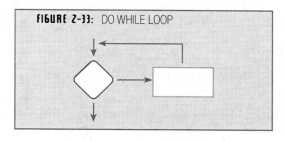

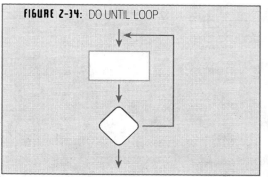

An important difference exists between these two structures. In a do while loop, you ask a question and, depending on the answer, you might or might not enter the loop to execute the loop's procedure. Conversely, in a **do until loop**, you ensure that the procedure executes at least once; then, depending on the answer to the controlling question, the loop may or may not execute additional times.

TIP □ □ □ □ | In a do while loop, the question that controls a loop comes at the beginning, or "top," of the loop body. In a do until loop, the question that controls the loop comes at the end, or "bottom," of the loop body.

You encounter examples of do until looping every day. For example:

```
do
        pay bills
until all bills are paid
```

and

```
do
        wash dishes
until all dishes are washed
```

In these examples, the activity (paying bills or washing dishes) must occur at least one time. You ask the question that determines whether you continue only after the activity has been executed at least one time.

You can duplicate the same series of events generated by any do until loop by creating a sequence followed by a do while loop. For example:

```
pay bills
while there are more bills to pay
        pay bills
endwhile
```

Consider the flowcharts and pseudocode in Figures 2-35 and 2-36.

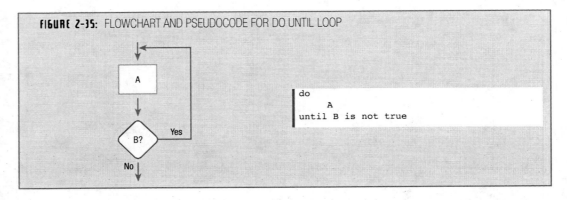

FIGURE 2-35: FLOWCHART AND PSEUDOCODE FOR DO UNTIL LOOP

```
do
     A
until B is not true
```

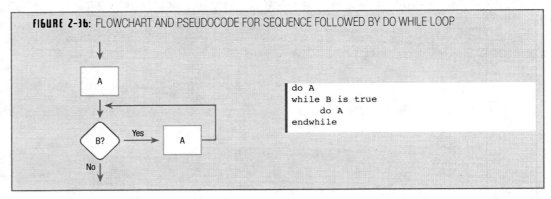

FIGURE 2-36: FLOWCHART AND PSEUDOCODE FOR SEQUENCE FOLLOWED BY DO WHILE LOOP

```
do A
while B is true
     do A
endwhile
```

In Figure 2-35, A is done, and then B is asked. If B is yes, then A is done and B is asked again. In Figure 2-36, A is done, and then B is asked. If B is yes, then A is done and B is asked again. In other words, both flowcharts and pseudocode segments do exactly the same thing.

Because programmers understand that a do until can be expressed with a sequence followed by a do while, most languages allow the do until. Again, you are never required to use a do until; you can always accomplish the same events with a sequence followed by a do while.

Figure 2-37 shows an unstructured loop. It is neither a do while loop (that begins with a decision and, after an action, returns to the decision), nor a do until loop (that begins with an action and ends with a decision that might repeat the action). Instead, it begins like a do until, with a process followed by a decision, but one branch of the decision does not repeat the initial process; instead, it performs an additional new action before repeating the initial process. If you need to use the logic shown in Figure 2-37—performing a task, asking a question, and perhaps performing an additional task before looping back to the first process—then the way to make the logic structured is to repeat the initial process within the loop, at the end of the loop. Figure 2-38 shows the same logic as Figure 2-37, but now it is structured logic, with a sequence of two actions occurring within the loop. Does this diagram look familiar to you? It uses the same technique of repeating a needed step that you saw earlier in this chapter, when you learned the rationale for the priming read.

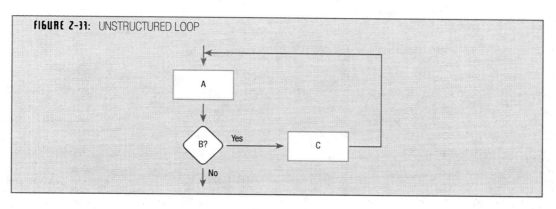

FIGURE 2-37: UNSTRUCTURED LOOP

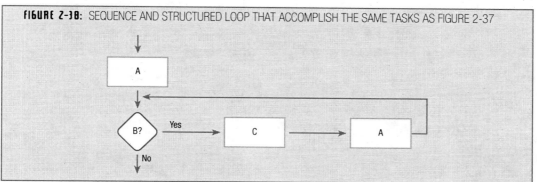

FIGURE 2-38: SEQUENCE AND STRUCTURED LOOP THAT ACCOMPLISH THE SAME TASKS AS FIGURE 2-37

TIP □ □ □ □   It is difficult for beginning programmers to distinguish between do while and do until loops. You can think of a do while loop as one that continues to execute while a condition remains true—for example, while not end of file is true, process records, or while hungry is true, eat food. On the other hand, a do until loop continues until some condition becomes false—for example, address envelopes until there are no more envelopes. When you use a do until loop, at least one performance of the action always occurs.

CHAPTER SUMMARY

- ☐ The popular name for snarled program statements is spaghetti code.

- ☐ Clearer programs can be constructed using only three basic structures: sequence, selection, and loop. These three structures can be combined in an infinite number of ways by stacking and nesting them. Each structure has one entry and one exit point; one structure can attach to another only at one of these entry or exit points.

- ☐ A priming read or priming input is the first read or data input statement prior to beginning a structured loop. The last step within the loop gets the next, and all subsequent, input values.

- ☐ You use structured techniques to promote clarity, professionalism, efficiency, and modularity.

- ☐ One way to straighten a flowchart segment that isn't structured is to imagine the flowchart as a bowl of spaghetti that you must untangle.

- ☐ You can use a case structure when there are several distinct possible values for a variable you are testing. When you write a series of decisions using the case structure, the computer still makes a series of individual decisions.

- ☐ In a do while loop, you ask a question and, depending on the answer, you might never enter the loop to execute the loop's procedure. In a do until loop, you ensure that the procedure executes at least once. You can duplicate the same series of events generated by any do until loop by creating a sequence followed by a do while loop.

KEY TERMS

Spaghetti code is snarled, unstructured program logic.

A structure is a basic unit of programming logic; each structure is a sequence, selection, or loop.

With a sequence structure, you perform an action or event, and then you perform the next action, in order. A sequence can contain any number of events, but there is no chance to branch off and skip any of the events.

With a selection, or decision, structure, you ask a question, and, depending on the answer, you take one of two courses of action. Then, no matter which path you follow, you continue with the next event.

An if-then-else is another name for a selection structure.

Dual-alternative ifs define one action to be taken when the tested condition is true, and another action to be taken when it is false.

Single-alternative ifs take action on just one branch of the decision.

The null case is the branch of a decision in which no action is taken.

With a loop structure, you ask a question; if the answer requires an action, you perform the action and ask the original question again.

Repetition and iteration are alternate names for a loop structure.

A do while is a loop in which a process continues while some condition continues to be true.

Attaching structures end-to-end is called stacking structures.

Placing a structure within another structure is called nesting the structures.

A block is a group of statements that execute as a single unit.

A priming read or priming input is the first read or data input statement in a program.

You can use the case structure when there are several distinct possible values for a single variable you are testing, and each requires a different course of action.

In a do until loop, you ensure that a procedure executes at least once; then, depending on the answer to the controlling question, the loop may or may not execute additional times.

REVIEW QUESTIONS

1. **Snarled program logic is called _____ code.**
   a. snake
   b. spaghetti
   c. string
   d. gnarly

2. **A sequence structure can contain _____.**
   a. only one event
   b. exactly three events
   c. no more than three events
   d. any number of events

3. **Which of the following is *not* another term for a selection structure?**
   a. decision structure
   b. if-then-else structure
   c. loop structure
   d. dual-alternative if structure

4. **The structure in which you ask a question, and, depending on the answer, take some action, then ask the question again can be called all of the following except _____.**
   a. if-then-else
   b. loop
   c. repetition
   d. iteration

5. **Placing a structure within another structure is called _____ the structures.**
   a. stacking
   b. nesting
   c. building
   d. untangling

6. **Attaching structures end-to-end is called _____.**
   a. stacking
   b. nesting
   c. building
   d. untangling

7. **The statement `if age >= 65 then seniorDiscount = "yes"` is an example of a _____.**
   a. single-alternative if
   b. loop
   c. dual-alternative if
   d. sequence

8. **The statement `while temperature remains below 60, leave the furnace on` is an example of a _____.**
   a. single-alternative if
   b. loop
   c. dual-alternative if
   d. sequence

9. **The statement `if age < 13 then movieTicket = 4.00 else movieTicket = 8.50` is an example of a _____.**
   a. single-alternative if
   b. loop
   c. dual-alternative if
   d. sequence

10. **Which of the following attributes do all three basic structures share?**
    a. Their flowcharts all contain exactly three processing symbols.
    b. They all contain a decision.
    c. They all begin with a process.
    d. They all have one entry and one exit point.

11. **The first input statement in a program _____.**
    a. is called a priming input
    b. cannot result in `eof`
    c. is the only part of a program allowed to be unstructured
    d. executes hundreds or even thousands of times in most business programs

12. **A group of statements that execute as a unit is a _____.**
    a. cohort
    b. family
    c. sequence
    d. block

13. **Which of the following is acceptable in a structured program?**
    a. placing a sequence within the true half of a dual-alternative decision
    b. placing a decision within a loop

c. placing a loop within one of the steps in a sequence

d. All of these are acceptable.

14. **Which of the following is *not* a reason for enforcing structure rules in computer programs?**

a. Structured programs are clearer to understand than unstructured ones.

b. Other professional programmers will expect programs to be structured.

c. Structured programs can be broken into modules easily.

d. Structured programs usually are shorter than unstructured ones.

15. **Which of the following is *not* a benefit of modularizing programs?**

a. Modular programs are easier to read and understand than nonmodular ones.

b. Modular components are reusable in other programs.

c. If you use modules, you can ignore the rules of structure.

d. Multiple programmers can work on different modules at the same time.

16. **Which of the following is true of structured logic?**

a. Any task can be described using the three structures.

b. You can use structured logic with newer programming languages, such as Java and C#, but not with older ones.

c. Structured programs require that you break the code into easy-to-handle modules.

d. All of these are true.

17. **The structure that you can use when you must make a decision with several possible outcomes, depending on the value of a single variable, is the _____.**

a. multiple-alternative if structure

b. case structure

c. do while structure

d. do until structure

18. **Which type of loop ensures that an action will take place at least one time?**

a. a do until loop

b. a do while loop

c. a do over loop

d. any structured loop

19. **A do until loop can always be converted to _____.**

a. a do while followed by a sequence

b. a sequence followed by a do while

c. a case structure

d. a selection followed by a do while

20. **Which of the following is never required by any program?**

a. a do while

b. a do until

c. a selection

d. a sequence

EXERCISES

1. **Match the term with the structure diagram. (Because the structures go by more than one name, there are more terms than diagrams.)**

   1. sequence   5. decision
   2. selection   6. if-then-else
   3. loop   7. iteration
   4. do while

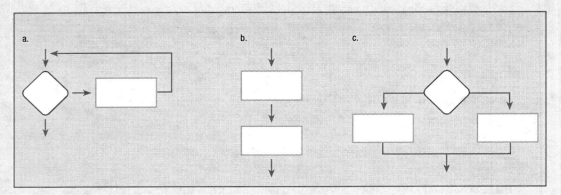

2. **Match the term with the pseudocode segment. (Because the structures go by more than one name, there are more terms than pseudocode segments.)**

   1. sequence   4. decision
   2. selection   5. if-then-else
   3. loop   6. iteration

   ```
   a. while not eof
          print theAnswer
      endwhile
   b. if inventoryQuantity  >  0 then
          do fillOrderProcess
      else
          do backOrderNotification
      endif
   c. do localTaxCalculation
      do stateTaxCalculation
      do federalTaxCalculation
   ```

3. Is each of the following segments structured, or unstructured? If unstructured, redraw it so that it does the same thing but is structured.

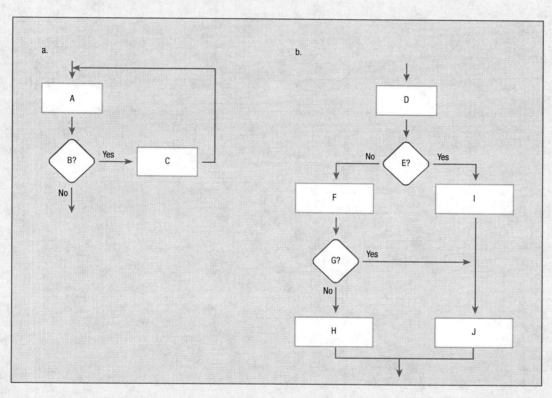

a.

b.

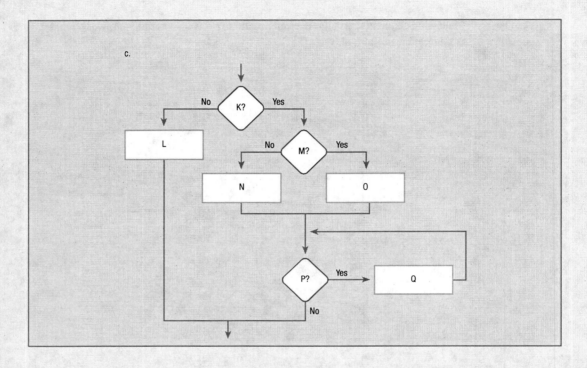

c.

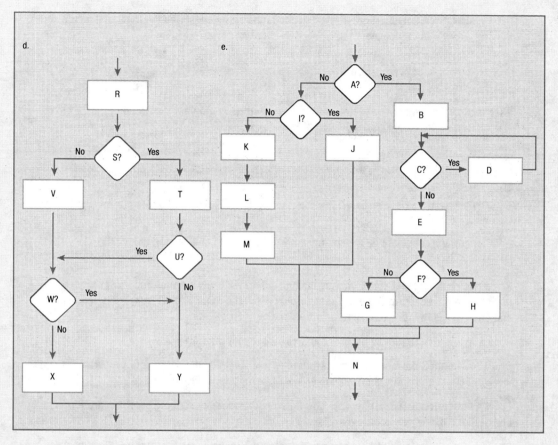

d.

e.

4.   **Write pseudocode for each example (a through e) in Exercise 3.**

5.   **Assume you have created a mechanical arm that can hold a pen. The arm can perform the following tasks:**

   ☐ Lower the pen to a piece of paper.
   ☐ Raise the pen from the paper.
   ☐ Move the pen one inch along a straight line. (If the pen is lowered, this action draws a one-inch line from left to right; if the pen is raised, this action just repositions the pen one inch to the right.)
   ☐ Turn 90 degrees to the right.
   ☐ Draw a circle that is one inch in diameter.

Draw a structured flowchart or write pseudocode that would describe the logic that would cause the arm to draw the following:

a. a one-inch square
b. a two-inch by one-inch rectangle
c. a string of three beads

Have a fellow student act as the mechanical arm and carry out your instructions.

6. **Assume you have created a mechanical robot that can perform the following tasks:**

   ☐ Stand up.
   ☐ Sit down.
   ☐ Turn left 90 degrees.
   ☐ Turn right 90 degrees.
   ☐ Take a step.

   Additionally, the robot can determine the answer to one test condition:

   ☐ Am I touching something?

   Place two chairs 20 feet apart, directly facing each other. Draw a structured flowchart or write pseudocode that describes the logic that would allow the robot to start from a sitting position in one chair, cross the room, and end up sitting in the other chair.

   Have a fellow student act as the robot and carry out your instructions.

7. **Draw a structured flowchart or write structured pseudocode describing your preparation to go to work or school in the morning. Include at least two decisions and two loops.**

8. **Draw a structured flowchart or write structured pseudocode describing your preparation to go to bed at night. Include at least two decisions and two loops.**

9. **Choose a very simple children's game and describe its logic, using a structured flowchart or pseudocode. For example, you might try to explain Musical Chairs; Duck, Duck, Goose; the card game War; or the elimination game Eenie, Meenie, Minie, Moe.**

10. **Draw a structured flowchart or write structured pseudocode describing how your paycheck is calculated. Include at least two decisions.**

11. **Draw a structured flowchart or write structured pseudocode describing the steps a retail store employee should follow to process a customer purchase. Include at least two decisions.**

3

MODULES, HIERARCHY CHARTS, AND DOCUMENTATION

After studying Chapter 3, you should be able to:

☐ Describe the advantages of modularization

☐ Modularize a program

☐ Understand how a module can call another module

☐ Explain how to declare variables

☐ Create hierarchy charts

☐ Understand documentation

☐ Create print charts

☐ Interpret file descriptions

☐ Understand the attributes of complete documentation

MODULES, SUBROUTINES, PROCEDURES, FUNCTIONS, OR METHODS

Programmers seldom write programs as one long series of steps. Instead, they break the programming problem down into reasonable units, and tackle one small task at a time. These reasonable units are called **modules**. Programmers also refer to them as **subroutines**, **procedures**, **functions**, or **methods**.

 The name that programmers use for their modules usually reflects the programming language they use. COBOL, RPG, and BASIC programmers are most likely to use "subroutine." Pascal and Visual Basic programmers use "procedure" (or "subprocedure"). C and C++ programmers call their modules "functions," whereas C#, Java, and other object-oriented language programmers are more likely to use "method."

The process of breaking a large program into modules is called **modularization**. You are never required to break a large program into modules, but there are at least four reasons for doing so:

- Modularization provides abstraction.
- Modularization allows multiple programmers to work on a problem.
- Modularization allows you to reuse your work.
- Modularization makes it easier to identify structures.

MODULARIZATION PROVIDES ABSTRACTION

One reason modularized programs are easier to understand is that they enable a programmer to see the big picture. **Abstraction** is the process of paying attention to important properties while ignoring nonessential details. Abstraction is selective ignorance. Life would be tedious without abstraction. For example, you can create a list of things to accomplish today:

```
Do laundry
Call Aunt Nan
Start term paper
```

Without abstraction, the list of chores would begin:

```
Pick up laundry basket
Put laundry basket in car
Drive to laundromat
Get out of car with basket
Walk into laundromat
Set basket down
Find quarters for washing machine
. . .and so on.
```

You might list a dozen more steps before you finish the laundry and move on to the second chore on your original list. If you had to consider every small, **low-level** detail of every task in your day, you would probably never make it out of bed in the morning. Using a higher-level, more abstract list makes your day manageable. Abstraction makes complex tasks look simple.

TIP ☐ ☐ ☐ ☐ | Abstract artists create paintings in which they see only the "big picture"—color and form—and ignore the details. Abstraction has a similar meaning among programmers.

Likewise, some level of abstraction occurs in every computer program. Fifty years ago, a programmer had to understand the low-level circuitry instructions the computer used. But now, newer **high-level** programming languages allow you to use English-like vocabulary in which one broad statement corresponds to dozens of machine instructions. No matter which high-level programming language you use, if you display a message on the monitor, you are never required to understand how a monitor works to create each pixel on the screen. You write an instruction like `print message` and the details of the hardware operations are handled for you.

Modules or subroutines provide another way to achieve abstraction. For example, a payroll program can call a module named `computeFederalWithholdingTax`. You can write the mathematical details of the function later, some-one else can write them, or you can purchase them from an outside source. When you plan your main payroll program, your only concern is that a federal withholding tax will have to be calculated; you save the details for later.

MODULARIZATION ALLOWS MULTIPLE PROGRAMMERS TO WORK ON A PROBLEM

When you dissect any large task into modules, you gain the ability to divide the task among various people. Rarely does a single programmer write a commercial program that you buy off the shelf. Consider any word-processing, spread-sheet, or database program you have used. Each program has so many options, and responds to user selections in so many possible ways, that it would take years for a single programmer to write all the instructions. Professional software developers can write new programs in weeks or months, instead of years, by dividing large programs into modules and assigning each module to an individual programmer or programming team.

MODULARIZATION ALLOWS YOU TO REUSE YOUR WORK

If a subroutine or function is useful and well-written, you may want to use it more than once within a program or in other programs. For example, a routine that checks the current month to make sure it is valid (not lower than 1 or higher than 12) is useful in many programs written for a business. A program that uses a personnel file containing each employee's birth date, hire date, last promotion date, and termination date can use the month-validation module four times with each employee record. Other programs in an organization can also use the module; these include programs that ship customer orders, plan employees' birthday parties, and calculate when loan payments should be made. If you write the month-checking instructions so they are entangled with other statements in a program, they are difficult to extract and reuse. On the other hand, if you place the instructions in their own module, the unit is easy-to-use and portable to other applications.

You can find many real-world examples of **reusability**. When you build a house, you don't invent plumbing and heating systems; you incorporate systems with proven designs. This certainly reduces the time and effort it takes to build a house. Assuming the plumbing and electrical systems you choose are also in service in other houses, they also improve the **reliability** of your house's systems—they have been tested under a variety of circumstances and have been proven to function correctly. Similarly, software that is reusable is more reliable, yet saves time and money. If you create the functional components of your programs as stand-alone modules and test them in your current programs, much of the work will already be done when you use the modules in future applications.

MODULARIZATION MAKES IT EASIER TO IDENTIFY STRUCTURES

When you combine several programming tasks into modules, it may be easier for you to identify structures. For example, you learned in Chapter 2 that the selection structure looks like Figure 3-1.

When you work with a program segment that looks like Figure 3-2, you may question whether it is structured. If you can modularize some of the statements and give them a more abstract group name, as in Figure 3-3, it is easier to see that the program involves a major selection and that the program segment is structured.

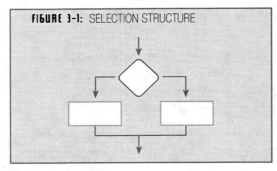

FIGURE 3-1: SELECTION STRUCTURE

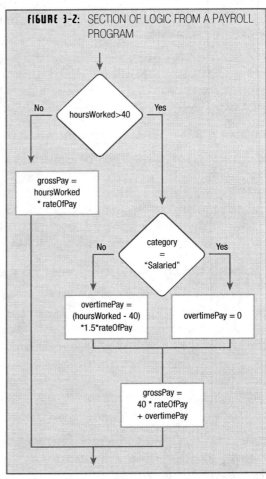

FIGURE 3-2: SECTION OF LOGIC FROM A PAYROLL PROGRAM

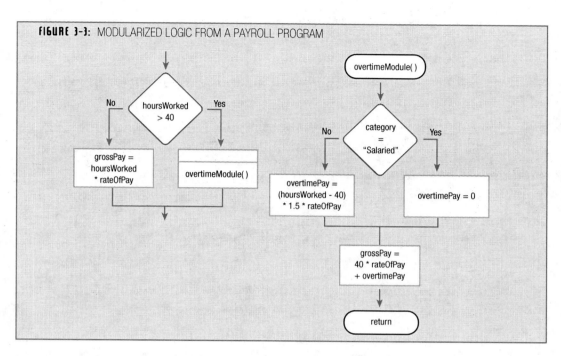

FIGURE 3-3: MODULARIZED LOGIC FROM A PAYROLL PROGRAM

The single program segment shown in Figure 3-2 accomplishes the same steps as the two program segments shown together in Figure 3-3; both program segments are structured. The structure may be more obvious in the program segments in Figure 3-3 because you can see two distinct parts—a decision structure calls a subroutine named `overtimeModule()`, and that module contains another decision structure, which is followed by a sequence. Neither of the program segments shown in Figures 3-2 and 3-3 is superior to the other in terms of functionality, but you may prefer to modularize to help you identify structures.

TIP □ □ □ □ A professional programmer will never modularize simply to *identify* whether a program is structured—he or she modularizes for reasons of abstraction, ease of dividing the work, and reusability. However, for a beginning programmer, being able to see and identify structure is important.

MODULARIZING A PROGRAM

When you create a module or subroutine, you give it a name. The rules for naming modules are different in every programming language, but they often are similar to the language's rules for variable names. In this text, module names follow the same two rules used for variable names:

- Module names must be one word.
- Module names should have some meaning.

Additionally, in this text, module names are followed by a set of parentheses. This will help you distinguish module names from variable names. This style corresponds to the way modules are named in many programming languages, such as Java, C++, C#, and Pascal.

Table 3-1 lists some possible module names for a module that calculates an employee's gross pay, and provides a rationale for the appropriateness of each one.

TABLE 3-1: VALID AND INVALID MODULE NAMES FOR A MODULE THAT CALCULATES AN EMPLOYEE'S GROSS PAY

Suggested module names for a module that calculates an employee's gross pay	Comments
calculateGrossPay()	Good
calculateGross()	Good—most people would interpret "Gross" to be short for "Gross pay"
calGrPy()	Legal, but cryptic
calculateGrossPayForOneEmployee()	Legal, but awkward
calculate gross()	Not legal—embedded space
calculategrosspay()	Legal, but hard to read without camel casing

TIP □ □ □ □ As you learn more about modules in specific programming languages, you will find that you sometimes place variable names within the parentheses of module names. Any variables enclosed in the parentheses contain information you want to send to the module. For now, the parentheses we use at the end of module names will be empty.

TIP □ □ □ □ Most programming languages require that module names begin with an alphabetic character. This text follows that convention.

TIP □ □ □ □ Although it is not a requirement of any programming language, it frequently makes sense to use a verb as all or part of a module's name, because modules perform some action. Typical module names begin with words such as get, compute, and print. When you program in visual languages that use screen components such as buttons and text boxes, the module names frequently contain verbs representing user actions, such as click and drag.

When a program uses a module, you can refer to the main program as the **calling program**, because it "calls" the module's name when it wants to use the module. The flowchart symbol used to call a subroutine is a rectangle with a bar across the top. You place the name of the module you are calling inside the rectangle.

TIP □ □ □ □ Instead of placing only the name of the module they are calling in the flowchart, many programmers insert an appropriate verb, such as "perform" or "do," before the module name.

TIP □ □ □ □ A module can call another module, and the called module can call another. The number of chained calls is limited only by the amount of memory available on your computer.

You draw each module separately with its own sentinel symbols. The symbol that is the equivalent of the `start` symbol in a program contains the name of the module. This name must be identical to the name used in the calling program. The symbol that is the equivalent of the `stop` symbol in a program does not contain "stop"; after all, the program is not ending. Instead, the module ends with a "gentler," less final term, such as `exit` or `return`. These words correctly indicate that when the module ends, the logical progression of statements will return to the calling program.

A flowchart and pseudocode for a program that calculates the arithmetic average of two numbers a user enters can look like Figure 3-4. Here the **main program**, or program that runs from start to stop and calls other modules, calls three modules named `getInput()`, `calculateAverage()`, and `printResult()`.

The logic of the program in Figure 3-4 proceeds as follows:

1. The main program starts.
2. The main program calls the `getInput()` module.
3. Within the `getInput()` module, the prompt "Enter a number" appears. A **prompt** is a message that is displayed on a monitor, asking the user for a response.
4. Within the `getInput()` module, the program accepts a value into the `firstNumber` variable.
5. Within the `getInput()` module, the prompt "Enter another number" appears.
6. Within the `getInput()` module, the program accepts a value into the `secondNumber` variable.
7. The `getInput()` module ends, and control returns to the main calling program.
8. The main program calls the `calculateAverage()` module.
9. Within the `calculateAverage()` module, a value for the variable `average` is calculated.
10. The `calculateAverage()` module ends, and control returns to the main calling program.
11. The main program calls the `printResult()` module.
12. Within the `printResult()` module, the value of `average` is displayed.
13. Within the `printResult()` module, a thank-you message is displayed.
14. The `printResult()` module ends, and control returns to the main calling program.
15. The main program ends.

Whenever a main program calls a module, the logic transfers to the module. When the module ends, the logical flow transfers back to the main calling program and resumes where it left off.

TIP □ □ □ □ | The computer keeps track of the correct memory address to which it should return after executing a module by recording the memory address in a location known as the *stack*.

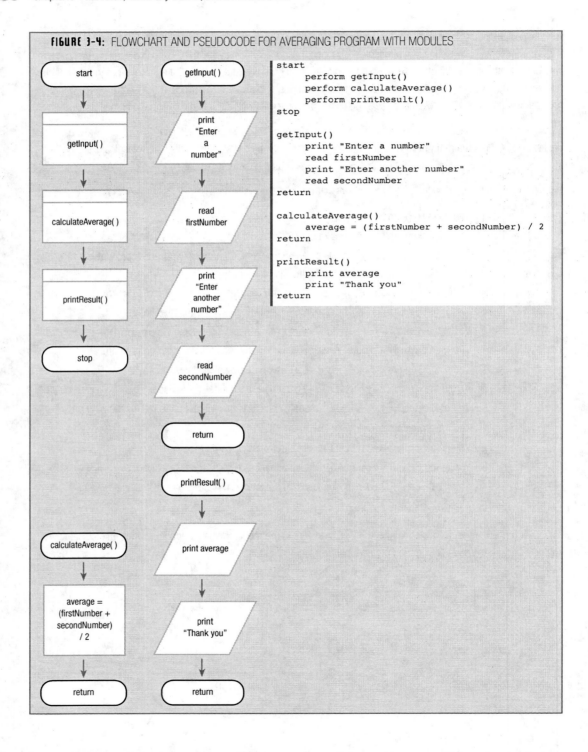

FIGURE 3-4: FLOWCHART AND PSEUDOCODE FOR AVERAGING PROGRAM WITH MODULES

```
start
    perform getInput()
    perform calculateAverage()
    perform printResult()
stop

getInput()
    print "Enter a number"
    read firstNumber
    print "Enter another number"
    read secondNumber
return

calculateAverage()
    average = (firstNumber + secondNumber) / 2
return

printResult()
    print average
    print "Thank you"
return
```

MODULES CALLING OTHER MODULES

Just as a program can call a module or subroutine, any module can call another module. For example, the program illustrated in Figure 3-4 can be broken down further, as shown in Figure 3-5.

FIGURE 3-5: FLOWCHART AND PSEUDOCODE FOR AVERAGING PROGRAM WITH SUBMODULES

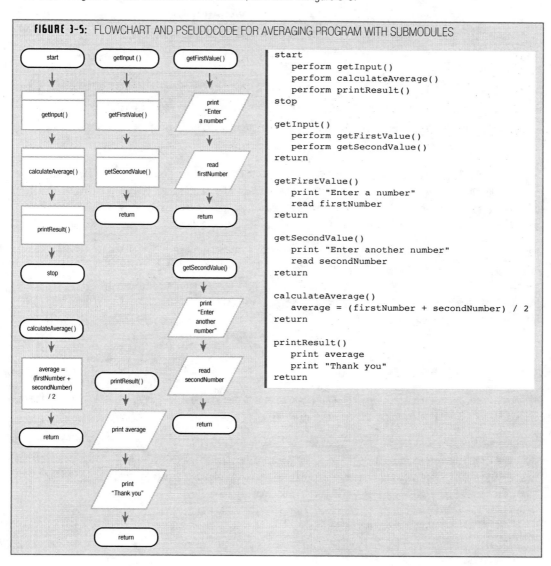

```
start
    perform getInput()
    perform calculateAverage()
    perform printResult()
stop

getInput()
    perform getFirstValue()
    perform getSecondValue()
return

getFirstValue()
    print "Enter a number"
    read firstNumber
return

getSecondValue()
    print "Enter another number"
    read secondNumber
return

calculateAverage()
    average = (firstNumber + secondNumber) / 2
return

printResult()
    print average
    print "Thank you"
return
```

After the program in Figure 3-5 begins:

1. The main program calls the `getInput()` module, and the logical flow transfers to that module.
2. From there, the `getInput()` module calls the `getFirstValue()` module, and the logical flow immediately transfers to the `getFirstValue()` module.
3. The `getFirstValue()` module displays a prompt and reads a number. When `getFirstValue()` ends, control passes back to `getInput()`, where `getSecondValue()` is called.
4. Control passes to `getSecondValue()`, which displays a prompt and retrieves a second value from the user. When this module ends, control passes back to the `getInput()` module.
5. When the `getInput()` module ends, control returns to the main program.
6. Then, `calculateAverage()` and `printResult()` execute as before.

Determining when to break down any particular module further into its own subroutines or submodules is an art. Programmers do follow some guidelines when deciding how far to break down subroutines, or how much to put in them. Some companies may have arbitrary rules, such as "a subroutine should never take more than a page," or "a module should never have more than 30 statements in it," or "never have a method or function with only one statement in it."

Rather than use such arbitrary rules, a better policy is to place together statements that contribute to one specific task. The more the statements contribute to the same job, the greater the **functional cohesion** of the module. A routine that checks the validity of a `month` variable's value, or one that prompts a user and allows the user to type in a value, are considered cohesive. A routine that checks date validity, deducts insurance premiums, and computes federal withholding tax for an employee would be less cohesive.

DECLARING VARIABLES

The primary work of most modules in most programs you write is to manipulate data—for example, to calculate the figures needed for a paycheck, customer bill, or sales report. You store your program data in variables.

Many program languages require you to declare all variables before you use them. **Declaring a variable** involves providing a name for the memory location where the computer will store the variable value, and notifying the computer of what type of data to expect. Every programming language requires that you follow specific rules when declaring variables, but all the rules involve identifying at least two attributes for every variable:

- You must declare a data type.
- You must give the variable a name.

You learned in Chapter 1 that different programming languages provide different variable types, but that all allow at least the distinction between character and numeric data. The rest of this book uses just two data types—`num`, which holds number values, and `char`, which holds all other values, including those that contain letters and combinations of letters and numbers.

Remember, you also learned in Chapter 1 that variable names must not contain spaces, so this book uses statements such as `char lastName` and `num weeklySalary` to declare two variables of different types.

TIP □ □ □ □ Although it is not a requirement of any programming language, it usually makes sense to give a variable a name that is a noun, because it represents a thing.

Some programming languages, such as Visual Basic, BASIC, and RPG, do not require you to name any variable until the first time you use it. However, other languages, including COBOL, C++, C#, Java, and Pascal, require that you declare variables with a name and a type. Some languages require that you declare all variables at the beginning of a program, before you write any executable statements; others allow you to declare variables at any point, but require the declaration before you can use the variable. For our purposes, this book follows the convention of declaring all variables at the beginning of a program.

In many modern programming languages, variables typically are declared within each module that uses them. Such variables are known as **local variables**. As you continue your study of programming logic, you will learn how to use local variables and understand their advantages. For now, this text will use **global variables**—variables that are given a type and name once, and then used in all modules of the program.

For example, to complete the averaging program shown in Figure 3-5 so that its variables are declared, you can redraw the main program flowchart to look like the one shown in Figure 3-6. Three variables are required: `firstNumber`, `secondNumber`, and `average`. The variables are declared as the first step in the program, before you use any of them, and each is correctly identified as numeric. They appear to the side of the "declare variables" step in an **annotation symbol** or **annotation box**, which is simply an attached box containing notes. You can use an annotation symbol any time you have more to write than you can conveniently fit within a flowchart symbol.

TIP □ □ □ □ Many programming languages support more specific numeric types with names like int (for integers or whole numbers), float or single (for single-precision, floating-point values; that is, values that contain one or more decimal-place digits), and double (for double-precision, floating-point values, which means more memory space is reserved). Many languages distinguish even more precisely. For example, in addition to whole-number integers, C++, C#, and Java allow short integers and long integers, which require less and more memory, respectively.
Many programming languages support more specific character types. Often, programming languages provide a distinction between single-character variables (such as an initial or a grade in a class) and string variables (such as a last name), which hold multiple characters.

Figure 3-6 also shows pseudocode for the same program. Because pseudocode is written and not drawn, you might choose to list the variable names below the `declare variables` statement, as shown.

Programmers sometimes create a **data dictionary**, which is a list of every variable name used in a program, along with its type, size, and description. When a data dictionary is created, it becomes part of the program documentation.

TIP □ □ □ □ After you name a variable, you must use that exact name every time you refer to the variable within your program. In many programming languages, even the case matters, so a variable name like firstNumber represents a different memory location than firstnumber or FirstNumber.

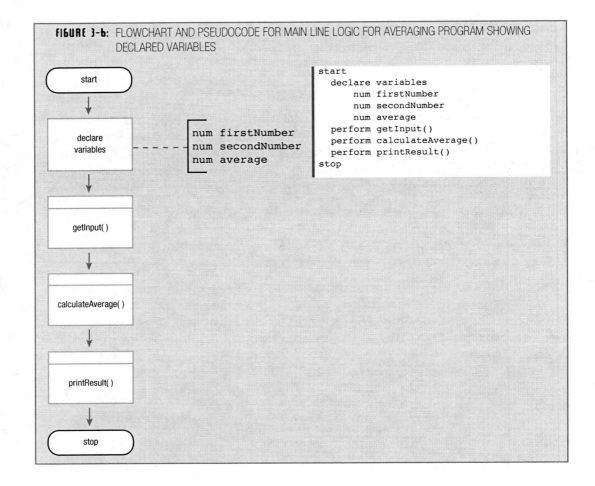

FIGURE 3-6: FLOWCHART AND PSEUDOCODE FOR MAIN LINE LOGIC FOR AVERAGING PROGRAM SHOWING DECLARED VARIABLES

CREATING HIERARCHY CHARTS

When a program has several modules calling other modules, programmers often use a tool besides flowcharts or pseudocode to show the overall picture of how these modules are related to one another. You can use a **hierarchy chart** to illustrate modules' relationships. A hierarchy chart does not tell you what tasks are to be performed within a module; it doesn't tell you *when* or *how* a module executes. It tells you only which routines exist within a program and which routines call which other routines.

The hierarchy chart for the last version of the number-averaging program looks like Figure 3-7, and shows which modules call which others. You don't know *when* the modules are called or *why* they are called; that information is in the flowchart or pseudocode. A hierarchy chart just tells you *which* modules are called by other modules.

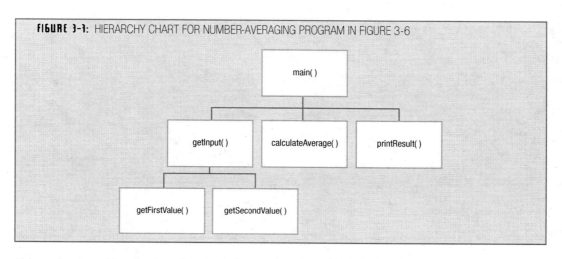

FIGURE 3-7: HIERARCHY CHART FOR NUMBER-AVERAGING PROGRAM IN FIGURE 3-6

You may have seen hierarchy charts for organizations, such as the one in Figure 3-8. The chart shows who reports to whom, not when or how often they report. Program hierarchy charts operate in an identical manner.

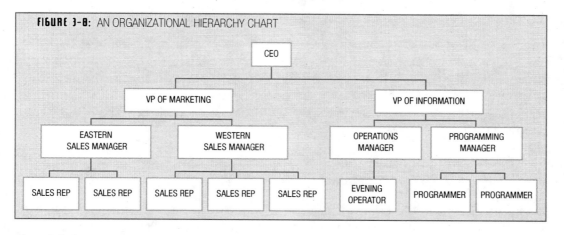

FIGURE 3-8: AN ORGANIZATIONAL HIERARCHY CHART

Figure 3-9 shows an example of a hierarchy chart for the billing program of a mail-order company. The hierarchy chart supplies module names only; it provides a general overview of the tasks to be performed, without specifying any details.

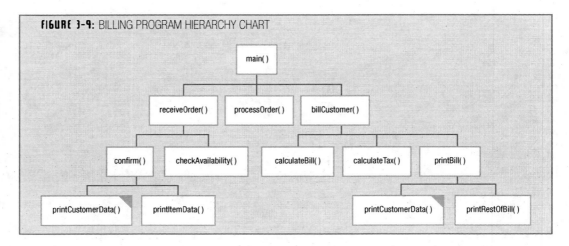

FIGURE 3-9: BILLING PROGRAM HIERARCHY CHART

Because program modules are reusable, a specific module may be called from several locations within a program. For example, in the billing program hierarchy chart in Figure 3-9, you can see that the `printCustomerData()` module is used twice. By convention, you blacken a corner of each box representing a module used more than once. This action alerts readers that any change to this module will affect more than one location.

The hierarchy chart can be a useful tool when a program must be modified months or years after the original writing. For example, if a tax law changes, a programmer might be asked to rewrite the `calculateTax()` module in the billing program diagrammed in Figure 3-9. As the programmer changes the `calculateTax()` routine, the hierarchy chart shows what other dependent routines might be affected. If a change is made to `printCustomerData()`, the programmer is alerted that changes will occur in multiple locations. A hierarchy chart is useful for "getting the big picture" in a complex program.

UNDERSTANDING DOCUMENTATION

Documentation refers to all of the supporting material that goes with a program. Two broad categories of documentation are the documentation intended for users and the documentation intended for programmers. People who use computer programs are called **end users**, or **users** for short. Most likely, you have been the end user of an application such as a word-processing program or a game. When you purchase software that other programmers have written, you appreciate clearly written instructions on how to install and use the software. These instructions constitute user documentation. In a small organization, programmers may write user documentation, but in most organizations, systems analysts or technical writers produce end-user instructions. These instructions may take the form of a printed manual, or may be presented online through a Web site or on a compact disc.

When programmers begin to plan the logic of a computer program, they require instructions known as **program documentation**. End users never see program documentation; rather, programmers use it when planning or modifying programs.

Program documentation falls into two categories: internal and external. **Internal program documentation** consists of **program comments**, or nonexecuting statements that programmers place within their code to explain program statements in English. The method for inserting comments within a program differs in each programming language, but every method provides a means for inserting clarifying comments that do not affect the running of a program. You will learn how to insert comments when you learn a specific programming language.

TIP ▫ ▫ ▫ ▫ | In the BASIC programming language, program comments begin with the letters REM (for REMark). In C++, C#, and Java, comments can begin with two forward slashes (//). An RPG program indicates that a line is a comment if there is an asterisk (*) in the sixth typed position in the line.

TIP ▫ ▫ ▫ ▫ | Some newer programming language such as C# and Java provide a tool that automatically converts the programmer's internal comments to external documentation.

External program documentation includes all the supporting paperwork that programmers develop before they write a program. Because most programs have input, processing, and output, usually there is documentation for all these functions.

OUTPUT DOCUMENTATION

Output documentation is usually the first to be written. This may seem backwards, but if you're planning a trip, which do you decide first: how to get to your destination or where you're going?

Most requests for programs arise because a user needs particular information to be output, so the planning of program output is usually done in consultation with the person or persons who will be using it. Only after the desired output is known can the programmer hope to plan the processes needed to produce the output.

Often the programmer does not design the output. Instead, the user who requests the output presents the programmer (or programming team) with an example or sketch of the desired result. Then the programmer might work with the user to refine the request, suggest improvements in the design, or clarify the user's needs. If you don't determine precisely what the user wants or needs at this point, you will write a program that the user soon wants redesigned and rewritten.

A very common type of output is a printed report. You can design a printed report on a **printer spacing chart**, which is also referred to as a **print chart** or a **print layout**. Figure 3-10 shows a printer spacing chart, which basically looks like graph paper. The chart has many boxes, and in each box the designer places one character that will be printed.

FIGURE 3-10: PRINTER SPACING CHART

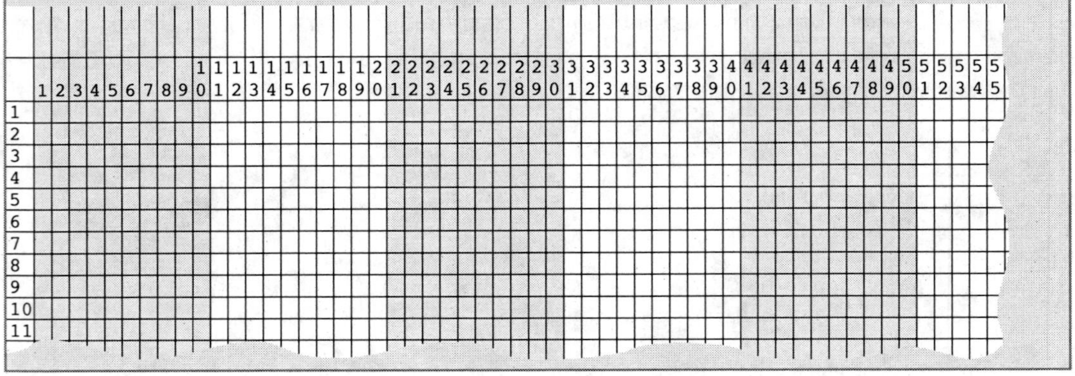

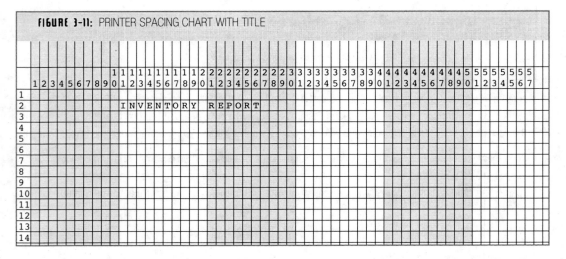

TIP ▫ ▫ ▫ ▫ | Besides using handwritten print charts, you can design report layouts on a computer using a word-processing program or other design software.

For example, if you want to create a printed report with the title INVENTORY REPORT, and you decide that the title looks best 11 spaces over from the left of the page and one line down, you would begin to create the printer spacing chart shown in Figure 3-11.

FIGURE 3-11: PRINTER SPACING CHART WITH TITLE

INVENTORY REPORT

You might want to skip a line and print the column headings ITEM NAME, PRICE, and QUANTITY IN STOCK, so the printer spacing chart would evolve into the one in Figure 3-12.

FIGURE 3-12: PRINTER SPACING CHART WITH TITLE AND COLUMN HEADINGS

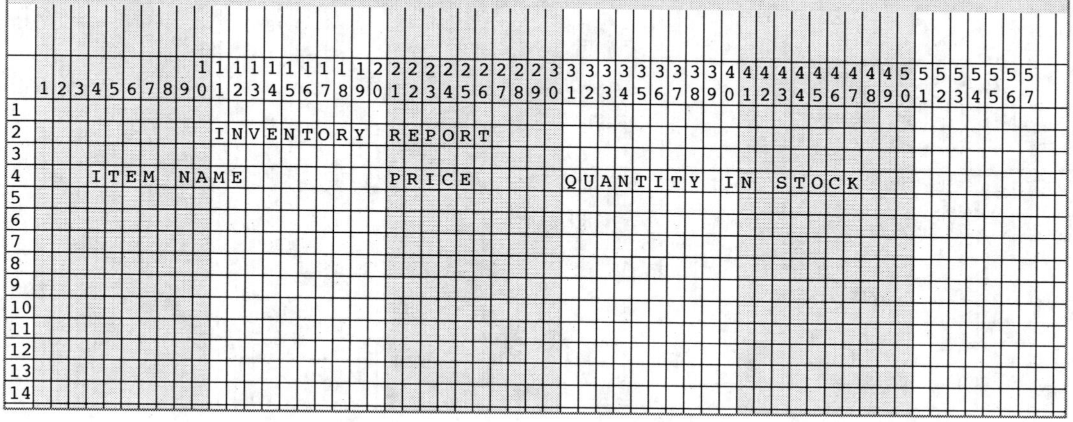

The title and column headings' values will be **constant**, or unchanging, on every page of the report. In other words, in this example, the title and column headings will not change based on the date, the number of pages that print, any input data, or any other conditions. Therefore, the title and column headings are written on the print chart exactly as they will appear on the report. The exact spacing and the use of upper- or lowercase characters make a difference. Notice that the constants used within a report do not need to follow the same rules as variable names. Within a report, constants like INVENTORY REPORT and ITEM NAME can contain spaces. These headings exist to help readers understand the information presented in the report—not for a computer to interpret.

A print layout typically shows how the variable data will appear on the report. Of course, the data will probably be different every time the report is run. Thus, instead of writing in actual item names and prices, the users and programmers usually use Xs to represent generic variable character data and 9s to represent generic variable numeric data. (Some programmers use Xs for both character and numeric data.) For example, Figure 3-13 shows how some data will look in the print chart.

Each line containing Xs and 9s representing data is a **detail line**, or a line that displays the data details. Detail lines typically appear many times per page, as opposed to **heading lines**, which contain the title and any column headings, and usually appear only once per page.

Even though an actual inventory report might eventually go on for hundreds or thousands of detail lines, writing two or three rows of Xs and 9s is sufficient to show how the data will appear. For example, if a report contains employee names and salaries, those data items will occupy the same print positions on output for line after line, whether the output eventually contains 10 employees or 10,000. A few rows of identically positioned Xs and 9s are sufficient to establish the pattern.

In any report layout, then, you write in constant data (such as headings) that will be the same on every run of this report. You write Xs and 9s to represent the variable data (such as the items, their prices, and their quantities) that will change from run to run.

FIGURE 3-13: PRINT CHART WITH GENERIC DATA

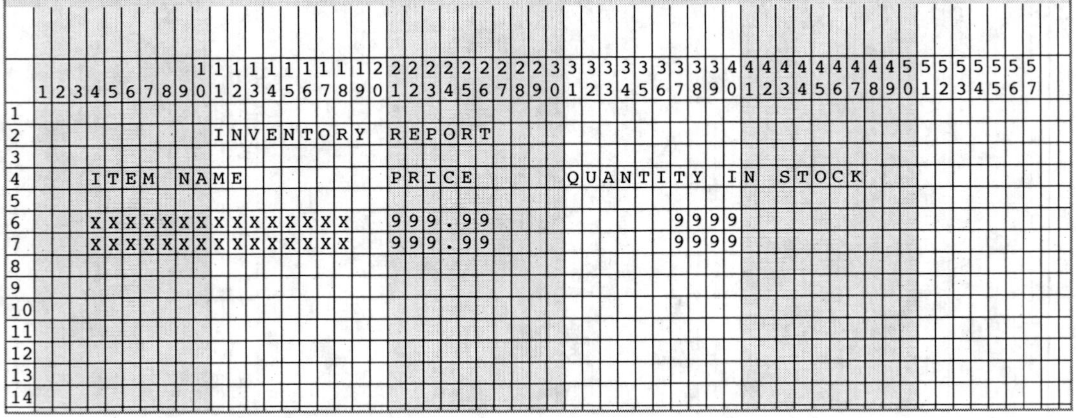

```
2          INVENTORY  REPORT
4     ITEM NAME        PRICE        QUANTITY  IN  STOCK
6     XXXXXXXXXXXXXX   999.99              9999
7     XXXXXXXXXXXXXX   999.99              9999
```

In the inventory report layout shown in Figure 3-13, the headings truly are constant, but you should not assume that all headings are completely constant. Let's say that your user decides to include the date in the inventory report heading. The report might now have a layout like that of Figure 3-14. Notice that now there is variable data, the date, in the report heading.

FIGURE 3-14: PRINT CHART CONTAINING VARIABLE DATA IN REPORT HEADING

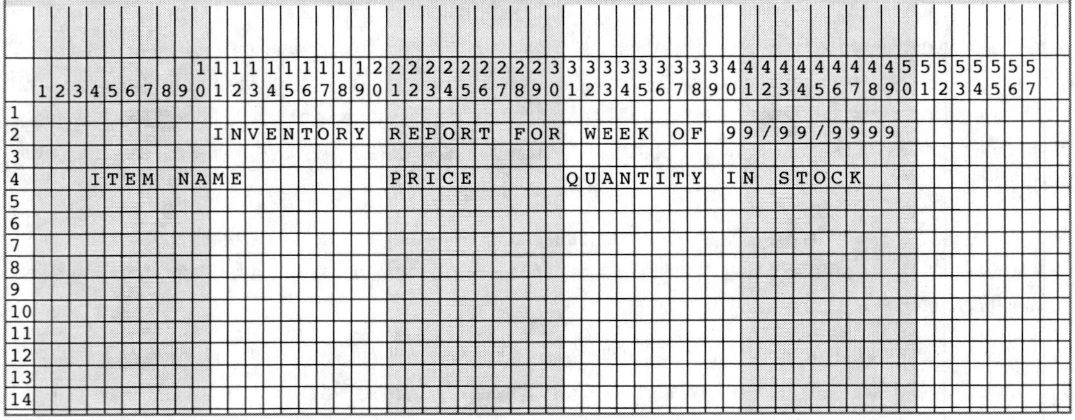

```
2          INVENTORY  REPORT  FOR  WEEK  OF  99/99/9999
4     ITEM NAME        PRICE        QUANTITY  IN  STOCK
```

For a long report that requires multiple pages, perhaps the user will also decide that the headings should appear at the top of every printed page, and that page numbers should also be added. Figure 3-15 shows how you might indicate page numbers.

FIGURE 3-15: PRINT CHART CONTAINING HEADING WITH PAGE NUMBERS

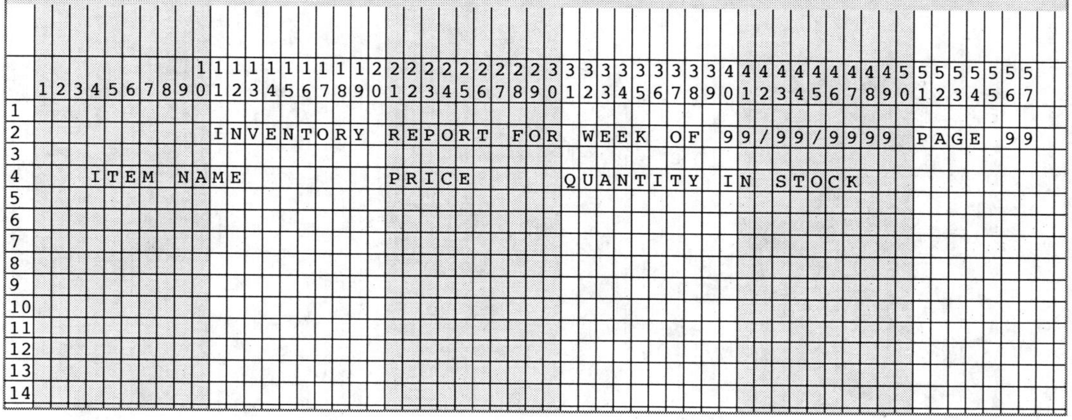

	1234567890123456789012345678901234567890123456789012345678901234567
1	
2	INVENTORY REPORT FOR WEEK OF 99/99/9999 PAGE 99
3	
4	ITEM NAME PRICE QUANTITY IN STOCK
5	
6	
7	
8	
9	
10	
11	
12	
13	
14	

Just as variable data might appear in a heading, constants might appear in the detail lines. For example, a company might choose to display a dollar sign to the left of every price listed on a report. In this case, the dollar sign would appear literally on each line, as shown in Figure 3-16.

FIGURE 3-16: PRINT CHART WITH DOLLAR SIGN IN EACH DETAIL LINE

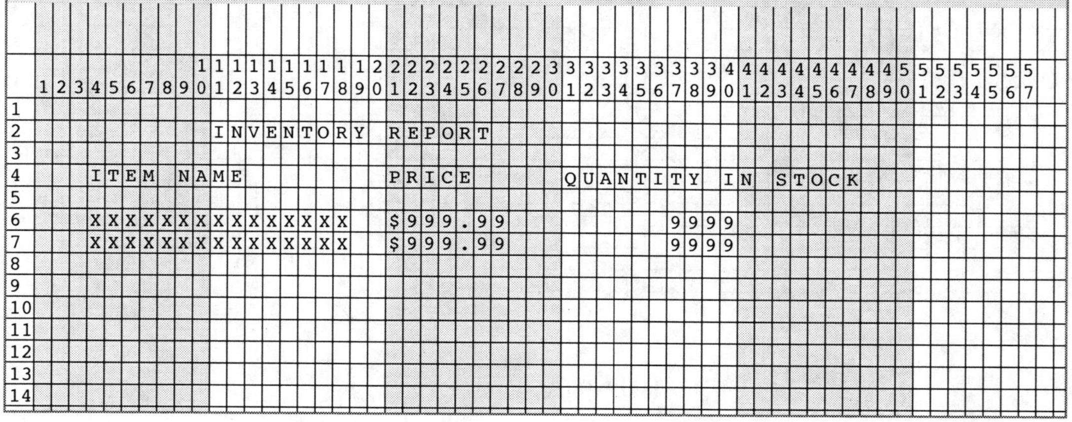

	1234567890123456789012345678901234567890123456789012345678901234567
1	
2	INVENTORY REPORT
3	
4	ITEM NAME PRICE QUANTITY IN STOCK
5	
6	XXXXXXXXXXXXXX $999.99 9999
7	XXXXXXXXXXXXXX $999.99 9999
8	
9	
10	
11	
12	
13	
14	

Besides header lines and detail lines, reports often include special lines at the end of a report. These may contain variable information only, as in Figure 3-17, or constant information only, as in Figure 3-18. Most often, however, reports will have both, as in Figure 3-19. Even though lines at the end of a report don't always contain numeric totals, they are usually referred to generically as **total lines** or **summary lines**.

FIGURE 3-17: REPORT WITH VARIABLE DATA AT END

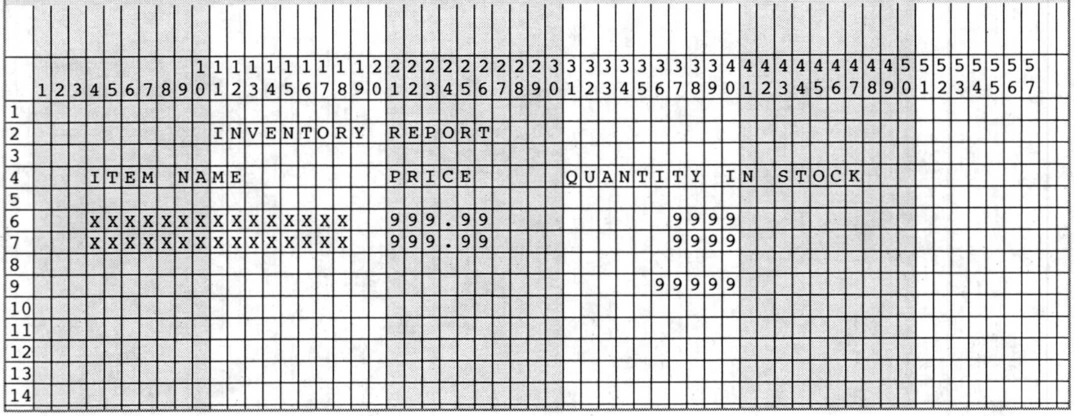

```
         111111111122222222223333333333444444444455555555
123456789012345678901234567890123456789012345678901234567
1
2            INVENTORY REPORT
3
4   ITEM NAME        PRICE       QUANTITY IN STOCK
5
6   XXXXXXXXXXXXXXX  999.99            9999
7   XXXXXXXXXXXXXXX  999.99            9999
8
9                                     99999
10
11
12
13
14
```

FIGURE 3-18: REPORT WITH CONSTANT DATA AT END

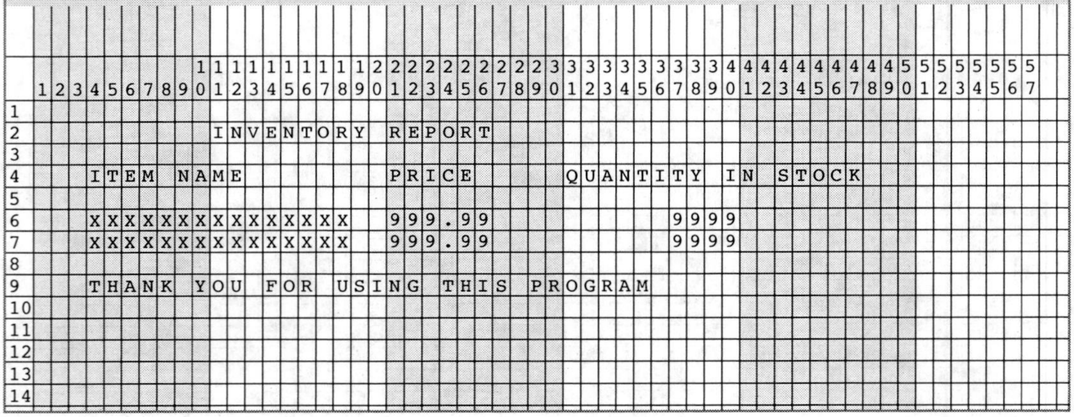

```
         111111111122222222223333333333444444444455555555
123456789012345678901234567890123456789012345678901234567
1
2            INVENTORY REPORT
3
4   ITEM NAME        PRICE       QUANTITY IN STOCK
5
6   XXXXXXXXXXXXXXX  999.99            9999
7   XXXXXXXXXXXXXXX  999.99            9999
8
9   THANK YOU FOR USING THIS PROGRAM
10
11
12
13
14
```

FIGURE 3-19: REPORT WITH COMBINED CONSTANT AND VARIABLE DATA AT END

	1 2 3 4 5 6 7 8 9	1 1 1 1 1 1 1 1 1 1 0 1 2 3 4 5 6 7 8 9	2 2 2 2 2 2 2 2 2 2 0 1 2 3 4 5 6 7 8 9	3 3 3 3 3 3 3 3 3 3 0 1 2 3 4 5 6 7 8 9	4 4 4 4 4 4 4 4 4 4 0 1 2 3 4 5 6 7 8 9	5 5 5 5 5 5 5 5 0 1 2 3 4 5 6 7
1						
2		INVENTORY	REPORT			
3						
4	ITEM	NAME	PRICE	QUANTITY	IN STOCK	
5						
6	XXXXXXX	XXXXXXXX	999.99	9999		
7	XXXXXXX	XXXXXXXX	999.99	9999		
8						
9			GRAND TOTAL:	999999		
10						
11						
12						
13						
14						

Printed reports do not necessarily contain detail lines. A report might contain only headers and summary lines. For example, a payroll report might contain only a heading and a total gross payroll figure for each department in the company, or a college might print a report showing how many students have declared each available major. These reports contain no detail—no information about individual employees or students—but they do contain summaries. Figure 3-20 shows an example of a print chart for a summary report.

FIGURE 3-20: PRINT CHART FOR PAYROLL SUMMARY REPORT

	1 2 3 4 5 6 7 8 9	1 1 1 1 1 1 1 1 1 1 0 1 2 3 4 5 6 7 8 9	2 2 2 2 2 2 2 2 2 2 0 1 2 3 4 5 6 7 8 9	3 3 3 3 3 3 3 3 3 3 0 1 2 3 4 5 6 7 8 9	4 4 4 4 4 4 4 4 4 4 0 1 2 3 4 5 6 7 8 9	5 5 5 5 5 5 5 5 0 1 2 3 4 5 6 7
1		PAYROLL	SUMMARY	REPORT		
2						
3		DEPT	TOTAL GROSS	PAYROLL		
4						
5		101	999,999,999.99			
6		102	999,999,999.99			
7		103	999,999,999.99			
8		104	999,999,999.99			
9		105	999,999,999.99			
10		106	999,999,999.99			
11		107	999,999,999.99			
12						
13						
14						

Not all program output takes the form of printed reports. If your program's output will appear on a monitor screen, particularly if you are working in a **GUI**, or graphical user interface environment like Windows, your design issues will differ. In a GUI program, the user sees a screen, and can typically make selections using a mouse or other pointing device. Instead of a print chart, your output design might resemble a sketch of a screen. Figure 3-21 shows how inventory records might be displayed in a graphical environment. On a monitor, you might choose to allow the user to see only one or a few records at a time, so one concern is providing a means for users to scroll through displayed records. In Figure 3-21, records are accessed using a single button that the user can click to read the next record; in a more sophisticated design, the user might be able to "jump" to the first or last record, or look up a specific record.

FIGURE 3-21: INVENTORY RECORDS DISPLAYED IN A GUI ENVIRONMENT

TIP ▫ ▫ ▫ ▫ | A printed report is also called a **hard copy**, whereas screen output is referred to as a **soft copy**.

TIP ▫ ▫ ▫ ▫ | Achieving good screen design is an art that requires much study and thought to master. Besides being visually pleasing, good screen design also requires ease of use and accessibility.

TIP ▫ ▫ ▫ ▫ | GUI programs often include several different screen formats that a user will see while running a program. In such cases, you would design several screens.

INPUT DOCUMENTATION

Once you have planned the design of the output, you need to know what input is available to produce this output. If you are producing a report from stored data, you frequently will be provided with a **file description** that describes the data contained in a file. You usually find a file's description as part of an organization's information systems documentation; physically, the description might be on paper in a binder in the Information Systems department, or it might be stored on a disk. If the file you will use comes from an outside source, the person requesting the report will have to provide you with a description of the data stored on the file. For example, Figure 3-22 shows an inventory file description for a file that could be used to produce the report described in Figure 3-13.

TIP ▫ ▫ ▫ ▫ | Not all programs use previously stored input files. Some use interactive input data supplied by a user during the execution of a program. Some programs produce an output file that is stored directly on a storage device, such as a disk. If your program produces file output instead of printed report output, you will create a file description for your output. Other programs then may use your output file description as an input description.

FIGURE 3-22: INVENTORY FILE DESCRIPTION

```
INVENTORY FILE DESCRIPTION
File name: INVTRY
FIELD DESCRIPTION      POSITIONS    DATA TYPE    DECIMALS
Name of item           1—15         Character
Price of item          16—20        Numeric      2
Quantity in stock      21—24        Numeric      0
```

The inventory file description in Figure 3-22 shows that each item's name occupies the first 15 bytes of each record in the file. A **byte** is a unit of computer storage that can contain any of 256 combinations of 0s and 1s that often represent a character. The code of 0s and 1s depends on the type of computer system you are using. Popular coding schemes include ASCII (American Standard Code for Information Interchange), EBCDIC (Extended Binary Coded Decimal Interchange Code), and Unicode. Each of these codes uses a different combination of 1s and 0s to represent characters—you can see a listing of each code's values in Appendix B. For example, in ASCII, an uppercase "A" is represented by 01000001. Programmers seldom care about the code used; for example, if an "A" is stored as part of a person's name, the programmer's only concern is that the "A" in the name appears correctly on output—not the combination of 0s and 1s that represents it. This book assumes that one stored character occupies one byte in an input file.

Some item names may require all 15 positions allowed for the name in the input file, for example "12 by 16 carpet", which contains exactly 15 characters, including spaces. Other item names require fewer than the allotted 15 positions, for example "door mat". In such cases, the remaining allotted positions remain blank. When only 15 storage positions are allowed for a name, some names might have to be truncated or abbreviated. For example, "hand woven carpet" might be stored as "hand woven carp". Whether the item name requires all 15 positions or not, you can see from the input file description in Figure 3-22 that the price for each item begins in position 16 of each input record.

The price of any item in the inventory file is allowed five positions, 16 through 20. It is natural to assume, therefore, that a price contains five digits. However, very often numeric values are stored on disk in a format that allows many more digits to be stored in a five-byte area. For convenience, this book assumes that a five-byte numeric storage location holds five digits, but keep in mind that, in reality, it would hold a much larger number in most systems.

TIP ▫ ▫ ▫ ▫   Some systems store numbers in a format called "unpacked," in which a number like 456 is stored in three bytes as +4, +5, and +6, and a number like –23789 is stored in five bytes as –2, –3, –7, –8, and –9. In each case, the sign (+ or –) occupies half a byte, and the digit occupies the other half of the byte. However, if a number is positive, the entire number is positive, and if a number is negative, the entire number is negative, so storing the sign with each digit is redundant. Therefore, some systems store numbers in a format called "packed." In these systems, the sign is stored only once with each multidigit number, and each digit occupies half a byte—so +456 occupies only two bytes (one for the + and the 4, and the other for the 5 and the 6), and –23789 requires only three bytes (containing – and 2, 3 and 7, and 8 and 9).

The input file description in Figure 3-22 shows that two of the positions in the price are reserved for decimal places. Typically, decimal points themselves are not stored in data files; they are **implied**, or **assumed**. Also typically, numeric data are stored with leading zeros so that all allotted positions are occupied. Thus, an item valued at $345.67 is stored as 34567, and an item valued at $1.23 is stored as 00123.

TIP □ □ □ □ Decimal points are implied in data files, but occupy positions on printed reports. Within data files, it is most efficient to save space. On printed reports, it is most important to represent information in a way that is easy for the reader to interpret. Leading zeros fill numeric fields within files, but are not used on printed reports. Within data files, numeric fields must be totally numeric, so spaces are not allowed within numeric fields. On printed reports, information must be easy for the reader to interpret; readers usually do not expect to see leading zeros in numeric data.

TIP □ □ □ □ Just as repetitious decimal points are not stored in numeric fields, data files often do not store other repeated characters whose position is assumed—for example, dashes in Social Security numbers or telephone numbers, or a period after a middle initial.

Typically, programmers create one program variable for each field that is part of the input file. In addition to the field descriptions contained in the input documentation, the programmer might be given specific variable names to use for each field, particularly if such variable names must agree with the ones that other programmers working on the project are using. In many cases, however, programmers are allowed to choose their own variable names. Therefore, you can choose `itemName`, `nameOfItem`, `itemDescription`, or any other reasonable one-word variable name when you refer to the item name within your program. The variable names you use within your program need not match constants printed on the report. Thus, the variable `itemName` might hold the characters that will print under the column heading NAME OF ITEM.

For example, examine the input file description in Figure 3-22. When this file is used for a project in which the programmer can choose variable names, he or she might choose the following variable declaration list:

```
char itemName
num itemPrice
num itemQuantity
```

Each data field in the list is declared using the data type that corresponds to the data type indicated in the file description, and has an appropriate, easy-to-read, single-word variable name.

TIP □ □ □ □ When a programmer uses an identifier like `itemName`, that variable identifier exists in computer memory only for the duration of the program in which the variable is declared. Another program can use the same input file and refer to the same field as `nameOfItem`. Variable names exist in memory during the run of a program—they are not stored in the data file. Variable names simply represent memory addresses at which pieces of data are stored while a program executes.

Recall the data hierarchy relationship introduced in Chapter 1:

- Database
- File
- Record
- Field
- Character

Whether the inventory file is part of a database or not, it will contain many records; each record will contain an item name, price, and quantity, which are fields. In turn, the field that holds the name of an item might contain up to 15 characters, for example "12 by 16 carpet", "blue miniblinds", or "diskette holder".

Organizations may use different forms to relay the information about records and fields, but the very least the programmer needs to know is:

- What is the name of the file?
- What data does it contain?
- How much room do the file and each of its fields take up?
- What type of data can be stored in each field—character or numeric?

Notice that a data field's position on the input file never has to correspond with the same item's position in an output file or in a print chart. For example, you can use the data file described in Figure 3-22 to produce the report shown in Figure 3-13. In the input data file, the item name appears in positions 1 through 15. However, on the printed report, the same information appears in columns 4 through 18. In an input file, data are "squeezed" together—no human being will read this file, and there is no need for it to be attractively spaced. However, on printed output, you typically include spaces between data items so they are legible as well as attractive. Figure 3-23 illustrates how input fields are read by the program and converted to output fields.

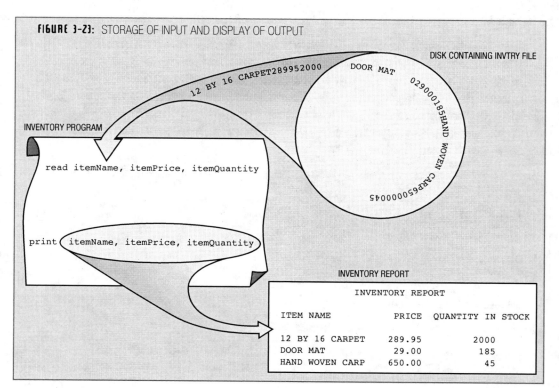

FIGURE 3-23: STORAGE OF INPUT AND DISPLAY OF OUTPUT

TIP ◻ ◻ ◻ ◻ You are never required to output all the available characters in a field that exist on input. For example, even though the item name in the input file description in Figure 3-22 shows that each item contains 15 stored characters, you might decide to display only 10 of them on output, especially if your output report contained many columns and you were "crunched" for space.

The inventory file description in Figure 3-22 contains all the information the programmer needs to create the output requested in Figure 3-13—the output lists each item's name, price, and quantity, and the input records clearly contain that data. Often, however, a file description more closely resembles the description in Figure 3-24.

FIGURE 3-24: EXPANDED INVENTORY FILE DESCRIPTION

```
INVENTORY FILE DESCRIPTION
File name: INVTRY
FIELD DESCRIPTION           POSITIONS    DATA TYPE      DECIMALS
Item number                 1—4          Numeric        0
Name of item                5—19         Character
Size                        20           Numeric        0
Manufacturing cost of item  21—25        Numeric        2
Retail price of item        26—30        Numeric        2
Quantity in stock           31—34        Numeric        0
Reorder point               35—38        Numeric        0
Sales rep                   39—48        Character
Amt sold last year          49—54        Numeric        0
```

The file description in Figure 3-24 contains nine fields. With this file description, it's harder to pinpoint the information needed for the report, but the necessary data fields are available, and you still can write the program. The input file contains more information than you need for the report you want to print, so you will ignore some of the input fields, such as Item number and Sales rep. These fields certainly may be used in other reports within the company. Typically, data input files contain more data than any one program requires. For example, your credit card company stores historical data about your past purchases, but these are not included on every bill. Similarly, your school records contain more data than are printed on each report card or tuition bill.

However, if the input file description resembles Figure 3-25, then there are not enough data to produce the requested report.

FIGURE 3-25: INSUFFICIENT INVENTORY FILE DESCRIPTION

```
INVENTORY FILE DESCRIPTION
File name: INVTRY
FIELD DESCRIPTION           POSITIONS    DATA TYPE      DECIMALS
Item number                 1—4          Numeric        0
Name of item                5—19         Character
Size                        20           Numeric        0
Manufacturing cost of item  21—25        Numeric        2
Retail price of item        26—30        Numeric        2
Reorder point               35—38        Numeric        0
Sales rep                   39—48        Character
Amt sold last year          49—54        Numeric        0
```

In Figure 3-25, there is no indication that the input file contains a figure for quantity in stock. If the user really needs (or wants) the report as requested, it's out of the programmer's hands until the data can be collected from some source and stored in a file the programmer can use.

Each field printed on a report does not need to exist on the input file. Assume that a user requests a report in the format shown in Figure 3-26, which includes a column labeled "PROFIT", and that the input file description is the one in Figure 3-25. In this case, it's difficult to determine whether you can create the requested report, because the input file does not contain a `profit` field. However, because the input data include the company's cost and selling price for each item, you can calculate the `profit` within your program by subtracting the cost from the price, and then produce the desired output.

FIGURE 3-26: REQUESTED PROFIT REPORT

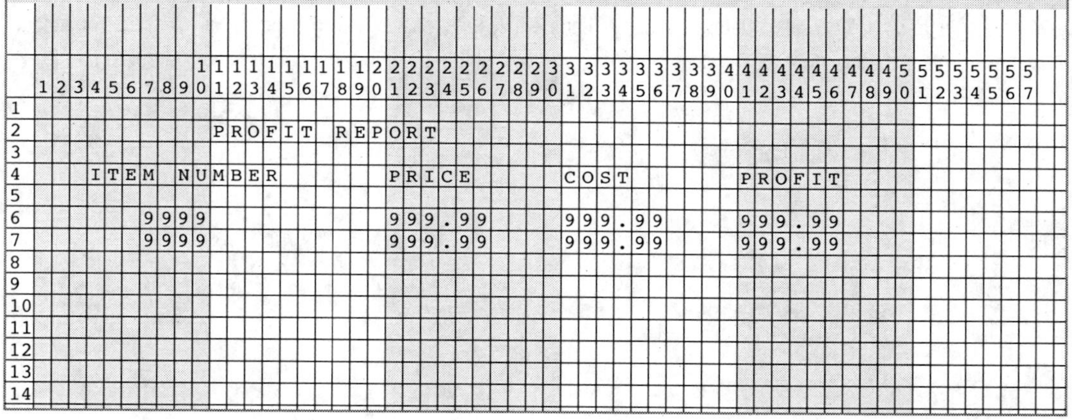

COMPLETING THE DOCUMENTATION

When you have designed the output and confirmed that it is possible to produce it from the input, then you can plan the logic of the program, code the program, and test the program. The original output design, input description, flowchart or pseudocode, and program code all become part of the program documentation. These pieces of documentation are typically stored together in a binder within the programming department of an organization, where they can be studied later, when program changes become necessary.

In addition to this program documentation, you typically must create user documentation. **User documentation** includes all the manuals or other instructional materials that nontechnical people use, as well as the operating instructions that computer operators and data-entry personnel need. It needs to be written clearly, in plain language, with reasonable expectations of the users' expertise. Within a small organization, the programmer may prepare the user documentation. In a large organization, user documentation is usually prepared by technical writers or systems analysts, who oversee programmers' work and coordinate programmers' efforts. These professionals consult with the programmer to ensure that the user documentation is complete and accurate.

The areas addressed in user documentation may include:

- How to prepare input for the program
- To whom the output should be distributed
- How to interpret the normal output
- How to interpret and react to any error message generated by the program
- How frequently the program needs to run

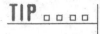 Complete documentation also might include operations support documentation. This type of documentation provides backup and recovery information, run-time instructions, and security considerations for computer center personnel who run large applications within data centers.

All these issues must be addressed before a program can be fully functional in an organization. When users throughout an organization can supply input data to computer programs and obtain the information they need in order to do their jobs well, then a skilled programmer has provided a complete piece of work.

CHAPTER SUMMARY

☐ Programmers break programming problems down into smaller, reasonable units called modules, subroutines, procedures, functions, or methods. Modularization provides abstraction, allows multiple programmers to work on a problem, makes it easy to reuse your work, and allows you to identify structures more easily.

☐ When you create a module or subroutine, you give the module a name that a calling program uses when the module is about to execute. The flowchart symbol used to call a subroutine is a rectangle with a bar across the top; the name of the module that you are calling is inside the rectangle. You draw a flowchart for each module separately, with its own sentinel symbols.

☐ A module can call other modules.

☐ Declaring a variable involves providing a name for the memory location where the computer will store the variable value, and notifying the computer of what type of data to expect.

☐ You can use a hierarchy chart to illustrate modules' relationships.

☐ Documentation refers to all of the supporting material that goes with a program.

☐ Output documentation is usually written first. You can design a printed report on a printer spacing chart to represent both constant and variable data.

☐ A file description lists the data contained in a file, including a description, size, and data type. Typically, numeric data are stored with leading zeros and without decimal points.

☐ In addition to program documentation, you typically must create user documentation, which includes the manuals or other instructional materials that nontechnical people use, as well as the operating instructions that computer operators and data-entry personnel may need.

KEY TERMS

Modules are small program units that you can use together to make a program. Programmers also refer to modules as subroutines, procedures, functions, or methods.

The process of breaking a program into modules is called **modularization**.

Abstraction is the process of paying attention to important properties while ignoring nonessential details.

Low-level details are small, nonabstract steps.

High-level programming languages allow you to use English-like vocabulary in which one broad statement corresponds to dozens of machine instructions.

Reusability is the feature of modular programs that allows individual modules to be used in a variety of applications.

Reliability is the feature of modular programs that assures you that a module has been tested and proven to function correctly.

A calling program is one that calls a module.

A main program runs from start to stop and calls other modules.

A prompt is a message that is displayed on a monitor, asking the user for a response.

The functional cohesion of a module is a measure of the degree to which all the module statements contribute to the same task.

Declaring a variable involves providing a name for the memory location where the computer will store the variable value, and notifying the computer of what type of data to expect.

Local variables are declared within each module that uses them.

Global variables are given a type and name once, and then are used in all modules of the program.

An annotation symbol or annotation box is a flowchart symbol that represents an attached box containing notes.

A data dictionary is a list of every variable name used in a program, along with its type, size, and description.

A hierarchy chart is a diagram that illustrates modules' relationships to each other.

Documentation refers to all of the supporting material that goes with a program.

End users, or users, are people who use computer programs.

Program documentation is the set of instructions that programmers use when they begin to plan the logic of a program.

Internal program documentation is documentation within a program.

Program comments are nonexecuting statements that programmers place within their code to explain program statements in English.

External program documentation includes all the supporting paperwork that programmers develop before they write a program.

A printer spacing chart, which is also referred to as a print chart or a print layout, is a tool for planning program output.

Constant output does not change based on any conditions.

A detail line on a report is a line that contains data details. Most reports contain many detail lines.

Heading lines on a report, which contain the title and any column headings, usually appear only once per page.

Total lines or summary lines contain end-of-report information.

A GUI, or graphical user interface environment, uses screens to display program output. Users interact with GUI programs with a device such as a mouse.

A hard copy is a printed copy.

A soft copy is a screen copy.

A file description is a document that describes the data contained in a file.

A byte is a unit of computer storage that can contain any of 256 combinations of 0s and 1s that often represent a character.

When pieces of data are implied or assumed, they do not exist explicitly.

User documentation includes all the manuals or other instructional materials that nontechnical people use, as well as the operating instructions that computer operators and data-entry personnel need.

REVIEW QUESTIONS

1. Which of the following is *not* a term used for modules in any programming language?

    a. structure
    b. procedure
    c. method
    d. function

2. Which of the following is *not* a reason to use modularization?

    a. Modularization provides abstraction.
    b. Modularization allows multiple programmers to work on a problem.
    c. Modularization allows you to reuse your work.
    d. Modularization eliminates the need for structure.

3. What is the name for the process of paying attention to important properties while ignoring nonessential details?

    a. structure
    b. iteration
    c. abstraction
    d. modularization

4. All modern programming languages that use English-like vocabulary to create statements that correspond to dozens of machine instructions are referred to as _____.

    a. high-level
    b. object-oriented
    c. modular
    d. obtuse

5. Modularizing a program makes it _____ to identify structures.

    a. unnecessary
    b. easier
    c. more difficult
    d. impossible

6. Programmers say that one module can _____ another, meaning that the first module causes the second module to execute.

    a. declare
    b. define
    c. enact
    d. call

7. **A message that appears on a monitor, asking the user for a response is a _____.**

   a. call
   b. prompt
   c. command
   d. declaration

8. **The more that a module's statements contribute to the same job, the greater the _____ of the module.**

   a. structure
   b. modularity
   c. functional cohesion
   d. size

9. **When you declare a variable, you must provide _____.**

   a. a name
   b. a name and a type
   c. a name, a type, and a value
   d. a name, a type, a value, and a purpose

10. **A _____ is a list of every variable name used in a program, along with its type, size, and description.**

    a. flowchart
    b. hierarchy chart
    c. data dictionary
    d. variable map

11. **A hierarchy chart tells you _____.**

    a. what tasks are to be performed within each program module
    b. when a module executes
    c. which routines call which other routines
    d. all of the above

12. **Two broad categories of documentation are the documentation intended for _____.**

    a. management and workers
    b. end users and programmers
    c. people and the computer
    d. defining variables and defining actions

13. **Nonexecuting statements that programmers place within their code to explain program statements in English are called _____.**

    a. comments
    b. pseudocode
    c. trivia
    d. user documentation

14. The first type of documentation usually created when writing a program pertains to _____.

    a. end users

    b. input

    c. output

    d. data

15. Lines of output that never change, no matter what data values are input, are referred to as _____.

    a. detail lines

    b. headers

    c. rigid

    d. constant

16. Report lines that contain the information stored in individual data records are known as _____.

    a. headers

    b. footers

    c. detail lines

    d. X-lines

17. Summary lines appear _____.

    a. at the end of every printed report

    b. at the end of some printed reports

    c. in printed reports, but never in screen output

    d. only when detail lines also appear

18. If an input file description allows 15 characters for a first name, and the stored name for the first record is "John", then typically _____.

    a. the actual field for the first record will be shortened to four characters

    b. the fields for first name in all subsequent records will be shortened to four characters

    c. the first name field in the first record will end with 11 zeros

    d. the first name field in the first record will end with 11 blanks

19. In most computer systems, when numbers that contain a decimal point are stored, _____.

    a. the decimal point is not stored; its position is assumed

    b. the decimal point occupies one byte of storage

    c. the decimal point occupies two bytes of storage

    d. Most systems cannot store numbers containing a decimal point.

20. A field holding a student's last name is stored in bytes 10 through 29 of each student record. Therefore, when you design a print chart for a report that contains each student's last name, _____.

    a. the name must print in positions 10 through 29 of the print chart

    b. the name must occupy exactly 20 positions on the print chart

    c. Both of these are true.

    d. Neither of these is true.

EXERCISES

1. **Redraw the following flowchart so that the decisions and compensation calculations are in a module.**

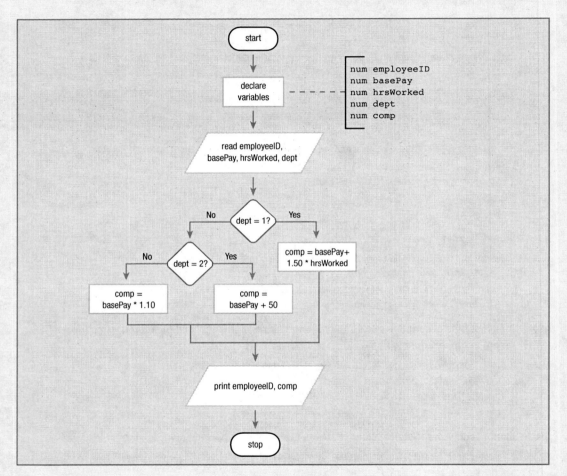

2.   **Rewrite the following pseudocode so the discount decisions and calculations are in a module.**

```
start
     read customerRecord
     if quantityOrdered > 100 then
          discount = .20
     else
          if quantityOrdered > 12 then
               discount = .10
          endif
      endif
      total = priceEach * quantityOrdered
      total = total - discount * total
      print total
stop
```

3.   **What are the final values of variables a, b, and c after the following program runs?**

```
start
     a = 2
     b = 4
     c = 10
     while c > 6
          perform changeBAndC()
     endwhile
     if a = 2 then
          perform changeA()
     endif
     if c = 10 then
          perform changeA()
     else
          perform changeBAndC()
     endif
     print a,b,c
stop

changeBAndC()
     b = b + 1
     c = c - 1
return

changeA()
     a = a + 1
     b = b - 1
return
```

4. **What are the final values of variables d, e, and f after the following program runs?**

```
start
    d = 1
    e = 3
    f = 100
    while e > d
        perform module1()
    endwhile
    if f > 0 then
        perform module2()
    else
        d = d + 5
    endif
    print d, e, f
stop

module1()
    f = f - 50
    e = e + 1
    d = d + 3
return

module2()
    f = f + 13
    d = d * 10
return
```

5. **Draw a typical hierarchy chart for a paycheck-producing program. Try to think of at least 10 separate modules that might be included. For example, one module might calculate an employee's dental insurance premium.**

6. **Design a print chart for a payroll roster that is intended to list the following items for every employee: employee's first name, last name, and salary.**

7. **Design a print chart for a payroll roster that is intended to list the following items for every employee: employee's first name, last name, hours worked, rate per hour, gross pay, federal withholding tax, state withholding tax, union dues, and net pay.**

8. Given the following input file description, determine if there is enough information provided to produce each of the requested reports:

```
INSURANCE PREMIUM LIST
File name: INSPREM
FIELD DESCRIPTION              POSITIONS    DATA TYPE      DECIMALS
Name of insured driver         1-40         Character
Birth date                     41-46        Numeric        0
Gender                         47           Character
Make of car                    48-57        Character
Year of car                    58-61        Numeric        0
Miles driven per year          62-67        Numeric        0
Number of traffic tickets      68-69        Numeric        0
Balance owed                   70-75        Numeric        2
```

a. a list of the names of all insured drivers

b. a list of very high-risk insured drivers, defined as male, under 25 years old, with more than two tickets

c. a list of low-risk insured drivers, defined as those with no tickets in the last three years, and over 30 years old

d. a list of insured drivers to contact about a special premium offer for those with a passenger car who drive under 10,000 miles per year

e. a list of the names of female drivers whose balance owed is more than $99.99

9. Given the **INSPREM** file description in Exercise 8, design a print chart to satisfy each of the following requests:

a. a list of every driver's name and make of car

b. a list of the names of all insured drivers who drive more than 20,000 miles per year

c. a list of the name, gender, make of car, and year of car for all drivers who have more than two tickets

d. a report that summarizes the number of tickets held by drivers who were born in 1940 or before, from 1941–1960, from 1961–1980, and from 1981 on

e. a report that summarizes the number of tickets held by drivers in the four birth-date categories listed in part d, grouped by gender

10. A program calculates the gown size that a student needs for a graduation ceremony. The program accepts as input a student's height in feet and inches and weight in pounds. It converts the student's height to centimeters and weight to grams. Then, it calculates the graduation gown size needed by adding ⅓ of the weight in grams to the height in centimeters. Finally, the program prints the results. There are 2.54 centimeters in an inch and 453.59 grams in a pound. Write the pseudocode that matches the following flowchart.

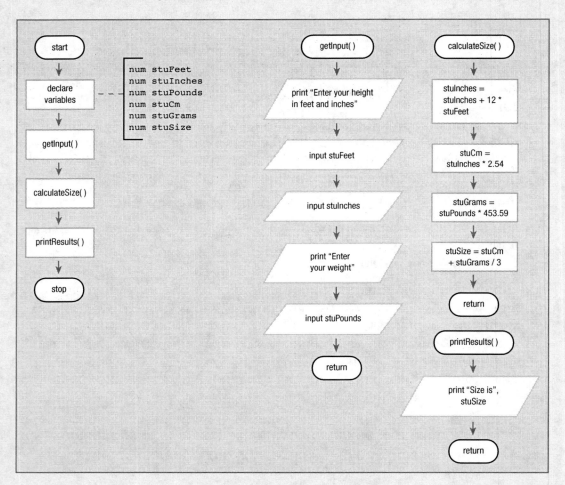

11. A program calculates the service charge a customer owes for writing a bad check. The program accepts a customer's name, the date the check was written (month, day, and year), the current date (month, day, and year), and the amount of the check in dollars and cents. The service charge is $20.00 plus 2% of the amount of the check, plus $5 for every month that has passed since the check was written. Draw the flowchart that matches the pseudocode.

(This pseudocode assumes that all checks entered are already written—that is, their dates are prior to today's date. Additionally, a check is one month late as soon as a new month starts—so a bad check written on September 30 is one month overdue on October 1.)

```
start                                    getDates()
    declare variables                        print "Enter the date of the check"
        char custName                        input checkMonth
        num checkMonth                       input checkDay
        num checkDay                         input checkYear
        num checkYear                        print "Enter today's date"
        num todayMonth                       input todayMonth
        num todayDay                         input todayDay
        num todayYear                        input todayYear
        num checkAmount                  return
        num serviceCharge
        num baseCharge                   calculateServiceCharge()
        num extraCharge                      baseCharge = 20.00
        num yearsLate                        extraCharge = .02 * checkAmount
        num monthsLate                       serviceCharge = baseCharge + extraCharge +
        num checkWorkField                       monthsLate * 5
        num todayWorkField               return
    perform getInput()
    perform calculateServiceCharge()     printResults()
    perform printResults()                   print custName, serviceCharge
stop                                     return

getInput()
    print "Enter customer name"
    input custName
    perform getDates()
    print "Enter check amount"
    input checkAmount
return
```

12. Draw the hierarchy chart that corresponds to the pseudocode presented in Exercise 11.

4

WRITING AND DESIGNING A COMPLETE PROGRAM

After studying Chapter 4, you should be able to:

Plan the mainline logic for a complete program

Describe typical housekeeping tasks

Describe tasks typically performed in the main loop of a program

Describe tasks performed in the end-of-job module

Understand the need for good program design

Appreciate the advantages of storing program components in separate files

Select superior variable and module names

Design clear module statements

Understand the need for maintaining good programming habits

UNDERSTANDING THE MAINLINE LOGICAL FLOW THROUGH A PROGRAM

You're ready to plan the logic for your first complete computer program. The output is an inventory report, as shown in Figure 4-1. The report lists inventory items along with the price, cost, and profit of each item.

FIGURE 4-1: PRINT CHART FOR INVENTORY REPORT

Figure 4-2 shows the input INVENTORY file description, Figure 4-3 shows some typical data that might exist in the input file, and Figure 4-4 shows how the output would actually look if the input file in Figure 4-3 were used.

FIGURE 4-2: INVENTORY FILE DESCRIPTION

```
INVENTORY FILE DESCRIPTION
File name: INVENTORY
FIELD DESCRIPTION        POSITIONS      DATA TYPE       DECIMALS
Item name                1-15           Character
Price                    16-20          Numeric         2
Cost                     21-25          Numeric         2
Quantity in stock        26-29          Numeric         0
```

FIGURE 4-3: TYPICAL DATA THAT MIGHT BE STORED IN INVENTORY FILE

```
cotton shirt    01995    01457    2500
wool scarf      01450    01125    0060
silk blouse     16500    04850    0525
cotton shorts   01750    01420    1500
```

TIP ☐ ☐ ☐ ☐   In some older operating systems, file names are limited to eight characters, in which case INVENTORY might be an unacceptable file name.

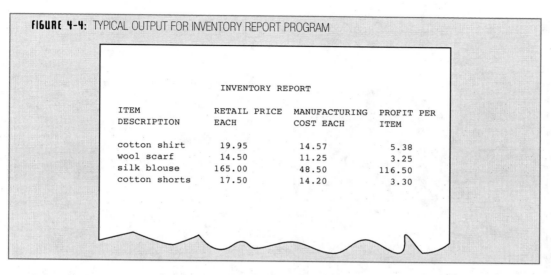

FIGURE 4-4: TYPICAL OUTPUT FOR INVENTORY REPORT PROGRAM

```
                     INVENTORY REPORT

ITEM              RETAIL PRICE  MANUFACTURING  PROFIT PER
DESCRIPTION       EACH          COST EACH      ITEM

cotton shirt        19.95          14.57          5.38
wool scarf          14.50          11.25          3.25
silk blouse        165.00          48.50        116.50
cotton shorts       17.50          14.20          3.30
```

Examine the print chart and the input file description. Your first task is to make sure you understand what the report requires; your next job is to determine whether you have all the data you need to produce the report. (Figure 4-5 shows this process.) The output requires the item name, price, and cost, and you can see that all three are data items on the input file. The output also requires a profit figure for each item; you need to understand how profit is calculated—which could be done differently in various companies. If there is any doubt as to what a term used in the output means or as to how a value is calculated, you must ask the **user**, or your **client**—the person who has requested this program and who will read and use this report to make management decisions. In this case, suppose you are told you can determine the profit by subtracting an item's cost from its selling price. The input record contains an additional field, "Quantity in stock." Input records often contain more data than an application needs, so you will ignore this field in your program. You have all the necessary data, so you can begin to plan the program.

FIGURE 4-5: STEPS TO CREATING A PROGRAM

Understand the user's needs. Examine input and output specifications.

Develop the logic that will produce the desired output.

```
private sub command()
    housekeeping()
    while not eof
```

Code the logic using a programming language.

TIP ☐ ☐ ☐ ☐ It is very common for input records to contain more data than an application uses. For example, although your doctor stores your blood pressure in your patient record, that field does not appear on your bill, and although your school stores your grades from your first semester, they do not appear on your report card for your second semester.

Where should you begin? It's wise to try to understand the big picture first. You can write a program that reads records from an input file and produces a printed report as a **procedural program**—that is, a program in which one procedure follows another from the beginning until the end. You write the entire set of instructions for a procedural program, and when the program executes, instructions take place one at a time, following your program's logic. The overall logic, or **mainline logic**, of almost every procedural computer program can follow a general structure that consists of three distinct parts:

1. Performing housekeeping, or initialization tasks. **Housekeeping** includes steps you must perform at the beginning of a program to get ready for the rest of the program.

2. Performing the main loop repeatedly within the program. The **main loop** contains the instructions that are executed for every record until you reach the end of the input of records, or eof.

3. Performing the end-of-job routine. The **end-of-job routine** holds the steps you take at the end of the program to finish the application.

TIP □ □ □ □ | Not all programs are procedural; some are object-oriented. A distinguishing feature of many (but not all) object-oriented programs is that they are event-driven: often the user determines the timing of events in the main loop of the program by using an input device such as a mouse. As you advance in your knowledge of programming, you will learn more about object-oriented techniques.

You can write any procedural program as one long series of programming language statements, but most programmers prefer to break their programs into at least three parts. The main program can call the three major modules, as shown in the flowchart and pseudocode in Figure 4-6. The module or subroutine names, of course, are entirely up to the programmer.

TIP □ □ □ □ | Reducing a large program into more manageable modules is sometimes called **functional decomposition**.

FIGURE 4-6: FLOWCHART AND PSEUDOCODE OF MAINLINE LOGIC

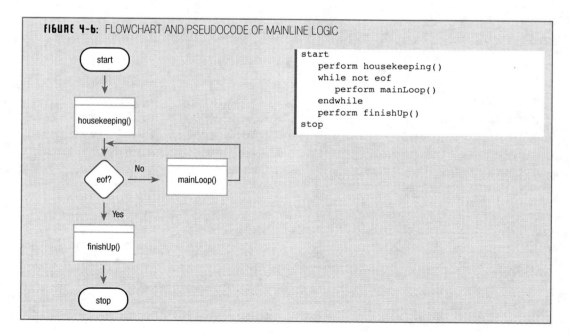

```
start
    perform housekeeping()
    while not eof
        perform mainLoop()
    endwhile
    perform finishUp()
stop
```

Figure 4-7 shows the hierarchy chart for this program.

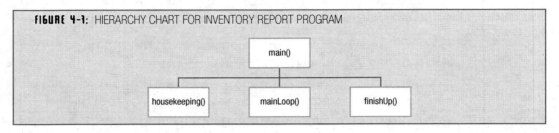

FIGURE 4-7: HIERARCHY CHART FOR INVENTORY REPORT PROGRAM

In summary, breaking down a big program into three basic procedures, or modularizing the program, helps keep the job manageable, allowing you to tackle a large job one step at a time. Dividing the work into routines also might allow you to assign the three major procedures to three different programmers, if you choose. It also helps you keep the program structured.

HOUSEKEEPING TASKS

Housekeeping tasks include all the steps that must take place at the beginning of a program. Very often, this includes four major tasks:

- You declare variables.
- You open files.
- You perform any one-time-only tasks that should occur at the beginning of the program, such as printing headings at the beginning of a report.
- You read the first input record.

DECLARING VARIABLES

Your first task in writing any program is to declare variables. When you declare variables, you assign reasonable names to memory locations, so you can store and retrieve data there. Declaring a variable involves selecting a name and a type. When you declare a variable in program code, the operating system reserves space in memory to hold the contents of the variable. It uses the type (`num` or `char`) to determine how to store the information; it stores numeric and character values in different formats.

For example, within the inventory report program, you need to supply variable names for the data fields that appear in each input record. You might decide on the variable names and types shown in Figure 4-8.

FIGURE 4-8: VARIABLE DECLARATIONS FOR THE INVENTORY FILE

```
char    invItemName
num     invPrice
num     invCost
num     invQuantity
```

TIP ▫ ▫ ▫ ▫ Some languages require that you provide storage size, in addition to a type and name, for each variable. Other languages provide a predetermined amount of storage based on the variable type; for example, four bytes for an integer or one byte for a character. Also, many languages require you to provide a length for strings of characters. For simplicity, this book just declares variables as either character or numeric.

You can provide any names you choose for your variables. When you write another program that uses the same input file, you are free to choose completely new variable names. Similarly, other programmers can write programs that use the same file and choose their own variable names. The variable names just represent memory positions, and are internal to your program. The files do not contain any variable names; files contain only data. When you read the characters "cotton shirt" from an input file, it doesn't matter whether you store those characters at a memory location named invItemName, nameOfItem, productDescription, or any other one-word variable name. The variable name is simply an easy-to-remember name for a specific memory address where those characters are stored.

TIP ▫ ▫ ▫ ▫ Programmers always must decide between descriptive, but long, variable names and cryptic, but short, variable names. In general, more descriptive names are better, but certain abbreviations are almost always acceptable in the business world. For example, SSN is commonly used as an abbreviation for Social Security number, and if you use it as a variable name, it will be interpreted correctly by most of your associates who read your program.

Each of the four variable declarations in Figure 4-8 contains a type (character or numeric) and a name. You can choose any one-word names for the variables, but a typical practice involves beginning similar variables with a common **prefix**, for example, inv. In a large program in which you eventually declare dozens of variables, the inv prefix will help you immediately identify a variable as part of the inventory file.

TIP ▫ ▫ ▫ ▫ Organizations sometimes enforce different rules for programmers to follow when naming variables. Some use a variable-naming convention called **Hungarian notation**, in which a variable's data type or other information is stored as part of the name.

Creating the inventory report as planned in Figure 4-1 involves using the invItemName, invPrice, and invCost fields, but you do not need to use the invQuantity field in this program. However, the information regarding quantity does take room in the input file. If you imagine the surface of a disk as pictured in Figure 4-9, you can envision how the data fields follow one another in the file.

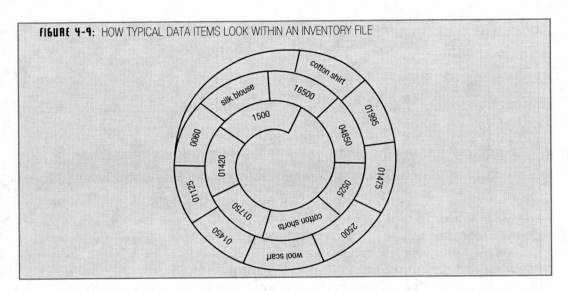

FIGURE 4-9: HOW TYPICAL DATA ITEMS LOOK WITHIN AN INVENTORY FILE

When you ask the program to read in an inventory record, four "chunks" of data will be transferred from the input device to the computer's main memory: name, price, cost, and quantity. When you declare the variables that represent the input data, you must provide a memory position for each of the four pieces of data, whether or not they all are used within this program.

TIP ☐ ☐ ☐ ☐ Some languages do not require you to use a unique name for each data field in an input record. For example, in COBOL, you can use the generic name FILLER for all unused data positions. This frees you from the task of creating variable names for items you do not intend to use. The examples in this book always provide a unique identifier for each variable in a file.

TIP ☐ ☐ ☐ ☐ Considering that dozens of programs within the organization might access the INVENTORY file, some organizations create the data file descriptions for you. This system is efficient because the description of variable names and types is stored in one location, and each programmer who uses the file simply imports the data file description into his or her own program. Of course, the organization must provide the programmer with documentation specifying and describing the chosen names.

In most programming languages, you can give a group of associated variables a **group name**. This allows you to handle several associated variables using a single instruction. Just as it is easier to refer to "The Andersons" than it is to list "Nancy, Bud, Jim, Tom, Julie, Jane, Kate, and John," the benefit of using a group name is the ability to reference several variables with one all-encompassing name. For example, writing `read invRecord` is simpler than writing `read invItemName`, `invPrice`, `invCost`, and `invQuantity`. The way you assign a group name to several variables differs in each programming language. This book follows the convention of underlining any group name and indenting the group members beneath, as shown in Figure 4-10.

FIGURE 4-10: VARIABLE DECLARATIONS FOR THE INVENTORY FILE INCLUDING A GROUP NAME

```
invRecord
       char    invItemName
       num     invPrice
       num     invCost
       num     invQuantity
```

TIP ☐ ☐ ☐ ☐   A group of variables is often called a *data structure*, or more simply, a *structure*. Some object-oriented languages refer to a group as a *class*, although a class often contains method definitions as well as variables.

TIP ☐ ☐ ☐ ☐   The ability to group variable names does not automatically provide you with the ability to perform every sort of operation with a group. For example, you cannot multiply or divide one invRecord by another (unless, with some languages, you write special code to do so). In this book, assume that you can use one input or output statement on a set of fields that constitute a record.

In addition to declaring variables, sometimes you want to provide a variable with an initial value. Providing a variable with a value when you create it is known as **initializing**, or **defining**, **the variable**. For example, for the inventory report print chart shown in Figure 4-1, you might want to create a variable named `mainHeading` and store the value "INVENTORY REPORT" in that variable. The declaration is `char mainHeading = "INVENTORY REPORT"`. This indicates that `mainHeading` is a character variable, and that the character contents are the words "INVENTORY REPORT".

TIP ☐ ☐ ☐ ☐   *Declaring* a variable provides it with a name and type. *Defining*, or initializing, a variable also provides it with a value.
In some programming languages, you can declare a variable such as `mainHeading` to be constant, or never changing. Even though `invItemName`, `invPrice`, and the other fields in the input file will hold a variety of values when a program executes, the `mainHeading` value will never change.

In many programming languages, if you do not provide an initial value when declaring a variable, then the value is unknown or **garbage**. Some programming languages do provide you with an automatic starting value; for example in Java, BASIC, or RPG, all numeric variables automatically begin with the value zero. However, in C++, C#, Pascal, and COBOL, variables do not receive any initial value unless you provide one. No matter which programming language you use, it is always clearest to provide a value for those variables that require them.

TIP ☐ ☐ ☐ ☐   Be especially careful to make sure all variables you use in calculations have initial values. If you perform arithmetic with garbage values, the result will also contain garbage.

When you declare the variables `invItemName`, `invPrice`, `invCost`, and `invQuantity`, you do not provide them with any initial value. The values for these variables will be assigned when the first file record is read into memory. It would be *legal* to assign a value to input file record variables—for example, `invItemName = "cotton shirt"`—but it would be a waste of time and might mislead others who read your program. The first `invItemName` will come from an input device, and may or may not be "cotton shirt."

The report illustrated in Figure 4-1 contains three individual heading lines. The most common practice is to declare one variable or constant for each of these lines. The three declarations are as follows:

```
char mainHeading = "INVENTORY REPORT"
char columnHead1 = "ITEM            RETAIL PRICE
       MANUFACTURING        PROFIT PER"
char columnHead2 = "DESCRIPTION   EACH
       COST EACH          ITEM"
```

Within the program, when it is time to write the heading lines to an output device, you will code:

```
print mainHeading
print columnHead1
print columnHead2
```

You are not required to create variables for your headings. Your program can contain the following statements, in which you use literal strings of characters instead of variable names. The printed results are the same either way.

```
print "INVENTORY REPORT"
print "ITEM          RETAIL PRICE  MANUFACTURING   PROFIT PER"
print "DESCRIPTION   EACH          COST EACH       ITEM"
```

Using variable names, as in `print mainHeading`, is usually more convenient than spelling out the heading's contents within the statement that prints, especially if you will use the headings in multiple locations within your program. Additionally, if the contents of all of a program's heading lines can be found in one location at the start of the program, it is easier to locate them all if changes need to be made in the future.

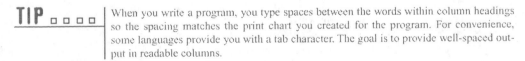

TIP □ □ □ □ When you write a program, you type spaces between the words within column headings so the spacing matches the print chart you created for the program. For convenience, some languages provide you with a tab character. The goal is to provide well-spaced output in readable columns.

Dividing the headings into three lines is not required either, but it is a common practice. In most programming languages, you could write all the headings in one statement, using a code that indicates a new line at every appropriate position. Alternately, most programming languages let you produce a character for output without advancing to a new line. You could write out the headings using separate print statements to display one character at a time, advancing to a new line only after all the line's characters had been individually printed, although this approach seems painstakingly detailed. Storing and writing one complete line at a time is a reasonable compromise.

Every programming language provides you with a means to physically advance printer paper to the top of a page when you print the first heading. Similarly, every language provides you with a means for producing double- and triple-spaced lines of text by sending specific codes to the printer or monitor. Because the methods and codes differ from language to language, examples in this book assume that if a print chart shows a heading that prints at the top of the page and then skips a line, any corresponding variable you create, such as `mainHeading`, will also print in this manner. You can add the appropriate language-specific codes to implement the `mainHeading` spacing when you write the actual computer program. Similarly, if you create a print chart that shows detail lines as double-spaced, assume your detail lines will double-space when you execute the step to write them.

Often, you must create dozens of variables when you write a computer program. If you are using a flowchart to diagram the logic, it is physically impossible to fit the variables in one flowchart box. Therefore, you might want to use an annotation symbol. The beginning of a flowchart for the `housekeeping()` module of the inventory report program is shown in Figure 4-11.

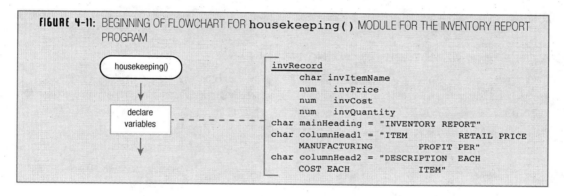

FIGURE 4-11: BEGINNING OF FLOWCHART FOR `housekeeping()` MODULE FOR THE INVENTORY REPORT PROGRAM

TIP ▢ ▢ ▢ ▢ You learned about the annotation symbol in Chapter 3.

Notice that the three heading variables defined in Figure 4-11 are not indented under `invRecord` as the `invRecord` fields are. This shows that although `invItemName`, `invPrice`, `invCost`, and `invQuantity` are part of the `invRecord` group, `mainHeading`, `columnHead1`, and `columnHead2` are not.

In Figure 4-11, notice that columnHead1 contains only the words that appear in the first line of column headings, in row 4 of the print chart in Figure 4-1: "ITEM   RETAIL PRICE   MANUFACTURING   PROFIT PER". Similarly, columnHead2 contains only the words that appear in the second row of column headings.

OPENING FILES

If a program will use input files, you must tell the computer where the input is coming from—for example, a specific disk drive, CD, or tape drive. This process is known as **opening a file**. Because a disk can have many files stored on it, the program also needs to know the name of the file being opened. In many languages, if no input file is opened, input is accepted from a default or **standard input device**, most often the keyboard.

If a program will have output, you must also open a file for output. Perhaps the output file will be sent to a disk or tape. Although you might not think of a printed report as a file, computers treat a printer as just another output device, and if output will go to a printer, then you must open the printer output device as well. Again, if no file is opened, a default or **standard output device**, usually the monitor, is used.

When you create a flowchart, you usually write the command to open the files within a parallelogram. You use the parallelogram because it is the input/output symbol, and you are opening the input and output devices. You can use an annotation box to list the files that you open, as shown in Figure 4-12.

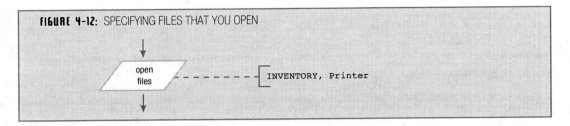

FIGURE 4-12: SPECIFYING FILES THAT YOU OPEN

open files —————— INVENTORY, Printer

A ONE-TIME-ONLY TASK—PRINTING HEADINGS

Within a program's housekeeping module, besides declaring variables and opening files, you perform any other tasks that occur only at the beginning of the program. A common housekeeping task involves printing headings at the top of a report. In the inventory report example, three lines of headings appear at the beginning of the report. In this example, printing the heading lines is straightforward:

```
print mainHeading
print columnHead1
print columnHead2
```

READING THE FIRST INPUT RECORD

The last task you execute in the `housekeeping()` module of most computer programs is to read the first data record into memory. When you read the four data fields for the inventory file data, you can write `read invItemName,` `invPrice, invCost, invQuantity`, but if you have declared a group name such as `invRecord`, it is simpler to write `read invRecord`. Using the group name is a shortcut for writing each field name.

The last task within the `housekeeping()` module is to read the first `invRecord`; the first task following `housekeeping()` is to check for `eof` on the file that contains the inventory records. An input device recognizes that it has reached the end of a file when it attempts to read a record and finds no records available. Recall the mainline logic of the inventory report program from Figure 4-6—`eof` is tested immediately after `housekeeping()` ends.

If the input file has no records, when you read the first record the computer recognizes the end-of-file condition and proceeds to the `finishUp()` module, never executing `mainLoop()`. More commonly, an input file does have records, and after the first `read` the computer determines that the `eof` condition is false, and the logic proceeds to the `mainLoop()`.

Immediately after reading from a file, the next step always should determine whether `eof` was encountered. Notice in Figure 4-6 that the `eof` question always follows both the `housekeeping()` module and the `mainLoop()` module. When the last instruction in each of these modules reads a record, then the `eof` question correctly follows each `read` instruction immediately.

Not reading the first record within the `housekeeping()` module is a mistake. If `housekeeping()` does not include a step to read a record from the input file, you must read a record as the first step in the `mainLoop()`, as shown on the left side of Figure 4-13. In this program, a record is read, a profit is calculated, and a line is printed. Then, if it is not `eof`, another record is read, a profit calculated, and a line printed. The program works well, reading records, calculating profits, and printing information until reaching a `read` command in which the computer encounters the `eof` condition. When this last read occurs, the next steps involve computing a profit and writing a line—but there isn't any data to process. Depending on the programming language you use, either garbage data will calculate and print, or a repeat of the data from the last record before `eof` will print.

TIP □ □ □ □ | Reading an input record in the `housekeeping()` section is an example of a priming read. You learned about the priming read in Chapter 2.
In some modern programming languages, such as Visual Basic, file `read` commands can look ahead to determine if the *next* record is empty. With these languages, the priming read is no longer necessary. Because most languages do not currently have this type of read statement, and because the priming read is always necessary when input is based on user response rather than reading from a file, this book uses the conventional priming read.

The flowchart in the lower part of Figure 4-13 shows correct record-reading logic. The appropriate place for the priming record `read` is at the end of the preliminary housekeeping steps, and the appropriate place for all subsequent reads is at the end of the main processing loop.

FIGURE 4-13: COMPARING FAULTY AND CORRECT RECORD-READING LOGIC

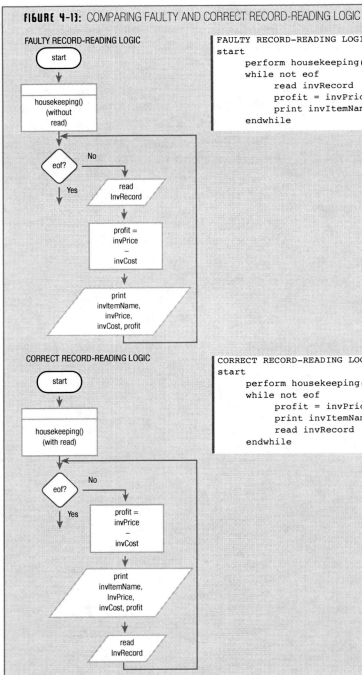

FAULTY RECORD-READING LOGIC

```
FAULTY RECORD-READING LOGIC
start
      perform housekeeping() (without read)
      while not eof
            read invRecord
            profit = invPrice - invCost
            print invItemName, invPrice, invCost, profit
      endwhile
```

CORRECT RECORD-READING LOGIC

```
CORRECT RECORD-READING LOGIC
start
      perform housekeeping() (with read)
      while not eof
            profit = invPrice - invCost
            print invItemName, invPrice, invCost, profit
            read invRecord
      endwhile
```

Figure 4-14 shows a completed `housekeeping()` routine for the inventory program in both flowchart and pseudocode versions.

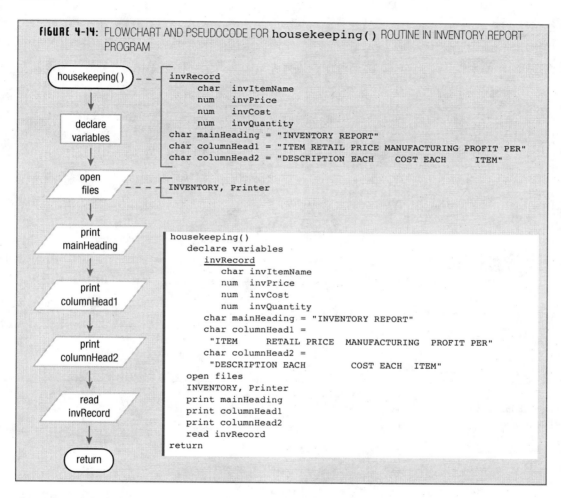

FIGURE 4-14: FLOWCHART AND PSEUDOCODE FOR `housekeeping()` ROUTINE IN INVENTORY REPORT PROGRAM

As an alternative to including `print mainHeading`, `print columnHead1`, and `print columnHead2` within the `housekeeping()` module, you can place the three heading line statements in their own subroutine. In this case, the flowchart and pseudocode for `housekeeping()` will look like Figure 4-15, with the steps in the newly created `headings()` module appearing in Figure 4-16. Either approach is fine; the logic of the program is the same whether or not the heading line statements are segregated into their own routine. The programmer can decide on the program organization that makes the most sense.

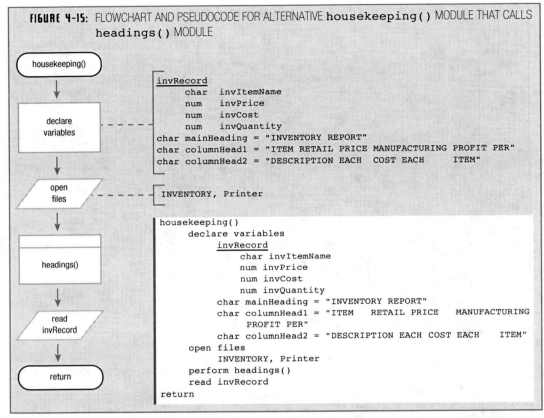

FIGURE 4-15: FLOWCHART AND PSEUDOCODE FOR ALTERNATIVE `housekeeping()` MODULE THAT CALLS `headings()` MODULE

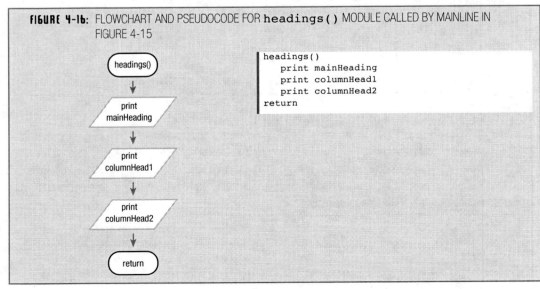

FIGURE 4-16: FLOWCHART AND PSEUDOCODE FOR `headings()` MODULE CALLED BY MAINLINE IN FIGURE 4-15

WRITING THE MAIN LOOP

After you declare the variables for a program and perform the housekeeping tasks, the "real work" of the program begins. The inventory report described at the beginning of this chapter and depicted in Figure 4-1 needs just one set of variables and one set of headings, yet there might be hundreds or thousands of inventory items to process. The main loop of a program, controlled by the eof decision, is the program's "workhorse." Each data record will pass once through the main loop, where calculations are performed with the data and the results printed.

TIP ▫ ▫ ▫ ▫ | If the inventory report contains more records than will fit on a page of output, you probably will want to print a new set of headings at the top of each page. You will learn how to do this in Chapter 7.

For the inventory report program to work, the mainLoop() module must include three steps:

1. Calculate the profit for an item.
2. Print the item information on the report.
3. Read the next inventory record.

At the end of housekeeping(), you read one data record into the computer's memory. As the first step in the mainLoop(), you can calculate an item's profit by subtracting its manufacturing cost from its retail price: profit = invPrice - invCost. The name profit is the programmer-created variable name for a new spot in computer memory where the value of the profit is stored. Although it is legal to use any variable name to represent profit, naming it invProfit would be misleading. Using the inv prefix would lead those who read your program to believe that profit was part of the input record, like the other variable names that start with inv. The profit is not part of the input record however; it represents a memory location used to store the arithmetic difference between two other variables.

TIP ▫ ▫ ▫ ▫ | Recall that the standard way to express mathematical statements is to assign values from the right side of an equal sign to the left. That is, profit = invPrice - invCost assigns a value to profit. The statement invPrice - invCost = profit is an illegal statement.

Because you have a new variable, you must add profit to the list of declared variables at the beginning of the program. Programmers often work back and forth between the variable list and the logical steps during the creation of a program, listing some of the variables they will need as soon as they start to plan, and adding others later as they think of them. Because profit will hold the result of a mathematical calculation, you should declare it as a numeric variable when you add it to the variable list, as shown in Figure 4-17. Notice that, like the headings, profit is not indented under invRecord. You want to show that profit is not part of the invRecord group; instead, it is a separate variable that you are declaring to store a calculated value.

TIP ▫ ▫ ▫ ▫ | You can declare mainHeading, columnHead1, columnHead2, and profit in any order. The important point is that none of these four variables is part of the invRecord group.

FIGURE 4-17: VARIABLE LIST FOR INVENTORY REPORT PROGRAM, INCLUDING PROFIT

```
invRecord
   char   invItemName
   num    invPrice
   num    invCost
   num    invQuantity
char mainHeading = "INVENTORY       REPORT"
char columnHead1 = "ITEM                 RETAIL PRICE   MANUFACTURING   PROFIT PER"
char columnHead2 = "DESCRIPTION          EACH           COST EACH       ITEM"
num profit
```

After you determine an item's profit, you can write a detail line of information on the inventory report: `print invItemName, invPrice, invCost, profit`. Notice that in the flowchart and pseudocode for the `mainLoop()` routine in Figure 4-15, the output statement is not `print invRecord`. For one thing, the entire `invRecord` is not printed—the quantity is not part of the report. Also, the calculated profit is included in the detail line—it does not appear on the input record. Even if the report detail lines listed each of the `invRecord` fields in the exact same order as on the input file, the print statement still would most often be written listing the individual fields to be printed. Usually, you would include a formatting statement with each printed field to control the spacing within the detail line. Because the way you space fields on detail lines differs greatly in programming languages, discussion of the syntax to space fields is not included in this book. However, the fields that are printed are listed separately, as you would usually do when coding in a specific programming language.

The last step in the `mainLoop()` module of the inventory report program involves reading in the next `invRecord`. Figure 4-18 shows the flowchart and pseudocode for `mainLoop()`.

Just as headings are printed one full line at a time, detail lines are also printed one line at a time. You can print each field separately, as in the following code, but it is clearer and most efficient to write one full line at a time, as shown in Figure 4-18.

```
print invItemName
print invPrice
print invCost
print profit
```

In most programming languages, you also have the option of calculating the profit and printing it in one statement, as in the following:

```
print invItemName, invPrice, invCost, invPrice - invCost
```

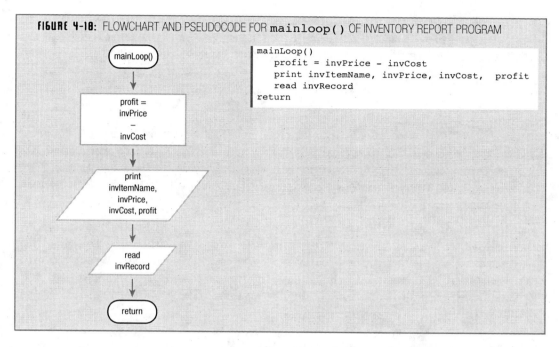

FI6URE 4-18: FLOWCHART AND PSEUDOCODE FOR `mainloop()` OF INVENTORY REPORT PROGRAM

```
mainLoop()
    profit = invPrice - invCost
    print invItemName, invPrice, invCost,  profit
    read invRecord
return
```

If the language you use allows this type of statement, in which a calculation takes place within the output statement, it is up to you to decide which format to use. Performing the arithmetic as part of the `print` statement allows you to avoid declaring a `profit` variable. However, if you need the `profit` figure for further calculations, then it makes sense to compute the profit and store it in a `profit` field. Using a separate **work variable** or **work field** such as `profit` to temporarily hold a calculation is never wrong, and often it's the clearest course of action.

TIP □ □ □ □ | As with performing arithmetic within a print statement, different languages often provide multiple ways to combine several steps into one. For example, many languages allow you to print multiple lines of output or read a record and check for end of file using one statement. This book uses only the most common combinations, such as performing arithmetic within a print statement.

TIP □ □ □ □ | Although a language may allow you to combine actions in a single statement, you are never required to do so. If the program is clearer using separate statements, then that is what you should do.

After the detail line containing the item name, price, cost, and profit has been written, the last step you take before leaving the `mainLoop()` module is to read the next record from the input file into memory. When you exit the `mainLoop()`, the logic flows back to the `eof` question in the mainline logic. If it is not `eof`—that is, if an additional data record exists—then you enter the `mainLoop()` again, compute profit on the second record, print the detail line, and read the third record.

Eventually, during an execution of the `mainLoop()`, the program will read a new record and encounter the end of the file. Then, when you ask the `eof` question in the main line of the program, the answer will be *yes*, and the program will not enter the `mainLoop()` again. Instead, the program logic will enter the `finishUp()` routine.

PERFORMING END-OF-JOB TASKS

Within any program, the end-of-job routine holds the steps you must take at the end of the program, after all input records are processed. Some end-of-job modules print summaries or grand totals at the end of a report. Others might print a message such as "End of Report," so readers can be confident that they have received all the information that should be included. Such end-of-job message lines often are called **footer lines**, or **footers** for short. Very often, end-of-job modules must close any open files.

The end-of-job module for the inventory report program is very simple. The print chart does not indicate that any special messages, such as "Thank you for reading this report", print after the detail lines end. Likewise, there are no required summary or total lines; nothing special happens. Only one task needs to be performed in the end-of-job routine that this program calls `finishUp()`. In `housekeeping()`, you opened files; in `finishUp()`, you close them. The complete `finishUp()` module is flowcharted and written in pseudocode in Figure 4-19.

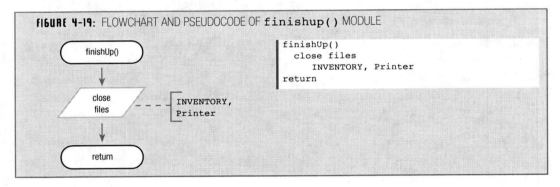

FIGURE 4-19: FLOWCHART AND PSEUDOCODE OF `finishup()` MODULE

Many programmers wouldn't bother with a subroutine for just one statement, but as you create more complicated programs, your end-of-job routines will get bigger, and it will make more sense to see the necessary job-finishing tasks together in a module.

For your convenience, Figure 4-20 shows the flowchart and pseudocode for the entire inventory report program. Make sure you understand the importance of each flowchart symbol and each pseudocode line. There is nothing superfluous—each is included to accomplish a specific part of the program that creates the completed inventory report.

FIGURE 4-20: FLOWCHART AND PSEUDOCODE FOR INVENTORY REPORT PROGRAM

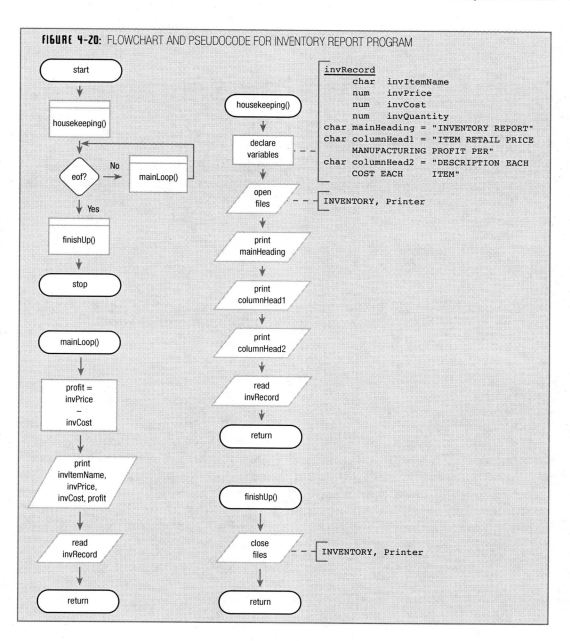

FIGURE 4-20: FLOWCHART AND PSEUDOCODE FOR INVENTORY REPORT PROGRAM (CONTINUED)

```
start                          housekeeping()
   perform housekeeping()         declare variables
   while not eof                     invRecord
       perform mainLoop()               char    invItemName
   endwhile                             num     invPrice
   perform finishUp()                   num     invCost
stop                                    num     invQuantity
                                  char mainHeading = "INVENTORY REPORT"
                                  char columnHead1 =
                                     "ITEM          RETAIL PRICE  MANUFACTURING  PROFIT PER"
                                  char columnHead2 =
                                     "DESCRIPTION EACH           COST EACH      ITEM"
                                  open files
                                     INVENTORY, Printer
                                  print mainHeading
                                  print columnHead1
                                  print columnHead2
                                  read invRecord
                               return


mainLoop()                                      finishUp()
   profit = invPrice - invCost                     close files
   print invItemName, invPrice, invCost,  profit      INVENTORY, Printer
   read invRecord                               return
return
```

UNDERSTANDING THE NEED FOR GOOD PROGRAM DESIGN

As your programs become larger and more complicated, the need for good planning and design increases. Think of an application you use, such as a word processor or a spreadsheet. The number and variety of user options are staggering. Not only would it be impossible for a single programmer to write such an application, but without thorough planning and design, the components would never work together properly. Ideally, each program module you design needs to work well as a stand-alone module and as an element of larger systems. Just as a house with poor plumbing or a car with bad brakes is fatally flawed, a computer-based application can be great only if each component is designed well.

STORING PROGRAM COMPONENTS IN SEPARATE FILES

When you start to work on professional programs, you will see that many of them are quite lengthy, with some containing hundreds of variables and thousands of lines of code. Earlier in this chapter, you learned you can manage lengthy procedural programs by breaking them into modules. Although modularization helps you to organize your programs, sometimes it is still difficult to manage all of a program's components.

Most modern programming languages allow you to store program components in separate files. If you write a module and store it in the same file as the program that uses it, your program files become large and hard to work with, whether you are trying to read them on a screen or on multiple printed pages. In addition, when you define a useful module, you might want to use it in many programs. Of course, you can copy module definitions from one file to another, but this method is time-consuming as well as prone to error. A better solution (if you are using a language that allows it) is to store your modules in individual files and use an instruction to include them in any program that uses them. The statement needed to access modules from separate files varies from language to language, but it usually involves using a verb such as *include*, *import*, or *copy*, followed by the name of the file that contains the module.

For example, suppose your company has a standard employee record definition, part of which is shown in Figure 4-21. Files with the same format are used in many applications within the organization—personnel reports, production reports, payroll, and so on. It would be a tremendous waste of resources if every programmer rewrote this file definition in multiple applications. Instead, once a programmer writes the statements that constitute the file definition, those statements should be imported in their entirety into any program that uses a record with the same structure. For example, Figure 4-22 shows how the data fields in Figure 4-21 would be defined in the C++ programming language. If the statements in Figure 4-22 are saved in a file named Employees, then any C++ program can contain the statement `#include Employees` and all the data fields are automatically defined.

TIP ▫ ▫ ▫ ▫ | The pound sign (#) is used with the include statement in C++ to notify the compiler that it is part of a special type of statement called a *pre-processor directive*.

FIGURE 4-21: PARTIAL EMPLOYEES FILE DESCRIPTION

EMPLOYEE FILE DESCRIPTION

FILE NAME: EMPLOYEES

Field description	Data type	Decimals
Employee ID	numeric	0
Last name	character	
First name	character	
Hire date	numeric	0
Hourly wage	numeric	2
Birth date	numeric	0
Termination date	numeric	0

FIGURE 4-22: DATA FIELDS IN FIGURE 4-21 DEFINED IN THE C++ LANGUAGE

```
class Employee
{
      int employeeID;
      string lastName;
      string firstName;
      long hireDate;
      double hourlyWage;
      long birthDate;
      long terminationDate;
};
```

TIP ▫ ▫ ▫ ▫ | Don't be concerned with the syntax used in the file description in Figure 4-22. The words *class*, *int*, *string*, *long*, and *double* are all part of the C++ programming language and are not important to you now. Simply concentrate on how the variable names reflect the field descriptions in Figure 4-21.

Suppose you write a useful module that checks dates to guarantee their validity. For example, the two digits that represent a month can be neither less than 01 nor greater than 12, and the two digits that represent the day can contain different possible values, depending on the month. Any program that uses the employee file description shown in Figure 4-21 might want to call the date-validating module several times in order to validate any employee's hire date, birth date, and termination date. Not only do you want to call this module from several locations within any one program, you want to call it from many programs. For example, programs used for company ordering and billing would each contain several dates. If the date-validating module is useful and well-written, you might even want to market it to other companies. By storing the module in its own file, you enable its use to be flexible. When you write a program of any length, you should consider storing each of its components in its own file.

Storing components in separate files can provide an advantage beyond ease of reuse. When you let others use your programs or modules, you often provide them with only the compiled (that is, machine-language) version of your code, not the **source code**, which is composed of readable statements. Storing your program statements in a separate, non-readable, compiled file is an example of **implementation hiding**, or hiding the details of how the program or module works. Other programmers can use your code, but cannot see the statements you used to create it. A programmer who cannot see your well-designed modules is more likely to use them simply as they were intended; the programmer also will not be able to attempt to make adjustments in your code, thereby introducing error. Of course, in order to work with your modules or data definitions, a programmer must know the names and types of data you are using. Typically, you provide programmers who use your definitions with written documentation of the data names and purposes.

TIP ▫ ▫ ▫ ▫ | Recall from Chapter 1 that when you write a program in a programming language, you must compile or interpret it into machine language before the computer can actually carry out your instructions.

SELECTING VARIABLE AND MODULE NAMES

An often-overlooked element in program design is the selection of good data and module names (sometimes generically called **identifiers**). In Chapter 1, you learned that every programming language has specific rules for the construction of names—some languages limit the number of characters, some allow dashes, and so on—but there are other general guidelines:

- Use meaningful names. Creating a data field named `someData` or a module named `firstModule()` makes a program cryptic. Not only will others find it hard to read your programs, but you will forget the purpose of these identifiers even within your own programs. All programmers occasionally use short, nondescriptive names such as `x` or `temp` in a quick program written to test a procedure; however, in most cases, data and module names should be meaningful. Programmers refer to programs that contain meaningful names as **self-documenting**. This means that even without further documentation, the program code explains itself to readers.

- Usually, you should use pronounceable names. A variable name like `pzf` is neither pronounceable nor meaningful. A name that looks meaningful when you write it might not be as meaningful when someone else reads it; for instance, `preparead()` might mean "Prepare ad" to you, but is "Prep a read" to others. Look at your names critically to make sure they are pronounceable. Very standard abbreviations do not have to be pronounceable. For example, most business people would interpret `ssn` as a Social Security number.

TIP □ □ □ □ Don't forget that not all programmers share your culture. An abbreviation whose meaning seems obvious to you might be cryptic to someone in a different part of the world.

- Be judicious in your use of abbreviations. You can save a few keystrokes when creating a module called `getStat()`, but is its purpose to find the state in which a city is located, output some statistics, or determine the status of some variables? Similarly, is a variable named `fn` meant to hold a first name, file number, or something else?

TIP □ □ □ □ To save typing time when you develop a program, you can use a short name like `efn`. After the program operates correctly, you can use an editor's Search and Replace feature to replace your coded name with a more meaningful name such as `employeeFirstName`. Some newer compilers support an automatic statement completion feature that saves typing time. After the first time you use a name like `employeeFirstName`, you need to type only the first few letters before the compiler editor offers a list of available names from which to choose. The list is constructed from all names you have used in the file that begin with the same characters.

- Usually, avoid digits in a name. Zeroes get confused with the letter "O", and lowercase "l"s are misread as the numeral 1. Of course, use your judgment: `budgetFor2005` is probably not going to be misinterpreted.

- Use the system your language allows to separate words in long, multiword variable names. For example, if the programming language you use allows dashes or underscores, then use a method name like `initialize-data()` or `initialize_data()`, which is easier to read than `initializedata()`. If you use a language that allows camel casing, then use `initializeData()`. If you use a language that is case sensitive, it is legal but confusing to use variable names that differ only in case, for example `empName`, `EmpName`, and `Empname`.

- Consider including a form of the verb *to be*, such as *is* or *are*, in names for variables that are intended to hold a status. For example, use `isFinished` as a flag variable that holds a "Y" or "N" to indicate whether a file is exhausted. The shorter name `finished` is likely to be confused with a module that executes when a program is done.

When you begin to write programs, the process of determining what data variables and modules you will need and what to name them all might seem overwhelming. The design process is crucial, however. When you acquire your first professional programming assignment, the design process might very well be completed already. Most likely, your first assignment will be to write or make modifications to one small member module of a much larger application. The more the original programmers stuck to these guidelines, the better the original design was, and the easier your job of modification will be.

DESIGNING CLEAR MODULE STATEMENTS

In addition to selecting good identifiers, you can use the following tactics to contribute to the clarity of the statements within your program modules.

- Avoid confusing line breaks.
- Use temporary variables to clarify long statements.
- Use constants where appropriate.

AVOIDING CONFUSING LINE BREAKS

Some older programming languages require that program statements be placed in specific columns. Most modern programming languages are free-form; you can arrange your lines of code any way you see fit. As in real life, with freedom comes responsibility; when you have flexibility in arranging your lines of code, you must take care to make sure your meaning is clear. With free-form code, programmers often do not provide enough line breaks, or they provide inappropriate ones.

Figure 4-23 shows an example of code (part of the housekeeping module from Figure 4-14) that does not provide enough line breaks for clarity. If you have been following the examples used throughout this book, the code in Figure 4-24 looks clearer to you; it will also look clearer to most other programmers.

FIGURE 4-23: PART OF A `housekeeping()` MODULE WITH INSUFFICIENT LINE BREAKS

```
open files   print mainHeading   print columnHead1
  print columnHead2   read invRecord
```

FIGURE 4-24: PART OF A `housekeeping()` MODULE WITH APPROPRIATE LINE BREAKS

```
open files
print mainHeading
print columnHead1
print columnHead2
read invRecord
```

Figure 4-24 shows that more, but shorter, lines usually improve your ability to understand a program's logic; appropriately breaking lines will become even more important as you introduce decisions and loops into your programs in the next chapters.

USING TEMPORARY VARIABLES TO CLARIFY LONG STATEMENTS

When you need several mathematical operations to determine a result, consider using a series of temporary variables to hold intermediate results. For example, Figure 4-25 shows two ways to calculate a value for a real estate `salespersonCommission` variable. Each method achieves the same result—the salesperson's commission is based on the square feet multiplied by the price per square foot plus any premium for a lot with special features, such as a wooded or waterfront lot. However, the second example uses two temporary variables, `sqFootPrice` and `totalPrice`. When the computation is broken down into less complicated, individual steps, it is easier to see how the total price is calculated. In calculations with even more computation steps, performing the arithmetic in stages would become increasingly helpful.

TIP ▫ ▫ ▫ ▫ Programmers might say using temporary variables, like the example in Figure 4-25, is *cheap*. When executing a lengthy arithmetic statement, even if you don't explicitly name temporary variables, the programming language compiler creates them behind the scenes, so declaring them yourself does not cost much in terms of program execution time.

FIGURE 4-25: TWO WAYS OF ACHIEVING THE SAME `salespersonCommission` RESULT

```
salespersonCommission = (sqFeet * pricePerSquareFoot + lotPremium) *
        commissionRate
```
```
sqFootPrice = sqFeet * pricePerSquareFoot
totalPrice = sqFootPrice + lotPremium
salespersonCommission = totalPrice * commissionRate
```

USING CONSTANTS WHERE APPROPRIATE

Whenever possible, use named values in your programs. If your program contains a statement like `salesTax = price * taxRate` instead of `salesTax = price * .06`, you gain two benefits:

- It is easier for readers to know that the price is being multiplied by a tax rate instead of a discount, commission, or some other rate represented by .06.
- When the tax rate changes, you make one change to the value where `taxRate` is defined, rather than searching through a program for every instance of .06.

For example, the program segment in Figure 4-26 uses the constants `tuitionPerCreditHour` and `athleticFee`. If the values of these variables change in the future, then the changes to the constants can be made in the declaration list, and the actual program code does not have to be disturbed.

FIGURE 4-26: PROGRAM SEGMENT THAT CALCULATES STUDENT BALANCE DUE USING DEFINED CONSTANTS

```
declare variables
    studentRecord
        num studentId
        num creditsEnrolled
    num tuitionDue
    num totalDue
    num tuitionPerCreditHour = 74.50
    num athleticFee = 25.00
read studentRecord
tuitionDue = creditsEnrolled * tuitionPerCreditHour
totalDue = tuitionDue + athleticFee
```

TIP ▫ ▫ ▫ ▫ | Some programmers refer to numeric constants that are hard coded into a program as "magic numbers." They feel that using magic numbers should always be avoided, and that you should provide a descriptive name for every numeric constant you use.

MAINTAINING GOOD PROGRAMMING HABITS

When you learn a programming language and begin to write lines of program code, it is easy to forget the principles you have learned in this text. Having some programming knowledge and a keyboard at your fingertips can lure you into typing lines of code before you think things through. But every program you write will be better if you plan before you code. If you maintain the habits of first drawing flowcharts or writing pseudocode, as you have learned here, your future programming projects will go more smoothly. If you walk through your program logic on paper (called **desk-checking**) before starting to type statements in C++, COBOL, Visual Basic, or Java, your programs will run correctly sooner. If you think carefully about the variable and module names you use, and design your program statements so they are easy for others to read, you will be rewarded with programs that are easier to get up and running, and are easier to maintain as well.

CHAPTER SUMMARY

☐ When you write a complete program, you first determine whether you have all the necessary data to produce the report. Then, you plan the mainline logic, which usually includes modules to perform housekeeping, a main loop that contains the steps that repeat for every record, and an end-of-job routine.

☐ Housekeeping tasks include all steps that must take place at the beginning of a program. These tasks include declaring variables, opening files, performing any one-time-only tasks—such as printing headings at the beginning of a report—and reading the first input record.

☐ The main loop of a program is controlled by the `eof` decision. Each data record passes once through the main loop, where calculations are performed with the data and results are printed.

☐ Within any program, the end-of-job module holds the steps you must take at the end of the program, after all the input records have been processed. Typical tasks include printing summaries, grand totals, or final messages at the end of a report, and closing all open files.

☐ As your programs become larger and more complicated, the need for good planning and design increases.

☐ Most modern programming languages allow you to store program components in separate files and use instructions to include them in any program that uses them. Storing components in separate files can provide the advantages of easy reuse and implementation hiding.

☐ When selecting data and module names, use meaningful, pronounceable names. Be judicious in your use of abbreviations, avoid digits in a name, and visually separate words in multiword names. Consider including a form of the verb *to be*, such as *is* or *are*, in names for variables and those that are intended to hold a status.

☐ When writing program statements, you should avoid confusing line breaks, use temporary variables to clarify long statements, and use constants where appropriate.

KEY TERMS

A user, or client, is a person who requests a program, and who will actually use the output of the program.

A procedural program is a program in which one procedure follows another from the beginning until the end.

The mainline logic of a program is the overall logic of the main program from beginning to end.

A housekeeping module includes steps you must perform at the beginning of a program, to get ready for the rest of the program.

The main loop of a program contains the steps that are repeated for every record.

The end-of-job routine holds the steps you take at the end of the program, to finish the application.

Functional decomposition is the act of reducing a large program into more manageable modules.

A prefix is a set of characters used at the beginning of related variable names.

Hungarian notation is a variable-naming convention in which a variable's data type or other information is stored as part of its name.

A group name is a name for a group of associated variables.

Initializing, or defining, a variable is the process of providing a variable with a value, as well as a name and a type, when you create it.

Garbage is the unknown value of an undefined variable.

Opening a file is the process of telling the computer where the input is coming from—for example, a specific disk drive, CD, or tape drive.

The standard input device is the default device from which input comes, most often the keyboard.

The standard output device is the default device to which output is sent, usually the monitor.

A work variable, or work field, is a variable you use to temporarily hold a calculation.

Footer lines, or footers, are end-of-job message lines.

Source code is the readable statements of a program, written in a programming language.

Implementation hiding is hiding the details of the way a program or module works.

Identifiers are the names of variables and modules.

Self-documenting programs are those that contain meaningful data and module names that describe the programs' purpose.

Desk-checking is the process of walking through a program's logic on paper.

REVIEW QUESTIONS

1. **Input records usually contain _____.**
    a. less data than an application needs
    b. more data than an application needs
    c. exactly the amount of data an application needs
    d. none of the data an application needs

2. **A program in which one operation follows another from the beginning until the end is a _____ program.**
    a. modular
    b. functional
    c. procedural
    d. object-oriented

3. **The mainline logic of many computer programs contains _____.**
    a. calls to housekeeping, record processing, and finishing routines
    b. steps to declare variables, open files, and read the first record
    c. arithmetic instructions that are performed for each record on the input file
    d. steps to print totals and close files

4. **Modularizing a program _____.**

   a. keeps large jobs manageable
   b. allows work to be divided easily
   c. helps keep a program structured
   d. all of the above

5. **Which of the following is not a typical housekeeping module task?**

   a. declaring variables
   b. printing summaries
   c. opening files
   d. performing a priming read

6. **When a programmer uses a data file and names the first field stored in each record `idNumber`, then other programmers who use the same file _____ in their programs.**

   a. must also name the field `idNumber`
   b. might name the field `idNumber`
   c. cannot name the field `idNumber`
   d. cannot name the field

7. **If you use a data file containing student records, and the first field is the student's last name, then you can name the field _____.**

   a. `stuLastName`
   b. `studentLastName`
   c. `lastName`
   d. any of the above

8. **If a field in a data file used for program input contains "Johnson", then the best choice from among the following names for a programmer to use when declaring a memory location for the data is _____.**

   a. Johnson
   b. n
   c. `lastName`
   d. A programmer cannot declare a variable name for this field; it is already called Johnson.

9. **The purpose of using a group name is _____.**

   a. to be able to handle several variables with a single instruction
   b. to eliminate the need for machine-level instructions
   c. to be able to use both character and numeric values within the same program
   d. to be able to use multiple input files concurrently

10. **Defining a variable means the same as _____ it.**

    a. declaring
    b. initializing
    c. deleting
    d. assigning

11. **In most programming languages, the initial value of unassigned variables is _____.**

    a. 0
    b. spaces
    c. 0 or spaces, depending on whether the variable is numeric or character
    d. unknown

12. **The types of variables you usually do not initialize are _____.**

    a. those that will never change value during a program
    b. those representing fields on an input file
    c. those that will be used in mathematical statements
    d. those that will not be used in mathematical statements

13. **The name programmers use for unknown variable values is _____.**

    a. default
    b. trash
    c. naive
    d. garbage

14. **Preparing an input device to deliver data records to a program is called _____ a file.**

    a. prompting
    b. opening
    c. refreshing
    d. initializing

15. **A computer system's standard input device is most often _____.**

    a. a mouse
    b. a floppy disk
    c. a keyboard
    d. a compact disc

16. **The last task performed in a housekeeping module is most often to _____.**

    a. open files
    b. close files
    c. check for eof
    d. read an input record

17. **Most business programs contain a _____ that executes once for each record on an input file.**

    a. housekeeping module
    b. main loop
    c. finish routine
    d. terminal symbol

18. Which of the following pseudocode statements is equivalent to this pseudocode:

```
salePrice = salePrice - discount
finalPrice = salePrice + tax
print finalPrice
```

a. `print salePrice + tax`
b. `print salePrice - discount`
c. `print salePrice - discount + tax`
d. `print discount + tax - salePrice`

19. Common end-of-job module tasks in programs include all of the following except _____.

a. opening files
b. printing totals
c. printing end-of-job messages
d. closing files

20. Which of the following is never performed in an end-of-job module?

a. closing files
b. checking for eof
c. printing the message "End of report"
d. adding two values

EXERCISES

1. A pet store owner needs a weekly sales report. The output consists of a printed report titled PET SALES, with column headings TYPE OF ANIMAL and PRICE. Fields printed on output are: type of animal and price. After all records print, a footer line END OF REPORT prints. The input file description is shown below.

```
File name: PETS
```

FIELD DESCRIPTION	POSITIONS	DATA TYPE	DECIMALS
Type of Animal	1-20	Character	
Price of Animal	21-26	Numeric	2

a. Design the print chart for this program.
b. Draw the hierarchy chart for this program.
c. Draw the flowchart for this program.
d. Write the pseudocode for this program.

2. An employer wants to produce a personnel report. The output consists of a printed report titled ACTIVE PERSONNEL. Fields printed on output are: last name of employee, first name of employee, and current weekly salary. Include appropriate column headings and a footer. The input file description is shown below.

```
File name: PERSONNEL
FIELD DESCRIPTION        POSITIONS      DATA TYPE      DECIMALS
Last Name                1-15           Character
First Name               16-30          Character
Soc. Sec. Number         31-39          Numeric        0
Department               40-41          Numeric        0
Current Salary           42-47          Numeric        2
```

a. Design the print chart for this program.
b. Draw the hierarchy chart for this program.
c. Draw the flowchart for this program.
d. Write the pseudocode for this program.

3. An employer wants to produce a personnel report that shows the end result if she gives everyone a 10 percent raise in salary. The output consists of a printed report entitled PROJECTED RAISES. Fields printed on output are: last name of employee, first name of employee, current weekly salary, and projected weekly salary. The input file description is shown below.

```
File name: PERSONNEL
FIELD DESCRIPTION        POSITIONS      DATA TYPE      DECIMALS
Last Name                1-15           Character
First Name               16-30          Character
Soc. Sec. Number         31-39          Numeric        0
Department               40-41          Numeric        0
Current Salary           42-47          Numeric        2
```

a. Design the print chart for this program.
b. Draw the hierarchy chart for this program.
c. Draw the flowchart for this program.
d. Write the pseudocode for this program.

4. A furniture store maintains an inventory file that includes data about every item it sells. The manager wants a report that lists each stock number, description, and profit, which is the retail price minus the wholesale price. The fields include a stock number, description, wholesale price, and retail price. The input file description is shown below.

```
File name: FURNITURE
FIELD DESCRIPTION        POSITIONS      DATA TYPE      DECIMALS
Stock Number             1-4            Numeric        0
Description              5-29           Character
Wholesale Price          30-35          Numeric        2
Retail Price             36-41          Numeric        2
```

a. Design the print chart for this program.
b. Draw the hierarchy chart for this program.

    c. Draw the flowchart for this program.

    d. Write the pseudocode for this program.

5. **A summer camp keeps a record for every camper, including first name, last name, birth date, and skill scores that range from 1 to 10 in four areas: swimming, tennis, horsemanship, and crafts. (The birth date is stored in the format MMDDYYYY without any punctuation.) The camp wants a printed report listing each camper's data, plus a total score that is the sum of the camper's four skill scores. The input file description is shown below.**

```
File name: CAMPERS
FIELD DESCRIPTION        POSITIONS      DATA TYPE      DECIMALS
First Name               1-15           Character
Last Name                16-30          Character
Birth Date               31-38          Numeric        0
Swimming Skill           39-40          Numeric        0
Tennis Skill             41-42          Numeric        0
Horsemanship Skill       43-44          Numeric        0
Crafts Skill             45-46          Numeric        0
```

    a. Design the print chart for this program.

    b. Draw the hierarchy chart for this program.

    c. Draw the flowchart for this program.

    d. Write the pseudocode for this program.

6. **An employer needs to determine how much tax to withhold for each employee. This withholding amount computes as 20 percent of each employee's weekly pay. The output consists of a printed report titled WITHHOLDING FOR EACH EMPLOYEE. Fields printed on output are: last name of employee, first name of employee, hourly pay, weekly pay based on a 40-hour work week, and withholding amount per week. The input file description is shown below.**

```
File name: EMPLOYEES
FIELD DESCRIPTION        POSITIONS      DATA TYPE      DECIMALS
Company ID               1-5            Numeric        0
First Name               6-17           Character
Last Name                18-29          Character
Hourly Rate              30-34          Numeric        2
```

    a. Design the print chart for this program.

    b. Draw the hierarchy chart for this program.

    c. Draw the flowchart for this program.

    d. Write the pseudocode for this program.

7. A baseball team manager wants a report showing her players' batting statistics. A batting average is computed as hits divided by at-bats, and it is usually expressed to three decimal positions, for example: .235. The output consists of a printed report titled TEAM STATISTICS. Fields printed on output are: player number, first name, last name, and batting average. The input file description is shown below.

```
File name: BASEBALL
FIELD DESCRIPTION        POSITIONS       DATA TYPE       DECIMALS
Player Number            1-2             Numeric         0
First Name               3-18            Character
Last Name                19-35           Character
At-bats                  36-38           Numeric         0
Hits                     39-41           Numeric         0
```

a. Design the print chart for this program.
b. Draw the hierarchy chart for this program.
c. Draw the flowchart for this program.
d. Write the pseudocode for this program.

5

MAKING DECISIONS

After studying Chapter 5, you should be able to:

- ☐ Evaluate Boolean expressions to make comparisons
- ☐ Use the logical comparison operators
- ☐ Understand AND logic
- ☐ Understand OR logic
- ☐ Use selections within ranges
- ☐ Understand precedence when combining AND and OR selections
- ☐ Understand the case structure
- ☐ Use decision tables

EVALUATING BOOLEAN EXPRESSIONS TO MAKE COMPARISONS

The reason people think computers are smart lies in the computer program's ability to make decisions. A medical diagnosis program that can decide if your symptoms fit various disease profiles seems quite intelligent, as does a program that can offer you different potential vacation routes based on your destination.

The selection structure (sometimes called a decision structure) involved in such programs is not new to you—it's one of the basic structures of structured programming. See Figures 5-1 and 5-2.

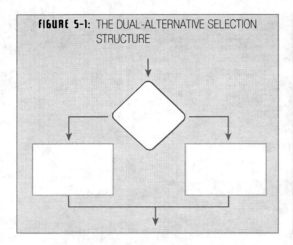

FIGURE 5-1: THE DUAL-ALTERNATIVE SELECTION STRUCTURE

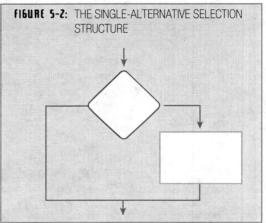

FIGURE 5-2: THE SINGLE-ALTERNATIVE SELECTION STRUCTURE

You can refer to the structure in Figure 5-1 as a **dual-alternative**, or **binary**, selection because there is an action associated with each of two possible outcomes. Depending on the answer to the question represented by the diamond, the logical flow proceeds either to the left branch of the structure or to the right. The choices are mutually exclusive; that is, the logic can flow only to one of the two alternatives, never to both. This selection structure is also called an **if-then-else** structure because it fits the statement:

```
if the answer to the question is yes, then
    do something
else
    do somethingElse
endif
```

The flowchart segment in Figure 5-2 represents a **single-alternative**, or **unary**, selection where action is required for only one outcome of the question. You call this form of the if-then-else structure an **if-then**, because no alternative or "else" action is necessary.

TIP ☐ ☐ ☐ ☐   You can call a single-alternative decision (or selection) a *single-sided decision*. Similarly, a dual-alternative decision is a *double-sided decision* (or selection).

For example, Figure 5-3 shows the flowchart and pseudocode for a typical if-then-else decision in a business program. Many organizations pay employees time and a half (one and one-half times their usual hourly rate) for hours in excess of 40 per week. The logic segments in the figure show this decision.

FIGURE 5-3: FLOWCHART AND PSEUDOCODE FOR OVERTIME PAY DECISION

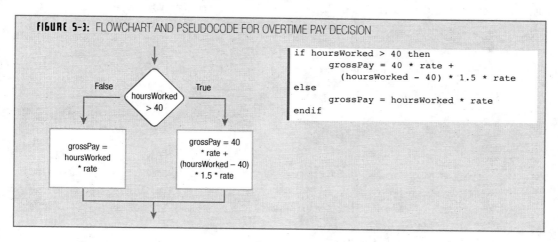

```
if hoursWorked > 40 then
      grossPay = 40 * rate +
          (hoursWorked - 40) * 1.5 * rate
else
      grossPay = hoursWorked * rate
endif
```

In the example in Figure 5-3, the longer calculation that adds a time-and-a-half factor to an employee's gross pay executes only when the expression `hoursWorked > 40` is true. The long calculation exists in the **if clause** of the decision—the part of the decision that holds the action or actions that execute when the tested condition in the decision is true. The shorter calculation, which produces `grossPay` by multiplying `hoursWorked` by `rate`, constitutes the **else clause** of the decision—the part that executes only when the tested condition in the decision is false.

The typical if-then decision in Figure 5-4 shows the employee's paycheck being reduced if the employee participates in the dental plan. No action is taken if the employee is not a dental plan participant.

FIGURE 5-4: FLOWCHART AND PSEUDOCODE FOR DENTAL PLAN DECISION

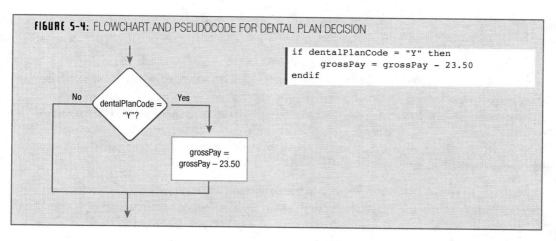

```
if dentalPlanCode = "Y" then
      grossPay = grossPay - 23.50
endif
```

The expressions `hoursWorked > 40` and `dentalPlanCode = "Y"` that appear in Figures 5-3 and 5-4 are Boolean expressions. A **Boolean expression** is one that represents only one of two states, usually expressed as true or false. Every decision you make in a computer program involves evaluating a Boolean expression. True/false evaluation is "natural" from a computer's standpoint, because computer circuitry consists of two-state, on-off switches, often represented by 1 or 0. Every computer decision yields a true-or-false, yes-or-no, 1-or-0 result.

TIP □ □ □ □ George Boole was a mathematician who lived from 1815 to 1864. He approached logic more simply than his predecessors did, by expressing logical selections with common algebraic symbols. He is considered the founder of symbolic logic, and Boolean (true/false) expressions are named for him.

USING THE LOGICAL COMPARISON OPERATORS

Usually, you can compare only values that are of the same type; that is, you can compare numeric values to other numeric values, and character values to other characters. You can ask every programming question by using one of only three types of comparison operators in a Boolean expression. For any two values that are the same type, you can decide whether:

- The two values are equal.
- The first value is greater than the second value.
- The first value is less than the second value.

TIP □ □ □ □ Usually, character variables are not considered to be equal unless they are identical, including the spacing and whether they appear in upper or lowercase. For example, "black pen" is *not* equal to "blackpen", "BLACK PEN", or "Black Pen".

TIP □ □ □ □ Some programming languages allow you to compare a character to a number. If this is the case, then a single character's numeric code value is used in the comparison. For example, most microcomputers use the ASCII coding system, in which an uppercase "A" is represented numerically as a 65, an uppercase "B" is a 66, and so on.

In any Boolean expression, the two values used can be either variables or constants. For example, the expression `currentTotal = 100?` compares a variable, `currentTotal`, to a numeric constant, 100. Depending on the `currentTotal` value, the expression is true or false. In the expression `currentTotal = previousTotal?`, both values are variables, and the result is also true or false depending on the values stored in each of the two variables. Although it's legal to do so, you would never use expressions in which you compare two constants, for example `20 = 20?` or `30 = 40?`. Such expressions are considered **trivial** because each will always evaluate to the same result: true for the first expression and false for the second.

Each programming language supports its own set of **logical comparison operators**, or comparison symbols, that express these Boolean tests. For example, many languages such as Visual Basic and Pascal use the equal sign (=) to express testing for equivalency, so `balanceDue = 0?` compares `balanceDue` to zero. COBOL programmers can use the equal sign, but they also can spell out the expression, as in `balanceDue equal to 0?`. RPG programmers use the two-letter operator `EQ` in place of a symbol. C#, C++, and Java programmers use two equal signs to test for equivalency, so they write `balanceDue == 0?` to compare the two values. Although each programming language supports its own syntax for comparing values' equivalency, all languages provide for the same logical concept of equivalency.

TIP ◻ ◻ ◻ ◻ | The reason some languages use two equal signs for comparisons is to avoid confusion with assignment statements such as `balanceDue = 0`. In C++ or Java, this statement only assigns the value 0 to `balanceDue`; it does not compare `balanceDue` to zero.

TIP ◻ ◻ ◻ ◻ | Whenever you use a comparison operator, you must provide a value on each side of the operator. Comparison operators are sometimes called *binary operators* because of this requirement.

Most languages allow you to use the algebraic signs for greater than (>) and less than (<) to make the corresponding comparisons. Additionally, COBOL, which is very similar to English, allows you to spell out the comparisons in expressions like `daysPastDue is greater than 30?` or `packageWeight is less than maximumWeightAllowed?`. RPG uses the two-letter abbreviations `GT` and `LT` to represent greater than or less than. When you create a flowchart or pseudocode, you can use any form of notation you want to express "greater than" and "less than." It's simplest to use the symbols > and < if you are comfortable with their meaning. As with equivalency, the syntax changes when you change languages, but the concepts of greater than and less than exist in all programming languages.

In addition to the three basic comparisons you can make, most programming languages provide three others. For any two values that are the same type, you can decide whether:

- The first is greater than or equal to the second.
- The first is less than or equal to the second.
- The two are not equal.

Most programming languages allow you to express "greater than or equal to" by typing a greater-than sign immediately followed by an equal sign (>=). When you are drawing a flowchart or writing pseudocode, you might prefer a greater-than sign with a line under it (≥) because mathematicians use that symbol to mean "greater than or equal to." However, when you write a program, you type >= as two separate characters, because no single key on the keyboard expresses this concept. Similarly, "less than or equal to" is written with two symbols, < immediately followed by =.

TIP ◻ ◻ ◻ ◻ | The operators >= and <= are always treated as a single unit; no spaces separate the two parts of the operator. Also, the equal sign always appears second. No programming language allows => or =< as a comparison operator.

Any logical situation can be expressed using just three types of comparisons: equal, greater than, and less than. You never need the three additional comparisons (greater than or equal to, less than or equal to, or not equal to), but using them often makes decisions more convenient. For example, assume you need to issue a 10 percent discount to any customer whose age is 65 or greater, and charge full price to other customers. You can use the greater-than-or-equal-to symbol to write the logic as follows:

```
if customerAge >= 65 then
        discount = 0.10
else
        discount = 0
endif
```

As an alternative, if you want to use only the three basic comparisons (=, >, and <) you can express the same logic by writing:

```
if customerAge < 65 then
        discount = 0
else
        discount = 0.10
endif
```

In any decision for which a >= b is true, then a < b is false. Conversely, if a >= b is false, then a < b is true. By rephrasing the question and swapping the actions taken based on the outcome, you can make the same decision in multiple ways. The clearest route is often to ask a question so the positive or true outcome results in the unusual action. When your company policy is to "provide a discount for those who are 65 and older," the phrase "greater than or equal to" comes to mind, so it is the most natural to use. Conversely, if your policy is to "provide no discount for those under 65," then it is more natural to use the "less than" syntax. Either way, the same people receive a discount.

Comparing two amounts to decide if they are *not* equal to each other is the most confusing of all the comparisons. Using "not equal to" in decisions involves thinking in double negatives, which makes you prone to include logical errors in your programs. For example, consider the flowchart segment in Figure 5-5.

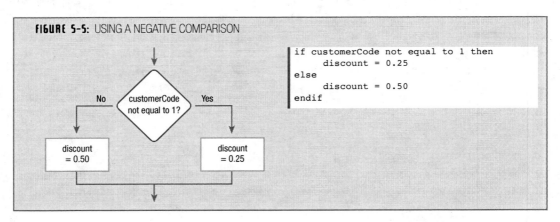

FIGURE 5-5: USING A NEGATIVE COMPARISON

```
if customerCode not equal to 1 then
        discount = 0.25
else
        discount = 0.50
endif
```

In Figure 5-5, if the value of `customerCode` *is* equal to 1, the logical flow follows the false branch of the selection. If `customerCode not equal to 1` is true, the `discount` is 0.25; if `customerCode not equal to 1` is not true, it means the `customerCode` *is* 1, and the `discount` is 0.50. Even using the phrase "`customerCode not equal to 1 is not true`" is awkward.

Figure 5-6 shows the same decision, this time asked in the positive. Making the decision `if customerCode is 1 then discount = 0.50` is clearer than trying to determine what `customerCode` is *not*.

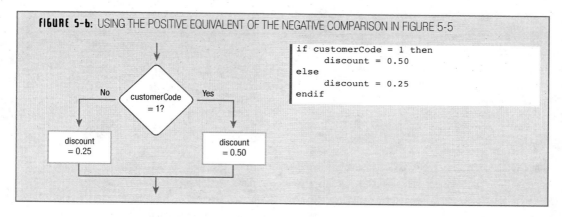

FIGURE 5-6: USING THE POSITIVE EQUIVALENT OF THE NEGATIVE COMPARISON IN FIGURE 5-5

```
if customerCode = 1 then
     discount = 0.50
else
     discount = 0.25
endif
```

Besides being awkward to use, the "not equal to" comparison operator is the one most likely to be different in the various programming languages you may use. COBOL allows you to write "not equal to"; Pascal uses a less-than sign followed immediately by a greater-than sign (<>); C#, C++, C, and Java use an exclamation point followed by an equal sign (!=). In a flowchart or in pseudocode, you can use the symbol that mathematicians use to mean "not equal," an equal sign with a slash through it (≠). When you program, you will not be able to use this symbol, because no single key on the keyboard produces it.

TIP □ □ □ □ Although NOT comparisons can be awkward to use, there are times when your meaning is clearest if you use one. Frequently, this occurs when you take action only when some condition is false. An example would be: if customerZipCode is not equal to localZipCode, then add deliveryCharge to total. The mainline logic of many programs, including those you have worked with in this book, includes a negative comparison that controls a loop. The pseudocode you have seen for almost every program includes a statement similar to: while not eof, perform mainLoop().

Figure 5-7 summarizes the six comparison operators and contrasts trivial (both true and false) examples with typical examples of their use.

FIGURE 5-7: LOGICAL COMPARISONS

Comparison	Trivial true example	Trivial false example	Typical example
Equal to	7 = 7?	7 = 4?	amtOrdered = 12?
Greater than	12 > 3?	4 > 9?	hoursWorked > 40?
Less than	1 < 8?	13 < 10?	hourlyWage < 5.65?
Greater than or equal to	5 >= 5?	3 >= 9?	customerAge >= 65?
Less than or equal to	4 <= 4?	8 <= 2?	daysOverdue <= 60?
Not equal to	16 <> 3?	18 <> 18?	customerBalance <> 0?

UNDERSTANDING AND LOGIC

Often, you need more than one selection structure to determine whether an action should take place. For example, suppose that your employer wants a report that lists workers who have registered for both insurance plans offered by the company: the medical plan and the dental plan. This type of situation is known as an **AND decision** because the employee's record must pass two tests—participation in the medical plan *and* participation in the dental plan—before you write that employee's information on the report. A compound, or AND, decision requires a **nested decision**, or a **nested if**—that is, a decision "inside of" another decision. The logic looks like Figure 5-8.

TIP □ □ □ □ You first learned about nesting structures in Chapter 2.

TIP □ □ □ □ A series of nested if statements can also be called a **cascading if statement**.

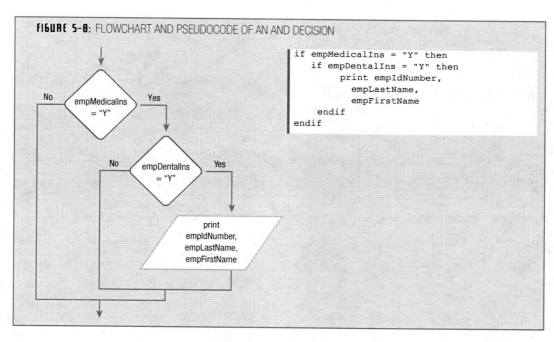

FIGURE 5-8: FLOWCHART AND PSEUDOCODE OF AN AND DECISION

```
if empMedicalIns = "Y" then
    if empDentalIns = "Y" then
        print empIdNumber,
            empLastName,
            empFirstName
    endif
endif
```

The AND decision shown in Figure 5-8 is part of a much larger program. To help you develop this program, suppose your employer provides you with the employee data file description shown in Figure 5-9, and you learn that the medical and dental insurance fields contain a single character, "Y" or "N", indicating each employee's participation status. With your employer's approval, you develop the print chart shown in Figure 5-10.

FIGURE 5-9: EMPLOYEE FILE DESCRIPTION

```
EMPLOYEE FILE DESCRIPTION
File Name: EMPFILE
FIELD DESCRIPTION   POSITIONS   DATA        DECIMALS   EXAMPLE
ID Number           1-4         Numeric     0          1234
Last Name           5-20        Character              Kroening
First Name          21-35       Character              Ginny
Department          36          Numeric     0          3
Hourly Rate         37-40       Numeric     2          17.50
Medical Plan        41          Character              Y
Dental Plan         42          Character              N
Number of           43-44       Numeric     0          2
  Dependents
```

FIGURE 5-10: PRINT CHART LISTING EMPLOYEES PARTICIPATING IN BOTH INSURANCE PLANS

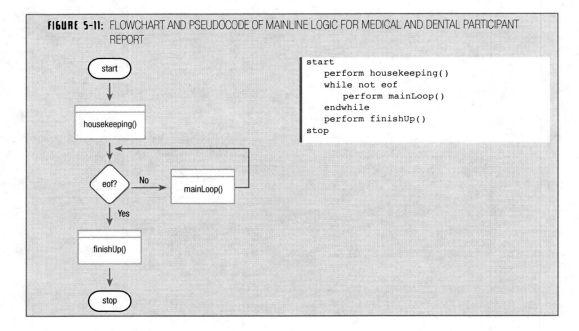

Print chart content:

- Row 2: Employees with Medical and Dental Insurance
- Row 4: ID number   Last name   First name
- Row 6: 9999   XXXXXXXXXXXXXXX   XXXXXXXXXXXXXXX
- Row 7: 9999   XXXXXXXXXXXXXXX   XXXXXXXXXXXXXXX

The mainline logic and `housekeeping()` routines for this program are diagrammed in Figures 5-11 and 5-12.

FIGURE 5-11: FLOWCHART AND PSEUDOCODE OF MAINLINE LOGIC FOR MEDICAL AND DENTAL PARTICIPANT REPORT

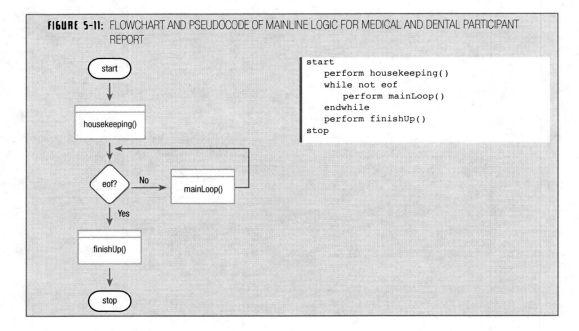

```
start
    perform housekeeping()
    while not eof
        perform mainLoop()
    endwhile
    perform finishUp()
stop
```

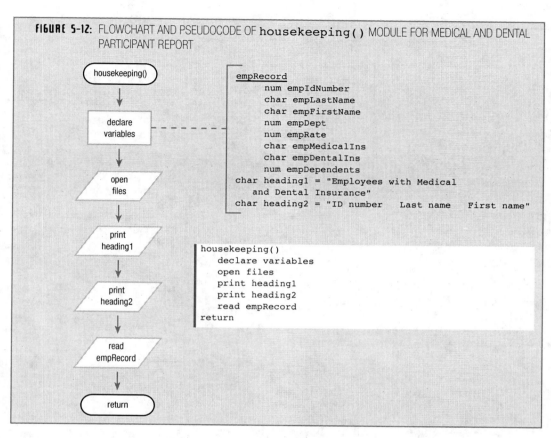

FIGURE 5-12: FLOWCHART AND PSEUDOCODE OF `housekeeping()` MODULE FOR MEDICAL AND DENTAL PARTICIPANT REPORT

```
empRecord
     num empIdNumber
     char empLastName
     char empFirstName
     num empDept
     num empRate
     char empMedicalIns
     char empDentalIns
     num empDependents
char heading1 = "Employees with Medical
    and Dental Insurance"
char heading2 = "ID number    Last name    First name"
```

```
housekeeping()
     declare variables
     open files
     print heading1
     print heading2
     read empRecord
return
```

At the end of the `housekeeping()` module, the first employee record is read into computer memory. Assuming that the `eof` condition is not yet met, the logical flow proceeds to the `mainLoop()`. If the program required data for all employees to be printed, you would simply print the information from the current record and get the next record. However, in this case, the output should contain only the names of those employees who participate in both the medical and dental insurance plans. Therefore, within the `mainLoop()` module of this program, you ask the questions that determine whether the current employee's record will print; if the employee's data meet the medical and dental insurance requirements, then you print the record. Whether or not you take the path that prints the record, the last thing you do in the `mainLoop()` is to read the next input record. Figure 5-13 shows the `mainLoop()` module.

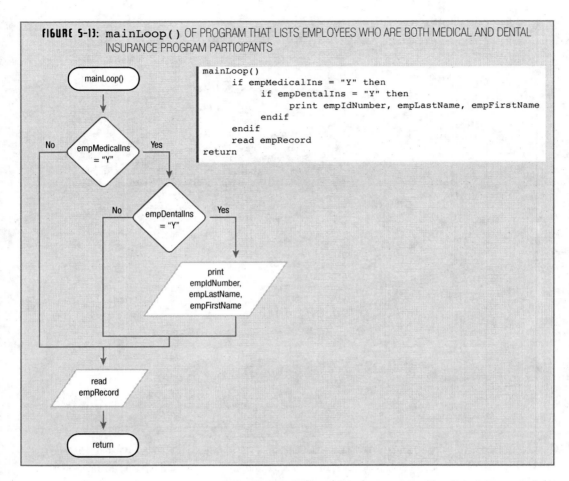

FIGURE 5-13: `mainLoop()` OF PROGRAM THAT LISTS EMPLOYEES WHO ARE BOTH MEDICAL AND DENTAL INSURANCE PROGRAM PARTICIPANTS

```
mainLoop()
     if empMedicalIns = "Y" then
          if empDentalIns = "Y" then
                print empIdNumber, empLastName, empFirstName
          endif
     endif
     read empRecord
return
```

The `mainLoop()` module works like this: If the employee has medical insurance, *then* and *only then*, test to see if the employee has dental insurance. If so, *then* and *only then*, print the employee's data. The dental insurance question is nested entirely within half of the medical insurance question structure. If an employee does not carry medical insurance, there is no need to ask about the dental insurance; the employee is already disqualified from the report. Pseudocode for the entire program is shown in Figure 5-14. Notice how the second (dental insurance) decision within the `mainLoop()` is indented within the first (medical insurance) decision. This technique shows that the second question is asked only when the result of the first comparison is true.

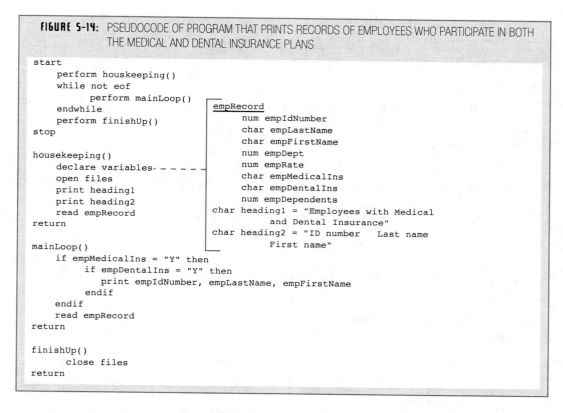

FIGURE 5-14: PSEUDOCODE OF PROGRAM THAT PRINTS RECORDS OF EMPLOYEES WHO PARTICIPATE IN BOTH THE MEDICAL AND DENTAL INSURANCE PLANS

```
start
    perform houskeeping()
    while not eof
        perform mainLoop()
    endwhile
    perform finishUp()
stop

housekeeping()
    declare variables
    open files
    print heading1
    print heading2
    read empRecord
return

mainLoop()
    if empMedicalIns = "Y" then
        if empDentalIns = "Y" then
            print empIdNumber, empLastName, empFirstName
        endif
    endif
    read empRecord
return

finishUp()
    close files
return
```

```
empRecord
    num empIdNumber
    char empLastName
    char empFirstName
    num empDept
    num empRate
    char empMedicalIns
    char empDentalIns
    num empDependents
char heading1 = "Employees with Medical
                and Dental Insurance"
char heading2 = "ID number    Last name
                First name"
```

WRITING NESTED AND DECISIONS FOR EFFICIENCY

When you nest decisions because the resulting action requires that two conditions be true, you must decide which of the two decisions to make first. Logically, either selection in an AND decision can come first. However, when there are two selections, you often can improve your program's performance by making an appropriate choice as to which selection to make first.

For example, Figure 5-15 shows the nested decision structure in the `mainLoop()` logic of the program that produces a report of employees who participate in both the medical and dental insurance plans.

FIGURE 5-15: FINDING MEDICAL AND DENTAL PLAN PARTICIPANTS

```
if empMedicalIns = "Y" then
    if empDentalIns = "Y" then
        print empIdNumber, empLastName, empFirstName
    endif
endif
```

Alternately, you can write the decision as in Figure 5-16.

FIGURE 5-16: FINDING DENTAL AND MEDICAL PLAN PARTICIPANTS

```
if empDentalIns = "Y" then
    if empMedicalIns = "Y" then
        print empIdNumber, empLastName, empFirstName
    endif
endif
```

Examine the decision statements in the preceding figures. If you want to print employees who participate in the medical AND dental plans, you can ask about the medical plan first, eliminate those employees who do not participate, and ask about the dental plan only for those employees who "pass" the medical insurance test. Or, you could ask about the dental plan first, eliminate those who do not participate, and ask about the medical plan only for those employees who "pass" the dental insurance test. Either way, the final list contains only those employees who have both kinds of insurance.

Does it make a difference which question is asked first? As far as the output goes, no. Either way, the same employee names appear on the report—those with both types of insurance. As far as program efficiency goes, however, it *might* make a difference which question is asked first.

Assume you know that out of 1,000 employees in your company, about 90 percent, or 900, participate in the medical insurance plan. Assume you also know that out of 1,000 employees, only about half, or 500, participate in the dental plan.

The medical and dental insurance program will ask the first question in the `mainLoop( )` 1,000 times during its execution—once for each employee record contained on the input file. If the program uses the logic in Figure 5-15, it asks the first question `empMedicalIns = "Y"`? 1,000 times. For approximately 90 percent of the employees, or 900 of the records, the answer is `true`, meaning the `empMedicalIns` field contains the character "Y". So 100 employees are eliminated, and 900 proceed to the next question about dental insurance. Only about half of the employees participate in the dental plan, so 450 out of the 900 will appear on the printed report.

Using the alternate logic in Figure 5-16, the program asks the first question `empDentalIns = "Y"`? 1,000 times. Because only about half of the company's employees participate, only 500 will "pass" this test and proceed to the medical insurance question. Then about 90 percent of the 500, or 450 employees, will appear on the printed report. Whether you use the logic in Figure 5-15 or 5-16, the same 450 employees who have both types of insurance appear on the report.

The difference lies in the fact that when you use the logic in Figure 5-15, the program must ask 1,900 questions to produce the report—the medical insurance question tests all 1,000 employee records, and 900 continue to the dental insurance question. If you use the logic in Figure 5-16 to produce the report, the program asks only 1,500 questions— all 1,000 records are tested for dental insurance, but only 500 proceed to the medical insurance question. By asking about the dental insurance first, you "save" 400 decisions.

The 400-question difference between the first set of decisions and the second set really doesn't take much time on most computers. But it will take *some* time, and if there are hundreds of thousands of employees instead of only 1,000, or if many such decisions have to be made within a program, performance time can be significantly improved by asking questions in the proper order.

In many AND decisions, you have no idea which of two events is more likely to occur; in that case, you can legitimately ask either question first. In addition, even though you know the probability of each of two conditions, the two events might not be mutually exclusive; that is, one might depend on the other. For example, if employees with dental insurance are significantly more likely to carry medical insurance than those who don't carry dental insurance, the order in which to ask the questions might matter less or not matter at all. However, if you do know the probabilities of the conditions, or can make a reasonable guess, the general rule is: *In an AND decision, first ask the question that is less likely to be true.* This eliminates as many records as possible from having to go through the second decision, which speeds up processing time.

COMBINING DECISIONS IN AN AND SELECTION

Most programming languages allow you to ask two or more questions in a single comparison by using a **logical AND operator**. For example, if you want to select employees who carry both medical and dental insurance, you can use nested `if`s, or you can include both decisions in a single statement by writing `empDentalIns = "Y" AND empMedicalIns = "Y"?`. When you use one or more AND operators to combine two or more Boolean expressions, each Boolean expression must be true in order for the entire expression to be evaluated as true. For example, if you ask, "Are you at least 18, and are you a registered voter, and did you vote in the last election?", the answer to all three parts of the question must be "yes" before the response can be a single, summarizing "yes". If any part of the question is false, then the entire question is false.

If the programming language you use allows an AND operator, you still must realize that the question you place first is the question that will be asked first, and cases that are eliminated based on the first question will not proceed to the second question. The computer can ask only one question at a time; even when your logic follows the flowchart segment in Figure 5-17, the computer will execute the logic in the flowchart in Figure 5-18.

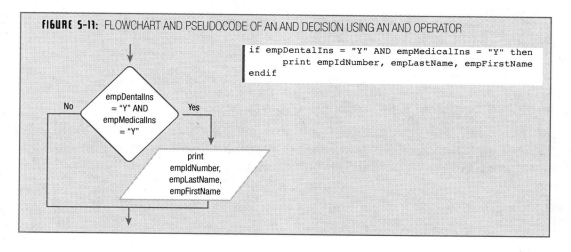

FIGURE 5-17: FLOWCHART AND PSEUDOCODE OF AN AND DECISION USING AN AND OPERATOR

```
if empDentalIns = "Y" AND empMedicalIns = "Y" then
        print empIdNumber, empLastName, empFirstName
endif
```

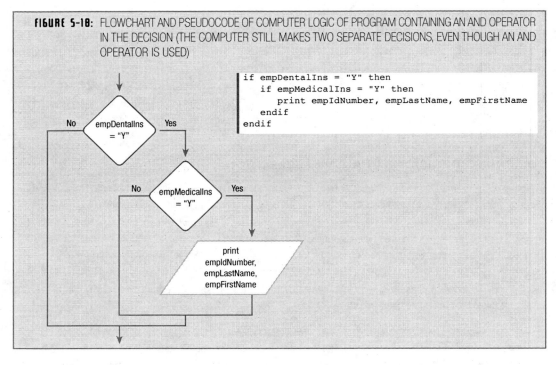

FIGURE 5-18: FLOWCHART AND PSEUDOCODE OF COMPUTER LOGIC OF PROGRAM CONTAINING AN AND OPERATOR IN THE DECISION (THE COMPUTER STILL MAKES TWO SEPARATE DECISIONS, EVEN THOUGH AN AND OPERATOR IS USED)

```
if empDentalIns = "Y" then
    if empMedicalIns = "Y" then
        print empIdNumber, empLastName, empFirstName
    endif
endif
```

TIP □ □ □ □ The AND operator in Java, C++, and C# consists of two ampersands, with no spaces between them (&&).

TIP □ □ □ □ Using an AND operator in a decision that involves multiple conditions does not eliminate your responsibility for determining which of the conditions to test first. Even when you use an AND operator, the computer makes decisions one at a time, and makes them in the order you ask them. If the first question in an AND expression evaluates to false, then the entire expression is false, and the second question will not even be tested.

AVOIDING COMMON ERRORS IN AN AND SELECTION

When you must satisfy two or more criteria to initiate an event in a program, you must make sure that the second decision is made entirely within the first decision. For example, if a program's objective is to print a report of those employees who carry both medical and dental insurance, then the program segment shown in Figure 5-19 contains three different types of logic errors.

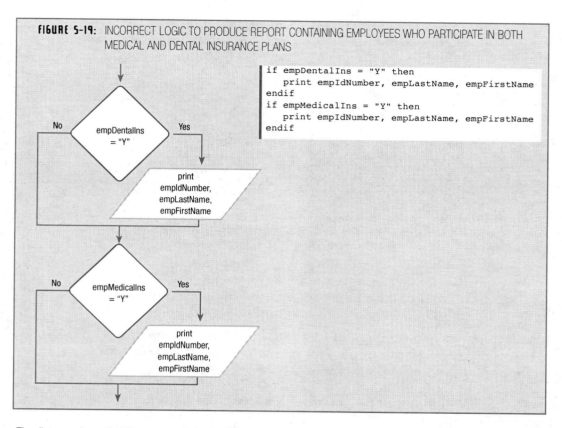

FIGURE 5-19: INCORRECT LOGIC TO PRODUCE REPORT CONTAINING EMPLOYEES WHO PARTICIPATE IN BOTH MEDICAL AND DENTAL INSURANCE PLANS

```
if empDentalIns = "Y" then
    print empIdNumber, empLastName, empFirstName
endif
if empMedicalIns = "Y" then
    print empIdNumber, empLastName, empFirstName
endif
```

The diagram shows that the program asks the dental insurance question first. However, if an employee participates in the dental program, the employee's record prints immediately. The employee record should not print, because the employee might not have the medical insurance. In addition, the program should eliminate an employee without dental insurance from the next selection, but every employee's record proceeds to the medical insurance question, where it might print, whether the employee has dental insurance or not. Additionally, any employee who has both medical and dental insurance, having passed each test successfully, will appear twice on this report. For many reasons, the logic shown in Figure 5-19 is *not* correct for this problem.

Beginning programmers often make another type of error when they must make two comparisons on the same field while using a logical AND operator. For example, suppose you want to list employees who make between $10.00 and $11.99 per hour, inclusive. When you make this type of decision, you are basing it on a **range** of values—every value between low and high limits. For example, you want to select employees whose empRate is greater than or equal to 10.00 AND whose empRate is less than 12.00; therefore, you need to make two comparisons on the same field. Without the logical AND operator, the comparison is:

```
if empRate >= 10.00 then
    if empRate < 12.00 then
```

```
                     print empIdNumber, empLastName, empFirstName
            endif
        endif
```

TIP ☐ ☐ ☐ ☐   To check for empRate values that are 10.00 and greater, you can use either empRate > 9.99? or empRate >= 10.00?. To check for empRate values under 12.00, you can write empRate <= 11.99? or empRate < 12.00?.

The correct way to make this comparison with the AND operator is as follows:

```
        if empRate >= 10.00 AND empRate < 12.00 then
            print empIdNumber, empLastName, empFirstName
        endif
```

You substitute the AND operator for the phrase `then if`. However, some programmers might try to make the comparison as follows:

```
        if empRate >= 10.00 AND < 12.00 then
            print empIdNumber, empLastName, empFirstName
        endif
```

In most languages, the phrase `empRate >= 10.00 AND < 12.00` is incorrect. The logical AND is usually a binary operator that requires a complete Boolean expression on each side. The expression to the right of the AND, `< 12.00`, is not a complete Boolean expression; you must indicate *what* is being compared to 12.00.

TIP ☐ ☐ ☐ ☐   In some programming languages, such as COBOL and RPG, you can write the equivalent of empRate >= 10.00 AND < 12.00? and the empRate variable is implied for both comparisons. Still, it is clearer, and therefore preferable, to use the two full expressions, empRate >= 10.00 AND empRate < 12.00?.

UNDERSTANDING OR LOGIC

Sometimes, you want to take action when one *or* the other of two conditions is true. This is called an **OR decision** because either one condition must be met *or* some other condition must be met, in order for an event to take place. If someone asks you, "Are you free Friday or Saturday?"only one of the two conditions has to be true in order for the answer to the whole question to be "yes"; only if the answers to both halves of the question are false is the value of the entire expression false.

For example, suppose your employer wants a list of all employees who participate in either the medical or dental plan. Assuming you are using the same input file described in Figure 5-9, the mainline logic and `housekeeping()` module for this program are identical to those used in Figures 5-11 and 5-12. You only need to change the heading on the print chart (Figure 5-10) and change the `heading1` variable in Figure 5-12 from `heading1 = "Employees with Medical and Dental Insurance"` to `heading1 = "Employees with Medical or Dental Insurance"`. The only substantial changes to the program occur in the `mainLoop()` module.

Figure 5-20 shows the possible logic for `mainLoop()` in this OR selection. As each record enters the `mainLoop()`, you ask the question `empMedicalIns = "Y"?`, and if the result is true, you print the employee data. Because the employee needs to participate in only one of the two insurance plans to be selected for printing, there is no need for further questioning after you have determined that an employee has medical insurance. If the employee does not participate in the medical insurance plan, only then do you need to ask if `empDentalIns = "Y"?`. If the employee does not have medical insurance, but does have dental, you want this employee information to print on the report.

FIGURE 5-20: FLOWCHART AND PSEUDOCODE FOR `mainLoop()` OF PROGRAM THAT PRINTS RECORDS OF EMPLOYEES WHO PARTICIPATE IN EITHER THE MEDICAL OR DENTAL INSURANCE PLAN

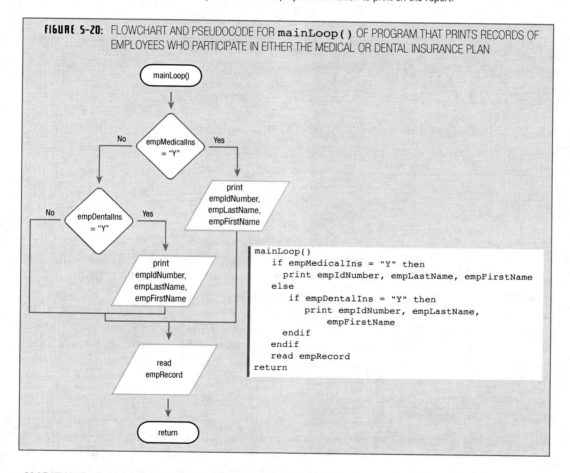

```
mainLoop()
   if empMedicalIns = "Y" then
      print empIdNumber, empLastName, empFirstName
   else
      if empDentalIns = "Y" then
         print empIdNumber, empLastName,
               empFirstName
      endif
   endif
   read empRecord
return
```

AVOIDING COMMON ERRORS IN AN OR SELECTION

You might have noticed that the statement `print empIdNumber, empLastName, empFirstName` appears twice in the flowchart and in the pseudocode shown in Figure 5-20. The temptation is to redraw the flowchart in Figure 5-20 to look like Figure 5-21. Logically, you can argue that the flowchart in Figure 5-21 is correct because the correct employee records print. However, this flowchart is not allowed because it is not structured.

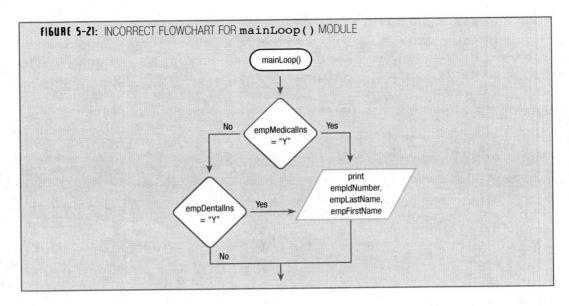

FIGURE 5-21: INCORRECT FLOWCHART FOR `mainLoop()` MODULE

TIP ▫ ▫ ▫ ▫ | If you do not see that Figure 5-21 is not structured, go back and review Chapter 2. In particular, review the example that begins at Figure 2-21.

An additional source of error that is specific to the OR selection stems from a problem with language and the way people use it too casually. When your boss needs a report of all employees who carry medical or dental insurance, she is likely to say, "I need a report of all the people who have medical insurance and all those who have dental insurance." The request contains the word "and," and the report contains people who have one type of insurance "and" people who have another. However, the records you want to print are those from employees who have medical insurance OR dental insurance OR both. The logical situation requires an OR decision. Instead of saying "people who have medical insurance and people who have dental insurance," it would be clearer if your boss asked for "people who have medical or dental insurance." In other words, it would be more correct to put the question-joining "or" conjunction between the insurance types held by each person than between the people, but bosses and other human beings often do not speak like computers. As a programmer, you have the job of clarifying what really is being requested, and determining that often a request for A *and* B means a request for A *or* B.

The way we casually use English can cause another type of error when you require a decision based on a value falling within a range of values. For example, a movie theater manager might say, "Provide a discount to patrons who are under 13 years old and those who are over 64 years old; otherwise charge the full price." Because the manager has used the word "and" in the request, you might be tempted to create the decision shown in Figure 5-22; however, this logic will not provide a discounted price for any movie patron. You must remember that every time the decision in Figure 5-22 is made, it is made using a single data record. If the age field in that record contains an age lower than 13, then it cannot possibly contain an age over 64. Similarly, if it contains an age over 64, then there is no way it can contain an age under that. Therefore, there is no value that could be stored in the age field of a movie patron record for which both parts of the AND question could be true—and the price will never be set to the `discountPrice` for any record. Figure 5-23 shows the correct logic.

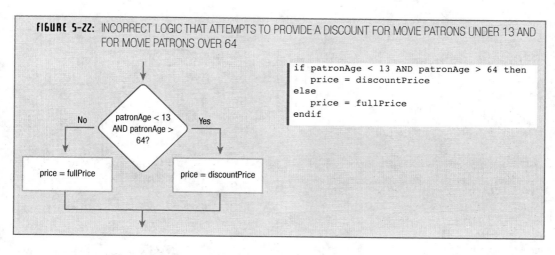

FIGURE 5-22: INCORRECT LOGIC THAT ATTEMPTS TO PROVIDE A DISCOUNT FOR MOVIE PATRONS UNDER 13 AND FOR MOVIE PATRONS OVER 64

```
if patronAge < 13 AND patronAge > 64 then
    price = discountPrice
else
    price = fullPrice
endif
```

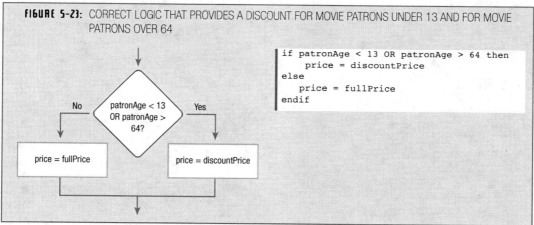

FIGURE 5-23: CORRECT LOGIC THAT PROVIDES A DISCOUNT FOR MOVIE PATRONS UNDER 13 AND FOR MOVIE PATRONS OVER 64

```
if patronAge < 13 OR patronAge > 64 then
    price = discountPrice
else
    price = fullPrice
endif
```

A similar error can occur in your logic if the theater manager says something like, "Don't give a discount—that is, charge full price—if a patron is over 12 or under 65." Because the word "or" appears in the request, you might plan your logic like that shown in Figure 5-24.

As in Figure 5-22, in Figure 5-24, no patron ever receives a discount, because every patron is either over 12 or under 65. Remember, in an OR decision, only one of the conditions needs to be true in order for the entire expression to be evaluated as true. So, for example, because a patron who is 10 is under 65, the full price is charged, and because a patron who is 70 is over 12, the full price also is charged. Figure 5-25 shows the correct logic for this decision.

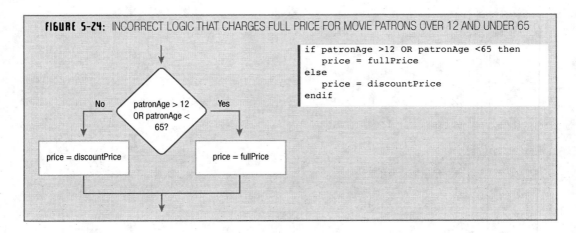

FIGURE 5-24: INCORRECT LOGIC THAT CHARGES FULL PRICE FOR MOVIE PATRONS OVER 12 AND UNDER 65

```
if patronAge >12 OR patronAge <65 then
    price = fullPrice
else
    price = discountPrice
endif
```

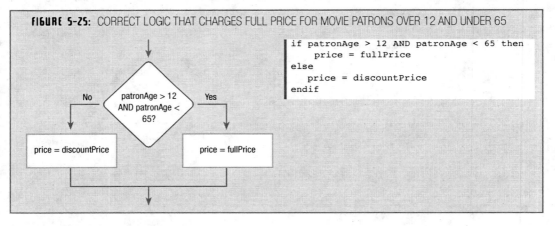

FIGURE 5-25: CORRECT LOGIC THAT CHARGES FULL PRICE FOR MOVIE PATRONS OVER 12 AND UNDER 65

```
if patronAge > 12 AND patronAge < 65 then
    price = fullPrice
else
    price = discountPrice
endif
```

TIP □ □ □ □ Using an OR operator in a decision that involves multiple conditions does not eliminate your responsibility for determining which of the conditions to test first. Even when you use an OR operator, the computer makes decisions one at a time, and makes them in the order you ask them. If the first question in an OR expression evaluates to true, then the entire expression is true, and the second question will not even be tested.

WRITING OR DECISIONS FOR EFFICIENCY

You can write a program that creates a report containing all employees who have either the medical or dental insurance by using the `mainLoop()` in either Figure 5-26 or Figure 5-27.

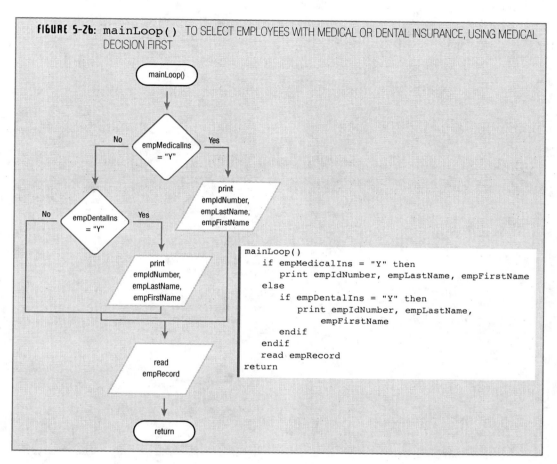

FIGURE 5-26: `mainLoop()` TO SELECT EMPLOYEES WITH MEDICAL OR DENTAL INSURANCE, USING MEDICAL DECISION FIRST

```
mainLoop()
    if empMedicalIns = "Y" then
        print empIdNumber, empLastName, empFirstName
    else
        if empDentalIns = "Y" then
            print empIdNumber, empLastName,
                empFirstName
        endif
    endif
    read empRecord
return
```

You might have guessed that one of these selections is superior to the other, if you have some background information about the relative likelihood of each condition you are testing. For example, once again assume you know that out of 1,000 employees in your company, about 90 percent, or 900, participate in the medical insurance plan, and about half, or 500, participate in the dental plan.

When you use the logic shown in Figure 5-26 to select employees who participate in either insurance plan, you first ask about medical insurance. For 900 employees, the answer is true; you print these employee records. Only about 100 records continue to the next question regarding dental insurance, where about half, or 50, fulfill the requirements to print. In the end, you print about 950 employees.

If you use Figure 5-27, you ask `empDentalIns = "Y"`? first. The result is true for 50 percent, or 500 employees, whose names then print. Five hundred employee records then progress to the medical insurance question, after which 90 percent, or 450, of them print.

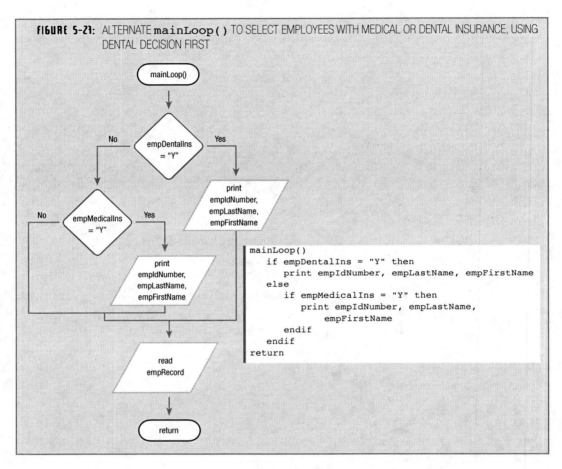

FIGURE 5-27: ALTERNATE `mainLoop()` TO SELECT EMPLOYEES WITH MEDICAL OR DENTAL INSURANCE, USING DENTAL DECISION FIRST

```
mainLoop()
    if empDentalIns = "Y" then
        print empIdNumber, empLastName, empFirstName
    else
        if empMedicalIns = "Y" then
            print empIdNumber, empLastName,
                empFirstName
        endif
    endif
return
```

Using either scenario, 950 employee records appear on the list, but the logic used in Figure 5-26 requires 1,100 decisions, whereas the logic used in Figure 5-27 requires 1,500 decisions. The general rule is: *In an OR decision, first ask the question that is more likely to be true*. Because a record qualifies for printing as soon as it passes one test, asking the more likely question first eliminates as many records as possible from having to go through the second decision. The time it takes to execute the program is decreased.

COMBINING DECISIONS IN AN OR SELECTION

When you need to take action when either one or the other of two conditions is met, you can use two separate, nested selection structures, as in the previous examples. However, most programming languages allow you to ask two or more questions in a single comparison by using a **logical OR operator**—for example, `empDentalIns = "Y" OR empMedicalIns = "Y"`. When you use the logical OR operator, only one of the listed conditions must be met for the resulting action to take place. If the programming language you use allows this construct, you still must realize that the question you place first is the question that will be asked first, and cases eliminated by the first question will not proceed to the second question. The computer can ask only one question at a time; even when you draw the flowchart in Figure 5-28, the computer will execute the logic in the flowchart in Figure 5-29.

TIP □ □ □ □ C#, C++, C, and Java use the symbol ‖ to represent the logical OR.

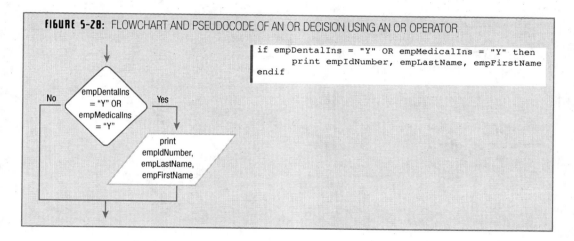

FIGURE 5-28: FLOWCHART AND PSEUDOCODE OF AN OR DECISION USING AN OR OPERATOR

```
if empDentalIns = "Y" OR empMedicalIns = "Y" then
        print empIdNumber, empLastName, empFirstName
endif
```

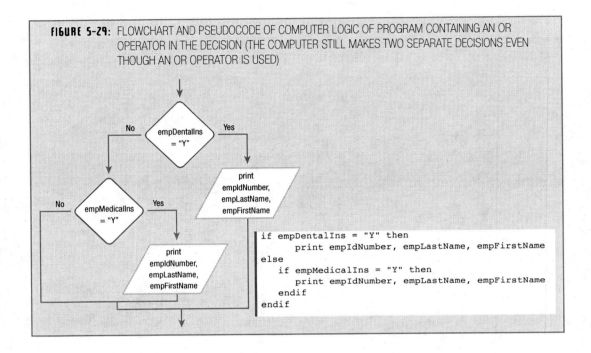

FIGURE 5-29: FLOWCHART AND PSEUDOCODE OF COMPUTER LOGIC OF PROGRAM CONTAINING AN OR OPERATOR IN THE DECISION (THE COMPUTER STILL MAKES TWO SEPARATE DECISIONS EVEN THOUGH AN OR OPERATOR IS USED)

```
if empDentalIns = "Y" then
        print empIdNumber, empLastName, empFirstName
else
    if empMedicalIns = "Y" then
        print empIdNumber, empLastName, empFirstName
    endif
endif
```

USING SELECTIONS WITHIN RANGES

Business programs often need to make selections based on a variable falling within a range of values. For example, suppose you want to print a list of all employees and the names of their supervisors. An employee's supervisor is assigned according to the employee's department number, as shown in Figure 5-30.

FIGURE 5-30: SUPERVISORS BY DEPARTMENT

DEPARTMENT NUMBER	SUPERVISOR
1-3	Dillon
4-7	Escher
8-9	Fontana

When you write the program that reads each employee's record, you could make nine decisions before printing the supervisor's name, such as `empDept = 1?`, `empDept = 2?`, and so on. However, it is more convenient to find the supervisor by using a range check.

When you use a **range check**, you compare a variable to a series of values between limits. To perform a range check, make comparisons using either the lowest or highest value in each range of values you are using. For example, to find each employee's supervisor as listed in Figure 5-30, either use the values 1, 4, and 8, which represent the low ends of each supervisor's department range, or use the values 3, 7, and 9, which represent the high ends.

Figure 5-31 shows the flowchart and pseudocode that represent the logic for choosing a supervisor name by using the high-end range values. You test the `empDept` value for less than or equal to the high end of the lowest range group. If the comparison evaluates as true, you know the `supervisorName`. If not, you continue checking.

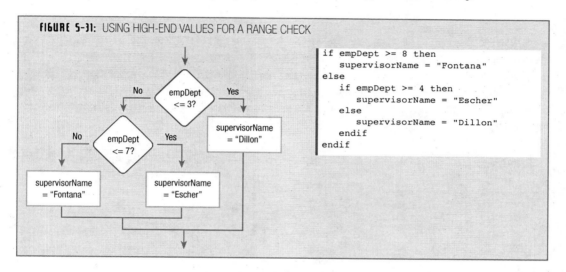

FIGURE 5-31: USING HIGH-END VALUES FOR A RANGE CHECK

```
if empDept >= 8 then
    supervisorName = "Fontana"
else
    if empDept >= 4 then
        supervisorName = "Escher"
    else
        supervisorName = "Dillon"
    endif
endif
```

TIP ▫ ▫ ▫ ▫ | In Figure 5-31, notice how each `else` aligns vertically with its corresponding `if`.

For example, consider records containing three different values for `empDept`, and compare how they would be handled by the set of decisions in Figure 5-31.

- First, assume that the value of `empDept` for a record is 2. Using the logic in Figure 5-31, the value of the Boolean expression `empDept <= 3` is true, the `supervisorName` is set to "Dillon", and the `if` structure ends. In this case, the second decision, `empDept <= 7`, is never made, because the `else` half of the `empDept <= 3` never executes.

- Next, assume that for another record, the value of `empDept` is 7. Then, `empDept <= 3` evaluates as false, so the `else` clause of the decision executes. There, `empDept <= 7` is evaluated, and found to be true, so `supervisorName` becomes "Escher".

- Finally, assume that the value of `empDept` is 9. In this case, the first decision, `empDept <= 3`, is false, so the `else` clause executes. Then, the second decision, `empDept <=7`, also evaluates as false, so the `else` clause of the second decision executes, and the `supervisorName` is set to "Fontana". In this example, "Fontana" can be called a **default value**, because if neither of the two decision expressions is true, the `supervisorName` becomes "Fontana" by default. A default value is the value assigned after a series of selections are all false.

TIP □ □ □ □ | Using the logic in Figure 5-31, the supervisorName becomes "Fontana" even if the empDept is a high, invalid value such as 10, 12, or even 300. The example is intended to be simple, using only two decisions. However, in a business application, you might consider amending the logic so an additional, third decision is made that compares empDept less than or equal to 9. Then, you could assign "Fontana" as the supervisor name if the empDept is less than or equal to 9, and issue an error message if the empDept is not. You might also want to insert a similar decision at the beginning of the program segment to make sure the empDept is not less than 1.

The flowchart and pseudocode for choosing a supervisor name using the reverse of this method, by comparing the employee department to the low end of the range values that represent each supervisor's area, appear in Figure 5-32. Using the technique shown in Figure 5-32, you compare empDept to the low end (8) of the highest range (8 to 9) first; if the empDept falls in the range, the supervisorName is known; otherwise, you check the next lower group. In this example, "Dillon" becomes the default value. That is, if the department number is not greater than or equal to 8, and it is also not greater than or equal to 4, then by default, the supervisor name is set to "Dillon".

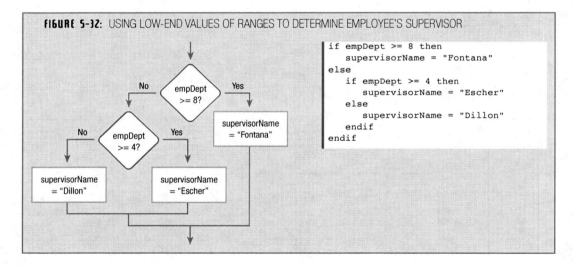

FIGURE 5-32: USING LOW-END VALUES OF RANGES TO DETERMINE EMPLOYEE'S SUPERVISOR

```
if empDept >= 8 then
    supervisorName = "Fontana"
else
    if empDept >= 4 then
        supervisorName = "Escher"
    else
        supervisorName = "Dillon"
    endif
endif
```

COMMON ERRORS USING RANGE CHECKS

Two common errors that occur when programmers perform range checks both entail doing more work than is necessary. Figure 5-33 shows a range check in which the programmer has asked one question too many. If you know that all empDept values are positive numbers, then if the empDept is not greater than or equal to 8, and it is also not greater than or equal to 4, then by default it must be greater than or equal to 1. Asking whether empDept is greater than or equal to 1 is a waste of time; no employee record can ever travel the logical path on the far left. You might say that the path that can never be traveled is a **dead** or **unreachable path**, and that the statements written there constitute dead or unreachable code. Providing such a path is always a logical error.

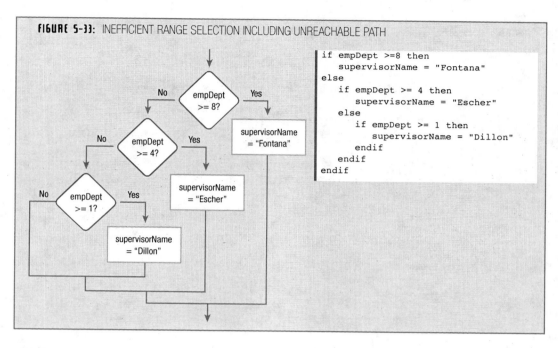

FIGURE 5-33: INEFFICIENT RANGE SELECTION INCLUDING UNREACHABLE PATH

```
if empDept >=8 then
    supervisorName = "Fontana"
else
    if empDept >= 4 then
        supervisorName = "Escher"
    else
        if empDept >= 1 then
            supervisorName = "Dillon"
        endif
    endif
endif
```

TIP □ □ □ □   When you ask questions of human beings, you sometimes ask a question to which you already know the answer. For example, in court, a good trial lawyer seldom asks a question if the answer will be a surprise. With computer logic, however, such questions are an inefficient waste of time.

Another error that programmers make when writing the logic to perform a range check also involves asking unnecessary questions. You should never ask a question if there is only one possible answer or outcome. Figure 5-34 shows an inefficient range selection that asks two unneeded questions. In the figure, if `empDept` is greater than or equal to 8, "Fontana" is the supervisor. If the `empDept` is not greater than or equal to 8, then it must be less than 8, so the next question does not have to check for less than 8. The computer logic will never execute the second decision unless the `empDept` is already less than 8—that is, unless it follows the false branch of the first selection. If you use the logic in Figure 5-34, you are wasting computer time asking a question that has previously been answered. Similarly, if the `empDept` is not greater than or equal to 8 and it is also not greater than or equal to 4, then it must be less than 4. Therefore, there is no reason to compare `empDept` to 4 to determine whether "Dillon" is the supervisor. If the logic makes it past the first two `if` statements in Figure 5-34, then the supervisor must be "Dillon".

TIP □ □ □ □   Beginning programmers sometimes justify their use of unnecessary questions as "just making really sure." Such caution is unnecessary when writing computer logic.

FIGURE 5-34: INEFFICIENT RANGE SELECTION INCLUDING UNNECESSARY QUESTION

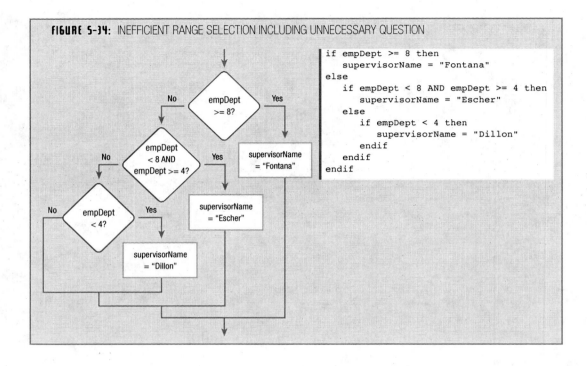

```
if empDept >= 8 then
   supervisorName = "Fontana"
else
   if empDept < 8 AND empDept >= 4 then
      supervisorName = "Escher"
   else
      if empDept < 4 then
         supervisorName = "Dillon"
      endif
   endif
endif
```

UNDERSTANDING PRECEDENCE WHEN COMBINING AND AND OR SELECTIONS

Most programming languages allow you to combine as many AND and OR operators in an expression as you need. For example, assume you need to achieve a score of at least 75 on each of three tests in order to pass a course. When multiple conditions must be true before performing an action, you can use an expression like the following:

```
if score1 >= 75 AND score2 >= 75 AND score3 >= 75 then
   classGrade = "Pass"
else
   classGrade = "Fail"
endif
```

On the other hand, if you need to pass only one test in order to pass the course, then the logic is as follows:

```
if score1 >= 75 OR score2 >= 75 OR score3 >= 75 then
   classGrade = "Pass"
else
   classGrade = "Fail"
endif
```

The logic becomes more complicated when you combine AND and OR operators within the same statement. When you combine AND and OR operators, the AND operators take **precedence**, meaning their Boolean values are evaluated first.

For example, consider a program that determines whether a movie theater patron can purchase a discounted ticket. Assume discounts are allowed for children (age 12 and under) and senior citizens (age 65 and older) who attend "G"-rated movies. The following code looks reasonable, but produces incorrect results, because the AND operator evaluates before the OR.

```
if age <= 12 OR age >= 65 AND rating = "G" then
    print "Discount applies"
```

For example, assume a movie patron is 10 years old and the movie rating is "R". The patron should not receive a discount—or be allowed to see the movie! However, within the previous `if` statement, the part of the expression containing the AND, `age >= 65 AND rating = "G"`, evaluates first. For a 10 year old and an "R" rated movie, the question is false (on both counts), so the entire `if` statement becomes the equivalent of the following:

```
if age <= 12 OR aFalseExpression
```

Because the patron is 10, `age <= 12` is true, so the original `if` statement becomes the equivalent of:

```
if aTrueExpression OR aFalseExpression
```

which evaluates as true. Therefore, the statement "Discount applies" prints when it should not.

Many programming languages allow you to use parentheses to correct the logic and force the expression `age <= 12 OR age >= 65` to evaluate first, as shown in the following pseudocode.

```
if (age <= 12 OR age >= 65) AND rating = "G" then
    print "Discount applies"
```

With the added parentheses, if the patron's age is 12 or under OR 65 or over, the expression is evaluated as:

```
if aTrueExpression AND rating = "G"
```

When the age value qualifies a patron for a discount, then the rating value must also be acceptable before the discount applies. This was the original intention of the statement.

You always can avoid the confusion of mixing AND and OR decisions by nesting `if` statements instead of using ANDs and ORs. With the flowchart and pseudocode shown in Figure 5-35, it is clear which movie patrons receive the discount. In the flowchart in the figure, you can see that the OR is nested entirely within the Yes branch of the `rating = "G"?` selection. Similarly, by examining the pseudocode in Figure 5-35, you can see by the alignment that if the rating is not "G", the logic proceeds directly to the last `endif` statement, bypassing any checking of the age at all.

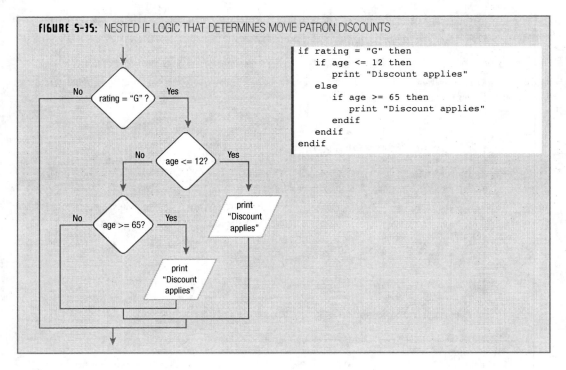

FIGURE 5-35: NESTED IF LOGIC THAT DETERMINES MOVIE PATRON DISCOUNTS

```
if rating = "G" then
   if age <= 12 then
      print "Discount applies"
   else
      if age >= 65 then
         print "Discount applies"
      endif
   endif
endif
```

TIP ▫ ▫ ▫ ▫   In every programming language, multiplication has precedence over addition in an arithmetic statement. That is, the value of 2 + 3 * 4 is 14 because the multiplication occurs before the addition. Similarly, in every programming language, AND has precedence over OR. That's because computer circuitry treats the AND operator as multiplication and the OR operator as addition. In every programming language, 1 represents true and 0 represents false. So, for example, aTrueExpression AND aTrueExpression results in true, because 1 * 1 is 1, and aTrueExpression AND aFalseExpression is false, because 1 * 0 is 0. Similarly, aFalseExpression OR aFalseExpression AND aTrueExpression evaluates to aFalseExpression because 0 + 0 * 1 is 0, whereas aFalseExpression AND aFalseExpression OR aTrueExpression evaluates to aTrueExpression result because 0 * 0 + 1 evaluates to 1.

UNDERSTANDING THE CASE STRUCTURE

When you have a series of decisions based on the value stored in a single variable, most languages allow you to use a case structure. You first learned about the case structure in Chapter 2. There, you learned that you can solve any programming problem using only the three basic structures—sequence, selection, and loop. You are never required to use a case structure—you can always substitute a series of selections. The **case structure** simply provides a convenient alternative to using a series of decisions when you must make choices based on the value stored in a single variable.

For example, suppose you work for a real estate developer who is selling houses that have one of three different floor plans. The logic segment of a program that determines the base price of the house might look like the logic shown in Figure 5-36.

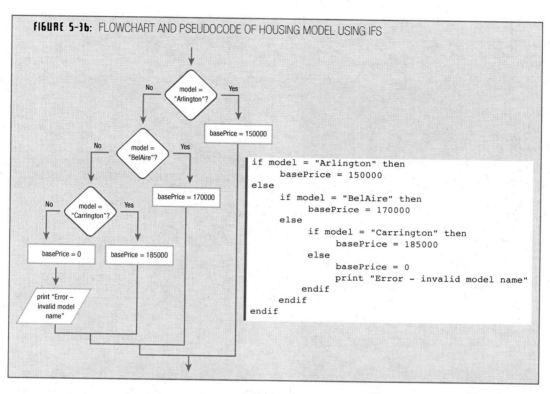

FIGURE 5-36: FLOWCHART AND PSEUDOCODE OF HOUSING MODEL USING IFS

```
if model = "Arlington" then
      basePrice = 150000
else
      if model = "BelAire" then
            basePrice = 170000
      else
            if model = "Carrington" then
                  basePrice = 185000
            else
                  basePrice = 0
                  print "Error - invalid model name"
            endif
      endif
endif
```

The logic shown in Figure 5-36 is completely structured. However, rewriting the logic using a case structure, as shown in Figure 5-37, might make it easier to understand. When using the case structure, you test a variable against a series of values, taking appropriate action based on the variable's value.

In Figure 5-37, the `model` variable is compared in turn with "Arlington", "BelAire", and "Carrington", and an appropriate `basePrice` value is set. The default case is the case that executes in the event no other cases execute. The logic shown in Figure 5-36 is identical to that shown in Figure 5-37; your choice of method to set the housing model prices is entirely a matter of preference.

TIP □ □ □ □   When you look at a nested `if-else` structure containing an outer and inner selection, if the inner nested `if` is within the `if` portion of the outer `if`, the program segment is a candidate for AND logic. On the other hand, if the inner `if` is within the `else` portion of the outer `if`, the program segment might be a candidate for the case structure.

TIP □ □ □ □   Some languages require a break statement at the end of each case selection segment. In those languages, once a case is true, all the following cases execute until a break statement is encountered. When you study a specific programming language, you will learn how to use break statements if they are required in that language.

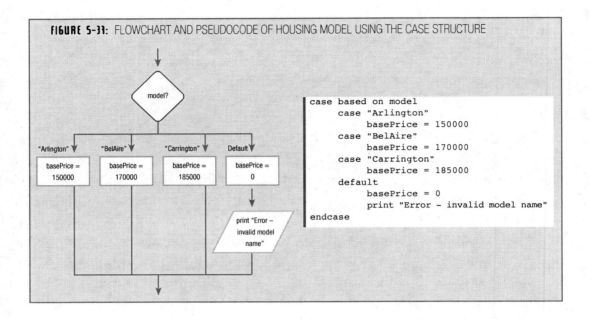

FIGURE 5-37: FLOWCHART AND PSEUDOCODE OF HOUSING MODEL USING THE CASE STRUCTURE

```
case based on model
     case "Arlington"
          basePrice = 150000
     case "BelAire"
          basePrice = 170000
     case "Carrington"
          basePrice = 185000
     default
          basePrice = 0
          print "Error - invalid model name"
endcase
```

USING DECISION TABLES

Some programs require multiple decisions to produce the correct output. Managing all possible outcomes of multiple decisions can be a difficult task, so programmers sometimes use a tool called a decision table to help organize the possible decision outcome combinations.

A **decision table** is a problem-analysis tool that consists of four parts:

- Conditions
- Possible combinations of Boolean values for the conditions
- Possible actions based on the conditions
- The specific action that corresponds to each Boolean value of each condition

For example, suppose a college collects input data like that shown in Figure 5-38. Each student's data record includes the student's age and a variable that indicates whether the student has requested a residence hall that enforces quiet study hours.

FIGURE 5-38: STUDENT FILE DESCRIPTION

```
STUDENT FILE DESCRIPTION
File Name: STURESFILE
FIELD DESCRIPTION         POSITION     DATA TYPE     DECIMALS      EXAMPLE
ID Number                 1–4          Numeric       0             5377
Last Name                 5–20         Character                   Bowers
First Name                21–35        Character                   Laurel
Age                       36–37        Numeric       0             19
Request for Hall          38           Character                   Y
  with Quiet Hours
```

Assume the residence hall director makes residence hall assignments based on the following rules:

- Students who are under 21 years old and who request a residence hall with quiet study hours are assigned to Addams Hall.
- Students who are under 21 years old and who do not request a residence hall with quiet study hours are assigned to Grant Hall.
- Students who are 21 years old and over and who request a residence hall with quiet study hours are assigned to Lincoln Hall.
- Students who are 21 years old and over and who do not request a residence hall with quiet study hours are also assigned to Lincoln Hall.

You can create a program that assigns each student to the appropriate residence hall and prints a list of students along with each student's hall assignment. The print chart for the report is shown in Figure 5-39. The mainline logic for this program appears in Figure 5-40. Most programs you write will contain the same basic mainline logic: Each performs start-up or housekeeping tasks, a main loop that acts repeatedly—once for each input record, and a finishing module that performs any necessary program-ending tasks, including closing the open files.

FIGURE 5-39: PRINT CHART FOR STUDENT RESIDENCE HALL ASSIGNMENTS REPORT

```
         11111111112222222222333333333344444444445555555555
12345678901234567890123456789012345678901234567890123456789
        Student Residence Hall Assignments


   Student ID    Assigned Hall


   9999         XXXXXXXX
   9999         XXXXXXXX
```

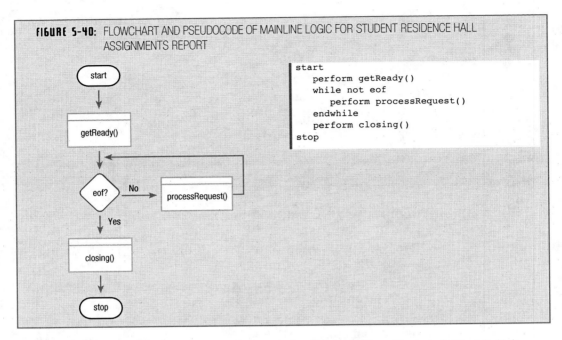

FIGURE 5-40: FLOWCHART AND PSEUDOCODE OF MAINLINE LOGIC FOR STUDENT RESIDENCE HALL ASSIGNMENTS REPORT

```
start
    perform getReady()
    while not eof
        perform processRequest()
    endwhile
    perform closing()
stop
```

The `getReady()` module for the program that produces the residence hall report is shown in Figure 5-41. It declares variables, opens the files, prints the report headings, and reads the first data record into memory.

Before you draw a flowchart or write the pseudocode for the `processRequest()` module, you can create a decision table to help you manage all the decisions. You can begin to create a decision table by listing all possible conditions. They are:

- stuAge < 21, or not
- stuQuietRequest = "Y", or not

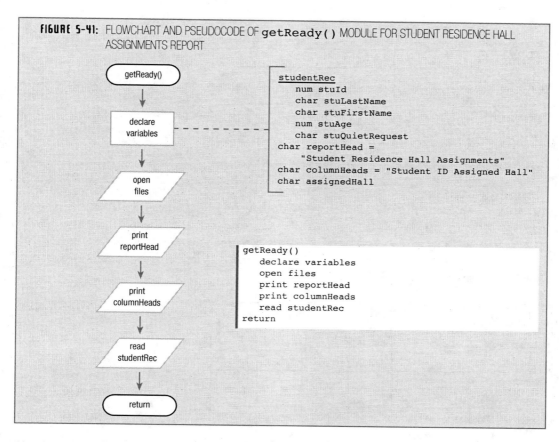

FIGURE 5-41: FLOWCHART AND PSEUDOCODE OF `getReady()` MODULE FOR STUDENT RESIDENCE HALL ASSIGNMENTS REPORT

```
studentRec
    num stuId
    char stuLastName
    char stuFirstName
    num stuAge
    char stuQuietRequest
char reportHead =
    "Student Residence Hall Assignments"
char columnHeads = "Student ID Assigned Hall"
char assignedHall
```

```
getReady()
    declare variables
    open files
    print reportHead
    print columnHeads
    read studentRec
return
```

Next determine how many possible Boolean value combinations exist for the conditions. In this case, there are four possible combinations, shown in Figure 5-42. A student can be under 21, request a residence hall with quiet hours, both, or neither. Because each condition has two outcomes and there are two conditions, there are 2 * 2, or four, possibilities. Three conditions would produce eight possibilities (2 * 2 * 2); four conditions would produce 16 possible outcome combinations (2 * 2 * 2 * 2), and so on.

FIGURE 5-42: POSSIBLE OUTCOMES OF RESIDENCE HALL REQUEST CONDITIONS

Condition	Outcome			
stuAge < 21	T	T	F	F
stuQuietRequest = "Y"	T	F	T	F

Next, add rows to the decision table to list the possible outcome actions. A student might be assigned to Addams, Grant, or Lincoln Hall. Figure 5-43 shows an expanded decision table that includes these three possible outcomes.

FIGURE 5-43: DECISION TABLE INCLUDING POSSIBLE OUTCOMES OF RESIDENCE HALL DECISIONS

Condition	Outcome			
stuAge < 21	T	T	F	F
stuQuietRequest = "Y"	T	F	T	F
assignedHall = "Addams"				
assignedHall = "Grant"				
assignedHall = "Lincoln"				

You choose one required outcome for each possible combination of conditions. As shown in Figure 5-44, you place an X in the Addams Hall row when `stuAge` is less than 21 and the student requests a residence hall with quiet study hours. You place an X in the Grant Hall row under the condition when a student is under 21 but does not request a residence hall with quiet hours. Finally, you place Xs in the Lincoln Hall row for both `stuQuietRequest` values when a student is not under 21 years old—only one residence hall is available for students 21 and over, whether they have requested a hall with quiet hours or not.

FIGURE 5-44: COMPLETED DECISION TABLE FOR RESIDENCE HALL SELECTION

Condition	Outcome			
stuAge < 21	T	T	F	F
stuQuietRequest = "Y"	T	F	T	F
assignedHall = "Addams"	X			
assignedHall = "Grant"		X		
assignedHall = "Lincoln"			X	X

The decision table is complete (count the Xs—there are four possible outcomes). Take a moment and confirm that each residence hall selection is the appropriate value based on the original specifications. Now that the decision table is complete, you can start to plan the logic.

If you choose to use a flowchart to express the logic, you start by drawing a path to the outcome shown in the first column. This result (which occurs when `stuAge < 21` and `stuQuietRequest = "Y"`) sets the residence hall to "Addams". Next, add the resulting action shown in the second column of the decision table, which occurs when `stuAge < 21` is true and `stuQuietRequest = "Y"` is false. In those cases, the residence hall becomes "Grant". See Figure 5-45.

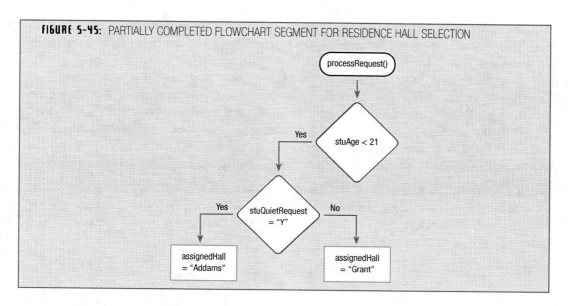

FIGURE 5-45: PARTIALLY COMPLETED FLOWCHART SEGMENT FOR RESIDENCE HALL SELECTION

Next, on the false outcome side of the `stuAge < 21` question, you add the resulting action shown in the third column of the decision table—set the residence hall to "Lincoln". This action occurs when `stuAge < 21` is false and `stuQuietRequest = "Y"` is true. Finally, add the resulting action shown in the fourth column of the decision table, which occurs when both conditions are false. When a student is not under 21 and does not request a hall with quiet study hours, then the assigned hall is "Lincoln". See Figure 5-46.

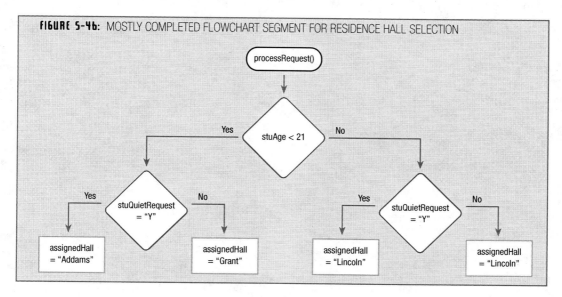

FIGURE 5-46: MOSTLY COMPLETED FLOWCHART SEGMENT FOR RESIDENCE HALL SELECTION

The decision making in the flowchart segment is now complete and accurately assigns each student to the correct residence hall. To finish it, all you need to do is tie up the loose ends of the decision structure, print a student's ID number and residence hall assignment, and read the next record. However, if you examine the two rightmost result boxes in Figure 5-46, you see that the assigned residence hall is identical—"Lincoln" in both cases. When a student is not under 21, whether the `stuQuietRequest` equals "Y" or not, the residence hall assignment is the same; therefore, there is no point in asking the `stuQuietRequest` question. Additionally, many programmers prefer that the True or Yes side of a flowchart decision always appears on the right side of a flowchart. Figure 5-47 shows the complete residence hall assignment program, including the redrawn `processRequest()` module, which has only one "Lincoln" assignment statement and True results to the right of each selection. Figure 5-47 also shows the pseudocode for the same problem.

Perhaps you could have created the final decision-making `processRequest()` module without creating the decision table first. If so, you need not use the table. Decision tables are more useful to the programmer when the decision-making process becomes more complicated. Additionally, they serve as a useful graphic tool when you want to explain the decision-making process of a program to a user who is not familiar with flowcharting symbols.

TIP □ □ □ □ In Appendix C, you can walk through the process used to create a larger decision table.

FIGURE 5-47: COMPLETE FLOWCHART AND PSEUDOCODE FOR RESIDENCE HALL SELECTION PROBLEM

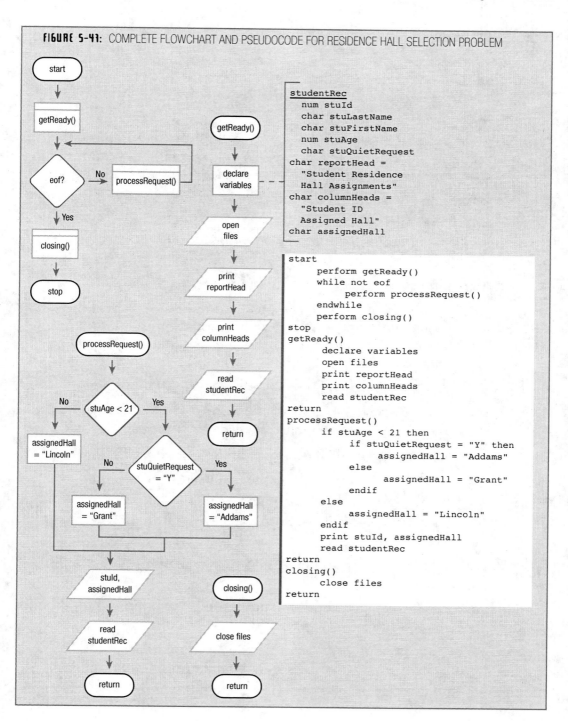

```
studentRec
    num stuId
    char stuLastName
    char stuFirstName
    num stuAge
    char stuQuietRequest
char reportHead =
    "Student Residence
    Hall Assignments"
char columnHeads =
    "Student ID
    Assigned Hall"
char assignedHall
```

```
start
    perform getReady()
    while not eof
        perform processRequest()
    endwhile
    perform closing()
stop
getReady()
    declare variables
    open files
    print reportHead
    print columnHeads
    read studentRec
return
processRequest()
    if stuAge < 21 then
        if stuQuietRequest = "Y" then
            assignedHall = "Addams"
        else
            assignedHall = "Grant"
        endif
    else
        assignedHall = "Lincoln"
    endif
    print stuId, assignedHall
    read studentRec
return
closing()
    close files
return
```

CHAPTER SUMMARY

☐ Every decision you make in a computer program involves evaluating a Boolean expression. You can use dual-alternative, or binary, selections or if-then-else structures to choose between two possible outcomes. You also can use single-alternative, or unary, selections or if-then structures when there is only one outcome for the question where action is required.

☐ For any two values that are the same type, you can use logical comparison operators to decide whether the two values are equal, the first value is greater than the second value, or the first value is less than the second value. The two values used in a Boolean expression can be either variables or constants.

☐ An AND decision occurs when two conditions must be true in order for a resulting action to take place. An AND decision requires a nested decision or a nested if.

☐ In an AND decision, first ask the question that is less likely to be true. This eliminates as many records as possible from the number that have to go through the second decision, which speeds up processing time.

☐ Most programming languages allow you to ask two or more questions in a single comparison by using a logical AND operator.

☐ When you must satisfy two or more criteria to initiate an event in a program, you must make sure that the second decision is made entirely within the first decision, and that you use a complete Boolean expression on both sides of the AND.

☐ An OR decision occurs when you want to take action when one or the other of two conditions is true.

☐ Errors occur in OR decisions when programmers do not maintain structure. An additional source of errors that are particular to the OR selection stems from people using the word AND to express OR requirements.

☐ In an OR decision, first ask the question that is more likely to be true.

☐ Most programming languages allow you to ask two or more questions in a single comparison by using a logical OR operator.

☐ To perform a range check, make comparisons with either the lowest or highest value in each range of values you are using.

☐ Common errors that occur when programmers perform range checks include asking unnecessary and previously answered questions.

☐ The case structure provides a convenient alternative to using a series of decisions when you must make choices based on the value stored in a single variable.

☐ A decision table is a problem-analysis tool that consists of conditions, possible combinations of Boolean values for the conditions, possible actions based on the conditions, and the action that corresponds to each Boolean value of each condition.

KEY TERMS

A dual-alternative, or binary, selection offers two actions, each associated with one of two possible outcomes. It is also called an if-then-else structure.

In a single-alternative, or unary, selection, action is required for only one outcome of the question. You call this form of the selection structure an if-then, because no "else" action is necessary.

An if clause of a decision holds the action that results when a Boolean expression in a decision is true.

The else clause of a decision holds the action or actions that execute only when the Boolean expression in the decision is false.

A Boolean expression is one that represents only one of two states, usually expressed as true or false.

A trivial Boolean expression is one that always evaluates to the same result.

Logical comparison operators are the symbols that express Boolean comparisons. Examples include =, >, <, >=, <=, and <>.

With an AND decision, two conditions must both be true for an action to take place. An AND decision requires a nested decision, or a nested if—that is, a decision "inside of" another decision. A series of nested if statements can also be called a cascading if statement.

A logical AND operator is a symbol that you use to combine decisions so that two (or more) conditions must be true for an action to occur.

A range of values encompasses every value between a high and low limit.

An OR decision contains two (or more) decisions; if at least one condition is met, the resulting action takes place.

A logical OR operator is a symbol that you use to combine decisions when any one condition can be true for an action to occur.

When you use a range check, you compare a variable to a series of values between limits.

A default value is one that is assigned after all test conditions are found to be false.

A dead or unreachable path is a logical path that can never be traveled.

When an operator has precedence, it is evaluated before others.

The case structure provides a convenient alternative to using a series of decisions when you must make choices based on the value stored in a single variable.

A decision table is a problem-analysis tool that consists of four parts: conditions, possible combinations of Boolean values for the conditions, possible actions based on the conditions, and the specific action that corresponds to each Boolean value of each condition.

REVIEW QUESTIONS

1. The selection statement `if quantity > 100 then discountRate = 0.20` is an example of a _____.

   a. single-alternative selection
   b. dual-alternative selection
   c. binary selection
   d. all of the above

2. The selection statement `if dayOfWeek = "S" then price = 5.00 else price = 6.00` is an example of a _____.

   a. unary selection
   b. single-alternative selection
   c. binary selection
   d. all of the above

3. All selection statements must have _____.

   a. an `if` clause
   b. an `else` clause
   c. both of these
   d. neither of these

4. An expression like `amount < 10` is a _____ expression.

   a. Gregorian
   b. Boolean
   c. unary
   d. binary

5. Usually, you compare only variables that have the same _____.

   a. value
   b. size
   c. name
   d. type

6. Symbols like > and < are known as _____ operators.

   a. arithmetic
   b. logical comparison
   c. sequential
   d. scripting accuracy

7. If you could use only three logical comparison operators, you could get by with _____.

   a. greater than, less than, and greater than or equal to
   b. less than, less than or equal to, and not equal to
   c. equal to, less than, and greater than
   d. equal to, not equal to, and less than

8. **If a > b is false, then which of the following is always true?**

   a. $a < b$

   b. $a <= b$

   c. $a = b$

   d. $a >= b$

9. **Usually, the most difficult comparison operator to work with is _____.**

   a. equal to

   b. greater than

   c. less than

   d. not equal to

10. **Which of the lettered choices is equivalent to the following decision?**

```
if x > 10 then
    if y > 10 then
        print "X"
    endif
endif
```

   a. `if x > 10 AND y > 10 then print "X"`

   b. `if x > 10 OR y > 10 then print "X"`

   c. `if x > 10 AND x > y then print "X"`

   d. `if y > x then print "X"`

11. **The Midwest Sales region of Acme Computer Company consists of five states—Illinois, Indiana, Iowa, Missouri, and Wisconsin. Suppose you have input records containing Acme customer data, including state of residence. To most efficiently select and display all customers who live in the Midwest Sales region, you would use _____.**

   a. five completely separate unnested `if` statements

   b. nested `if` statements using AND logic

   c. nested `if` statements using OR logic

   d. Not enough information is given.

12. **The Midwest Sales region of Acme Computer Company consists of five states—Illinois, Indiana, Iowa, Missouri, and Wisconsin. About 50 percent of the regional customers reside in Illinois, 20 percent in Indiana, and 10 percent in each of the other three states. Suppose you have input records containing Acme customer data, including state of residence. To most efficiently select and display all customers who live in the Midwest Sales region, you would ask first about residency in _____.**

   a. Illinois

   b. Indiana

   c. Wisconsin

   d. either Iowa, Missouri, or Wisconsin—it does not matter which one is first

13. The Boffo Balloon Company makes helium balloons. Large balloons cost $13.00 a dozen, medium-sized balloons cost $11.00 a dozen, and small balloons cost $8.60 a dozen. About 60 percent of the company's sales are the smallest balloons, 30 percent are the medium, and large balloons constitute only 10 percent of sales. Customer order records include customer information, quantity ordered, and size. When you write a program to determine price based on size, for the most efficient decision, you should ask first whether the size is _____.

   a. large
   b. medium
   c. small
   d. It does not matter.

14. The Boffo Balloon Company makes helium balloons in 3 sizes, 12 colors, and with a choice of 40 imprinted sayings. As a promotion, the company is offering a 25-percent discount on orders of large, red "Happy Valentine's Day" balloons. To most efficiently select the orders to which a discount applies, you would use _____.

   a. three completely separate unnested `if` statements
   b. nested `if` statements using AND logic
   c. nested `if` statements using OR logic
   d. Not enough information is given.

15. Radio station FM-99 keeps a record of every song played on the air in a week. Each record contains the day, hour, and minute the song started, and the title and artist of the song. The station manager wants a list of every title played during the important 8 a.m. commute hour on the two busiest traffic days, Monday and Friday. Which logic would select the correct titles?

   a.
   ```
   if day = "Monday" OR day = "Friday" OR hour = 8 then
         print title
   endif
   ```
   b.
   ```
   if day = "Monday" then
         if hour = 8 then
            print title
         else
            if day = "Friday" then
               print title
            endif
         endif
   endif
   ```
   c.
   ```
   if hour = 8 AND day = "Monday" OR day = "Friday" then
         print title
   endif
   ```
   d.
   ```
   if hour = 8 then
         if day = "Monday" OR day = "Friday" then
            print title
         endif
   endif
   ```

16. **In the following pseudocode, what percentage raise will an employee in Department 5 receive?**

```
if department < 3 then
   raise = 25
else
   if department < 5 then
     raise = 50
   else
     raise = 75
   endif
endif
```

   a. 25
   b. 50
   c. 75
   d. impossible to tell

17. **In the following pseudocode, what percentage raise will an employee in Department 8 receive?**

```
if department < 5 then
   raise = 100
else
   if department < 14 then
     raise = 250
   else
      if department < 9 then
        raise = 375
      endif
   endif
endif
```

   a. 100
   b. 250
   c. 375
   d. impossible to tell

18. **In the following pseudocode, what percentage raise will an employee in Department 10 receive?**

```
if department < 2 then
   raise = 1000
else
   if department < 6 then
     raise = 2500
   else
      if department < 10 then
        raise = 3000
      endif
   endif
endif
```

    a. 1000

    b. 2500

    c. 3000

    d. impossible to tell

19. **When you use a range check, you compare a variable to the _____ value in the range.**

    a. lowest

    b. middle

    c. highest

    d. lowest or highest

20. **Which of the following is not a part of a decision table?**

    a. conditions

    b. declarations

    c. possible actions

    d. specific actions that will take place under given conditions

EXERCISES

1. **Assume the following variables contain the values shown:**

    numberRed = 100   numberBlue = 200   numberGreen = 300

    wordRed = "Wagon"   wordBlue = "Sky"   wordGreen = "Grass"

    For each of the following Boolean expressions, decide whether the statement is true, false, or illegal.

    a. numberRed = numberBlue?

    b. numberBlue > numberGreen?

    c. numberGreen < numberRed?

    d. numberBlue = wordBlue?

    e. numberGreen = "Green"?

    f. wordRed = "Red"?

    g. wordBlue = "Blue"?

    h. numberRed <= numberGreen?

    i. numberBlue >= 200?

    j. numberGreen >= numberRed + numberBlue?

2. **A candy company wants a list of its best-selling items, including item number and name of candy. Best-selling items are those that sell over 2,000 pounds per month. Input records contain fields for the item number (three digits), the name of the candy (20 characters), the price per pound (four digits, two assumed decimal places), and the quantity in pounds sold last month (four digits, no decimals).**

    a. Design the print chart for this program.

    b. Draw the hierarchy chart for this program.

    c. Draw the flowchart for this program.

    d. Write the pseudocode for this program.

3. The same candy company described in Exercise 2 wants a list of its high-priced, best-selling items. Best-selling items are those that sell over 2,000 pounds per month. High-priced items are those that sell for $10 per pound or more.

    a. Design the print chart for this program.
    b. Draw the hierarchy chart for this program.
    c. Draw the flowchart for this program.
    d. Write the pseudocode for this program.

4. The Literary Honor Society needs a list of English majors who have a grade point average of 3.5 or higher. The student record file includes students' last names and first names (15 characters each), major (10 characters, for example "History" or "English"), and grade point average (two digits, one assumed decimal place, for example 3.9 or 2.0).

    a. Design the print chart for this program.
    b. Draw the hierarchy chart for this program.
    c. Draw the flowchart for this program.
    d. Write the pseudocode for this program.

5. A telephone company charges 10 cents per minute for all calls outside the customer's area code that last over 20 minutes. All other calls are 13 cents per minute. The phone company has a file with one record for every call made in one day. (In other words, a single customer might have many such records on file.) Fields for each call include customer area code (three digits), customer phone number (seven digits), called area code (three digits), called number (seven digits), and call time in minutes (four digits). The company wants a report listing one detail line for each call, including the customer area code and number, the called area code and number, the minutes, and the total charge.

    a. Design the print chart for this program.
    b. Draw the hierarchy chart for this program.
    c. Create a decision table to use while planning the logic for this program.
    d. Draw the flowchart for this program.
    e. Write the pseudocode for this program.

6. A nursery maintains a file of all plants in stock. Each record contains the name of a plant, its price, and fields that indicate the plant's light and soil requirements. The light field contains either "sunny", "partial sun", or "shady". The soil field contains either "clay" or "sandy". Only 20 percent of the nursery stock does well in shade, and 50 percent does well in sandy soil. Customers have requested a report that lists the name and price of each plant that would be appropriate in a shady, sandy yard.

    a. Design the print chart for this program.
    b. Draw the hierarchy chart for this program.
    c. Create a decision table to use while planning the logic for this program.
    d. Draw the flowchart for this program.
    e. Write the pseudocode for this program.

7. You have declared variables for an insurance company program as follows:

FIELD	POSITIONS	EXAMPLE
num custPolicyNumber	1-6	223356
char custLastName	7-20	Falkenburg

```
num custAge           21-23         25
num custDueMonth      24-25         06
num custDueDay        26-27         24
num custDueYear       28-31         2005
num custAccidents     32-34         2
```

Draw the flowchart or write the pseudocode for the selection structures that print the `custPolicyNumber` **and** `custLastName` **for customers whose data satisfy the following requests for lists of policyholders:**

a. over 35 years old

b. at least 21 years old

c. no more than 30 years old

d. due no later than March 15 any year

e. due up to and including January 1, 2005

f. due by April 27, 2008

g. due as early as December 1, 2004

h. fewer than 11 accidents

i. no more than 5 accidents

j. no accidents

8. **Student files contain an ID number (four digits), last and first names (15 characters each), and major field of study (10 characters). Plan a program that lists ID numbers and names for all French or Spanish majors.**

a. Design the print chart for this program.

b. Draw the hierarchy chart for this program.

c. Create a decision table to use while planning the logic for this program.

d. Draw the flowchart for this program.

e. Write the pseudocode for this program.

9. **A florist wants to send coupons to her best customers, so she needs a list of names and addresses for customers who placed orders more than three times last year or spent more than $200 last year. The input file description follows:**

```
File name: FLORISTCUSTS
FIELD DESCRIPTION     POSITIONS     TYPE          DECIMALS
Customer ID           1-3           Numeric       0
First Name            4-16          Character
Last Name             17-30         Character
Street Address        31-51         Character
Orders Last Year      52-55         Numeric       0
Amount Spent          56-62         Numeric       2
  Last Year
```

(Note: To save room, don't include city or state. Assume all the florist's best customers are in town.)

a. Design the print chart for this program.

b. Draw the hierarchy chart for this program.

c. Create a decision table to use while planning the logic for this program.

d. Draw the flowchart for this program.

e. Write the pseudocode for this program.

10. **A carpenter needs a program that computes the price of any desk a customer orders, based on the following input fields: order number, desk length and width in inches (three digits each, no decimals), type of wood (20 characters), and number of drawers (two digits). The price is computed as follows:**

☐ The charge for all desks is a minimum $200.

☐ If the surface (length * width) is over 750 square inches, add $50.

☐ If the wood is "mahogany", add $150; for "oak", add $125. No charge is added for "pine".

☐ For every drawer in the desk, there is an additional $30 charge.

a. Design the print chart for this program.

b. Draw the hierarchy chart for this program.

c. Create a decision table to use while planning the logic for this program.

d. Draw the flowchart for this program.

e. Write the pseudocode for this program.

11. **A company is attempting to organize carpools to save energy. Each input record contains an employee's name and town of residence. Ten percent of the company's employees live in Wonder Lake. Thirty percent of the employees live in Woodstock. Because these towns are both north of the company, the company wants a list of employees who live in either town, so it can recommend that these employees drive to work together.**

a. Design the print chart for this program.

b. Draw the hierarchy chart for this program.

c. Create a decision table to use while planning the logic for this program.

d. Draw the flowchart for this program.

e. Write the pseudocode for this program.

12. **A supervisor in a manufacturing company wants to produce a report showing which employees have increased their production this year over last year, so that she can issue them a certificate of commendation. She wants to have a report with three columns: last name, first name, and either the word "UP" or blanks printed under the column heading PRODUCTION. "UP" is printed when this year's production is a greater number than last year's production. Input exists as follows:**

```
PRODUCTION FILE DESCRIPTION
File name: PRODUCTION
```

FIELD DESCRIPTION	POSITIONS	DATA TYPE	DECIMALS
Last Name	1-20	Character	
First Name	21-30	Character	
Last Year's Production	31-34	Numeric	0
This Year's Production	35-38	Numeric	0

    a. Design the print chart for this program.

    b. Draw the hierarchy chart for this program.

    c. Create a decision table to use while planning the logic for this program.

    d. Draw the flowchart for this program.

    e. Write the pseudocode for this program.

13. **A supervisor in the same manufacturing company as described in Exercise 12 wants to produce a report from the PRODUCTION input file showing bonuses she is planning to give based on this year's production. She wants to have a report with three columns: last name, first name, and bonus. The bonuses will be distributed as follows.**

    If this year's production is:

      ☐ 1,000 units or fewer, the bonus is $25

      ☐ 1,001 to 3,000 units, the bonus is $50

      ☐ 3,001 to 6,000 units, the bonus is $100

      ☐ 6,001 units and up, the bonus is $200

    a. Design the print chart for this program.

    b. Draw the hierarchy chart for this program.

    c. Create a decision table to use while planning the logic for this program.

    d. Draw the flowchart for this program.

    e. Write the pseudocode for this program.

14. **Modify Exercise 13 to reflect the following new facts, and have the program execute as efficiently as possible:**

      ☐ Only employees whose production this year is higher than it was last year will receive bonuses. This is true for approximately 30 percent of the employees.

      ☐ Sixty percent of employees produce over 6,000 units per year; 20 percent produce 3,001 to 6,000; 15 percent produce 1,001 to 3,000 units; and only 5 percent produce fewer than 1,001.

    a. Design the print chart for this program.

    b. Draw the hierarchy chart for this program.

    c. Create a decision table to use while planning the logic for this program.

    d. Draw the flowchart for this program.

    e. Write the pseudocode for this program.

15. **The Richmond Riding Club wants to assign the title of Master or Novice to each of its members. A member earns the title of Master by accomplishing two or more of the following:**

   ☐ Participating in at least eight horse shows

   ☐ Winning a first or second place ribbon in at least two horse shows, no matter how many shows the member has participated in

   ☐ Winning a first, second, third, or fourth place ribbon in at least four horse shows, no matter how many shows the member has participated in

   Create a report that prints each club member's name along with the designation "Master" or "Novice". Input exists as follows:

   ```
   PRODUCTION FILE DESCRIPTION
   File name: RIDING
   ```

FIELD DESCRIPTION	POSITIONS	DATA TYPE	DECIMALS
Last Name	1-15	Character	
First Name	16-25	Character	
Number of shows	26-28	Numeric	0
First Place Ribbons	29-31	Numeric	0
Second Place Ribbons	32-34	Numeric	0
Third Place Ribbons	35-37	Numeric	0
Fourth Place Ribbons	38-40	Numeric	0

   a. Design the print chart for this program.
   b. Draw the hierarchy chart for this program.
   c. Create a decision table to use while planning the logic for this program.
   d. Draw the flowchart for this program.
   e. Write the pseudocode for this program.

LOOPING

After studying Chapter 6, you should be able to:

☐ Understand the advantages of looping

☐ Control a **while** loop using a loop control variable

☐ Increment a counter to control a loop

☐ Loop with a variable sentinel value

☐ Control a loop by decrementing a loop control variable

☐ Avoid common loop mistakes

☐ Use a **for** loop

☐ Use a **do until** loop

☐ Recognize the characteristics shared by all loops

☐ Nest loops

☐ Use a loop to accumulate totals

UNDERSTANDING THE ADVANTAGES OF LOOPING

If making decisions is what makes computers seem intelligent, it's looping that makes computer programming worthwhile. When you use a loop within a computer program, you can write one set of instructions that operates on multiple, separate sets of data. Consider the following set of tasks required for each employee in a typical payroll program:

- Determine regular pay.
- Determine overtime pay, if any.
- Determine federal withholding tax based on gross wages and number of dependents.
- Determine state withholding tax based on gross wages, number of dependents, and state of residence.
- Determine insurance deduction based on insurance code.
- Determine Social Security deduction based on gross pay.
- Subtract federal tax, state tax, Social Security, and insurance from gross pay.

In reality, this list is too short—companies deduct stock option plans, charitable contributions, union dues, and other items from checks in addition to the items mentioned in this list. Also, they might pay bonuses and commissions and provide sick days and vacation days that must be taken into account and handled appropriately. As you can see, payroll programs are complicated.

The advantage of having a computer perform payroll calculations is that all of the deduction instructions need to be written *only once* and can be repeated over and over again for each paycheck, using a **loop**, the structure that repeats actions while some condition continues.

USING A WHILE LOOP WITH A LOOP CONTROL VARIABLE

Recall the loop, or do-while structure, that you learned about in Chapter 2. (See Figure 6-1.) In Chapter 4, you learned that almost every program has a **main loop**, or a basic set of instructions that is repeated for every record. The main loop is a typical loop—within it, you write one set of instructions that executes repeatedly while records continue to be read from an input file. Several housekeeping tasks execute at the start of most programs, and a few clean-up tasks execute at the end. However, most of a program's tasks are located in a main loop; these tasks repeat over and over for many records (sometimes hundreds, thousands, or millions).

FIGURE 6-1: THE `while` LOOP

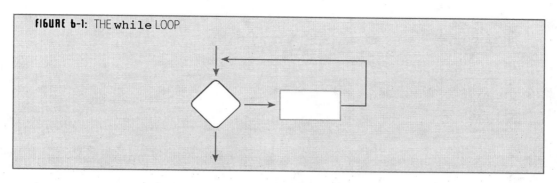

In addition to this main loop, loops also appear within subroutines. They are used any time you need to perform a task several times and don't want to write identical or similar instructions over and over. Suppose, for example, as part of a much larger program, you want to print a warning message on the computer screen when the user has made a potentially danger-ous menu selection (for example, "Delete all files"). To get the user's attention, you want to print the message four times. You can write this program segment as shown in Figure 6-2, but using a loop, as shown in Figure 6-3, is much more efficient.

FIGURE 6-2: PRINTING FOUR WARNING MESSAGES IN SEQUENCE

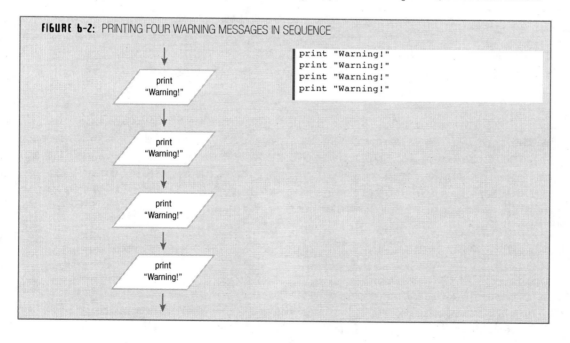

```
print "Warning!"
print "Warning!"
print "Warning!"
print "Warning!"
```

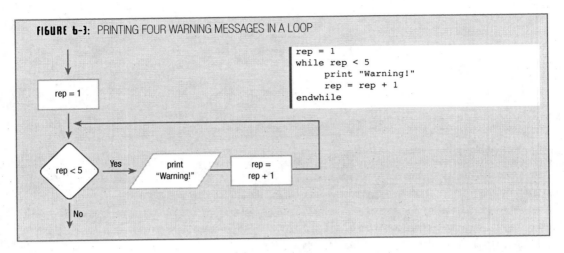

FIGURE 6-3: PRINTING FOUR WARNING MESSAGES IN A LOOP

```
rep = 1
while rep < 5
      print "Warning!"
      rep = rep + 1
endwhile
```

The flowchart and pseudocode segments in Figure 6-3 show three steps that must occur in every loop:

1. You must initialize a variable that will control the loop. The variable in this case is named `rep`.
2. You must compare the variable to some value that controls whether the loop continues or stops. In this case, you compare `rep` to the value 5.
3. Within the loop, you must alter the variable that controls the loop. In this case, you alter `rep` by adding 1 to it.

On each pass through the loop, the value in the `rep` variable determines whether the loop will continue. Therefore, variables like `rep` are known as **loop control variables**. Any variable that determines whether a loop will continue is a loop control variable. To stop a loop, you compare the loop control value to a **sentinel value** (also known as a limit, or ending value), in this case the value 5. The decision that controls every loop is always based on a Boolean comparison. You can use any of the six comparison operators that you learned about in Chapter 5 to control a loop—equal to, greater than, less than, greater than or equal to, less than or equal to, and not equal to.

TIP □ □ □ □   Just as with a selection, the Boolean comparison that controls a `while` loop must compare same-type values: numeric values are compared to other numeric values, and character values to other character values.

The statements that execute within a loop are known as the **loop body**. The body of a loop might contain any number of statements, including subroutine calls, decisions, and other loops. Once your program enters the body of a structured loop, the entire loop body must execute. Your program can leave a structured loop only at the comparison that tests the loop control variable.

USING A COUNTER TO CONTROL LOOPING

Suppose you own a factory and have decided to place a label on every product you manufacture. The label contains the words "Made for you personally by" followed by the first name of one of your employees. For one week's production, you need 100 personalized labels for each employee.

Assume you already have a personnel file that can be used for input. This file has more information than you'll need for this program: an employee last name, first name, Social Security number, address, date hired, and salary. The important feature of the file is that it does contain each employee's name stored in a separate record. The input file description appears in Figure 6-4.

FIGURE 6-4: EMPLOYEE DATA FILE DESCRIPTION

```
File Name: EMPLOYEES
FIELD DESCRIPTION          POSITIONS     DATA TYPE      DECIMALS
Employee Last Name         1-20          Character
Employee First Name        21-35         Character
Social Security Number     36-44         Numeric        0
Address                    45-60         Character
Date Hired                 61-68         Numeric        0
Hourly Salary              69-72         Numeric        2
```

In the main line of this program, you call three modules: a housekeeping module (`housekeep()`), a main loop (`mainLoop()`), and a finish routine (`finishUp()`). See Figure 6-5.

FIGURE 6-5: MAINLINE LOGIC FOR LABEL-MAKING PROGRAM

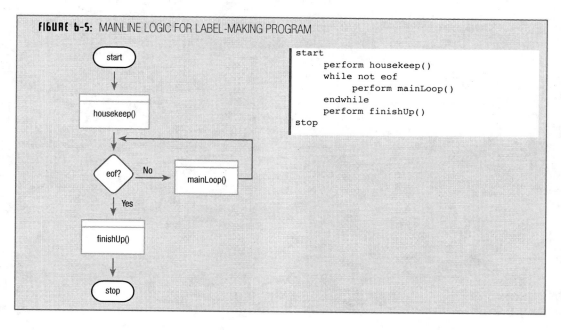

```
start
    perform housekeep()
    while not eof
        perform mainLoop()
    endwhile
    perform finishUp()
stop
```

The first task for the label program involves naming the fields on the input record so you can refer to them within the program. As a programmer, you can choose any variable names you like, for example: `inLastName`, `inFirstName`, `inSSN`, `inAddress`, `inDate`, and `inSalary`.

TIP □ □ □ □ | In Chapter 4 you learned that starting all field names in the input record with the same prefix, such as in, is a common programming technique to help identify these fields in a large program and differentiate them from work areas and output areas that will have other names. Another benefit to using a prefix like in is that some language compilers also produce a dictionary of variable names when you compile your program. These dictionaries show at which lines in the program each data name is referenced. If all your input field names start with the same prefix, they will be together alphabetically in the dictionary, and perhaps be easier to find and work with.

You also can set up a variable to hold the characters "Made for you personally by" and name it `labelLine`. You eventually will print this `labelLine` variable followed by the employee's first name (`inFirstName`).

You will need one more variable: a location called a counter. A **counter** is any numeric variable you use to count the number of times an event has occurred; in this example, you need a counter to keep track of how many labels have been printed at any point. Each time you read an employee record, the counter variable is set to 0. Then every time a label is printed, you add 1 to the counter. Adding 1 to a variable is called **incrementing** the variable. Before the next employee label is printed, the program checks the variable to see if it has reached 100 yet. When it has, that means 100 labels have been printed, and the job is done for that employee. While the counter remains below 100, you continue to print labels. As with all variables, the programmer can choose any name for a counter; this program uses `labelCounter`. In this example, `labelCounter` is the loop control variable.

The `housekeep()` routine for the label program, shown in Figure 6-6, includes a step to open the files: the employee file and the printer. Unlike a program that produces a report, this program has no headings, so the next and last task performed in `housekeep()` is to read the first input record.

TIP □ □ □ □ | Remember, you can give any name you like to subroutines within your programs. This program uses `housekeep()` for its first routine, but `housekeeping()`, `startUp()`, `prep()`, or any other name with the same general meaning could be used.

TIP □ □ □ □ | If you don't know why the first record is read in the `housekeep()` module, go back and review the concept of the priming read, presented in Chapter 2.

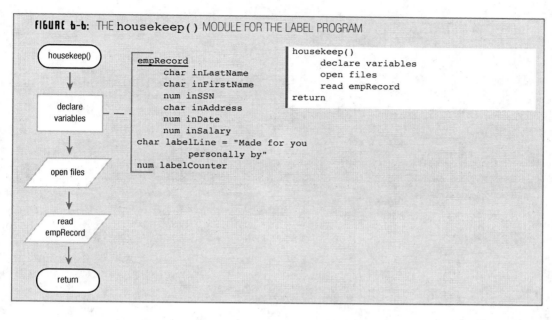

FIGURE 6-6: THE `housekeep()` MODULE FOR THE LABEL PROGRAM

TIP □ □ □ □   In previous chapters, the list of declared variables was shown with both the flowchart and the pseudocode. To save space in the rest of the chapters in this book, the variable list will be shown only with the flowchart.

When the `housekeep()` module is done, the logical flow returns to the `eof` question in the main line. If you attempt to read the first record at the end of `housekeep()` and for some reason there is no record, the answer to `eof`? is Yes, so then the `mainLoop()` is never entered; instead, the logic of the program flows directly to the `finishUp()` module.

Usually, however, employee records will exist and the program will enter the `mainLoop()` module, which is shown in Figure 6-7. When this happens, the first employee record is sitting in memory waiting to be processed. During one execution of the `mainLoop()` module, 100 labels will be printed for one employee. As the last event within the `mainLoop()` module, the program reads the next employee record. Control of the program then returns to the `eof` question. If the new read process has not resulted in the `eof` condition, control reenters the `mainLoop()` module, where 100 more labels print for the new employee.

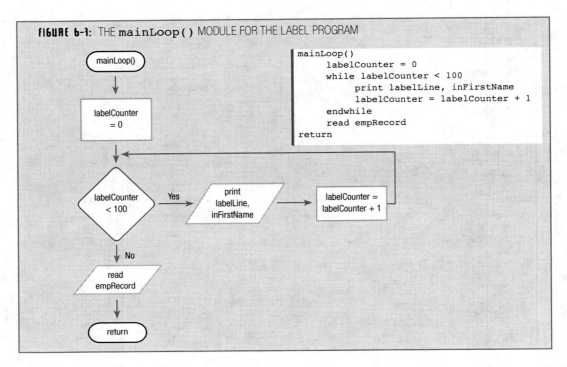

FIGURE 6-1: THE `mainLoop()` MODULE FOR THE LABEL PROGRAM

```
mainLoop()
    labelCounter = 0
    while labelCounter < 100
        print labelLine, inFirstName
        labelCounter = labelCounter + 1
    endwhile
    read empRecord
return
```

The `mainLoop()` of this label program contains three parts:

- Set the `labelCounter` to 0.
- Compare the `labelCounter` to 100.
- While the `labelCounter` is less than 100, print the `labelLine` and the `inFirstName`, and add 1 to the `labelCounter`.

When the first employee record enters the `mainLoop()` module, the `labelCounter` is set to 0. Comparing the `labelCounter` to 100 results in a true condition, so the record enters the label-making loop. One label prints for the first employee, the `labelCounter` increases by one, and the logical flow returns to the question `labelCounter < 100?`. After the first label is printed, the `labelCounter` holds a value of only 1. It is nowhere near 100 yet, so the value of the Boolean expression is true, and the loop is entered for a second time, thus printing a second label.

After the second printing, `labelCounter` holds a value of 2. After the third printing, it holds a value of 3. Finally, after the 100th label prints, `labelCounter` has a value of 100. When the question `labelCounter < 100?` is asked, the answer will finally be No, and the loop will exit.

Before leaving `mainLoop()`, and after the program prints 100 labels for an employee, there is one final step: the next input record is read from the EMPLOYEES file. When `mainLoop()` is over, control returns to the `eof` question in the main line of the logic. If it is not `eof` (if another employee record is present), the program enters `mainLoop()` again, resets `labelCounter` to 0, and prints 100 new labels with the next employee's name.

TIP □ □ □ □ Setting the labelCounter to 0 when the mainLoop() is entered is important. With each new record, the labelCounter must begin at 0 if 100 labels are to print. When the first employee's set of labels is complete, labelCounter holds the value 100. If it is not reset to 0 for the second employee, then no labels will ever print for that employee.

At some point while attempting to read a new record, the program encounters the end of the file, the mainLoop() is not entered again, and control passes to the finishUp() module. In this program the finishUp() module simply closes the files. See Figure 6-8.

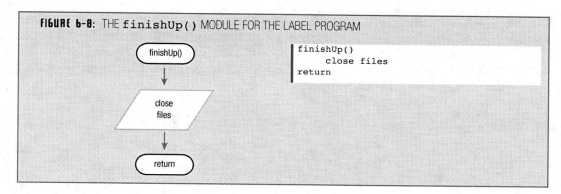

FIGURE 6-8: THE finishUp() MODULE FOR THE LABEL PROGRAM

```
finishUp()
     close files
return
```

LOOPING WITH A VARIABLE SENTINEL VALUE

Sometimes you don't want to be forced to repeat every pass through a loop the same number of times. For example, instead of printing 100 labels for each employee, you might want to vary the number of labels based on how many items a worker actually produces. That way, high-achieving workers won't run out of labels, and less productive workers won't have too many. Instead of printing the same number of labels for every employee, a more sophisticated program prints a different number of labels for each employee, depending on that employee's previous week's production. For example, you might decide to print enough labels to cover 110% of each employee's production rate from the previous week; this ensures that the employee will have enough labels for the week, even if his or her production level improves.

For example, assume that employee production data exists in an input file called EMPPRODUCTION in the format shown in Figure 6-9.

FIGURE 6-9: EMPLOYEE PRODUCTION FILE DESCRIPTION

File Name: EMPPRODUCTION

FIELD DESCRIPTION	POSITIONS	DATA TYPE	DECIMALS
Last Name	1–20	Character	
First Name	21–35	Character	
Production Last Week	36–38	Numeric	0

A real-life production file would undoubtedly have more fields in each record, but these fields supply more than enough information to produce the labels. You need the first name to print on the label, and you need the field that holds production for the last week in order to calculate the number of labels to print for each employee. This field can contain any number from 0 through 999.

To write a program that produces an appropriate number of labels for each employee, you can make some minor modifications to the original label-making program. For example, the input file variables have changed; you must declare a variable for an `inLastProduction` field. Additionally, you might want to create a numeric field named `labelsToPrint` that can hold a value equal to 110% of a worker's `inLastProduction`.

The major modification to the original label-making program is in the question that controls the label-producing loop. Instead of asking if `labelCounter < 100`, you now can ask if `labelCounter < labelsToPrint`. The sentinel or limit value can be a variable like `labelsToPrint` just as easily as it can be a constant like 100. See Figure 6-10 for the flowchart as well as the pseudocode.

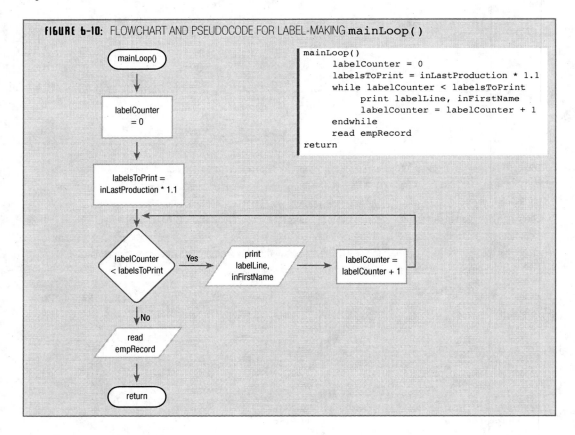

FIGURE 6-10: FLOWCHART AND PSEUDOCODE FOR LABEL-MAKING `mainLoop()`

```
mainLoop()
    labelCounter = 0
    labelsToPrint = inLastProduction * 1.1
    while labelCounter < labelsToPrint
        print labelLine, inFirstName
        labelCounter = labelCounter + 1
    endwhile
    read empRecord
return
```

The statement `labelsToPrint = inLastProduction * 1.1` calculates `labelsToPrint` as 110% of `inLastProduction`. Alternately, you can perform the calculation as `labelsToPrint = inLastProduction + 0.10 * inLastProduction`. The mathematical result is the same.

LOOPING BY DECREMENTING

Rather than increasing a loop control variable until it passes some sentinel value, sometimes it is more convenient to reduce a loop control variable on every cycle through a loop. For example, again assume you want to print enough labels for every worker to cover 110% production. As an alternative to setting a `labelCounter` variable to 0 and increasing it after each label prints, you initially can set `labelCounter` equal to the number of labels to print (`inLastProduction * 1.1`), and subsequently reduce the `labelCounter` value every time a label prints. You continue printing labels and reducing the `labelCounter` until you have counted down to zero. Decreasing a variable by one is called **decrementing** the variable.

For example, when you write the following, you produce enough labels to equal 110% of `inLastProduction`:

```
labelCounter = inLastProduction * 1.1
while labelCounter > 0
     print labelLine, inFirstName
     labelCounter = labelCounter - 1
endwhile
```

When you decrement, you can avoid declaring a special variable for the `labelsToPrint`. The `labelCounter` variable starts with a value that represents the labels to print, and works its way down to zero.

Yet another alternative allows you to eliminate the `labelCounter` variable. You could use the `inLastProduction` variable itself to keep track of the labels. For example, the following pseudocode segment also produces a number of labels equal to 110% of each worker's `inLastProduction` value:

```
inLastProduction = inLastProduction * 1.1
while inLastProduction > 0
     print labelLine, inFirstName
     inLastProduction = inLastProduction - 1
endwhile
```

In this example, `inLastProduction` is first increased by 10%. Then, while it remains above 0, there are more labels to print; when it is eventually reduced to hold the value 0, all the needed labels will have been printed. With this method, you do not need to create any new counter variables such as `labelCounter`, because `inLastProduction` itself acts as a counter. However, you can't use this method if you need to use the value of `inLastProduction` for this record later in the program. By decrementing the variable, you are changing its value on every cycle through the loop; when you have finished, the original value in `inLastProduction` has been lost.

TIP □ □ □ □ | Do not think the value of inLastProduction is gone forever when you alter it. The original value still exists within the data file. It is the main memory location called inLastProduction that is being reduced.

AVOIDING COMMON LOOP MISTAKES

The mistakes programmers make most often with loops are:

- Neglecting to initialize the loop control variable
- Neglecting to alter the loop control variable
- Using the wrong comparison with the loop control variable
- Including statements inside the loop that belong outside the loop
- Initializing a variable that does not require initialization

NEGLECTING TO INITIALIZE THE LOOP CONTROL VARIABLE

It is always a mistake to fail to initialize a loop's control variable. For example, assume you remove the statement labelCounter = 0 from the program illustrated in Figure 6-10. When labelCounter is compared to labelsToPrint at the start of the while loop, it is impossible to predict whether any labels will print. Because uninitialized values contain unknown, unpredictable garbage, comparing such a variable to another value is meaningless. Even if you initialize labelCounter to 0 in the housekeep() module of the program, you must reset labelCounter to 0 for each new record that is processed within the while loop. If you fail to reset the labelCounter, it never surpasses 100 because after it reaches 100, the answer to the question labelCounter < 100 is always No, and the logic never enters the loop where a label can be printed.

NEGLECTING TO ALTER THE LOOP CONTROL VARIABLE

A different sort of error occurs if you remove the statement that adds 1 to the labelCounter from the program in Figure 6-10. This error results in the following code:

```
while labelCounter < labelsToPrint
    print labelLine, inFirstName
endwhile
```

Following this logic, if labelCounter is 0 and labelsToPrint is, for example, 110, then labelCounter will be less than labelsToPrint forever. Nothing in the loop changes either variable, so when labelCounter is less than labelsToPrint once, then labelCounter is less than labelsToPrint forever, and labels will continue to print. A loop that never stops executing is called an **infinite loop**. It is always incorrect to create a loop that cannot terminate.

USING THE WRONG COMPARISON WITH THE LOOP CONTROL VARIABLE

Programmers must be careful to use the correct comparison in the statement that controls a loop. Although there is only a one-keystroke difference between the following two code segments, one performs the loop 10 times and the other performs the loop 11 times.

```
counter = 0
while counter < 10
     perform someModule()
     counter = counter + 1
endwhile
```

and

```
counter = 0
while counter <= 10
     perform someModule()
     counter = counter + 1
endwhile
```

The seriousness of the error of using <= or >= when only < or > is needed depends on the actions performed within the loop. For example, if such an error occurred in a loan company program, each customer might be charged a month's additional interest; if the error occurred in an airline's program; it might overbook a flight; and if it occurred in a pharmacy's drug-dispensing program, each patient might receive one extra (and possibly harmful) unit of medication.

INCLUDING STATEMENTS INSIDE THE LOOP THAT BELONG OUTSIDE THE LOOP

When you run a computer program that uses the loop in Figure 6-10, hundreds or thousands of employee records might pass through the `mainLoop()`. If there are 100 employee records, then `labelCounter` is set to 0 exactly 100 times; it must be reset to 0 once for each employee, in order to count each employee's labels correctly. Similarly, `labelsToPrint` is reset (to 1.1 times the current `inLastProduction` value) once for each employee.

If the average employee produces 100 items during a week, then the loop within the `mainLoop()`, the one controlled by the statement `while labelCounter < labelsToPrint`, executes 11,000 times—110 times each for 100 employees. This number of repetitions is necessary in order to print the correct number of labels.

A repetition that is *not* necessary would be to execute 11,000 separate multiplication statements to recalculate the value to compare to `labelCounter`. See Figure 6-11.

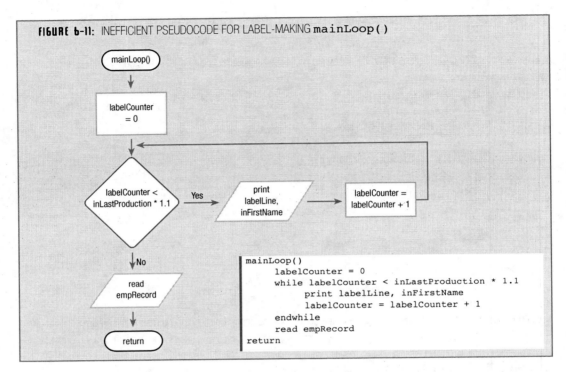

FIGURE 6-11: INEFFICIENT PSEUDOCODE FOR LABEL-MAKING `mainLoop()`

```
mainLoop()
    labelCounter = 0
    while labelCounter < inLastProduction * 1.1
        print labelLine, inFirstName
        labelCounter = labelCounter + 1
    endwhile
    read empRecord
return
```

Although the logic shown in Figure 6-11 will produce the correct number of labels for every employee, the statement `while labelCounter < inLastProduction * 1.1` executes an average of 110 times for each employee. That means the arithmetic operation that is part of the question—multiplying `inLastProduction` by 1.1—occurs 110 separate times for each employee. Performing the same calculation that results in the same mathematical answer 110 times in a row is inefficient. Instead, it is superior to perform the multiplication just once for each employee and use the result 110 times, as shown in the original version of the program in Figure 6-10. In the pseudocode in Figure 6-10, you still must recalculate `labelsToPrint` once for each record, but not once for each label, so you have improved the program's efficiency.

The modules illustrated in Figures 6-10 and 6-11 do the same thing: print enough labels for every employee to cover 110% of production. As you become more proficient at programming, you will recognize many opportunities to perform the same tasks in alternative, more elegant, and more efficient ways.

INITIALIZING A VARIABLE THAT DOES NOT REQUIRE INITIALIZATION

Another common error made by beginning programmers involves initializing a variable that does not require initialization. When declaring variables for the label-making program, you might be tempted to declare `num labelsToPrint = inLastProduction * 1.1`. It seems as though this declaration statement indicates that the value of the `labelsToPrint` will always be 110% of the `inLastProduction` figure. However, this approach is incorrect for two reasons. First, at the time `labelsToPrint` is declared, the first employee record has not yet been read into memory, so the value of `inLastProduction` is garbage; therefore, the result in `labelsToPrint` after multiplication will also be garbage. Second, even if you read the first `empRecord` into memory before declaring the `labelsToPrint` variable, the mathematical calculation of the `labelsToPrint` within the `housekeep()` module would be valid for the first record only. The value of `labelsToPrint` must be recalculated for each employee record in the input file. Therefore, calculation of the `labelsToPrint` correctly belongs within the `mainLoop()`, as shown in Figure 6-10.

USING THE FOR LOOP

The label-making programs discussed in this chapter each contain two loops. For example, Figures 6-12 and 6-13 show the loop within the mainline program as well as the loop within the `mainLoop()` module for a program that produces exactly 100 labels for each employee.

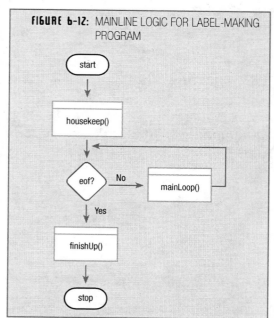

FIGURE 6-12: MAINLINE LOGIC FOR LABEL-MAKING PROGRAM

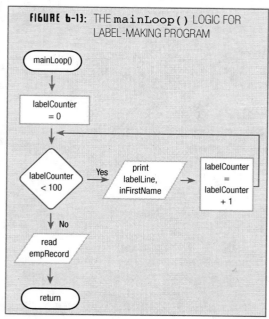

FIGURE 6-13: THE `mainLoop()` LOGIC FOR LABEL-MAKING PROGRAM

Entry to the `mainLoop()` in the mainline logic is controlled by the `eof` decision. Within the `mainLoop()`, label production is controlled by the `labelCounter` decision. When you execute the mainline logic, you cannot predict how many times the `mainLoop()` module will execute. Depending on the size of the input file, any number of records might be processed; while the program runs, you don't know what the total number of records finally will be. Until you attempt to read a record and encounter the end of the file, you don't know if more records are going to become available. Of course, not being able to predict the number of input records is valuable—it allows the program to function correctly no matter how many employees exist from week to week or year to year. Because you can't determine ahead of time how many records there might be and, therefore, how many times the loop might execute, the mainline loop in the label-making program is called an **indeterminate**, or **indefinite**, **loop**.

With some loops, you know exactly how many times they will execute. If every employee needs 100 printed labels, then the loop within the `mainLoop()` module executes exactly 100 times for each employee. This kind of loop, in which you definitely know the repetition factor, is a **definite loop**.

Every high-level computer programming language contains a **while statement** that you can use to code any loop, including indefinite loops (like the mainline loop) and definite loops (like the label-printing loop). You can write statements like the following:

```
while not eof
     perform mainLoop()
endwhile
```

and

```
while labelCounter < 100
     print labelLine, inFirstName
     labelCounter = labelCounter + 1
endwhile
```

In addition to the `while` statement, most computer languages also support a `for` statement. You can use the **for statement**, or **for loop**, with definite loops—those for which you know how many times the loop will repeat. The `for` statement provides you with three actions in one compact statement. The `for` statement uses a loop control variable that it automatically:

- initializes
- evaluates
- increments

The `for` statement usually takes the form:

```
for initialValue to finalValue
     do something
endfor
```

For example, to print 100 labels you can write:

```
for labelCounter = 0 to 99
     print labelLine, inFirstName
endfor
```

This `for` statement accomplishes several tasks at once in a compact form:

- The `for` statement initializes the `labelCounter` to 0.
- The `for` statement checks the `labelCounter` against the limit value 99 and makes sure that the `labelCounter` is less than or equal to that value.
- If the evaluation is true, the `for` statement body that prints the label executes.
- After the `for` statement body executes, the `labelCounter` increases by 1 and the comparison to the limit value is made again.

TIP □ □ □ □   As an alternative to using the loop for `labelCounter = 0 to 99`, you can use for `labelCounter = 1 to 100`. You can use any combination of values, as long as there are 100 whole number values between (and including) the two limits.

You are never required to use a `for` statement; the label loop executes correctly using a `while` statement with `labelCounter` as a loop control variable. However, when a loop is based on a loop control variable progressing from a known starting value to a known ending value in equal increments, the `for` loop presents you with a convenient shorthand.

TIP □ □ □ □   The programmer needs to know neither the starting nor the ending value for the loop control variable; only the program must know those values. For example, you don't know the value of a worker's `inLastProduction`, but when you tell the program to read a record, the program knows. To use this value as a limit value, you can write a `for` loop that begins for `labelCounter = 1 to inLastProduction`.

TIP □ □ □ □   In most programming languages, you can provide a `for` loop with a step value. A step value is a number you use to increase a loop control variable on each pass through a loop. In most programming languages, the default loop step value is 1. You specify a step value when you want each pass through the loop to change the loop control variable by a value other than 1.

USING THE DO UNTIL LOOP

When you use either a `while` or a `for` loop, the body of the loop may never execute. For example, in the mainline logic in Figure 6-5, the last action in the `housekeep()` module is to read an input record. If the input file contains no records, the result of the `eof` decision is true, and the program executes the `finishUp()` module without ever entering the `mainLoop()` module.

Similarly, when you produce labels within the `mainLoop()` module shown in Figure 6-10, labels are produced `while labelCounter < labelsToPrint`. Suppose an employee record contains a 0 in the `inLastProduction` field—for example, in the case of a new employee or an employee who was on vacation during the previous week. In such a case, the value of `labelsToPrint` would be 0, and the label-producing body of the loop would never execute. With a `while` loop, you evaluate the loop control variable prior to executing the loop body, and the evaluation might indicate that you can't enter the loop.

When you want to ensure that a loop's body executes at least one time, you can use a do until loop. In a do until loop, the loop control variable is evaluated after the loop body executes instead of before. Therefore, the body always executes at least one time.

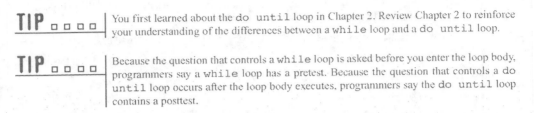

TIP ▫ ▫ ▫ ▫ | You first learned about the do until loop in Chapter 2. Review Chapter 2 to reinforce your understanding of the differences between a while loop and a do until loop.

TIP ▫ ▫ ▫ ▫ | Because the question that controls a while loop is asked before you enter the loop body, programmers say a while loop has a pretest. Because the question that controls a do until loop occurs after the loop body executes, programmers say the do until loop contains a posttest.

For example, suppose you want to produce one label for each employee to wear as identification, before you produce enough labels to cover 110% of last week's production. You can write the do until loop that appears in Figure 6-14.

In Figure 6-14, the labelCounter variable is set to 0 and labelsToPrint is calculated. Suppose labelsToPrint is computed to be 0. The do loop will be entered, a label will print, 1 will be added to the labelCounter, and then and only then will labelCounter be compared to labelsToPrint. Because labelCounter is now 1 and labelsToPrint is only 0, the loop is exited, having printed a single identification label and no product labels.

As a different example using the logic in Figure 6-14, suppose that for a worker labelsToPrint is calculated to be 1. In this case, the loop is entered, a label prints, and 1 is added to labelCounter. Now, the value of labelCounter is not yet greater than the value of labelsToPrint, so the loop repeats, a second label prints, and labelCounter is incremented again. This time labelCounter (with a value of 2) does exceed labelsToPrint (with a value of 1), so the loop ends. This employee gets an identification label as well as one product label.

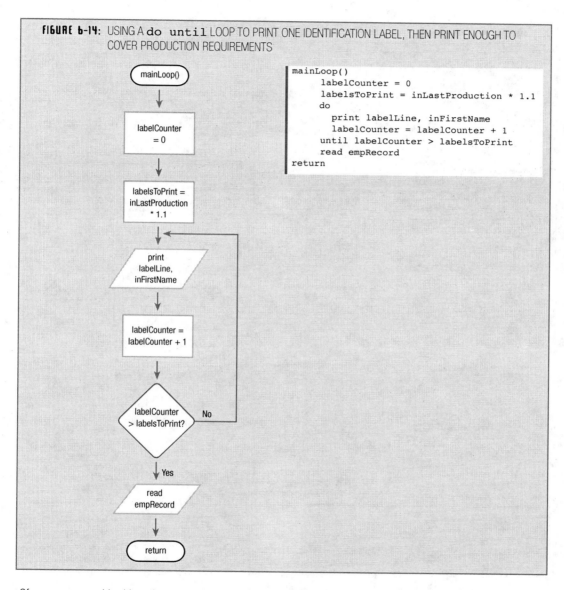

FIGURE 6-14: USING A `do until` LOOP TO PRINT ONE IDENTIFICATION LABEL, THEN PRINT ENOUGH TO COVER PRODUCTION REQUIREMENTS

```
mainLoop()
    labelCounter = 0
    labelsToPrint = inLastProduction * 1.1
    do
      print labelLine, inFirstName
      labelCounter = labelCounter + 1
    until labelCounter > labelsToPrint
    read empRecord
return
```

Of course, you could achieve the same results by printing one label, then entering a `while` loop, as in Figure 6-15. In this example, one label prints before `labelCounter` is compared to `labelsToPrint`. No matter what the value of `labelsToPrint` is, one identification label is produced.

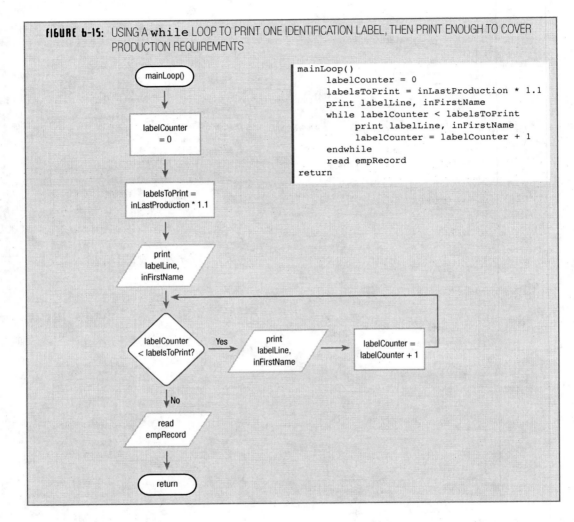

FIGURE 6-15: USING A `while` LOOP TO PRINT ONE IDENTIFICATION LABEL, THEN PRINT ENOUGH TO COVER PRODUCTION REQUIREMENTS

```
mainLoop()
    labelCounter = 0
    labelsToPrint = inLastProduction * 1.1
    print labelLine, inFirstName
    while labelCounter < labelsToPrint
        print labelLine, inFirstName
        labelCounter = labelCounter + 1
    endwhile
    read empRecord
return
```

TIP □ □ □ □ The logic in Figure 6-15, in which you print one label, then test a value to determine whether you will print more, takes the same form as the mainline logic in most of the programs you have worked with so far. When you read records from a file, you read one record (the priming read) and then test for eof before continuing. In effect, the first label printed in Figure 6-15 is a "priming label."

The results of the programs shown in Figures 6-14 and 6-15 are the same. Using either, every employee will receive an identification label and enough labels to cover production. Each module works correctly, and neither is logically superior to the other. There is almost always more than one way to solve the same programming problem. As you learned in Chapter 3, a `do until` loop can always be replaced by pairing a sequence and a `do while` loop. Which method you choose depends on your (or your instructor's or supervisor's) preferences.

TIP ☐ ☐ ☐ ☐ | There are several additional ways to approach the logic shown in the programs in Figures 6-14 and 6-15. For example, after calculating `labelsToPrint`, you could immediately add 1 to the value. Then, you could use the logic in Figure 6-14, as long as you change the loop-ending question to `labelCounter >= labelsToPrint` (instead of only `>`). Alternatively, using the logic in Figure 6-15, after adding 1 to `labelsToPrint`, you could remove the lone first label-printing instruction; that way, one identification label would always be printed, even if the last production figure was 0.

RECOGNIZING THE CHARACTERISTICS SHARED BY ALL LOOPS

You can see from Figure 6-15 that you are never required to use a `do until` loop. The same results always can be achieved by performing the loop body steps once before entering a `while` loop. If you follow the logic of either of the loops shown in Figures 6-14 and 6-15, you will discover that when an employee has an `inLastProduction` value of 3, then exactly four labels print. Likewise, when an employee has an `inLastProduction` value of 0, then in both cases exactly one label prints. You can accomplish the same results with either type of loop; the `do until` loop is simply a convenience when you need a loop to execute at least one time.

TIP ☐ ☐ ☐ ☐ | In some languages, the `do until` loop is called a `repeat until` loop.

TIP ☐ ☐ ☐ ☐ | If you can express the logic you want to perform by saying "while a is true, keep doing b," you probably want to use a `while` loop. If what you want to accomplish seems to fit the statement "do a until b is true," you can probably use a `do until` loop.

As you examine Figures 6-14 and 6-15, notice that with the `do until` loop, the loop-controlling question is placed at the *end* of the sequence of the steps that repeat. With the `while` loop, the loop-controlling question is placed at the *beginning* of the steps that repeat. All structured loops share these characteristics:

- The loop-controlling question provides either entry to or exit from the repeating structure.
- The loop-controlling question provides the *only* entry to or exit from the repeating structure.

You should also notice the difference between *unstructured* loops and the structured `do until` and `while` loops. Figure 6-16 diagrams the outline of two unstructured loops. In each case, the decision labeled X breaks out of the loop prematurely. In each case, the loop control variable (labeled `LC`) does not provide the only entry to or exit from the loop.

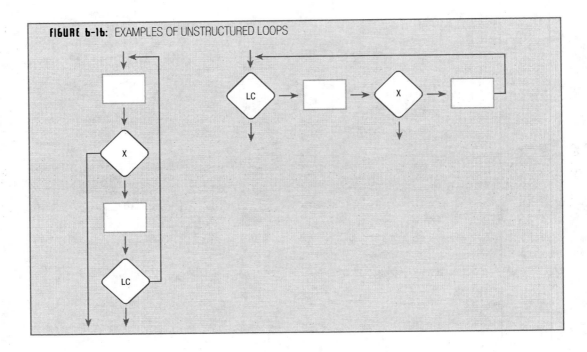

FIGURE 6-16: EXAMPLES OF UNSTRUCTURED LOOPS

NESTING LOOPS

Program logic gets more complicated when you must use loops within loops, or **nesting loops**. When one loop appears inside another, the loop that contains the other loop is called the **outer loop**, and the loop that is contained is called the **inner loop**. For example, suppose you work for a company that pays workers twice per month. The company has decided on an incentive plan to provide each employee with a one-fourth of one percent raise for each pay period during the coming year, and it wants a report like that shown in Figure 6-17. A list will be printed for each employee showing the exact paycheck amounts for each of the next 24 pay periods—two per month for 12 months. As an example of how the report looks for one employee, see Figure 6-18. A description of each employee input record is shown in Figure 6-19.

FIGURE 6-17: PRINT CHART FOR PROJECTED PAYROLL REPORT

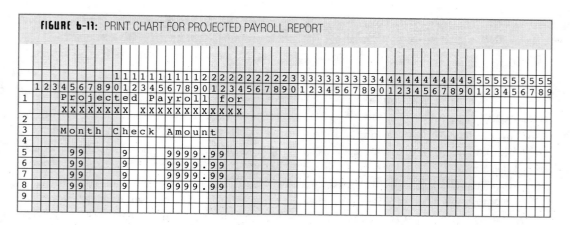

FIGURE 6-18: SAMPLE PROJECTED PAYROLL REPORT FOR ONE EMPLOYEE

Projected Payroll for
Roberto Martinez

Month	Check	Amount
1	1	501.25
1	2	502.50
2	1	503.76
2	2	505.02
3	1	506.28

FIGURE 6-19: EMPLOYEE PAYROLL RECORD DATA FILE DESCRIPTION

File Name: EMPPAY

FIELD DESCRIPTION	POSITIONS	DATA TYPE	DECIMALS
Employee Last Name	1-12	Character	
Employee First Name	13-20	Character	
Weekly salary at start of year	21-26	Numeric	2

To produce the Projected Payroll report, you need to maintain two separate counters to control two separate loops. One counter will keep track of the month (1 through 12), and another will keep track of the pay period within the month (1 through 2). When nesting loops, you must maintain individual loop control variables—one for each loop—and alter each at the appropriate time.

Figure 6-20 shows the mainline, `housekeeping()`, and `finish()` logic for the program. These modules are standard. Besides the input file variables and the headers that print for each employee, the list of declared variables includes two counters. One, named `monthCounter`, keeps track of the month that is currently printing. The other, named `checkCounter`, keeps track of which check within the month is currently printing. Three additional declarations hold the number of months in a year (12), the number of checks in a month (2), and the rate of increase (0.0025). Declaring these variables is not required; the program could just use the numeric constants 12, 2, and 0.0025, but providing those values with names serves two purposes. First, the program becomes more **self-documenting**—that is, it describes itself to the reader. When other programmers read a program and encounter a number like 2, they might wonder about the meaning. Instead, if the value is named `numberOfChecksInMonth`, the meaning of the value is much clearer. Second, after the program is in production, the company might choose to change one of the values, for example, by going to an 11-month year, producing more or fewer paychecks in a month, or changing the raise rate. In those cases, the person who modifies the program would not have to search for appropriate spots to make those changes, but would simply redefine the values assigned to the appropriate variables.

FIGURE 6-20: MAINLINE LOGIC, `housekeeping()`, AND `finish()` MODULES FOR PROJECTED PAYROLL REPORT PROGRAM

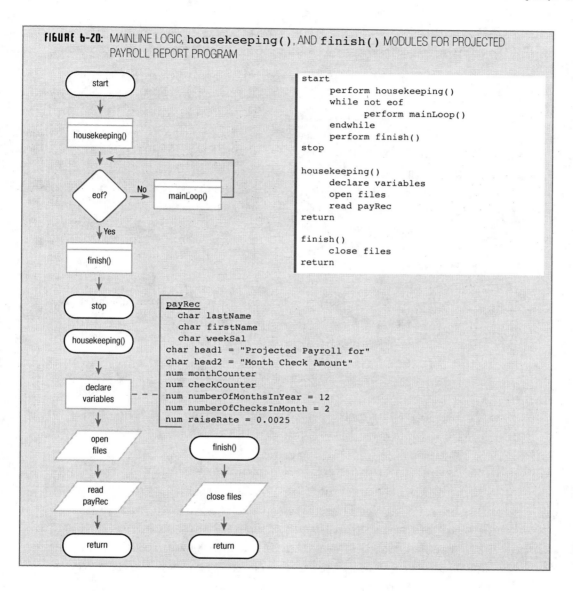

```
start
    perform housekeeping()
    while not eof
        perform mainLoop()
    endwhile
    perform finish()
stop

housekeeping()
    declare variables
    open files
    read payRec
return

finish()
    close files
return
```

```
payRec
    char lastName
    char firstName
    char weekSal
char head1 = "Projected Payroll for"
char head2 = "Month Check Amount"
num monthCounter
num checkCounter
num numberOfMonthsInYear = 12
num numberOfChecksInMonth = 2
num raiseRate = 0.0025
```

At the end of the `housekeeping()` module in Figure 6-20, the first employee record is read into main memory. Figure 6-21 shows how the record is processed in the `mainLoop()` module. The program proceeds as follows:

1. The first heading prints, followed by the employee name and the column headings.

2. The `monthCounter` variable is set to 1; the `monthCounter` variable is the loop control variable for the outer loop, and this step provides it with its initial value.

3. The `monthCounter` is compared to the number of months in a year, and because the comparison evaluates as true, the outer loop is entered. Within this loop, the `checkCounter` variable is used as a loop control variable for an inner loop.

4. The `checkCounter` is initialized to 1, and then compared to the number of checks in a month. Because this comparison evaluates as true, the inner loop is entered.

5. Within this inner loop, the employee's weekly salary is increased by one-quarter of one percent (the old salary plus 0.0025 of the old salary).

6. The month number (currently 1), check number (also currently 1), and newly calculated salary are printed.

7. The check number is increased (to 2), and the inner loop reaches its end; this causes the logical control to return to the top of the inner loop, where the `while` condition is tested again. Because the check number (2) is still less than or equal to the number of checks in a month, the inner loop is entered again.

8. The pay amount increases, and the month (still 1), the check number (2), and the new salary are printed.

9. Then, the check number becomes 3. Now, when the loop condition is tested for the third time, the check number is no longer less than or equal to the number of checks in a month, so the inner loop ends.

10. As the last step in the outer loop, the `monthCounter` becomes 2.

11. After the `monthCounter` increases to 2, control returns to the entry point of the outer loop.

12. The `while` condition is tested, and because 2 is not greater than the number of months in a year, the outer loop is entered for a second time.

13. The `checkCounter` is reset to 1 so that it will correctly count two checks for this month.

14. Because the newly reset `checkCounter` is not more than the number of checks in a month, the salary is increased, and the amount prints for month 2, check 1.

15. The `checkCounter` increases to 2 and another value is printed for month 2, check 2 before the inner loop ends and the `monthCounter` is increased to 3.

16. Then, month 3, check 1 prints, followed by month 3, check 2.

FIGURE 6-21: THE `mainLoop()` MODULE FOR THE PROJECTED PAYROLL REPORT PROGRAM

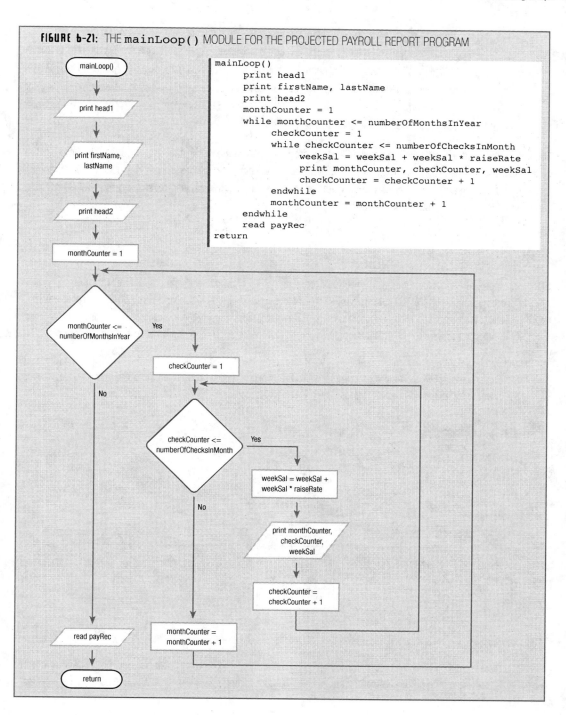

```
mainLoop()
     print head1
     print firstName, lastName
     print head2
     monthCounter = 1
     while monthCounter <= numberOfMonthsInYear
          checkCounter = 1
          while checkCounter <= numberOfChecksInMonth
               weekSal = weekSal + weekSal * raiseRate
               print monthCounter, checkCounter, weekSal
               checkCounter = checkCounter + 1
          endwhile
          monthCounter = monthCounter + 1
     endwhile
     read payRec
return
```

17. The `mainLoop()` continues printing two check amounts for each of 12 months before the outer loop is finished, when the `monthCounter` eventually exceeds 12. Only then is the next employee record read into memory, and control leaves the `mainLoop()` module and returns to the mainline logic where the end of file is tested. If a new record exists, control returns to the `mainLoop()` for the new employee, for whom headings are printed, and the `monthCounter` is set to 1 to start the set of 24 calculations for this employee.

There is no limit to the number of loop-nesting levels a program can contain. For instance, suppose that in the projected payroll example, the company wanted to provide a slight raise each hour or each day of each pay period in each month for each of several years. No matter how many levels deep the nesting goes, each loop must still contain a loop control variable that is initialized, tested, and altered.

USING A LOOP TO ACCUMULATE TOTALS

Business reports often include totals. The supervisor requesting a list of employees who participate in the company dental plan is often as much interested in *how many* such employees there are as in *who* they are. When you receive your telephone bill at the end of the month, you are usually more interested in the total than in the charges for the individual calls. Some business reports list no individual detail records, just totals. Such reports are called **summary reports**.

For example, a real estate broker might maintain a file of company real estate listings. Each record in the file contains the street address and the asking price of a property for sale. The broker wants a listing of all the properties for sale; she also wants a total value for all the company's listings. The print chart appears in Figure 6-22.

FIGURE 6-22: PRINT CHART FOR REAL ESTATE REPORT

```
                    1 1 1 1 1 1 1 1 1 1 2 2 2 2 2 2 2 2 2 2 3 3 3 3 3 3 3 3 3 3 4 4 4 4 4 4 4 4 4 4 5 5 5 5 5 5 5 5 5 5 6 6
  1 2 3 4 5 6 7 8 9 0 1 2 3 4 5 6 7 8 9 0 1 2 3 4 5 6 7 8 9 0 1 2 3 4 5 6 7 8 9 0 1 2 3 4 5 6 7 8 9 0 1 2 3 4 5 6 7 8 9 0 1
1
2                   P R O P E R T I E S   F O R   S A L E
3
4       S T R E E T   A D D R E S S       A S K I N G   P R I C E
5
6
7       X X X X X X X X X X X X X X           9 , 9 9 9 , 9 9 9
8       X X X X X X X X X X X X X X           9 , 9 9 9 , 9 9 9
9
10            T O T A L   V A L U E         9 9 , 9 9 9 , 9 9 9
11
12
13
14
```

When you read a real estate listing record, besides printing it you must add its value to an accumulator. An **accumulator** is a variable that you use to gather or accumulate values. An accumulator is very similar to a counter. The difference lies in the value that you add to the variable; usually, you add just one to a counter, whereas you add some other value to an accumulator. If the real estate broker wants to know how many listings the company holds, you count them. When she wants to know total real estate value, you accumulate it.

In order to accumulate total real estate prices, you declare a numeric variable at the beginning of the program, as shown in the `housekeep()` module in Figure 6-23. You must initialize the accumulator, `accumValue`, to zero. In Chapter 4, you learned that when using most programming languages, declared variables do not automatically assume any particular value; the unknown value is called garbage. When you read the first real estate record, you will add its value to the accumulator. If the accumulator contains garbage, the addition will not work. Some programming languages issue an error message if you don't initialize a variable you use for accumulating; others let you accumulate, but the results are worthless because you start with garbage.

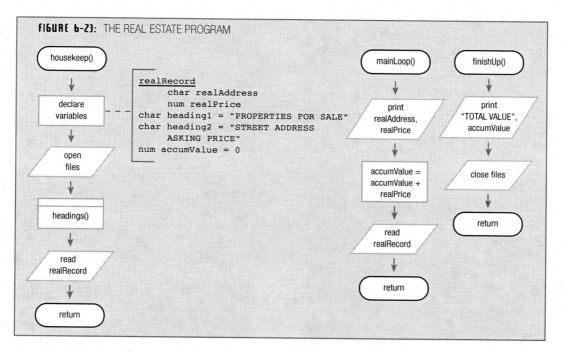

FIGURE 6-23: THE REAL ESTATE PROGRAM

If you name the input record fields `realAddress` and `realPrice`, then the `mainLoop()` module of the real estate listing program can be written as shown in Figure 6-23. For each real estate record, you print it and add its value to the accumulator `accumValue`. Then you can read the next record.

After the program reaches the end of the file, the accumulator will hold the grand total of all the real estate values. When you reach the end of the file, the `finishUp()` module executes, and it is within the `finishUp()` module that you print the accumulated value, `accumValue`. After printing the total, you can close both the input and the output files and return to the main line where the program ends.

New programmers often want to reset the `accumValue` to zero after printing it. Although you *can* take this step without harming the execution of the program, it does not serve any useful purpose. You cannot set `accumValue` to zero in antici-pation of having it ready for the next program, or even for the next time you execute this program. Program variables exist only for the life of the program, and even if a future program happens to contain a variable named `accumValue`, the variable will not necessarily occupy the same memory location as this one. Even if you run the program a second time, the variables might occupy physical memory locations different from those they occupied during the first run. At the beginning of the program, it is the programmer's responsibility to initialize all variables that must start with a specific value. There is no benefit to changing a variable's value when it will never be used again during the current execution of the program.

It is especially important to avoid changing the value of a variable unnecessarily when the change occurs within a loop. One extra, unnecessary statement in a loop that executes hundreds of thousands of times can significantly slow a program's performance speed.

CHAPTER SUMMARY

☐ When you use a loop within a computer program, you can write one set of instructions that operates on multiple, separate sets of data.

☐ Three steps must occur in every loop: You must initialize a loop control variable, compare the variable to some value that controls whether the loop continues or stops, and alter the variable that controls the loop.

☐ A counter is a numeric variable you use to count the number of times an event has occurred. You can count occurrences by incrementing a variable.

☐ You can use a variable sentinel value to control a loop.

☐ Sometimes, it is convenient to reduce or decrement a loop control variable on every cycle through a loop.

☐ The two mistakes programmers make most often with loops are neglecting to initialize the loop control variable, and neglecting to alter the loop control variable. Additionally, when a calculation can be performed once before entering a loop, it is inefficient to place the calculation within the loop. It is incorrect to attempt to initialize a variable by using data values that have not been read into memory yet.

☐ Most computer languages support a `for` statement or `for` loop that you can use with definite loops when you know how many times a loop will repeat. The `for` statement uses a loop control variable that it automatically initializes, evaluates, and increments.

☐ When you want to ensure that a loop's body executes at least one time, you can use a `do until` loop, in which the loop control variable is evaluated after the loop body executes.

☐ All structured loops share these characteristics: The loop-controlling question provides either entry to or exit from the repeating structure, and the loop-controlling question provides the *only* entry to or exit from the repeating structure.

☐ When you must use loops within loops, you use nesting loops. When nesting loops, you must maintain two individual loop control variables and alter each at the appropriate time.

☐ Business reports often include totals. Summary reports list no detail records—only totals. An accumulator is a variable that you use to gather or accumulate values.

KEY TERMS

A loop is a structure that repeats actions while some condition continues.

A main loop is a basic set of instructions that is repeated for every record.

A loop control variable is a variable that determines whether a loop will continue.

A sentinel value is a limit, or ending, value.

A loop body is the set of statements that executes within a loop.

A counter is any numeric variable you use to count the number of times an event has occurred.

Adding 1 to a variable is called incrementing the variable.

Decreasing a variable by one is called decrementing the variable.

A loop that never stops executing is called an infinite loop.

An indeterminate, or indefinite, loop is one for which you cannot predetermine the number of executions.

A loop for which you definitely know the repetition factor is a definite loop.

A while statement can be used to code any loop.

A for statement, or for loop, can be used to code definite loops. It contains a loop control variable that it automatically initializes, evaluates, and increments.

Nesting loops are loops within loops.

When one loop appears inside another, the loop that contains the other loop is called the outer loop, and the loop that is contained is called the inner loop.

A self-documenting program is one that describes itself to the reader.

A summary report lists only totals, without individual detail records.

An accumulator is a variable that you use to gather or accumulate values.

REVIEW QUESTIONS

1. **The structure that allows you to write one set of instructions that operates on multiple, separate sets of data is the _____.**

   a. sequence
   b. selection
   c. loop
   d. case

2. **Which of the following is not a step that must occur in every loop?**

   a. Initialize a loop control variable.
   b. Compare the loop control value to a sentinel.
   c. Set the loop control value equal to a sentinel.
   d. Alter the loop control variable.

3. **The statements executed within a loop are known collectively as the _____.**

   a. sentinels
   b. loop controls
   c. sequences
   d. loop body

4. **A counter keeps track of _____.**

   a. the number of times an event has occurred
   b. the number of machine cycles required by a segment of a program
   c. the number of loop structures within a program
   d. a total that prints at the end of a summary report

5. **Adding 1 to a variable is also called _____.**

   a. digesting
   b. incrementing
   c. decrementing
   d. resetting

6. **In the following pseudocode, what is printed?**

```
a = 1
b = 2
c = 5
while a < c
      a = a + 1
      b = b + c
endwhile
print a, b, c
```

   a. 1 2 5
   b. 5 22 5
   c. 5 6 5
   d. 6 22 9

7. **In the following pseudocode, what is printed?**

```
d = 4
e = 6
f = 7
while d > f
      d = d + 1
      e = e - 1
endwhile
print d, e, f
```

   a. 7 3 7
   b. 8 2 8
   c. 4 6 7
   d. 5 5 7

8. **When you decrement a variable, you _____.**

   a. set it to 0

   b. reduce it by one-tenth

   c. subtract 1 from it

   d. remove it from a program

9. **In the following pseudocode, what is printed?**

   ```
   g = 4
   h = 6
   while g < h
        g = g + 1
   endwhile
   print g, h
   ```

   a. nothing

   b. 4 6

   c. 5 6

   d. 6 6

10. **Most programmers use a `for` loop _____.**

    a. for every loop they write

    b. when they know the exact number of times a loop will repeat

    c. when they do not know the exact number of times a loop will repeat

    d. when a loop will not repeat

11. **Unlike a `do while` loop, you use a `do until` loop when _____.**

    a. you can predict the exact number of loop repetitions

    b. the loop body might never execute

    c. the loop body must execute exactly one time

    d. the loop body must execute at least one time

12. **Which of the following is a characteristic shared by `while` loops and `do until` loops?**

    a. Both have one entry and one exit.

    b. Both have a body that executes at least once.

    c. Both compare a loop control variable at the top of the loop.

    d. All of these are true.

13. **A comparison with a loop control variable provides _____.**

    a. the only entry to a `while` loop

    b. the only exit from a `do until` loop

    c. both of the above

    d. none of the above

14. When two loops are nested, the loop that is contained by the other is the _____ loop.

    a. inner
    b. outer
    c. unstructured
    d. captive

15. In the following pseudocode, how many times is "Hello" printed?

```
j = 2
k = 5
m = 6
n = 9
while j < k
     while m < n
          print "Hello"
          m = m + 1
     endwhile
     j = j + 1
endwhile
```

    a. zero
    b. three
    c. six
    d. nine

16. In the following pseudocode, how many times is "Hello" printed?

```
j = 2
k = 5
n = 9
while j < k
     m = 6
     while m < n
          print "Hello"
          m = m + 1
     endwhile
     j = j + 1
endwhile
```

    a. zero
    b. three
    c. six
    d. nine

17. **In the following pseudocode, how many times is "Hello" printed?**

```
p = 2
q = 4
while p < q
      print "Hello"
      r = 1
      while r < q
          print "Hello"
          r = r + 1
      endwhile
      p = p + 1
endwhile
```

 a. zero
 b. four
 c. six
 d. eight

18. **A report that lists no details about individual records, but totals only, is a(n) _____ report.**

 a. accumulator
 b. final
 c. summary
 d. detailless

19. **Typically, the value added to a counter variable is _____.**

 a. 0
 b. 1
 c. 10
 d. 100

20. **Typically, the value added to an accumulator variable is _____.**

 a. zero
 b. one
 c. smaller than a value added to a counter variable
 d. larger than a value added to a counter variable

EXERCISES

1. **Design the logic for a module that would print every number from 1 through 10.**

   a. Draw the flowchart.
   b. Design the pseudocode.

2. **Design the logic for a module that would print every number from 1 through 10 along with its square and cube.**

   a. Draw the flowchart.
   b. Design the pseudocode.

3. **Design a program that reads credit card account records and prints payoff schedules for customers. Input records contain an account number, customer name, and balance due. For each customer, print the account number and name; then print the customer's projected balance each month for the next 10 months. Assume that there is no finance charge on this account, that the customer makes no new purchases, and that the customer pays off the balance with equal monthly payments, which are 10% of the original bill.**

   a. Design the print chart for this program.
   b. Design the hierarchy chart for this program.
   c. Design the flowchart for this program.
   d. Write pseudocode for this program.

4. **Design a program that reads credit card account records and prints payoff schedules for customers. Input records contain an account number, customer name, and balance due. For each customer, print the account number and name; then print the customer's payment amount and new balance each month until the card is paid off. Assume that when the balance reaches $10 or less, the customer can pay off the account. At the beginning of every month, 1.5% interest is added to the balance, and then the customer makes a payment equal to 5% of the current balance. Assume the customer makes no new purchases.**

   a. Design the print chart for this program.
   b. Design the hierarchy chart for this program.
   c. Design the flowchart for this program.
   d. Write pseudocode for this program.

5. **Assume you have a bank account that compounds interest on a yearly basis. In other words, if you deposit $100 for two years at 4% interest, at the end of 1 year you will have $104. At the end of 2 years, you will have the $104 plus 4% of that, or $108.16. Create the logic for a program that would (1) read in records containing a deposit amount, a term in years, and an interest rate, and (2) for each record, print the running total balance for each year of the term.**

   a. Design the print chart for this program.
   b. Design the hierarchy chart for this program.
   c. Design the flowchart for this program.
   d. Write pseudocode for this program.

6. **A school maintains class records in the following format:**

```
CLASS FILE DESCRIPTION
File name: CLASS
```

FIELD DESCRIPTION	POSITIONS	DATA TYPE	DECIMALS	EXAMPLE
Class Code	1-6	Character		CIS111
Section No.	7-9	Numeric	0	101
Teacher	10-29	Character		Gable
Enrollment	30-31	Numeric	0	24
Room	32-35	Character		A213

There is one record for each class section offered in the college. Design the program that would print as many stickers as a class needs to provide one for each enrolled student, plus one for the teacher. Each sticker would leave a blank for the student's (or teacher's) name like this:

Hello!

My name is _____

Class: XXXXXX Section: 999

This border is preprinted, but you must design the program to print all the text you see on the sticker. (You do not need to design a print chart—the image of the sticker serves as a print chart.)

a. Design the hierarchy chart for this program.
b. Design the flowchart for this program.
c. Write pseudocode for this program.

7. **A mail-order company often sends multiple packages per order. For each customer order, print enough mailing labels to use on each of the separate boxes that will be mailed. The mailing labels contain the customer's complete name and address, along with a box number in the form "Box 9 of 9". For example, an order that requires three boxes produces three labels: Box 1 of 3, Box 2 of 3, and Box 3 of 3. The file description is as follows:**

```
SHIPPING FILE DESCRIPTION
File name: ORDERS
```

FIELD DESCRIPTION	POSITIONS	DATA TYPE	DECIMALS	EXAMPLE
Title	1-3	Character		Ms
First Name	4-14	Character		Kathy
Last Name	15-25	Character		Lewis
Street	26-40	Character		847 Pine
City	41-51	Character		Aurora
State	52-53	Character		IL

| Boxes | 54-55 | Numeric | 0 | 3 |
| Balance Due | 56-61 | Numeric | 2 | 129.95 |

a. Design the print chart for this program.
b. Design the hierarchy chart for this program.
c. Design the flowchart for this program.
d. Write pseudocode for this program.

8. A secondhand store is having a seven-day sale during which the price of any unsold item drops 10% each day. The inventory file includes an item number, description, and original price on day one. For example, an item that costs $10.00 on the first day costs 10% less, or $9.00, on the second day. On the third day, the same item is 10% less than $9.00, or $8.10. Produce a report that shows the price of the item on each day, one through seven.

a. Design the print chart for this program.
b. Design the hierarchy chart for this program.
c. Design the flowchart for this program.
d. Write pseudocode for this program.

9. The state of Florida maintains a census file in which each record contains the name of a county, the current population, and a number representing the rate at which population is increasing per year. The governor wants a report listing each county and the number of years it will take for the population of the county to double, assuming the present rate of growth remains constant.

CENSUS FILE DESCRIPTION
File name: CENSUS

FIELD DESCRIPTION	POSITIONS	DATA TYPE	DECIMALS	EXAMPLE
County Name	1-20	Character		Dade
Current				
Population	21-28	Numeric	0	525000
Rate of Growth	29-30	Numeric	2	.07

a. Design the print chart for this program.
b. Design the hierarchy chart for this program.
c. Design the flowchart for this program.
d. Write pseudocode for this program.

10. A Human Resources Department wants a report that shows its employees the benefits of saving for retirement. Produce a report that shows 12 predicted retirement account values for each employee—the values if the employee saves 5, 10, or 15% of his or her annual salary for 10, 20, 30, or 40 years. The department maintains a file in which each record contains the name of an employee and the employee's current annual salary. Assume that savings grow at a rate of 8% per year.

a. Design the print chart for this program.
b. Design the hierarchy chart for this program.
c. Design the flowchart for this program.
d. Write pseudocode for this program.

11. **Randy's Recreational Vehicles pays its salespeople once every three months. Salespeople receive one-quarter of their annual base salary plus 7% of all sales made in the last three-month period. Randy creates an input file with four records for each salesperson. The first of the four records contains the salesperson's name and annual salary, while each of the three records that follow contains the name of a month and the monthly sales figure. For example, the first eight records in the file might contain the following data:**

Kimball	20000
April	30000
May	40000
June	60000
Johnson	15000
April	65000
May	78000
June	135500

Because the two types of records contain data in the same format, a character field followed by a numeric field, you can define one input record format containing two variables that you use with either type of record. Design the logic for the program that reads a salesperson's record, and if not at `eof`, reads the next three records in a loop, accumulating sales and computing commissions. For each salesperson, print the quarterly base salary, the three commission amounts, and the total salary, which is the quarterly base plus the three commission amounts.

   a. Design the print chart for this program.
   b. Design the hierarchy chart for this program.
   c. Design the flowchart for this program.
   d. Write pseudocode for this program.

12. **Mr. Furly owns 20 apartment buildings. Each building contains 15 units that he rents for $800 per month each. Design the logic for the program that would print 12 payment coupons for each of the 15 apartments in each of the 20 buildings. Each coupon should contain the building number (1 through 20), the apartment number (1 through 15), the month (1 through 12), and the amount of rent due.**

   a. Design the print chart for this program.
   b. Design the hierarchy chart for this program.
   c. Design the flowchart for this program.
   d. Write pseudocode for this program.

13. Mr. Furly owns 20 apartment buildings. Each building contains 15 units that he rents. The usual monthly rent for apartments numbered 1 through 9 in each building is $700; the monthly rent is $850 for apartments numbered 10 through 15. The usual rent is due every month except July and December; in those months Mr. Furly gives his renters a 50% credit, so they owe only half the usual amount. Design the logic for the program that would print 12 payment coupons for each of the 15 apartments in each of the 20 buildings. Each coupon should contain the building number (1 through 20), the apartment number (1 through 15), the month (1 through 12), and the amount of rent due.

   a. Design the print chart for this program.
   b. Design the hierarchy chart for this program.
   c. Design the flowchart for this program.
   d. Write pseudocode for this program.

CONTROL BREAKS

After studying Chapter 7, you should be able to:

- ☐ Understand control break logic
- ☐ Perform single-level control breaks
- ☐ Use control data within a heading in a control break module
- ☐ Use control data within a footer in a control break module
- ☐ Perform control breaks with totals
- ☐ Perform multiple-level control breaks
- ☐ Perform page breaks

UNDERSTANDING CONTROL BREAK LOGIC

A **control break** is a temporary detour in the logic of a program. In particular, programmers refer to a program as a **control break program** when a change in the value of a variable initiates special actions or causes special or unusual processing to occur. You usually write control break programs to organize output for programs that handle data records that are organized logically in groups based on the value in a field. As you read in records, you examine the same field in each record, and when you encounter a record that contains a different value from the ones that preceded it, you perform a special action. If you have ever read a report that lists items in groups, with each group followed by a subtotal, then you have read a type of **control break report**. Some other examples of control break reports produced by control break programs include:

- All employees listed in order by department number, with a new page started for each department
- All company clients listed in order by state of residence, with a count of clients after each state's client list
- All books for sale in a bookstore in order by category (such as reference or self-help), with a dollar total following each category of book for the value of all books
- All items sold in order by date of sale, with a different ink color for each new month

Each of these reports shares two traits:

- The records used in each report are listed in order by a specific variable: department, state, category, or date.
- When that variable changes, the program takes special action: starts a new page, prints a count or total, or switches ink color.

To generate a control break report, your input records must be organized in sequential order based on the field that will cause the breaks. In other words, if you are going to write a program that prints employee records on separate pages based on their departments, then the records must be arranged in department-number order before you begin processing. As you grow more proficient in programming logic, you will learn techniques for writing programs that sort records before you proceed with control break logic. Programs that **sort** records take records that are not in order and rearrange them so that they are in order. For now, assume that a sorting program has already been used to presort your records before you begin the part of a program that requires control breaks.

TIP ▫ ▫ ▫ ▫ | You will learn techniques for processing unsorted records in Chapter 8.

PERFORMING A SINGLE-LEVEL CONTROL BREAK TO START A NEW PAGE

Suppose you want to print a list of employees, advancing to a new page for each department. Figure 7-1 shows the input file description, from which you can see that the employee department is a two-digit numeric field, and that the file has been presorted so that the records will arrive in a program in employee-department-number order. Figure 7-2 shows the desired output—a simple list of employee names.

FIGURE 7-1: EMPLOYEE FILE DESCRIPTION

```
File name: EMPSBYDEPT
Sorted by: Department
FIELD DESCRIPTION     POSITIONS     DATA TYPE      DECIMALS
Department            1-2           Numeric        0
Last Name             3-14          Character
First Name            15-26         Character
```

FIGURE 7-2: PRINT CHART FOR EMPLOYEES LISTED BY DEPARTMENT

	1	2	3	4	5	6	7	8	9	10	11	12	13	14	15	16	17	18	19	20	21	22	23	24	25
2	E	M	P	L	O	Y	E	E	S		B	Y		D	E	P	A	R	T	M	E	N	T		
4		L	A	S	T		N	A	M	E							F	I	R	S	T		N	A	M	E
6	X	X	X	X	X	X	X	X	X	X	X						X	X	X	X	X	X	X	X	X	X
7	X	X	X	X	X	X	X	X	X	X	X						X	X	X	X	X	X	X	X	X	X
8	X	X	X	X	X	X	X	X	X	X	X						X	X	X	X	X	X	X	X	X	X

The basic logic of the program works like this: Each time you read an employee record from the input file, you will determine whether the employee belongs to the same department as the previous employee. If so, you simply print the employee record and read another record, without any special processing. If there are 20 employees in a department, these steps are repeated 20 times in a row—read an employee record in and print the employee record out. However, eventually you will read in an employee who does not belong to the same department. At that point, before you print the employee who is in the new department, you must print headings on the top of a new page. Then, you can proceed to read and print employees who belong to the new department, and you continue to do so until the next time you encounter an employee in a different department. This type of program contains a **single-level control break**, a break in the logic of the program (pausing or detouring to print new headings) that is based on the value of a single variable (the department number).

However, there is a slight problem you must solve before you can determine whether a newly input record contains the same department number as the previously input record. When you read a record from an input file, the data items that represent department, last name, and first name occupy specific physical locations in computer memory. For each new record, new data must occupy the same positions, and the previous set of data is lost. For example, if you read a record containing data for Alan Andrews in Department 1, when you read the next record for Barbara Bailey in Department 2, "Barbara" replaces "Alan", "Bailey" replaces "Andrews", and 2 replaces 1. After you read in a new record, there is no way to look back at the previous record to determine whether that record had a different department number. The previous record's data has been replaced by the new record's data.

The technique you must use to "remember" the old department number is to create a special variable, called a **control break field**, to hold the previous department number. With a control break field, every time you read in a record and print it, you also can save the crucial part of the record that will signal the change or control the program break. In this case, you want to store the department number in this specially created variable. Comparing the new and old department-number values will determine when it is time to print headings at the top of a new page.

The mainline logic for the Employees by Department report is the same as the mainline logic for all the other programs you've analyzed so far. It performs a `housekeeping()` module, after which an `eof` question controls execution of a `mainLoop()`. At `eof`, a `finish()` module executes. See Figure 7-3.

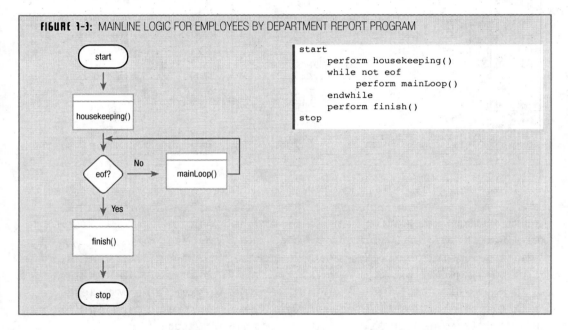

FIGURE 7-3: MAINLINE LOGIC FOR EMPLOYEES BY DEPARTMENT REPORT PROGRAM

```
start
        perform housekeeping()
        while not eof
                perform mainLoop()
        endwhile
        perform finish()
stop
```

The `housekeeping()` module begins similarly to others you have seen. You declare variables as shown in Figure 7-4, including those you will use for the input data: `empDept`, `empLast`, and `empFirst`. You can also declare variables to hold the headings, and an additional variable that is named `oldDept` in this example. The purpose of `oldDept` is to serve as the control break field. Every time you read a record, you can save its department number in `oldDept` before you read the next record.

Note that it would be incorrect to initialize `oldDept` to the value of `empDept` when you declare `oldDept` in the `housekeeping()` module. When you declare variables at the beginning of the `housekeeping()` module, you have not yet read in the first record; therefore, `empDept` does not yet have any usable value. You use the value of the first `empDept` at the end of the module, only after you read the first input record.

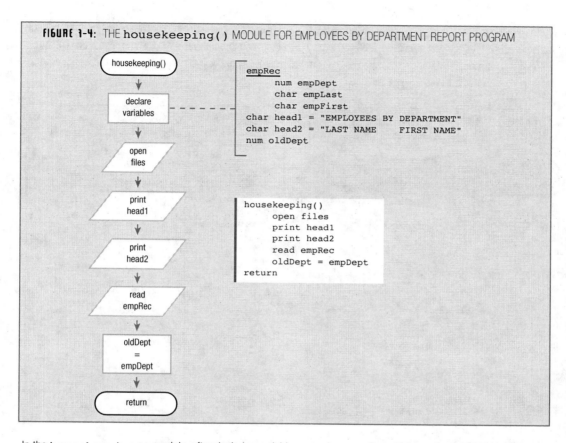

FIGURE 7-4: THE `housekeeping()` MODULE FOR EMPLOYEES BY DEPARTMENT REPORT PROGRAM

In the `housekeeping()` module, after declaring variables, you also open files, print headings, and read the first input record. Before you leave the `housekeeping()` module, you can set the `oldDept` variable to equal the `empDept` value in the first input record. You will write the `mainLoop()` of the program to check for any change in department number; that's the signal to print headings at the top of a new page. Because you just printed headings and read in the first record, you do not want to print headings again for this first record, so you want to ensure that the `empDept` and `oldDept` are equal when you enter the `mainLoop()`.

TIP ▫ ▫ ▫ ▫ As an alternative to the `housekeeping()` logic shown here, you can remove printing headings from the `housekeeping()` module and set the `oldDept` to any impossible value, for example, –1. Then, in the `mainLoop()`, the first record will force the control break, and the headings will print in the `newPage()` control break routine.

The first task within the `mainLoop()` module is to check whether the `empDept` holds the same value as `oldDept`. For the first record, on the first pass through the `mainLoop()`, the values are equal; you set them to be equal in the `housekeeping()` module. Therefore, you proceed without performing the `newPage()` module, printing the first employee's record and reading a second record. At the end of the `mainLoop()` shown in Figure 7-5, the logical flow returns to the mainline logic shown in Figure 7-3. If it is not `eof`, the flow travels back into the `mainLoop()` module.

There, you compare the second record's `empDept` to `oldDept`. If the second record holds an employee from the same department as the first employee, then you simply print that second employee's record, and read a third record into memory. As long as each new record holds the same `empDept` value, you continue reading and printing, never pausing to perform the `newPage()` module.

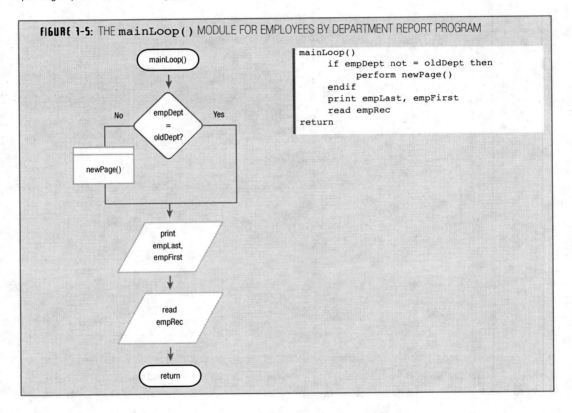

FIGURE 7-5: THE `mainLoop()` MODULE FOR EMPLOYEES BY DEPARTMENT REPORT PROGRAM

```
mainLoop()
    if empDept not = oldDept then
        perform newPage()
    endif
    print empLast, empFirst
    read empRec
return
```

TIP □ □ □ □   In the flowchart in Figure 7-5, you could change the question to `empDept <> oldDept` or `empDept not = oldDept`. Then, the Yes branch of the decision structure would perform the `newPage()` module, and the No branch would be null. This format would more closely resemble the pseudocode in Figure 7-5, but the logic would be identical to the version shown here, in which the question is asked in the positive rather than the negative.

Eventually, you will read in an employee whose `empDept` is not the same as `oldDept`. That's when the control break routine, `newPage()`, executes. The `newPage()` module must perform two tasks:

- It must print headings at the top of a new page.
- It must update the control break field.

Figure 7-6 shows the `newPage()` module.

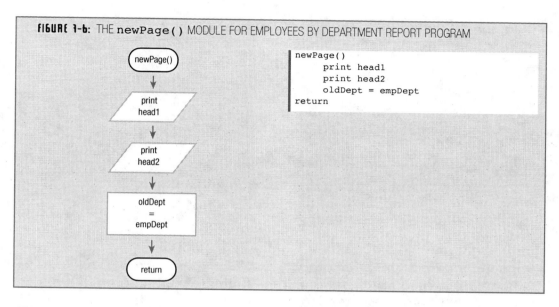

FIGURE 7-6: THE `newPage()` MODULE FOR EMPLOYEES BY DEPARTMENT REPORT PROGRAM

```
newPage()
     print head1
     print head2
     oldDept = empDept
return
```

TIP □ □ □ □ In Chapter 4, you learned that specific programming languages each provide you with a means to physically advance printer paper to the top of a page. Usually, you insert a language-specific code just before the first character in the first heading that will appear on a page. For this book, if a print chart shows a heading printing at the top of the page, then you can assume that printing the heading causes the paper in the printer to advance to the top of a new page. The appropriate language-specific codes can be added when you code the program.

When you read an employee whose `empDept` is not the same as `oldDept`, you cause a break in the normal flow of the program. The new employee record must "wait" while headings print and the control break field `oldDept` acquires a new value. After the `oldDept` field has been updated, and before the `mainLoop()` module ends, the waiting employee record prints on the new page. When you read the *next* employee record (and it is not `eof`), the `mainLoop()` module is reentered and the next employee's `empDept` is compared to the updated `oldDept`. If the new employee works in the same department as the one just preceding, then normal processing continues with the print-and-read statements.

The `newPage()` module in the employee report program performs two tasks required in all control break modules:

- It performs any necessary processing for the new group—in this case, it prints headings.
- It updates the control break field—in this case, the `oldDept` field.

TIP □ □ □ □ As an alternative to updating the control break field within the control break routine, you could set the `oldDept` equal to `empDept` just before you read each record. However, if there are 200 employees in Department 55, then you set the `oldDept` to the same value 200 times. It's more efficient to set `oldDept` to a different value only when there is a change in the value of the department.

The `finish()` module for the Employees by Department report program requires only that you close the files. See Figure 7-7.

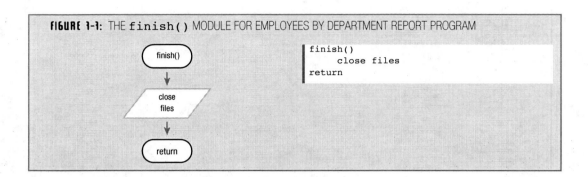

FIGURE 7-7: THE `finish()` MODULE FOR EMPLOYEES BY DEPARTMENT REPORT PROGRAM

USING CONTROL DATA WITHIN A HEADING IN A CONTROL BREAK MODULE

In the Employees by Department report program example, the control break module printed constant headings at the top of each new page; in other words, each page heading was the same. However, sometimes you need to use control data within the heading. For example, consider the report layout shown in Figure 7-8.

FIGURE 7-8: PRINT CHART FOR EMPLOYEES BY DEPARTMENT REPORT THAT DISPLAYS THE DEPARTMENT NUMBER IN THE HEADING

| | 1 | 2 | 3 | 4 | 5 | 6 | 7 | 8 | 9 | 1 0 | 1 1 | 1 2 | 1 3 | 1 4 | 1 5 | 1 6 | 1 7 | 1 8 | 1 9 | 2 0 | 2 1 | 2 2 | 2 3 | 2 4 | 2 5 | 2 6 | 2 7 | 2 8 | 2 9 | 3 0 | 3 1 | 3 2 | 3 3 | 3 4 | 3 5 | 3 6 | 3 7 | 3 8 | 3 9 | 4 0 | 4 1 | 4 2 | 4 3 | 4 4 | 4 5 | 4 6 | 4 7 | 4 8 | 4 9 | 5 0 | 5 1 | 5 2 | 5 3 | 5 4 | 5 5 | 5 6 | 5 7 | 5 8 | 5 9 |

1																					
2		E	M	P	L	O	Y	E	E	S		F	O	R		D	E	P	A	R	T	M	E	N	T		9	9
3																					
4		L	A	S	T		N	A	M	E							F	I	R	S	T		N	A	M	E
5																					
6		X	X	X	X	X	X	X	X	X	X	X	X				X	X	X	X	X	X	X	X	X	X	X	X
7		X	X	X	X	X	X	X	X	X	X	X	X				X	X	X	X	X	X	X	X	X	X	X	X
8		X	X	X	X	X	X	X	X	X	X	X	X				X	X	X	X	X	X	X	X	X	X	X	X

The difference between Figure 7-2 and Figure 7-8 lies in the heading. Figure 7-8 shows variable data in the heading—a different department number prints at the top of each page of employees. To create this kind of program, you must make two changes in the existing program. First, you modify the `newPage()` module, as shown within the `newPage()` module in Figure 7-9. Instead of printing a fixed heading on each new page, you print a heading that contains two parts: a constant beginning ("EMPLOYEES FOR DEPARTMENT") and a variable ending (the department number for the employees who appear on the page). Notice that you use the `empDept` number that belongs to the employee record that is waiting to be printed while this control break module executes. Additionally, you must modify the `housekeeping()` module to ensure that the first heading on the report prints correctly. As Figure 7-9 shows, you must modify the `housekeeping()` module from Figure 7-4 so that you read the first `empRec` prior to printing the headings. The reason is that you must know the first employee's department number before you can print the heading for the top of the first page.

FIGURE 7-9: MODIFIED `newPage()` AND `housekeeping()` MODULES FOR EMPLOYEES BY DEPARTMENT REPORT THAT DISPLAYS THE DEPARTMENT NUMBER IN THE HEADING

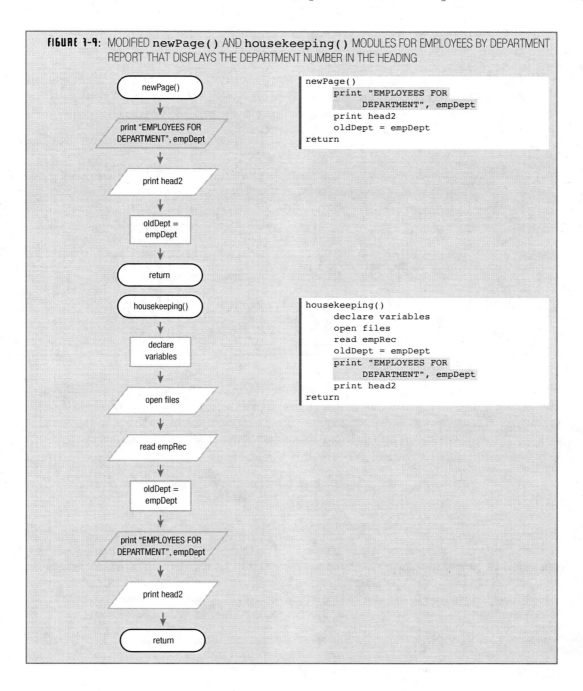

```
newPage()
    print "EMPLOYEES FOR
        DEPARTMENT", empDept
    print head2
    oldDept = empDept
return
```

```
housekeeping()
    declare variables
    open files
    read empRec
    oldDept = empDept
    print "EMPLOYEES FOR
        DEPARTMENT", empDept
    print head2
return
```

USING CONTROL DATA WITHIN A FOOTER IN A CONTROL BREAK MODULE

In the previous section, you learned how to use control break data in a heading. Figure 7-10 shows a different print chart. For this report, the department number prints *following* the employee list for the department. A message that prints at the end of a page or other section of a report is called a **footer**. Headings usually require information about the *next* record; footers usually require information about the *previous* record.

FIGURE 7-10: PRINT CHART FOR EMPLOYEES BY DEPARTMENT REPORT IN WHICH DEPARTMENT NUMBERS APPEAR IN A FOOTER

Figure 7-11 shows a program that prints a list of employees by department, including a footer that displays the department number at the end of each department's list. When you write a program that produces the report shown in Figure 7-10, you continuously read records with `empLast`, `empFirst`, and `empDept` fields. Each time an `empDept` does not equal the `oldDept`, it means that you have reached a department break and that you should perform the `newPage()` module. The `newPage()` module has three tasks:

- It must print the footer for the previous department at the bottom of the employee list.
- It must print headings at the top of a new page.
- It must update the control break field.

When the `newPage()` module prints the footer at the bottom of the old page, you must use the `oldDept` number. For example, assume you have printed several employees from Department 12. When you read a record with an employee from Department 13 (or any other department), the first thing you must do is print "END OF DEPARTMENT 12". You print the correct department number by accessing the value of the `oldDept`, not `empDept`. Then, you can print the other headings at the top of a new page and update `oldDept` to the current `empDept`, which in this example is 13.

The `newPage()` module in Figure 7-11 performs three tasks required in all control break routines:

- It performs any necessary processing for the previous group—in this case, it prints the footer.
- It performs any necessary processing for the new group—in this case, it prints headings.
- It updates the control break field.

FIGURE 7-11: PROGRAM THAT LISTS EMPLOYEES BY DEPARTMENT, INCLUDING DEPARTMENT NUMBER IN THE FOOTER

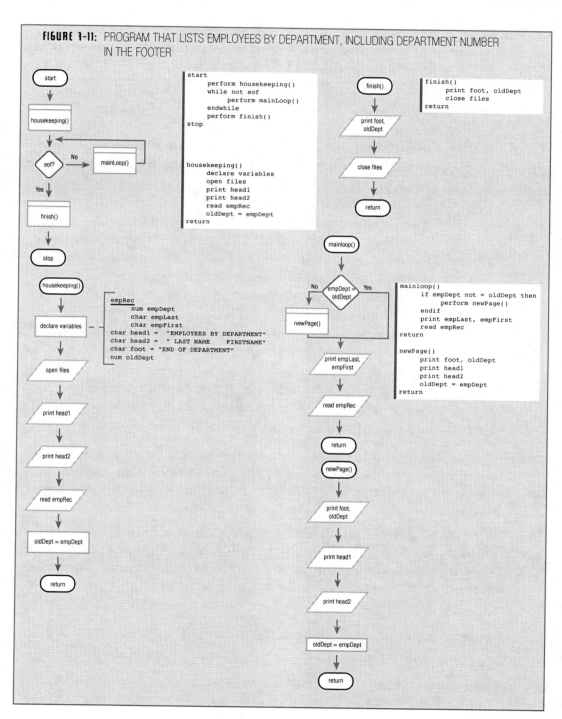

When you printed the department number in the header in the example in the previous section, you needed a special step in the `housekeeping()` module. When you print the department number in the footer, the `finish()` module requires an extra step. Imagine that the last five records on the input file include two employees from Department 78, Amy and Bill, and three employees from Department 85, Carol, Don, and Ellen. The logical flow proceeds as follows:

1. After the first Department 78 employee (Amy) prints, you read in the second Department 78 employee (Bill).
2. At the top of the `mainLoop()` module, Bill's department is compared to `oldDept`. The departments are the same, so the second Department 78 employee (Bill) is printed. Then, you read in the first Department 85 employee (Carol).
3. At the top of the `mainLoop()`, Carol's `empDept` and the `oldDept` are different, so you perform the `newPage()` module, while Carol's record waits in memory.
4. In the `newPage()` module, you print "END OF DEPARTMENT 78". Then, you print headings at the top of the next page. Finally, you set `oldDept` to 85, and then return to the `mainLoop()`.
5. Back in the `mainLoop()`, you print a line of data for the first Department 85 employee (Carol), whose record waited while `newPage()` executed. Then, you read in the record for the second Department 85 employee (Don).
6. At the top of `mainLoop()`, you compare Don's department number to `oldDept`. The numbers are the same, so you print Don's employee data and read in the last Department 85 employee (Ellen).
7. At the top of `mainLoop()`, you determine that Ellen has the same department number, so you print Ellen's data and attempt to read from the input file, where you encounter `eof`.
8. The `eof` decision in the mainline logic sends you to the `finish()` module.

You have printed the last Department 85 employee (Ellen), but the department footer for Department 85 has not printed. That's because every time you attempt to read an input record, you don't know whether there will be more records. The mainline logic checks for the `eof` condition, but if it determines that it is `eof`, the logic does not flow back into the `mainLoop()` where the `newPage()` module can execute.

To print the footer for the last department, you must print a footer one last time within the `finish()` routine. The `finish()` module that is part of the complete program in Figure 7-11 illustrates this. Taking this action is similar to printing the first heading in the `housekeeping()` module. The very first heading prints separately from all the others at the beginning; the very last footer must print separately from all the others at the end.

PERFORMING CONTROL BREAKS WITH TOTALS

Suppose you run a bookstore, and one of the files you maintain is called BOOKFILE, which has one record for every book title that you carry. Each record has fields such as `bookTitle`, `bookAuthor`, `bookCategory` (fiction, reference, self-help, and so on), `bookPublisher`, and `bookPrice`, as shown in the file description in Figure 7-12.

FIGURE 7-12: BOOKFILE FILE DESCRIPTION

```
File name: BOOKFILE
Sorted by: Category
FIELD DESCRIPTION      POSITIONS      DATA TYPE      DECIMALS
Title                  1-30           Character
Author                 31-46          Character
Category               47-56          Character
Publisher              57-72          Character
Price                  73-77          Numeric         2
```

Suppose you want to print out a list of all the books that your store carries, with a total number of books at the bottom of the list, as shown in Figure 7-13. You can use the logic shown in Figure 7-14. In the main loop module, named `bookListLoop()`, you print a book title, add 1 to the `grandTotal`, and read the next record. At the end of the program, in the `closeDown()` module, you print the `grandTotal` before you close the files.

FIGURE 7-13: PRINT CHART FOR BOOK LIST

As you can see from the pseudocode in Figure 7-14, the `bookListLoop()` module performs three major tasks:

- Prints a book title
- Adds 1 to the `grandTotal`
- Reads in the next book record

The `closeDown()` module prints the `grandTotal`. You can't print `grandTotal` any earlier in the program because the `grandTotal` value isn't complete until the last record has been read.

The logic of the preceding program is pretty straightforward. Suppose, however, that you decide you want a count for each category of book rather than just one grand total. For example, if all the book records contain a category that is either fiction, reference, or self-help, then the book records might be sorted to be in alphabetical order by category, and the output would consist of a list of all fiction books first, followed by a count; then all reference books, followed by a count; and finally all self-help books, followed by a count. The report is a control break report, and the control break field is the `bookCategory`.

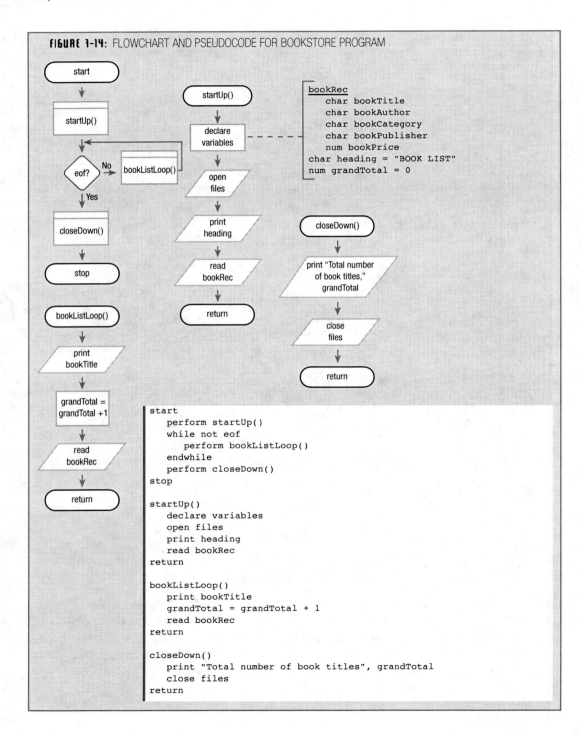

FIGURE 7-14: FLOWCHART AND PSEUDOCODE FOR BOOKSTORE PROGRAM

```
start
   perform startUp()
   while not eof
      perform bookListLoop()
   endwhile
   perform closeDown()
stop

startUp()
   declare variables
   open files
   print heading
   read bookRec
return

bookListLoop()
   print bookTitle
   grandTotal = grandTotal + 1
   read bookRec
return

closeDown()
   print "Total number of book titles", grandTotal
   close files
return
```

To produce the report with subtotals by category, you must declare two new variables: `previousCategory` and `categoryTotal`. Every time you read in a book record, you compare `bookCategory` to `previousCategory`; when there is a category change, you print the count of books for the previous category. The `categoryTotal` variable holds that count. See Figure 7-15.

TIP □ □ □ □   When you draw a flowchart, it usually is clearer to ask questions positively, as in "`bookCategory = previousCategory?`", and draw appropriate actions on the Yes or No side of the decision. In pseudocode, when action occurs only on the No side of a decision, it is usually clearer to ask negatively, as in "`bookCategory not equal to previousCategory?`". Figure 7-15 uses these tactics.

When you read the first record from the input file in the `startUp()` module of the program in Figure 7-15, you save the value of `bookCategory` in the `previousCategory` variable. Every time a record enters the `bookListLoop()` module, the program checks to see if the current record represents a new category of work, by comparing `bookCategory` to the variable called `previousCategory`. When you process the first record, the categories match, so the book title prints, the `categoryTotal` increases by one, and you read the next record. If this next record's `bookCategory` value matches the `previousCategory` value, processing continues as usual with printing a line and adding 1 to the `categoryTotal`.

At some point, the `bookCategory` for an input record does not match the `previousCategory`. At that point, you perform the `categoryChange()` module. Within the `categoryChange()` module, you print the count of the previous category of books. Then, you add the `categoryTotal` to the `grandTotal`. Adding a total to a higher-level total is called **rolling up the totals**.

You could write the `bookListLoop()` so that as you process each book, you add one to the `categoryTotal` and add one to the `grandTotal`. Then, there would be no need to roll totals up in the `categoryChange()` module. If there are 120 fiction books, you add 1 to `categoryTotal` 120 times; you also would add 1 to `grandTotal` 120 times. This technique would yield correct results, but you can eliminate executing 119 addition instructions by waiting until you have accumulated all 120 category counts before adding the total figure to `grandTotal`.

This control break report containing totals performs the five tasks required in all control break routines that include totals:

- It performs any necessary processing for the previous group—in this case, it prints the `categoryTotal`.
- It rolls up the current-level totals to the next higher level—in this case, it adds `categoryTotal` to `grandTotal`.
- It resets the current level's totals to zero—in this case, the `categoryTotal` is set to zero.
- It performs any necessary processing for the new group—in this case, there is none.
- It updates the control break field—in this case, `previousCategory`.

FIGURE 7-15: FLOWCHART AND PSEUDOCODE FOR BOOKSTORE PROGRAM CONTAINING A COUNT AFTER EACH BOOK CATEGORY GROUP

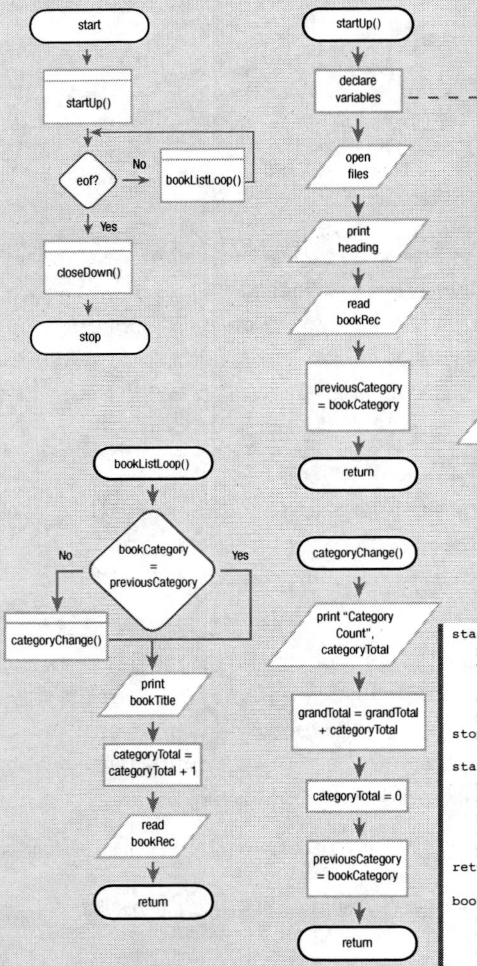


```
bookRec
   char bookTitle
   char bookAuthor
   char bookCategory
   char bookPublisher
   num bookPrice
char heading = "BOOK LIST"
num grandTotal = 0
num categoryTotal = 0
char previousCategory
```

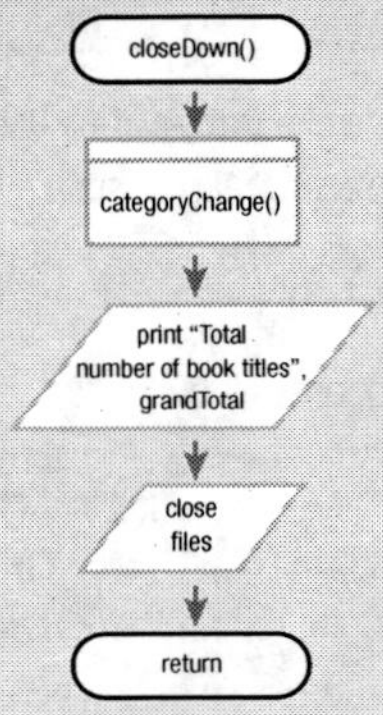


```
start
   perform startUp()
   while not eof
      perform bookListLoop()
   endwhile
   perform closeDown()
stop

startUp()
   declare variables
   open files
   print heading
   read bookRec
   previousCategory = bookCategory
return

bookListLoop()
   if bookCategory not equal to previousCategory then
      perform categoryChange()
   endif
   print bookTitle
   categoryTotal = categoryTotal + 1
   read bookRec
return

categoryChange()
   print "Category count", categoryTotal
   grandTotal = grandTotal + categoryTotal
   categoryTotal = 0
   previousCategory = bookCategory
return

closeDown()
   perform categoryChange()
   print "Total number of book titles", grandTotal
   close files
return
```

The `closeDown()` routine for this type of program is more complicated than it might first appear. It seems as though you should print the `grandTotal`, close the files, and return to the mainline logic. However, when you read the last record, the mainline `eof` decision sends the logical flow to the `closeDown()` routine. You have not printed the last `categoryTotal`, nor have you added the count for the last category into the `grandTotal`. You must take care of both these tasks before printing the `grandTotal`. You can perform these two tasks as separate steps in `closeDown()`, but it is often simplest just to remember to perform the control break routine `categoryChange()` one last time. The `categoryChange()` module already executes after every previous category completes—that is, every time you encounter a new category during the execution of the program. You also can execute this module after the final category completes, at end of file. Encountering the end of the file is really just another form of break; it signals that the last category has finally completed. The `categoryChange()` module prints the category total and rolls the totals up to the `grandTotal` level.

TIP ▫ ▫ ▫ ▫ | When you call the `categoryChange()` module from within `closeDown()`, it performs a few tasks you don't need, such as setting the value of `previousCategory`. You have to weigh the convenience of calling the already-written `categoryChange()` module, and executing a few unneeded statements, against taking the time to write a new module that would execute only the statements that are absolutely necessary.

It is very important to note that this control break program works whether there are three categories of books or 300. Note further that it does not matter what the categories of books are. For example, the program never asks `bookCategory = "fiction"?`. Instead, the control of the program breaks when the category field *changes*, and it is in no way dependent on *what* that change is.

PERFORMING MULTIPLE-LEVEL CONTROL BREAKS

Let's say your bookstore from the last example is so successful that you have a chain of them across the country. Every time a sale is made, you create a record with the fields `bookTitle`, `bookPrice`, `bookCity`, and `bookState`. You want a report that prints a summary of books sold in each city and each state, similar to the one shown in Figure 7-16. A report such as this one, which does not include any information about individual records, but instead includes only group totals, is a **summary report**.

This program contains a **multiple-level control break**—that is, the normal flow of control (reading records and counting book sales) breaks away to print totals in response to more than just one change in condition. In this report, a control break occurs in response to either (or both) of two conditions: when the contents of the `bookCity` variable changes as well as when the contents of the `bookState` variable changes.

Just as the file you use to create a single-level control break report must be presorted, so must the input file you use to create a multiple-level control break report. The input file that you use for the book sales report must be sorted by `bookCity` *within* `bookState`. That is, all of one state's records, for example all records from IA, come first; then all the records from another state, such as IL, follow. Within any one state, all of one city's records come first, then all of the next city's records follow. For example, the input file that produces the report shown in Figure 7-16 contains 200 records for book sales in Ames, IA, followed by 814 records for book sales in Des Moines, IA. The basic processing entails reading a book sale record, adding one to a counter, and reading the next book sale record. At the end of any city's records, you print a total for that city; at the end of a state's records, you print a total for that state.

FIGURE 7-16: SAMPLE RUN OF BOOK SALES BY CITY AND STATE REPORT

BOOK SALES BY CITY AND STATE

Ames	200
Des Moines	814
Iowa City	291
Total for IA	1305
Chicago	1093
Crystal Lake	564
McHenry	213
Springfield	365
Total for IL	2235
Springfield	289
Worcester	100
Total for MA	389
Grand Total	3929

The `housekeeping()` module of the Book Sales by City and State report program looks similar to the `housekeeping()` module in the previous control break program, in which there was a single control break for change in category of book. In each program, you declare variables, open files, and read the first record. This time, however, there are multiple fields to save and compare to the old fields. Here, you declare two special variables, `prevCity` and `prevState`, as shown in Figure 7-17. In addition, the Book Sales report shows three kinds of totals, so you declare three new variables that will serve as holding places for the total in the Book Sales report: `cityCounter`, `stateCounter`, and `grandTotal`, which are all initialized to zero.

This program prints both `bookState` and `bookCity` totals, so you need two control break modules, `cityBreak()` and `stateBreak()`. Every time there is a change in the `bookCity` field, the `cityBreak()` routine performs these standard control break tasks:

- It performs any necessary processing for the previous group—in this case, it prints totals for the previous city.
- It rolls up the current-level totals to the next higher level—in this case, it adds the city count to the state count.
- It resets the current level's totals to zero—in this case, it sets the city count to zero.
- It performs any necessary processing for the new group—in this case, there is none.
- It updates the control break field—in this case, it sets `prevCity` to `bookCity`.

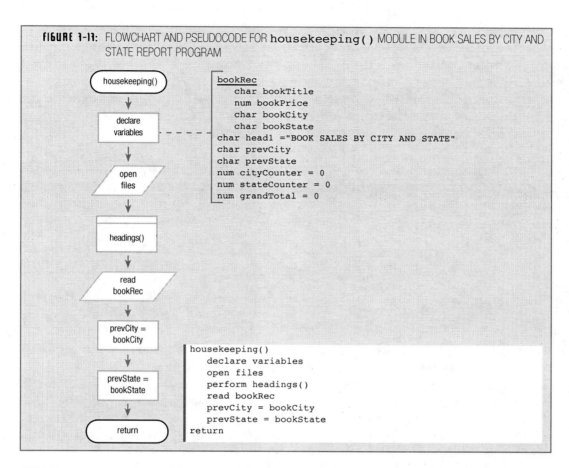

FIGURE 7-17: FLOWCHART AND PSEUDOCODE FOR `housekeeping()` MODULE IN BOOK SALES BY CITY AND STATE REPORT PROGRAM

Within the `stateBreak()` module, you must perform one new type of task, as well as the control break tasks you are familiar with. The new task is the first task: Within the `stateBreak()` module, you must first perform a `cityBreak()` automatically (because if there is a change in the state, there must also be a change in the city). The `stateBreak()` module does the following:

- It processes the lower-level break—in this case, `cityBreak()`.
- It performs any necessary processing for the previous group—in this case, it prints totals for the previous state.
- It rolls up the current-level totals to the next higher level—in this case, it adds the state count to the grand total.
- It resets the current level's totals to zero—in this case, it sets the state count to zero.
- It performs any necessary processing for the new group—in this case, there is none.
- It updates the control break field—in this case, it sets `prevState` to `bookState`.

The `mainLoop()` of this multiple-level control break program checks for any change in two different variables: `bookCity` and `bookState`. When the `bookCity` changes, a city total is printed, and when the `bookState` changes, a state total is printed. As you can see from the sample report in Figure 7-16, all city totals for each state print before the state total for the same state, so it might seem logical to check for a change in `bookCity` before checking for a change in `bookState`. However, the opposite is true. For the totals to be correct, you must check for any `bookState` change first. You do so because when a `bookCity` changes, the `bookState` also *might* be changing, but when the `bookState` changes, it means the `bookCity` *must* be changing.

Consider the sample input records shown in Figure 7-18, which are sorted by `bookCity` within `bookState`:

FIGURE 7-18: SAMPLE DATA FOR BOOK SALES BY CITY AND STATE REPORT

TITLE	PRICE	CITY	STATE
A Brief History of Time	20.00	Iowa City	IA
The Scarlet Letter	15.99	Chicago	IL
Math Magic	4.95	Chicago	IL
She's Come Undone	12.00	Springfield	IL
The Joy of Cooking	2.50	Springfield	IL
Walden	9.95	Springfield	MA
A Bridge Too Far	3.50	Springfield	MA

When you get to the point in the program where you read the first Illinois record (*The Scarlet Letter*), "Iowa City" is the value stored in the field `prevCity`, and "IA" is the value stored in `prevState`. Because the values in the `bookCity` and `bookState` variables on the new record are both different from the `prevCity` and `prevState` fields, both a city and state total will print. However, consider the problem when you read the first record for Springfield, MA (*Walden*). At this point in the program, `prevState` is IL, but `prevCity` is the same as the current `bookCity`; both contain Springfield. If you check for a change in `bookCity`, you won't find one at all, and no city total will print, even though Springfield, MA, is definitely a different city from Springfield, IL.

Cities in different states can have the same name; when cities with the same name but in different states follow each other, if you have written your control break program to check for a change in city name first, the program will not recognize that you are working with a new city. Instead, you should always check for the major-level break first. If the records are sorted by `bookCity` within `bookState`, then a change in `bookState` causes a **major-level break**, and a change in `bookCity` causes a **minor-level break**. When the `bookState` value "MA" is not equal to the `prevState` value "IL", you force a `cityBreak()`, printing a city total for Springfield, IL, before a state total for IL and before continuing with the Springfield, MA, record. You check for a change in `bookState` first, and if there is one, you perform a `cityBreak()`. In other words, if there is a change in `bookState`, there is an implied change in `bookCity`, even if the cities happen to have the same name.

TIP □ □ □ □ | If you needed totals to print by `bookCity` within a field defined as `bookCounty` within `bookState`, you could say you have minor-, intermediate-, and major-level breaks.

Figure 7-19 shows the `mainLoop()` for the Book Sales by City and State Report program. You check for a change in the `bookState` value. If there is no change, you check for a change in the `bookCity` value. If there is no change there either, you add 1 to the counter for the city and read the next record. When there is a change in the `bookCity` value, you print the city total and add the city total to the state total. When there is a change in the `bookState` value, you perform the break routine for the last city in the state, then you print the state total and add it to the grand total.

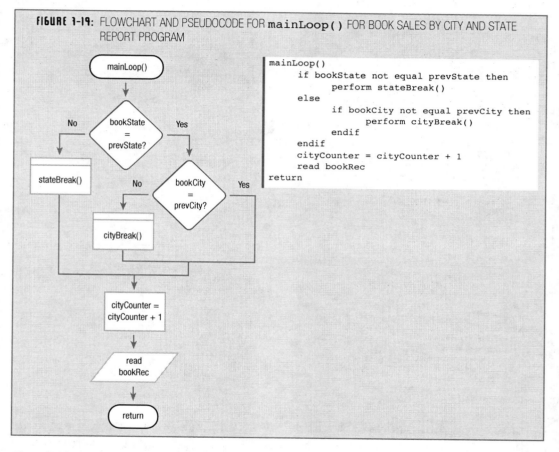

FIGURE 7-19: FLOWCHART AND PSEUDOCODE FOR `mainLoop()` FOR BOOK SALES BY CITY AND STATE REPORT PROGRAM

```
mainLoop()
    if bookState not equal prevState then
            perform stateBreak()
    else
            if bookCity not equal prevCity then
                    perform cityBreak()
            endif
    endif
    cityCounter = cityCounter + 1
    read bookRec
return
```

Figures 7-20 and 7-21 show the `stateBreak()` and `cityBreak()` modules. The two modules are very similar; the `stateBreak()` routine contains just one extra type of task. When there is a change in `bookState`, you perform the `cityBreak()` automatically before you perform any of the other necessary steps to change states.

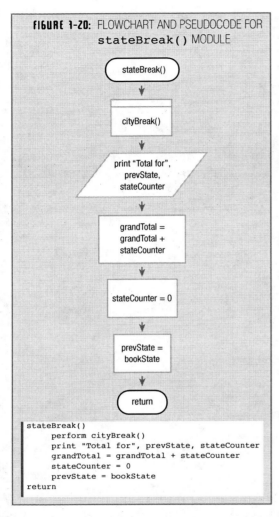

FIGURE 7-20: FLOWCHART AND PSEUDOCODE FOR `stateBreak()` MODULE

```
stateBreak()
    perform cityBreak()
    print "Total for", prevState, stateCounter
    grandTotal = grandTotal + stateCounter
    stateCounter = 0
    prevState = bookState
return
```

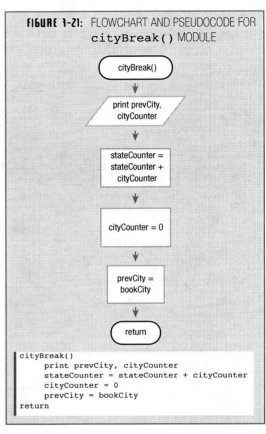

FIGURE 7-21: FLOWCHART AND PSEUDOCODE FOR `cityBreak()` MODULE

```
cityBreak()
    print prevCity, cityCounter
    stateCounter = stateCounter + cityCounter
    cityCounter = 0
    prevCity = bookCity
return
```

The sample report containing book sales by city and state shows that you print the grand total for all book sales, so within the `closeDown()` module, you must print the `grandTotal` variable. Before you can do so, however, you must perform both the `cityBreak()` and the `stateBreak()` modules one last time. You can accomplish this by performing `stateBreak()`, because the first step within `stateBreak()` is to perform `cityBreak()`.

Consider the sample data shown in Figure 7-18. While you continue to read records for books sold in Springfield, MA, you continue to add to the `cityCounter` for that city. At the moment you attempt to read one more record past the end of the file, you do not know whether there will be more records; therefore, you have not yet printed either the `cityCounter` for Springfield or the `stateCounter` for MA. In the `closeDown()` module, you perform `stateBreak()`, which immediately performs `cityBreak()`. Within `cityBreak()`, the count for Springfield prints and rolls up to the `stateCounter`. Then, after the logic transfers back to the `stateBreak()` module, the total for MA prints and rolls up to the `grandTotal`. Finally, you can print the `grandTotal`, as shown in Figure 7-22.

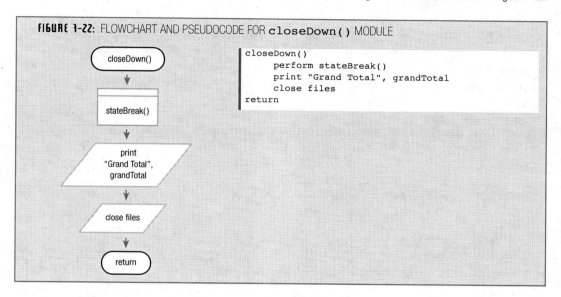

FIGURE 7-22: FLOWCHART AND PSEUDOCODE FOR `closeDown()` MODULE

```
closeDown()
     perform stateBreak()
     print "Grand Total", grandTotal
     close files
return
```

Every time you write a program where you need control break routines, you should check whether you need to complete each of the following tasks within the modules:

- Performing the lower-level break, if any
- Performing any control break processing for the previous group
- Rolling up the current-level totals to the next higher level
- Resetting the current level's totals to zero
- Performing any control break processing for the new group
- Updating the control break field

PERFORMING PAGE BREAKS

Many business programs use a form of control break logic to start a new page when a printed page fills up with output. In other words, you might want the change to a new page to be based on the number of lines already printed, rather than on the contents of an input field, such as department number. The logic in these programs involves counting the lines printed, pausing to print headings when the counter reaches some predetermined value, and then going on. This common business task is just another example of providing a break in the usual flow of control.

TIP ▫ ▫ ▫ ▫ Some programmers may prefer to reserve the term *control break* for situations in which the break is based on the contents of one of the fields in an input record, rather than on the contents of a work field such as a line counter.

Let's say you have a file called CUSTOMERFILE containing 1,000 customers, with two character fields that you have decided to call `custLast` and `custFirst`. You want to print a list of these customers, 60 detail lines to a page, in the format shown in Figure 7-23. The mainline logic of the program is familiar. The only new feature is a variable called a line counter. You will use a **line-counter** variable to keep track of the number of printed lines, so that you can break to a new page after printing 60 lines. See Figure 7-24.

TIP ▫ ▫ ▫ ▫ You first learned about detail lines in Chapter 3. Detail lines contain individual record data, as opposed to summary lines, which typically contain counts, totals, or other group information culled from multiple records.

FIGURE 7-23: PRINT CHART FOR CUSTOMER REPORT

	1	2	3	4	5	6	7	8	9	0	1	2	3	4	5	6	7	8	9	0	1	2	3	4	5	6	7	8	9	0	1	2	3	4	5	6	7	8	9	0	1	2	3	4	5	6	7	8	9	0	1	2	3	4	5	6	7	8	9
1																																																												
2																C	u	s	t	o	m	e	r		L	i	s	t																																
3																																																											
4		L	A	S	T		N	A	M	E											F	I	R	S	T		N	A	M	E																													
5																																																											
6		X	X	X	X	X	X	X	X	X	X	X									X	X	X	X	X	X	X	X	X	X	X	X																											
7		X	X	X	X	X	X	X	X	X	X	X									X	X	X	X	X	X	X	X	X	X	X	X																											
8		X	X	X	X	X	X	X	X	X	X	X									X	X	X	X	X	X	X	X	X	X	X	X																											

TIP ▫ ▫ ▫ ▫ When creating a printed report, you need to clarify whether the user wants a specific number of *total* lines per page, including headings, or a specific number of *detail* lines per page following the headings.

Within the `getReady()` module (Figure 7-25), you declare the variables, open the files, print the headings, and read the first record. Within the `produceReport()` module (Figure 7-26), you compare the `lineCounter` to 60. When you process the first record, the `lineCounter` is zero, so you print the record, add one to the `lineCounter`, and read the next record.

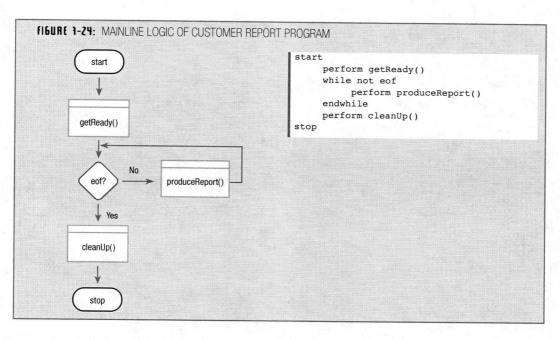

FIGURE 7-24: MAINLINE LOGIC OF CUSTOMER REPORT PROGRAM

```
start
     perform getReady()
     while not eof
          perform produceReport()
     endwhile
     perform cleanUp()
stop
```

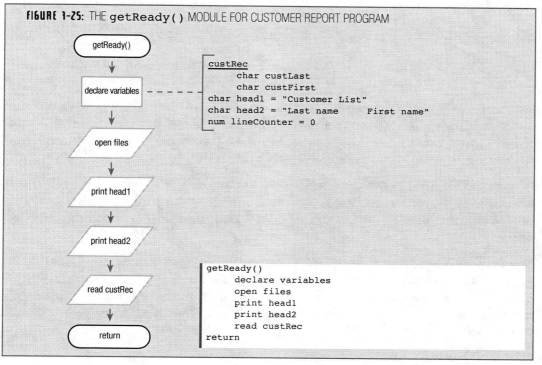

FIGURE 7-25: THE `getReady()` MODULE FOR CUSTOMER REPORT PROGRAM

```
custRec
     char custLast
     char custFirst
char head1 = "Customer List"
char head2 = "Last name     First name"
num lineCounter = 0
```

```
getReady()
     declare variables
     open files
     print head1
     print head2
     read custRec
return
```

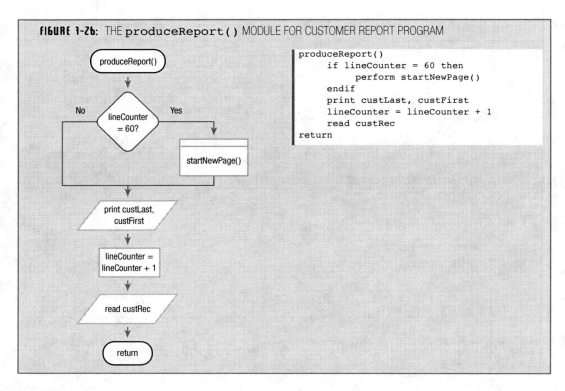

FIGURE 7-26: THE `produceReport()` MODULE FOR CUSTOMER REPORT PROGRAM

```
produceReport()
    if lineCounter = 60 then
        perform startNewPage()
    endif
    print custLast, custFirst
    lineCounter = lineCounter + 1
    read custRec
return
```

TIP ▢ ▢ ▢ ▢   In Figure 7-25, instead of printing head1 and head2, you could perform a module that starts a new page. Figure 7-27 shows a startNewPage() module that the getReady() module could call.

On every cycle through the `produceReport()` module, you check the line counter to see if it is 60 yet. When the first record is written, `lineCounter` is 1. You read the second record, and if there is a second record (that is, if it is not `eof`), you return to the top of the `produceReport()` module. In that module, you compare `lineCounter` to 60, print another line, and add 1 to `lineCounter`, making it equal to 2.

After 60 records read and write, `lineCounter` holds a value of 60. When you read the sixty-first record (and if it is not `eof`), you enter the `produceReport()` module for the 61st time. The answer to the question `lineCounter = 60?` is yes, and you break to perform the `startNewPage()` module. The `startNewPage()` module is a control break routine.

The `startNewPage()` module, shown in Figure 7-27, must print the headings that appear at the top of a new page, and it must also set the `lineCounter` back to zero. If you neglect to reset the `lineCounter`, its value will increase with each successive record and never be equal to 60 again. When resetting the `lineCounter` for a new page, you force execution of the `startNewPage()` module after 60 more records (120 total) print.

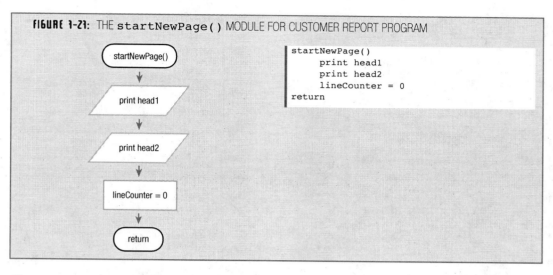

FIGURE 7-27: THE `startNewPage()` MODULE FOR CUSTOMER REPORT PROGRAM

```
startNewPage()
    print head1
    print head2
    lineCounter = 0
return
```

The `startNewPage()` module is simpler than many control break modules because no record counters or accumulators are being maintained. In fact, the `startNewPage()` module must perform only two of the tasks you have seen required by control break routines.

- It does not perform the lower-level break, because there is none.
- It does not perform any control break processing for the previous group, because there is none.
- It does not roll up the current-level totals to the next higher level, because there are no totals.
- It does not reset the current level's totals to zero, because there are no totals (other than the `lineCounter`, which is the control break field).
- It does perform control break processing for the new group by printing headings at the top of the new page.
- It does update the control break field—the line counter.

You might want to employ one little trick that you can use to remove the statements that print the headings from the `getReady()` module. If you initialize `lineCounter` to 60 when defining the variables at the beginning of the program, on the first pass through `mainLoop()`, you can "fool" the computer into printing the first set of headings automatically. When you initialize the `lineCounter` to 60, you can remove the statements `print head1` and `print head2` from the `getReady()` module. With this change, when you enter the `produceReport()` module for the first time, `lineCounter` is already set to 60, and the `startNewPage()` module prints the headings and resets the `lineCounter` to zero before processing the first record from the input file. Figure 7-28 shows the entire program.

As with control break report programs that break based on the contents of one of a record's fields, in any program that starts new pages based on a line count, you always must update the line-counting variable that causes the unusual action. Using page breaks or control breaks (or both) within reports adds a new degree of organization to your printed output and makes it easier for the user to interpret and use.

FIGURE 7-28: THE COMPLETE CUSTOMER REPORT PROGRAM

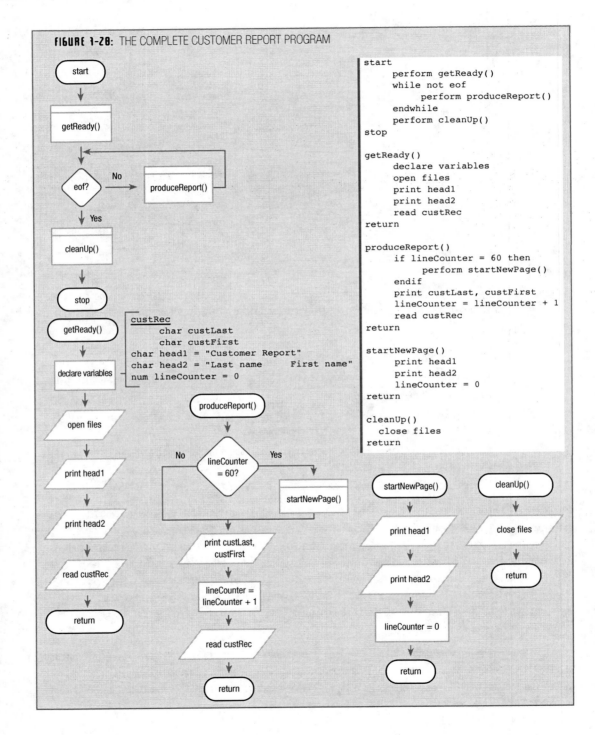

```
start
    perform getReady()
    while not eof
        perform produceReport()
    endwhile
    perform cleanUp()
stop

getReady()
    declare variables
    open files
    print head1
    print head2
    read custRec
return

produceReport()
    if lineCounter = 60 then
        perform startNewPage()
    endif
    print custLast, custFirst
    lineCounter = lineCounter + 1
    read custRec
return

startNewPage()
    print head1
    print head2
    lineCounter = 0
return

cleanUp()
  close files
return
```

```
custRec
     char custLast
     char custFirst
char head1 = "Customer Report"
char head2 = "Last name      First name"
num lineCounter = 0
```

CHAPTER SUMMARY

☐ A control break is a temporary detour in the logic of a program; programmers refer to a program as a control break program when a change in the value of a variable initiates special actions or causes special or unusual processing to occur. To generate a control break report, your input records must be organized in sorted order based on the field that will cause the breaks.

☐ You use a control break field to hold data from a previous record. You decide when to perform a control break routine by comparing the value in the control break field to the corresponding value in the current record. At minimum, the simplest control break routines perform necessary processing for the new group and update the control break field.

☐ Sometimes, you need to use control data within a control break module, such as in a heading that requires information about the next record, or in a footer that requires information about the previous record. The very first heading prints separately from all the others at the beginning; the very last footer must print separately from all the others at the end.

☐ A control break report contains and prints totals for the previous group, rolls up the current-level totals to the next higher level, resets the current level's totals to zero, performs any other needed control break processing, and updates the control break field.

☐ In a program containing a multiple-level control break, the normal flow of control breaks away for special processing in response to a change in more than one field. You should always test for a major-level break before a minor-level break, and include a call to the minor break routine within the major break module.

☐ Every time you write a program in which you need control break routines, you should check whether you need to perform each of the following tasks within the routines: any lower-level break, any control break processing for the previous group, rolling up the current-level totals to the next higher level, resetting the current level's totals to zero, any control break processing for the new group, and updating the control break field.

☐ To perform page breaks, you count the lines printed and pause to print headings when the counter reaches some predetermined value.

KEY TERMS

A control break is a temporary detour in the logic of a program.

A control break program is one in which a change in the value of a variable initiates special actions or causes special or unusual processing to occur.

A control break report lists items in groups. Frequently, each group is followed by a subtotal.

Programs that sort records take records that are not in order and rearrange them so that they are in an order based on some field.

A single-level control break is a break in the logic of a program based on the value of a single variable.

A control break field is a variable that holds the value that signals a break in a program.

A footer is a message that prints at the end of a page or other section of a report.

Rolling up the totals is the process of adding a total to a higher-level total.

A summary report is one that does not include any information about individual records, but instead includes only group totals.

A multiple-level control break is one in which the normal flow of control breaks away for special processing in response to a change in more than one field.

A major-level break is a break in the flow of logic that is caused by a change in the value of a higher-level field.

A minor-level break is a break in the flow of logic that is caused by a change in the value of a lower-level field.

A line counter is a variable that keeps track of the number of printed lines on a page.

REVIEW QUESTIONS

1. **A control break occurs when a program _____.**

   a. takes one of two alternate courses of action for every record

   b. pauses to perform special processing based on the value of a field

   c. ends prematurely, before all records have been processed

   d. passes logical control to a module contained within another program

2. **Which of the following is an example of a control break report?**

   a. a list of all employees in a company, with a message "Retain" or "Dismiss" following each employee record

   b. a list of all students in a school, arranged in alphabetical order, with a total count at the end of the report

   c. a list of all customers of a business in ZIP code order, with a count of the number of customers who reside in each ZIP code

   d. a list of some of the patients of a medical clinic—those who have not seen a doctor for at least two years

3. **Placing records in sequential order based on the value in one of the fields is called _____.**

   a. sorting

   b. collating

   c. merging

   d. categorizing

4. **In a program with a single-level control break, _____.**

   a. the input file must contain a variable that contains a single digit

   b. the hierarchy chart must contain a single level below the main level

   c. special processing occurs based on the value in a single field

   d. the control break module must not contain any submodules

5. **A control break field _____.**

   a. always prints prior to any group of records on a control break report

   b. always prints after any group of records on a control break report

   c. never prints on a report

   d. causes special processing to occur

6. **The value stored in a control break field _____.**

   a. can be printed at the end of each group of records

   b. can be printed with each record

   c. both of these

   d. neither of these

7. **Within any control break module, you must _____.**

   a. declare a control break field

   b. set the control break field to zero

   c. print the control break field

   d. update the value in the control break field

8. **An insurance agency employs 10 agents and wants to print a report of claims based on the insurance agent who sold each policy. The agent's name should appear in a heading prior to the list of each agent's claims. In the housekeeping module for this program, you should _____.**

   a. read the first record before printing the first heading

   b. print the first heading before reading the first record

   c. read all the records that represent clients of the first agent before printing the heading

   d. print the first heading, but do not read the first record until the main loop

9. **In contrast to using control break data in a heading, when you use control break data in a footer, you usually need data from the _____ record in the input data file.**

   a. previous

   b. next

   c. first

   d. priming

10. **An automobile dealer wants a list of cars sold, grouped by model, with a total dollar amount sold at the end of each group. The program contains four modules, appropriately named `housekeeping()`, `mainLoop()`, `modelBreak()`, and `finish()`. The total for the last car model group should be printed in the _____.**

    a. `mainLoop()` module, after the last time the control break module is called

    b. `mainLoop()` module, as the last step in the module

    c. `modelBreak()` module when it is called from within the `mainLoop()` module

    d. `modelBreak()` module when it is called from within the `finish()` module

11. The Hampton City Zoo has a file that contains information about each of the animals it houses. Each animal record contains such information as the animal's ID number, date acquired by the zoo, and species. The zoo wants to print a list of animals, grouped by species, with a count after each group. As an example, a typical summary line might be "Species: Giraffe   Count: 7". Which of the following happens within the control break module that prints the count?

    a. The previous species count prints, and then the previous species field is updated.
    b. The previous species field is updated, and then the previous species count prints.
    c. Either of these will produce the desired results.
    d. Neither of these will produce the desired results.

12. Adding a total to a higher-level total is called _____ the totals.

    a. sliding
    b. advancing
    c. rolling up
    d. replacing

13. The Academic Dean of Creighton College wants a count of the number of students who have declared each of the college's 45 major courses of study, as well as a grand total count of students enrolled in the college. Individual student records contain each student's name, ID number, major, and other data, and are sorted in alphabetical order by major. A control break module executes when the program encounters a change in student major. Within this model, what must occur?

    a. The total count for the previous major prints.
    b. The total count for the previous major prints, and the total count is added to the grand total.
    c. The total count for the previous major prints, the total count for the major is added to the grand total, and the total count for the major is reset to zero.
    d. The total count for the previous major prints, the total count for the major is added to the grand total, the total count for the major is reset to zero, and the grand total is reset to zero.

14. In a control break program containing printed group totals and a grand total, the final module that executes must _____.

    a. print the group total for the last group
    b. roll up the total for the last group
    c. both of these
    d. neither of these

15. A summary report _____.

    a. contains detail lines
    b. contains total lines
    c. both of these
    d. neither of these

16. The Cityscape Real Estate Agency wants a list of all housing units sold last year that includes a subtotal of sales that occurred each month. Within each month group, there are also subtotals of each type of property—single-family homes, condominiums, commercial properties, and so on. This report is a _____ control break report.

    a. single-level
    b. multiple-level
    c. semilevel
    d. trilevel

17. The Packerville Parks Commission has a file that contains picnic permit information for the coming season. They need a report that lists each day's picnic permit information, including permit number and name of permit holder, starting on a separate page each day of the picnic season. (Figure 7-29 shows a sample page of output for the Packerville Parks report.) Within each day's permits, they want subtotals that count permits in each of the city's 30 parks. The permit records have been sorted by park name within date. In the main loop of the report program, the first decision should check for a change in _____.

FIGURE 7-29:

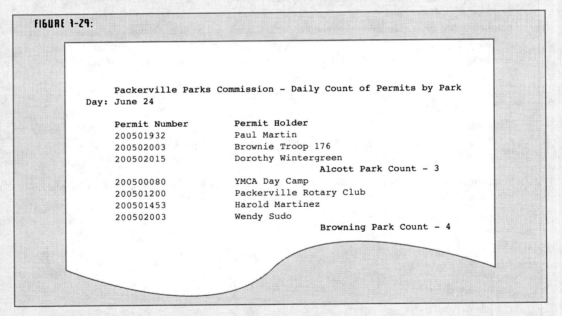

```
           Packerville Parks Commission - Daily Count of Permits by Park
      Day: June 24

           Permit Number          Permit Holder
           200501932              Paul Martin
           200502003              Brownie Troop 176
           200502015              Dorothy Wintergreen
                                           Alcott Park Count - 3
           200500080              YMCA Day Camp
           200501200              Packerville Rotary Club
           200501453              Harold Martinez
           200502003              Wendy Sudo
                                           Browning Park Count - 4
```

    a. park name
    b. date
    c. permit number
    d. any of these

18. Which of the following is *not* a task you need to complete in any control break module that has multiple levels and totals at each level?

    a. Perform lower-level breaks.
    b. Roll up the totals.
    c. Update the control break field.
    d. Reset the current-level totals to the previous-level totals.

19. The election commission for the state of Illinois maintains a file that contains the name of each registered voter, the voter's county, and precinct within the county. The commission wants to produce a report that counts the voters in each precinct and county. The file should be sorted in _____.

    a. county order within precinct
    b. last name order within precinct
    c. last name order within county
    d. precinct order within county

20. A variable that determines when a new page should start based on the number of detail lines printed on a page is a(n) _____.

    a. detail counter
    b. line counter
    c. page counter
    d. break counter

EXERCISES

1. What fields might you want to use as the control break fields to produce a report that lists all inventory items in a grocery store? (For example, you might choose to group items by grocery store department.) Design the print chart for the report.

2. What fields might you want to use as the control break fields to produce a report that lists all the people you know? (For example, you might choose to group friends by city of residence.) Design the print chart for the report.

3. Cool's Department Store keeps a record of every sale in the following format:

   ```
   DEPARTMENT STORE SALES FILE DESCRIPTION
   File name: DEPTSALES
   Sorted by: Department
   ```

FIELD DESCRIPTION	POSITIONS	DATA TYPE	DECIMALS	EXAMPLE
Transaction Number	1-7	Numeric	0	2615441
Amount	8-13	Numeric	2	012599
Department	14-16	Numeric	0	501

   Create the logic for a program that would print each transaction's details, with a total at the end of each department.

   a. Create the print chart.
   b. Create the hierarchy chart.
   c. Create the flowchart.
   d. Create the pseudocode.

4. A used-car dealer keeps track of sales in the following format:

   ```
   AUTO SALES FILE DESCRIPTION
   File name: AUTO
   Sorted by: Salesperson
   ```

FIELD DESCRIPTION	POSITIONS	DATA TYPE	DECIMALS	EXAMPLE
Salesperson	1-20	Character		Miller
Make of Car	21-30	Character		Ford
Vehicle Type	31-40	Character		Sedan
Sale Price	41-45	Numeric	0	12500

   By the end of the week, a salesperson may have sold no cars, one car, or many cars. Create the logic of a program that would print one line for each salesperson, with that salesperson's total sales for the week and commission earned, which is 4% of the total sales.

   a. Create the print chart.
   b. Create the hierarchy chart.
   c. Create the flowchart.
   d. Create the pseudocode.

5. A community college maintains student records in the following format:

```
STUDENT FILE DESCRIPTION
File name: STUDENTS
Sorted by: Hour of First Class
FIELD DESCRIPTION        POSITIONS      DATA TYPE      DECIMALS      EXAMPLE
Student Name             1-20           Character                    Amy Lee
City                     21-30          Character                    Woodstock
Hour of First Class      31-32          Numeric        0             08
Phone Number             33-42          Numeric        0             8154379823
```

The records have been sorted by hour of the day. The Hour of First Class is a two-digit number based on a 24-hour clock (that is, a 1 p.m. first class is recorded as 13).

Create a report that students can use to organize carpools. The report lists the names and phone numbers of students from the city of Huntley. Note that some students come from cities other than Huntley; these students should not be listed on the report.

Start a new page for each hour of the day, so that all students starting classes at the same hour are listed on the same page. Include the hour that each page represents in the heading for that page.

a. Create the print chart.
b. Create the hierarchy chart.
c. Create the flowchart.
d. Create the pseudocode.

6. The Stanton Insurance Agency needs a report summarizing the counts of life, health, and other types of insurance policies it sells. Input records contain policy number, name of insured, policy value, and type of policy, and have been sorted in alphabetical order by type of policy. At the end of the report, display a count of all the policies.

a. Create the print chart.
b. Create the hierarchy chart.
c. Create the flowchart.
d. Create the pseudocode.

7. If a university is organized into colleges (such as Liberal Arts), divisions (such as Languages), and departments (such as French), what would constitute the major, intermediate, and minor control breaks in a report that prints all classes offered by the university?

8. A zoo keeps track of the expense of feeding the animals it houses. Each record holds one animal's ID number, name, species (elephant, rhinoceros, tiger, lion, and so on), zoo residence (pachyderm house, large cat house, and so on), and weekly food budget. The records take the following form:

```
ANIMAL FEED RECORDS
File name: ANIMFOOD
Sorted by: Species within house
```

FIELD DESCRIPTION	POSITIONS	DATA TYPE	DECIMALS	EXAMPLE
Animal ID	1-4	Numeric	0	4116
Animal Name	5-29	Character		Elmo
Species	30-45	Character		Elephant
House	46-55	Character		Pachyderm
Weekly Food	56-59	Numeric	0	0075
Budget in Dollars				

Design a report that lists each animal's ID, name, and budgeted food amount. At the end of each species group, print a total budget for the species. At the end of each house (for example, the species lion, tiger, and leopard are all in the large cat house), print the house total. At the end of the report, print the grand total.

a. Create the print chart.
b. Create the hierarchy chart.
c. Create the flowchart.
d. Create the pseudocode.

9. A soft-drink manufacturer produces several flavors of drink—for example, cola, orange, and lemon. Additionally, each flavor has several versions such as regular, diet, and caffeine-free. The manufacturer operates factories in several states.

Assume you have input records that list version, flavor, yearly production in gallons, and state (for example: Regular Cola 5000 Kansas). The records have been sorted in alphabetical order by version within flavor within state. Design the report that lists each version and flavor, with minor total production figures for each flavor and major total production figures for each state.

a. Create the print chart.
b. Create the hierarchy chart.
c. Create the flowchart.
d. Create the pseudocode.

10. An art shop owner maintains records for each item in the shop, including the title of the work, the artist who made the item, the medium (for example, watercolor, oil, or clay), and the monetary value. The records are sorted by artist within medium. Design a report that lists all items in the store, with a minor total value following each artist's work, and a major total value following each medium. Allow only 40 detail lines per page.

    a. Create the print chart.

    b. Create the hierarchy chart.

    c. Create the flowchart.

    d. Create the pseudocode.

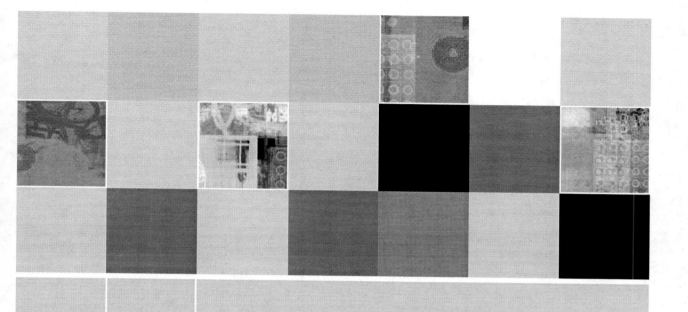

16

USING RELATIONAL DATABASES

After studying Chapter 16, you should be able to:

- ☐ Understand relational database fundamentals
- ☐ Create databases and table descriptions
- ☐ Identify primary keys
- ☐ Understand database structure notation
- ☐ Understand the principles of adding, deleting, updating, and sorting records within a table
- ☐ Write queries
- ☐ Understand relationships between tables and functional dependence between columns
- ☐ Recognize poor table design
- ☐ Understand anomalies, normal forms, and the normalization process
- ☐ Understand the performance and security issues connected to database administration

UNDERSTANDING RELATIONAL DATABASE FUNDAMENTALS

When you store data items for use within computer systems, they are often stored in what is known as a data hierarchy, where the smallest usable unit of data is the character, often a letter or number. Characters are grouped together to form fields, such as firstName, lastName, and socialSecurityNumber. Related fields are often grouped together to form records—groups of fields that go together because they represent attributes of some entity, such as an employee, a customer, an inventory item, or a bank account. Files are composed of related records—for example, a file might contain a record for each employee in a company or each account at a bank.

TIP □ □ □ □ | You first learned about the data hierarchy in Chapter 1 of this book. The terms *character*, *field*, *record*, and *file* were defined there, and you have been using these terms throughout this book.

Most organizations store many files that contain the data they need to operate their businesses; for example, businesses often need to maintain files containing data about employees, customers, inventory items, and orders. Many organizations use database software to organize the information in these files. A **database** holds a group of files that an organization needs to support its applications. In a database, the files often are called **tables** because you can arrange their contents in rows and columns. Real-life examples of database-like tables abound. For example, consider the listings in a telephone book. Each listing in a city directory might contain four columns, as shown in Figure 16-1—last name, first name, street address, and phone number. Although your local phone directory might not store its data in the rigid columnar format shown in the figure, it could. You can see that each column represents a field and that each row represents one record. You can picture a table within a database in the same way.

FIGURE 16-1: A TELEPHONE BOOK TABLE

Last name	First name	Address	Phone
Abbott	William	123 Oak Lane	490-8912
Ackerman	Kimberly	467 Elm Drive	787-2781
Adams	Stanley	8120 Pine Street	787-0129
Adams	Violet	347 Oak Lane	490-8912
Adams	William	12 Second Street	490-3667

TIP □ □ □ □ | One record or row is also called an **entity**. One column can also be called an **attribute**.

Figure 16-1 includes five records, each representing a unique person. It is relatively easy to scan this short list of names to find the phone number for a person you want; of course, most telephone books contain many more records. Some telephone book users, such as telemarketers, or even the phone company, might prefer to look up a number in a book in which the records are organized in telephone-number order. Others, such as door-to-door salespeople, might prefer a telephone book in which the records are organized in street-address order. Most people, however, prefer a telephone book in which the records are organized as shown, in alphabetical order by last name. Similarly, it is convenient for different users when computerized databases can sort records in various orders based on the contents of different columns.

Unless you are reading a telephone book for a very small town, a last name alone often is not sufficient to identify an individual. In the example in Figure 16-1, three people have the last name of Adams. For these records, you need to examine the first name before you can determine the correct phone number. In a large city, many people might have the same first and last names; in that case, you might also need to examine the street address to identify an individual. As with the telephone book, in most computerized database tables, it is important to have a way to uniquely identify each record, even if it means using multiple columns. A field or column that uniquely identifies a record is called a **primary key**, or a **key** for short. Key fields often are defined as a single table column, but as with the telephone book, keys can be constructed from multiple columns; a key constructed from multiple columns is a **compound key**.

TIP □ □ □ □ You learn more about key fields and compound keys later in this chapter.

Telephone books are republished periodically because changes have occurred—new people have moved into the city and become telephone customers, and others have left, canceled service, or changed numbers. With computerized database tables, you also need to add, delete, and modify records, although usually far more frequently than phone books are published.

Telephone books often contain thousands of records. Computerized database tables also frequently contain thousands of records, or rows, and each row might contain entries in dozens of columns. Handling and organizing all the data contained in an organization's tables requires sophisticated software. **Database management software** is a set of programs that allows users to:

- Create table descriptions.
- Identify key fields.
- Add, delete, and update records within a table.
- Organize the records within a table into different sorted orders.
- Write questions that select specific records from a table for viewing.
- Write questions that combine information from multiple tables. This is possible because the database management software establishes and maintains relationships between the columns in the tables. A group of database tables from which you can make these connections is a **relational database**.
- Create reports that allow users to easily interpret your data, and create forms that allow users to view and enter data using an easy-to-manage interactive screen.
- Keep data secure by employing sophisticated security measures.

If you have used different word-processing or spreadsheet programs, you know that each version works a little differently, although each carries out the same types of tasks. Like other computer programs, each database management software package operates differently; however, with each, you need to perform the same types of tasks.

CREATING DATABASES AND TABLE DESCRIPTIONS

Creating a useful database requires a lot of planning and analysis. You must decide what data will be stored, how that data will be divided between tables, and how the tables will interrelate. Before you physically create any tables, you must create the database itself. With most database software packages, creating the database that will hold the tables requires nothing more than providing a name for the database and indicating the physical location, perhaps a hard disk drive, where the database will be stored. When you save a table, it is conventional to provide it with a name that begins with the prefix `tbl`, for example, `tblCustomers`. Your databases often become filled with a variety of objects—tables, forms that users can use for data entry, reports that organize the data for viewing, queries that select subsets of data for viewing, and so on. Using naming conventions, such as beginning each table name with a prefix that identifies it as a table, helps you to keep track of the various objects in your system.

TIP □ □ □ □ Many database management programs suggest that you use a generic name such as `Table1` when you save a table description. Usually, a more descriptive name is more useful to you as you continue to create objects.

Before you can enter any data into a database table, you must design the table. At minimum, this involves two tasks:

- You must decide what columns your table needs, and provide names for them.
- You must provide a data type for each column.

For example, assume you are designing a customer database table. Figure 16-2 shows some column names and data types you might use.

FIGURE 16-2: CUSTOMER TABLE DESCRIPTION

Column	Data type
customerID	text
lastName	text
firstName	text
streetAddress	text
balanceOwed	numeric

TIP □ □ □ □ A table description closely resembles the record descriptions you have used with data files throughout this book.

The table description in Figure 16-2 uses just two data types—text and numeric. Text columns can hold any type of characters—letters or digits. Numeric columns can hold numbers only. Depending on the database management software you use, you might have many more sophisticated data types at your disposal. For example, some database software divides the numeric data type into several subcategories such as integer (whole number only) values and double-precision numbers (numbers that contain decimals). Other options might include special categories for currency numbers (representing dollars and cents), dates, and Boolean columns (representing true or false). At the least, all database software recognizes the distinction between text and numeric data.

TIP ☐ ☐ ☐ ☐ | You have been aware of the distinction that computers make between character and numeric data throughout this book. Because of the way computers handle data, every type of software observes this dichotomy.

TIP ☐ ☐ ☐ ☐ | Unassigned variables within computer programs might be empty, containing a null value, or might contain unknown or garbage values. Similarly, columns in database tables might also contain null or unknown values.

The table description in Figure 16-2 uses one-word column names and camel casing, in the same way that variable names have been defined throughout this book. Many database software packages do not require that data column names be single words without embedded spaces, but many database table designers prefer single-word names because they resemble variable names in programs. In addition, when you use a single word to label each database column, it is easier to understand whether just one column is being referenced, or several.

The `customerID` column in Figure 16-2 is defined as a text field or column. If `customerID` numbers are composed entirely of digits, this column could also be defined as numeric. However, many database designers feel that columns should be defined as numeric only if they need to be—that is, only if they might be used in arithmetic calculations. The description in Figure 16-2 follows this convention by declaring `customerID` to be a text column.

Many database management software packages allow you to add a narrative description of each data column to a table. This allows you to make comments that become part of the table. These comments do not affect the way the table operates; they simply serve as documentation for those who are reading a table description. For example, you might want to make a note that the `customerID` should consist of five digits, or that the `balanceOwed` should not exceed a given limit. Some software allows you to specify that a certain column is required—the user cannot create a record without providing data for this column. In addition, you might be able to indicate value limits on a column—high and low numbers between which the column contents must fall.

IDENTIFYING PRIMARY KEYS

In most tables you create for a database, you want to identify a column, or possibly a combination of columns, as the table's key column or field, also called the primary key. The primary key in a table is the column that makes each record different from all others. For example, in the customer table in Figure 16-2, the logical choice for a primary key is the `customerID` column—each customer record that is entered into the customer table has a unique value in this column. Many customers might have the same first name or last name, or both, and multiple customers also might have the same street address or balance due. However, each customer possesses a unique ID number.

Other typical examples of primary keys include:

- A student ID number in a table that contains college student information
- An item number in a table that contains inventory items
- A Social Security number in a table that contains employee information

In each of these examples, the primary key uniquely identifies the row. For example, each student has a unique ID number assigned by the college. Other columns in a student table would not be adequate keys—many students have the same last name, first name, home town, and major.

TIP □ □ □ □ It is no coincidence that each of the preceding examples of a key is a number, such as a student ID number or item number. Usually, assigning a number to each row in a table is the simplest and most efficient method of obtaining a useful key.

The primary key is important for several reasons:

- You can configure your database software to prevent multiple records from containing the same value in this column, thus avoiding data-entry errors.
- You can sort your records in this order before displaying or printing them.
- You use this column when setting up relationships between this table and others that will become part of the same database.
- In addition, you need to understand the concept of the primary key when you normalize a database—a concept you will learn more about later in this chapter.

TIP □ □ □ □ In some database software packages, such as Microsoft Access, you indicate a primary key simply by selecting a column name and clicking a button that is labeled with a key icon.

In some tables, when no identifying number has been assigned to the rows, more than one column is required to construct a primary key. A multicolumn key is a compound key. For example, consider Figure 16-3, which might be used by a residence hall administrator to store data about students living on a university campus. Each room in a building has a number and two students, each assigned to either bed A or bed B.

FIGURE 16-3: TABLE CONTAINING RESIDENCE HALL STUDENT RECORDS

hall	room	bed	lastName	firstName	major
Adams	101	A	Fredricks	Madison	Chemistry
Adams	101	B	Garza	Lupe	Psychology
Adams	102	A	Liu	Jennifer	CIS
Adams	102	B	Smith	Crystal	CIS
Browning	101	A	Patel	Sarita	CIS
Browning	101	B	Smith	Margaret	Biology
Browning	102	A	Jefferson	Martha	Psychology
Browning	102	B	Bartlett	Donna	Spanish
Churchill	101	A	Wong	Cheryl	CIS
Churchill	101	B	Smith	Madison	Chemistry
Churchill	102	A	Patel	Jennifer	Psychology
Churchill	102	B	Jones	Elizabeth	CIS

In Figure 16-3, no single column can serve as a primary key. Many students live in the same residence hall, and the same room numbers exist in the different residence halls. In addition, some students have the same last names, first names, and majors. It is even possible that two students with the same first name, last name, and major are assigned to the same room. In this case, the best primary key is a multicolumn key that combines residence hall, room number, and bed number. "Adams 101 A" identifies a single room and student, as does "Churchill 102 B."

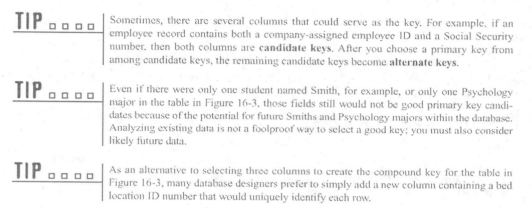

TIP □ □ □ □ | Sometimes, there are several columns that could serve as the key. For example, if an employee record contains both a company-assigned employee ID and a Social Security number, then both columns are **candidate keys**. After you choose a primary key from among candidate keys, the remaining candidate keys become **alternate keys**.

TIP □ □ □ □ | Even if there were only one student named Smith, for example, or only one Psychology major in the table in Figure 16-3, those fields still would not be good primary key candidates because of the potential for future Smiths and Psychology majors within the database. Analyzing existing data is not a foolproof way to select a good key; you must also consider likely future data.

TIP □ □ □ □ | As an alternative to selecting three columns to create the compound key for the table in Figure 16-3, many database designers prefer to simply add a new column containing a bed location ID number that would uniquely identify each row.

Usually, after you have identified the necessary fields and their data types, and identified the primary key, you are ready to save your table description and begin to enter data.

UNDERSTANDING DATABASE STRUCTURE NOTATION

A shorthand way to describe a table is to use the table name followed by parentheses containing all the field names, with the primary key underlined. Thus, when a table is named `tblStudents` and contains columns named `idNumber`, `lastName`, `firstName`, and `gradePointAverage`, and `idNumber` is the key, then you can reference the table using the following notation:

```
tblStudents(idNumber, lastName, firstName, gradePointAverage)
```

Although this shorthand notation does not provide you with information about data types or range limits on values, it does provide you with a quick overview of the structure of a table.

TIP □ □ □ □ | Some database designers insert an asterisk after the key instead of underlining it.

TIP □ □ □ □ | The key does not have to be the first attribute listed in a table reference, but frequently it is.

ADDING, DELETING, AND UPDATING RECORDS WITHIN TABLES

Entering data into an already created table is not difficult, but it requires a good deal of time and accurate typing. Depending on the application, the contents of the tables might be entered over the course of many months or years by any number of data-entry personnel. Entering data of the wrong type is not allowed. In addition, you might have set up your table to prevent duplicate data in specific fields, or to prevent data entry outside of specified bounds in other fields. With some database software, you type data into rows representing each record, and columns representing each field in each record, much as you would enter data into a spreadsheet. With other software, you can create on-screen forms to make data entry more user-friendly. Some software does not allow you to enter a partial record.

TIP ☐ ☐ ☐ ☐ | Computer professionals use the acronym GIGO, which stands for "garbage in, garbage out." It means that if you enter invalid input data into an application, the output results will be worthless.

Deleting records from and modifying records within a database table are also relatively easy tasks. In most organizations, most of the important data are in a constant state of change. Maintaining the data records so they are up-to-date is a vital part of any database management system.

SORTING THE RECORDS IN A TABLE

Database management software generally allows you to sort a table based on any column, letting you view your data in the way that is most useful to you. For example, you might want to view inventory items in alphabetical order, or from the most to the least expensive. You also can sort by multiple columns—for example, you might sort employees by first name within last name (so that Aaron Black is listed before Andrea Black), or by department within first name within last name (so that Aaron Black in Department 1 is listed before another Aaron Black in Department 6).

After rows are sorted, they also usually can be grouped. For example, you might want to sort customers by their ZIP codes, or employees by the departments in which they work; in addition, you might want counts or subtotals at the end of each group. Database software provides the means to create displays in the formats that suit your present information needs.

TIP ☐ ☐ ☐ ☐ | When a database program includes counts or totals at the end of each sorted group, it is creating a control break report. You learned about control break reports in Chapter 7.

CREATING QUERIES

Data tables often contain hundreds or thousands of rows; making sense out of that much information is a daunting task. Frequently, you want to cull subsets of data from a table you have created. For example, you might want to view only those customers with addresses in a specific state, only those inventory items whose quantity in stock has fallen below the normal reorder point, or only those employees who participate in an insurance plan. Besides limiting records, you might also want to limit the columns that you view. For example, student records might contain dozens of fields, but a school administrator might only be interested in looking at names and grade point averages. The questions that cause the database software to extract the appropriate records from a table and specify the fields to be viewed are called queries; a **query** is simply a question asked using the syntax that the database software can understand.

Depending on the software you use, you might create a query by filling in blanks (a process called **query by example**) or by writing statements similar to those in many programming languages. The most common language that database administrators use to access data in their tables is **Structured Query Language**, or **SQL**. The basic form of the SQL command that retrieves selected records from a table is SELECT-FROM-WHERE. The **SELECT-FROM-WHERE** SQL statement:

- Selects the columns you want to view
- From a specific table
- Where one or more conditions are met

For example, suppose a customer table named `tblCustomer` contains data about your business customers and that the structure of the table is `tblCustomer(custId, lastName, state)`. Then, a statement such as:

```
SELECT custId, lastName FROM tblCustomer WHERE state = "WI"
```

would display a new table containing two columns—`custId` and `lastName`—and only as many rows as needed to hold those customers whose `state` column contains "WI". Besides using = to mean "equal to," you can use the comparison conditions > (greater than), < (less than), >= (greater than or equal to), and <= (less than or equal to). As you have already learned from working with programming variables throughout this book, text field values are always contained within quotes, whereas numeric values are not.

TIP □ □ □ □ Conventionally, SQL keywords such as SELECT appear in all uppercase; this book follows that convention.

To select all fields for each record in a table, you can use the asterisk as a wildcard; a wildcard is a symbol that means "any" or "all". For example, `SELECT * from tblCustomer WHERE state = "WI"` would select all columns for every customer whose state is "WI", not just specifically named columns. To select all customers from a table, you can omit the WHERE clause in a SELECT-FROM-WHERE statement. In other words, `SELECT * FROM tblCustomer` selects all columns for all customers.

You learned about making selections in computer programs much earlier in this book, and you have probably noticed that SELECT-FROM-WHERE statements serve the same purpose as programming decisions. As with decision statements in programs, when using SQL, you can create compound conditions using AND or OR operators. In addition, you can precede any condition with a NOT operator to achieve a negative result. In summary, Figure 16-4 shows a database table named `tblInventory` with the following structure: `tblInventory(itemNumber, description, quantityInStock, price)`. The table contains five records. Figure 16-5 lists several typical SQL SELECT statements you might use with the `tblInventory`, and explains each.

FIGURE 16-4: THE `tblInventory` TABLE

itemNumber	description	quantityInStock	price
144	Pkg 12 party plates	250	14.99
231	Helium balloons	180	2.50
267	Paper streamers	68	1.89
312	Disposable tablecloth	20	6.99
383	Pkg 20 napkins	315	2.39

FIGURE 16-5: SAMPLE SQL STATEMENTS AND EXPLANATIONS

SQL statement	Explanation
SELECT itemNumber, price FROM tblInventory	Shows only the item number and price for all five records.
SELECT * FROM tblInventory WHERE price > 5.00	Shows all fields from only those records where price is over $5.00—items 144 and 312.
SELECT itemNumber FROM tblInventory WHERE quantityInStock > 200 AND price > 10.00	Shows item number 144—the only record that has a quantity greater than 200 as well as a price greater than $10.00.
SELECT description, price FROM tblInventory WHERE description = "Pkg 20 napkins" OR itemNumber < 200	Shows the description and price fields for the package of 12 party plates and the package of 20 napkins. Each selected record must satisfy only one of the two criteria.
SELECT itemNumber FROM tblInventory WHERE NOT price < 14.00	Shows the item number for the only record where the price is not less than $14.00—item 144.

UNDERSTANDING TABLE RELATIONSHIPS

Most database applications require many tables, and these applications also require that the tables be related. The connection between two tables is a **relationship**, and the database containing the relationships is called a relational database. Connecting two tables based on the values in a common column is called a **join operation**, or more simply, a **join**; the column on which they are connected is the **join column**. A virtual, or imaginary, table that is displayed as the result of the query takes some of its data from each joined table. For example, in Figure 16-6, the customerNumber column is the join column that could produce a virtual image when a user makes a query. When a user asks to see the name of a customer associated with a specific order number, or a list of all of the names of customers who have ordered a specific item, then a joined table is produced. The three types of relationships that can exist between tables are:

- One-to-many
- Many-to-many
- One-to-one

FIGURE 16-6: SAMPLE CUSTOMERS AND ORDERS

tblCustomers

customerNumber	customerName
214	Kowalski
215	Jackson
216	Lopez
217	Thompson
218	Vitale

tblOrders

orderNumber	customerNumber	orderQuantity	orderItem	orderDate
10467	215	2	HP203	10/15/2005
10468	218	1	JK109	10/15/2005
10469	215	4	HP203	10/16/2005
10470	216	12	ML318	10/16/2005
10471	214	4	JK109	10/16/2005
10472	215	1	HP203	10/16/2005
10473	217	10	JK109	10/17/2005

UNDERSTANDING ONE-TO-MANY RELATIONSHIPS

A **one-to-many relationship** is one in which one row in a table can be related to many rows in another table. It is the most common type of relationship between tables. Consider the following tables:

```
tblCustomers(customerNumber, customerName)
tblOrders(orderNumber, customerNumber, orderQuantity, orderItem, orderDate)
```

The tblCustomers table contains one row for each customer, and customerNumber is the primary key. The tblOrders table contains one row for each order, and each order is assigned an orderNumber, which is the primary key in this table.

In most businesses, a single customer can place many orders. For example, in the sample data in Figure 16-6, customer 215 has placed three orders. One row in the tblCustomers table can correspond to, and can be related to, many rows in the tblOrders table. This means that there is a one-to-many relationship between the two tables tblCustomers and tblOrders. The "one" table (tblCustomers) is the **base table** in this relationship, and the "many" table (tblOrders) is the **related table**.

When two tables are related in a one-to-many relationship, the relationship occurs based on the values in one or more columns in the tables. In this example, the column, or attribute, that links the two tables together is the customerNumber attribute. In the tblCustomers table, the customerNumber is the primary key, but in the tblOrders table, the customerNumber is not a key—it is a **non-key attribute**. When a column that is not a key in a table contains an attribute that is a key in a related table, the column is called a **foreign key**. When a base table is linked to a related table in a one-to-many relationship, it is always the primary key of the base table that is related to the foreign key in the related table. In this example, the customerNumber of the tblOrders table is a foreign key.

TIP □ □ □ □ A key in a base table and the foreign key in the related table do not need to have the same name; they only need to contain the same type of data. Some database management software programs automatically create a relationship for you if the columns in two tables you select have the same name and data type. However, if this is not the case (for example, if the column is named customerNumber in one table and custID in another), you can explicitly instruct the software to create the relationship.

UNDERSTANDING MANY-TO-MANY RELATIONSHIPS

Another example of a one-to-many relationship is depicted with the following tables:

- tblItems(<u>itemNumber</u>, itemName, itemPurchaseDate, itemPurchasePrice, itemCategoryId)

- tblCategories(<u>categoryId</u>, categoryName, categoryInsuredAmount)

Assume you are creating these tables to keep track of all the items in your household for insurance purposes. You want to store data about items such as your sofa, stereo, refrigerator, and so on. The tblItems table contains the name, purchase date, and purchase price of each item. In addition, this table contains the ID number of the item category (Appliance, Jewelry, Antique, and so on) to which the item belongs. You need the category of each item because your insurance policy has specific insurance coverage limits for different types of property. For example, with many insurance policies, antiques might have a different insurance coverage limit than appliances, or jewelry might have a different limit than furniture. Sample data for these tables are shown in Figure 16-7.

FIGURE 16-7: SAMPLE ITEMS AND CATEGORIES

tblItems

itemNumber	itemName	itemPurchaseDate	itemPurchasePrice	itemCategoryId
1	Sofa	1/13/2001	$6500	5
2	Stereo	2/10/2003	$1200	6
3	Refrigerator	5/12/2003	$750	1
4	Diamond ring	2/12/2004	$42000	2
5	TV	7/11/2004	$285	6
6	Rectangular pine coffee table	4/21/2005	$300	5
7	Round pine end table	4/21/2005	$200	5

tblCategories

categoryId	categoryName	categoryInsuredAmount
1	Appliance	$30,000
2	Jewelry	$15,000
3	Antique	$10,000
4	Clothing	$25,000
5	Furniture	$5,000
6	Electronics	$2,500
7	Miscellaneous	$5,000

The primary key of the `tblItems` table is `itemNumber`, a unique identifying number that you have assigned to each item that you own. (You might even prepare labels with these numbers and stick a label on each item in an inconspicuous place.) The `tblCategories` table contains the category names and the maximum insured amounts for the specific categories. For example, one row in this table may have a `categoryName` of "Jewelry" and a `categoryInsuredAmount` of $15,000. The primary key for the `tblCategories` table is `categoryId`, which is simply a uniquely assigned value for each property category.

The two tables in Figure 16-7 are related in a one-to-many relationship. Which is the "one" table and which is the "many" table? Or, asked in another way, which is the base table, and which is the related table? You have probably determined that the `tblCategories` table is the base table (the "one" table) because one category can describe many items that you own. Therefore, the `tblItems` table is the related table (the "many" table); that is, there are many items that fall into each category. The two tables are linked with the `categoryId` attribute, which is the primary key in the base table (`tblCategories`) and a foreign key in the related table (`tblItems`).

In the tables in Figure 16-7, one row in the `tblCategories` table relates to multiple items you own. The opposite is not true—that is, one item in the `tblItems` table cannot relate to multiple categories in the `tblCategories` table. The row in the `tblItems` table that describes the "rectangular pine coffee table" relates to one specific category in the `tblCategories` table—the Furniture category. However, what if you own a rectangular pine coffee table that has a built-in DVD player, or a diamond ring that is an antique, or a stereo that could also be worn as a hat on a rainy day? Even though this last example is humorous, it does bring up an important consideration.

The structure of the tables shown in Figure 16-7 and the relationship between those tables is designed to support a particular application—keeping track of possessions for insurance purposes. If you acquired a sofa with a built-in CD player and speakers, what would you do? For guidance, you probably would call your insurance agent. If the agent said, "Well, for insurance purposes that item is considered to be a piece of furniture," then the existing table structures and relationships are adequate.

However, if the insurance agent said, "Well, actually a sofa with a CD player is considered to be a special type of hybrid item, and that category of property has a specific maximum insured amount," then you could simply create a new row in the `tblCategories` table to describe this special hybrid category—perhaps Electronic Furniture. This new category would acquire a category number, and then you could associate the CD-sofa to the new category using the foreign key in the `tblItems` table.

However, what if your insurance agent said, "You know, that's a good question. We've never had that come up before—a sofa with a CD player. What we would probably do if you filed a claim because the sofa was damaged is to take a look at it to try to determine whether the sofa is mostly a piece of furniture or mostly a piece of electronics." This answer presents a problem to your database. You may want to categorize your new sofa as both a furniture item *and* an electronic item. The existing table structures, with their one-to-many relationship, would not support this because the current design limits any specific item to one and only one category. When you insert a row into the `tblItems` table to describe the new CD-sofa, you can assign the Furniture code to the foreign key `itemCategory`, or you can assign the Electronics code, but not both.

If you want to assign the new CD-sofa to both categories (Furniture and Electronics), you have to change the design of the table structures and relationships, because there is no longer a one-to-many relationship between the two tables.

Now, there is a **many-to-many relationship**—one in which multiple rows in each table can correspond to multiple rows in the other. That is, in this example, one row in the `tblCategories` table (for example, Furniture) can relate to many rows in the `tblItems` table (for example, sofa and coffee table) *and* one row in the `tblItems` table (for example, the sofa with the built-in CD player) can relate to multiple rows in the `tblCategories` table.

The `tblItems` table contains a foreign key named `itemCategoryId`. If you want to change the application so that one specific row in the `tblItems` table can link to many rows (and, therefore, many `categoryIds`) in the `tblCategories` table, you cannot continue to maintain the foreign key `itemCategoryId` in the `tblItems` table, because one item may be assigned to many categories. You could change the structure of the `tblItems` table so that you can assign multiple `itemCategoryIds` to one specific row in that table, but as you will learn later in this chapter, that approach leads to many problems using the data and, therefore, is not an option.

The simplest way to support a many-to-many relationship between the `tblItems` and `tblCategories` tables is to remove the `itemCategoryId` attribute (what was once the foreign key) from the `tblItems` table, producing:

`tblItems(`<u>`itemNumber`</u>`, itemName, itemPurchaseDate, itemPurchasePrice)`

The `tblCategories` table structure remains the same. That is:

`tblCategories(`<u>`categoryId`</u>`, categoryName, categoryInsuredAmount)`

With just the preceding two tables, there is no way to know that any specific row(s) in the `tblItems` table link(s) to any specific row(s) in the `tblCategories` table, so you create a new table called `tblItemsCategories` that contains the primary keys from the two tables that you want to link in a many-to-many relationship. This table is depicted as:

`tblItemsCategories(`<u>`itemNumber`</u>`, `<u>`categoryId`</u>`)`

Notice that this new table contains a compound primary key—both `itemNumber` and `categoryId` are underlined. The `itemNumber` value of 1 might be associated with many `categoryIds`. Therefore, `itemNumber` alone cannot be the primary key because the same value may occur in many rows. Similarly, a `categoryId` might relate to many different `itemNumbers`; this would disallow using just the `categoryId` as the primary key. However, a combination of the two attributes `itemNumber` and `categoryId` results in a unique primary key value for each row of the `tblItemsCategories` table.

The purpose of all this is to create a many-to-many relationship between the `tblItems` and `tblCategories` tables. The `tblItemsCategories` table contains two attributes; together, these attributes are the primary key. In addition, each of these attributes separately is a foreign key to one of the two original tables. The `itemNumber` attribute in the `tblItemsCategories` table is a foreign key that links to the primary key of the `tblItems` table. The `categoryId` attribute in the `tblItemsCategories` table links to the primary key of the `tblCategories` table. Now, there is a one-to-many relationship between the `tblItems` table (the "one," or base table) and the `tblItemsCategories` table (the "many," or related table) and a one-to-many relationship between the `tblCategories` table (the "one," or base table) and the `tblItemsCategories` table (the "many," or related table). This in effect implies a many-to-many relationship between the two base tables (`tblItems` and `tblCategories`).

Figure 16-8 shows the new tables holding a few items. The sofa (`itemNumber` 1) in the `tblItems` table is associated with the Furniture category (`categoryId` 5) in the `tblCategories` table because the first row of the `tblItemsCategories` table contains a 1 and a 5. Similarly, the stereo (`itemNumber` 2) in the `tblItems` table is associated with the Electronics category (`categoryId` 6) in the `tblCategories` table because in the `tblItemsCategories` table there is a row containing the values 2, 6.

FIGURE 16-8: SAMPLE ITEMS, CATEGORIES, AND ITEMCATEGORIES

tblItems

itemNumber	itemName	itemPurchaseDate	itemPurchasePrice
1	Sofa	1/13/2001	$6500
2	Stereo	2/10/2003	$1200
3	Sofa with CD player	5/24/2005	$8500
4	Table with DVD player	6/24/2005	$12000
5	Granpa's pocket watch	12/24/1927	$100

tblItemsCategories

itemNumber	categoryId
1	5
2	6
3	5
3	6
4	5
4	6
5	2
5	3

tblCategories

categoryId	categoryName	categoryInsuredAmount
1	Appliance	$30,000
2	Jewelry	$15,000
3	Antique	$10,000
4	Clothing	$25,000
5	Furniture	$5,000
6	Electronics	$2,500
7	Miscellaneous	$5,000

The fancy sofa with the built-in CD player (`itemNumber` 3 in the `tblItems` table) occurs in two rows in the `tblItemsCategories` table, once with a `categoryId` of 5 (Furniture) and once with a `categoryId` of 6 (Electronics). Similarly, the table with the DVD player and Grandpa's pocket watch both belong to multiple categories. It is the `tblItemsCategories` table, then, that allows the establishment of a many-to-many relationship between the two base tables, `tblItems` and `tblCategories`.

UNDERSTANDING ONE-TO-ONE RELATIONSHIPS

In a **one-to-one relationship**, a row in one table corresponds to exactly one row in another table. This type of relationship is easy to understand, but is the least frequently encountered. When one row in a table corresponds to a row in another table, the columns could be combined into a single table. A common reason you create a one-to-one relationship is security. For example, Figure 16-9 shows two tables, `tblEmployees` and `tblSalaries`. Each employee in the `tblEmployees` table has exactly one salary in the `tblSalaries` table. The salaries could have been added to the `tblEmployees` table as an additional column; the salaries are separate only because you want some clerical workers to be allowed to view only names, addresses, and other nonsensitive data, so you give them permission to access only the `tblEmployees` table. Others, who work in payroll or administration, can create queries that allow them to view joined tables that include the salary information.

TIP ▫ ▫ ▫ ▫ | Another reason to create tables with one-to-one relationships is to avoid lots of empty columns, or **nulls**, if a certain subset of columns is applicable only to specific types of rows in the main table.

FIGURE 16-9: SAMPLE EMPLOYEES AND SALARIES

tblEmployees

empId	empLast	empFirst	empDept	empHireDate
101	Parker	Laura	3	4/07/1998
102	Walters	David	4	1/19/1999
103	Shannon	Ewa	3	2/28/2003

tblSalaries

empId	empSalary
101	42,500
102	28,800
103	36,000

TIP ▫ ▫ ▫ ▫ | You learn more about security issues later in this chapter.

RECOGNIZING POOR TABLE DESIGN

As you create database tables that will hold the data an organization needs, you will encounter many occasions when the table design, or structure, is inadequate to support the needs of the application. In other words, even if a table contains all the attributes required by a specific application, the structural design of the table may make the application cumbersome to use (you will see examples of this later) and prone to data errors.

For example, assume that you have been hired by an Internet-based college to design a database to keep track of its students. After meeting with the college administrators, you determine that you need to know the following information:

- Students' names
- Students' addresses
- Students' cities
- Students' states

■ Students' ZIP codes

■ ID numbers for classes in which students are enrolled

■ Titles for classes in which students are enrolled

TIP ▫ ▫ ▫ ▫ | Of course, in a real-life example you could probably think of many other data requirements for the college, in addition to those listed here. The number of attributes is small here for simplicity.

Figure 16-10 contains the Students table. Assume that because the Internet-based college is new, only three students have already enrolled. Besides the columns you identified as being necessary, notice the addition of the `studentId` attribute. Given the earlier discussions, you probably recognize that this is the best choice to use as a primary key, because many students can have the same names and even addresses. Although the table in Figure 16-10 contains a column for each of the data requirements decided upon with the college administration, the table is poorly designed and will create many problems for the users of the database.

FIGURE 16-10: STUDENTS TABLE BEFORE NORMALIZATION PROCESS

studentId	name	address	city	state	zip	class	classTitle
1	Rodriguez	123 Oak	Schaumburg	IL	60193	CIS101	Computer Literacy
						PHI150	Ethics
						BIO200	Genetics
2	Jones	234 Elm	Wild Rose	WI	54984	CHM100	Chemistry
						MTH200	Calculus
3	Mason	456 Pine	Dubuque	IA	52004	HIS202	World History

What if a college administrator wanted to view a list of courses the Internet-based college offers? Can you answer that question by reviewing the table? Well, you can see six courses listed for the three students, so you can assume that at least six courses are offered. But, is it possible that there is also a Psychology course, or a class whose code is CIS102? You can't determine this from the table because no students have enrolled in those classes. Wouldn't it be nice to know all the classes that are offered by your institution, regardless of whether any students have enrolled in them?

Consider another potential problem: What if student Mason withdraws from the school, and, therefore, his row is deleted from the table? You would lose some valuable information that really has nothing to do specifically with student Mason, but that is very important for running the college. For instance, if Mason's row is deleted from the table, you no longer know, from the remaining data in the table, whether the college offers any History classes, because Mason was the only student enrolled in the HIS202 class.

Why is it so important to discuss the deficiencies of the existing table structure? You have probably heard the saying, "Pay me now or pay me later." This is especially true as it relates to table design. If you do not take the time to ensure well-designed table structures when you are initially designing your database, then you (or the users of your database) will surely spend lots of time later fixing data errors, typing the same information multiple times, and being frustrated by the inability to cull important subsets of information from the database. If you were really hired to create this database and this table structure was your solution to the college's needs, then it is unlikely you would be hired for future database projects.

UNDERSTANDING ANOMALIES, NORMAL FORMS, AND THE NORMALIZATION PROCESS

Database management programs can maintain all the relationships you need. As you add records to, delete records from, and modify records within your database tables, the software keeps track of all the relationships you have established, so that you can view any needed joins any time you want. The software, however, can only maintain useful relationships if you have planned ahead to create a set of tables that supports all the applications you will need. The process of designing and creating a set of database tables that satisfies the users' needs and avoids many potential problems is **normalization**.

The normalization process helps you reduce data redundancies and anomalies. **Data redundancy** is the unnecessary repetition of data. An **anomaly** is an irregularity in a database's design that causes problems and inconveniences. Three common types of anomalies are:

- Update anomalies
- Delete anomalies
- Insert anomalies

If you look ahead to the college database table in Figure 16-11, you will see an example of an **update anomaly**, or a problem that occurs when the data in the table need to be altered. Because the table contains redundant data, if student Rodriguez moves to a new residence, you have to change the values stored as `address`, `city`, `state`, and `zip` in more than one location. Of course, this table example is small; imagine if additional data were stored about Rodriguez, such as birth date, e-mail address, major field of study, previous schools attended, and so on.

The database table in Figure 16-10 contains a **delete anomaly**, or a problem that occurs when a row is deleted. If student Jones withdraws from the college, and his entries are deleted from the table, important data regarding the classes CHM100 and MTH200 are lost.

With an **insert anomaly**, problems occur when new rows are added to a table. In the table in Figure 16-10, if a new student named Ramone has enrolled in the college, but has not yet registered for any specific classes, then you can't insert a complete row for student Ramone; the only way to do so would be to "invent" at least one phony class for him. It would certainly be valuable to the college to be able to maintain data on all enrolled students regardless of whether those students have registered for specific classes—for example, the college might want to send catalogs and registration information to these students.

When you normalize a database table, you walk through a series of steps that allows you to remove redundancies and anomalies. The normalization process involves altering a table so that it satisfies one or more of three **normal forms**, or rules, for constructing a well-designed database. The three normal forms are:

- **First normal form**, also known as **1NF**, in which you eliminate repeating groups
- **Second normal form**, also known as **2NF**, in which you eliminate partial key dependencies
- **Third normal form**, also known as **3NF**, in which you eliminate transitive dependencies

Each normal form is structurally better than the one preceding it.

TIP ☐ ☐ ☐ ☐ In a 1970 paper titled, "A Relational Model of Data for Large Shared Data Banks," Dr. E. F. Codd listed seven normal forms. For business applications, 3NF is usually sufficient, and so only 1NF through 3NF are discussed in this chapter.

FIRST NORMAL FORM

A table that contains repeating groups is **unnormalized**. A **repeating group** is a subset of rows in a database table that all depend on the same key. A table in 1NF contains no repeating groups of data.

The table in Figure 16-10 violates this 1NF rule. The `class` and `classTitle` attributes repeat multiple times for some of the students. For example, student Rodriguez is taking three classes; her `class` attribute contains a repeating group. To remedy this situation, and to transform the table to 1NF, you simply repeat the rows for each repeating group of data. Figure 16-11 contains the revised table.

FIGURE 16-11: STUDENTS TABLE IN 1NF

studentId	name	address	city	state	zip	class	classTitle
1	Rodriguez	123 Oak	Schaumburg	IL	60193	CIS101	Computer Literacy
1	Rodriguez	123 Oak	Schaumburg	IL	60193	PHI150	Ethics
1	Rodriguez	123 Oak	Schaumburg	IL	60193	BIO200	Genetics
2	Jones	234 Elm	Wild Rose	WI	54984	CHM100	Chemistry
2	Jones	234 Elm	Wild Rose	WI	54984	MTH200	Calculus
3	Mason	456 Pine	Dubuque	IA	52004	HIS202	World History

The repeating groups have been eliminated from the table in Figure 16-11. However, as you look at the table, you will notice a problem—the primary key, `studentId`, is no longer unique for each row in the table. For example, the table in Figure 16-11 now contains three rows with `studentId` 1. You can fix this problem, and create a primary key, by simply adding the `class` attribute to the primary key, creating a compound key. The table's key, then, becomes a combination of `studentId` and `class`. By knowing the `studentId` *and* the `class`, you can identify one, and only one, row in the table—for example, a combination of `studentId` 1 and `class` BIO200 identifies a single row. Using the notation discussed earlier in this chapter, the table in Figure 16-11 can be described as:

tblStudents(<u>studentId</u>, name, address, city, state, zip, <u>class</u>, classTitle)

Both the `studentId` and `class` attributes are underlined, showing that they are both part of the key.

TIP ☐ ☐ ☐ ☐ When you combine two columns to create a compound key, you are **concatenating the columns**.

The table in Figure 16-11 is now in 1NF because there are no repeating groups and the primary key attributes are defined. Satisfying the "no repeating groups" condition is also called making the columns **atomic**; that is, making them as small as possible, containing an undividable piece of data. In 1NF, all values for an intersection of a row and column must be atomic. Recall the table in Figure 16-10 in which the `class` attribute for `studentId` 1 (Rodriguez) contained three entries: CIS101, PHI150, and BIO200. This violated the 1NF atomicity rule because these three classes represented a set of values rather than one specific value. The table in Figure 16-11 does not repeat this problem because, for each row in the table, the `class` attribute contains one and only one value. The same is true for the other attributes that were part of the repeating group.

Now, think back to the earlier discussion about why we want to normalize tables in the first place. Look at Figure 16-11. Are there still redundancies? Are there still anomalies? Yes to both questions. Recall that you want to have your tables at 3NF before actually defining them to the database. Currently, the table in Figure 16-11 is only in 1NF.

In Figure 16-11, notice that Student 1, Rodriguez, is taking three classes. If you were the college employee who was responsible for typing the data into this table, would you want to type this student's name, address, city, state, and zip for each of the three classes Rodriguez is taking? It is very probable that you may, for one of her classes, type her name as "Rodrigues" instead of "Rodriguez." Or, you might misspell the city of "Schaumburg" as "Schamburg" for one of Rodriguez's classes. A college administrator looking at the table might not know whether Rodriguez's correct city of residence is Schaumburg or Schamburg. If you queried the database to select or count the number of classes being taken by students residing in "Schaumburg," one of Rodriguez's classes would be missed.

TIP □ □ □ □ | Misspelling the student name "Rodriguez" is an example of a data integrity error. You learn more about this type of error later in this chapter.

Consider the student Jones who is taking two classes. If Jones changes his residence, how many times will you need to retype his new `address`, `state`, `city`, and `zip`? What if Jones is taking six classes?

SECOND NORMAL FORM

To improve the design of the table and bring the table in Figure 16-11 to 2NF, you need to eliminate all **partial key dependencies**; that is, no column should depend on only part of the key. Restated, this means that for a table to be in 2NF, it must be in 1NF and all non-key attributes must be dependent on the entire primary key.

In the table in Figure 16-11, the key is a combination of `studentId` and `class`. Consider the `name` attribute. Does the name "Rodriguez" depend on the entire primary key? In other words, do you need to know that the `studentId` is 1 *and* that the class is CIS101 to determine that the name is "Rodriguez"? No, it is sufficient to know that the `studentId` is 1 to know that the name is "Rodriguez." Therefore, the `name` attribute is only partially dependent on the primary key, and so, the table violates 2NF. The same is true for the other attributes of `address`, `city`, `state`, and `zip`. If you know, for example, that the `studentId` is 3, then you also know that the student's `city` is "Dubuque"; you do not need to know any `class` codes.

Similarly, examine the `classTitle` attribute in the first row in the table in Figure 16-11. This attribute has a value of "Computer Literacy." In this case, you do not need to know both the `studentId` and the `class` to predict the `classTitle` "Computer Literacy." Rather, just the `class` attribute, which is only part of the compound key, is required. Looked at in another way, `class` "PHI150" will always have the associated `classTitle` "Introduction to Philosophy" regardless of the particular students who are taking that class. So, `classTitle` represents a partial key dependency.

You bring a table into 2NF by eliminating the partial key dependencies. To accomplish this, you can create multiple tables so that each non-key attribute of each table is dependent on the *entire* primary key for the specific table within which the attribute occurs. If the resulting tables are still in 1NF and there are no partial key dependencies, then those tables will also be in 2NF.

Figure 16-12 contains three tables: `tblStudents`, `tblClasses`, and `tblStudentClasses`. To create the `tblStudents` table, you simply take those attributes from the original table that depend on the `studentId` attribute, and group them into a new table; `name`, `address`, `city`, `state`, and `zip` all can be determined by the `studentId` alone. The primary key to the `tblStudents` table is `studentId`. Similarly, you can create the `tblClasses` table by simply grouping the attributes from the 1NF table that depend on the `class` attribute. In this application, only one attribute from the original table, the `classTitle` attribute, depends on the `class` attribute. The first two Figure 16-12 tables can be notated as:

```
tblStudents(studentId, name, address, city, state, zip)
tblClasses(class, className)
```

FIGURE 16-12: STUDENTS TABLE IN 2NF

tblStudents

studentId	name	address	city	state	zip
1	Rodriguez	123 Oak	Schaumburg	IL	60193
2	Jones	234 Elm	Wild Rose	WI	54984
3	Mason	456 Pine	Dubuque	IA	52004

tblClasses

class	classTitle
CIS101	Computer Literacy
PHI150	Ethics
BIO200	Genetics
CHM100	Chemistry
MTH200	Calculus
HIS202	World History

tblStudentClasses

studentId	class
1	CIS101
1	PHI150
1	BIO200
2	CHM100
2	MTH200
3	HIS202

The `tblStudents` and `tblClasses` tables contain all the attributes from the original table. Remember the prior redundancies and anomalies. Several improvements have occurred:

- You have eliminated the update anomalies. The name "Rodriguez" occurs just once in the `tblStudents` table. The same is true for Rodriguez's `address`, `city`, `state`, and `zip`. The original table contained three rows for student Rodriguez. By eliminating the redundancies, you have fewer anomalies. If Rodriguez changes her residence, you only need to update one row in the `tblStudents` table.

- You have eliminated the insert anomalies. With the new configuration, you can insert a complete row into the `tblStudents` table even if the student has not yet enrolled in any classes. Similarly, you can add a complete row for a new class offering to the `tblClasses` table even though no students are currently taking it.

- You have eliminated the delete anomalies. Recall from the original table that student Mason was the only student taking HIS202. This caused a delete anomaly because the HIS202 class would disappear if student Mason was removed. Now, if you delete Mason from the `tblStudents` table in Figure 16-12, the HIS202 class remains in the `tblClasses` list.

If you create the first two tables shown in Figure 16-12, you have eliminated many of the problems associated with the original version. However, if you have those two tables alone, you have lost some important information that you originally had while at 1NF—specifically, which students are taking which classes. Or, alternately, which classes are being taken by which students. When breaking up a table into multiple tables, you need to consider the type of relationship among the resulting tables—you are designing a *relational* database, after all.

You know that the Internet-based college application requires that you keep track of which students are taking which classes. This implies a relationship between the `tblStudents` and `tblClasses` tables. Your job is to determine what type of relationship exists between the two tables. Recall from earlier in the chapter that the two most common types of relationships are one-to-many and many-to-many. This specific application requires that one specific student can enroll in many different classes, and that one specific class can be taken by many different students. Therefore, there is a many-to-many relationship between the tables `tblStudents` and `tblClasses`.

As you learned in the earlier example of categorizing insured items, you create a many-to-many relationship between two tables by creating a third table that contains the primary keys from the two tables that you want to relate. In this case, you create the `tblStudentClasses` table in Figure 16-12 as:

$$tblStudentClasses(\underline{studentId}, \underline{class})$$

If you examine the rows in the `tblStudentClasses` table, you can see that the student with `studentId` 1, Rodriguez, is enrolled in three classes; `studentId` 2, Jones, is taking two classes; and `studentId` 3, Mason, is enrolled in only one class. Finally, the table requirements for the Internet-based college have been fulfilled.

Or have they? Earlier, you saw the many redundancies and anomalies that were eliminated by structuring the tables into 2NF, and it is certainly true that the 2NF table structures result in a much "better" database application than the 1NF structures. But look again at the Figure 16-12 `tblStudents` table. What if, as the college expands, you need to add 50 new students to this table, and all of the new students reside in Schaumburg, IL? If you were the data-entry person, would you want to type the city of "Schaumburg", the state of "IL", and the ZIP code of "60193" fifty times? This data is redundant, and you can improve the design of the tables to eliminate this redundancy.

THIRD NORMAL FORM

3NF requires that a table be in 2NF and that it have no transitive dependencies. A **transitive dependency** occurs when the value of a non-key attribute determines, or predicts, the value of another non-key attribute. Clearly, the `studentId` attribute of the Figure 16-12 `tblStudents` table is a determinant—if you know a particular `studentId` value, you can also know that student's `name`, `address`, `city`, `state`, and `zip`. But this is not considered a transitive dependency because the `studentId` attribute is the primary key for the `tblStudents` table, and, after all, the primary key's job is to determine the values of the other attributes in the row.

There is a problem, however, if a non-key attribute determines another non-key attribute. In the Figure 16-12 `tblStudents` table, there are five non-key attributes: `name`, `address`, `city`, `state`, and `zip`.

The `name` is a non-key attribute. If you know the value of `name` is "Rodriguez", do you also know the one specific address where Rodriguez resides? In other words, is this a transitive dependency? No, it isn't. Even though only one student is named "Rodriguez" now, there may be many more in the future. So, though it may be tempting to consider that the `name` attribute is a determinant of `address`, it isn't. Looked at another way, if your boss said, "Look at the `tblStudents` table and tell me Jones' address," you wouldn't be able to do so if you had ten students named "Jones".

The `address` attribute is a non-key attribute. Does it predict anything? If you know the value of an address is "20 N. Main Street", can you, for instance, determine the name of the student who is associated with that address? No, because in the future, you might have many students who live at "20 N. Main Street," but they might live in different cities, or you might have two students who live at the same address in the same city. Therefore, `address` does not cause a transitive dependency.

Similarly, the `city` and `state` attributes are not keys, but they also are not determinants because knowing their values alone is not sufficient to predict another non-key attribute value. You might argue that if you know a city's name, you know the state, but many states contain cities named, for example, Union or Springfield.

But what about the non-key attribute `zip`? If you know, for example, that the ZIP code is 60193, can you determine the value of any other non-key attributes? Yes, a ZIP code of 60193 indicates that the `city` is Schaumburg and the `state` is IL. This is the "culprit" that is causing the redundancies with regard to the `city` and `state` attributes. The attribute `zip` is a determinant because it determines `city` and `state`; therefore, the `tblStudents` table contains a transitive dependency and is not in 3NF.

To convert the `tblStudents` table to 3NF, simply remove the attributes that depend upon, or are **functionally dependent** on, the `zip` attribute. For example, if attribute `zip` determines attribute `city`, then attribute `city` is considered to be functionally dependent on attribute `zip`. So, as Figure 16-13 shows, the new `tblStudents` table is defined as:

> tblStudents(<u>studentId</u>, name, address, zip)

TIP □ □ □ □ | A functionally dependent relationship is sometimes written using an arrow that extends from the depended-upon attribute to the dependent attribute, for example `zip → city`.

FIGURE 16-13: THE COMPLETE STUDENTS DATABASE

tblStudents

studentId	name	address	zip
1	Rodriguez	123 Oak	60193
2	Jones	234 Elm	54984
3	Mason	456 Pine	52004

tblZips

zip	city	state
60193	Schaumburg	IL
54984	Wild Rose	WI
52004	Dubuque	IA

tblClasses

class	classTitle
CIS101	Computer Literacy
PHI150	Ethics
BIO200	Genetics
CHM100	Chemistry
MTH200	Calculus
HIS202	World History

tblStudentClasses

studentId	class
1	CIS101
1	PHI150
1	BIO200
2	CHM100
2	MTH200
3	HIS202

Figure 16-13 also shows the `tblZips` table, which is defined as:

```
tblZips(zip, city, state)
```

The new `tblZips` table is related to the `tblStudents` table by the `zip` attribute. Using the two tables together, you can determine, for example, that `studentId` 3, Mason, in the `tblStudents` table resides in the city of Dubuque and the state of IA, attributes stored in the `tblZips` table. When you encounter a table with a functional dependence, you almost always can reduce data redundancy by creating two tables, as in Figure 16-13. With the new configuration, a data-entry operator must still type a ZIP code for each student, but the drudgery of typing and the possibility of introducing data-entry errors in city and state names for each student are eliminated.

Is the students-to-ZIP-codes relationship a one-to-many relationship, a many-to-many relationship, or a one-to-one relationship? You know that one row in the `tblZips` table can relate to many rows in the `tblStudents` table—that is, many students can reside in ZIP 60193. However, the opposite is not true—one row in the `tblStudents` table (a particular student) cannot relate to many rows in the `tblZips` table, because a particular student can only reside in one `zip`. Therefore, there is a one-to-many relationship between the base table, `tblZips`, and the related table `tblStudents`. The link to the relationship is the `zip` attribute, which is a primary key in the `tblZips` table and a foreign key in the `tblStudents` table.

This was a lot of work, but it was worth it. The tables are in 3NF, and the redundancies and anomalies that would have contributed to an unwieldy, error-prone, inefficient database design have been eliminated.

Recall that the definition of 3NF is 2NF plus no transitive dependencies. What if you were considering changing the structure of the `tblStudents` table by adding an attribute to hold the student's Social Security number (`ssn`)? If you know a specific `ssn` value, you also know a particular student name, address, and so on; in other words, a specific value for `ssn` determines one and only one row in the `tblStudents` table. No two students have the same Social Security numbers (ruling out identity theft, of course). However, `studentId` is the primary key; `ssn` is a non-key determinant, which, by definition, seems to violate the requirements of 3NF. However, if you add `ssn` to the `tblStudents` table, the table is still in 3NF because a determinant is allowed in 3NF if the determinant is also a candidate key. Recall that a candidate key is an attribute that could qualify as the primary key but has not been used as the primary key. In the example concerning the `zip` attribute of the `tblStudents` table (Figure 16-11), `zip` was a determinant of the `city` and `state` attributes. Therefore, the `tblStudents` table was not in 3NF because many rows in the `tblStudents` table can have the same value for `zip`, meaning `zip` is not a candidate key. The situation with the `ssn` column is different because `ssn` could be used as a primary key for the `tblStudents` table.

TIP □ □ □ □ | In general, you try to create a database in the highest normal form. However, when data items are stored in multiple tables, it takes longer to access related information than when it is all stored in a single table. So, sometimes, for performance, you might **denormalize** a table, or reduce it to a lower normal form, by placing some repeated information back into the table. Deciding on the best form in which to store a body of data is a sophisticated art.

In summary:

- A table is in first normal form when there are no repeating groups.
- A table is in second normal form if it is in first normal form and no non-key column depends on just part of the primary key.
- A table is in third normal form if it is in second normal form and the only determinants are candidate keys.

TIP ▫ ▫ ▫ ▫ | Not every table starts out denormalized. For example, a table might already be in third normal form when you first encounter it. On the other hand, a table might not be normalized, but after you put it in 1NF, you may find that it also satisfies the requirements for 2NF and 3NF.

DATABASE PERFORMANCE AND SECURITY ISSUES

Frequently, a company's database is its most valuable resource. If buildings, equipment, or inventory are damaged or destroyed, they can be rebuilt or re-created. However, the information contained in a database is often irreplaceable. A company that has spent years building valuable customer profiles cannot re-create them at the drop of a hat; a company that loses billing or shipment information might not simply lose the current orders, it might also lose the affected customers forever as they defect to competitors who can serve them more accurately. Keeping an organization's data secure is often the most economically valuable responsibility in the company.

You can study entire books to learn all the details involved in data security. The major issues include:

- Providing data integrity
- Recovering lost data
- Avoiding concurrent update problems
- Providing authentication and permissions
- Providing encryption

PROVIDING DATA INTEGRITY

Database software provides the means to ensure that data integrity is enforced; a database has **data integrity** when it follows a set of rules that make the data accurate and consistent. For example, you might indicate that a quantity in an inventory record can never be negative, or that a price can never be higher than a predetermined value. In addition, you can enforce integrity between tables; for example, you might prohibit entering an insurance plan code for an employee if the insurance plan code is not one of the types offered by the organization.

RECOVERING LOST DATA

An organization's data can be destroyed in many ways—legitimate users can make mistakes, hackers or other malicious users can enter invalid data, and hardware problems can wipe out records or entire databases. Recovery is the process of returning the database to a correct form that existed before an error occurred.

Periodically making a backup copy of a database and keeping a record of every transaction together provide one of the simplest approaches to recovery. When an error occurs, you can replace the database with an error-free version that was saved at the last backup. Usually, there have also been changes to the database, called transactions, since the last backup; if so, you must then reapply those transactions.

TIP ▫ ▫ ▫ ▫ | Many organizations keep a copy of their data off-site so that if a disaster such as a fire or flood destroys data, the remotely stored copy can serve as a backup.

AVOIDING CONCURRENT UPDATE PROBLEMS

Large databases are accessible by many users at a time. The database is stored on a central computer, and users work at terminals in diverse locations. For example, several order takers might be able to update customer and inventory tables concurrently. A **concurrent update problem** occurs when two database users need to make changes to the same record at the same time. Suppose two order processors take a phone order for item number 101 in an inventory file. Each gets a copy of the quantity in stock, for example 25, loaded into the memory of her terminal. Each accepts her customer's order, and subtracts 1 from inventory. Now, in each local terminal, the quantity is 24. One order gets written to the central database, then the other, and the final inventory is 24, not 23 as it should be.

Several approaches can be used to avoid this problem. With one approach, a lock can be placed on one record the moment it is accessed. While one order taker makes a change, the other cannot access the record. Potentially, a customer on the phone with the second order taker could be inconvenienced while the first order taker maintains the lock, but the data in the inventory table would remain accurate.

Another approach to preventing the concurrent update problem is to not allow the users to update the original database at all, but to have them store transactions, which then can be applied to the database all at once, or in a batch, at a later time—perhaps once or twice a day or after business hours. The problem with this approach is that as soon as the first transaction occurs and until the batch processing takes place, the original database is out-of-date. For example, if several order takers place orders for the same item, the item might actually be out of stock. However, none of the order takers will realize the item is unavailable because the database will not reflect the orders until it is updated with the current batch of transactions.

PROVIDING AUTHENTICATION AND PERMISSIONS

Most database software can authenticate that those who are attempting to access an organization's data are legitimate users. **Authentication techniques** include storing and verifying passwords or even using physical characteristics such as fingerprints or voice recognition before users can view data. When a user is authenticated, the user typically receives authorization to all or part of the database. The **permissions** assigned to a user indicate which parts of the database the user can view, and which parts he or she can change or delete. For example, an order taker might not be allowed to view or update personnel data, whereas a clerk in the personnel office might not be allowed to alter inventory data.

PROVIDING ENCRYPTION

Database software can be used to encrypt data. **Encryption** is the process of coding data into a format that human beings cannot read. If unauthorized users gain access to database files, the data will be in a coded format that is useless to them. Only authorized users see the data in a readable format.

CHAPTER SUMMARY

☐ A database holds a group of files that an organization needs to support its applications. In a database, the files often are called tables because you can arrange their contents in rows and columns. A field or column that uniquely identifies a record is called a key field, or a key for short. Database management software is a set of programs that allows users to create table descriptions; identify key fields; add records to, delete records from, and update records within a table; organize the records within a table into different sorted orders; write questions that select specific records from a table for viewing; write questions that combine information from multiple tables; create reports and forms; and keep data secure by employing sophisticated security measures.

☐ Creating a useful database requires a lot of planning and analysis. You must decide what data will be stored, how that data will be divided between tables, and how the tables will interrelate.

☐ In most tables you create for a database, you want to identify a column, or possibly a combination of columns, as the table's key column or field, also called the primary key. The primary key is important because you can configure your software to prevent multiple records from containing the same value in this column, thus avoiding data-entry errors. In addition, you can sort your records in primary key order before displaying or printing them, and you need to use this column when setting up relationships between the table and others that will become part of the same database.

☐ A shorthand way to describe a table is to use the table name followed by parentheses containing all the field names, with the primary key underlined.

☐ Entering data into an already created table requires a good deal of time and accurate typing. Depending on the application, the contents of the tables might be entered over the course of many months or years by any number of data-entry personnel. Deleting records from and modifying records within a database table are relatively easy tasks. In most organizations, most of the important data are in a constant state of change.

☐ Database management software generally allows you to sort a table based on any column, letting you view your data in the way that is most useful to you. After rows are sorted, they also usually can be grouped.

☐ Frequently, you want to cull subsets of data from a table you have created. The questions that cause the database software to extract the appropriate records from a table and specify the fields to be viewed are called queries. Depending on the software you use, you might create a query by filling in blanks, a process called query by example, or by writing statements similar to those in many programming languages. The most common language that database administrators use to access data in their tables is Structured Query Language, or SQL.

☐ Most database applications require many tables, and these applications also require that the tables be related. The three types of relationships are one-to-many, many-to-many, and one-to-one.

□ As you create database tables that will hold the data an organization needs, you will encounter many situations in which the table design, or structure, is inadequate to support the needs of the application.

□ The process of designing and creating a set of database tables that satisfies the users' needs and avoids many potential problems is normalization. The normalization process helps you reduce data redundancies, update anomalies, delete anomalies, and insert anomalies. The normalization process involves altering a table so that it satisfies one or more of three normal forms, or rules, for constructing a well-designed database. The three normal forms are first normal form, also known as 1NF, in which you eliminate repeating groups; second normal form, also known as 2NF, in which you eliminate partial key dependencies; and third normal form, also known as 3NF, in which you eliminate transitive dependencies.

□ Frequently, a company's database is its most valuable resource. Major security issues include providing data integrity, recovering lost data, avoiding concurrent update problems, providing authentication and permissions, and providing encryption.

KEY TERMS

A database holds a group of files, or tables, that an organization needs to support its applications.

A database table contains data in rows and columns.

An entity is one record or row in a database table.

An attribute is one field or column in a database table.

A primary key, or key for short, is a field or column that uniquely identifies a record.

A compound key is a key constructed from multiple columns.

Database management software is a set of programs that allows users to create table descriptions; identify key fields; add records to, delete records from, and update records within a table; organize the records within a table into different sorted orders; write questions that select specific records from a table for viewing; write questions that combine information from multiple tables; create reports and forms; and keep data secure by employing sophisticated security measures.

A relational database contains a group of tables from which you can make connections to produce virtual tables.

Candidate keys are columns or attributes that could serve as a primary key in a table.

After you choose a primary key from among candidate keys, the remaining candidate keys become alternate keys.

A query is a question asked using syntax that the database software can understand. Its purpose is often to display a subset of data.

Query by example is the process of creating a query by filling in blanks.

Structured Query Language, or SQL, is a commonly used language for accessing data in database tables.

The SELECT-FROM-WHERE SQL statement is the command that selects the fields you want to view from a specific table where one or more conditions are met.

A relationship is a connection between two tables.

A join operation, or a join, connects two tables based on the values in a common column.

A join column is the column on which two tables are connected.

A one-to-many relationship is one in which one row in a table can be related to many rows in another table. It is the most common type of relationship among tables.

The base table in a one-to-many relationship is the "one" table.

The related table in a one-to-many relationship is the "many" table.

A non-key attribute is any column in a table that is not a key.

A foreign key is a column that is not a key in a table, but contains an attribute that is a key in a related table.

A many-to-many relationship is one in which multiple rows in each of two tables can correspond to multiple rows in the other.

In a one-to-one relationship, a row in one table corresponds to exactly one row in another table.

Nulls are empty columns.

Normalization is the process of designing and creating a set of database tables that satisfies the users' needs and avoids redundancies and anomalies.

Data redundancy is the unnecessary repetition of data.

An anomaly is an irregularity in a database's design that causes problems and inconveniences.

An update anomaly is a problem that occurs when the data in the table need to be altered; the result is repeated data.

A delete anomaly is a problem that occurs when a row in a table is deleted; the result is loss of related data.

An insert anomaly is a problem that occurs when new rows are added to a table; the result is incomplete rows.

Normal forms are rules for constructing a well-designed database.

First normal form, also known as 1NF, is the normalization form in which you eliminate repeating groups.

Second normal form, also known as 2NF, is the normalization form in which you eliminate partial key dependencies.

Third normal form, also known as 3NF, is the normalization form in which you eliminate transitive dependencies.

An unnormalized table contains repeating groups.

A repeating group is a subset of rows in a database table that all depend on the same key.

To concatenate columns is to combine columns to produce a compound key.

Atomic attributes or columns are as small as possible so as to contain an undividable piece of data.

A partial key dependency occurs when a column in a table depends on only part of the table's key.

A transitive dependency occurs when the value of a non-key attribute determines, or predicts, the value of another non-key attribute.

An attribute is functionally dependent on another if it can be determined by the other attribute.

You might denormalize a table, or place it in a lower normal form, by placing some repeated information back into it.

A database has data integrity when it follows a set of rules that makes the data accurate and consistent.

A concurrent update problem occurs when two database users need to make changes to the same record at the same time.

Authentication techniques include storing and verifying passwords or even using physical characteristics such as fingerprints or voice recognition before users can view data.

The permissions assigned to a user indicate which parts of the database the user can view, and which parts he or she can change or delete.

Encryption is the process of coding data into a format that human beings cannot read.

REVIEW QUESTIONS

1. A field or column that uniquely identifies a row in a database table is a(n) _____.

   a. variable
   b. identifier
   c. principal
   d. key

2. Which of the following is *not* a feature of most database management software?

   a. sorting records in a table
   b. creating reports
   c. preventing poorly designed tables
   d. relating tables

3. Before you can enter any data into a database table, you must do all of the following except _____.

   a. determine the attributes the table will hold
   b. provide names for each attribute
   c. provide data types for each attribute
   d. determine maximum and minimum values for each attribute

4. Which of the following is the best key for a table containing a landlord's rental properties?

   a. numberOfBedrooms
   b. amountOfMonthlyRent
   c. streetAddress
   d. tenantLastName

5. A table's notation is: `tblClients(`<u>`socialSecNum`</u>`, lastName, firstName, clientNumber, balanceDue)`. You know that _____.

    a. the primary key is `socialSecNum`
    b. the primary key is `clientNumber`
    c. there are four candidate keys
    d. there is at least one numeric attribute

6. You can extract subsets of data from database tables using a(n) _____.

    a. query
    b. sort
    c. investigation
    d. subroutine

7. A database table has the structure `tblPhoneOrders(`<u>`orderNum`</u>`, custName, custPhoneNum, itemOrdered, quantity)`. Which SQL statement could be used to extract all attributes for orders for item AB333?

    a. `SELECT * FROM tblPhoneOrders WHERE itemOrdered = "AB3333"`
    b. `SELECT tblPhoneOrders WHERE itemOrdered = "AB3333"`
    c. `SELECT itemOrdered FROM tblPhoneOrders WHERE = "AB3333"`
    d. Two of these are correct.

8. Connecting two database tables based on the value of a column producing a virtual view of a new table is a _____ operation.

    a. merge
    b. concatenate
    c. join
    d. met

9. Heartland Medical Clinic maintains a database to keep track of patients. One table can be described as: `tblPatients(`<u>`patientId`</u>`, name, address, primaryPhysicianCode)`. Another table contains physician codes along with other physician data; it is described as `tblPhysicians(`<u>`physicianCode`</u>`, name, officeNumber, phoneNumber, daysOfWeekInOffice)`. In this example, the relationship is _____.

    a. one-to-one
    b. one-to-many
    c. many-to-many
    d. impossible to determine

10. **Edgerton Insurance Agency sells life, home, health, and auto insurance policies. The agency maintains a database containing a table that holds customer data—each customer's name, address, and types of policies purchased. For example, customer Michael Robertson holds life and auto policies. Another table contains information on each type of policy the agency sells—coverage limits, term, and so on. In this example, the relationship is _____.**

    a. one-to-one
    b. one-to-many
    c. many-to-many
    d. impossible to determine

11. **Kratz Computer Repair maintains a database that contains a table that holds job information about each repair job the company agrees to perform. The jobs table is described as: tblJobs(jobId, dateStarted, customerId, technicianId, feeCharged). Each job has a unique ID number that serves as a key to this table. The customerId and technicianId columns in the table each link to other tables where customer information, such as name, address and phone number, and technician information, such as name, office extension, and hourly rate, are stored. When the tblJobs and tblCustomers tables are joined, which is the base table?**

    a. tblJobs
    b. tblCustomers
    c. tblTechnicians
    d. a combination of two tables

12. **When a column that is not a key in a table contains an attribute that is a key in a related table, the column is called a _____.**

    a. foreign key
    b. merge column
    c. internal key
    d. primary column

13. **The most common reason to construct a one-to-one relationship between two tables is _____.**

    a. to save money
    b. to save time
    c. for security purposes
    d. so that neither table is considered "inferior"

14. **The process of designing and creating a set of database tables that satisfies the users' needs and avoids many potential problems is _____.**

    a. purification
    b. normalization
    c. standardization
    d. structuring

15. **The unnecessary repetition of data is called data _____.**

   a. amplification
   b. echoing
   c. redundancy
   d. mining

16. **Problems with database design are caused by irregularities known as _____.**

   a. glitches
   b. anomalies
   c. bugs
   d. abnormalities

17. **When you place a table into first normal form, you have eliminated _____.**

   a. transitive dependencies
   b. partial key dependencies
   c. repeating groups
   d. all of the above

18. **When you place a table into third normal form, you have eliminated _____.**

   a. transitive dependencies
   b. partial key dependencies
   c. repeating groups
   d. all of the above

19. **If a table contains no repeating groups, but a column depends on part of the table's key, the table is in _____ normal form.**

   a. first
   b. second
   c. third
   d. fourth

20. **Which of the following is not a database security issue?**

   a. providing data integrity
   b. recovering lost data
   c. providing normalization
   d. providing encryption

EXERCISES

1. The Lucky Dog Grooming Parlor maintains data about each of its clients in a table named `tblClients`. Attributes include each dog's name, breed, and owner's name, all of which are text attributes. The only numeric attributes are an ID number assigned to each dog and the balance due on services. The table structure is `tblClients(`<u>`dogID`</u>`, name, breed, owner, balanceDue)`. Write the SQL statement that would select each of the following:

   a. name and owner of all Great Danes
   b. owner of all dogs with balance due over $100
   c. all attributes of dogs named "Fluffy"
   d. all attributes of Poodles whose balance is no greater than $50

2. Consider the following table with the structure `tblRecipes(`<u>`recipeName`</u>`, timeToPrepare, ingredients)`. If necessary, redesign the table so it satisfies each of the following:

   a. 1NF
   b. 2NF
   c. 3NF

recipeName	timeToPrepare	ingredients
Baked lasagna	1 hour	1 pound lasagna ½ pound ground beef 16 ounces tomato sauce ½ pound ricotta cheese ½ pound parmesan cheese 1 onion
Fruit salad	10 minutes	1 apple 1 banana 1 bunch grapes 1 pint blueberries
Marinara sauce	30 minutes	16 ounces tomato sauce ¼ pound parmesan cheese 1 onion

3. Consider the following table with the structure `tblFriends(`<u>`lastName`</u>`, `<u>`firstName`</u>`, address, birthday, phoneNumbers, emailAddresses)`. If necessary, redesign the table so it satisfies each of the following:

   a. 1NF
   b. 2NF
   c. 3NF

lastName	firstName	address	birthday	phoneNumbers	emailAddresses
Gordon	Alicia	34 Second St.	3/16	222-4343 349-0012	agordon@mail.com
Washington	Edward	12 Main St.	12/12	222-7121	ewash@mail.com coolguy@earth.com
Davis	Olivia	55 Birch Ave.	10/3	222-9012 333-8788 834-0112	olivia@abc.com

4. You have created the following table to keep track of your DVD collection. The structure is `tblDVDs(movie, year, stars)`. If necessary, redesign the table so it satisfies each of the following:

   a. 1NF
   b. 2NF
   c. 3NF

movie	year	stars
Jerry McGuire	1996	Tom Cruise Renee Zellweger
Chicago	2002	Renee Zellweger Catherine Zeta-Jones Richard Gere
Risky Business	1983	Tom Cruise Rebecca DeMornay

5. The Midtown Ladies Auxiliary is sponsoring a scholarship for local high-school students. They have constructed a table with the structure `tblScholarshipApplicants(appId, lastName, hsAttended, hsAddress, gpa, honors, clubsActivities)`. The `hsAttended` and `hsAddress` attributes represent high school attended and its street address, respectively. The `gpa` attribute is a grade point average. The `honors` attribute holds awards received, and the `clubsActivities` attribute holds the names of clubs and activities in which the student participated. If necessary, redesign the table so it satisfies each of the following:

   a. 1NF
   b. 2NF
   c. 3NF

appId	lastName	hsAttended	hsAddress	gpa	honors	clubsActivities
1	Wong	Central	1500 Main	3.8	Citizenship award Class officer Soccer MVP	Future teachers Model airplane Newspaper
2	Jefferson	Central	1500 Main	4.0	Valedictorian Citizenship award Homecoming court Football MVP	Pep Yearbook
3	Mitchell	Highland	200 Airport	3.6	Class officer Homecoming court	Pep Future teachers
4	O'Malley	St. Joseph	300 Fourth	4.0	Valedictorian	Pep Chess
5	Abel	Central	1500 Main	3.7	Citizenship award Class officer	Yearbook

6. **Assume you want to create a database to store information about your music collection. You want to be able to query the database for each of the following attributes:**

☐ A particular title (for example, *Tapestry* or Beethoven's Fifth Symphony)

☐ Artist (for example, Carole King or the Chicago Symphony Orchestra)

☐ Format of the recording (for example, CD or tape)

☐ Style of music (for example, rock or classical)

☐ Year recorded

☐ Year acquired as part of your collection

☐ Recording company

☐ Address of the recording company

Design the tables you would need so they are all in third normal form. Create at least five sample data records for each table you create.

7. Design a group of database tables for the St. Charles Riding Academy. The Academy teaches students to ride by starting them on horses that have been ranked as to their manageability, using a numeric score from 1 to 4. The data you need to store includes the following attributes:

☐ Student's last name

☐ Student's first name

☐ Student's address

☐ Student's age

☐ Student's emergency contact information—name and phone number

☐ Student's riding level—1, 2, 3, or 4

☐ Each horse's name

☐ Horse's age

☐ Horse's color

☐ Horse's manageability level—1, 2, 3, or 4

☐ Horse's veterinarian's name

☐ Horse's veterinarian's phone number

Design the tables you would need so they are all in third normal form. Create at least five sample data records for each table you create.

Guide to
Linux Shell Script Programming

Todd Meadors

THOMSON

COURSE TECHNOLOGY

Australia • Canada • Mexico • Singapore • Spain • United Kingdom • United States

1

INTRODUCTION TO THE OPERATING SYSTEM ENVIRONMENT

In this chapter, you will:
- ♦ Understand operating systems
- ♦ Define the Unix and Linux operating systems
- ♦ Understand classifications of software
- ♦ Understand data
- ♦ Understand the user roles
- ♦ Understand basic Linux commands
- ♦ Create shell scripts

The operating system is a set of software instructions that run the computer. When you write shell script programs, you combine Linux operating system commands and programming logic to create automated tasks. In this chapter, you will learn about the major operating systems as well as features specific to the Linux operating system. You will learn about the types of users in a Linux environment, which will help you determine the type of access and type of scripts individuals need. Some of the common basic Linux commands will be discussed. You can use these commands in scripts to make a user's job easier. Finally, to get you started with shell programming, you will create a few shell scripts.

UNDERSTANDING OPERATING SYSTEMS

Software is a set of instructions that are processed by the computer system. The **operating system** is software that governs computer systems. The components in a computer system are the users, the applications, and the hardware. The operating system acts as a liaison between these components. It is the operating system that allows you to save a file to disk, retrieve a file from disk, run a spreadsheet application, print a file, compile a program, point and click with your mouse, enter text commands, or navigate the graphical user interface (GUI). Think of the operating system as the software "brains" of the computer system. Figure 1-1 highlights the relationship between the operating system and the other components in a computer system.

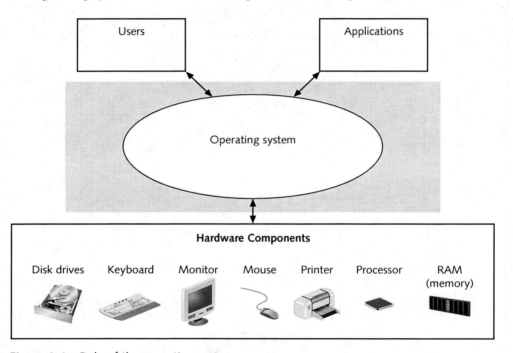

Figure 1-1 Role of the operating system

 The terms "software" and "programs" are synonymous in the computer industry.

There are many different operating systems running many different computer systems both for business and home use. Operating systems run large mainframe computers, server-based networks, PC (personal computer) systems, laptops, and even small handheld devices.

Mainframe operating systems are designed to handle the input/output (I/O), processing, and storage requirements for many users. These operating systems run mainframe computers and are generally used in large corporations. An example of a mainframe operating system is the IBM Multiple Virtual Storage (MVS) system.

Network operating systems allow computers to share resources over a network. A **resource** is a hardware device, a software program, or a file. A printer that can be used by multiple users is an example of a shared resource. In the past a **network** was defined as a group of computers and printers connected by cables. However, with the advent of newer technology, computers and printers can communicate via wireless transmission as well. Network operating systems use **protocol software** to facilitate the communication among computers throughout a network. TCP/IP is the most common protocol used today. **Transmission Control Protocol/Internet Protocol (TCP/IP)** allows you to connect to the Internet and browse Web sites, perform searches, or shop online. Each computer, called a **host**, must have an **IP (Internet Protocol) address** to communicate with other computers on the network. The host may also have a **Domain Name Service (DNS) name** such as Redhat.com. This is sometimes called its "friendly name." The DNS name is used so people won't have to remember the IP address of a host.

In a network, **servers** are computers that allow other computers to connect to the server's shared resources. **Clients** are the computers that use the resources made available by the servers. The **client/server** model is when a server computer handles the requests made by the client computer. There are usually more clients than servers in a network. Because the server has to handle numerous client requests, the server typically has more memory, hard drive space, and processing capability than the clients. Examples of operating systems that run on servers are Novell NetWare, Microsoft Windows NT Server, 2000 Server, and UNIX/Linux. Windows 95, Windows 98, Windows NT Workstation, Windows 2000 Professional, and Windows XP are examples of client operating systems. You can also run UNIX/Linux as a client. Servers and clients must use the same protocol in order to communicate with one another. Even if clients are using different operating systems, the use of a common protocol allows communication to occur. In Figure 1-2, you can see the server and clients in a network environment.

Server computer

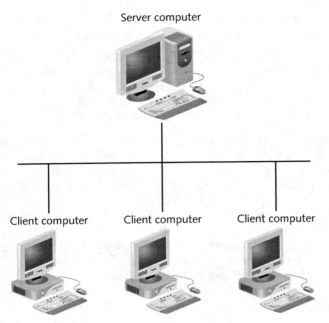

Client computer   Client computer   Client computer

Figure 1-2   Client/server model in a network

DEFINING THE UNIX AND LINUX OPERATING SYSTEMS

The UNIX operating system goes back to the 1960s. Several employees working for AT&T developed an operating system based on the C language and called it UNIX. The initial version was called AT&T System Release V. The operating system code was freely distributed to major universities where changes were made to it. So, unlike proprietary operating systems such as Microsoft Windows, Novell, and IBM, a single vendor has not developed UNIX. There have been numerous versions of the initial operating system, and many vendors have customized UNIX to fit their own platforms. IBM has written a version of UNIX called Advanced Interactive Executive (AIX), Sun has written Solaris, and Hewlett-Packard has written HP-UX, and there are many others. Recently, software vendors who have traditionally developed their own operating systems for their own hardware are beginning to use the Linux operating system.

The Linux operating system was developed from another version of UNIX called MINIX. It comes with many built-in features, a full compliment of programming languages, compilers, and system administration tools, and is available at a very reasonable cost. Table 1-1 shows a listing of some of the versions of the Linux operating system and the associated Web sites for researching them. This book focuses on the Linux operating system.

Table 1-1   Versions of Linux and their Web sites

Version	Web Site
Debian	www.debian.org
OpenLinux	www.calderasystems.com
SuSe	www.suse.com
Slackware	www.slackware.com
Mandrake	www.mandrake.com
Red Hat	www.redhat.com

Let's look at some of the features the Linux operating systems offers. They are as follows:

- Multiuser capability
- Portability
- Multitasking
- Ability to use multiple processors
- Multiple modes of operation

Multiuser Capability

A **multiuser** operating system is one capable of handling multiple requests by a variety of users. Many companies run Linux as their mainstay operating system for their business because it provides a multiple user platform. They can install their applications on a Linux server and have client computers access the application on the server over the network. Some operating systems are single-user platforms (only one user can use the computer), such as Windows 95 and 98.

 A platform comprises both the hardware and software combination on which a given system runs. For example, if Linux version 8.0 is the software running on an Intel-based hardware system, then the two combined are called the platform.

Portability

Portability allows you to carry the Linux operating system to another hardware system, recompile it, and run the operating system. Of course, this is always easier said than done because installing an operating system can be an arduous task. Many operating systems are written for a specific processor. Each processor has its own **instruction set**, which is the set of instructions the processor uses to operate. The instruction sets of different processors are typically not compatible. You can think of an instruction set as being the language specific to the processor.

There are two general types of processors. A **complex instruction set computer (CISC)** has a large set of instructions in its instruction set. A **reduced instruction set computer (RISC)** has a reduced number of instructions in its instruction set but relies on hardware to perform the tasks not provided by the instruction set. Because of the enhanced hardware, a RISC processor is faster, yet more expensive, than a CISC processor. The processor in most PCs is a CISC processor. Windows 98 runs only on CISC-based Intel processors. Red Hat Linux can run on both CISC and RISC processors. The portability of the Linux operating system gives you more hardware options on which to run the operating system because you can choose to run Linux on either type of processor.

Multitasking

Multitasking is when the operating system can handle multiple jobs at seemingly the same time. When a program executes, it is known as a job or process. Technically, the operating system performs only one job at a time. However, through time slicing, the operating system gives each job a little bit of time. The jobs take turns being processed in a round-robin manner. Let's look at an example. Assume the operating system gives each job only one minute of CPU time. If a job exceeds the one-minute time slice, it is sent to the swap file. Then the next job in line begins processing. If this job finishes in less than a minute, then the system can retrieve the next job in the process queue or continue processing the first job that was sent to the swap file. This is done for all jobs until there is no more work to be done. The advantage of this is that one large job lasting 15 minutes or so won't slow down the whole system and keep smaller jobs that require less processing time from being completed.

The Linux operating system employs preemptive multitasking as opposed to cooperative multitasking. With **preemptive multitasking**, the operating system has the ability to take control of the system from an application. With **cooperative multitasking**, the application takes control of the system resources. The advantage of preemptive multitasking is that if an application fails, the whole system won't necessarily crash. In cooperative operating systems, a failed application can cause the whole computer to freeze or crash.

Ability to Use Multiple Processors

The ability to have several processors to improve overall throughput, or the amount of work that can be put through the system, is another advantage of the Linux operating system, and Linux can accommodate up to 32 processors. Linux also uses **multithreading** which allows for a program to be split across several processors, with each processor working on a different piece of the program at the same time.

1

Symmetrical multiprocessing (SMP) facilitates multithreading. SMP greatly enhances throughput because several processors handle one large task instead of a single processor handling the same task alone. SMP is typical on systems with a large number of users where throughput demands are great.

Multiple Modes of Operation

The Linux operating system operates in two modes. They are as follows:

- Graphical user interface (GUI)
- Text

Graphical User Interface (GUI) Mode

The GUI program, called X Windows, offers a Windows look and feel to the Linux environment. What you see on your screen is called the **desktop** because it includes the tools you need to perform daily functions. Some of the tools provided as part of the desktop are a GUI file manager, a Desktop manager and an Internet Web browser. Figure 1-3 shows a screenshot of the Linux Gnome desktop.

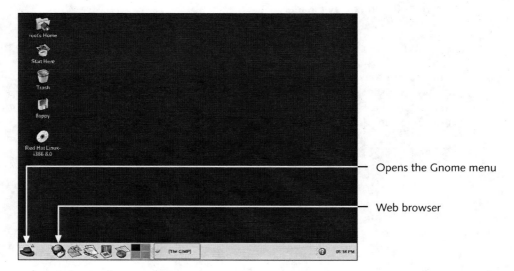

Figure 1-3 The Linux Gnome desktop

 Linux also gives you access to the Internet by utilizing the necessary hardware to run Netscape Communicator, Web browser software, and TCP/IP.

Figure 1-4 shows a screen shot of the Linux file manager open on the desktop.

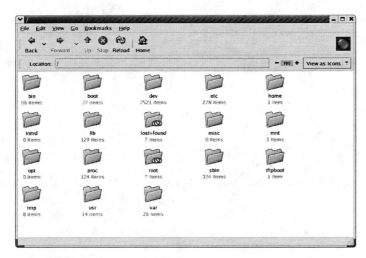

Figure 1-4   Linux file manager

Text Mode

Linux also provides you with a text mode interface. In this interface you use commands to navigate the Linux system and write your shell scripts. You will need to use text or graphical editors to write shell script programs. Figure 1-5 shows a screenshot of the Linux text mode open on the desktop of the GUI.

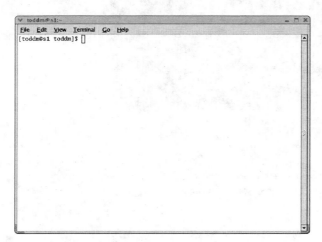

Figure 1-5   Linux text mode

You access the text mode in the Linux operating system via a shell. Acting as an interpreter, the **shell** accepts commands from the keyboard and either executes the command or displays an error if the command encounters a problem. Technically, the shell is a language, so you must adhere to its syntax, or rules. A few of the shells available on Linux are listed in Table 1-2.

Table 1-2 Various shell interpreters available on Linux

Shell Name	Description
sh	The original shell written by Steven Bourne, also known as the Bourne Shell
bash	Publicly licensed Bourne-Again Shell compatible with the original Bourne Shell; this is the default shell you get at login
csh	C-shell which uses a C-like syntax
ksh	Publicly licensed Korn shell written by David Korn

UNDERSTANDING CLASSIFICATIONS OF SOFTWARE

It is always a good idea to know what software is running on your system. This way, you are better equipped to troubleshoot in case a problem occurs. Also, software can be under a software contract, so you may be able to contact someone if problems arise.

Software is divided into the following categories:

- System software
- Application software

System Software

System software includes the core components of the system that must be present in order for the computer to operate. Examples of system software are:

- The kernel
- Job management software
- Memory management software
- Programming languages
- Device drivers
- Software utilities

The Kernel

The kernel is the "heart" of the operating system. When any computer system boots, a set of program instructions are loaded from the hard drive and kept in memory. Many programs are kept, or cached, in memory for speedy access, but the **kernel** is the core of any operating system that occupies memory as long as the computer remains on. It controls all other software activity. Only the most important and widely used programs are part of the kernel. The kernel calls upon other programs that are held on disk or in other areas of memory by interfacing with other operating system programs with the hardware of the computer system. Most operating systems have a kernel that remains in memory. Examples include Linux, Novell NetWare, Windows NT, Windows 2000, and Windows XP.

The kernel is cached in memory. Caching means to keep programs in memory for quick access. Because memory access is faster than retrieving files from a hard disk or network, cached programs are retrieved quicker.

Customizing your Linux kernel allows you to give your computer system different capabilities. You can modify your kernel by adding or removing support of different features such as the ones shown in Figure 1-6.

Job Management

It is the function of the operating system to manage processes that are executing. In general, when a program executes it is known as a **job** or **process**.

▾ Linux Kernel Configuration		_ ☐ ✕
Code maturity level options	ATA/IDE/MFM/RLL support	Crypto Hardware support
Loadable module support	SCSI support	File systems
Processor type and features	Fusion MPT device support	Console drivers
Processor type and features	IEEE 1394 (FireWire) support (EXPERIMENTAL)	Sound
Binary emulation of other systems	I2O device support	USB support
Memory Technology Devices (MTD)	Network device support	Bluetooth support
Parallel port support	Amateur Radio support	Kernel hacking
Plug and Play configuration	IrDA (infrared) support	Library routines
Block devices	ISDN subsystem	
Multi-device support (RAID and LVM)	Old CD-ROM drivers (not SCSI, not IDE)	Save and Exit
Cryptography support (CryptoAPI)	Input core support	Quit Without Saving
Networking options	Character devices	Load Configuration from File
Telephony Support	Multimedia devices	Store Configuration to File

Figure 1-6   Kernel features you can customize

A daemon is a job that runs in the background waiting for work. Many of the system programs are jobs run as daemons.

Prior to job execution, a job is placed in a job process queue. A **job process queue** is a holding area for the job while it waits its turn for execution. A running process has CPU and memory resources bound to it. The Linux operating system uses **a process tree** to keep track of the processes on the system. When a program or command executes, it is assigned a number, called the **process ID (PID)**. The PID is used for internal purposes by the operating system. The operating system uses the PID when communicating with the process. The process name is much like your own name and the PID is much like your Social Security number.

Each process is created from a parent. Linux uses the term **spawning** to describe one process starting from another. At times, a process may encounter problems causing it to consume excessive CPU time or to become orphaned. For instance, if process A spawns process B, then process A encounters a problem and is killed and removed from the process tree, process B, which is still running, is said to have been "orphaned."

Memory Management

Memory management software allows you to manage all of memory—including both physical memory and virtual memory. **Virtual memory** is the concept of the system utilizing physical memory as well as a section of hard disk space for accommodating multiple processes. The use of virtual memory facilitates the multiuser and multitasking features and capabilities of an operating system.

 The area on the hard disk reserved for virtual memory is sometimes called the page file or swap file. The swap file is created during the installation of the operating system.

Here is how virtual memory works. Programs are loaded into physical memory, also known as **random access memory (RAM)**. Programs are allocated a certain amount of time, called a time slice. When memory utilization reaches a certain threshold or when a process's time is up, the system sends the program and its data to the hard drive. Here the program is in a wait state and is placed temporarily on hold. When the system is ready to process the program and data that is currently on hold, the program's data is sent back to physical memory for main processing.

Mainframe operating systems and some network operating systems, such as Novell NetWare, UNIX, Linux, and Windows platforms, utilize virtual memory. One way to speed up your computer system is to add more memory to it. Another way is to increase the size of your swap file by allocating more disk space to it.

Programming Languages

Software programs are written in languages such as C, C++, Java, Visual BASIC, COBOL, FORTRAN or Assembly. Languages are divided into two major classifications:

- High-level
- Low-level

High-level Programming Languages High-level programming languages are designed with people in mind. They tend to be similar to English in style and are much easier for the programmer to read and comprehend than low-level programming languages. For example, review the following excerpt of a COBOL programming language statement:

```
IF HOURS > 40 THEN
      PERFORM CALCULATE-OVER-TIME
ELSE
      PERFORM CALCULATE-REGULAR-TIME
END-IF
```

In the example, if the hours exceed 40, then overtime is calculated. If the hours are under and including 40, then regular time is calculated. You can clearly see how this sample COBOL program is very much like English. Examples of high-level programming languages include: Perl, COBOL, C, BASIC, Visual BASIC, and FORTRAN. High-level programming languages must be converted from their human-readable form into computer- or machine-readable form. This conversion can be done through either compiling or interpreting. The compiler or interpreter is software that is written to perform the conversion.

With **compiling**, the entire program is converted into an executable program. Once it is free of errors and compiled, the program is capable of being run or executed. On many systems, it is just a matter of clicking an icon representing the program. Examples of compiled languages are: C, C++, COBOL, and FORTRAN.

In the case of **interpreting**, each line is converted into machine-readable form as it is executed. The statements within the program are still converted into machine-readable form; it's just done line by line. Think of an interpretive language as being one where a minicompile is done for each statement. Some examples of interpretive languages are: Visual BASIC (however you can compile the code), Perl, BASIC, and shell programs.

Low-level Programming Languages Each processor has its own programming language, often called a low-level programming language. The term "low-level" is used because the language is native to the processor instead of being similar to English. Examples of these are the Assembly language statements that are specific to every computer system. So, you could not take an Assembly language program and run it on just any system. However, you are more likely to take a high-level program and run it on another system with maybe only a few modifications. Take a look at the following excerpt from an Assembly language program:

```
L  1,X
A  1,Y
A  1,Z
ST 1,T
```

The above programming code simply adds up a set of three variables, X, Y, and Z, and stores them in a variable named T. It is not like English, and it greatly differs from the COBOL program example you saw earlier.

Device Drivers

Keep in mind that if you have a piece of hardware, such as a printer or scanner, you must have software that governs it. **Device drivers** are software instructions that manage a particular device. You must configure the correct driver for the type of hardware you install. Unfortunately, it's not uncommon to install a device driver incorrectly. Take a printer driver for example. A possible symptom of an incorrectly installed printer driver is that the printer's output is garbled and unreadable. Another symptom is the printer prints one line on a page and then advances to the next page to print the next line.

 Remember, you must use the device driver that goes with the device. In other words, if you are using a brand X, model Y device, you must use a brand X, model Y device driver or the device will not function properly.

Software Utilities

Software utilities are commands that help augment the functionality of the operating system. They are especially important because they can be used in combination with shell script programming logic to automate certain tasks.

The following are some software utilities:

- Backup and restore
- Compression and uncompression
- Printer management

Backup and Restore   One of the most important aspects of any job is backing up your data. Whether you back it up to a floppy disk, CD, hard drive, or tape, you should always back up your data. Although many organizations use redundant servers in case one goes down, or they use redundant disks storage, they still require their personnel to perform backups.

Backups typically occur during off-hours when users are not working with application files. The reason being that if you back up files during business hours, you cannot guarantee the backup has indeed backed up the data that is being processed at that moment by the application. Also, some backup utilities do not backup files that are in use.

The restore process is the copying of the data that was backed up to either its original storage location or another one. The backup and restore processes should be tested to verify they work in case a real emergency ever occurs.

Compression and Uncompression   Most every file has something in it that is repeated. For example, one of the most common words is the word "the," which occurs in many documents and books, such as this one. **Compression** is the process of removing those repeating portions of a file, thereby making a new smaller file. Compression varies based on the amount of data that is duplicated and the compression algorithm that is used. At times, compression can yield between a 75% and 90% savings. You would generally compress a file that is to be downloaded over the Internet. It takes less time to download a compressed file because it is smaller. Another advantage of compression is that it saves disk space because of the reduced file size. However, in order to utilize the file, you must uncompress it first.

Printer Management   The Linux printing system uses the concept of print queues to temporarily hold print jobs. When a user sends a print job to a printer, the print job is spooled to a directory for the printer where it waits.

 The term "spool" is an acronym that comes from IBM mainframe terminology. It stands for Simultaneous Peripheral Operations OnLine.

Simply stated, it means the system can send a print job to the printer software concurrent with other system activities. If the printer is busy or not turned on, the print job waits in the print queue until the printer is ready to accept the request. When the printer is ready to print, the print management software looks in the printer's directory, or queue, and prints the next job. It then deletes the print job request from the print queue.

Application Software

Application software is software that assists users in performing typical office work such as writing letters and business proposals, managing numeric information, and organizing large amounts of data. As such, application software is generally divided into these major categories:

- Word processing
- Spreadsheet
- Database

Word-Processing Software

Word-processing software has been around since the early 1980s. Word-processing software allows you to create, modify, delete, save, and print office-quality documents. Word-processing software also includes the enhanced capabilities of spell checker, dictionary, and a thesaurus. Today, Microsoft makes Word and Sun Microsystems offers a word-processing package as part of the Star Office software package suite. Star Office runs on the Linux operating system.

Spreadsheet Software

Also during the early 1980s, a group of students taking an accounting class grew tired of making numerous changes to the accounting sheets when only one number changed. These students eventually started the Lotus Corporation, one of the first companies to create spreadsheet software for PCs. Spreadsheet programs allow you to manage numeric data on a large scale. Spreadsheets hold data in cells, which are much like storage locations. When one cell changes, all cells referencing the original cell also change. Cells are labeled consecutively starting with A1 and continuing as far as your data demands. Letters represent the columns and numbers represent the rows.

Spreadsheet programs are extremely powerful and can include programming logic. They also include built-in functions. **Functions** are miniprograms that do the work when you supply the data, such as performing a mathematical calculation.

 You will learn how to use shell script programs to create functions in Chapter 8.

In this spreadsheet example, =AVERAGE(A1:A20), you can see the power of a spreadsheet function. The AVERAGE function is given, or passed, two values—the beginning cell in a cell range, A1, and the ending cell in a cell range, A20. Whatever values are held in any of the 20 cells in column A are included in the average. If a value in any cell in the range changes, the average changes too.

Database Software

Database programs allow you to manipulate and manage data, create tables of data for organization, and join or combine data from multiple tables to create views or subsets of tables. Data held in databases can be accessed quickly via a unique identifier called a key field. Ashton-Tate Corporation developed one of the first database programs on the market for PCs in the 1980s called dBASE. Other companies such as IBM, Microsoft, Oracle, and Sun Microsystems have also developed database software. Linux comes with a database product called MySQL. It allows you to add, delete, and modify data within databases.

UNDERSTANDING DATA

In order to successfully write shell script programs, you must understand what data is as well as the structure of data. **Data** is made up of raw facts that are not much use until they are processed into information. Consider the number 75. This is considered data. You cannot look at the number 75 and tell if it is an exam grade, the outdoor temperature, or someone's age. Only when a program, in conjunction with the computer's processor, processes the number can it become information. The programmer's job is to write program code to turn data into useful information. Think of data as a hierarchy or a pyramid. Figure 1-7 shows the data pyramid.

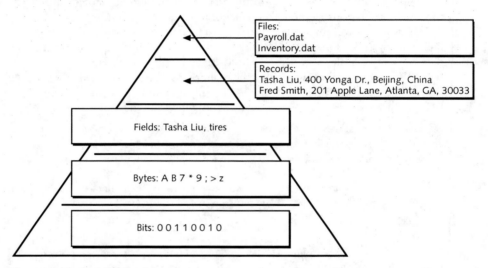

Figure 1-7   Data pyramid

At the lowest level of the data hierarchy are bits. The term bit stands for binary digit and is either a zero (0) or a one (1). Each computer system has a character set that maps all the letters on the keyboard to its appropriate bit sequence. American Standard Code for Information Interchange (ASCII) is a character set common among most computer environments including all Windows operating systems and the Linux operating system. Although you don't typically use anything as small as a bit in your daily dealings with computers, you do need to understand the concept.

In the computer industry, the term **byte** refers to eight bits taken in sequence. Another synonym for the term byte is alphanumeric character. An alphanumeric character is defined as any of the letters A through Z, numbers 0 through 9, and special symbols. Although it is up one notch on the data hierarchy, a character is generally the lowest level of the data hierarchy that people process.

1

A group of bytes is called a **field**. For example, if you've ever filled out a job or college admission application, or even your 1040 tax forms, you know that you must fill in little boxes or blank lines with your personal data. Each of the boxes or blank lines is entered into an application screen to be processed by a program. These boxes and blank lines are considered fields. Fields are labeled, or given names, so that you may refer to the data contained within them. For instance, a field called NAME, may have the following data: Tasha Lui. If you wanted to print the NAME field, it would print the name Tasha Lui. Notice also that a field is comprised of characters or bytes.

A group of related fields makes up a **record**. For example, consider the employee records containing the field names and data shown in Table 1-3. There are three records with six fields each. In this case, you can think of a record as a row and think of a field as a column.

Table 1-3   Sample employee records

Name	Address	City	State	Zip	Phone
Sarah Togar	214 Scott Way	Concord	NH	03301	555-5550
Xin Chun Liu	428 Aubrey Way	Lilburn	GA	30047	555-5551
Molly Obakin	1027 Michelle Lane	Tulsa	OK	74101	555-5557

In most application systems, there is one unique identifying field in a record called the **primary key field**. This field is used to access the remaining fields in the records. The purpose of the primary key is to locate the data in the record efficiently. When a bank teller asks you for your bank account number, the account number is used as the primary key. Your Social Security number is used as a primary key when you fill out your tax returns or an employment application.

To help you understand the primary key concept, think about how the index in the back of this book works. If you want to look up a term, you go to the index and look through the alphabetical listing until you locate the page number reference for the term. Then, you go to the actual page number that describes the term. The primary key is analogous to the term you seek in the index. In an application, the primary key field is used to locate the record containing the rest of the data.

A grouping of related records is called a **file**. A file has a name and location for where the data is housed. A file can contain two major types of data, executable, or binary data, and nonexecutable data.

Executable or **binary files** are files that have been compiled and perform some type of operation or task. They are written using text editors following the strict syntax of the language and then they are compiled. The compilation process creates the executable code. The commands that you'll use in this book are executable files.

Nonexecutable files are generally data that the executable files operate on. The user runs an application or program that creates data files. Data files can also be created automatically by programs that run without user intervention. Examples of nonexecutable files are text files, word-processing document files, spreadsheet files, database files, or picture files.

UNDERSTANDING USER ROLES

In the Linux computing environment, there are several types of users, each with differing roles. Understanding the role of a user is important because it helps you decide the type of shell scripts that person might need on the job. Additionally, the role governs the type of access the user has to the system. Here is a list of the typical user types:

- Standard user
- System Administrator or root user
- Shell programmer

Standard Users

The **standard user**, sometimes just called "user," is the person who uses the Linux operating system on a daily basis. Users may also have access to commands via the text mode and other programs in the GUI. They also use the system to access applications. The applications they need depend upon their functions in the organization. Consider this example of typical users' needs. An accounting manager may need access to the accounting application, an engineer may need access to a computer aided design/computer aided manufacturing (CAD/CAM) program, an insurance agent may need access to the insurance adjustment application, and a travel agent may need access to the travel booking application.

Users access the Linux system by logging in using a user account. Generally, a computer specialist, such as a System Administrator who has authority to create the accounts, generates the user accounts. The user account should also have a password that is assigned to it. Once the users log in, they usually set their own passwords.

System Administrator

The **System Administrator** is a computer specialist who is responsible for the operations of the computer systems and network. Depending upon the size of the operation, there may be more than one System Administrator in an organization. They are completely responsible for ensuring that the systems, the networks, and the applications are available to the users during the hours needed by the users.

System Administrators perform a variety of tasks including upgrading applications and installing system software, changing user passwords, monitoring the network for bottlenecks, and in some cases, changing printer toner cartridges. Some have to be on call 24 hours a day to provide support for multiple shift operations.

System Administrators also maintain security, making sure users have the right access to application files and folders on the computer system. The goal is to give each user just what is needed to do the job, but no more.

At times, a System Administrator may have to log in to a special user account that has the ability to perform system administrative work, such as add a print queue, change another user's password, or backup a system file; standard user accounts don't have the ability to do these things. In Linux, the name of the user with complete administrative capability is called **root**. The root user has access to programs and configuration files that standard users don't.

 You must use caution when logging in as the root user because you can delete or modify configuration files and programs that are unrecoverable without completely reinstalling the operating system.

Depending upon the organization, the System Administrator may be responsible for writing shell scripts, or the responsibility could be relegated to a shell programmer.

Shell Programmer

A **shell programmer** is responsible for writing shell scripts. A **shell script** is a program that is written to automate a process in the Linux operating system. A shell programmer writes the script using an editor, tests the script, and when the script passes the tests, makes the script available to users. The shell programmer must have an understanding of programming concepts as well as the Linux commands in order to successfully write scripts. For example, a shell programmer may need to write a script that uses system commands and decision logic for a System Administrator who needs a way to automate the backup process. Or a shell programmer may need to create a menu so several users can run Linux commands without entering the complete syntax of the command. Typically, a shell programmer logs in using a regular user account unless the task requires them to use the root user account.

At times a shell programmer may have to **debug** scripts or remove any syntax or logic error from scripts or programs. A **syntax error** is one that does not conform to the rules of the language. An example of a syntax error is a misspelled command. A compiler or interpreter usually displays an error message when it encounters a syntax error. A script or program can not run until it is syntax-error free. Shell programmers must learn the syntax of the shell to prevent syntax errors.

 The term debug was coined in the 1940s when a moth short-circuited electrical components in a mainframe computer system causing a system failure. By removing the moth, the system was "debugged."

A **logic error** is an error that does not meet the requirements of the programming logic as decided upon by the users and management. These are typically more difficult for the shell programmer to identify because the scripts are most likely syntactically correct. The compiler or interpreter does not display a message indicating the error and the program appears to run normally. An example of a logic error would be using a less-than symbol instead of a greater-than symbol in an overtime calculation script. In the following set of COBOL statements, a logic error occurs because the less-than symbol is used in place of the greater-than symbol. In the example, a person working more than 40 hours will have their pay calculated on regular time. The program would run because the use of the less-than symbol is syntactically correct, but the output of the code would be undesirable. Compare this example to the earlier COBOL example where use of the greater-than symbol (> 40) is logically correct.

```
IF HOURS < 40 THEN
      PERFORM CALCULATE-OVER-TIME
ELSE
      PERFORM CALCULATE-REGULAR-TIME
END-IF
```

UNDERSTANDING BASIC LINUX COMMANDS

The Linux operating system contains numerous commands. Some are only available to System Administrators and not to standard users, while other commands are available to everyone. You need to learn about the commands that are available to all users because they may also be used in shell scripts.

Logging In and Logging Out

One of the first things you need to know is how to log in to the Linux system. You need a username and password. (To complete the activities and projects in this book, you may need to ask your instructor for your username and password.)

There are two ways of logging in to a Linux system. First, you can physically sit in front of the system and enter you username and password. Second, you can use the `telnet` command to log in to the Linux system. This requires the host to have an IP address or DNS name.

Next you will log in using the second method just discussed. You will use the `ping` command to verify the Linux computer is accessible on the network and the `telnet` command to connect to it if it is. You will access the Linux system from a Windows-based system that is running TCP/IP.

To verify the Linux host is accessible and connect to the Linux system if it is:

1. Start Windows on your computer (any version of Windows will work).

2. Click the **Start** button, and then click **Run**. The Run dialog box opens.

3. Type **command**, and then click **OK**. The Windows command prompt opens.

4. Type **ping** *hostname/hostaddress*, and then press **Enter**. Be sure to substitute your correct host's name or IP address. If the command succeeded, you should see a "Reply from" message. If so, proceed to Step 6.

5. If you received an error, such as "Request timed out," it means the host is inaccessible. See your instructor. Do not go to the next step.

6. Type **telnet** *hostname/hostaddress*, and then press **Enter**. Be sure to substitute your correct host's name or IP address. The Linux login prompt appears. Figure 1-8 includes the logging-in process to the Linux system from the Windows command prompt.

7. Type your **username**, and then press **Enter**. Your username appears on the screen, and you are prompted for a password.

8. Type your **password**, and then press **Enter**. Your password will not appear on the screen for security reasons. You have now successfully logged in and have access to the Linux system.

9. To log out, type **logout**, and then press **Enter**. Your connection to the Linux host is terminated, and you return to the Windows command prompt.

 Another way to log out is to press Ctrl+D instead of typing logout.

```
F:\WINNT\System32\cmd.exe - telnet 160.100.100.1
Red Hat Linux release 8.0 (Psyche)
Kernel 2.4.18-14 on an i686
login: root
Password:
Last login: Wed Oct  9 17:47:14 from 160.100.100.20
You have mail.
[root@s1 root]#
```

Figure 1-8   Logging in to a Linux system from a Windows-based PC

The `cal` Command

Once you've successfully logged in to the Linux system, you can use other Linux commands. The `cal` command displays the current calendar month. However, you can use the `cal` command to display a variety of months and years. Here is the general format of the command:

    cal *month year*

The *month* is an optional number between one and 12 representing the numeric number for the month. You can only display the month if you include the *year* option. The *year* is an optional number between one and 9999 reflecting the year. So, for example, if you want to display the current month's calendar, you would run this command: `cal`. To display the calendar for the whole year, you would run the `cal` command with the year only. For example, the following statement displays the calendar for the first nine months for the year 2004.

```
cal 2004
```

Figure 1-9 shows the partial calendar for the year 2004.

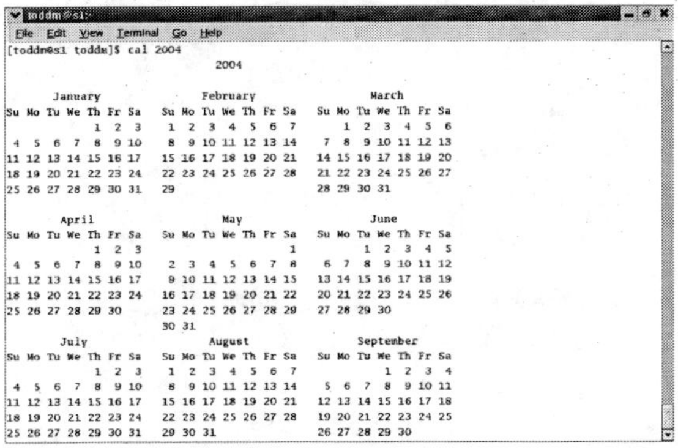

Figure 1-9   The results of the `cal 2004` command

The cat Command

The `cat` command allows you to display the contents of text files very easily. You simply type in the command followed by the filename; the text displays on your screen. After the command completes its task, your prompt returns.

The `cat` command is derived from the term concatenate which means to join or fuse together. The `cat` command concatenates the contents of a file on your disk with the screen. The command takes the following form:

```
cat option filename
```

Here is an example that displays the contents of the sales file:

```
cat sales
```

The `cat` command not only allows you to display text on the screen, but also allows you to create a file. To do this you use the greater-than redirection operator, `>`. At this point, all you need to understand is that the output of the `cat` command is redirected to a file instead of your screen. This results in the creation of a new file.

The concept of redirection will be fully discussed in Chapter 4.

Next you will create a file using the `cat` command and the redirection operator, and then display the file's contents.

To redirect text to a file using the `cat` command:

1. Log in to the Linux system as a user.

2. Right-click a blank area of the desktop, and then click **New Terminal**. The Terminal emulation program window appears with your prompt.

3. Type `cat > file2.txt`, and then press **Enter**. Notice that the cursor moves to the beginning of the next line and that there is no prompt on that line.

4. Type the following code exactly as it is shown, being sure to press **Enter** at the completion of each line:

   ```
   Shell Programming will help me on the job.
   Linux is fun!
   ```

When creating a file with the `cat` command, once you've pressed Enter at the end of a line, you cannot go back to that line and edit it. Creating a file using the `cat` command is for quick tasks. To edit the file, you need to use one of the editors discussed later in this chapter.

5. Press **Ctrl+D** to send an end-of-file (EOF) character to the `cat` command. The cursor moves to the next line and your prompt returns.

6. To display the contents of the file, type `cat file2.txt`, and then press **Enter**. Figure 1-10 shows the contents of the file you just created as well as your creation of that file.

7. To exit the window, type `exit`, and then press **Enter**.

8. Log out.

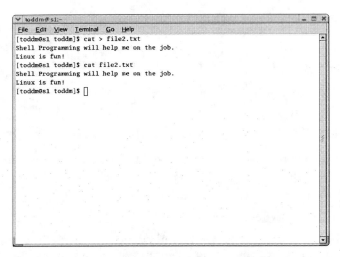

Figure 1-10   The cat command to create a file

The date Command

The **date** command displays or sets the system date and time. Here is the general syntax of the command:

        date *option* +*format*

Table 1-4 provides a listing of available formats for the **date** command.

Table 1-4   Options for the date command

Option	Description	Example
%D	Displays the date in MM/DD/YY format; this is where MM is the two-digit month, DD is the two-digit day, and YY is the last two digits of the year	date +%D
%d	Displays the two-digit day	date +%d
%Y	Displays the four-digit year	date +%Y
%H	Displays the two-digit hour	date +%H
%h	Displays the three-letter month	date +%h
%T	Displays the time	date +%T
%j	Displays the numeric day from 001 to 366; this is sometimes called the Julian date	date +%j
%m	Displays the two-digit month	date +%m

Figure 1-11 shows a screenshot of the `date` command run using various formats shown in Table 1-4.

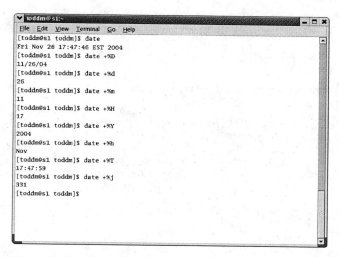

Figure 1-11 The `date` command run with different formats

The echo Command

You use the `echo` command to display text on the screen. As such, the `echo` command is a very useful debugging tool that can help you troubleshoot shell script programs. The `echo` command takes the form of the following:

```
echo "Text to display"
```

While not required on all versions of Linux, on some versions you do need the quotes. However, it is good practice to enclose text that includes spaces in quotes. You will learn more about use of quotes in Chapter 3. Consider this example:

```
echo "How are you doing?"
```

You can use the `echo` command to create a file. However, using the `echo` command to do this is only recommended when you only need a small file consisting of just a few lines. To do this you use the greater-than operator, `>`, to redirect the output from the screen to a file. Redirection will be discussed in Chapter 4.

In the following example, the output of the `echo` statement is sent to a file called sales:

```
echo "March sales exceed projections for the Houston Branch
office." > sales
```

Next you will use the `echo` command to redirect text to the sales file, and then use the `cat` command to display the contents of the file.

To redirect text to a file using the echo command:

1. Log in to the Linux system as a user.

2. Right-click a blank area of the desktop, and then click **New Terminal**. The Terminal emulation program window appears with your prompt.

3. To redirect the output to a file named sales, type the following code, and then press **Enter**:

   ```
   echo "March sales exceed projections for the Houston Branch
   office." > sales
   ```

   The command executes but returns no output to the screen because the output is redirected to the sales file.

4. To display the contents of the sales file to your screen type **cat sales**. Figure 1-12 shows a screenshot of the creation of the sales file using the echo command and it's displayed using the cat command.

5. To exit the window, type **exit**.

6. Log out.

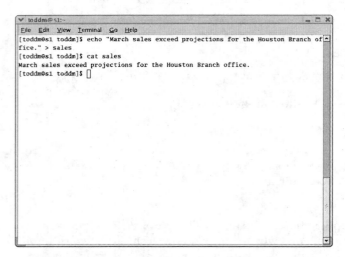

Figure 1-12   The echo command used to create the sales file

The history Command

If you want to see the commands you've already entered, you can run the history command. This command is useful for saving keystrokes. You can use your up and down arrows to go up and down through your history list to locate a command you previously entered. Once you locate the command you can use the backspace key to modify it, or you can press Enter to rerun the command as is.

Here is the general format of the command `history`:

```
history option
```

If you enter the `history` command without any options, it displays the last 1,000 commands you've entered. Used without any options, it can provide you with more information than you may be prepared to deal with. Here are a few ways you can use the `history` command.

The `history` command feature allows you to enter a recently executed command by placing the ! operator prior to the command. So, to rerun the most recently executed `cal` command, enter:

```
!cal
```

 You don't have to enter the complete command when using the ! operator. For example, if you entered, `!da`, the most recently executed command that begins with the letters "da" is executed. If the `date` command was the most recently executed command, then it would be rerun.

The `history` command displays numbers to the left of each command in its list. If you see a command in the history list that you want to rerun, you can enter the ! operator followed by the number of the command in the list. So, to rerun the 1031st command in the list, enter:

```
!1031
```

Figure 1-13 shows a screenshot of running the `history` command using the ! operator.

```
 toddm@s1:~                                                    _ □ ×
File  Edit  View  Terminal  Go  Help
 1025  clear
 1026  history
 1027  clear
 1028  history
 1029  date
 1030  clear
 1031  cal 12 2004
 1032  clear
 1033  pwd
 1034  history
[toddm@s1 toddm]$ !1031
cal 12 2004
     December 2004
Su Mo Tu We Th Fr Sa
          1  2  3  4
 5  6  7  8  9 10 11
12 13 14 15 16 17 18
19 20 21 22 23 24 25
26 27 28 29 30 31

[toddm@s1 toddm]$ !da
date
Fri Nov 26 17:52:16 EST 2004
[toddm@s1 toddm]$ ▊
```

Figure 1-13   The `history` command using the ! operator

The lpr Command

The lpr command places a file in the print queue for printing. You use this command to send a document to the printer.

The format of the command lpr is:

```
lpr option filename
```

To print the sales file you created in an earlier exercise, you enter the following code:

```
lpr sales
```

Although the lpr command prints to the default printer set up by the System Administrator, it can also be used to print to a specific printer using the –P option. For example, to print the sales file to a printer named LinuxPrinter, enter lpr –P LinuxPrinter sales.

 Most commands allow you to enter options. However, because each command has a different function, the formats of their options are usually different. For the most part, an option is preceded by either one or two dashes, as in –t.

The man Command

The man command allows you to display the manual, or help, pages for a command. You run this command to see a description of a command and its options, if it has any. The general form is:

```
man command
```

To use the man command to display the manual pages for the echo command, enter man echo. Figure 1-14 shows a screenshot of the man pages for the echo command.

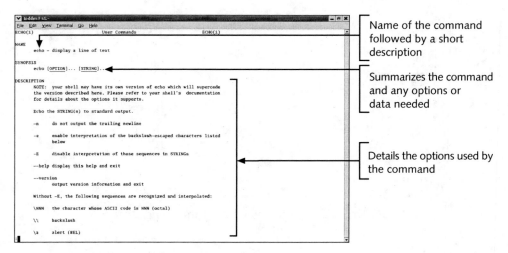

Figure 1-14   The man echo command

The `touch` Command

The main purpose of the `touch` command is to update the modification date and time stamp of a file. This is particularly useful when writing shell script programs. For example, if you had a shell script program that ran overnight or anytime when you weren't available to check on it, you can ensure the script ran or the file was updated by running the `touch` command for the file. The `touch` command takes the following form:

> touch *filename*

You can also use the `touch` command to create an empty file and set the modification date and time on that file using the same form.

The `who` Command

The `who` command allows you to display the list of users who are currently logged on to the Linux system. The form of the command is as follows:

> who *options*

You can also display a count of the total number of users logged in using the `-q` option. Figure 1-15 shows a sample screenshot of both the `who` and `who -q` commands.

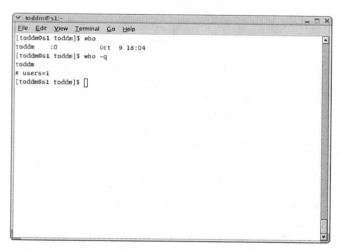

Figure 1-15   The who and who –q commands

Refer to Table 1-5 for a listing of the common basic Linux commands.

Table 1-5   Basic Linux commands

Command	Description
cal	Displays a calendar
cat	Displays the contents of a file
clear	Clears the screen
date	Displays or sets the date and time
echo	Displays text
history	Displays previously entered commands
login and logout	Allows you to log in and log out
lpr	Prints a file
man	Displays manual (help) pages for a command
ping	Determines if another TCP/IP system is available
telnet	Connects to a TCP/IP computer
touch	Updates the modification date and time of a file
who	Displays the currently logged on users

CREATING SHELL SCRIPTS

Because the shell is a command interpreter that makes use of programming capabilities, it allows you to use traditional programming concepts. Here are some of the traditional programming concepts the shell allows you to perform with scripts:

- Make decisions based upon conditions
- Perform arithmetic operations
- Create a menu using looping statements
- Use functions to perform very specific tasks
- Manipulate data using an array

 The terms "script" and "program" are synonymous.

A shell script performs one other function that traditional programming languages do not typically support; the shell script runs operating system commands. Like other programming languages, you write your shell script, and then you execute it. Next you will create a simple shell script.

To create and execute a simple shell script:

1. Log in to the Linux system as a user.

2. Right-click a blank area of the desktop, and then click **New Terminal**. The Terminal emulation program window appears with your prompt.

3. Type `cat > script1`, and then press **Enter** to create a file called script1.

4. Type the following code to add text to script1:

```
echo "Welcome to my shell script."
echo "This is one of my first shell scripts!"
echo "Shell script programming is a tool for helping users
 automate their tasks."
```

5. Press **Crl+D** to terminate the line. Your prompt returns.

6. To execute the script, type **bash script1**, and then press **Enter**. Your screen should look like Figure 1-16 which shows the script you have input as well as the resulting output.

7. To exit the Terminal emulation program, type **exit**, and then press **Enter**.

8. Log out.

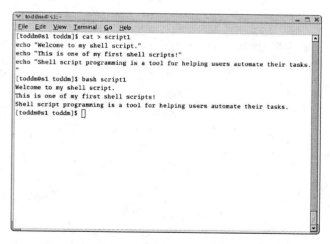

Figure 1-16   script1 and resulting output

To reinforce what you've already learned about using commands and creating shell scripts, next you will create a shell script that displays the calendar for the current month, the current time on the screen, and the usernames of the users currently logged in.

To create a shell script which displays the calendar, the current time, and the usernames of those users currently logged in:

1. Log in to the Linux system as a user.

2. Right-click a blank area of the desktop, and then click **New Terminal**. The Terminal emulation program window appears with your prompt.

3. Type **cat > script2**, and then press **Enter** to create a new file named script2.

4. Type **cal**, and then press **Enter** to include the current calendar.

5. Type **date**, and then press **Enter** to include the current date.

6. Type **who**, and then press **Enter** to display the users that are currently logged in. Press **Crl+D** to terminate the line. The prompt returns.

7. To execute the script, type **bash script2**, and then press **Enter**. Your screen should look like Figure 1-17 which displays the script you have input as well as the resulting output.

8. Record the output.

9. To exit the Terminal emulation program, type **exit**, and then press **Enter**.

10. Log out.

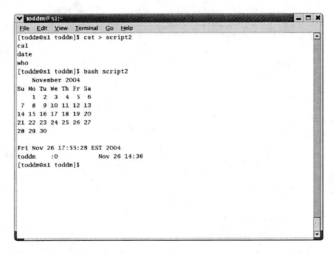

Figure 1-17   script2 and resulting output

CHAPTER SUMMARY

❑ The operating system is the software "brains" that manage the computer system. The operating system interacts with users, the applications, and the hardware. All computer systems must have an operating system in order for the system to run.

❑ The Linux operating system is a portable, multiuser, multitasking, and multiprocessing system. Linux supports both a graphical user interface (through the use of X Windows) or a text mode interface. There are numerous versions of Linux in the marketplace. The Linux shell interprets shell scripts.

❑ Software can be classified into systems software and application software. System software includes the kernel, job management software, memory management software, and device drivers. System utilities include backup and restore software, compression and uncompression software, file system management software, and printer management software. The kernel is the nucleus of the operating system. It remains in memory and controls other software components.

❑ Data is made up of raw facts. Information is processed data. A bit is either a binary zero or one. A byte is a group of eight bits. A field is a group of bytes. A record is a group of fields. A primary key field is a special field that allows you to quickly access a record in a file. A file is a group of records. There are two types of files: executable, or binary, and nonexecutable. Examples of executable files are commands and programs. Examples of nonexecutable files are picture files or text files.

❑ It is important to understand the user roles in a Linux environment so you can create appropriate scripts and access to the system for the user. A standard user is a person who uses the application and system on a daily basis to perform a certain job function such as payroll, accounting, marketing, finance, or engineering. A System Administrator is responsible for maintaining, monitoring, upgrading, and troubleshooting the system and network so users can do their jobs. A shell programmer writes shell programs for users. Shell programmers apply their knowledge of programming logic and Linux commands to create scripts for users.

❑ Linux allows you to interact with the operating system via commands. There are literally hundreds of commands. Most have multiple options that augment the command in some way. You use the manual pages for the command you want to learn more about.

❑ Shell script programming combines programming logic structures with operating system commands to automate routine tasks. The shell runs commands in the shell program.

REVIEW QUESTIONS

1. _____ is the software that remains in memory and controls other activity.
   a. Kernel
   b. Software utilities
   c. Backup software
   d. Job management software

2. Shell script programs usually run in the _____ mode of Linux.
   a. X Windows
   b. MS Windows
   c. graphical
   d. text

3. Which of the following is an interpreted language?
   a. COBOL
   b. C
   c. C++
   d. Bourne-Again Shell (bash)

4. A spreadsheet is an example of _____ software.
   a. backup
   b. application
   c. print management
   d. assembly language

5. A group of fields is also known as a _____.
   a. byte
   b. character
   c. record
   d. table

6. How many bits are in a byte?
   a. 1
   b. 2
   c. 4
   d. 8

7. What company first developed UNIX?

   a. Microsoft

   b. Linux

   c. Red Hat

   d. AT&T

8. _____ is another name for a process.

   a. Job

   b. Disk drive

   c. Folder

   d. X Windows

9. Which command allows you to display the manual pages for a command?

   a. `man`

   b. `pages`

   c. `who`

   d. `lpr`

10. When was UNIX developed?

   a. 1960s

   b. 1970s

   c. 1980s

   d. 1990s

11. Which command allows you to display the two-digit day?

   a. `date +%Y`

   b. `date +%T`

   c. `date +%d`

   d. `date +%D`

12. _____ is raw facts?

   a. Information

   b. Job

   c. Data

   d. Daemon

13. _____ is a background job.

    a. Information

    b. Job

    c. Data

    d. Daemon

14. The _____ command sends a document to the printer.

    a. `lpr`

    b. `printit`

    c. `date`

    d. `echo "Hi" > file4.txt`

15. A _____ is a group of related records.

    a. field

    b. file

    c. bit

    d. character

16. A _____ is a person who uses the system on a daily basis to do his specific job, such as manufacturing, accounting, or payroll.

    a. System Administrator

    b. standard user

    c. shell programmer

    d. daemon

17. A _____ is a person responsible for making sure the systems and networks are available to the users when needed.

    a. System Administrator

    b. standard user

    c. shell programmer

    d. job

18. A picture file is an example of a _____ file.

    a. binary

    b. executable

    c. nonexecutable

    d. job management

19. A command is an example of a _____ file.
    a. binary
    b. nonexecutable
    c. print queue
    d. X Windows

20. A _____ is a person who writes scripts as his or her main job function.
    a. System Administrator
    b. standard user
    c. shell programmer
    d. print queue

HANDS-ON PROJECTS

Project 1-1

In this project, you will visit an organization that uses the Linux operating system and discuss the type of hardware and software it uses. You'll also record if the organization uses any scripts, and if so, for what purpose.

1. Locate an organization that uses the Linux operating system as the main operating system for their organization.
2. Record the name of the organization.
3. Interview one of the System Administrators or other persons responsible for the computer system. Record the type of hardware used.
4. Record the version of Linux used.
5. Record the application software used.
6. Record the shell interpreter used by their users.

Project 1-2

In this project, you will visit various Linux vendor Web sites and record your findings. To complete this project, you will need Internet access.

1. Open your Web browser, then go to the **redhat.com** Web site.
2. Spend some time browsing this Web site.
3. Record information about cost, hardware requirements, software version, and product offerings of the Red Hat version of Linux.

4. Change the address location to the **calderasystems.com** Web site.

5. Spend some time browsing this Web site.

6. Record information about cost, hardware requirements, software version, and product offerings of the Linux version offered by Caldera.

7. Change the address location to the **mandrake.com** Web site.

8. Spend some time browsing this Web site.

9. Record information about cost, hardware requirements, software version, and product offerings of the Linux version offered by Mandrake.

Project 1-3

In this project, you will execute basic Linux commands to help you understand how to interact with the operating system shell.

1. Log in to the Linux system as a user.

2. Open a Terminal emulation window.

3. Type **who**, and then record the output.

4. Type **cal**, and then record the output.

5. Type **date**, and then record the output.

6. Type **history**, and then record the output.

7. Type **!#** where **#** is a number in the history list of a command you want to execute.

8. Record the command that was used.

9. Use the up and down arrow keys to scroll back and forth in the history list of recently executed commands, and press **Enter** to execute a command.

10. Record the command.

11. To exit the Terminal emulation program, type **exit**.

12. Log out.

Project 1-4

In this project, you will execute different variations of the commands to help you understand how to run commands using different options.

1. Log in to the Linux system as a user.

2. Open a Terminal emulation window.

3. Type **date +%h**, and then record the output.

4. Type **date +%T**, and then record the output.

5. Type **date +%m**, and then record the output.

6. Type **who -q**, and then record the output.

7. Type **cal *month year*** where *month* is your two-digit birth month and *year* is your four-year birth year, and then record the day of the week you were born on.

8. To exit the Terminal emulation program, type **exit**.

9. Log out.

Project 1-5

In this project, you will write a small shell script to display text on the screen.

1. Log in to the Linux system as a user.

2. Open a Terminal emulation window.

3. Type **cat > Project1-5**.

4. Type the following code to insert text into the Project1-5 script:

```
echo "Welcome to my shell script."
echo "This is one of my first shell scripts."
echo "Shell script programming is a tool for helping System
Administrators."
```

5. Send an end-of-file (EOF) character to the **cat** command.

6. To execute the script, type **bash Project1-5**.

7. To print your script to the default printer, type **lpr Project1-5**. If you don't have access to a printer, record what displays on the screen on a separate sheet of paper.

8. To exit the Terminal emulation program, type **exit**.

9. Log out.

Project 1-6

In this project, you will write a shell script to display the current Julian date and the number of users currently logged in.

1. Log in to the Linux system as a user.

2. Open a Terminal emulation window.

3. Type **cat > Project1-6**.

4. Type **date +%j**.

5. Type **who -q**.

6. Send an end-of-file (EOF) character to the **cat** command.

7. To execute the script, type **bash Project1-6**.

8. Record the output.

9. To print your script to a specific printer, type **lpr —P *printer-name* Project1-6** where ***printer-name*** is the name of the printer. You may have to get the printer name from your instructor.

10. Close your Terminal emulation window.

11. Log out.

Project 1-7

In this project, you will use the manual pages to help you locate a particular option.

1. Log in to the Linux system as a user, and then open a Terminal emulation window.

2. Type **man cat**.

3. Locate the option to number all output lines, and then record the letter for that option.

4. To use the option, type **cat —*option* Project1-6** where *option* is the letter you recorded in the previous step. (Line numbers display to the left of the commands in the previous script for the previous project.)

5. Type **man lpr**.

6. Read through the man pages and find a new option for the **lpr** command that has not been discussed in this chapter, and then record the option and its description.

7. Type **man touch**.

8. Read through the man pages and find an option for the **touch** command, and then record the option and its description.

9. Run the command using the option you chose, and then record the command and the option you chose.

10. Close your Terminal emulation window.

11. Log out.

Project 1-8

In this project, you will create a script containing three statements. You will insert different versions of the **date** command using various options.

1. Log in to the Linux system as a user, and then open a Terminal emulation window.

2. Use the **cat** command to create a file named **Project1-8**. (*Hint:* You need to use the redirection symbol.)

3. Using the correct option from Table 1-4, insert the **date** command so it displays the date in MM/DD/YY format.

4. Using the correct option from Table 1-4, insert the **date** command so it only displays the current time.

5. Send an end-of-file (EOF) character to the **cat** command.

6. Display the contents of the Project1-8 script, using the **cat** command.

7. Record the contents of the script.

8. Execute the script using the **bash** command.

9. Print your script. If you do not have access to a printer, record what displays on your screen on a separate sheet of paper.

10. Record the command needed to print the script.

11. Close the Terminal emulation window.

12. Log out.

Case Projects

Case 1-1

TMI Corporation is currently running mainframe computers in a distributed environment. There are about 25 users connecting via dumb terminals to the main office, located in Lawrenceville, Georgia. They use manufacturing, inventory, and personnel applications written in COBOL. Their programmers are willing to learn other languages but have not yet had the chance because they've been too busy maintaining the current applications. The company has outgrown its computing resources. It is in the process of selecting an entirely new computer system—from hardware to software.

Write a proposal to the company's chief information officer (CIO) convincing her to choose the Linux operating system. Include specifications for the TMI Corporation, accounting for enough computers to service the current number of users, two servers, and five printers. Indicate the programming language the new applications should be written in and support your decision. Include a rationale for sending two System Administrators to attend Linux administration classes.

Case 1-2

The Daisy Mae Woo Haberdashery Corporation currently is running a proprietary UNIX operating system from the XYZ Corporation vendor. The XYZ Corporation is going out of business because of a downturn in the economy. The Daisy Mae Woo Haberdashery's business is thriving, but they are worried about the potential lack of support in the future. The Daisy Mae Woo Haberdashery has five remote offices located within 10 miles of its main office. The Daisy Mae Woo Haberdashery has financial applications running in C and many of the System Administration tools are written in the Bourne Shell. Many times, the software locks up the computer system causing it to halt. So, a new operating system is needed. The current version of UNIX is compatible with versions of MINIX.

The Daisy Mae Woo Haberdashery Corporation has decided to go with a new vendor, the Alpha Firm, for consulting services. Write a proposal to The Daisy Mae Woo Haberdashery Corporation as if you were a vice president for the Alpha Firm. Include in your proposal which version of Linux you would recommend, the shell you would support, and how you would go about migrating the current programs to the new system. Defend your decision on paper.

2

UNDERSTANDING THE LINUX FILE SYSTEM

In this chapter, you will:

♦ Understand the Linux tree hierarchy
♦ Navigate the tree hierarchy
♦ Understand directory management commands
♦ Use editing commands
♦ Understand file management commands

In this chapter, you will gain an understanding of the Linux file system. You will learn its purpose and how to navigate and manipulate it. You will also learn about some editors you can use to accomplish a variety of tasks, as well as various Linux commands you need to accomplish these goals.

UNDERSTANDING THE LINUX TREE HIERARCHY

The Linux file system is based upon a tree hierarchy. Like other hierarchies, an order exists within the tree. There is a top level with other sublevels branching beneath it. The tree hierarchy offers storage and quick access.

Storage

Storage within the Linux file system is accomplished with two main elements: directories and files. **Directories** are considered holding areas or containers. From a user's standpoint, directories can contain files and other directories, sometimes called subdirectories. Files contain data—text, binary information, picture images, and other types of information. Files are stored in directories. Typically, files that are alike are stored within one directory. While a directory can contain multiple directories and files, files themselves cannot contain directories or other files.

 The Linux operating system treats every storage component such as a directory or a file as a *file*. Files contain the data you need. Directories are simply a means of grouping the files.

At the top of the Linux tree is a single directory called root. The root directory is where all other files and directories in the file system stem from. The root directory is created during installation of the operating system and cannot be changed or deleted without losing the operating system and related files. The symbol for the root directory is the forward slash (/). You must use this symbol when accessing the root, or top-level, directory.

 Both files and directories are ultimately stored on disk.

Quick Access

Generally, when you create directories, you group and store similar files together. This directly benefits you and also translates to quicker access when you need to find a file. If you know what type of file you are looking for, you can go straight to the directory in which it is located. Consider this example. You work in the payroll department for Townsend Toyota and you are responsible for making sure payroll goes out on a monthly basis. Because the company pays its employees monthly, you have twelve payroll files. The files are named "Jan.dat," "Feb.dat," "Mar.dat," and so on. How would you organize these in the tree? You could put them in separate directories or even scattered in a directory with other unrelated files.

However, when you try to locate them, you may not be able to find them quickly because they are not organized in a central location. A better design is to create a directory named Payroll and place all the monthly payroll files in it. Then, near payday, you simply look in the Payroll directory, find the files you need, and process the payroll data.

As another example, if you had several files dealing with your personal information, you might create a directory called Personal and place your resume, sample cover letters, school documents, and e-mail messages in that directory. Ultimately, it is easier for you to find the files because you have organized them.

The "Garden Store Tree" Analogy

The Linux file system hierarchy is analogous to an actual tree you might purchase at a garden store that has its root system wrapped in canvas. If you turn that garden store tree upside down in your mind, you have the concept of the Linux tree hierarchy. The root system is now at the top, just like the Linux root directory. The branches and leaves stem from the root. A directory in Linux is analogous to a branch on the garden store tree. A leaf is analogous to a file because a leaf cannot contain branches or other leaves just as a file cannot contain directories or other files; however, a file does have contents. Just as a directory can contain other subdirectories and files, a branch can contain other branches and leaves.

Consider this example. Townsend Toyota has a Linux system which contains files and directories. It has created directories to represent its business departments. There are files within the directories that contain business-related data. Figure 2-1 shows the tree structure of Townsend Toyota. The `tree` command displays a hierarchical listing of the directory. Notice that the root, (/), directory is near the upper-left corner. The directories and files are organized into logical groupings beneath the directory named TownsendToyota which is immediately beneath the root, (/). The directories named Accounting, IT, Marketing, and Production are on the same level, falling immediately within the TownsendToyota directory. Look at the Accounting directory and see the four directories beneath it—AccountsPayable, AccountsReceivable, GeneralLedger, and Payroll. Recall that the directory named Payroll contains the payroll files mentioned in the previous example.

 You can use the `tree` command to show a snapshot of a subdirectory too. If you want to see the tree structure just for the directory named Marketing, you enter `tree Marketing`.

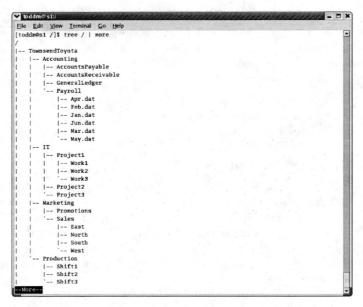

```
[toddm@s1 /]$ tree / | more
/
|-- TownsendToyota
|   |-- Accounting
|   |   |-- AccountsPayable
|   |   |-- AccountsReceivable
|   |   |-- GeneralLedger
|   |   `-- Payroll
|   |       |-- Apr.dat
|   |       |-- Feb.dat
|   |       |-- Jan.dat
|   |       |-- Jun.dat
|   |       |-- Mar.dat
|   |       `-- May.dat
|   |-- IT
|   |   |-- Project1
|   |   |   |-- Work1
|   |   |   |-- Work2
|   |   |   `-- Work3
|   |   |-- Project2
|   |   `-- Project3
|   |-- Marketing
|   |   |-- Promotions
|   |   `-- Sales
|   |       |-- East
|   |       |-- North
|   |       |-- South
|   |       `-- West
|   `-- Production
|       |-- Shift1
|       |-- Shift2
|       `-- Shift3
--More--
```

Figure 2-1   Tree hierarchy for Townsend Toyota

The **tree** command is useful for showing the tree structure; however, when writing shell programs, you need to understand how to get to those file or directories within the tree. If you wanted to access the May.dat file from the root directory, you would have to follow the lines in Figure 2-1 down and over to the right until you finally got to the file. You would end up going through the TownsendToyota, Accounting, and Payroll directories, respectively.

 You can think of the output of the **tree** command as a map to get to a file or directory. A map shows you towns you must go through to get to your destination. The **tree** command shows you the directories you must go through to get to your files.

Linux System Directories

Linux stores many of its system files in various subdirectories beneath the root directory. These are created during installation of the operating system and should not be deleted or renamed. You need understand the purpose of the Linux system directories, shown in Table 2-1, in case your scripts refer to commands or files contained within them.

Table 2-1   Some of the Linux system directories

Directory	Purpose
/bin	Holds many binary executable programs
/boot	Holds the Linux kernel
/dev	Contains device files for all the devices in the Linux file system
/etc	Holds configuration files; many are written using shell script programs. Configuration files are files that various programs read in order to know what they are supposed to do.
/home	Default location which contains user directories; when users log in to a Linux system, their current directory is /home/*username*. For example, a user named Marissa has a home directory of /home/marissa.
/lib	Contains files and executable programs used by the system
/mnt	Contains mounted drives
/root	The Linux superuser, or root user's home directory
/sbin	Contains additional binary executable programs normally used by the root user
/tmp	Used for temporary file and directory storage
/usr	Contains other subdirectories for applications, such as X11 (for X Windows on Linux), HTML files, library files, and games; also included are header files for C programs. Two of the most widely used subdirectories within /usr are usr/bin and /usr/sbin. These contain directories and binary executables.
/var	Contains both files and directories; typically, the type of files in /var vary in size, such as the log files for various processes located in /var/log. The system log file, /var/log/messages, is also held here.

NAVIGATING THE TREE HIERARCHY

Now that you understand how the hierarchy is set up, you need to learn how to navigate the Linux file system. Look at the sample hierarchy tree shown in Figure 2-2, the top-level directory is root, shown by the forward slash symbol, (/). Other directories branch beneath it. Under the user's home directory, represented by the variable $HOME, the directories named dirA and dirB exist. A variable is used for flexibility, so that users and shell scripts can refer to $HOME, and it equates to their individual home directory. Beneath each of these are other directories. Ultimately, files are stored at the bottom of the tree. Directories on the same level and having the same parent directory are considered **sibling directories**. Said another way, dirA and dirB are **child directories** of $HOME, their parent.

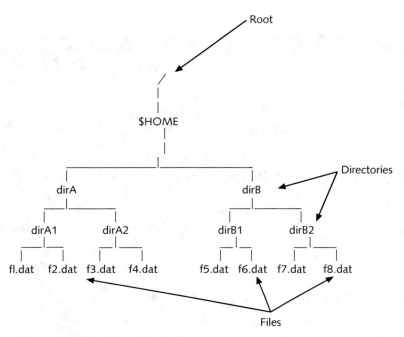

Figure 2-2   A sample tree hierarchy

When a user account is created, a home directory is automatically created for that user. The home directory is usually located in /home as described in Table 2-1. The system uses a variable named $HOME which equates to your home directory.

The contents of the variable named $HOME is different for each user. It is just a method of saying your own home directory. For example, Mary Phan's $HOME may literally be equal to /home/maryphan; while Harold Patel's $HOME directory may literally be equal to /home/haroldpatel.

Your **current directory** denotes where you are within the file system. Think of it as where you are in a building when looking at a building evacuation map. The makers of the map assume you are in a certain room when they created the evacuation plan. They even have a red "You Are Here" dot with a red arrow representing a path showing how to exit the building. The Linux tree operates similarly. The "You Are Here" dot represents your current directory and the long red arrow represents how to get to another location, such as another directory.

When navigating you need to know two things—where you are and where you want to go within the tree hierarchy.

Changing Directory Locations

If you want to change your current position to the root directory, you have to use the cd command. This command allows you to "change directory" locations within the tree to another directory. It takes the general form:

    cd *directory*

Think of the cd command as changing your "You Are Here" location in the tree.

The *directory* is a directory location within the tree that you want to go to.

To help you navigate through the tree, you need to understand the terms full path and partial path. The **full path** specifies the complete path from root. A full path always begins from the root directory. The **partial path** specifies a certain point in the directory path, which is simply the name of the directory that you would like to change to relative to your current location. It never begins at root.

The full or partial path can be used with most any command.

Imagine someone asks you for directions from his house to your house. You would give him directions that would take him from his front door to yours. Essentially, you would be providing him with the full path. If that same person was already on the way to your house and perhaps became lost, you wouldn't give them the full path directions, instead you would provide directions relative to where he currently is located, in other words, the partial path.

Changing Directory Locations to the / Directory

Assume your current directory is dirA in Figure 2-2. In order to change to the root directory using a full path, you would issue this command:

    cd /

Figure 2-3 shows changing directory locations to the root directory. Notice that the before the cd command is performed, the user is in the toddm directory.

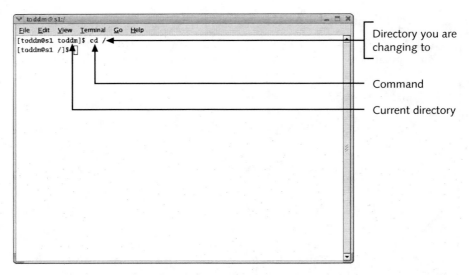

Figure 2-3   Running the cd to change the root directory

Changing Directory Locations to a Parent Directory

In order to change to a parent directory, you use a special notation. In Linux, the parent directory is represented by the use of two dots (**..**) notation. Let's say your current directory is dirA1 as shown in Figure 2-2. The command to navigate to the parent directory, dirA is:

```
cd ..
```

The use of the two dots, **..**, is an example of a partial path. Every directory, except the root directory, has a parent directory, or **..** The root directory cannot have a parent directory because it is the top directory. A way you can remember this is that you have two parents, one mom and one dad, and in the tree hierarchy, they are collectively referred to as the "parent." Figure 2-4 shows changing directory locations to the parent directory.

Changing Directory Locations to a Child Directory

In order to change directory locations to a child directory, you refer to the child by its name. Here is the general form:

```
cd child-directory
```

This is where **child-directory** is the name of the child directory you want to change directory locations to. If you want to change from the current directory of dirA to one of its child directories, such as dirA1, as shown in Figure 2-2, you would issue this command:

```
cd dirA1
```

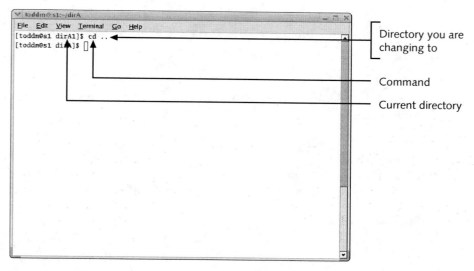

Figure 2-4   Running the `cd ..` command to navigate to a parent directory

Figure 2-5 shows changing directory locations to a child directory

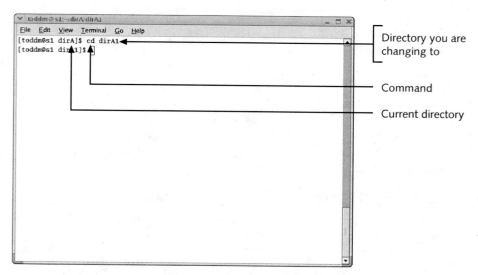

Figure 2-5   Changing to a child directory using the `cd` command

Changing Directory Locations to a Sibling Directory

A sibling directory is a peer directory of your current directory. In Figure 2-2, the directories dirA and dirB are sibling directories. Also, dirA1 and dirA2 are siblings, as well as dirB1 and dirB2. However, even though dirA1 and dirA2 are on the same level as dirB1 and dirB2 they are not siblings because they have different parents.

To change to any sibling directory, the syntax is:

```
cd ../sibling
```

Assume your current directory is dirB, and you want to change directory locations to dirA. You would use the code:

```
cd ../dirA
```

In the command, `cd ../dirA`, the two dots represent the parent directory, in this case `$HOME`, and the forward slash is a separator between the parent and child levels of root and dirA. Figure 2-6 shows changing directory locations to a sibling directory.

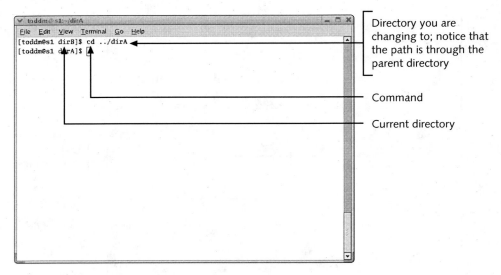

Figure 2-6   Changing to a sibling directory using the `cd` command

Changing Directory Locations Across Multiple Levels

In order to change directory locations across multiple levels you refer to each parent in the hierarchy tree. Here is the syntax:

```
cd ../../directory
```

If your current directory is dirA1 as in Figure 2-2, you navigate to dirB as follows:

```
cd ../../dirB
```

The first pair of dots represents the parent of dirA1 which is dirA. The second pair of dots represents the parent of dirA which is `$HOME`. This happens to be the grandparent of dirA1. Finally, you include the directory name you want to navigate to that is multiple levels away, which in this case is dirB. Figure 2-7 shows changing directory locations across multiple levels.

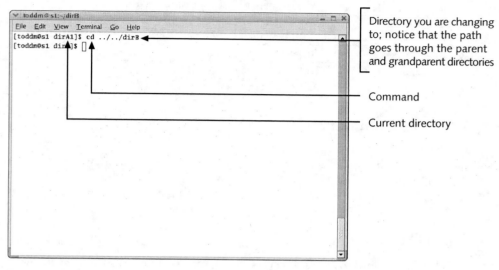

Figure 2-7 Changing directories across multiple levels

UNDERSTANDING DIRECTORY MANAGEMENT COMMANDS

In order to be a proficient Linux System Administrator, you must be aware of many of the commands used to manage the Linux file system. Each command executes and generates one of the following:

- *No output*—The command worked successfully.
- *Output*—The command worked successfully.
- *An error*—The command did not work correctly.

The Linux commands are divided into three main categories:

- *Directory commands*—Commands that work with directories
- *Editor commands*—Commands that allow you to manipulate the file system
- *File commands*—Commands that work with files

The main commands that deal with directories are summarized in Table 2-2. These are the most commonly used commands relating to the file system. It is important that you learn these commands because they allow you to manage the Linux file system, and understanding them gives you greater control over the file system.

Table 2-2   Directory commands

Directory Command	Purpose
pwd	Displays the name of your current directory
ls	Displays both files and directories; by default, it displays the files and directories in the current directory
cd	Changes directory locations
mkdir	Creates or makes a directory
rmdir	Deletes or removes a directory

The pwd Command

The pwd command displays your current working directory and returns output to the screen. Although it does not have very many practical options, it is one of the most important commands because it lets you know where you are in the tree hierarchy. To execute the command, you simply type pwd on the command line, and then press Enter. This displays your current directory location on the screen.

The ls Command

The ls command lists a directory's contents. You use this command to determine what is in a directory. The ls command has a variety of uses and many different options for listing directories. For example, if you wanted to see the size of a file in bytes, you would attach the appropriate option to the ls command. Like the other directory commands, the command is written:

> ls *option path-name*

The symbol for indicating an option is typically either a single dash (-) or a double-dash (--), and it is followed by the option. So, the -l option when attached to the ls command as in ls -l gives additional information about the files and directories—such as the size of the files and the permissions.

The command ls -l uses a lowercase letter l (as in lucky), not the numeral one. Don't make the mistake of putting a one after the dash symbol; it results in an error.

The path name is optional. If you leave it off, the ls command default is to show you the contents of the current directory.

The -l Option on the ls Command

One of the most common options for the ls command is -l which is short for long listing. The term "long listing" means that more information—type of file, permissions, links, owner, group, size in bytes, date and time, and name—is displayed on the screen when you use this option than if you don't. Figure 2-8 shows the output of the ls command with the -l option. Table 2-3 provides an overview of the various fields represented in the figure.

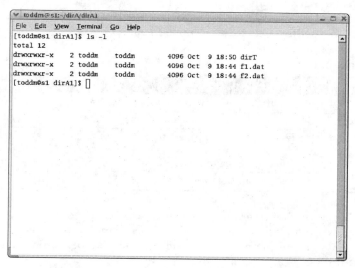

Figure 2-8   Output of the ls -l command

Table 2-3   Table of the column fields in a long listing

Type	Permissions	Links	Owner	Group	Size in Bytes	Date and Time	Name
d	rwxrwxr-x	2	toddm	toddm	4096	Aug 30 20:52	dirT
-	rw-rw-r--	1	toddm	toddm	37	Aug 31 6:48	f1.dat
-	rw-rw-r--	1	toddm	toddm	102	Aug 31 6:48	f2.dat

The Type Column   The first field of the long listing format is the Type field. Table 2-4 provides a listing of the various types of items that can appear here.

Table 2-4   Possible values of the type field of the long listing

Type Value	Description
d	File is a directory
-	File is a file
c	File is a character device
b	File is a block device

The Permissions Column   The next nine characters after the file type represent permissions for the file or directory. These are grouped into three sets of three. The first three characters represent permissions for the owner, the second set of three characters represents permissions for the group, and the last set of three characters represents permissions for other users, commonly known as the world. Table 2-5 provides comprehensive definitions of the permissions.

Table 2-5   Permissions

Letter Abbreviation	Description
r	Indicates that the file or directory can be read
w	Indicates that the file or directory can be written to
x	Indicates that the file can be executed; shell scripts always have the x permission turned on. An x permission for a directory indicates that you can take a directory listing of the directory to see its subdirectories and files.
-	Indicates the permission is not granted

Note that the permissions are positional. They are always in this order: read, write, and execute. If a dash exists in place of the permission, then the permission is turned off or not available. For example, if the permissions are r-x, then the permissions are for read and execute, but no write permission is given.

Additional Columns   The remaining six columns are a bit more straightforward in their presentation. The Links column represents the number of links or shortcuts to the file or directory. The Owner column represents the actual user who owns the file. Generally, this is the person who created it. Notice that "toddm" is the owner. The owner of the file or directory receives the owner set of permissions (the first set of read, write, and execute permissions after the Type field). The Group column represents the group membership. If a user is a member of the group, they get the group set of permissions (the middle set of read, write, and execute permissions) in the permissions fields. If you are not the owner or a member of the group, then you get the last set of permissions.

The Date and Time column is the date and time stamp the file or directory was created. The Size in bytes column is the size of the file or directory. And finally, the Name column is the Linux name used when referring to the file. A Linux filename can be no more than 256 characters long.

The -a Option on the ls Command

The -a option is used to display all files and directories. What makes it different from the -l option is that it is used to display hidden files in your own directory. Hidden files begin with a dot or period. Knowing how to list hidden files can be very useful. You may find it necessary to hide files in order to protect them from being deleted or seen by a user. There are several hidden files that are created by default when a user account is created. When you use the `ls -1` command, you'll notice a directory named dot (.) and one named dot dot (..). The single dot represents your current directory—every directory has one of these. The two dots represent the parent. The existence of a directory named dot dot is why you can issue the `cd ..` command to navigate to your parent directory.

Next you will use these two options with the `ls` command.

To execute the `ls` command:

1. Log in to the Linux system as a user, and then open a Terminal emulation window.

2. Type `ls -1`, and then press **Enter**. A long listing of your current directory appears.

3. Record the number of directories and files.

4. Record the permissions for one of the files.

5. Type `ls -a`, and then press **Enter**. A listing of hidden files in your current directory appears.

6. Record the number of hidden files.

7. Now, combine these options on one line. Type `ls -al`, and then press **Enter**. A listing of hidden files in your current directory appears as well as all other files. (The order of the options does not matter. So, `ls -la` would work, too.)

8. Record the permissions of just the hidden files.

9. To exit the Terminal emulation program, type **exit**, and then press **Enter**.

10. Log out.

The `mkdir` and `rmdir` Commands

The `mkdir` command, which creates a new directory, normally returns no output to the screen. The `mkdir` command takes the following form:

```
mkdir directory
```

The path can be either full or partial. For example, to create a directory called paychecks, you would execute the following command:

```
mkdir paychecks
```

Conversely, you use the `rmdir` command to remove an empty directory. The `rmdir` command takes the following form:

```
rmdir directory
```

The path can be either full or partial.

 When removing a directory with the rmdir command, the directory must be empty and your current directory cannot be the directory you are trying to remove.

To remove the paychecks directory just shown you would use the **rmdir** command:

    rmdir paychecks

Next you will create a directory named Class, and then remove it.

To create and remove a directory:

1. Log in to the Linux system as a user, and then open a Terminal emulation window.

2. Type **pwd**, and then press **Enter**. Your current working directory is displayed.

3. Type **mkdir Class**, and then press **Enter** to create a new directory named Class.

4. To remove the directory you just created, type **rmdir Class**, and then press **Enter**.

5. Create the Class directory again using the **mkdir** command.

6. Navigate to the Class directory, by typing **cd Class**, and then press **Enter**.

7. Type **pwd**, and then press **Enter**. Notice that Class directory is your present working directory.

8. Type **rmdir Class**, and then press **Enter**. An error message results. Figure 2-9 shows a result of attempting to remove your present directory.

9. To navigate to the parent directory, type **cd ..**, and press **Enter**.

10. Type **pwd**, and then press **Enter**. Your current working directory is displayed. Record it now.

11. Type **rmdir Class**, and then press **Enter**. You are now able to remove the Class directory because it is no longer your current working directory.

12. To exit the Terminal emulation program window, type **exit**, and then press **Enter**.

13. Log out.

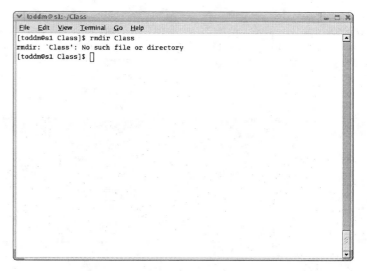

Figure 2-9   Message displays when you attempt to remove your parent directory

USING EDITING COMMANDS

In the Linux system you use editors to create shell script programs. **Editors** are programs that allow you to create, copy, and remove text within a file. Editors are similar to word-processing software. There are several different editors, so you need to try out a variety of them in order to determine the one that fits your needs and style best. It is important that you familiarize yourself with these programs because you occasionally need to use them within shell script programs.

Table 2-6 lists the most commonly used editor programs.

Table 2-6   Editor programs

Editor Program	Purpose
vi	Allows you to create a new file; it is somewhat more difficult to navigate than most graphical word-processing programs. The vi editor is the most commonly used editor on Linux systems.
gedit	User-friendly graphical text editor

The vi Program

Visual Interface or **vi**, as it's more commonly called, operates in several modes. While the **vi editor** is not as user-friendly as some of the other editors, particularly the graphical ones, it is the most commonly used editor on most Linux platforms. It operates in two modes. **Command mode** is when you input commands, telling the vi editor what you want to do. **Text mode** is when you type in your text or code. Because you use the keyboard to enter commands and text, the Escape key allows you to toggle back and forth between command mode and text mode. It is important to remember that you must issue one of the commands listed in Table 2-7 before you enter any text.

Table 2-7   Common vi commands

Command	Description
I	Inserts or moves the cursor to the beginning of the current line and allows you to enter text there
i	Inserts text at the current location of the cursor
O	Opens or adds a new blank line above the current line
o	Opens or adds a new blank line below the current line
A	Appends a new blank line to the end of the current line
a	Appends a new blank line immediately after the current location of the cursor
R	Represents the replace command mode; characters you type replace current characters starting at the location of the cursor
r	Replaces the character at the location of the cursor
k or UP ARROW	Moves up one line
j or DOWN ARROW	Moves down one line
h or LEFT ARROW	Moves one character position to the left
l or RIGHT ARROW	Moves one character position to the right
w	Moves the cursor to the next word
b	Moves the cursor to the previous word (b for back)
Shift+G	Moves the cursor to the end of the file
N followed by Shift+G	Moves the cursor to the Nth line (where N represents a number) in the file. For example, 3 followed by Shift+G, takes you to the third line.
D	Deletes text from the current cursor position to the end of the current line
de or dw	Deletes the current word
db	Deletes the previous word (b for back)
d(	Deletes all the text from the current cursor location to the beginning of the line
d)	Deletes all the text from the current cursor location to the end of the line
dh	Deletes the previous letter
dl or x	Deletes the current letter
dd	Deletes the current line
dw	Deletes the current word

Table 2-7 Common `vi` commands (continued)

Command	Description
u	Undoes the previous command
yy	Yanks, or copies, one line into the vi buffer; the buffer is simply an area of memory for holding data
p	Puts or pastes lines previously yanked and residing in the vi buffer to a new location
Nyy	Yanks, or copies, N lines (where N represents a number) into the vi buffer
:wq!	Writes and then quits vi

You can run the `vi` editor by simply typing the command `vi` in the Terminal emulation window. Then, you can enter your text and save it to a file. However, `vi` is normally executed with the file's path, as in this example:

> `vi payroll`

Next you will use the `vi` editor to create a file and manage text and code within that file.

To use `vi` to create and manage a file:

1. Log in to the Linux system as a user, and then open a Terminal emulation window.

2. Type **vi file42.txt**, and then press **Enter**. A screen like the one shown in Figure 2-10 appears. The `vi` editor opens the file named file42.txt. (Note that the ~ symbol is called the tilde.)

3. To insert text, press **Esc**, and then type **i**. You are now in the text mode.

4. Enter the following text (be sure to press Enter at the end of each line). Note: If you make a mistake when typing in the text, you'll need to use the Escape key to toggle back and forth between text and command mode. Refer to the commands in Table 2-7.

   ```
   Line 1 of the vi editor.
   Line 2 of the vi editor.
   Line 3 of the vi editor.
   Last line of the vi editor.
   ```

5. To copy the first two lines and place them at the end of the file, move your cursor to the first character on the first line. Press **Esc**, type **2**, and then type **y** twice. This yanks or copies, the first two lines and places them in the `vi` buffer.

6. Move your cursor to the end of the file by pressing **Shift+G**. The cursor moves to the first character on the last line.

7. To put or paste the two previously yanked lines, type **p**. Notice that this places a copy of the two lines at the end of the file.

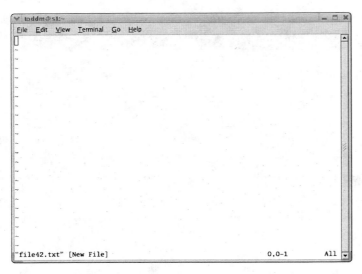

Figure 2-10   The vi command changes

8. To delete the first two lines, move the cursor to the first character on the first line by pressing **1** followed by **Shift+G**. Your cursor moves to the first line.

9. Press **d** twice to delete the first line of text.

10. Repeat Step 9 to delete the second line of text. When complete, the file should look like Figure 2-11.

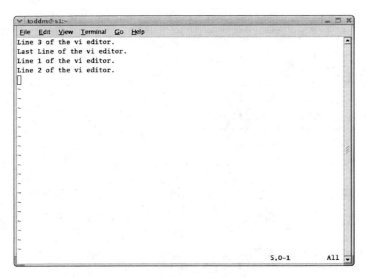

Figure 2-11   The output of the vi command

11. Type **:wq!**, and then press **Enter**. The file is saved and your prompt is returned.

12. Close your window, and then log out.

2

UNDERSTANDING FILE MANAGEMENT COMMANDS

File management commands help you manipulate files. While you use the editor commands to manipulate file content, you use file management commands to manipulate the files themselves such as when you create copies of existing files, move or rename existing files, or even merge text from multiple files. It is important to understand these commands because you will use them on a daily basis. They can also be used in shell scripts. Table 2-8 includes some of the more commonly used file management commands.

Table 2-8   File management commands

cp	Creates a copy of an existing file
mv	Moves or renames an existing file
sort	Sorts a file's fields in either ascending or descending order
cut	Pulls text out of a file; the original text within the file remains intact
paste	Merges the text from multiple files
diff	Displays the differences between two files; this is useful for verifying the integrity of a file against a master file
rm	Removes a file
uniq	Removes duplicate records from a sorted file

The cp Command

The **cp** command allows you to make a copy of a file. It takes the general form:

> cp *option source destination*

This is where *source* is the source file—the file you want to copy. The source file must exist or the **cp** command generates an error. The *destination* is the file to where you want to copy the source data. The destination file does not have to exist. It is user defined, meaning that the user can change the destination filename. When you use the **cp** command with the **-i** option for interactive mode, if the destination file *does* exist, a message is displayed asking whether or not you would like to overwrite the file.

The cp Command with a Full or Partial Path for Both the Source and Destination Filenames

The **cp** command accepts any combination of full and partial paths for the source and destination files. Let's look at an example. Refer back to Figure 2-1 of the Townsend Toyota tree structure. In order to copy the Apr.dat file from the Payroll directory to the

/TownsendToyota/IT/Project3 directory, you can execute the following command using full paths:

```
cp /TownsendToyota/Accounting/Payroll/Apr.dat/
TownsendToyota/IT/Project3/Apr.dat
```

Once successfully completed, you have a copy of Apr.dat in both the /TownsendToyota/Accounting/Payroll and /TownsendToyota/IT/Project3 directories.

In order to copy the Feb.dat file, located in the /TownsendToyota/Accounting/Payroll to another file called Febbackup.dat within the same directory, you would issue this partial path:

```
cp Feb.dat Febbackup.dat
```

Once successfully completed, you have two files: the original, Feb.dat and the duplicate copy, Febbackup.dat. Both are in the same directory.

Using the cp Command to Copy a File to the Parent Directory or a Sibling Directory

In order to copy the May.dat file to the parent directory, you use a partial path for the destination file as shown in this example:

```
cp May.dat ../May.dat
```

Once successfully completed, you have a copy of May.dat in the parent directory.

In order to copy the Jun.dat file, located in the /TownsendToyota/Accounting/Payroll to the sibling directory named /TownsendToyota/Accounting/GeneralLedger, you can use a partial path on the destination as shown in this example:

```
cp Jun.dat ../GeneralLedger/Jun.dat
```

Once successfully completed, you have a copy of Jun.dat in the /TownsendToyota/Accounting/GeneralLedger sibling directory.

The mv Command

The mv command allows you to move, or rename, a file or directory. It takes the following form:

```
mv source destination
```

As with the cp command, the source file must exist. The destination can be user defined.

 While you use the mv command to both move and rename files and directories, the term move is used when the source path and the destination path are in different directories. The term rename is used when the source path and the destination path is in the same directory.

Like the **cp** command, if you use the **-i** option with the **mv** command, it prompts you before it moves a source file to an existing destination file.

The source and destination paths can be either a full or partial path to a file or a directory. However, the source and destination cannot be identical—you cannot move a file to itself.

Using the mv Command to Rename a File or Move a File to Another Directory

To rename a file, consider the following example where a file called x.file is changed to the new name y.file. The contents of the newly changed filename remain the same. Because you are renaming and not copying, the original file named x.file no longer exists.

```
mv x.file y.file
```

You can also use the mv command to change the location of the file. As in the previous example, the contents remain the same, but the file is moved and has a new name. Think of the move as if you were physically moving something from one place to another. Its location changes but the contents do not. In the following example, the x2.file is moved to the dirA directory and renamed y2.file.

```
mv x2.file /dirA/y2.file
```

Using the mv Command When the Source and Destination Have the Same Name

The only time the source and destination file can have the same name is when you are moving it to another directory. As previously noted, you cannot rename a file to its same name. Yet, in this example, mv /dirB/x2.file /dirA/x2.file, the actual filename stays the same—x2.file. This is because the directory name of the source, dirB, and the directory name of the destination, dirA, are different. This results in two completely different paths, hence two completely different filenames as far as Linux is concerned.

Next you will use the **cp** and mv commands to become familiar with how they work.

To copy and move files:

1. Log in to the Linux system as a user, and then open a Terminal emulation window.

2. Type **mkdir dirA1**, and then press **Enter**.

3. First, you need to create a file to duplicate. Use **vi** to create a file named **f1.dat**.

4. Type **cp f1.dat f8.dat**, and then press **Enter** to copy the file you created in the previous step.

5. Type **ls**, and then press **Enter**. Notice that the listing of files includes the file you just created as well as the copy of that file.

6. Type **cp -i f1.dat f8.dat**, and then press **Enter**. The command interactively prompts you asking if you want to overwrite the file.

7. Type **y**, and then press **Enter**.

8. Type **mv f1.dat f9.dat**, and then press **Enter**. The f1.dat file is moved to f9.dat.

9. Type **mv -i f8.dat f9.dat**, and then press **Enter**. The command interactively prompts you, asking if you want to overwrite the file.

10. Type **y**, and then press **Enter**.

11. Type **ls**, and then press **Enter**. Notice that the f9.dat file no longer exists, but the f1.dat file does. Now look at Figure 2-12; it shows the commands as you've used them in this exercise. You can see a listing displaying the files in the directory, in this case dirA1, before they are copied or moved. You can also see the message generated from the **-i** option when it is used with the **cp** and **mv** commands.

12. To exit the Terminal emulation program, type **exit**, and then press **Enter**.

```
toddm@s1: ~/dirA/dirA1                                    _  □  X
File  Edit  View  Terminal  Go  Help
[toddm@s1 dirA1]$ ls
dirT  f1.dat
[toddm@s1 dirA1]$ cp f1.dat f8.dat
[toddm@s1 dirA1]$ ls
dirT  f1.dat  f8.dat
[toddm@s1 dirA1]$ cp -i f1.dat f8.dat
cp: overwrite `f8.dat'? y
[toddm@s1 dirA1]$ ls
dirT  f1.dat  f8.dat
[toddm@s1 dirA1]$ mv f1.dat f9.dat
[toddm@s1 dirA1]$ mv -i f8.dat f9.dat
mv: overwrite `f9.dat'? y
[toddm@s1 dirA1]$ ls
dirT  f9.dat
[toddm@s1 dirA1]$ []
```

Figure 2-12   The output of the cp and mv commands

The sort Command

The **sort** command is used to sort data either in ascending or descending order. For example, if you want to alphabetically sort a file containing employee names, you use this command. Or, if you want to sort a numeric field in descending order, you also use the `sort` command. The basic syntax of the `sort` command is:

```
sort filename
```

In order to run the `sort` command for a file named unsort.dat, you enter the following command:

```
sort unsort.dat
```

When you use the `sort` command, the default is for the output to be displayed on your screen. However, you can redirect the output to a file by using the greater-than operator, `>`. The following example sorts a file named unsort.dat and places the output to a new file named sort.dat. The original file remains intact. There is no output to the screen because it is being redirected to a file. The name of the file following the greater-than symbol is user defined.

```
sort unsort.dat > sort.dat
```

By default, the `sort` command sorts in ascending order, or lower to higher. You can sort in descending order, called reverse order, using the `-r` option as in this command:

```
sort -r filename
```

The cut Command

The `cut` command allows you to strip text out of files and display the cut text on the screen or redirect the text to another file. This command is most often used to cut fields within a file. The data is not permanently cut from the file. The command does not alter the original file and it automatically opens the file for you. The basic syntax for the `cut` command is:

```
cut options filename
```

You need to be aware of two important options. The `-d` option is used to identify the delimiter in the file. The colon is generally used as a separator or **delimiter** between fields, letting programs know where one field begins and one ends. For example, `-d:` identifies the colon as a delimiter. The `-f` option is used to identify which field you want based on the delimiter. For example, consider the following record for an animal clinic:

```
1001:King Pup:Dog
```

The first field, "1001," represents the ID, the second field, "King Pup," represents the animal's name, and the third field, "Dog," represents the type of animal. Colons are used to delimit the fields in this example. You use a colon, or some other character, instead of a space to separate fields. The space can not be used because it may actually separate words in a field, such as "King Pup."

Assuming the file is named animal.dat, the command to display the first field is: `cut -d: -f1 animal.dat`. The command to display the first and third fields would be: `cut -d: -f1,3 animal.dat`.

Next you will create a file with several employee records in it. Each record will consist of two fields—an employee number followed by a colon and the employee name.

To use the cut command in a file:

1. Log in to the Linux system as a user, and then open a Terminal emulation window.

2. Create a file named **unsort.dat** using the vi editor.

3. Enter the data in two fields. Note in the data below, that the format is *number:name* where *number* represents the first field and *name* represents the second field. The colon (:) is the delimiter. Place the following data in the file noting that there are duplicate 3:Jessie records. (You will use these two records later when you learn about the uniq command.) After you enter the data make sure you press Enter at the end of each line, save the file, and then exit the vi editor.

   ```
   3:Jessie James Garcia
   3:Jessie James Garcia
   2:Zachary Scott Pheng
   4:Lorenzo Todd Von Schloss
   1:Micki McSunday-Washington
   ```

4. To cut the first field, type **cut -d: -f1 unsort.dat**, and then press **Enter**. See Figure 2-13; the first field appears on your screen, but the data has not been removed from the original file.

5. To cut the second field, the names, and then send the output to a file named name.dat, type **cut -d: -f2 unsort.dat > name.dat**, and then press **Enter**. See Figure 2-13.

6. To display the contents of the new file, type **cat name.dat**, and then press **Enter**. See Figure 2-13; notice that the new file only has the names in it.

7. To ensure that the original contents of unsortcut.dat have not been literally cut, type **cat unsort.dat**, and then press **Enter**. The original contents that were created in Step 3 appear unchanged on your screen as shown in Figure 2-13.

8. To exit, type **exit**, and then press **Enter**.

9. Log out.

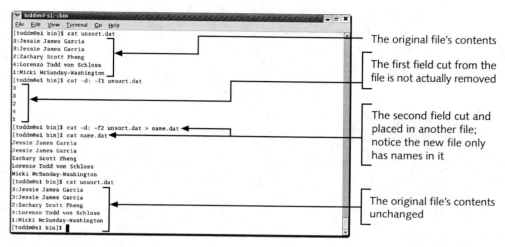

The original file's contents

The first field cut from the file is not actually removed

The second field cut and placed in another file; notice the new file only has names in it

The original file's contents unchanged

Figure 2-13   Demonstrating the cut command

The paste Command

Whereas the cut command cuts file fields, the paste command pastes, or merges, data from one file to another. The data can then be merged into a new file. The basic syntax of the paste command is:

    paste filename_one filename_two

The above code merges each line from file two with each line of file one. For example, assume you had two files each containing name data. The last.dat file contents are Smith Jones Adams, and the first.dat file contents are Joe Mary Sue. If you enter the command paste first.dat last.dat, then your output to the screen would be:

    Joe Smith
    Mary Jones
    Sue Adams

If you had entered the command paste last.dat first.dat, then your output would be:

    Smith Joe
    Jones Mary
    Adams Sue

The contents of the original files remain the same. You can also create an altogether new file using the redirect output (>) symbol. If you enter the command paste first.dat last.dat > first_last.dat, you would create a new file called first_last.dat with the pasted data from the first.dat and last.dat files.

Suppose that Mama's Hardware Store maintains two separate files. One file is called product and contains the names of top selling sale items, and the other file is called quantity and contains the amount of the sales items that have been ordered. The owners would like the information to appear in one file named orders. To do that, you need to paste these files together. Figure 2-14 shows the contents of the two original files as well as the use of the **paste** command to merge these files and redirect the contents to the new file.

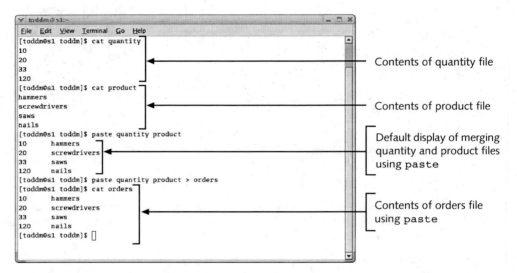

Figure 2-14   The **paste** command for Mama's Hardware Store

The **rm** Command

The **rm** command is used to remove a file permanently from the file system tree hierarchy. There is no way to recover a removed file. The basic syntax of the command is:

    rm *filename*

In the following example, the file named resume.dat is removed.

    rm resume.dat

Some versions of Linux ask you to verify that you really want to remove a file before it is removed. Other versions simply remove the file without asking. Use caution and consider testing this concept by removing a test file before removing any files from your file hierarchy.

The uniq Command

The uniq command is to used to find duplicate lines from a sorted file. This is a particularly helpful programming technique to use if redundant records happen to exist in a file. The uniq command does not remove the duplicate lines; it just displays them on the screen. The uniq command opens the file for you. The basic syntax of this command is:

```
uniq filename
```

The output defaults to the screen, displaying the duplicates. You can also redirect the output to a user-defined filename using the following command:

```
uniq duplicates.dat > uniq.dat
```

In this case, the repeating lines from the duplicates.dat file are redirected to the uniq.dat file. You use redirection when you want to refer to the original data file. In this case, you would process the uniq.dat file because any redundant records have already been removed from the file.

The uniq command has a useful option for counting the number of occurrences of a line in a file. This is helpful when you want to identify the number of duplicates you have in a file. The following uniq command with the attached -c option accomplishes this:

```
uniq -c duplicates.dat
```

Next you will use the uniq command to remove duplicate items from a grocery list where several people in the household have added redundant items.

To use the uniq command to remove duplicates from a file:

1. Log in to the Linux system as a user, and then open a Terminal emulation window.

2. Create a file named **grocery.dat** using the vi editor.

3. Enter the following data. As you enter the data, make sure you press Enter at the end of each line. Save the file, and then exit the vi editor.

```
soup
soup
pizza
turkey
lettuce
lettuce
lettuce
apples
bananas
grapes
grapes
```

4. To remove the duplicate grocery items, type **uniq grocery.dat**, and then press **Enter**. See Figure 2-15.

5. To redirect this to a file that you can take to the grocery store, type **uniq grocery.dat > list.dat**, and then press **Enter**.

6. To display the contents of the new list, type **cat list.dat**, and then press **Enter**. See Figure 2-15. Notice that now the items are part of the list.dat file.

7. To exit, type **exit**, and then press **Enter**.

8. Log out.

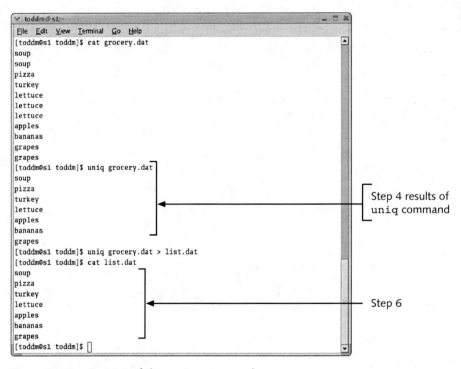

Figure 2-15   Output of the uniq command

2

Chapter Summary

❏ The Linux file system is designed for storage and quick access. Directories contain other directories or files. Files contain only data. The Linux file system is hierarchical, or treelike, in nature. In the Linux file system, the root directory (/) is the top of the tree. All files and folders branch from the root directory. The system directories are created during the installation of the Linux operating system, and they should not be modified or deleted.

❏ When navigating the tree hierarchy, you need to be aware of where you are, or what your current directory is. With the hierarchy structure, there is a parent-child relationship. The parent directory is referred to as dot dot (..). A child directory is referred to by name. Siblings have the same parent. A full path begins at the root directory. A partial path does not include the root directory.

❏ Directory management commands deal with manipulating and displaying the directories in the tree. The most commonly used commands are **cd** for changing the current directory location, **pwd** for displaying the current directory location, and **ls** for displaying the contents of a directory.

❏ Editors and editor commands allow you to manipulate the contents in a file. The most commonly used editor is **vi**. It can be used to add, copy, delete, insert, or modify data within a file.

❏ The file management commands allow you to manipulate the actual files within the tree. The **cp** command is used for copying an existing file to another file, creating two files. The **mv** command is used for moving or renaming an existing file; however, you end up with just one file when you use this command. The **rm** is used to remove a file.

Review Questions

1. Use the _____ command to change directory locations.

   a. **cd**

   b. **rm**

   c. **mkdir**

   d. **cut**

2. Which of the following are considered full paths? (Choose all that apply.)

   a. /dirA

   b. ../dir2

   c. payroll

   d. /

3. Use the _____ command to delete a directory.

   a. `delete_dir`

   b. `mkdir`

   c. `rmdir`

   d. `cat`

4. Which of the following are considered partial paths? (Choose all that apply.)

   a. `/dirA`

   b. `../dir2`

   c. `payroll`

   d. `/`

5. Which of the following are text editors? (Choose all that apply.)

   a. `vi`

   b. `emacs`

   c. `ls`

   d. `cat`

6. The _____ command sorts data in descending order.

   a. `sort -r`

   b. `sort`

   c. `mkdir`

   d. `reverse`

7. To change the working directory location to a sibling directory named dir2, you enter the _____ command.

   a. `cd /`

   b. `cd \`

   c. `cd ..\dir2`

   d. `cd ../dir2`

8. The _____ directory holds mounted drives.

   a. `/root`

   b. `/boot`

   c. `/mnt`

   d. `/var`

2

9. The _____ file system holds files and directories that vary in size.

   a. /root

   b. /boot

   c. /mnt

   d. /var

10. The _____ command creates a directory named winchester in the root directory.

   a. `mkdir /winchester`

   b. `mkdir ../winchester`

   c. `mkdir \winchester`

   d. `md /winchester`

11. The _____ option for the `ls` command displays a long listing.

   a. `-i`

   b. `-a`

   c. `-l`

   d. `-c`

12. Which of the following represents your parent directory?

   a. `..`

   b. `.`

   c. `/`

   d. `\`

13. The _____ command allows you to change directory locations to a child directory named child1.

   a. `mkdir child1`

   b. `cd ../child1`

   c. `cd child1`

   d. `cd /`

14. In `vi`, the command to change to insert mode is:

   a. `o`

   b. `O`

   c. `i`

   d. `d`

15. The _____ command deletes a file.

   a. `rmdir`

   b. `cd`

   c. `rm`

   d. `pwd`

16. The _____ command displays your present working directory.

   a. `cat`

   b. `cd`

   c. `touch`

   d. `pwd`

17. The _____ system directory contains the Linux kernel.

   a. /boot

   b. /root

   c. /dev

   d. /var

18. The _____ in the `vi` editor allows you to save and quit the program.

   a. `:wq`

   b. `q!`

   c. `w!`

   d. `!`

19. The command to rename a file is _____.

   a. `mv`

   b. `cp`

   c. `del`

   d. `rename`

20. The _____ command makes a duplicate of a file.

   a. `mv`

   b. `cp`

   c. `del`

   d. `rename`

HANDS-ON PROJECTS

Project 2-1

In this project, you will compare your own family tree to the Linux file system. Research your family tree no further than your grandparents. Draw your family tree on a separate piece of paper, and then explain how your family tree compares to what you've learned about the Linux file system in this chapter.

Project 2-2

In this project, you will compare a building's evacuation plan for one room to the use of paths in the Linux file system. You will first need to get a copy of a building evacuation plan for one room from your local church, school, or work. Then, write a description of how the evacuation plan relates to a path in the Linux file system hierarchy.

Project 2-3

In this project, you will execute various commands in your home directory.

1. Log in to the Linux computer as a user, and then open a Terminal emulation window.
2. Type **touch file1.dat**, and then press **Enter**.
3. Repeat Step 2 three additional times; however, change the number at the end of the filename each time, e.g., file2.dat, file3.dat, file4.dat.
4. Create a hidden file by typing **touch .hiddenfile.txt**, and then press **Enter**.
5. Issue a long listing of all the files in the directory by typing **ls -al**, and then press **Enter**.
6. On a separate sheet of paper, label and identify each column that is displayed.
7. Close your window, and then log off.

Project 2-4

In this project, you will search the Red Hat Web site for information on various Linux commands in order to learn how to use the Web site as a research tool. You will need access to the Internet.

1. Open a Web browser.
2. In the Address or location box on your browser, type *http://www.redhat.com*, and then press **Enter**. The Red Hat Web site appears.

3. In the Search Red Hat: text box, type **ls**, and then click the **Go** button. The screen displays a listing of the links to documents related to the **ls** command.

4. Click one of the documents and review it. Keep checking documents until you locate one that gives you additional insight into the **ls** command.

5. Based on your findings at this Web site, identify something new you've learned about the **ls** command.

6. Repeat Steps 3 through 5 for the **pwd** command.

7. Repeat Steps 3 through 5 for the **cp** command.

8. Repeat Steps 3 through 5 for the **vi** editor.

9. Close your Web browser.

Project 2-5

In this project, you will execute commands, and then draw the resulting tree structure.

1. Log in to the Linux system as a user, and then open a Terminal emulation window.

2. Type **mkdir Project2-5**, and then press **Enter**.

3. Type **cd Project2-5**, and then press **Enter**.

4. Type **mkdir R**, and then press **Enter**.

5. Type **mkdir S**, and then press **Enter**.

6. Type **mkdir T**, and then press **Enter**.

7. Type **cd T**, and then press **Enter**.

8. Type **touch t1.dat**, and then press **Enter**.

9. Type **touch t2.dat**, and then press **Enter**.

10. Type **touch t3.dat**, and then press **Enter**.

11. Type **cd ../R**, and then press **Enter**.

12. Type **touch r1.dat**, and then press **Enter**.

13. Type **touch r2.dat**, and then press **Enter**.

14. Type **cd ../S**, and then press **Enter**.

15. Type **touch s1.dat**, and then press **Enter**.

16. Type **touch s2.dat**, and then press **Enter**.

17. Type **cd ..**, and then press **Enter**.

18. Draw the resulting tree structure.

19. Close your window, and then log out.

Project 2-6

In this project, you will create a directory tree based on the output of the **tree** command shown in Figure 2-16.

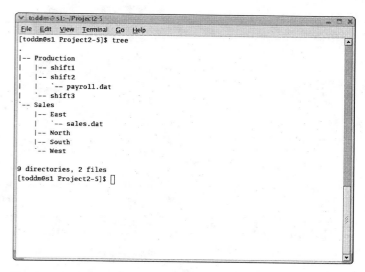

Figure 2-16 Tree you will create for Project 2-6

1. Log in to the Linux system as a user, and then open a Terminal emulation window.
2. Create the directory tree shown in Figure 2-16. You need to use these commands to complete this project: **cd**, **pwd**, **mkdir**, and **rmdir**.
3. Record the order in which you used each command to create the tree.
4. Close your window, and then log out.

Project 2-7

In this project, you will create the directory shown in Figure 2-17 in order to reinforce your understanding of the Linux file system hierarchy. You will need to use these commands to complete this project: **cd**, **pwd**, **mkdir**, and **rmdir**. Finally, record the commands in the order in which you used them to create the tree.

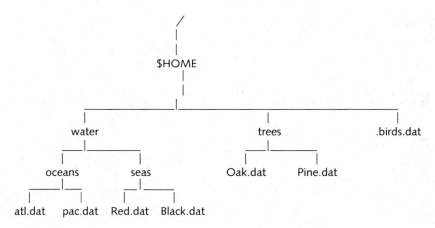

Figure 2-17 Tree you will create for Project 2-7

Project 2-8

In this project, you will use the tree structure from Project 2-5 to manipulate the files and directories created. Project 2-8 requires completion of Project 2-5.

1. Log in to the Linux system as a user, and then open a Terminal emulation window.

2. Type **cd Project2-5**, and then press **Enter**.

3. Type **cd T**, and then press **Enter**.

4. Type **ls**, press **Enter**, and then record the output.

5. Type **cp t1.dat t11.dat**, and then press **Enter**.

6. Type **cp t2.dat t22.dat**, and then press **Enter**.

7. Type **ls**, press **Enter**, and then record the output.

8. Type **mv t3.dat t33.dat**, and then press **Enter**.

9. Type **ls**, press **Enter**, and then record the output.

10. Record the difference between the **cp** and **mv** commands.

11. Type **cd ../S**, and then press **Enter**.

12. Type **ls**, press **Enter**, and then record the output.

13. Type **cp s1.dat ../R/r5.dat**, press **Enter**, and then record what this command does.

14. Type **cd ../R**, and then press **Enter**.

15. Type **ls**, press **Enter**, and then record the output.

16. Close your window, and then log out.

Project 2-9

In this project, you will use **vi** to create a data file with records. You will then sort the data.

1. Log in to the Linux system as a user, and then open a Terminal emulation window.

2. Type **mkdir Project2-9**, and then press **Enter**.

3. Type **cd Project2-9**, and then press **Enter**.

4. Type **vi infile.dat**, and then press **Enter**. The **vi** editor opens.

5. To insert text, press **Esc**, and then type **i**.

6. Enter the following text and make sure you press Enter at the end of each line. (Each row is considered an employee record with colons separating the fields. The first field is the employee number. The second field is the employee name, and the third field is the employee salary.)

```
401:Sue Fanglee Tuen:$34000
104:Sammy Jones:$55402
207:Tammy Phang:$50040
214:Zoe Buhari-Jones:$56000
505:James Brongan:$50500
```

7. To save the file, press **Esc**, and then type the colon symbol (**:**). The cursor moves to the bottom of the screen with a colon to its left.

8. To write the file, type **wq!**, and then press **Enter**. The prompt returns.

9. Sort the data in ascending order by typing **sort infile.dat**, press **Enter**, and then record the output.

10. Sort the data in descending order by typing **sort -r infile.dat**, press **Enter**, and then record the output.

11. Sort the data in descending order and redirect the output to another file by typing **sort -r infile.dat > reverse_sort.dat**, and then press **Enter**.

12. Sort the data in ascending order, redirect the output to another file, and then record the command you used.

13. Close your window, and then log out.

Project 2-10

In this project, you will use the files created in Project 2-9. Project 2-10 requires completion of Project 2-9.

1. Log in to the Linux system as a user, and then open a Terminal emulation window.

2. Type **cd Project2-9**, and then press **Enter**.

3. Cut the first field.

4. Cut the second field.

5. Cut the third field.

6. Cut both the first and third field and redirect the output to a new file named **salary.dat**.

7. Make a duplicate of infile.dat by typing `cp infile.dat infile2.dat`, and then press **Enter**.

8. Open the file named **infile2.dat**, and add five additional records. Add a sixth record that has your name. Also, create a fictitious employee number and employee salary to complete your record.

9. Type `diff infile.dat infile2.dat`, and then press **Enter**. Record the output.

10. Close your window, and then log out.

CASE PROJECTS

Case 2-1

You have been hired by TMI to design an application using shell script programs. TMI needs you to design and create a new directory structure.

The company has several departments: accounting, sales, manufacturing, information technology, and headquarters. The accounting department has accounts receivable, accounts payable, and payroll functions within it. The manufacturing department runs three shifts and a weekend shift. The information technology department has five projects in progress. The sales department has offices located in the West, East, North, and South.

First, design the Linux file system hierarchy on paper. Keep in mind that the departments, functions, shifts, regions, and projects need to translate into directories. Next, you need to create this hierarchy on the Linux system. Create at least one empty file in each directory. Use the department, function, shift, region, or project name as the filename and include an extension of .dat.

Case 2-2

Zonka Corp. has sales offices in five countries: the United States, Canada, Spain, Singapore, and France. Design your directory structure on paper and then implement it. Make sure that each country is represented by a directory. Next, create two files in each directory named first.dat and last.dat. These will be used to hold employees' names with an employee's first and last names split between two files. In the file named first.dat, add the first name of five employees. In the file named last.dat, add the corresponding last name of the same five employees. Then, using the `paste` command, merge the first two files together into a new file. For each employee, the new file must have the first name followed by the last name on one line. Then, merge the first two files into another file. For each employee, this file must have the last name followed by the first name on one line. Finally, make backup copies of the newly merged files.

3

SHELL BASICS

In this chapter, you will:

- ◆ Understand the shell login and logout files
- ◆ Learn about shell variables
- ◆ Become familiar with the shell environment
- ◆ Learn about shell builtin commands
- ◆ Learn about shell grammar
- ◆ Understand command types

The Linux shell is the program that acts as the interface between you and the operating system kernel. The shell accepts input in the form of your commands, and then gives the commands over to the processor for execution. You see evidence of the shell when you log in and go to a command prompt. In this chapter, you will learn how the shell is executed and understand the purpose of the shell and shell grammar. Redirection will also be discussed.

UNDERSTANDING THE SHELL LOGIN AND LOGOUT FILES

When you log in, a shell is executed and provides you with a shell prompt. You type your commands to the right of the prompt. From your previous experience, you know that you need a username to log in and interact with the operating system. However, when a user account is created, it is given a default shell, which is what allows you to access the operating system. For Red Hat Linux, the default shell is **bash**.

As you know from Chapter 1, there are several different shells. This book focuses on the bash shell.

The bash shell is an Institute of Electrical and Electronic Engineers (IEEE) Portable Operating Systems Interface standard (POSIX) developed by the Free Software Foundation. This means it is a standard that comes free with the operating system.

The /etc/profile Script File

There are startup files in the Linux directory hierarchy, which are used to set up default settings for the user's environment. The startup files are read and executed in a specific order as the user logs in. The logout file is read and executed as the user logs out.

The shell reads and executes commands in the /etc/profile file, if it is present. Figure 3-1 shows what's included in this file. This file is actually a script. It is important because it is executed for every user. However, your file content may differ. If you wanted all users to have a script execute when they log in or if you wanted to display a message that all would see as they log in, you would modify this file accordingly. You typically place any statements at the end of this file so you won't interfere with other statements already contained within it. The permissions on this file are read and write for the root user and read for all other users; therefore, you must be logged in as root to modify this file. Users cannot modify it. Although you may not understand all the code at this point, it will become clear as you work your way through this book.

Let's look at a statement in the /etc/profile script to give you an idea of what happens with this script. Recall from Chapter 1 that the `history` command allows you to keep up to 1,000 commands. If you look at Figure 3-1, you notice a `HISTSIZE=1000` statement. This sets the number of commands that the `history` command keeps to 1,000. As root user, you could change it to 10,000 or even just 100. If you increase it, you keep more commands in the history list. This is helpful because you can see previous commands in cases where you want to verify the exact syntax of a command. However, if you increase the size of this file, the file that keeps the history list, called ~/.bash_history, will also increase over time. This means you will use more disk space for the enlarged history list.

3

```
# /etc/profile
# System wide environment and startup programs
# Functions and aliases go in /etc/bashrc
if ! echo $PATH | /bin/grep -q "/usr/X11R6/bin" ; then
  PATH="$PATH:/usr/X11R6/bin"
fi
ulimit -S -c 1000000 > /dev/null 2>&1
if [ `id -gn` = `id -un` -a `id -u` -gt 14 ]; then
        umask 002
else
        umask 022
fi
USER=`id -un`
LOGNAME=$USER
MAIL="/var/spool/mail/$USER"
HOSTNAME=`/bin/hostname`
HISTSIZE=1000
REPLY="Y"
if [ -z "$INPUTRC" -a ! -f "$HOME/.inputrc" ]; then
        INPUTRC=/etc/inputrc
fi
export PATH USER LOGNAME MAIL HOSTNAME HISTSIZE INPUTRC REPLY
```

Figure 3-1   The /etc/profile script file

You can also see that a variable called $LOGNAME is set in this file. The $LOGNAME equates to the user account of the user that is currently logged in. As a System Administrator you might use this information for auditing purposes.

The ~/.bash_profile Script File

After the shell executes the /etc/profile script file for all users, another script executes; it is called ~/.bash_profile. However, this file, in each user's home directory, is hidden (notice the dot prior to the filename). The file is hidden so you won't accidentally delete it. The permissions for this file are read and write for the owner and read for all other users; that way each user can customize this file. Figure 3-2 shows what's included in this file. Again, your content may vary. This file exists so that users can customize their own login processes. They can modify this script and place their own commands in the file. For example, if a user wants to display a calendar or the date on the screen each time he or she logs in, it can be done by changing this file. This script file also adds the directory $HOME/bin to the PATH so that users can execute their own scripts without entering a full path.

The tilde, ~, is used to represent the user's home directory. The ~ symbol and $HOME are equivalent. Thus ~/.bash_profile is a hidden file in each user's home directory.

```
# .bash_profile
# Get the aliases and functions
if [ -f ~/.bashrc ]; then
. ~/.bashrc
fi
# User specific environment and startup programs
PATH=$PATH:$HOME/bin
BASH_ENV=$HOME/.bashrc
export BASH_ENV PATH
unset USERNAME
```

Figure 3-2   The ~/.bash_profile script file

Next you will modify and test the ~/.bash_profile file to become more familiar with its operation.

To modify and test the ~/.bash_profile file:

1. Log in to the Linux system as a user, and then open a Terminal emulation window.

2. Type **vi .bash_profile**, and then press **Enter**. The shell script is displayed on the screen. You don't need to include the tilde for your home directory because when you log in, your position in the Linux tree already is your own home directory.

3. Press **Shift+G**. Your cursor moves to the bottom of the screen.

4. Type **o** to open a line of text in vi.

5. Type **echo "Hello"**, and then press **Enter**.

6. Save the file, and then close the editor.

7. In order to test .bash_profile, type **bash .bash_profile**, and then press **Enter**. The text "Hello" appears on the screen.

8. To exit the Terminal emulation program, type **exit**, and then press **Enter**.

9. Log out.

The ~/.bash_profile executes another hidden file, called ~/.bashrc, if it exists on the system. The ~/.bashrc script in turn executes another script that sets your prompt; it is called /etc/bashrc and can only be modified by the root user. Remember that the ~/.bashrc is able to be changed by the user, but that the /etc/bashrc file can only be changed by the root user.

3

The ~/.bash_logout Script File

There is another hidden file located in each user's home directory, which is read and executed each time a user logs out of the Linux system; it is named .bash_logout. A practical use of the ~/.bash_logout file is to check when a user logs off by redirecting the output of the date command to a file. Then, you can determine exactly when a user logged off the system.

Next you will perform an exercise where you change the ~/.bash_logout file, and then test it. The goal of this exercise is to have you modify the file to understand what happens when you change it.

To modify and test the ~/.bash_logout file:

1. Log in to the Linux system as a user, and then open a Terminal emulation window.

2. Type **vi .bash_logout**, and then press **Enter**. The shell script is displayed on the screen.

3. Press **Shift+G**. Your cursor moves to the bottom of the screen.

4. Type **o** to open a line of text in vi.

5. To ensure that you are properly logging out, you can add a closing response by typing **echo "Good Bye!"**, and then press **Enter**.

6. Save the file, and then close the editor.

7. In order to test the **.bash_logout** file, type **bash .bash_logout**, and then press **Enter**. The text "Good Bye!" appears on the screen.

8. To exit the Terminal emulation program, type **exit**, and then press **Enter**.

9. Log out.

Another way to invoke the shell is by entering bash at the command prompt. It is located in the /bin directory.

LEARNING ABOUT SHELL VARIABLES

A **shell variable** is a keyword that is set by the shell for a specific use. It is typically entered in all uppercase letters. This is different from most commands, which are entered in lowercase. Each shell variable is used for a different purpose. Notice some of the shell variables, such as PATH and HOSTNAME in Figures 3-1 and 3-2.

You can display the contents of an individual variable by using the echo command and placing a dollar sign ($) prior to the variable's name. For example echo $HOME displays the home directory. Note that echo ~ also displays the home directory.

A few of the shell variables are listed in Table 3-1. You can refer to the man pages on bash for others.

Table 3-1   Some of the important shell variables

Shell Variable	Description
PWD	The most recent current working directory set with the cd command
OLDPWD	The previous working directory set by the cd command
BASH	The full path name used to invoke the bash shell
RANDOM	Generates a random integer between 0 and 32,767
HOSTNAME	The current hostname of the system running Linux
IFS	IFS or Internal Field Separator, used as a separator between words in the shell or shell scripts
PATH	Contains a list of directories that are used to search for commands within the Linux tree hierarchy
HOME	The home directory of the current user. Each user has a home directory when his or her account is created. This is the default location for storing files and directories for a user.
PS1	Represents the prompt
PS3	Represents the prompt for the select statement
TMOUT	Represents the amount of time the shell waits, without user input, before exiting the current shell; TMOUT means to "timeout" the user's session after a specific amount of time passes

Next you will display the contents of a few shell variables so you can understand how to access them in case you need to retrieve them either at the shell prompt or in a shell script.

To display the contents of shell variables:

1. Log in to the Linux system as a user, and then open a Terminal emulation window.

2. Type **echo $PWD**, and then press **Enter**. The current working directory is displayed. See Figure 3-3.

3. Type **echo $BASH**, and then press **Enter**. The full path of the default shell, bash, is displayed. See Figure 3-3.

4. Type **echo $RANDOM**, and then press **Enter**. A random number is displayed on the screen. See Figure 3-3; notice that the number is 22,178. You might use the RANDOM shell variable in a program that creates random passwords for users.

5. Type **echo $PATH**, and then press **Enter**. The command search path is displayed on the screen. See Figure 3-3. Here the path is quite long and includes many directories.

6. To exit the Terminal emulation program, type **exit**, and then press **Enter**.

7. Log out.

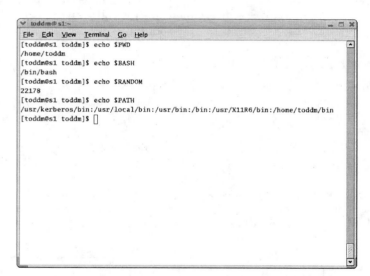

Figure 3-3   Contents of a few shell variables

 The contents of a variable set in the ~/.bash_profile file override the contents of a variable in the /etc/profile script file.

BECOMING FAMILIAR WITH THE SHELL ENVIRONMENT

When you enter a command using a partial path, such as cp, how does the shell know how to execute it? When a partial path is used when executing a command, the shell looks at the contents of the PATH variable until it finds the directory in which the command is located. Look again at Figure 3-3 and you see the contents of the PATH shell variable for the user toddm. Notice that a delimiter, in this case a colon, separates each of the directories in the path listing. When searching for the directory that a command is in, the shell searches each directory, separated by the delimiter in the path list starting from left and moving to the right. If the directory where the command is located is found in the PATH variable, the command is executed from that directory. Otherwise, the shell generates an error message indicating the command could not be found.

When executing a command using its full path, such as /bin/cp, the shell does not refer to the PATH contents. Instead it goes directly to the command using the specified path. For the command /bin/cp, the shell moves directly to the /bin directory, which is one of the system directories that you learned about in Chapter 2.

The File System Hierarchy Standard

Red Hat supports the **File System Hierarchy Standard**, which has been developed to standardize some of the system directories on computers running the Linux operating system. One important aspect of the standard is to use the /usr/local/bin directory to store all of your shell scripts that need to be available to many users. Note that only the root user can place scripts here, but all others can read and execute scripts within it. If users want to create their own scripts, they can place the script in a $HOME/bin directory, but they have to create the $HOME/bin directory first. This directory does not exist unless a user creates it. If you look at the PATH listing in Figure 3-3, you notice that each of these directories—/usr/local/bin and /home/toddm/bin ($HOME/bin)— are listed with the displaying of the shell variable, $PATH.

LEARNING ABOUT SHELL BUILTIN COMMANDS

A **builtin command** is a command that is part of the shell program, hence the term "builtin." These commands are actually compiled into the shell, thereby making the shell an executable command containing other commands. You cannot modify or delete builtin commands, and in fact, they are not available in any system directory. The only way you can find out more about these commands is to refer to man on bash. Table 3-2 shows the common builtin commands. You have seen some of these commands in Chapters 1 and 2. You need to understand these commands because they are used at the command line and in shell scripts.

Table 3-2   Some common shell builtin commands

Builtin Command	Description	Example(s)
`. filename`	Reads and executes commands from specified filename in the current shell environment	`. script1`
`cd`	Changes the current directory (See Chapter 2 for additional coverage)	`cd /`
`declare` or `typeset`	Declares a variable; the -r option makes the variable read-only	`declare var2` `declare —r ReadOnlyVar2`
`echo`	Displays output on the screen	`echo$ y echo "Hello"`
`exec`	Causes a command to replace the current shell; no new process is created	`exec ls`
`exit`	Causes the shell to exit with a status	`exit 1`
`export`	Exports the variable to a spawned shell; this allows a parent shell to set a variable that can be used by a child shell	`export x="Howdy!"`
`history`	Displays history of commands previously entered	`history`
`kill`	Sends a signal to a PID. If you run `kill —l`, you can see all the kill signals. You use this option to kill or stop background processes or daemons.	`kill 1409`
`let`	Evaluates an arithmetic expression	`let x=5`
`local`	Creates a local variable	`local x=5`
`logout`	Exits a login shell	`logout`
`pwd`	Displays current working directory (See Chapter 2 for additional coverage)	`pwd`
`read`	Reads characters from the keyboard	`read x`
`readonly`	Reads characters from the keyboard; once a variable is declared readonly, it cannot be changed	`readonly y`
`return`	Causes a function to exit with a certain value; a return value of 1 indicates failure and a return value of 0 indicates success	`return 1`
`set`	Sets and displays shell variables.	`set —xv`

3

Table 3-2   Some common shell builtin commands (continued)

Builtin Command	Description	Example(s)
`shift`	Shifts positional parameters	`shift 1`
`test`	Evaluates expressions. This works the same as the `[[expression]]` command. Also, you can use the `[[expression]]` command in place of the `test` command.	`test -d fileA.txt`
`trap`	Catches a signal sent to the shell; displays the message "Trapped signal 3" when signal 3 is sent to the shell	`trap "Trappedsignal 3" 3`

LEARNING ABOUT SHELL GRAMMAR

Shell grammar is defined as the rules that must be followed for proper operation of the shell. Basically, for the shell to function correctly, a specific set of syntax rules must be maintained just like in any spoken language. There are several fundamental building blocks in shell grammar. You need to understand these building blocks to best comprehend how the shell interprets the commands given to it. A thorough understanding can help you when you encounter shell errors. The building blocks of shell grammar are as follows:

- Blank
- Word
- Name
- Metacharacter
- Control operator
- Reserved word

A **blank** is defined as a space or a tab and is used to separate items in the shell. A **word** is defined as a sequence of characters that is considered a single unit by the shell. A word is also commonly known as a **token**. A **name** is a word that consists only of letters, numbers and the underscore. A **metacharacter** is a character that is used for a specific purpose by the shell; each purpose is unique to the character. A metacharacter is used to separate words. For example, you have seen the greater-than symbol, >, used as a metacharacter to redirect the output of a command. Table 3-3 contains the metacharacters used by the shell.

3

Table 3-3   Shell metacharacter symbols

Metacharacter Symbol(s)	Metacharacter Name	Purpose
|	The pipe symbol	Allows you to pass command output to another command
&	Ampersand	Allows you to run a job in the background
;	Semicolon	Allows you to sequence commands on the command line
( )	Left and right parentheses	Allows you to run a command in a subshell
<	Less-than symbol	Allows you to redirect input
>	Greater-than symbol	Allows you to redirect output and create a new file
Space	Spacebar	Allows you to separate words

Let's look at an example to help you understand how shell grammar works. In the following statement, echo "This is the production file">production.txt, the command echo is a word. The space immediately following this command is a blank that is used to separate this word from the next. The next word is literally "This is the production file". Next, the redirection operator, >, appears and is a metacharacter. Although most of the time you surround the redirection operator with a space, it is not mandatory because a metacharacter separates words. The redirection operator separates the text being echoed and the filename which is a name.

A **control operator** is a token that performs a specific control function. It modifies how the shell processes commands. Table 3–4 contains the control operator symbols.

Table 3-4   Shell control operators

Symbol(s)	Name	Function
||	Two pipe symbols	Causes one command to execute depending upon the failure of another
&&	Two ampersand symbols	Causes one command to execute depending upon the successful completion of another
&	Single ampersand	Allows you to run a job in the background
;	Semicolon	Allows you to run commands in a sequence
( )	Left and right parentheses	Allows you to run a command in a subshell
|	Pipe symbol	Allows you to pass command output to another command

In the next example, each command is executed from left to right in sequence:

```
echo "howdy" ; who ; pwd ; date
```

If you enter the commands in sequence without the semicolon, you would receive an error. Next you will perform an exercise to help you understand the importance of shell operators.

To use a shell control operator:

1. Log in to the Linux system as a user, and then open a Terminal emulation window.

2. Run the following commands, and then record the output.

   ```
   ls ; pwd ; who ; date ; cal 12 2005
   ```

3. Run the following commands, and then record the output.

   ```
   ls pwd who date cal 12 2005
   ```

4. Run the following commands, and then record the output.

   ```
   (ls; pwd; who; date; cal 12 2005;)
   ```

5. Run the following commands, and then record the output.

   ```
   pwd && date
   ```

6. Run the following commands, and then record the output.

   ```
   date & who
   ```

7. To exit the Terminal emulation program, type **exit**, and then press **Enter**.

8. Log out.

A **reserved word** is defined as a word that has special meaning to the shell. Such words cannot be used for any other purpose unless it is in quotes or not the first word in a command. Reserved words have specific syntax that must be followed; each is different. For example, the `if`, `then`, `else`, and `fi` statements are reserved to test conditions in a decision and you could not use them to accomplish something else. As another example, the `while`, `do`, and `done` statements are reserved for processing loops. You will learn the purpose of most of the remaining reserved words as you work your way through the remaining chapters.

UNDERSTANDING COMMAND TYPES

Now, that you have learned about the building blocks of shell grammar, you need to understand the major components, specifically, command types. Having a solid working knowledge of command types gives you the ability to properly structure commands in your shell scripts. The major components of shell grammar are listed in descending order of complexity of the command type.

- Compound commands
- Lists

- Pipelines
- Simple commands

Think of the command types as being structured in a pyramid in terms of complexity, with simple commands at the bottom and compound commands at the top of the pyramid. Refer to Figure 3-4 for the pyramid view of the command types.

3

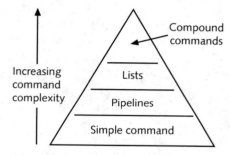

Figure 3-4   Command types pyramid

Simple Commands

A **simple command** is a set of words separated by blanks. It is also the most basic type of operation you can do within the shell. A shell control operator terminates a simple command. A simple command takes the general form:

```
command –options arguments
```

As you already know, the *command* is the name of the command; the hyphen (–) signifies that one or more options are to follow. An *option* adds extra features or characteristics to the command. An *argument* is usually one or more filenames that the command is going to use.

A synonym for argument is parameter.

Not all commands have options, nor do they all take filenames as arguments. Because each command has its own purpose and particular syntax, you should refer to the man pages for a given command to see specific information about the command's syntax.

Below are a few examples of simple commands. You have been executing simple commands since Chapter 1, so these types of commands should be familiar to you.

```
ls —l /etc
touch file1.txt
pwd
echo "Hi"
cd /usr/sbin
clear
```

Each command returns an exit status to the shell once the command completes. An exit status of zero indicates that the command succeeded. A nonzero exit status indicates that the command failed. The concept of an exit status will become important in later chapters when you want to test whether or not a command completed successfully or not.

Pipelines

The next level up in the command-type pyramid is the pipeline command. A **pipeline** is a sequence of simple commands separated by the pipe symbol character (|).

 Although the pipe symbol (|) prints as a solid vertical bar, it is shown as a broken vertical bar on most keyboards. You will usually find it above Enter on the same key as the backslash. The term pipe and pipeline are synonymous.

The pipeline allows data to be passed between processes. A pipeline takes the following general form:

```
command1 | command2 | command3 ...
```

This is where *command1*, *command2*, and *command3* are Linux commands separated by the pipe (|) symbol. The presence of the three dots implies you can add several pipelines. Below are examples of commands using the pipe symbol:

```
ls | more
ls | sort
who | sort | more
history | sort | more
```

To understand the pipeline process you need to realize that the output of the command on the left side of the pipe symbol is used as input for the command on the right side of the pipe symbol. The command on the right modifies the output in some way prior to displaying the output on the screen. For example, the command ls | more directs the output of the ls command as input to the more command. The more command then displays one page at a time on the screen. By combining these two commands together, the ls | more pipeline causes a directory listing to be displayed one page at a time. If you entered just ls, and the output was more than a page, the output would scroll off the screen and you would be unable to see the portion that scrolled. Here is another example: ls | sort | more. This pipeline sorts a directory listing before displaying it one page at a time.

A good analogy for pipelines is a water-filtering system. Some people have filters beneath their kitchen sinks to purify drinking water. Water, representing data, flows from the outside pipes as input to the filtering system, representing a command. The physical pipe represents the Linux pipeline. The filter purifies the water, or in the case of a pipeline, modifies its input. The output of the filter is input into your glass—the output you see on your screen.

Next you will perform an exercise to help you better understand the use of the pipe symbol.

To use the pipe symbol:

1. Log in to the Linux system as a user, and then open a Terminal emulation window.

2. Type **ls | more**, and then press **Enter**. The listing is displayed on the screen. Depending upon the number of files and directories to list, the listing may appear one page at a time.

3. Type **cat .bash_history | more**, and then press **Enter**. The file .bash_history appears on the screen one page at a time.

4. Type **who | sort | more**, and then press **Enter**. The output of the who command is sorted and displayed on the screen. Depending upon the number of users logged in, the output may appear one page at a time.

5. To exit the Terminal emulation program, type **exit**, and then press **Enter**.

6. Log out.

List

Up one level from a pipeline is a list. A **list** is a sequence of one pipeline or multiple pipelines which are separated by one of these operators: ;, &, &&, or ||. A list is terminated by either a ;, &, or a newline character. Each of these operators will be discussed next.

The ; Operator

Like pipelines, commands separated by a **semicolon** (;) are executed sequentially by the shell. Use of the ; operator takes the following general form on the command line:

    command1; command2

This is where *command1* and *command2* are Linux commands, executed in sequence, separated by the semicolon symbol. After the first command completes its execution, the shell executes the next command in sequence. Unlike pipes where the commands execute as parts of one process, each command separated by the semicolon is a separate process, and is given its own PID. Let's look at an example of a list using the ; operator. The command list **ls ; pwd** executes the **ls** command first. When it completes, the shell executes the **pwd** command. The subsequent command executes whether or not the previous command executed successfully.

The & Operator

If a command is followed by the **& operator**, it is executed in the background in a subshell. A **subshell** is a shell that is spawned, or generated, from the current shell. A **background process** is a process that can neither read from nor write to the terminal. Because of this, the shell does not wait for the background process to complete before returning the prompt. The shell normally executes a command as a **foreground process**—process that can read from or be written to the terminal. The shell must wait for a foreground process to complete before returning the prompt.

Normally, if a command executes in the foreground, you can stop it by pressing Ctrl+C. However, you cannot stop a background process by pressing Ctrl+C. Instead, you need to issue the `kill` command to stop a background process. Use of the **&** operator takes the following general form on the command line:

```
command1 & command2
```

This is where *command1* and *command2* are Linux commands, executed concurrently and separated by the ampersand symbol. *command1* is executed in a subshell at the same time that *command2* is executed in the current shell. Using the **&** symbol allows both commands to be executed at the same time. Note *command2* is optional. If you leave it off, then the shell simply executes *command1* in the background as in: *command1* **&**.

Here is an example using the **&** operator. In the command list `ls & pwd`, the `ls` command executes in the background, while the `pwd` command executes in the foreground. Because they are not executed sequentially, the `ls` command may actually complete after the `pwd`, even though it is listed first. In this list command example, the command completion sequence would be determined by the number of directories and files in the current directory.

The && Operator

The **&& operator** causes the shell to execute a command only if the immediately preceding command completes successfully (exit status of zero). This is different from the **&** operator. With the **&&** operator, the commands are executed sequentially in the same shell—not concurrently in a subshell. Use of the **&&** operator takes the following general form on the command line:

```
command1 && command2
```

This is where *command1* and *command2* are Linux commands separated by two ampersand symbols. The command specified as *command2* only executes if *command1* executes successfully (with an exit status of zero).

 With the **&** operator, even if the first one fails, the second command executes. With the **&&** operator, if the first command fails, the second command will *never* execute.

For example, in the list `rm file1.txt && pwd`, the `rm file1.txt` command executes first. If it completes successfully, the `pwd` executes after it. If `rm file1.txt` fails (exit status is nonzero), because the file to be removed does not exist, the `pwd` never executes.

Let's look at another example. In the list `lsxxx && pwd`, the `pwd` command never executes because the `lsxxx` command does not exist and returns a nonzero exit status.

The || Operator

The **|| operator** causes the shell to execute a secondary command in the event that the first command fails. Use of the || operator takes the following general form on the command line:

    command1 || command2

This is where *command1* and *command2* are Linux commands separated by two pipe symbols. Even though the || operator uses two pipe symbols, its use here is unrelated to the functionality of a single pipe symbol in pipelines. The command specified as *command2* only executes if *command1* executes unsuccessfully (with an exit status not equal to zero).

For example, in the list `rm file1.txt || pwd`, if the `rm file1.txt` command fails to execute successfully (nonzero exit status), the second command, `pwd`, executes. If the first command in the list, `rm file1.txt || pwd`, completes successfully, the `pwd` command never executes. In the following list, `lsxxx || pwd`, the `lsxxx` command does not exist and returns a nonzero exit status for being unsuccessful, so the `pwd` command executes.

Combining Commands and Operators

The shell allows you to combine operators on the command line. When using the && and || operators, the commands in the list are executed sequentially. In a list that includes both the && and || operators, equal precedence exists between the two operators. The operator that appears first, from left to the right, is executed first. In a list that only includes both the ; and & operators, equal precedence exists between these two as well. The operator appearing first, in left to right order, is executed first. However, in a list that includes all four operators, the && and || operators are evaluated before the ; and & operators.

Let's combine a few of these operators to see how they work together. In the list example, `date; pwd && who | more`, there are two simple commands, `date` and `pwd`, separated by the control operator, `;`. Then the && operator is used with the `who | more` pipeline. This list executes the `who | more` pipeline only if the preceding commands, `date; pwd` complete successfully. Thus, the `date` command runs first. Then, the `pwd` command executes. Next, the shell must determine if the preceding command failed. If so, it stops and processes no other statements. If the commands have succeeded, then the `who | more` command executes. Refer to the first command list in Figure 3-5. You can see that both commands on the left and right side of the && operator executed.

In the preceding example, all commands should execute. However, in the command, `date; pwdx && who | more` where `pwdx` is misspelled, only the `date` command executes. The `pwdx` fails because it is invalid. Because the sequence of commands on the left side of the `&&` operator failed, the pipeline on the right side does not execute.

Consider this list example, `date; pwd || who | more` which uses the `||` operator. Here the `who | more` pipeline only executes if the preceding commands, `date; pwd`, do *not* complete successfully. Figure 3-5 shows a sample screen shot of this list.

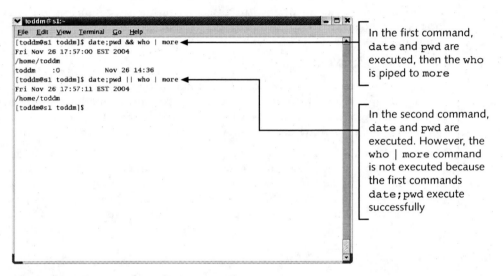

In the first command, date and pwd are executed, then the who is piped to more

In the second command, date and pwd are executed. However, the who | more command is not executed because the first commands date;pwd execute successfully

Figure 3-5   Output of two list commands

Compound Commands

At the top of the command-type pyramid, is the compound command; thus, it is the most powerful of the command types. **Compound commands** allow you to perform calculations, assign variables, perform decision tests, and create loops. A compound command can include any of the previous command types plus the following types:

- Group commands
- Expressions
- Decision constructs
- Looping constructs

Group commands and expressions will be discussed here. Decision and looping constructs will be discussed in Chapters 6 and 7, respectively.

Group Commands

A **group command** is a list of commands either executing in a subshell or the current shell. A group command is made up of one of the following formats:

- `(list)`
- `{ list; }`

The `(list)` Group Command

With a `(list)` group command, the list of commands is executed in a subshell. Because the commands in the list are executed in a subshell, any variables assigned within the list do not remain intact once the list completes. Let's look at an example. In Figure 3-6, the variable assignment `y=5` sets y to the value of 5. Next the `echo $y` command displays the contents of the variable "y," which is 5. In the next statement, which is a list group command, `(y=50)`, "y" is set to the value of 50 in a subshell. However, the result of the last `echo $y` command shows that "y" is still set to 5. This is because the commands in the `(list)` group command are executed in a shell spawned from the current shell. The current shell is not affected by commands executed in the shell spawned from it. You would use this group command when you wanted a variable to remain unaffected by a command in the current shell.

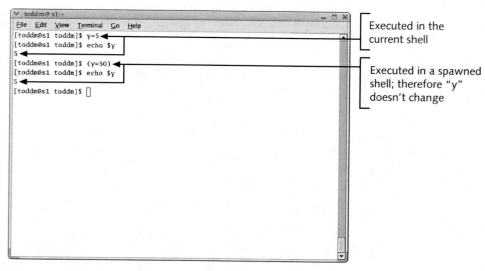

Figure 3-6   Use of the `(list)` group command

A variable is assigned by inputting a name, the equal sign, and then the value. For example, y=5 assigns the value 5 to the variable "y." You must precede a variable name with a dollar sign in order to use the contents. For example, in the command echo $y the dollar sign immediately prior to the variable name, "y," is required. If you left off the dollar sign, as in, echo y, the shell would literally display the letter "y."

You could also use the (list) group command structure if you wanted to execute multiple commands in the background. Using the & operator causes a command to be executed in the background as in who &. However, you can only place one command before the & operator. With the group command, you can execute multiple commands in the background. For example, the group command (pwd; who; ls) & causes each command within the parentheses to be executed collectively in the background. They will take only one PID.

When a subshell is spawned, it takes on a unique PID. Its PPID is the PID of the parent shell that spawned it.

The { list; } Group Command

With a {list; } group command, the list of commands is executed in the current shell. The list must be terminated with a semicolon ; or newline. Because the commands in the list are executed in the same shell, any variables assigned within the list remain once the list completes.

This type of group command is useful when you want to apply other operators to the commands in the list as a whole. For example, if you execute the who and ls -l commands, their output may scroll off the screen. You could use the pipe operator and the more command to scroll the output one screenful at a time. You could enter the commands as a group command, { who; ls -l;} | more. Then, the collective output of the commands between the { } symbols would be piped to the more command. Figure 3-7 shows a screenshot of the previous group command. Notice that the collective output is piped to the more command.

Let's look at another example dealing with variables. In Figure 3-8, the variable assignment y=5 sets "y" to the value of 5. Next the echo $y command displays the contents of the variable "y," which is 5. In the next statement, { y=50; }, "y" is set to the value of 50 in the current shell. The result of the last echo $y command shows that "y" now possesses the new value—50. Again, this is because the commands in the list execute in the current shell.

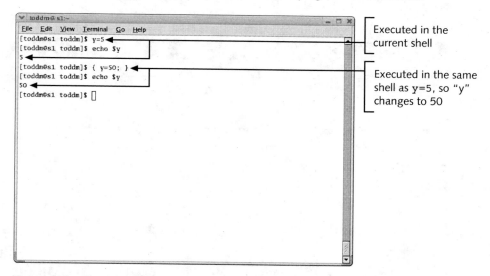

```
[toddm@s1 bin]$ { who; ls -l;} | more
toddm     :0          Oct 20 08:29
total 1384
-rw-rw-r--    1 toddm      toddm       463 Oct 19 09:42 \
-rwxrwxrwx    1 toddm      toddm       406 Oct 15 19:26 AF1
-rwxrwxrwx    1 toddm      toddm       397 Oct 15 19:26 AirFare
-rwxrwxrwx    1 toddm      toddm       211 Oct 15 19:26 alphatest1
-rwxrwxrwx    1 toddm      toddm       499 Oct 15 19:26 alphatest10
-rw-xrwxrwx   1 toddm      toddm       362 Oct 15 19:26 AnimalSearch
-rwxrwxrwx    1 toddm      toddm        29 Oct 15 19:26 awk1
-rwxrwxrwx    1 toddm      toddm       426 Oct 15 19:26 awk10
-rwxrwxrwx    1 toddm      toddm       426 Oct 15 19:26 awk11
-rwxrwxrwx    1 toddm      toddm        13 Oct 15 19:26 awk12
-rwxrwxrwx    1 toddm      toddm        20 Oct 15 19:26 awk13
-rwxrwxrwx    1 toddm      toddm        54 Oct 15 19:26 awk15
-rwxrwxrwx    1 toddm      toddm        47 Oct 15 19:26 awk16
-rwxrwxrwx    1 toddm      toddm        33 Oct 15 19:26 awk2
-rwxrwxrwx    1 toddm      toddm       463 Oct 15 19:26 awk20
-rwxrwxrwx    1 toddm      toddm       105 Oct 15 19:26 awk25
-rwxrwxrwx    1 toddm      toddm        89 Oct 15 19:26 awk3
-rwxrwxrwx    1 toddm      toddm       112 Oct 15 19:26 awk30
-rwxrwxrwx    1 toddm      toddm       160 Oct 15 19:26 awk31
-rwxrwxrwx    1 toddm      toddm       219 Oct 15 19:26 awk32
--More--
```

Figure 3-7   Use of the `{list;l;}` command grouping several commands

```
[toddm@s1 toddm]$ y=5                          Executed in the
[toddm@s1 toddm]$ echo $y                       current shell
5

[toddm@s1 toddm]$ { y=50; }                     Executed in the same
[toddm@s1 toddm]$ echo $y                        shell as y=5, so "y"
50                                               changes to 50
[toddm@s1 toddm]$
```

Figure 3-8   The use of the `{list;}` group command

If you look again at Figure 3-6 and compare it with Figure 3-8, you see that in the (y=5) group command, the value of "y" does not change because the statement is executed in a subshell and does not affect the current value of "y." In Figure 3-8, the { y=50; } group command does change it because it is performed in the same shell.

Expressions

An **expression** is used when you want to assign a value to a variable, perform an arithmetic calculation using variables, or test for values meeting certain conditions. An expression is made up of one of these formats:

- ((expression))
- [[expression]]

The ((expression)) command

You use the ((expression)) compound command to evaluate an arithmetic operation. The expression generally takes one of the following forms:

```
((variable-name = value1 operator value2))
((value1 operator value2))
```

This is where *value1* and *value2* are variable assignments or integers. The term *operator* represents an arithmetic operation that is performed on the values. A partial list of operators is shown in Table 3-5. The first statement of the expression is used for variable assignment, as in: ((y=5 + 6)). Note that *variable-name* is a variable assigned by you.

Table 3-5 Various operators used with the ((expression)) compound command

Operator	Name	Example
Variable-name++	The increment operation	((t = x++))
Variable-name--	The decrement operation	((t = x--))
**	Exponentiation	((x = 2**3))
*	Multiply	((x = 4*5))
/	Division	((x = 10 / 2))
+	Addition	((x = 10+2))
–	Subtraction	((x = 10 – 2))
%	Remainder	((r = 100 % 4))
= =	Equal to	(($x = = 2))
! =	Not equal to	(($x ! = 2))
>=	Greater than or equal to	(($x >= $y))
<=	Less than or equal to	(($t <= 10))
>	Greater than	(($x > 5))
<	Less than	(($t < $x))
&&	AND operation	(($y = = 5 && $t = = 5))
||	OR operation	(($y = =$r || $t = = 5))

You can use `let "expression"` instead of `((expression))` for arithmetic operations. The `"expression"` in the `let "expression"` statement uses the same syntax as `((expression))`. For example, `((y=500))` is equivalent to `let "y=500"`.

3

Next you will become familiar with the syntax of expressions because you will use expressions in future chapters.

To understand expressions:

1. Log in to the Linux operating system as a user, and then open a Terminal emulation window.

2. To multiply two numbers, type `((x=5 * 6))`, and then press **Enter**. The variable "x" now contains the number 30. However, nothing is displayed yet.

3. To add a variable and a number, type `((y=$x+4))`, and then press **Enter**. The variable "y" now contains the number 34. Again, nothing is displayed yet.

4. To display the contents of the two variables, type **echo $x $y**, and then press **Enter**. The numbers 30 and 34 are displayed on your screen.

5. To exit the Terminal emulation program, type **exit**, and then press **Enter**.

6. Log out.

The Increment and Decrement Operators

Now, look at the increment and decrement operators listed in Table 3-5. These are extremely useful operators because they allow you to add one to a value or subtract one from a value efficiently in a script. Two addition symbols, + +, are used as the increment operator. Two subtraction symbols, – –, are used as the decrement operator. Let's say you wanted to increment the value of a variable named **value1**, by 1; you could use the increment operator as follows:

```
((value1++))
```

 The increment operator can be used in a script as a counter when you want to count items you have processed. Other ways to increment a value are: `((value1=value1+1))`, `let "value1++"`, or `let "value1=value1+1"`

Figure 3-9 illustrates the use of the increment operator to increment a value. In the figure, value1 is set to 100 and then incremented using the **value1++** statement. Notice the **echo** statements result in 100 before and 101 after the value is incremented.

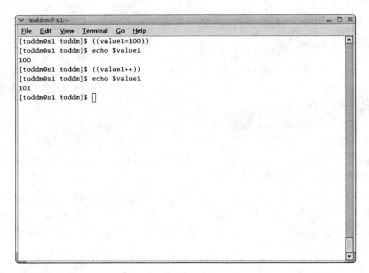

Figure 3-9   Using the increment operator to increment a value

Now, suppose you wanted to decrement the value of the variable named **value1** by 1. You could use the decrement operator as follows:

```
((value1--))
```

Figure 3-10 illustrates the use of the decrement operator to decrement a value. You can see the variable with a value of 100 is displayed before it is decremented and then the value changes to 99 after the variable contents are decremented.

The Exponentiation, Multiplication, Division, Addition, Subtraction, and Remainder Operators   You are probably familiar with the mathematical concepts of exponentiation, multiplication, division, addition, and subtraction. The idea of placing the remainder into a variable may be new to you; it will be covered at the end of this section. First, look at how these operators are set up in examples so you can understand how to implement them in shell scripts. These operators are important because they allow the shell to perform calculations and can be used in scripts.

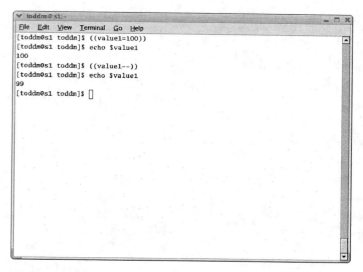

Figure 3-10   Using the decrement operator to decrement a value

First consider exponentiation—raising a number to a power. To do this, you use two asterisks, **. Look at an example:

```
((x = 4))
((y = 2**x))
```

In this example, the variable "x" is set to 4. In the expression, ((y=2**x)), the variable "y" is equal to 2 raised to the power of "x" which is 4. Thus, the answer is "y" equals 16.

Here are some multiplication, division, addition, subtraction, and remainder examples to consider. Figure 3-11 shows the results of these expressions.

```
((x = 4))
((y = 2))
((m=x*y))
((d=x/y))
((a=x+y))
((s=x-y))
((r= x%y))
```

```
┌─ toddm@sl:~ ──────────────────────────────────────────── _ □ ✕ ┐
│ File  Edit  View  Terminal  Go  Help                             │
│ [toddm@sl toddm]$ ((x=4))                                      ▲ │
│ [toddm@sl toddm]$ ((y=2))                                        │
│ [toddm@sl toddm]$ ((m=x*y))                                      │
│ [toddm@sl toddm]$ ((d=x/y))                                      │
│ [toddm@sl toddm]$ ((a=x+y))                                      │
│ [toddm@sl toddm]$ ((s=x-y))                                      │
│ [toddm@sl toddm]$ ((r=x%y))                                      │
│ [toddm@sl toddm]$ echo $x                                        │
│ 4                                                                │
│ [toddm@sl toddm]$ echo $y                                        │
│ 2                                                                │
│ [toddm@sl toddm]$ echo $m                                        │
│ 8                                                                │
│ [toddm@sl toddm]$ echo $d                                        │
│ 2                                                                │
│ [toddm@sl toddm]$ echo $a                                        │
│ 6                                                                │
│ [toddm@sl toddm]$ echo $s                                        │
│ 2                                                                │
│ [toddm@sl toddm]$ echo $r                                        │
│ 0                                                                │
│ [toddm@sl toddm]$ []                                             │
│                                                                ▼ │
└──────────────────────────────────────────────────────────────── ┘
```

Figure 3-11   The results of various arithmetic expressions

 When using the % operator, the variable to the left of the % operator is divided by the variable to the right of the % operator. Then, the remainder of this division is placed into the variable name. So, in ((x=10%2)), "x" equals zero, and in ((x=11%2)), "x" has a remainder value of 1.

Arithmetic expressions follow precedence. The order of what takes precedence is listed in Table 3-6. Operators listed within the same cell of the table have equal precedence, so if two operators with equal precedence are given in an expression, they are evaluated from left to right. For example, the increment and decrement operators have equal precedence and are evaluated before anything else.

Table 3-6   Precedence of arithmetic operations listed in descending order

Operators
Variable-name++, *Variable-name*--
**, *, /, %
+, -
<=, >=, <, >
= =, ! =
&&
‖

You can alter the order by placing parentheses around lower-precedence operations so that they are evaluated before higher ones. If you have multiple parentheses, the operations within the innermost parentheses are performed first. For example, in the statement

3

((y=5+3*2)), the multiplication operation is evaluated first. So, the number 3 is multiplied by the number 2, resulting in 6. Then, the number 5 is added to the number 6, and "y" is set to 11. However, if you placed parentheses around the addition operation, as in ((y=(5+3)*2)), it would evaluate first. So, 5 is added to 3 resulting in 8. Then, the number 8 is multiplied by the number 2, and "y" is set to 16.

Next you will complete an exercise to help you understand the use of parentheses in expressions.

To understand the use of parentheses in expressions:

1. Log in to the Linux system as a user, and then open a Terminal emulation window.

2. Type **((x=100-3**2))**, and then press **Enter** to change the value of "x" by first raising 3 to the power of 2 and then subtracting the result from 100.

3. Type **((y=(100-3)**2))**, and then press **Enter** to change the value of "y" by first subtracting 3 from 100 and then raising that result to the power of 2.

4. Type **echo $x $y**, and then press **Enter**. The numbers 91 and 9409, are displayed on the screen respectively.

5. To exit the Terminal emulation program, type **exit**, and then press **Enter**.

6. Log out.

 Expressions operate only on integers. Division by zero results in an error.

The [[expression]] command You can use the [[expression]] command, or the **test** command, to test attributes of a file or directory, perform character string comparisons, and perform numeric comparisons. A **string** is a set of one or more alphanumeric characters—either a number or a character. The [[expression]] commands have several formats. You would use the **if** command to make decisions with the [[expression]] command. The **if** command is covered in Chapter 6.

CHAPTER SUMMARY

❑ The shell can be invoked by either logging in or by entering the name of the shell at the shell prompt. The shell uses startup files to customize the user's environment. The login files are /etc/profile, ~/.bash_profile, and ~/.bashrc. The /etc/profile script file is read and executed for all users as they log in. The root user account can only change this script file. The other two, ~/.bash_profile and ~/.bashrc, located in each user's home directory, are executed if they exist. Each user can change these files. The ~/.bash_logout is executed when a user logs out and can be modified by the user.

❑ The shell has its own variables that are reserved specifically for its use. They must be entered in uppercase. The **PATH** shell variable contains a list of directories the shell searches when attempting to locate a script or command. To display the contents of a shell variable, precede it with a dollar sign, as in this example: **$PATH**.

❑ The File System Hierarchy Standard supports placing scripts used by all users in the /usr/local/bin directory and having users place their own scripts in ~/bin. The ~/bin directory must be created before any scripts can be placed in it.

❑ Shell builtin commands are commands that are compiled as part of the shell. You can't find them in any directory, and you have to refer to the man pages for the shell instead of for an individual command.

❑ It is important to understand the grammar of the shell because the shell is a language and a strong understanding of the fundamentals can help you troubleshoot problems when you are entering commands. The basic building blocks of shell grammar are: blanks, words, names, metacharacters, control operators, and reserved words. A blank is a space or tab and is used to separate items entered at the shell prompt. A word is a sequence of characters the shell uses as a unit. A name is a word consisting only of letters, numbers, and the underscore. A metacharacter is a character that has a special purpose to the shell. A control operator modifies how the shell processes commands. A reserved word is a word that is used by the shell and is generally a command.

❑ The shell provides for several command types. These include simple commands, pipelines, lists, and compound commands. You need to understand these different types in order to properly construct commands to accomplish a certain task without the threat of generating an error. A simple command is a set of words separated by blanks. A pipeline is used to process data between commands. A list is a series of pipelines separated by a control operator. A compound command allows you to assign variables, perform computations, and execute decisions and loop structures.

REVIEW QUESTIONS

1. _____ is the login startup file that is read first.

   a. /etc/profile

   b. ~/.bash_logout

   c. ~/.bash_profile

   d. ~/.bashrc

3

2. Which term is used to define a space or tab in shell grammar?

   a. metacharacter

   b. word

   c. name

   d. blank

3. A _____ process always executes in a subshell.

   a. foreground

   b. background

   c. simple command

   d. control operator

4. The _____ script file is read and executed when the user terminates his session.

   a. /etc/profile

   b. ~/.bash_logout

   c. ~/.bash_profile

   d. ~/.bashrc

5. Which term is used to describe a character that has special meaning to the shell?

   a. token

   b. word

   c. blank

   d. metacharacter

6. A _____ process can read data from the terminal.

   a. foreground

   b. background

   c. control operator

   d. token

7. Which is the name of the symbol that allows the output of one command to be filtered as input to another?

   a. greater-than

   b. pipe

   c. double greater-than

   d. less-than

8. _____ is the symbol used for executing a job in the background of the shell.

   a. &

   b. <

   c. ;

   d. ?

9. _____ is the symbol used to separate commands in a list, which are executed sequentially.

   a. ;

   b. <

   c. >>

   d. ?

10. _____ is the operator that is used when you want one command to execute only if another command executes successfully.

    a. *

    b. ||

    c. &&

    d. <

11. Which group command executes commands in a subshell?

    a. ((n++))

    b. ((expression))

    c. { list };

    d. (list)

12. You use the _____ group command to execute commands in the current shell.

    a. ((n++))

    b. ((expression))

    c. { list };

    d. (list)

13. Which group command is used to evaluate arithmetic operations?

    a. [list]

    b. ((expression))

    c. { list };

    d. (list)

14. Which of the following is an example of the increment operator?

    a. {{n++}}

    b. ((n--))

    c. ((n++))

    d. ((+n+))

15. The remainder symbol is _____.

    a. *

    b. /

    c. &

    d. %

16. Which command is synonymous with the `[[ expression ]]` command?

    a. `pwd`

    b. `test`

    c. `((expression))`

    d. `{list}`

17. Which term describes a set of one or more alphanumeric characters?

    a. token

    b. string

    c. list

    d. blank

18. A command that is part of the shell is called a _____ command.

    a. export

    b. import

    c. builtin

    d. inherent

19. Which command is used to send a signal to a PID?

    a. `pwd`

    b. `kill`

    c. `ls`

    d. `signal`

3

20. The _____ shell variable is used to locate the directory a command is stored in.

    a. `$path`

    b. `$PATH`

    c. /etc/profile

    d. `$TMOUT`

HANDS-ON PROJECTS

Project 3-1

In this project, you will change the ~/.bash_profile file so you can see it execute as part of the login process. This will help reinforce your understanding of its role in the login process.

1. Log in to the Linux system as a user, and then open a Terminal emulation window.

2. Type **vi .bash_profile**, and then press **Enter**. The shell script is displayed on the screen. Note there will be other commands currently there.

3. Press **Shift+G** to move the cursor to the bottom of the file.

4. Type **o** to open a line of text in **vi**, and then input the following lines of code to change the ~/.bash_profile file:

```
echo "Executing the .bash_profile login file."
echo "A list of current users:"
who
echo "The current directory is:"
pwd
echo "The end of the .bash_profile login file."
```

5. Save the file, and then close the editor.

6. Execute the script.

7. Record the output.

8. Delete the lines of code in the ~/.bash_profile file that you added.

9. Close your window, and then log out.

Project 3-2

In this project, you will change the ~/.bashrc file so you can see it execute as part of the login process.

1. Log in to the Linux system as a user, and then open a Terminal emulation window.

2. Type **vi .bashrc**, and then press **Enter**. The shell script is displayed on the screen.

3. Go to the end of the file and append the following lines of code:

```
echo "Executing the .bashrc login file."
date
echo "The end of the .bashrc login file."
```

4. Telnet to your system.

5. As you are logging in, notice the screen, and record what occurs.

6. Compare the execution of Project 3-1 and this project. Which script executes first?

7. Delete the lines in the ~/.bashrc file that you added.

8. Save the file, and then close the editor.

9. Close your window, and then log out.

Project 3-3

In this project, you will create a shell script and change the .bash_logout file to execute that shell script. You will display the user's login name set in the /etc/profile, as well as display the host name followed by the date. Finally, you will test the script. The goal of this project is to reinforce your knowledge of the login and logout shell script files.

1. Log in to the Linux system as a user, and then open a Terminal emulation window.

2. Type **vi LogOut**, and then press **Enter**.

3. Insert the following lines to display the user's login name, hostname, date, and time the user logged out:

```
echo -n $LOGNAME "logged out" $HOSTNAME "at"
date
```

4. Save the file, and then close the editor.

5. Open the **.bash_logout** file, and then insert the LogOut script you just created at the bottom of the screen.

6. Press **Shift+G** to move the cursor to the bottom of the file.

7. Type **o** to open a line of text in vi.

8. Type **bash LogOut**, and then press **Enter**.

9. Save the file, and then close the editor.

10. Telnet to your system.

11. Log out, notice the screen, and then record the results.

12. Close all windows.

Project 3-4

In this project, you will reinforce your understanding of shell variables.

1. Log in to the Linux system as a user, and then open a Terminal emulation window.

2. Create a shell script named **Project3-4** located in a directory supported by the File System Hierarchy Standard.

3. You need to perform the steps shown in pseudocode in the order shown:

```
Change to the /tmp directory
Change to your home directory
Display the previous working directory using a shell
variable
Display your home directory using a shell variable
Display your home directory using an alternate method to
using a shell variable
Display the amount of time the shell will wait for user
input before the current shell is terminated using a shell
variable
Set the previous variable to 120
Display the amount of time the shell will wait for user
input before the current shell is terminated using a
shell variable
Set the previous variable to 0
```

4. Save the file, and then close the editor.

5. Execute the script.

6. Record the commands used, and then record or print your script.

7. Close your window, and then log out.

Project 3-5

In this project, you will reinforce your understanding of what happens to variables when using group commands. You will also see how a formula changes when parentheses are added or removed from an arithmetic expression.

1. Log in to the Linux system as a user, and then open a Terminal emulation window.

2. Create a shell script named **Project3-5** located in a directory supported by the File System Hierarchy Standard that contains the following lines of code:

```
a=100
b=10
y=0
echo $a $b $y
( ((y=($a+4)*$b)); echo $y )
echo $y
( ((y=$a+4*$b)); echo $y)
echo $y
{ ((y=($a+4)*$b)); echo $y; }
echo $y
{ ((y=$a+4*$b)); echo $y; }
echo $y
```

3. Print the script.

4. Save the file, and then close the editor.

5. Execute the script.

6. Write down the output to the right of each command that executes. Why does the value of "y" either change or remain the same after each of the echo $y statements that are on a line by themselves?

7. Close your window, and then log out.

Project 3-6

In this project, you will use the increment operator as a counter. You will also use the decrement operator to reinforce your understanding of the use of expressions.

1. Log in to the Linux system as a user, and then open a Terminal emulation window.

2. Create a shell script named **Project3-6** located in a directory supported by the File System Hierarchy Standard.

3. The script needs to perform the following pseudocode in the order shown:

```
Set a variable named "n" to 10
Display the contents of "n"
Use the correct expression to increase "n" by 1
Display the contents of "n"
Use the correct expression to decrease "n" by 1
Display the contents of "n"
Increase the variable "n" again using a different
expression
Display the contents of "n"
Decrease the variable "n" again using a different
expression
Display the contents of "n"
```

4. Save the file, and then close the editor.

5. Execute the script, and then record the command used.

6. Record or print your script.

7. Close your window, and then log out.

Project 3-7

In this project, you use additional arithmetic operators in the ((expression)) commands. The goal of this project is to reinforce your understanding of arithmetic operations.

1. Log in to the Linux system as a user, and then open a Terminal emulation window.

2. Create a shell script named **Project3-7** located in a directory supported by the File System Hierarchy Standard.

3. The script needs to perform the following pseudocode in the order shown:

```
Set a variable named "x" to 10
Set a variable named "y" to 100
Display the result of dividing "y" by "x" and place the
result into variable "t"
Display the result of dividing "y" by 0
Display the result of multiplying "y" by "x" and place the
result into variable "t"
Display the result of adding "y" and "x" and place the
result into variable "t"
Display the result of subtracting "x" from "y" and place the
result into variable "t"
Display the result of raising "y" to the power of 2 and
place the result into variable "t"
Display the result of taking the remainder of "y" divided
by "x" and place the result into variable "t"
```

4. Save the file, and then close the editor.

5. Execute the script, and then record the commands used.

6. Record or print your script.

7. Close your window, and then log out.

Project 3-8

In this project, you will gain an understanding of how to use various command types at the command line.

1. Log in to the Linux system as a user, and then open a Terminal emulation window.

2. Create a shell script named **Project3-8** located in a directory supported by the File System Hierarchy Standard.

3. The script needs to perform the following pseudocode in the order shown:

```
Display the list of current users sequentially followed by
the current directory
Display the list of current users as a background process
Update the modification time of a file named cactus.dat
Issue the command to display a message indicating a file
named cactus.dat was removed only if the command to remove
it succeeds
Issue the command to display a message indicating a file
named cactus.dat was not removed only if the command to
remove it fails
Display a long listing of the /tmp directory one screen at
a time
```

4. Save the file, and then close the editor.

5. Execute the script, and then record or print your script.

6. Close your window, and then log out.

CASE PROJECTS

Case 3-1

TMI has hired your consulting firm to assist their Linux users. You get a call from Marge who is just learning the Linux system. She has saved up several questions and needs you to respond to these issues:

1. She needs to locate additional documentation on the **cd**, **pwd**, and the **history** commands, but she is having difficulty finding anything.

2. She has a script that one of the programmers wrote. It takes a long time to execute. She wants to be able to execute it and have the prompt immediately return.

3. She would like to add a message to all users as they log in. She would like a different message added for her own account.

Case 3-2

The Santiago Law Firm has recently purchased a Linux computer system. You interview the users and determine a shell script is needed to exit a user's process when he or she has not pressed a key after 60 seconds. When each user logs in, a list should be displayed of current users so everyone can see who is logged in and presumably, working. Additionally, the Santiago Law Firm wants each user to see what system he or she is logged on to. Also, the firm would like a calendar for the current month to be displayed. (*Hint:* This requires modification to the ~/.bash_profile file. The **TMOUT** shell variable must be set and exported to 60 seconds.) Finally, the ~/.bash_logout file needs to display the message "Exiting the Santiago system" when a user exits a Terminal emulation window.

4

THE SHELL ENVIRONMENT

In this chapter, you will:
- ◆ Understand redirection
- ◆ Understand pattern matching
- ◆ Understand the use of quoting
- ◆ Understand expansion
- ◆ Learn additional commands

In this chapter, you will understand how to redirect the flow of a command's input or output. You will also learn how to match specific patterns to access a subset of the files in a given directory and how to use quoting to protect certain metacharacters. You will see how various commands and operators expand into additional items. Finally, you will learn some additional commands that will help you perform your job better in a Linux operating system environment.

Understanding Redirection

Redirection means to direct the flow from one place to another. In Linux, you can redirect the flow of input or output from their normal default location. Why would you want to do this? Redirection gives you flexibility in terms of where your data is either coming from (input) or going to (output). For example, you might redirect output if you wanted to save the result of a command. Because output redirection typically results in a file being generated, you are able to review the file that contains the output of the command, either presently or at a later date. Input redirection is used less often than output redirection. With input redirection, the default location for a command's input is changed. However, most of the commands that accept filenames as part of their syntax usually don't require the input redirection operator.

Linux refers to **standard input (stdin)** as the default location for inputting commands. The default location for standard input is the keyboard. Linux refers to **standard output (stdout)** as the default location for outputting commands. Standard output defaults to the display screen. The term **standard error (stderr)** is the default location of errors generated from commands. Standard errors also default to the display screen. Redirection allows you to change the default locations of standard input, standard output, and standard error.

Linux uses the term **file descriptor** to describe a number that refers to a file. Each time a command runs, it has three file descriptors—one for stdin, stdout, and stderr. It uses these to handle input and output operations as well as error handling. Table 4-1 shows the file descriptors for standard input, output, and error.

Table 4-1   File descriptors for standard input, output, and error

File	File Descriptor	Location
Standard input	0	/dev/stdin
Standard output	1	/dev/stdout
Standard error	2	/dev/stderr

 Linux treats the keyboard and the display screen as files. Linux also treats other hardware devices such as tape backup devices, floppy devices, and CD-ROM devices similarly. If you execute the ls command in the /dev directory, you will see the device files.

Redirecting Standard Input

Redirecting input causes a program to read from a file instead of the keyboard. The symbol to redirect input is the less-than symbol (<). The arrow points toward the command for redirecting input. The general form is:

```
command < filename
```

This is where *command* is a command, and *filename* is a Linux file. For example, the sort command typed in without any options sorts the data from standard input, or the keyboard. However, you can sort a file if you use a redirection symbol, for example, sort < personnel.txt. This command takes the input for the sort command directly from the personnel.txt file instead of the keyboard. The original file remains intact and the output is sent to standard output, or the screen.

Next you will learn how to redirect input. In this exercise, you will enter employee names in a payroll file. You will use the sort command to sort the payroll file, which will be redirected as input to it.

To redirect input:

1. Log in to the Linux system as a user, and then open a Terminal emulation window.

2. Create a file named **pay.dat** in your **$HOME/bin** directory that includes the following records:

   ```
   Smith, Jay
   Patel, Arnie
   Trang, Vingh
   Adams, Claude
   DeRue, Jacques
   ```

3. Save the file, and then close the editor.

4. To redirect input, type **sort < pay.dat**, and then press **Enter**. See Figure 4-1. The data is sorted on the screen. The original pay.dat file is intact.

5. To verify the original file has not changed, type **cat pay.dat**. See Figure 4-1. Notice the order of employee names is the same as you originally input it in Step 2.

6. Close the window, and then log out.

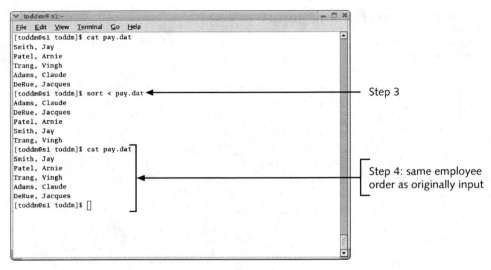

Figure 4-1 Input redirection

Redirecting Standard Output

Redirecting output causes the command to redirect its output from the display screen to a file. Redirecting output is useful when you want to keep the output of a command for later review. There are two forms of redirecting standard output. They are redirecting output to create a new file and redirecting output to append to an existing file.

Redirecting Output to Create a New File

Using the single greater-than (>) symbol to redirect output allows you to send the output of a command to a file. If the file exists, its current contents are overwritten. If the file does not exist, it is created. Notice that the arrow points away from the command for redirecting output. You might redirect output to a new file if you wanted to keep the listing of a command for later review. The general form is:

```
command > filename
```

For example, the `ls` command displays a directory listing to standard output, or the display screen. You can redirect standard output to a file named lslist.txt by typing `ls > lslist.txt`. This results in standard output being redirected to the specified file. When you use a single greater-than symbol, it causes a new file to be created as long as a file by that name doesn't already exist. If the file exists, then that file is overwritten.

Let's look at an example.

```
ls > file2.txt
cat file2.txt
who > file2.txt
cat file2.txt
```

The `ls > file2.txt` command causes the output of the `ls` command to be redirected to a file named file2.txt. The output is placed at the beginning of the file. If file2.txt already exists, any previous data in that file is lost. The second command, `cat file2.txt`, proves the output has been redirected. The third command, `who > file2.txt`, causes the output of the `who > file2.txt` command to be redirected to the same file, overwriting any previous data. Again, the output is placed at the beginning of the file. Ultimately, you only end up with the output from the `who > file2.txt` command as is proven by the last command, `cat file2.txt`. Figure 4-2 shows the results of the previous commands.

4

Figure 4-2   Output redirection to create a new file

 You can redirect input and output in a single command. For example, the command `sort -r < input.txt > output.txt` sorts the file input.txt in reverse sort order, and then redirects that output to a file named output.txt.

Redirecting Output to Append to a File

You use two greater than symbols to append output to a file. If the file exists, the output of the command adds its output just below the last line of the existing file. If the file does not exist, it is created. You perform the redirect append (>>) operation if you want to preserve the current contents of a file. You perform the redirect create (>) operation if you want to remove the previous contents of the output file. The general form is:

```
command > filename
```

Consider what happens if you issue the following sequence of commands:

```
ls > file2.txt
cat file2.txt
who >> file2.txt
cat file2.txt
```

The first command's output is redirected to the file; the second command's output is placed after the first. In this case, you would have the output of both commands in one file. Figure 4-3 shows a screenshot of these commands.

Figure 4-3   Redirecting output and appending it to a file

Compare Figures 4-2 and 4-3 and notice how they differ. In Figure 4-2, file2.txt contains just the output of the very last command. In Figure 4-3, file2.txt contains the output of both commands.

Next you will redirect output.

To redirect output:

1. Log in to the Linux system as a user, and then open a Terminal emulation window.

2. To redirect output and create a new file, type **ls -l > file3.txt**, and then press **Enter**. The output of the **ls -l** command does not appear on the screen because it was sent to the file named file3.txt.

3. To redirect output and append to a file, type **pwd >> file3.txt**, and then press **Enter**. The output of the **pwd** command does not appear on the screen because it was sent to the file named file3.txt.

4. To redirect output and append to a file, type **date >> file3.txt**, and then press **Enter**. The output of the **date** command does not appear on the screen because it was sent to the file named file3.txt.

5. To redirect output and append to a file, type **echo "The End" >> file3.txt**, and then press **Enter**. Again, the output of the **echo** command does not appear on the screen.

6. To display the contents of the file, type **cat file3.txt**, and then press **Enter**. See Figure 4-4; notice that the output that was redirected in Steps 2 through 5 now appears on the screen.

7. To exit the Terminal emulation program, type **exit**, and then press **Enter**.

8. Log out.

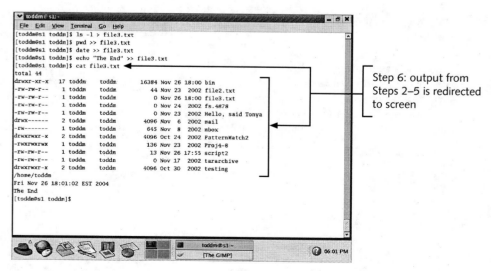

Figure 4-4   Redirecting output to both create and append to a file

Redirecting Standard Error

Most commands also send their error messages to the screen. If you want to capture that output to a file for later review, you can redirect standard error. Let's say you are working on the Linux help desk for a company, and a customer calls saying she is getting an error message. One solution is to have the customer redirect standard error to a file, and then send the file to you for inspection. Redirecting standard error is similar to redirecting standard output except you must refer to the file descriptor, 2, for standard error to redirect it. The general form is:

```
2>filename
```

For example, if you want an error message from the `rm` command to be redirected, you enter `rm 2>rmlist.err`. Then, you can issue the `cat rmlist.err` command to display the contents of the rmlist.err file.

Typically, standard error is combined with standard output. However, to redirect standard output and standard error to different files, you enter `rm >rmlist.txt 2>rmlist.err`. You implement this form of redirection if you want to send standard output and standard error to different files.

You typically redirect both standard output and standard error if a command runs automatically, for example, at night when you are not there to see the output on the screen. In this case, you would want to have the output sent to a file for review the next day.

 Setting up scripts to run automatically will be discussed in Chapter 12.

If you want standard output and standard error to go to the same file, the general form is:

```
&>filename
```

The use of the ampersand (`&`) tells the shell to redirect standard error and standard output to a file other than the default; you use the ampersand method with the redirection symbol. If you want to redirect both standard output and standard error in one file, you also use the method using the ampersand. For example, the following command tells the shell to redirect both standard output and standard error to the same filename.

```
rm &>rmlisting.txt
```

Next you will learn how to redirect standard output and standard error.

To redirect standard output and standard error:

1. Log in to the Linux system as a user, and then open a Terminal emulation window.

2. To redirect standard output and standard error to different files, type **(ls -l; who; rm t5) >listing.txt 2> errlisting.txt**, and then press **Enter**. There is no output displayed to the screen. (*Note:* The file t5, if it exists, should be removed prior to performing this step so an error will be generated.)

3. To display the contents of the listing.txt file, type **cat listing.txt**, and then press **Enter**. See Figure 4-5. The output is displayed on the screen.

4. To display the contents of the errlisting.txt file, type **cat errlisting.txt**, and then press **Enter**. See Figure 4-5. The output is displayed on the screen.

5. To combine standard output and error to a single file, type **(ls -l; who; rm t5) &>combolist.txt**, and then press **Enter**.

6. To display the contents of the combolist.txt file, type **cat combolist.txt**, and then press **Enter**. See Figure 4-6. The output is displayed on the screen.

7. Close the window, and then log out.

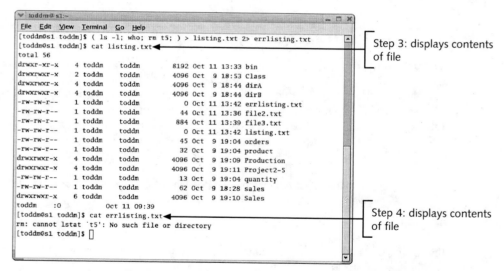

Figure 4-5   Redirecting standard output and standard error to separate files

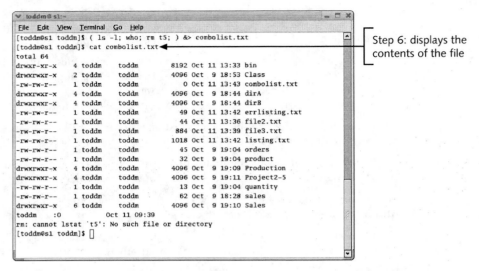

Step 6: displays the contents of the file

Figure 4-6   Redirecting standard output and standard error to the same file

UNDERSTANDING PATTERN MATCHING

Pattern matching is a technique that uses metacharacters to match characters based upon a certain pattern. For example, you use pattern-matching techniques to list all files that started with a "j." Or, if you want to match all characters with a .dat extension, you can use pattern-matching techniques. Pattern matching usually results in a subset of the total number of items available. For example, if you want to display all files beginning with a "j," then this would most likely be a subset of the total number of files in the given directory.

You can think of pattern matching as "searching" for specific files or directories in a given directory.

There are several methods for matching various patterns of characters. The pattern-matching techniques are as follows:

- To match any character use the (*) symbol
- To match a single character use the (?) symbol
- To match any one of several characters use the ([...]) symbol

Matching Any Character

You use the asterisk symbol to match any character. This type of pattern matching usually concludes in the largest number of results returned because it matches any character. You use this pattern-matching technique if you want to match patterns that match a lot of characters. The asterisk symbol matches any character position. For example, the command `cp *.dat /dirA` tells the shell to copy all files with a "dat" extension in the filename to the directory named dirA. The command `ls -l t*` tells the shell to list all of the files that begin with a lowercase "t." The command `rm G*.txt` tells the shell to remove all files that begin with an uppercase "G" and that have a "txt" extension.

Next you will learn how to match any character.

To match any character:

1. Log in to the Linux system as a user, and then open a Terminal emulation window.

2. Create a directory named **PatternMatch1** in the **$HOME** directory.

3. Change directory locations to **PatternMatch1**.

4. Use the `touch` command to create these files in the PatternMatch1 directory: **file1.dat**, **GreatBig.txt**, **file2.dat**, **file3.dat**, **file5.txt**, and **file6.txt**, and then list all the files with the `ls` command.

5. To list all files that begin with the letter "f," type `ls f*`, and then press **Enter**. See Figure 4-7. Only files beginning with an "f" are displayed.

6. To list all files that begin with the letter "G," type `ls G*`, and then press **Enter**. See Figure 4-7. Only files beginning with a "G" are displayed.

7. To list all files with an extension of "txt," type `ls *.txt`, and then press **Enter**. See Figure 4-7. Only files with an extension of "txt" are displayed.

8. To list all files that begin with the letter "f" and have an extension of "txt," type `ls f*.txt`, and then press **Enter**. See Figure 4-7. Only files beginning with an "f" *and* having an extension of "txt" are displayed.

9. Close your window, and then log out.

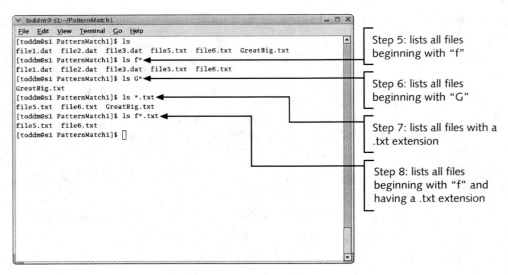

Figure 4-7 Pattern matching of any character

 Another term that is used to describe the concept of matching any character is "wildcard." Sometimes an asterisk is called the wildcard symbol. The term comes from playing with a deck of cards where a card can be any card the player chooses. Thus, pattern matching is synonymous with wildcarding.

Match a Single Character

To match a single character position, you use the question mark symbol. This type of pattern matching is usually more restrictive than matching any character because you can actually control which character position to match. For example, if you wanted to display only files that had a "2" in their fourth character position regardless of what follows the fourth character position, you would enter `ls ???2*`. If you had entered `ls *2*`, the result would be any file with a "2" anywhere in the filename, so the use of `?` is required to establish proper placement of the character for which you are searching.

Next you will perform a search to match a single character.

To match a single character:

1. Log in to the Linux system as a user, and then open a Terminal emulation window.

2. Create a directory named **PatternMatch2** in the **$HOME** directory.

3. Change directory locations to **PatternMatch2**.

4. Use the **touch** command to create these files in the **PatternMatch2** directory: **filemonkey.txt**, **filesilly.dat**, **file123.dat**, **t1.dat**, **t2.dat**, **t3.dat**, **tell.dat**, **telecommute.dat**, and **tv.txt**.

5. List all the files with the **ls** command.

6. To list all files that begin with a "t," are followed by a single character, and have a "dat" extension, type **ls t?.dat**, and then press **Enter**. See Figure 4-8. Notice that only the matching files are listed.

7. To list all files that begin with a "t," followed by a single character and have three characters in the extension, type **ls t?.???**, and then press **Enter**. See Figure 4-8. Notice that only matching files are listed.

8. To match files containing four characters with a three-character extension, type **ls ????.???**, and then press **Enter**. See Figure 4-8; notice that only the matching file is listed.

9. To remove all files that begin with a "t," have only one remaining character in the second character position, and have a three-character extension, type **rm t?.???**, and then press **Enter**. See Figure 4-8; notice that only the matching files, in this case, t1.dat, t2.dat, t3.dat, and tv.txt are removed.

 In some versions of Linux you may receive an interactive prompt from the **rm** command asking if you want to delete each file. To remove the files in question, you must answer in the affirmative.

10. List all the files using the **ls** command.

11. To list the files previously removed, type **ls t?.???**, and then press **Enter**. See Figure 4-8. A message appears indicating there are no such files.

12. Close your window, and then log out.

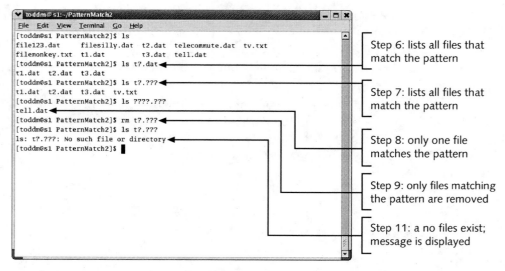

Figure 4-8 Pattern matching a single character

Match Any One of Several Characters

The use of square brackets allows you to match any one of the characters contained within the square brackets. You use this type of pattern matching for matching files containing uppercase and lowercase filenames. Linux filenames are case sensitive, meaning that the following files are considered different: FUN.DAT, Fun.Dat, fun.dat, FuN.DaT and fuN.dAt. Consequently, if you want to match any files beginning with either an uppercase "T" or a lowercase "t," you would enter ls [Tt]*. Like the question mark symbol, use of square brackets is positional.

This pattern-matching technique also allows you to match a range of characters. For example, if you want to list all files that begin with any of the uppercase letters "L" through "P," you enter ls [L-P]*. To match these same lowercase characters, you enter ls [l-p]*.

Next you will use pattern matching to match one of several characters.

To match one of several characters:

1. Log in to the Linux system as a user, and then open a Terminal emulation window.

2. Change to the **PatternMatch2** directory.

3. Use the **touch** command to create these additional files in the **PatternMatch2** directory: **zorro.txt**, **pecan.dat**, **apples.dat**, **water.dat**, and **bread.txt**.

4. List all the files.

5. To list all files beginning with either an "f" or "t," type ls [ft]*, and then press **Enter**. See Figure 4-9. Only matching files are listed.

6. To list all files beginning with "tel" and having either an "l" or an "e" in the fourth character position, type ls tel[le]*, and then press **Enter**. See Figure 4-9; notice that only the telecommute.dat and tell.dat files are displayed.

7. To list all files that begin with a letter in the range of "f" through "z," type ls [f-z]*, and then press **Enter**. See Figure 4-9. Notice that only matching files beginning with any letter starting with "f" through the letter "z" are listed.

8. To list all files that begin with "file" with the letters "m" through "s" as the fifth character position, type ls file[m-s]*, and then press **Enter**. See Figure 4-9. Only matching files are displayed.

9. Close your window, and then log out.

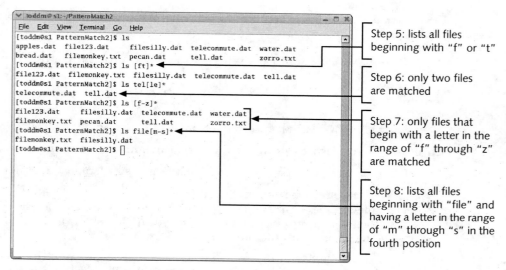

Step 5: lists all files beginning with "f" or "t"

Step 6: only two files are matched

Step 7: only files that begin with a letter in the range of "f" through "z" are matched

Step 8: lists all files beginning with "file" and having a letter in the range of "m" through "s" in the fourth position

Figure 4-9   Matching more than one character

UNDERSTANDING THE USE OF QUOTING

If you have to use one of the metacharacters discussed in Chapter 3, or one of the pattern-matching characters, you need a way to distinguish between the literal symbol and the symbol's use as a metacharacter or pattern-matching character. This is called **quoting** and it allows you to distinguish between the literal value of the symbol and the symbols used as code. To do this, you must use one of these three symbols:

- Backslash (\)

- Single quote (')

- Double quote (")

A Backslash (\)

A backslash is also called the **escape character**. When you use the backslash symbol when you are quoting, it allows you to preserve only the character immediately following it, with the exception of a newline character. For example, consider the greater-than symbol. You know that the greater-than symbol is a shell metacharacter that redirects output to create a new file. To stop the shell from interpreting the greater-than symbol as the redirection symbol, you need to protect it. If you want to create a file named "tools>," you do so by entering the following command: touch tools\>. In this example, it is the backslash symbol that preserves the literal meaning of the greater-than symbol. If you enter touch tools>, the shell generates an error because the shell uses the greater-than symbol as a redirection operator, and it is expecting a filename to follow this operator.

 In general, it is not advisable to use metacharacters as symbols when naming a file.

Next you will use the backslash symbol to preserve the meaning of a metacharacter.

To use the backslash to preserve the literal meaning of a metacharacter:

1. Log in to the Linux system as a user, and then open a Terminal emulation window.

2. Type **touch TimeKeeper>**, and then press **Enter**. An error message is displayed on the screen. This is because the backslash was not included in the filename, so the shell tried to interpret the greater-than symbol as a redirection operator and failed because a filename was not following the greater-than symbol.

3. To create a file with the greater-than metacharacter in the filename, type **touch TimeKeeper\>**, and then press **Enter**. The prompt returns.

4. Type **ls TimeKeeper>**, and then press **Enter**. Again, you receive an error because the **ls** command could not handle the greater-than metacharacter correctly.

5. To list the file with the greater-than metacharacter in the filename, type **ls TimeKeeper\>**, and then press **Enter**. Notice that this time, the file is displayed.

6. To exit the Terminal emulation program, type **exit**, and then press **Enter**.

7. Log out.

A Single Quote (')

Like the backslash, a single quote is used to protect the literal meaning of metacharacters. However, it differs from the backslash in that it can protect all characters within the single quotes. The only character it cannot protect is itself. Usually, you use single quotes if you want to display a quote from someone. For example, the command echo 'Joe said "Have fun!"' results in the shell placing double quotes around the text "Have fun!".

A single quote cannot occur with other single quotes even if preceded by a backslash. For example, the command echo 'Joe said 'Have fun'' would not result in the shell placing single quotes around the text 'Have fun'. Instead, the shell simply displays Joe said Have fun. To display the quotes, you enter echo 'Joe said "Have fun" '.

Next you will protect text and metacharacters using single quotes.

To use the single quotes to preserve the literal meaning of characters within the quotes:

1. Log in to the Linux system as a user, and then open a Terminal emulation window.

2. Type `touch ' "Hello", said Tonya'`, and then press **Enter** to create a file with this unusual name.

3. List this file with the `ls ' "Hello", said Tonya'` command. The file is listed on the screen.

4. Insert the following lines of code to create and display the file:

   ```
   touch ''Hello', said Tonya'
   ls ''Hello', said Tonya'
   ```

   The text Hello does not have quotes around it when the filename is displayed. Remember, you cannot embed single quotes within single quotes.

5. Close your window, and then log out.

A Double Quote (")

You use double quotes to protect all symbols and characters within the double quotes. However, double quotes will not protect these literal symbols: $, ', and \, even though they are metacharacters. Recall that single quotes will protect these symbols. If you want to display these characters or have them as part of a filename, you need to use single quotes. For example, the command `echo '$5.00'` displays the text $5.00 correctly.

If you want to display a single quote, as an apostrophe, then you need to use double quotes. For example, to display the text, Ross' Farms, Inc., you use double quotes because single quotes cannot contain single quotes. To create a file named "Micki's file", you enter `touch "Micki's file"`.

Next you will preserve the literal meaning of a metacharacter using double quotes.

To use double quotes:

1. Log in to the Linux system as a user, and then open a Terminal emulation window.

2. To correctly display the text **I've gone fishin'**, enter `echo "I've gone fishin'"`, and then press **Enter**. Notice that the text is correctly displayed on the screen.

3. To correctly display the text **Jake won $500.00**, enter `echo 'Jake won $500.00'`, and then press **Enter**. Again, the text is correctly displayed on the screen. You could have entered it this way too: `echo Jake won '$'500.00` because you only need to protect the dollar sign.

4. To correctly display the text **You've earned $5.00**, enter `echo "You've" earned '$5.00'`, and then press **Enter**. You are required to form the statement this way because the apostrophe (a single quote) in the contraction

must be protected with double quotes. The dollar sign must be protected with the single quotes.

5. Close your window, and then log out.

UNDERSTANDING EXPANSION

Expansion is the process of changing metacharacters and special symbols into something else. The shell uses special symbols to expand or substitute words that are entered on the command line. You have already seen expansion as it applies to the shell variables in previous chapters. For example, $HOME expands, or turns, into your home directory. The $PATH variable expands into the list of directories the shell uses to search for locating commands. Expansion occurs when you use these variables. There are several types of expansion but only a few will be discussed in this chapter. They are listed below:

- Tilde
- Parameter and variable
- Command substitution

Tilde Expansion

A **tilde-prefix** is the part of a command that begins with the tilde symbol (~) and is followed by additional characters. The tilde (~) expands to the user's login name home directory. For example, if you execute the cd ~ command, your current directory changes to your home directory. If you enter the command cp ~/victory.dat /tmp, the file named "victory.dat" from your home directory would be copied to the /tmp directory.

If the tilde-prefix is part of the ~+ command, then the value of the shell variable PWD is substituted for the tilde-prefix. For example, if you enter the command echo ~+, your current working directory is displayed. In this case, the tilde-prefix with the plus sign achieve the same results as the pwd command.

If the tilde-prefix is part of the ~− command, then the value of the shell variable OLDPWD is substituted for the tilde-prefix and hyphen. If you enter the command echo ~−, your previous working directory is displayed.

Parameter (or Variable) Expansion

Parameter expansion, in general, substitutes values for parameter or variable names. Parameters and variables are discussed further in Chapter 5. For now, think of them as names that can contain values. The dollar sign ($) is used for parameter expansion. For example, you can set the variable Text1 to be "Please enter menu selection: " with the command Text1="Please enter menu selection: ". However, in order to access the contents, you must precede the variable with the dollar sign. So, echo $Text1 displays the contents of Text1 on the screen. In this example, the variable $Text1 is substituted with its contents, "Please enter menu selection:". There are a variety of ways you can achieve parameter substitution depending upon the expansion command you choose to use.

Use of the ${name} method

The use of braces is designed to allow you to mix variables and numbers in the shell. For the most part their use is not needed, but there are some circumstances where braces are required. This type of expansion takes the following general form:

```
${name}
```

For example, suppose you work for an international bank and you want to display a currency value symbol that you have stored in a variable named currency. You also want to display a credit transaction by a customer to show "Credit $500.00." To do so, you enter the following statements:

```
currency='$'
echo "Credit" ${currency}500.00
```

These commands display what you intended on the screen–"Credit $500." If you don't include the braces around the variable, you get unexpected results. Here the variable currency is equal to the number 500. Figure 4-10 demonstrates this use of braces for parameter substitution from the previous example. Notice the second example in Figure 4-10 does not contain braces. Without them, the dollar sign and the number are not displayed.

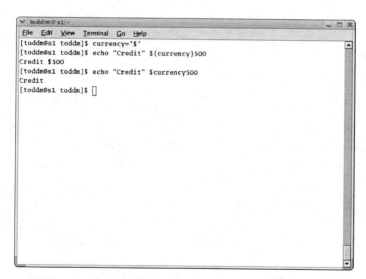

Figure 4-10   Use of braces in parameter substitution

Specifying Part of a Value Using ${name:offset:length}

You can use parameter expansion to specify a portion of a parameter's value by using the following form:

```
${name:offset:length}
```

The *name* value is the name of the variable. The *offset* position is the beginning position within the value you want, and the *length* number is the number of positions of the value you want. The *offset* position begins at zero. The use of braces is required. If you leave them off, you get unexpected results. Consider an example where you have a parameter named "p" that contained the value "abcde." Letter "a" is in position, or offset, zero; letter "b" is in position, or offset, one; and so on. If you want to specify the third and fourth character positions for "c" and "d," then you use the statement echo ${p:2:2}. The first "2" is the offset and the second "2" is the length. If you want to display the first four positions, you use the statement echo ${p:0:4}. A practical use of this type of parameter expansion might be using a portion of your Social Security Number (SSN) as a password. Many systems set your initial password to the last four digits of your SSN. So, the statement, password=${SSN:5:4} initially sets the password to the last four digits of your SSN.

Specifying a Variable's Length

There may be times when you want to determine the length of a variable. For instance, if you want to determine if a user has entered the appropriate number of characters in a field on the screen. To determine the length of a variable you use the following general form:

```
${#variable}
```

To display the length for a variable named "T," you type echo ${#T}.

Next you will complete an exercise to increase your understanding of parameter expansion.

To understand parameter expansion:

1. Log in to the Linux system as a user, and then open a Terminal emulation window.

2. To set a variable for use, type p="56789", and then press **Enter**.

3. To display the first two character positions of "p," type echo ${p:0:2}, and then press **Enter**. See Figure 4-11. The characters, "5" and "6," are displayed.

4. To display two character positions of "p" starting with the third position, type echo ${p:2:2}, and then press **Enter**. See Figure 4-11. The characters, "7" and "8" are displayed.

5. To display the last character position of "p," type echo ${p:4:1}, and then press **Enter**. See Figure 4-11. The last character is displayed.

6. To verify the need for braces, type **echo $p:4:1**, and then press **Enter**. See Figure 4-11. Notice that the text "56789:4:1" is displayed, which is not what you intended.

7. To display the length of "p," type **echo ${#p}**, and then press **Enter**. See Figure 4-11. The numeral five is displayed indicating that the length of the variable is five positions.

8. Close your window, and then log out.

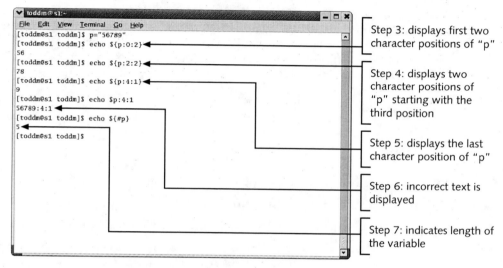

Figure 4-11   Use of parameter expansion

Command Substitution

Command substitution allows you to substitute the output of a command in place of the command itself. This is typically used in combination with parameter or variable substitution. For example, you know that the **pwd** command displays your current working directory. What if you want to keep this information? You can use command substitution to set a variable to equal the output of the **pwd** command. Then, you can display the contents of the variable using parameter substitution. There are two forms of command substitution. They are:

- $(*command*)
- \`*command*\`

In both cases, *command* is a Linux command. The $(*command*) is the newer of the two forms of command substitution and treats everything within the parentheses as part of the command.

The single back quote (`` ` ``) is used in `` `command` ``. It is on the same key as the tilde symbol.

Let's look at an example. If you enter the `t=`ls`` command, followed by the `echo $t` command, the contents of the variable named "t" are the output of the `ls` command. If you choose to use the other syntax, you enter `t=$(ls)`.

You can also nest command substitutions. Nesting means placing a command substitution with another command substitution. The innermost nested command executes first. For example, in the `t=$(ls $(pwd))` command, the content of the variable "t" first contains a listing of the current working directory, which is the output of the `$(pwd)` command that is substituted first. Next, the output of the `ls` command is substituted. Ultimately, the contents of "t" are the directory listing of the current directory in this example.

You cannot use the single back quotes when nesting. You will get unexpected results.

Next you will complete an exercise to help you understand command substitution.

To understand command substitution:

1. Log in to the Linux system as a user, and then open a Terminal emulation window.

2. Type **echo "User" $(whoami) "is on system" $(hostname)**, and then press **Enter**. The text "User *username* is on system *system-name*" is displayed on the screen. See Figure 4-12. Note that toddm is the username shown and the system name is s1. Your *username* and *system-name* will be different.

3. Type **echo "Your current directory is: " $(pwd)**, and then press **Enter**. The text "Your current directory is: *directory-name*" is displayed on the screen. In Figure 4-12 the current directory shown is /home/toddm/Ch4. Your *directory-name* will be different.

4. To implement an alternate form of command substitution, type **echo "Your current directory is: " `pwd`**, and then press **Enter**. See Figure 4-12. Notice that the results are the same for this step and the previous one.

5. To display the date, type **echo "Today is" `date`**, and then press **Enter**. The text "Today is *current-date*" is displayed on the screen. Your *current-date* will be different than what is shown in Figure 4-12.

6. To display the current year, type **echo "The year is" `date +%Y`**, and then press **Enter**. The text "The year is *current-year*" is displayed on the screen. Your *current-year* will be different than what is shown in Figure 4-12.

7. Close your window, and then log out.

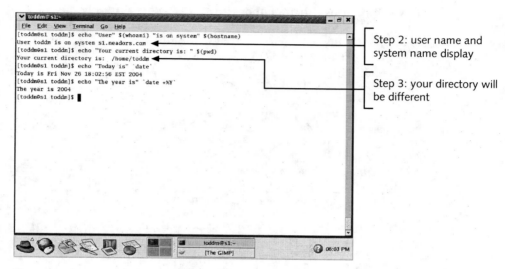

Figure 4-12   Use of command substitution

LEARNING ADDITIONAL COMMANDS

In this section, you will learn several additional Linux commands. These commands will help enhance your Linux skills; they are highly useful commands when implemented in shell scripts. The following is a list of additional commands:

- find
- tr
- tee
- mail

The find Command

The find command allows you to search for files in the directory tree. You use this command when you do not know where a file is located. This command locates the directory the file is in. You can also use this command with options to find files that are a certain size, owned by a specific user, or older than a specified number of days. The find command locates the files in the directory tree based upon the criteria specified in the options. While the `find` command has numerous options, only a few will be covered in this section. If you want to find out about additional options, refer to the `man` pages for the `find` command. The `find` command takes this general form:

> `find` *path* *expression*

This is where *path* is either a full or partial path. Note that only the current directory is searched if you do not specify a path. An *expression* can be comprised of options, tests, and actions. Only tests will be discussed in this section. There are several available actions, but the default action is to display text to the screen. Table 4-2 shows a list of some of the more important *find* tests.

Table 4-2 A few `find` tests

Test	Description	Example
`-mtime` *number-of-days*	Finds files modified a specified *number-of-days* ago	`find -mtime 5`
`-name` *pattern*	Searches for a directory based upon a specified *pattern*	`find -name ltml`
`-size` *number*	Finds files that are a minimum size. The *number* specifies the size used to compare. After the number, you can use a term. Some valid terms are: "k" for kilobytes "c" for bytes	`find -size 1k`
`-type`	Finds files of a certain type. Some valid types: "d"=directory "f"= file	`find -type d`
`-user` *username*	Find files owned by *username*	`find -user toddm`

Consider the example shown in the table used for finding a specific file named ltm1, `find -name ltm1`. The output returned for this example is the full path to the file in the tree. You don't have to be in the directory the file is located in to use the `find` command. The `find` command looks in all directories starting in the current directory. This is a particularly useful command when you don't know where a file is located.

You can use pattern matching techniques with the `find` command, too. For example, to find all files with a first character in the range of "a-c", you enter `find [a-c]*`.

If you want to locate all files that have not been modified in the last seven days, you enter `find -mtime 7`. A list of files not modified in the last seven days appears. The `find` command searches all subdirectories. Use of the modification option is very helpful when you want to clean up your system by deleting "older" files.

Another application of the `find` command is listing all files as opposed to directories. To do so you enter `find -type f`, and a listing of all files along with their full paths is displayed. To locate only directories, you enter `find -type d`, and a listing of all directories is displayed. The `find` command is also useful for finding files created by a particular user. To display all files owned by a user named "Sally," you enter `find -user Sally`, and all of her files are displayed.

You can even locate files that are a specific size. To find all files that are at least 10 kilobytes (10,000 characters), you enter `find -size 10k`. This application is useful for locating large files in the directory tree that might be occupying a lot of disk space.

Next you will complete an exercise to help you understand the `find` command.

To understand the `find` command:

1. Log in to the Linux system as a user, and then open a Terminal emulation window.

2. To locate all files and directories in the current directory, type **find**, and then press **Enter**. All files and directories appear on the screen.

3. To locate directories, type **find -type d**, and then press **Enter**. This time, only directories appear on the screen.

4. To locate files, type **find -type f**, and then press **Enter**. Now, only files appear on the screen.

5. To find files over 1 kilobyte, type **find -size 1k**, and then press **Enter**. Only files at least 1 kilobyte in size appear.

6. To find files owned by a user, type **find -user *username***. Replace *username* with your own name. All files that you own are displayed.

7. Close your window, and then log out.

The `tr` Command

The `tr` command translates or deletes characters. It is very useful for translating lowercase characters to uppercase when testing for user input in a shell script. It takes the following general form:

```
tr option set1 set2
```

This is where *set1* are either characters or classes of characters that are to be translated into characters or classes of characters specified in *set2*. The original characters in *set1* are translated into the characters in *set2*. If you wanted to translate all lowercase letters to uppercase using a class of characters, you enter `tr [:lower:] [:upper:]`. Or, you could reverse the two and convert uppercase to lowercase as in `tr [:upper:] [:lower:]`.

From a programming standpoint, translating characters gives you greater control over the characters because fewer possible variations exist. As a shell programmer, there may be times when you request a user to input data at a prompt. You can use the `tr` command to translate all the characters to uppercase, and continue your script based on uppercase input data. For example, suppose you wrote a shell script that checked whether a user entered a "Y," for "Yes," in order to perform a certain task. What if the user entered a lowercase "y"? Remember that uppercase and lowercase letters are different. One option is to write a script that accounts for all the possibilities, or you could just translate the lowercase "y" to an uppercase "Y," and then check for this.

 You can use the "-d" option to delete characters.

Next you will use the `tr` command to translate uppercase and lowercase letters.

To understand the `tr` command:

1. Log in to the Linux system as a user, and then open a Terminal emulation window.

2. To translate lowercase characters to uppercase, type `tr [:lower:]` `[:upper:]`, and then press **Enter**. The cursor moves to the beginning of the next line. The `tr` command is awaiting your input.

3. At the beginning of the next line, type **linux is fun!**, and then press **Enter**. See Figure 4-13. The characters are translated to uppercase.

4. Press **Ctrl+D** to terminate the command.

5. To translate uppercase characters to lowercase, type `tr [:upper:]` `[:lower:]`, and then press **Enter**. The cursor moves to the beginning of the next line. The `tr` command is awaiting your input.

6. At the beginning of the next line, type **THIS is cool.**, and then press **Enter**. See Figure 4-13. The uppercase characters are translated to lowercase. The already existing lowercase characters do not change.

7. Press **Ctrl+D** to terminate the command.

8. To translate just one character, type `tr y Y`, and then press **Enter**.

9. At the beginning of the next line, type **The answer is "y".**, and then press **Enter**. See Figure 4-13. The only character translated is "y." It is translated from lowercase to uppercase.

10. Press **Ctrl+D** to terminate the command.

11. Close your window, and then log out.

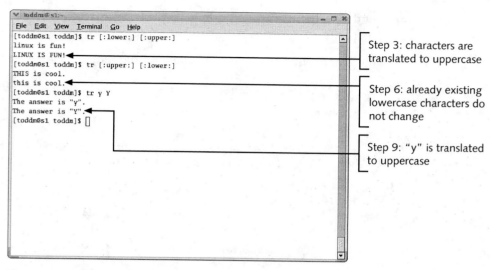

Step 3: characters are
translated to uppercase

Step 6: already existing
lowercase characters do
not change

Step 9: "y" is translated
to uppercase

Figure 4-13   Use of the `tr` command

The tee Command

The `tee` command is a useful command because it reads from standard input and writes both to standard output and to files. You use this command if you want to see the output of a command as well as keep the output of the command in a file for later review. The following is the general form:

```
tee option file
```

The `tee` command only has a few options; the most important one is the −a option used for appending. Consider a possible use for this command. One example might be displaying the output of the `who` command on the screen and then capturing that same output to a file for later review. You can use the `tee` command to accomplish this. Suppose you enter the `who | tee wholist.txt` command. Recall that the vertical bar is the pipe symbol discussed in Chapter 2. The output goes to the screen, and then the `tee` command sends the output to the wholist.txt file. This differs from redirection because with the `tee` command you get output in two places—the screen and a file. With (or without) redirection, you only get output in one place—either the screen or a file.

Next you will use the `tee` command to send output to two places.

To understand the `tee` command:

1. Log in to the Linux system as a user, and then open a Terminal emulation window.

2. To display the list of current users and send the output to a file named "output.txt," type **`who | tee output.txt`**, and then press Enter. Figure 4-14 shows possible results of this command. Your results will differ.

3. Display the content of the output file.

4. To display the list of current users and append the output to the output.txt file, type **`who | tee -a output.txt`**, and then press **Enter**. The listing of users should be similar to what was displayed in Step 2.

5. Display the contents of the output file. See Figure 4-14. Notice that the `cat` command is used to display the output.txt file. The original output that was sent to this file in Step 2 as well as the output appended in Step 4 is shown. Your results will differ.

6. To display the current directory, and then append the output to the output.txt file, type **`pwd | tee -a output.txt`**, and then press **Enter**. Your present working directory is displayed.

7. Display the contents of the output.txt file. See Figure 4-14. Notice that the information from Steps 2 and 4 is included as well as the result of the `pwd` command from Step 6. Your results will differ.

8. Close the window, and then log out.

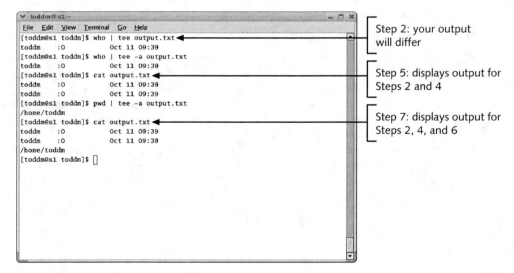

Figure 4-14 Use of the `tee` command

The mail Command

The mail command is used to send and receive electronic messages. To run the mail command, simply type mail at the command prompt. Because most people are already familiar with the concepts of sending and receiving e-mail, you will next perform an exercise to show you how it works on the Linux operating system.

To use the mail command:

1. Log in to the Linux system as a user, and then open a Terminal emulation window.

2. To send an e-mail to a user, type **mail *username***, and then press **Enter**. Be sure to replace *username* with your own username. The mail command displays a Subject: line.

3. On the Subject: line, type **Price Quote**, and then press **Enter**. The cursor moves to the beginning of the next line. This is one of the message lines where you will enter the text you want to send.

4. On the first message line, type **The price quote for customer 1001A for Purchase Order 1122-EG is $199.99.**, and then press **Enter**. On the next message line, type **Thanks,**, and then press **Enter**. The cursor moves to the beginning of the next message line. See Figure 4-15.

5. Press **Ctrl+D**. The Cc: line appears. This is for "Courtesy copy" in case you want to send this message to another user.

6. Press **Enter**. The Linux prompt returns.

7. Wait a few minutes for the mail daemon to send the message. To receive your mail, type **mail**, and then press **Enter**. An ampersand appears. This is the mail prompt. See Figure 4-15. One or more lines are displayed indicating you have a message. You should see the letter "N" for "New" message and a number to the right of the "N." This is the message number used for referencing the message.

8. Type in the message number of your new message, and then press **Enter**. The message appears. In Figure 4-15, the message number is "1."

9. Review the message, press **q**, and then press **Enter** to quit mail.

10. Close your window, and then log out.

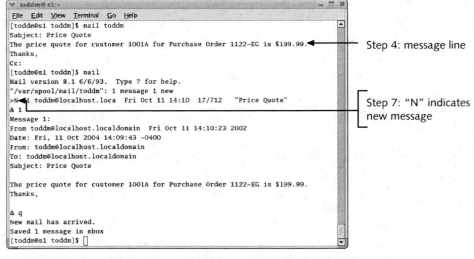

Figure 4-15   Use of the mail command

CHAPTER SUMMARY

❑ Redirection changes the default locations of standard input, standard output, and standard error. The symbol for redirecting standard input is the less-than symbol (<). The symbol for redirecting standard output and creating a new file is the single greater-than symbol (>). The symbol for redirecting standard output and appending it to a file is made up of two greater-than symbols (>).

❑ Pattern matching can be used to find characters. The symbol to match zero or more characters is the asterisk (*). The symbol to match a single character position is the question mark (?). To match several characters, you enclose a list or range of characters to be matched within brackets, ([. . .]).

❑ The use of quotes preserves the literal meaning of metacharacters. The backslash, \, preserves the meaning of the character immediately following it. Using two single quotes, ' . . . ', protects characters within the quotes. Single quotes preserve the meaning of all characters within them with the exception of another single quote. The use of two double quotes, " . . . ", preserves the meaning of all characters within double quotes with the exception of $, ', and \.

❑ Expansion is the process of changing the metacharacters into something else. The shell uses special symbols known as metacharacters to expand words or substitute values. The types of expansion discussed in this chapter include tilde, parameter, or variable, and command. Tilde expansion converts the metacharacter ~ into your home directory. Parameter, or variable, expansion allows you to use metacharacters to combine numbers and characters. To work with portions of a parameter, you use the (${*name:offset:length*}) form. To determine the length of a parameter, you use the (${*#name*}) form.

❏ The `find` command allows you to locate files and directories within the Linux tree based upon size, owner, age, and other criteria. The `tr` command translates and deletes characters. The `tee` command sends output both to the screen and to a file. The `mail` command allows you to send and receive e-mail messages.

4

REVIEW QUESTIONS

1. Which command is used to locate files?

   a. `who`

   b. `find`

   c. `tr`

   d. `mail`

2. Which command is used to send and receive messages?

   a. `who`

   b. `find`

   c. `tr`

   d. `mail`

3. You use _____ to redirect input.

   a. `>>`

   b. `<`

   c. `>`

   d. `$(...)`

4. The file descriptor for standard error is _____.

   a. 1

   b. 0

   c. 9

   d. 2

5. You use _____ to redirect output and create a new file.

   a. `>>`

   b. `<`

   c. `>`

   d. `$(...)`

6. You use _____ to redirect output and add data to the end of a file.

 a. `>>`

 b. `<`

 c. `>`

 d. `$(...)`

7. The _____ option on the **tee** command allows you to append to a file.

 a. `-o`

 b. `-a`

 c. `>`

 d. `>>`

8. The default location for standard input is the _____.

 a. printer

 b. hard disk

 c. screen

 d. keyboard

9. Which is used to perform command substitution?

 a. `'...'`

 b. `<`

 c. `>`

 d. `` `...` ``

10. The _____ command translates uppercase letters to lowercase letters.

 a. `tr`

 b. `tee`

 c. `mail`

 d. `find`

11. The _____ metacharacter preserves all characters except a single quote.

 a. `\`

 b. `"`

 c. `` ` ``

 d. `'`

12. The _____ metacharacter preserves all characters except the dollar sign, the single back quote, and the backslash.

    a. \

    b. "

    c. `

    d. '

13. The _____ metacharacter preserves the character following it.

    a. \

    b. "

    c. `

    d. '

14. To nest using command substitution, you use the _____ form.

    a. '...'

    b. "..."

    c. `...`

    d. $(...)

15. To locate files that are 2 kilobytes, you use the _____ command.

    a. `ls -l 2k`

    b. `find -size 2k`

    c. `find -length 2k`

    d. `find -size 2c`

16. To locate files owned by Marge, you use the _____ command.

    a. `ls -owner=Marge`

    b. `find -who Marge`

    c. `find -owner Marge`

    d. `find -user Marge`

17. To convert the letter "v" to uppercase, you use the _____ command.

    a. `tr v V`

    b. `tr V v`

    c. `ls v | tee -a out.txt`

    d. `tr [:upper:] [:lower:]`

18. To redirect standard error of the **pwd** command to a file named Error.txt, use the _____ command.

    a. pwd &>2

    b. pwd 2>error.lst

    c. pwd 2>Error.txt

    d. pwd > Error.txt

19. To redirect standard output and standard error of the **who** command to a file named wholist.txt, use the _____ command.

    a. who &>1 & 2

    b. who>>wholist.txt

    c. who 2>wholist.txt

    d. who &> wholist.txt

20. To display the output of the **ls** command to the screen and to a file named lslisting.txt you use the _____ command.

    a. ls | tr lslisting.txt

    b. find -name lslisting.txt

    c. ls | tee -a lslisting.dat

    d. ls | tee lslisting.txt

HANDS-ON PROJECTS

Project 4-1

In this project, you will reinforce your knowledge of redirecting input and output. The goal of this project is to use redirection to alter where the input of a command is coming from or where the output of a command is going to.

1. Log in to the Linux system as a user, and then open a Terminal emulation window.

2. To redirect output, type **who > x.dat**, and then press **Enter**.

3. To redirect and append output, type **ls >> x.dat**, and then press **Enter**.

4. To redirect and append output, type **pwd >> x.dat**, and then press **Enter**.

5. To redirect and append output, type **date >> x.dat**, and then press **Enter**.

6. To redirect and append output, type **echo "The end" >> x.dat**, and then press **Enter**.

7. To display the contents of the output file, type **cat x.dat | more**, and then press **Enter**.

8. Record the output.

9. To overwrite the output file previously used by redirecting the output and creating a new file, type **echo "Oops" > x.dat**, and then press **Enter**.

10. To display the contents of the output file, type **cat x.dat**, and then press **Enter**.

11. Record the reason for difference in this output compared with the output you recorded in Step 8.

12. To redirect standard input, you first need to create a file to work with. Create a file named **unsort.dat** with the following data:

    3

    1

    2

13. To redirect input, type **sort < unsort.dat**, and then press **Enter**.

14. Record the output.

15. To redirect input and output, type **sort < unsort.dat > sort.dat**, and then press **Enter**.

16. Type **cat unsort.dat**, and then press **Enter**.

17. Record the output.

18. Type **cat sort.dat**, and then press **Enter**.

19. Record the output.

20. Record the reason the two previous files differ.

21. Close your window, and then log out.

Project 4-2

In this project, you will reinforce your knowledge of redirecting standard output and standard error. The goal of this project is to use redirection to alter where the output of a command and any resulting error messages are sent.

1. Log in to the Linux system as a user, and then open a Terminal emulation window.

2. Create a file named **P4-2.dat**.

3. To redirect standard output and standard error to different files, type **ls P4-2.dat > List.txt 2> ListError.txt**, and then press **Enter**.

4. Display the contents of both files.

5. Remove the file named **P4-2.dat**, so you can generate an error in the next command.

6. To see what happens when an error is generated, repeat Step 3.

7. Display the contents of both files.

8. Record the output and the reason for the output.

9. To redirect standard output and error to the same file named both.txt, type **ls P4-2.dat &>both.txt**, and then press **Enter**.

10. Display the contents of the file named **both.txt**.

11. Record the output and the reason for the output.

12. Close your window, and then log out.

Project 4-3

In this project, you will reinforce your knowledge of the concept of pattern matching. The goal of this project is to create several files, and then write a script to perform pattern matching techniques for the listing of files.

1. Log in to the Linux system as a user, and then open a Terminal emulation window.

2. Create the following files in the same directory: **pay042004.dat, pay022004.dat, pay122004.dat, pay042003.dat, pay062004.dat, pay102004.dat, sales012004.dat, sales052004.dat, sales102004.dat,** and **sales042004.dat.** The files have a three character name followed by a two digit month and a four digit year. The file extension is "dat."

3. Create a script named **Project4-3** in the **$HOME/bin** directory.

4. List all files beginning with any letter in the range "a"–"r."

5. List all files beginning with an "s."

6. List all sales files that include the year 2004.

7. List all pay files for April.

8. List all files with a "txt" extension.

9. Save the script, and then close the editor.

10. Run the script, record the commands used in Steps 9–12, and then record or print the script.

11. Close your window, and then log out.

Project 4-4

In this project, you will reinforce your knowledge of the concepts of redirection and pattern matching. The goal of this project is to use the files created in Project 4-3, then write a script to perform both redirection and use pattern-matching techniques.

1. Log in to the Linux system as a user, and then open a Terminal emulation window.

2. Create a script named **Project4-4** in the **$HOME/bin** directory.

3. List all files beginning with "pay," and then redirect output to a file named PayList.txt.

4. List all sales files for August, redirect output to a file named AugList.txt, and then redirect standard error to ErrorList.txt.

5. List all pay files with a .txt extension, and then redirect both standard output and error to PayTxtList.txt.

6. List all files beginning in the range of "a–z," and then redirect both standard output and error to azList.txt.

7. Save the script, and then close the editor.

8. Run the script, record the commands used in Steps 3–6, record the command used, and then record or print the script.

9. Close your window, and then log out.

Project 4-5

In this project, you will reinforce your knowledge of the concept of quoting. The goal of this project is to have you write a script that quotes metacharacters, and then redirect that output to a file. By combining the quoting and redirection in one project, you will see the importance of quoting. (*Hint*: If you don't put the correct quoting characters in the correct place, you could end up with errors.)

1. Log in to the Linux system as a user, and then open a Terminal emulation window.

2. Create a script named **Project4-5** in the **$HOME/bin** directory.

3. Insert the following lines of code:

```
echo "This file has single quotes 'see'." > echolist.txt
echo "I've earned '$'500.00 "in sales this week." >> echolist.txt
echo "James' " '$'Money'$' "list" >> echolist.txt
echo The prompt on some systems has this symbol \>.  >> echolist.txt
```

4. Save the script, and then close the editor.

5. Run the script, record the commands used in Step 3, and then record or print the script.

6. Close your window, and then log out.

Project 4-6

In this project, you will reinforce your knowledge of expansion. The goal of this project is to help you understand the concepts of tilde expansion, parameter or variable expansion, and command substitution.

1. Log in to the Linux system as a user, and then open a Terminal emulation window.

2. To display your current working directory using tilde expansion, type **echo ~+**, and then press **Enter**.

3. To display your previous working directory using tilde expansion, type **echo ~-**, and then press **Enter**.

4. To use tilde expansion to change to your home directory, type **cd ~**, and then press **Enter**.

5. To set a value to be used with parameter expansion, type **Value="ABC123"**, and then press **Enter**.

6. To display the last three character positions, type **echo ${Value:3:3}**, and then press **Enter**.

7. To display the last (sixth) character position, type **echo ${Value:5:1}**, and then press **Enter**.

8. To display the length of the variable Value, type **echo ${#Value}**, and then press **Enter**.

9. To use command substitution to set a variable equal to the output of the previous command, type **len=$(echo ${#Value})**, and then press **Enter**.

10. Display the contents of the variable named len.

11. To use command substitution to set a variable named password equal to the last three characters in the value, type **password=$(echo ${Value:3:3})**, and then press **Enter**.

12. Display the contents of the variable named password.

13. Close your window, and then log out.

Project 4-7

The goal of this project is to help reinforce your understanding of the **find** command.

1. Log in to the Linux system as a user, and then open a Terminal emulation window.

2. To locate directories and redirect the output to a file, type **find -type d > dirlist.txt**, and then press **Enter**.

3. To locate files that are 3k (kilobyte) in size or larger and redirect the output, type **find -size 3k > ThreeK.txt**, and then press **Enter**.

4. To locate files that haven't been modified in seven days and redirect the output to a file, type **find -mtime 7 > SevenDays.txt**, and then press **Enter**.

5. To locate files that haven't been modified in three days and that are 1k in size, type **find -type f -size 1k -mtime 3**, and then press **Enter**.

6. To locate files that haven't been modified in 30 days, that are 10k in size, that are owned by your username, and then to redirect standard output and error to a file, type **find -type f -size 10k -mtime 30 -user *username* &> findlist.txt**, and then press **Enter**. Replace *username* with your own user name.

7. Close your window, and then log out.

Project 4-8

The goal of this project is to help reinforce your understanding of the **tee** command.

1. Log in to the Linux system as a user, and then open a Terminal emulation window.

2. Create a script named **Project4-8** in the **$HOME/bin** directory.

3. Run the correct command to display a long listing to the screen, and then place the results of the long listing in a file named **Project4-8list.txt**.

4. Run the correct command to display the currently logged in users to the screen, and then append the results to a file named **Project4–8list.txt**.

5. Run the correct command to find only files in the current directory and display them on the screen, and then append the results to a file named **Project4–8list.txt**.

6. Run the correct command to find only files in the current directory that begin with letters in the range "a–z" and display them on the screen, and then append the results to a file named **Project4–8list.txt**.

7. Save the script and then close the editor.

8. Run the script, record the command used, and then record or print the script.

9. Close your window, and then log out.

CASE PROJECTS

Case 4-1

You have been hired by TMI to create a shell script using pattern-matching techniques. The payroll department needs the following files created and then placed in the Payroll directory that you created in Case 2-1:

jan07.dat	dec04.dat	jul04.dat	feb06.dat	apr06.dat	dec06.dat
jan02.dat	feb14.txt	jun06.dat	feb16.dat	aug06.txt	jun04.dat
jan03.dat	jul04.txt	jul13.txt	feb26.dat	may06.txt	jun06.txt
oct27.txt	feb07.dat	dec07.dat	apr28.dat	mar06.dat	apr09.txt

Because the IT staff has a limited knowledge of the Linux operating system, they want you to help them perform the following tasks. Run the commands at the command line to make sure you get them to work properly. Once they are correct, place these commands in a shell script. Then, test and run the script.

The script must include a Linux statement for each step below:

1. Display all files with an extension of "dat."

2. Display only files for "January."

3. Display all files that begin with a "j" and have an extension of "dat."

4. Display all files only for the seventh of every month.

5. Display all files that begin with the letter "j" or the letter "d."

Case 4-2

Jenny's Motorcycle and Sidecar Shop has a Linux system used to run their main sales shop and two satellite sales offices. Recently, their Linux System Administrator left, and they need you to write a script for them. The script must perform the following and redirect output and errors to one or more files in your home directory:

❏ Find all files that are at least 10 kilobytes.

❏ Find all files owned by root that are 100 kilobytes in length.

❏ Use the **man** pages to construct the correct command to locate only files with the permissions of read, write, and execute for all files owned by root.

❏ Display the contents of the output file(s), and then translate all lowercase letters to uppercase.

❏ Print the output file(s) within the script.

5

SHELL SCRIPT PROGRAMMING CONCEPTS

In this chapter, you will:

♦ Understand the sequential flow of shell scripting
♦ Manage shell scripts
♦ Understand the basic components of a shell script
♦ Understand parameters
♦ Create interactive scripts
♦ Understand debugging

This chapter gives you an overview of shell script programming. You need to understand the flow of shell scripting in order to effectively write shell scripts. You will learn how to manage shell scripts, which entails changing the permissions on a script to allow you to execute it by simply entering the script name. You will also learn how the shell executes a script. By placing the script in a directory which is on the search path, you will be able to run the script from any directory location. You will learn the basic components of a script which include adding comments to a script and adding a usage clause which indicates to the user how to run the script. Allowing your script to accept values from the command line or interact with the user will also be discussed. Finally, you will learn how to debug and troubleshoot your script to handle any execution errors you may run into.

UNDERSTANDING THE SEQUENTIAL FLOW OF SHELL SCRIPTING

Shell scripts allow you to combine programming logic with operating system commands to automate parts of your job. The term **sequential**, as it applies to shell scripting, means one command executes at a time. All programming languages execute their statements in sequential order. You can alter this order with decision statements, looping structures, and functions. These concepts are discussed in later chapters.

Let's look at an example taken from most everyone's day—getting ready for school or work. This overall task can be set up in a series of sequential steps in pseudocode. As an example, here is the list of steps that one could use to get ready for school or work:

1. *Turn alarm clock off.*

2. *Get out of bed.*

3. *Shower and clean up.*

4. *Dress.*

5. *Eat breakfast.*

6. *Brush teeth.*

7. *Drive to school or work.*

Granted, some steps in this list can be done in a different order. You might say that you eat breakfast before you shower and dress. Or, you may be late so you skip eating breakfast and brushing your teeth. However, you must do some of these steps prior to others. You must get out of bed before you dress or even drive to school or work. And, if you complete the list of steps in the order shown, then you have a routine, or program, for getting ready for school or work everyday.

The getting-ready-for-school-or-work routine parallels the concept of a sequential flow of a shell script. In the above example, each of the individual steps is equal to a command. The collective steps are considered the program. In shell scripts like the getting-ready-for-school-or-work program, some commands may be executed before other commands, and there are some commands that must be executed before others.

 A shell script is a program.

In order to help understand the sequential flow of shell scripting, you will create a simple three-line shell script. The following steps are the pseudocode for the shell script. As you may already know, pseudocode allows you to concentrate on the logic of your program instead of being concerned about the specific syntax. Review the following pseudocode:

1. Change directory locations to root.

2. Run a listing on the directory.

3. Display the current working directory.

Next you will turn this pseudocode into a shell script.

To create a shell script from pseudocode:

1. Log in to the Linux system as a user, and then open a Terminal emulation window.

2. To change to the bin directory, type **cd bin**, and then press **Enter**.

3. To create the shell script with the name ListRoot, type **vi ListRoot**, and then press **Enter**.

4. Type **i** to insert a line of text. The text "—INSERT—"appears at the bottom of the window.

5. To mirror the pseudocode statements, insert the following lines of code to the ListRoot script:

```
cd /
ls
pwd
```

6. In order to save the script, press **Esc**, type **:wq!**, and then press **Enter**.

7. In order to execute the ListRoot script, type **bash ListRoot**, and then press **Enter**. The shell script executes and performs the statements you added in Step 4—specifically, changes to the root directory, performs a directory listing, and then displays the present, or current, working directory. Figure 5-1 shows the ListRoot script and its execution.

8. Close your window, and then log out.

When you create a shell script, you must arrange the commands in a logical order. The logical order depends upon the task you are trying to accomplish. In the ListRoot script, if you placed the **pwd** command before the **ls** command, the order of processing would change. In this case, the **ls** would execute last. Although this is a minor change in this shell script, in some cases, if you place the commands out of order, it can create unexpected results. Take for example, a shell script that redirects output to a file.

You learned in Chapter 4 the difference between using a single greater-than symbol and two greater-than symbols to redirect output. The single greater-than symbol overwrites the current contents of the file. Using two greater-than symbols appends to a file.

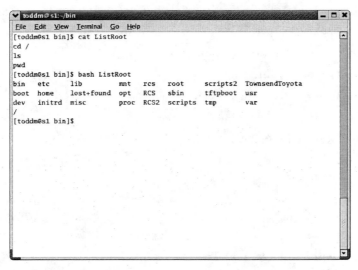

Figure 5-1   The ListRoot script

In the following sequence of commands, the first **echo** command is redirecting the text "output" to a file named **output.txt**. Any previous data is overwritten. The next two **echo** statements are appending to the same filename.

```
echo "output" > output.txt
echo "more output" >> output.txt
echo "even more output" >> output.txt
```

What would happen if you placed the first line at the end of the list of commands? In other words, if you used the following code instead of the previous code:

```
echo "more output" >> output.txt
echo "even more output" >> output.txt
echo "output" > output.txt
```

The answer to this question is that any previous data in the file would be lost. Although the first two commands are appending output, thus preserving any previous data in the file; the last statement is using a single greater-than symbol to overwrite the file, thus resulting in any prior data being lost. What you will have in the file, after the last statement is executed, is simply the text "output" in the file—nothing else. This is a problem if you want to keep any existing data.

The best way to ensure the correctness of your shell script is to write the logic on paper as pseudocode. Then, if possible, have your instructor review it. Next, convert the pseudocode statements into commands using an appropriate Linux editor. Finally, run the shell script.

MANAGING SHELL SCRIPTS

In this section, you will learn how to manage shell scripts. When you manage a shell script, you are making the script executable in a location where the users will be able to run it. Managing shell scripts involves the following:

- Modification of a shell script's file access permission
- Placement of shell scripts

Modification of the File Access Permission of a Shell Script

5

As you have learned, you can execute a shell script by entering the shell's name, such as bash, followed by the script's name. For example, to execute a shell script named paychecks, you enter **bash paychecks** at the command line. However, if you use a script frequently, there is a method that is more streamlined and that is widely used among programmers. Instead of entering the name of the shell (in this case bash) you can modify the permissions of your script so you can execute it by simply entering the script's name. The chmod command allows you to modify the file access permission on a file or directory. Recall that you learned about permissions in Chapter 2. The permissions are read, write, and execute for the user who owns the file, the group ownership of the file, and others. When a file is first created, it has certain default permissions. For nonroot users, the default file permissions are read and write for the user who owns the file as well as the group membership on the file, and just read for others. For the root user, the permissions are read and write for the owner and read for the group and others. The chmod command takes the following general form:

```
chmod ugo +-= rwx filename
```

In this syntax, u represents the user or owner of the file, g represents the group permissions on the file, and the o represents the other users. The + sign means to add a permission to the current permission set, the – sign means to remove a permission from the current permission set, and the = sign creates a new permission set. Recall that r, w, and x stand for read, write, and execute. The command syntax places the *filename* after the permissions. You can use any or all of these symbols to achieve the necessary level of permission you seek for your file. Next you will change the execute permission using the letter notation of the chmod command so you can simply enter the shell script name at the command line.

To modify the execute permissions of a file using letter notation so you can simply enter the script's name:

1. Log in to the Linux system as a user, and then open a Terminal emulation window.

2. Move **ListRoot** to the **~/bin** directory.

3. Change directory locations to the **~/bin** directory.

4. Type **chmod ugo+x ListRoot**, and then press **Enter**. The prompt returns.

5. To verify that the execute permission has been set, type **ls —l ListRoot**, and then press **Enter**. Notice that the execute permission has been added.

6. Run the script by simply entering **ListRoot**. Notice that the command executes just by entering the script's name.

7. Close your window, and then log out.

Now that you know how to modify the permissions of a script in order to make it executable, you will utilize this concept in subsequent exercises and labs as well as on the job.

Another method of changing permissions with the **chmod** command is to use numbers to represent the permissions for the user, group, and other users. This method takes the general form:

```
chmod nnn filename
```

Here, *n* represents a number from 0 to 7. Each *n* represents the permission number for the user owner, group, and other users. Table 5-1 shows the permissions and numbers to which they refer.

Table 5-1   Permission numbers for the **chmod** command

Permissions	Number
– – –	0
– –x	1
–w–	2
–wx	3
r– –	4
r–x	5
rw–	6
rwx	7

The best way to use this table is to look for the permission you want and then look to the right to find the appropriate number you need. The three permission columns represent a 4, 2, and 1 for read (**r**), write (**w**), and execute (**x**), respectively for the user owner, group, and other users. You add up the numbers for the permissions you want. For example, if you want read-only, you simply need 4 for the permission. If you want read and write, you would add 4 and 2 to get the number 6. If you want read, write and execute, you add up 4, 2, and 1 to get the number 7.

So, if a file named program1 needed to have read, write and execute for the user owner, read and execute permissions for the group, and no permissions for all others, you would enter `chmod 750 program1`.

Next you will perform an activity using the `chmod` command with the number notation. The end result is the same as the letter notation of the `chmod` command—to be able to execute a script by entering just the name on the command line. However, you can use the `chmod` command to modify other permissions.

To modify the execute permissions of a file using number notation:

1. Log in to the Linux system as a user, and then open a Terminal emulation window.

2. Change to the **bin** directory.

3. Create a shell script that displays the current date and a list of users logged on the system. (*Hint*: use the `date` command followed by the `who` command.) Be sure to save the script with the name **LoggedOn** in the **bin** subdirectory of your home directory, and then close `vi`.

4. The current permissions are `rw-` for user owner and group and `r- -` for all others. To add execute permission for all three permission sets, type **chmod 775 LoggedOn**, and then press **Enter**. By using "775," you are setting the permissions to `rwx` for the user owner and group and `r-x` for all others. You are only adding execute.

5. To verify the permissions type `ls -l LoggedOn`, and then press **Enter**.

6. Execute the script named **LoggedOn**.

7. Close your window, and then log out.

Some users find the number method easier to enter from the keyboard once they understand its methodology. As a user writing shell scripts, you need to understand both methods. One reason is that there are process startup scripts located in the /etc/rc.d/init.d directory that use both methods. You will need to understand the startup scripts in order to troubleshoot the Linux system. For example, if you execute the command `grep chmod *` in the /etc/rc.d/init.d directory you will see scripts that use either method. The `grep` command allows you to search for text in files and will be covered in Chapter 10. The command given above searches for the text "chmod" in all files.

 Exercise caution when using the `chmod` command. You don't want to inadvertently give group owners or other users excess permissions. For example, if a file named fileA.txt is created, it would have default permissions of `rw-rw- - r- -`. If you executed `chmod 777 fileA.txt`, then everyone on the system would have all permissions, including write. This would give anyone access to modify or even delete fileA.txt whether you intended this or not.

Placement of Shell Scripts

When you create a script or want to find an existing script, it's a good idea to understand how the shell locates scripts that are to be executed. Here's how it works. If you enter a command or script name using its full path, the shell attempts to locate the command in the specified directory. Say you entered the following command at the shell prompt:

    /scripts/script1

Assuming the script is executable, how does the shell know how to locate the script named script1 in order to execute it? Simply put, the shell attempts to locate the shell script named script1 in the /scripts directory because you told it to look there when you entered the full path on the command line. If the shell script is not present, the shell generates an error message indicating the shell script file cannot be found.

Now, if you enter the command or script name using the partial path instead of the full path, the shell attempts to locate the directory the script is in a little differently. Say you executed the same script as above but left off the root symbol and directory location as follows:

    script1

How does the shell know in which directory the script is located? The shell searches each element of the **PATH** shell variable for a directory containing the script file. If the directory is located that houses script1, the file is executed. Otherwise, an error is displayed. Figure 5-2 displays the contents of the **PATH** variable. The command used to display the contents of the **PATH** variable is `echo $PATH`. This variable is often called the search path.

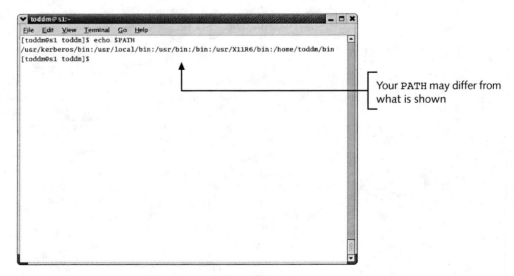

Your PATH may differ from what is shown

Figure 5-2   Contents of the PATH shell variable

In this example, you can see that there are six directories on the search path. Your actual search path may be different if a System Administrator changed the setting of the PATH variable. Changing the PATH is typically done in one of the startup files for the user account. In Figure 5-3 you can see the first directory listed is searched first. The next directory in the list is searched only if the script file is not found in the first directory. This process continues until the directory containing the file is found or the last directory is reached. If the shell cannot locate the script in any of the directories listed, then an error appears indicating the shell cannot find the script.

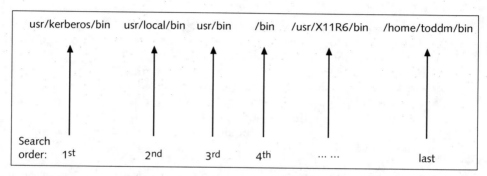

Figure 5-3   Search order of the search path

 You can also display the contents of the PATH shell variable using the env command. This command displays all variables for a given user account. The important thing to note here is that this command shows a colon separating each directory for the PATH variable.

The main reason for the search path is to make your job easier. It is much easier on you, the Linux user, if you can just enter the script name without having to enter the directory in which it is located. There is less to enter at the keyboard, resulting in fewer typos and errors. In order to run a shell script without using the full path name, you follow one of two methods. First, you can create a directory, place the shell scripts in the directory, and then add the directory to the search path. This method is useful when you have a shell script that needs to be used by many users or when you have a set of scripts you want to test. Next, you will see how this method works by creating a directory named testing where you will later place shell scripts that you are testing and don't want other users to access.

To create a directory and place it on the search path:

1. Log in to the Linux system as a user, and then open a Terminal emulation window.

2. Create a directory in your home directory named **testing**.

3. Type **PATH=$PATH:$HOME/testing**, and then press **Enter**. This command appends the current path, $PATH, with the directory, $HOME/testing. The text PATH= sets the path.

4. Change your current directory to the **$HOME/testing** directory.

5. Use the **vi** editor to create a shell script, named **display_hi** that displays the text "Hi."

6. Save the script, and then close **vi**.

7. Change to the **$HOME** directory to demonstrate the search path is used.

8. Type **bash display_hi**. The text "Hi" should appear on the screen.

9. Close your window, and then log out.

Another method for running the script without using the full path name is to place your shell script in one of the directories listed in the current search path. When you install the Linux operating system, there are a few directories that are used for the purpose of customization. For example, you can place your scripts in the /usr/local/bin directory or the **$HOME/bin** directory because both of these directories are on the search path. You can also place your scripts in the **$HOME/bin** directory as you have already done in previous exercises in this chapter. Either method works fine, but if you want to separate your scripts for testing, you should create a separate directory and place the directory name in the search path.

 The naming of scripts should be meaningful and unique. The script name must not duplicate the name of some other executable in the user's current path unless it will always be run using the full path name or an appropriate partial path name.

UNDERSTANDING THE BASIC COMPONENTS OF A SHELL SCRIPT

In this section, you will learn about the basic components of a shell script. All shell scripts can be broken down into the following list of components:

- Command interpreters
- Comments
- Variables

Specifying the Command Interpreter

You should place a statement that refers to the command interpreter that is being used in the very first line of your script. Remember from Chapter 1 that several shells, or command interpreters, exist in the Linux environment. Each shell has its own syntax rules, so commands that work in one script may not work in another. If you have multiple scripts that use different shells, you should place statements referencing the command interpreters at the beginning of each script. The advantage of specifying the command, or shell, interpreter in your program is that you ensure that later statements execute in the shell you want.

To specify the shell that is used to process subsequent commands in your script, place the statement #!, followed by the full path to the shell, as the very first line of your script. Consider the following example:

```
#!/bin/bash
# Comments
pwd
```

The first line references the command interpreter, the second includes any additional comments, and finally the third line contains the command statements.

There are no spaces in the statement #!/bin/bash and no spaces or characters follow the #! symbols.

Table 5-2 provides a list of the common Linux shells and their full paths.

Table 5-2   Full paths of common Linux shells

Shell	Path
Bash	/bin/bash
Ksh	/usr/bin/ksh
Sh	/bin/sh
Csh	/bin/csh

You can use the which command to determine the full path of the shells, or any commands. For example, which bash displays the full path of the bash shell.

Consider the script named MAIN shown in Figure 5-4. MAIN is written in the bash shell. However, it references other scripts written in different shells. Each of these scripts references the appropriate shell to be used for processing the commands within it. As each script completes, it returns to the MAIN script. Then, the next command or script in sequence executes.

Comments

Comments are placed in shell scripts so you and others understand what the programmer was thinking when he created the script. Anyone who has write permission to the script can place comments in it. This way, when the time comes for modification, you have a complete understanding of the programming that has already taken place. Accurate comments are essential to the programming process. Inaccurate comments are worse than no comments at all because they lead you to think one way when the program is doing something completely different. You implement or place comments by using the # symbol anywhere on a line. Commands or text following the # symbol will *not* be executed.

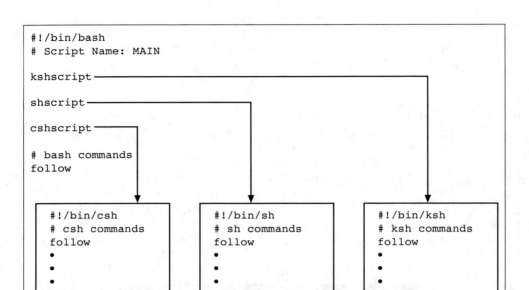

Figure 5-4   Specifying command interpreters in scripts

The use of **#** for comments causes the shell to ignore the line. You can place comments prior to a command to cause the shell to ignore the command. This can be useful if you are testing new statements in a script but are not sure if these statements will work as you've planned. For example, **#** **pwd** causes the shell to treat the **pwd** command as part of the comment text following the **#** symbol. If the **#** symbol were removed, the **pwd** command would execute normally.

In general, there should be a comment section at the beginning of every script so it is the first thing someone opening your script sees. Comments should contain the author of the script, a description of the script, the name and version number of the script, required parameters, the date modified, and a description of the modification. Figure 5-5 shows a script that uses comments. Note this is only a partial script.

At times, you may want to place comments close to actual code statements. In the following example, a comment is placed prior to each statement indicating what the next statement will do.

```
# Computes the new salary for the sales representatives
((Salary=$Salary+$Bonus))
# Displays the output to the screen
echo "Salary for $SalesPerson is $Salary and bonus amount is $Bonus"
```

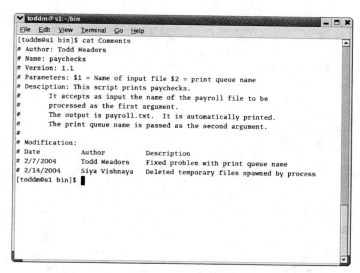

```
[toddm@s1 bin]$ cat Comments
# Author: Todd Meadors
# Name: paychecks
# Version: 1.1
# Parameters: $1 = Name of input file $2 = print queue name
# Desciption: This script prints paychecks.
#        It accepts as input the name of the payroll file to be
#        processed as the first argument.
#        The output is payroll.txt.  It is automatically printed.
#        The print queue name is passed as the second argument.
#
# Modification:
# Date          Author          Description
# 2/7/2004      Todd Meadors    Fixed problem with print queue name
# 2/14/2004     Siya Vishnaya   Deleted temporary files spawned by process
[toddm@s1 bin]$
```

Figure 5-5   Use of comments in a script

In this next example, comments are placed to the right of commands. Each command executes normally because the # symbol follows, rather than *precedes* the command. You see this approach used often in shell scripts because it saves space in the script file and places the comment closer to the actual command it references.

```
pwd      # Prints current directory
ls -l    # Displays a long listing
```

Although time consuming, the use of comments can reduce the time it takes to make modifications to the script. Even if you are the only one modifying the script, you should use comments. It's not unheard of for experienced System Administrators or programmers to sometimes forget why they wrote something a certain way when they created the script. Although placing comments in your script may take some time now, it will save a lot of time later when you need to remember why you did something.

Variables

A **variable** is used to represent data. It is composed of the variable name and the data, or contents. For example, the variable name "x" may have the number 5 as its data. The variable can be assigned by setting x to 5 as in the statement **x=5**. The contents of a variable are held in memory while in use. You can think of a variable as a cell in a spreadsheet.

A variable is sometimes called a field or a data name. To refer to the contents of a variable in the bash shell script, you precede the variable name with a dollar sign, $, as in $NetPay. For example, the command echo $NetPay displays the contents of the variable named NetPay.

Programmers try to assign variable names that describe the data they contain. For example, if the data contains a net pay amount, then a descriptive name assignment would be NetPay or NET_PAY. Programmers also make the variable names readable. For example, the variable named inventoryquantityonhand is not very easy to read. Unfortunately, most programming languages, including shell scripts, do not allow you to place a space or a hyphen between the words in the variable name. The variable names Net Pay and Net-Pay are not allowed. So, a programmer places underscores between the words of the name, uses common abbreviations, or capitalizes the first letter of each word to make the variable easier to read when reviewing a script. Thus, the following variable names would be acceptable: InventoryQuantityOnHand, InvQtyOnHand, QuantityOnHand, or Qty_On_Hand.

You can also indicate the type of data that a variable can contain as well as the size of the data. For example, if you have a variable such as NetPay and you know it should contain only numbers, you can indicate that NetPay is a numeric or an integer data type. For variables that only contain characters, you define them as a character string. When you define the size of the variable, you need to make the size large enough to hold all of the data. For example, if you define a character field to be five characters, and you try to store data with more than five characters, the data would be truncated on the right.

Variable declaration is the act of specifically defining the variable name and type. When you declare a variable, memory space is allocated for the variable's name and type. It is a good idea to define your variables near the beginning of your script or just prior to using them in a script. There are two commands that allow you to declare a variable in a script. They are the `declare` command and the `typeset` command. Their functions are identical. For example, to declare a variable as an integer for arithmetic evaluation and another variable as integer and read-only, you enter the following:

```
declare -i TotalSales
declare -i -r InterestRate
```

The shell dynamically creates variables for you if you don't declare them. However, you have much greater control over the type of data they can contain, when you declare them manually.

Initialization is the act of setting a variable to a beginning value. Although not required, it is advisable to set your variables to initial values so you know what they contain prior to using them. In the case of setting integer variables, you will most likely set your initial values to zero, for example, `NetPay=0`. You can either initialize your variable in an initialization section at the beginning of your script or in the script prior to using the variable.

A variable that has been initialized, or set, can be unset with the shell unset command. For example, to unset the variable named MonthlySales that has previously been set to a value, you enter unset MonthlySales.

Next you will create a script that contains comments, variable declarations, and initialization statements to further your understanding of these topics.

To understand how to implement comments, variable declarations, and initialization statements in a script:

1. Log in to the Linux system as a user, and then open a Terminal emulation window.

2. Create a script named **BasicComponents** in the $HOME/bin directory.

3. Insert the following lines of code to initialize the shell interpreter, add comments, declare and set a variable, and display a variable's contents. (*Note*: put your name in place of *your_name* and today's date in place of *today's_date*):

```
#!/bin/bash
# Author: your_name
# Date: today's_date
declare SalesRegion
SalesRegion="Eastern"
echo "The sales region is:" $SalesRegion
```

4. Make sure you save the script, close vi, and change permissions so you can execute the script by name.

5. Execute the script. The script displays "The sales region is: Eastern" on the screen.

6. Close your window and then log out.

UNDERSTANDING PARAMETERS

It is important to understand parameters because they allow you to provide a script with data. This allows you to make your scripts much more flexible because you can vary the data that goes into the script. Also, parameters give you information such as the status of a statement or the number of parameters entered. A **parameter** is a name, number, or special character that stores a value. A parameter is considered to be set if it has a value and can be set to a number, letters, or the null value. Null means the variable is set to no value.

There are two types of parameters used by the shell:

- Positional parameters
- Special parameters

5

Positional Parameters

You can make a shell script more flexible using positional parameters to apply values within your script. The parameters are called "positional" because they refer to the numeric position of the value in the list that follows the script's name. Once the values are given to the script, you can use these values within the script itself. You use positional parameters by entering the shell script name followed by multiple values on the command line. The general form for using positional parameters is:

```
script-name value1 value2 value3...value9
```

This is where *value1*, *value2*, *value3*, and so forth are positional values given, or passed, to the shell script. The positional parameters are called by number—1, 2, 3 and so on, and respectively represent *value1*, *value2*, *value3*, through *value9*.

> You will learn how to pass more than nine parameters using additional commands later in this chapter.

If you want to refer to the contents of a parameter, you precede the parameter with a dollar sign ($) followed by its positional number. So, the positional parameter $1 receives the value specified as *value1*. The positional parameter $2 receives the value specified as *value2*. The name of successive parameters is incremented by one until you reach $9. The $0 parameter takes the value of the actual script name itself.

> You cannot use $0 for passing values to the script.

Look at the following single line shell script named display_it below:

```
echo $1 $2
```

The display_it shell script displays two positional parameters in this example. The programmer does not know what the data is at the time the script is written. That is what makes positional parameters so flexible. The programmer does need to know how many parameters to account for. To enter the values for this shell script, you enter the following:

```
display_it a b
```

The first value, "a," is passed to the script as $1. The second value, "b," is passed to the script as $2. When executed, this shell script displays the values "a" and "b" on the screen. Figure 5-6 offers further explanation of this example.

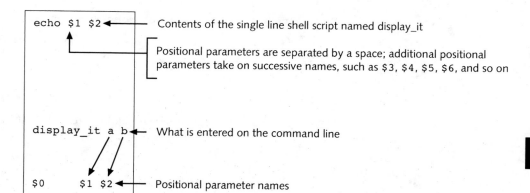

Figure 5-6 Understanding positional parameters

The benefit of using positional parameters is that you are able to write scripts that refer to parameters regardless of the value. This is a powerful feature of shell scripting. You can give a script many values and refer to the positional parameter name to get the actual value. You could rerun the previous script as `display_it The End` to display the text "The" and "End" on the screen. This is just an example. You could execute the script to display any two values as long as you separated them on the command line by a space.

You can also use positional parameters in conjunction with commands. For example, you can create a script to display the contents of a directory and pass the directory name as a positional parameter on the command line. The following code demonstrates how you can modify the ListRoot script to accept any directory as the first positional parameter.

```
cd $1
ls
pwd
```

For example, to execute this script and pass the /tmp directory to it, you enter `ListRoot /tmp`. The first positional parameter is /tmp. Thus, the script changes directory locations to /tmp, displays a listing of that directory, and then displays the present working directory.

 The shell knows when one value ends and the other begins by using the builtin variable named `IFS`, which stands for Internal Field Separator. It is set to space, tab, and newline and uses these as default separators. So, by entering `display_it The End` on the command line, the shell looks for either a space, tab, or newline to delimit each value. That's why "The" sets to $1 and "End" sets to $2.

Next, you will use your knowledge of expression from Chapter 3 to create a script that adds any two numbers passed to it.

To create a script that accepts and sums two positional parameters:

1. Log in to the Linux system as a user, and then open a Terminal emulation window.

2. Change to the $HOME/bin directory.

3. Open the vi editor.

4. Type the following lines of code to create a variable named Sum1 that is the sum of two positional parameters, and then display the Sum1 on the screen:

```
((Sum1 = $1 + $2))
echo $Sum1
```

5. Save the script as **AddThem**, and then exit **vi**.

6. To make it executable, type **chmod ugo+x AddThem**, and then press **Enter**.

7. To execute the script, type **AddThem 10 5**, and then press **Enter**. The sum of 15 is displayed.

8. Rerun the script and pass the values 500 and 200 respectively. The sum of 700 is displayed.

9. Close your window, and then log out.

Now, you have created a shell script that is flexible in terms of data that can be passed to it.

Next, you need to understand what happens when you have more than nine positional parameters that you want to pass to a shell script. To accomplish this you use the shift command. The shift command allows you to use more values in the shell by shifting them around. The general form is:

```
shift n
```

This is where *n* is a number that indicates how many positional parameters to shift. Take a look at the following shell script named ShiftThem:

```
echo $1 $2 $3 $4 $5 $6 $7 $8 $9
shift 1
echo $1 $2 $3 $4 $5 $6 $7 $8 $9
```

If you executed the script as follows:

```
ShiftThem 1 2 3 4 5 6 7 8 9 10
```

The output would be:

```
1 2 3 4 5 6 7 8 9
2 3 4 5 6 7 8 9 10
```

Figure 5-7 shows the flow of the shift command in action.

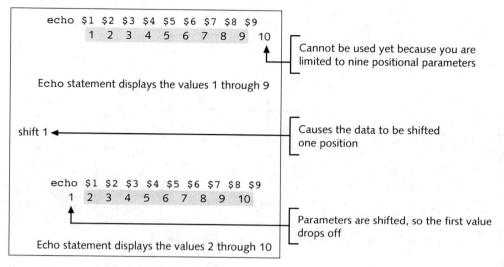

Figure 5-7   An explanation of the `shift` command

Figure 5–8 displays the script called ShiftThem along with the output of its execution.

```
[toddm@s1 bin]$ cat ShiftThem
echo $1 $2 $3 $4 $5 $6 $7 $8 $9
shift 1
echo $1 $2 $3 $4 $5 $6 $7 $8 $9
[toddm@s1 bin]$ ShiftThem 1 2 3 4 5 6 7 8 9 10
1 2 3 4 5 6 7 8 9
2 3 4 5 6 7 8 9 10
[toddm@s1 bin]$
```

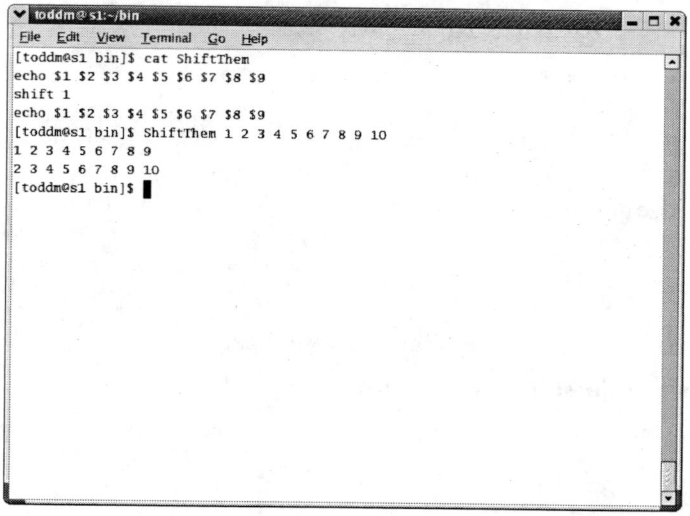

Figure 5-8   The ShiftThem script and the output of its execution

What would happen if you shifted the positional parameters more than one number, for instance, three positions? The answer is that the positional parameters shift the number you specify, or three in this case. Figure 5-9 shows a breakdown of shifting three parameters.

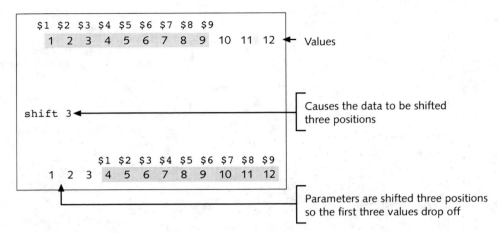

Figure 5-9 Explanation of shifting more than one parameter

Let's take a look at a practical implementation using the shift command. Imagine you need to add together 10 donations raised at a charity auction. Because you can only pass nine arguments to a script at one time, you have to shift the values to different positional parameters. The script, named DonatedSum, follows:

```
((DonatedSum=$1 + $2 + $3 + $4 + $5 + $6 + $7 + $8 + $9 ))
shift 9
((DonatedSum=$DonatedSum + $1))
echo $DonatedSum
```

In this sample code, the variable named DonatedSum is equal to the summation of the first nine positional parameters. Next, the shift 9 command shifts the parameters to the right nine positions so the new value of $1 becomes the 10th parameter. The parameter $1 no longer contains the first value. Figure 5-10 shows the DonatedSum script with output. The variable sum contains the summation of the values of all of the positional parameters.

Next you will create a script that uses shifting positional parameters.

To create a script that shifts positional parameters:

1. Log in to the Linux system as a user, and then open a Terminal emulation window.

2. Change to the **$HOME/bin** directory.

3. Open the **vi** editor.

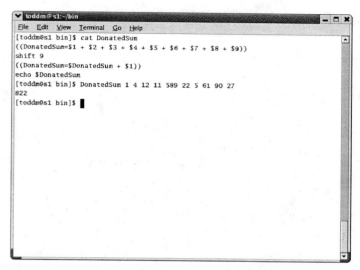

Figure 5-10   The DonatedSum script with output

4. Type the following lines of code to create a script that shifts the parameters two times:

```
echo $1 $2 $3 $4 $5 $6 $7 $8 $9
shift 5
echo $1 $2 $3 $4 $5 $6 $7 $8 $9
shift 2
echo $1 $2 $3 $4 $5 $6 $7 $8 $9
```

5. Save the file as **ShiftThemAgain**, and then close vi.

6. Type **chmod ugo+x ShiftThemAgain**, and then press **Enter**.

7. To execute the script, type **ShiftThemAgain 1 2 3 4 5 6 7 8 9 10 11 12 13 14 15 16**, and then press **Enter**.

8. Rerun the script and pass 16 different values to it on the command line.

9. Close your window, and then log out.

Now you have created a script for passing and shifting values. You can modify it as you see fit. Consider the potential tasks for which you could use this script. How might you modify it to make it best serve your needs?

As you can see, it is an advantage to be able to pass parameters to a script. However, the names of the positional parameters do not describe the data they contain, and this can seem like a complication whether you are using two parameters or several. Fortunately, you can have positional parameters take on more descriptive names. For example, if $1 represented someone's name and $2 represented his salary, you could write a shell script that set the variables to the positional parameters. Review the shell script, named NameSalary:

```
Name=$1
Salary=$2
echo $Name
echo $Salary
```

You could execute the script as **NameSalary "Jose Cruz" 50000**. In the above script, the first statement, the variable named "Name" contains the contents of the first parameter, which is "Jose Cruz." Quotes are required so the shell knows that both the first and last name represents the first positional parameter. If you leave the quotes off, the shell interprets "Jose" as **$1** and "Cruz" as **$2**, or Salary.

In the second statement, the variable named Salary contains the contents of the second parameter. Finally, the two **echo** statements display the contents of the Name and Salary variables, respectively.

The benefit of setting a descriptive name to equal the contents of a positional parameter is you can reference the data by using a variable that actually describes the data. In other words, **$Name**, brings to mind someone's name, whereas **$1** does not. You can later refer to Name and feel confident this variable contains someone's name, and this makes modifications to your script easier. Figure 5-11 shows the NameSalary script as well as two executions of that script and their output. The first command, **cat NameSalary**, displays the contents of the script. The second command, **NameSalary "Jose Dutch" 50000**, executes it correctly because quotes are included around the name. However, the third command, **NameSalary Jose Dutch 50000**, executes the script incorrectly; notice there are no quotes around the name Jose Dutch.

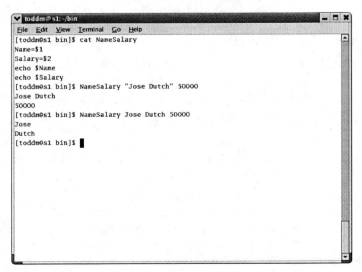

Figure 5-11   NameSalary script along with two executions and their respective output

Special Parameters

The shell uses special parameters to perform specific tasks such as referring to such items as the number of positional parameters given to a script, the name of the script, the PID of the shell, or the status of a command. Special parameters cannot be assigned values by you. You can only reference the contents of special parameters using the special parameter symbols. The actual symbols expand into other values. Some of the special parameters used by the shell are described in Table 5-3.

Table 5-3   Description of some of the special parameters used by the shell

Special Parameter	Description
@	Expands into all of the positional parameters starting at 1
#	Expands to the number of positional parameters
?	Expands to the exit status of the command previously executed as a foreground process
$	Expands to the PID of the shell
!	Expands to the PID of the previously executed background process

As with positional parameters, in order to reference a special parameter, you must precede it with the dollar sign ($). For example, if you wanted to display the current PID of your shell, you would enter `echo  $$` at the command line. By combining text with special parameters you can create more user-friendly scripts. For example, if you place the command `echo "The number of parameters is:"  $#` in a script, the command displays the text "The number of parameters is:" followed by the actual number of parameters passed to the script.

Take a look at the code for the sample script named ExitStatus shown in Figure 5-12, which utilizes the special parameter `$?` to determine the exit status of a previously executed command. Notice also that Figure 5-12 includes a breakdown of how each line of code functions.

Recall that an exit status of zero indicates success, and a nonzero exit status indicates failure. Thus, the second `rm payroll.dat` will fail because the file was previously removed. Figure 5-13 shows the output of this script, showing both the successful and failed exit statuses.

Of course, this is merely an example, you would not place two `rm` statements in tandem that remove the same file. However, what you can learn from this is that you can use the exit status to determine if a command failed or not. If the script did fail, you could send a message to the user, append the message to a file, or both.

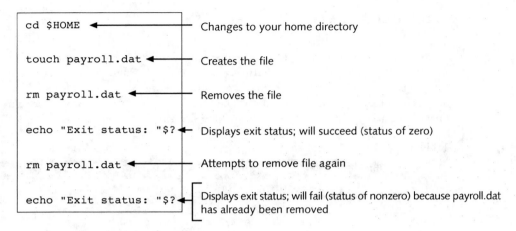

Figure 5-12   Code and its explanation for the ExitStatus script

Figure 5-13   The ExitStatus script and its output

Next you will further your understanding of special parameters.

To understand special parameters:

1. Log in to the Linux system as a user, and then open a Terminal emulation window.

2. Create a script named **SpecialParams** in the **$HOME/bin** directory.

3. Insert the following lines of code, noting that the command named `pwdx` intentionally fails and the resulting exit status reflects this:

```
pwd
echo "Exit status of last command is:" $?
pwdx
echo "Exit status of last command is:" $?
echo "Script name is:" $0
echo "The number of parameters passed is:" $#
```

4. Save the script, close `vi`, and then change the file permissions so you can execute the script by name.

5. Execute the script. The script executes and displays an exit status of zero for the command that runs correctly and displays a nonzero exit status for the invalid or incorrect command. Figure 5-14 shows the contents of the SpecialParams script followed by its output.

6. Close your window, and then log out.

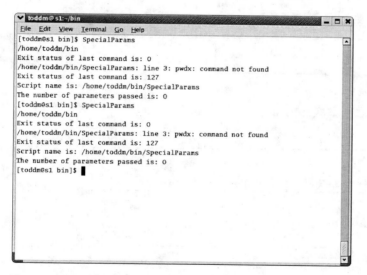

Figure 5-14   The contents of the SpecialParams script and its output

Using a Usage Clause

You can use the special parameter `$#` to determine if the appropriate number of parameters are entered by the user. This implementation is called a usage clause. A **usage clause** is a statement that displays a message indicating how to execute the script if it is executed incorrectly. Usage clauses are typically used with positional parameters that are entered on the command line following the script name. For example, if a script requires three positional parameters, and you only enter two of them, the script can detect that only two were entered, and then display a usage clause indicating how to execute the script successfully. The special parameter $#, used to reference the total number of positional parameters, is used in an if statement. (The details of if statements are covered in Chapter 6.) The following example checks to see if three positional parameters have been entered on the command line. The special parameter contains the actual number of positional parameters entered, in this case three. If a programmer enters less than three parameters, then a usage clause message is displayed. Finally, any subsequent statements execute.

```
if [ $# -lt 3 ]
then
        echo "Usage $0 value1 value2 value3"
fi
```

Figure 5-15 shows a sample script that contains the components used in this section.

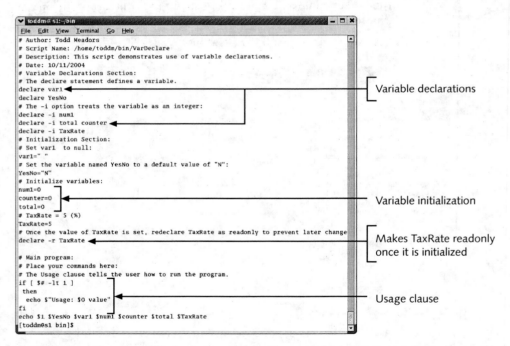

Figure 5-15   Sample script displaying comments, variable declaration, initialization, and a usage clause

CREATING INTERACTIVE SCRIPTS

Although you can use positional parameters to input data into a script, there is another approach that allows you to prompt the user for data called the **interactive method**. The interactive method uses the **read** command to prompt for user input.

The benefit of using the **read** command is that you can prompt users for input at the time you need the input. With positional parameters, all of the input must be known prior to command execution. With the **read** command, you can create a descriptive variable name to contain the data without having to rename it as you saw in an earlier section of this chapter. Later, in the script, you can refer to the data by using the variable name. There are no positional parameter names to worry about.

A common use of the **read** command in scripts is when you want a user to respond with either "Yes" or "No" to a prompt such as "Do you want to continue?". The **read** command follows the general format:

```
read variable-name
```

This is where *variable-name* is the name of a variable, not a positional parameter. Once you read data in the variable name, you can display the data by referencing the variable by name. Look at this simple example.

```
read value1
echo $value1
```

In this script there are two statements. The first statement reads data from the keyboard and places it into a variable named value1. The shell waits for the user input data followed by Enter. The second statement displays the variable's content on the screen.

You can make the script a bit more user-friendly by indicating the type of data you are requesting from the user. If you precede the **read** statement with the **echo -n** statement, you can display a message, thereby letting the user know what he or she needs to enter. The **-n** option of the **echo** statement suppresses a newline, so the cursor does not move to the next line. Next, you will use the **read** command to accept data.

To understand the read command:

1. Log in to the Linux system as a user, and then open a Terminal emulation window.

2. Create a script named **ReadHobby** in the **$HOME/bin** directory

3. Type the following lines of code to display a message statement, read the value entered, and then display the value:

```
echo -n "Enter your favorite hobby:"
read hobby
echo "You entered:" $hobby
```

4. Save the script, close **vi**, change the file permissions so you can execute the script by name, and then execute the script. Refer to Figure 5-16 and you see the contents of the script and execution with the text "Weight Lifting" entered into the script. Once entered, the text is displayed.

5. Modify the script to remove the **-n** option of the **echo** statement.

6. Execute the script again noticing the difference when using the **-n** option and not using it.

7. Close your window, and then log out.

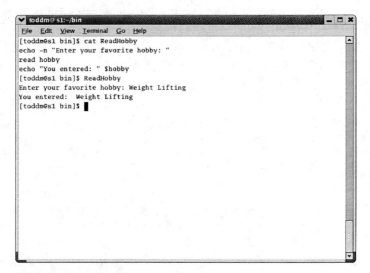

Figure 5-16 ReadHobby script and its output

Like many of the other commands that you've learned about, the **read** command has some important options. They are listed in Table 5-4.

Table 5-4 Some options used by the **read** command

Option	Description
-p *prompt*	Use to display *prompt* as a text message to prompt the user for input; this is an alternative to using the **echo** **-n** statement
-s	Use to suppress echoing characters on the screen; useful for suppressing passwords
-t *timeout*	Use to time out, or expire, the command once *timeout* seconds have been exceeded
-a *array-name*	Use to read data into an array (arrays are discussed in Chapter 8)

Let's use a few of these options in the following script:

```
read -t 3 -s -p "Enter password:" password
echo $password
```

In the first statement of this script, the **read** command displays the text "Enter password:" on the screen which is the text for the prompt that follows the **-p** option. The **-s** option suppresses the characters displayed on the screen when the user enters characters in response to the prompt. The data is placed in the variable named password. The **-t** 3 option specifies that if a key is not pressed within three seconds, the command times out, or stops. Processing then continues with the next statement.

 You don't have to use all of the options on the **read** command at the same time. You can use each option individually.

Protecting a Variable

Once you have set a variable, there may be times when you don't want it to change. What can you do to protect the contents of your variable against accidental change once its value has been set? You can use the **readonly** command to ensure that another user cannot change the variable.

The advantage of using the **readonly** command is that you are able to protect the contents of a variable. This can prove useful for constant values you don't want to change once set. An example might be the tax rate. You may want the user to enter a tax rate for different states. If the tax rate is entered as 5, for 5%, you don't want this to be changed to a different value later in the script. Use of the **readonly** command in this case serves to protect the value of the variable. Look at the following sample code for a script named ZipCode:

```
read -p "Enter Zip Code: " Zip
echo "Zip Code is: " $Zip
readonly Zip
read -p "Attempting to change Zip Code: " Zip
echo "Zip Code is: " $Zip
```

Figure 5-17 displays the ZipCode script output. Notice the value is initially set to "30044." Next, the variable is set to read-only. Then, there is an attempt to set it to "60505," resulting in an error because the variable is read-only. The last statement displays the original value, "30044."

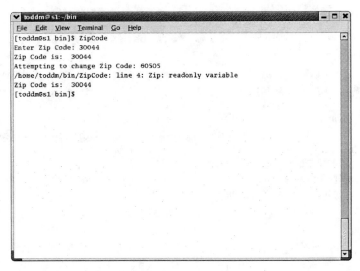

```
[toddm@s1 bin]$ ZipCode
Enter Zip Code: 30044
Zip Code is:  30044
Attempting to change Zip Code: 60505
/home/toddm/bin/ZipCode: line 4: Zip: readonly variable
Zip Code is:  30044
[toddm@s1 bin]$
```

Figure 5-17   The ZipCode script output

UNDERSTANDING DEBUGGING

One important aspect of learning any programming language is understanding how to debug a program. **Debugging** is troubleshooting errors that may occur during the execution of a script. You need to understand debugging techniques so you can quickly and effectively locate an error and correct it. The following two commands can help you debug a shell script:

- echo
- set

Using echo

The simplest method you can utilize for debugging is to use the echo statement to display the contents of a variable at different points in the script. Recall the ZipCode script; the echo statement is used there to display the contents of a variable. First, the data is entered, and then it is displayed on the screen. If you are only using the echo statement for debugging purposes, you should consider removing it once the user works with the script to keep your script clean and to the point. While displaying additional values may help you, especially when you are debugging, these values may just confuse other users.

Although the echo statement can show you the value in a variable or parameter, it cannot very easily show you the flow in a script. To accomplish this, you use the set command.

Using set

Another approach to debugging is to use the **set** command. The **set** command is a shell builtin command that has numerous options. Two of its options used in combination allow you to see line by line what is going on in the script. You want to use this approach if you need to understand the logical flow of a script. The **-v** option prints each line as it is read. The **-x** option displays the command and its arguments. You can arrange the options in any order with the **set** command.

 You should not keep the **set** options on for users. The **set** command gives them too much detail and may result in unnecessary phone calls asking for help.

The minus sign allows you to use the options. You turn the options off using the plus sign. For example, **set -xv**, turns the options on while **set +xv** turns them off. Although this may seem contradictory, it is how they work.

Generally, you place the statement **set -xv** at the beginning of the script or immediately prior to the statement you want to begin debugging. You place the statement **set +xv** at the end of the script or someplace in the script where you are certain you no longer need it. Next you will use the **set** command to debug the ZipCode script.

To understand the set statements in order to debug:

1. Log in to the Linux system as a user, and then open a Terminal emulation window.

2. Create a script named **ZipCode** in the **$HOME/bin** directory. This is the same code that is used to create the results shown in Figure 5-17.

3. To set debugging on, enter the following statement as the first line of the script:

   ```
   set -xv
   ```

4. Now, enter the code for the script:

   ```
   read -p "Enter Zip Code: " Zip
   echo "Zip Code is: " $Zip
   readonly Zip
   read -p "Attempting to change Zip Code: " Zip
   echo "Zip Code is: " $Zip
   ```

5. To set debugging off, enter the following statement as the last line of the script:

   ```
   set +xv
   ```

6. Save the script, and then close **vi**.

7. Change the file permissions so you can execute the script by name, and then execute the script. Type **30044** at the first prompt for setting the value of Zip. Type **44440** at the second prompt where you attempt to change the Zip Code.

The result is you cannot change the value at the second prompt. Also, extra text is displayed due to debugging. Figure 5-18 shows the ZipCode script with debugging options. The first statement simply displays the contents of the ZipCode script. The second statement is the script's execution. Notice as the script runs, the two plus symbols, ++, are located to the left of the statement as it is executing.

8. Close your window, and then log out.

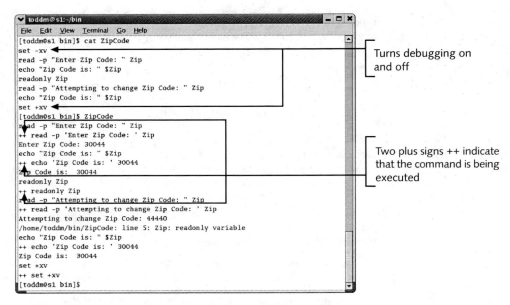

Figure 5-18   The contents of the ZipCode script using the set command

 You can also use a command named `script` for debugging purposes. You run the command prior to executing the script. When the script is finished, press Ctrl+D to terminate the `script` command. The output is contained in a file named "typescript." This is very similar to using the `set` command.

CHAPTER SUMMARY

❐ Programs execute statements sequentially, or one after the other. Because a shell script is a program, it follows the same rule. You can break down the logic of a problem's solution into pseudocode using statements that are not specific to the programming language. A pseudocode statement describes what is needed to accomplish a task without being concerned with the actual syntax of the language.

❐ In managing shell scripts, you must be aware of two factors: modifying the permissions of a script and placement of the script. You use the **chmod** command to modify a script's permissions. In order to execute the script by simply specifying the script's name on the command line, you need to give the script execute permission and place the script in a directory that is on the search path. The **$PATH** variable contains a list of directories that are searched when the shell attempts to locate a command.

❐ To have a complete understanding of the basic components of a script you need to be familiar with how to use comments, specify the command interpreter, manage variables, and use a usage clause. You should place comments in your script to describe the goal of the script. The comments should include your name, the date, the name of the script, required positional parameters, and any modifications you make to your script. Comments tell others what your script is doing. You should also specify the command interpreter to ensure that all commands are running in the correct shell. Variable names need to describe their contents. You should declare and initialize all variables used in your program. Also, you should use a usage clause when using positional parameters in a script.

❐ The shell uses two types of parameters—positional parameters and special parameters. Positional parameters allow you to place values on the command line following the script's name. This data can be used inside the script. The positional parameters range from 0 to 9. The $0 positional parameter represents the script's name. If you have more than nine, you must shift the parameters using the **shift** command. The shell uses special parameters to accomplish tasks such as displaying the exit status of a command or displaying the number of parameters passed to a script. You cannot change special parameters. The most useful special parameter is **?** which is used for checking exit status.

❐ You can create scripts that allow for user interaction by using the **read** command. This allows you more control over the variable names because you can define their names at the time you ask for input. You can use the **readonly** command to prevent a variable's contents from changing.

❐ You can debug your script with the **set -xv** command. This command displays each line and variable as it is executed. The **set +xv** command turns off debugging. You can also use the **echo** command to display the contents of variables. However, make sure you delete or comment out the **echo** statement when you no longer need them for debugging purposes.

REVIEW QUESTIONS

1. _____ describes a set of statements that establish the logic of actual program code.

   a. Script

   b. Machine code

   c. Pseudocode

   d. Binary executable

2. Which of the following uses the bash shell for the command interpreter in a script?

   a. `/bin/bash`

   b. `# /bin/bash`

   c. `!/bin/bash`

   d. `#!/bin/bash`

3. What is the name of the directory located in your home directory that is usually on the search path? (If a script is in this directory, it can be executed without entering the full path name of the script.)

   a. `$HOME/bin`

   b. /bin

   c. /usr/local/bin

   d. `$PATH`

4. What is the name of the shell builtin variable that is used for searching directories when you enter a command or script name?

   a. `$HOME`

   b. `$ENV`

   c. `$$`

   d. `$PATH`

5. What does the positional parameter `$0` reference?

   a. the first parameter following the script name

   b. the exit status of the previous command

   c. the name of the script

   d. the very last positional parameter

6. _____ is the concept of setting a variable to a beginning value.

   a. Declaration

   b. Initialization

   c. Usage clause

   d. A signal

7. The _____ command is used to set and unset permissions.

   a. `trap`

   b. `kill`

   c. `echo`

   d. `chmod`

8. The _____ command allows you to use more than nine positional parameters.

   a. `trap`

   b. `kill`

   c. `shift`

   d. `chmod`

9. What special parameter is used to determine the exit status of a previously executed command?

   a. `*`

   b. `?`

   c. `#`

   d. `0`

10. What command sets the permissions of a file named payroll.dat to be read, write, and execute for the owner; read and execute for the group; and no access for others?

   a. `chmod 750 payroll.dat`

   b. `chmod 742 payroll.dat`

   c. `chmod 057 payroll.dat`

   d. `chmod 776 payroll.dat`

11. You can implement _____ to indicate to a user how many positional parameters to pass to a script.

   a. a declaration of an integer

   b. an initialization of a variable

   c. a usage clause

   d. pseudocode

12. You use the _____symbol to mark the beginning of a comment in a script.

    a. !

    b. #

    c. $

    d. <

13. What command sets the permissions of a directory named HumanResources to be read, write, and execute for the owner; read and write for the group; and read for others?

    a. `chmod 764 HumanResources`

    b. `chmod 744 HumanResources`

    c. `chmod 742 HumanResources`

    d. `chmod 706 HumanResources`

14. You can use the _____ command to retrieve data interactively in a script.

    a. `readonly`

    b. `read`

    c. `echo $1`

    d. `shift`

15. What command is used to define a variable as an integer?

    a. `declare -i`

    b. `define -i`

    c. `shift`

    d. `readonly`

16. The _____ command is used to prevent a variable from changing.

    a. `read`

    b. `declare`

    c. `shift`

    d. `readonly`

17. What is the result of the following script?

    ```
    #!/bin/bash
    # echo $1 $2
    echo $3
    echo $?
    ```

    a. The positional parameters, $1, $2, and $3, and the total number of positional parameters are displayed.

    b. The positional parameters, $1, $2, and $3, and the exit status are displayed.

c. The positional parameter $3 and the exit status are displayed.

d. The positional parameter $3 and the number of positional parameters are displayed.

18. You use the _____ command to determine the PID of a process.

   a. ps

   b. declare

   c. grep

   d. readonly

19. You use the _____ command to debug a script.

   a. set -xv

   b. set +xv

   c. grep

   d. read

20. What special parameter is used to determine the number of positional parameters passed to a script?

   a. *

   b. ?

   c. #

   d. 0

HANDS-ON PROJECTS

Project 5-1

In this project, you will turn pseudocode into an actual shell script.

1. Log in to the Linux system as a user, and then open a Terminal emulation window.

2. Create a shell script named **Project5-1** in your **$HOME/bin** directory for the following pseudocode:

   Turn debugging on.
   Place a reference to the bash shell interpreter in the script.
   Place some appropriate comments at the beginning of your script.
   Redirect the date to a new file named /tmp/list.txt.
   Append a listing of the current users to the same file.
   Append the contents of the search path variable to this same file.
   Copy /tmp/list.txt to your home directory and name it $HOME/Project5-1.txt.
   Remove the file named /tmp/list.txt.
   Turn debugging off.

3. Save the script, close the editor, make the script executable, and then execute your script.

4. Close your window, and then log out.

Project 5-2

In this project, you will write a script that calculates an average of five values passed as positional parameters.

1. Log in to the Linux system as a user, and then open a Terminal emulation window.
2. Create a script named **Project5-2** in the **$HOME/bin** directory.
3. Insert a reference to the bash shell, appropriate comments, and your name as author.
4. Accept five positional parameters from the command line.
5. Display all five values on the screen.
6. Display a usage clause if the incorrect number of values is entered.
7. Display an average of the five values.
8. Save the script, close the editor, make the script executable, and then execute the script.
9. Record the output.
10. Close your window, and then log out.

Project 5-3

In this project, you will shift positional parameters. You will pass 13 numbers to a script, and then display their sum. You will also modify one of the scripts, named sum1, used as an exercise in this chapter. You will use sum1 as a guide to complete this project.

1. Log in to the Linux system as a user, and then open a Terminal emulation window.
2. Copy **sum1** to **Project5-3** in the **$HOME/bin** directory.
3. Insert a reference to the bash shell with the appropriate comments, including your name as the author. Indicate that this is a modification of the original script, the date of modification, and a description of the modification (see Steps 4 through 8).
4. Clear the screen with the **clear** command.
5. Display the script name. (*Hint*: Use $0.)
6. Display today's date.
7. Allow the script to accept 13 values.
8. Display the sum of the 13 values.
9. Save the script, close the editor, make the script executable, and then execute the script.
10. Close your window, and then log out.

Project 5-4

In this project, you will perform calculations in interactive scripts using the **read** command to accept variables from the keyboard and display their average. You will modify the script created in Project 5-2 to read three numbers from the keyboard.

1. Log in to the Linux system as a user, and then open a Terminal emulation window.
2. Create a script named **Project5-4** in the **$HOME/bin** directory.
3. Read three values from the keyboard.
4. Declare the variables as integers, initialize the variables to zero, and then once the variables are read, make them read-only.
5. Set a timeout value of five seconds for each variable.
6. Display the contents of the variables.
7. Attempt to change them again.
8. Save the script, close the editor, make the script executable, and then execute the script.
9. Close your window, and then log out.

Project 5-5

In this project, you will perform exponentiation in interactive scripts using the **read** command to accept two variables and then raise one to the power of the other. Once the answer is displayed, you will unset all variables using the **unset** command.

1. Log in to the Linux system as a user, and then open a Terminal emulation window.
2. Create a script named **Project5-5** in the **$HOME/bin** directory.
3. Declare three variables as integer, x, y, and A. Read x and y in from the keyboard. Compute the answer, A, as x raised to the yth power, and then display the answer.
4. Unset the variable with the **unset** command.
5. Save the script, close the editor, make the script executable, and then execute the script.
6. Close your window, and then log out.

Project 5-6

In this project, you will create a script that accepts a variable. The variable will be suppressed, thereby emulating password entry. You will use the **read** command to accept a variable from the keyboard. When the variable is read, the characters must not be displayed back to the user on the screen.

1. Log in to the Linux system as a user, and then open a Terminal emulation window.
2. Create a script named **Project5-6** in the **$HOME/bin** directory.
3. Clear the screen, and then display the message "Enter password:" on the screen.

4. Read the variable for the password, but suppress characters from displaying on the screen as the user types them. Use a timeout value of your choosing to limit the amount of time the user has to enter the value.

5. Save the script, close the editor, make the script executable, and then execute the script.

6. Close the window, and then log out.

Project 5-7

In this project, you will perform computations on positional parameters as well as implement a usage clause by creating a script that calculates a net amount based on sales (less costs).

1. Log in to the Linux system as a user, and then open a Terminal emulation window.

2. Create a script named **Project5-7** in the **$HOME/bin** directory, and be sure to include the appropriate comments.

3. Set up the script to accept two positional parameters from the command line and display a usage clause if the incorrect number of values is entered.

4. Store the positional parameters as declared integers as follows:

```
Sales=$1
Costs=$2
```

5. Declare a variable named **Net** as an integer. It will contain the difference between Sales and Costs.

6. Calculate the difference between Sales and Costs using the variable named Net to display an appropriate message indicating the difference.

7. Save the script, close the editor, make the script executable, and then execute the script.

8. Close your window, and then log out.

Project 5-8

In this project, you will properly protect data on the command line when it is passed to a script by creating a script where you will pass positional parameters.

1. Log in to the Linux system as a user, and then open a Terminal emulation window.

2. Create a script named **Project5-8** in the **$HOME/bin** directory, and be sure to include the appropriate comments.

3. Clear the screen.

4. To accept name, address, city, state, phone number, fax number, and e-mail account from the command line, use the following positional parameters:

```
$1=name, $2=address, $3=city, $4=state, $5=phone number,
$6=fax number, and $7=email account.
```

Remember you are required to use double quotes in order to assign the value to the correct positional parameters.

5. Display a usage clause if the incorrect number of values is entered.

6. Display all parameters.

7. Save the script, close the editor, make the script executable, and then execute the script.

8. Run the script using the following data:

   Name: Rachael Sing

   Address: 100 East Windam Street

   City: Atlanta

   State: Georgia

   Phone: 555-555-5550

   Fax: 555-555-5551

   Email: rsing@domainname.com

9. Rerun the script with different data of your own choosing.

10. Record the output.

11. Close your window, and then log out.

CASE PROJECTS

Case 5-1

TMI needs help writing a script that calculates net pay. The script needs to support the 11 items of data that are listed below. (*Note:* you must use whole-number amounts.)

- ❑ Employee ID
- ❑ Gross Pay
- ❑ Federal Tax Amount
- ❑ Social Security Amount
- ❑ 401K Deduction Amount
- ❑ Medical Insurance
- ❑ Dental Insurance
- ❑ Vision Insurance
- ❑ Disability Insurance
- ❑ Legal Insurance
- ❑ Stock Purchase

To complete this case you need to write the pseudocode logic for this script, write the script using positional parameters where all parameters must have an amount even if it is 0, use integers only when inputting the data, use comments, reference the shell, include variable declaration and initialization, and add a usage clause where appropriate. Display the Employee's ID, the Gross Pay, all of the deductions and the Net Pay in an appropriate manner. (*Hint*: the Net Pay is the Gross Pay after all the deductions have been accounted for.)

Case 5-2

The Antonio Czechos Drywall Firm has hired you to help implement a directory structure for them based on Figure 5-19. Because you were called out of town to aid another customer, you cannot go to the site. In the meantime, you decide to write a script that will create the structure for them. To create the directory structure, complete the following tasks:

1. Write the pseudocode.
2. Write a script to create the directory structure shown in Figure 5-19.
3. The directory structure should start from the AC_Drywall directory from within your home directory.
4. Other issues:
   a. If the item has an extension, treat it as a file. Otherwise, consider it a directory.
   b. Note the hidden file.
   c. The Manager1.txt file must only have these permissions: read and write for the user owner and the group owners. Others should have no access.
   d. The Emp1.txt file must have all permissions turned on.

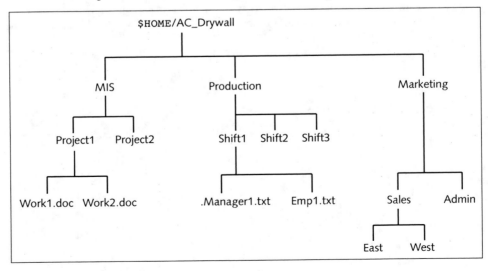

Figure 5-19   AC Drywall directory structure

6

DECISION STRUCTURES

In this chapter, you will:

♦ Understand decision-structure theory
♦ Understand `if` statements
♦ Use logical operators
♦ Use the `elif` clause in an `if` statement
♦ Nest `if` statements
♦ Understand the `case` statement

You learned in Chapter 5 that each statement in a shell script is executed sequentially. There are programming structures, which allow you to change the sequential flow. Decision structures test for a condition and, based upon the result of that test, execute one set of statements or another, but not both. Shell scripts use the `if` statement and the `case` statement for decision making.

UNDERSTANDING DECISION-STRUCTURE THEORY

Before you learn about the decision statements, you need to understand how decision theory works in scripts. A **decision** is a choice made from possible alternatives based on some condition. You make decisions on a daily basis—deciding what to wear, choosing which movie to see, and scheduling time to study for a test. Once you've made your decisions, there is usually no turning back. For example, if you have just enough money for one movie, and you purchase a ticket for a specific one, you cannot go back and purchase another ticket for a different movie. You made your decision.

Here's another example. You probably have more than one route you can take from your home to your school. Let's say you are driving to school, but you are running a little late for the final exam for your programming class. You notice that the road ahead is blocked due to an accident. At this point, you must make a decision. Do you wait for the accident to clear, or do you take an alternate route? Let's say that the logic is that if the road is blocked, you will take the alternate route. Once your decision is made, you need to follow through on the chosen path.

A decision has one entry point and one exit point. In other words only one set of instructions can be followed based on the decision.

This type of decision making can be implemented in shell scripts as well. In writing your shell scripts, you may need to have the script make a decision about a condition before it takes a course of action. Once a decision is made, the script executes only one set of statements. In Linux you use the `if` statement as a form of decision making. It takes the following general form:

If condition then

    Do activity if condition is true

End-if

This is where *condition* is evaluated as either true or false. If the *condition* evaluates as true, then the activity immediately following it is performed. If the *condition* evaluates as false, then no *activity* is performed. The clause *End-if* is used to terminate the *if* logic in this pseudocode sample. Also, the term **clause** refers to words that are used in conjunction with a statement, such as *then* or *End-if*. The clause *then* is required in shell scripts as well as many other programming languages.

When referring to decision structures, the term "statement," or "command," is used to refer to an actual decision statement, such as `if`.

The `if` structure applies to all programming languages. As you are aware, you cannot implement the above logic in a shell script without converting it into the specific syntax for the shell's implementation of the `if` statement.

Here's how you can turn a decision into pseudocode logic. In the previous example, if the road is indeed blocked, you plan to take the alternate route. Otherwise, you continue on your normal path. Here is the pseudocode that demonstrates this decision:

Get ready for school

Drive to school

If road is blocked then

> *Take alternate route*

End-if

Take final exam

Statements that come before or after the `if` are unaffected by the condition it tests. Here is what happens. All statements are executed sequentially prior to the `if` statement. The `if` statement is then executed. Once the condition is evaluated, statements that follow `if` are executed sequentially as normal. For example, you *Get ready for school* and *Drive to school* in that order, before you deal with the *if* statement. Once the decision has been made regarding an alternate route, you still *Take final exam* once you arrive at school, regardless of the route taken. What would happen in the previous statement if the road were not blocked? The answer is that the condition of *If road is blocked then* would evaluate false. You would not take the alternate route but you would still take the final exam.

Flowcharts and Decision Making

In programming, one of the tools used to help you understand the logic of decisions is the flowchart. The **flowchart** uses symbols to help you understand the overall flow of a program. The flowchart symbols and their use are listed in Table 6-1.

Table 6-1 Description of the flowchart symbols

Name	Symbol	Usage
Oval		Used to indicate where the flowchart begins and ends
Parallelogram		Used to represent the input and output of data
Square		Used to represent a processing activity
Diamond		Used to represent a decision

Figure 6-1 shows a flowchart for the decision made while driving to school.

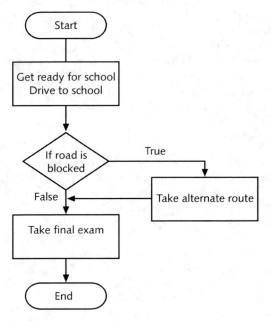

Figure 6-1 Flowchart of the decision made while driving to school

Understanding the *else* Decision Structure

What would you do if you wanted to perform an activity for the false condition of an *if* statement? Because the *if* statement tests for a true condition, you need to add logic to your *if* statement that handles the false condition. To do this, you use the *else* clause.

Here's how the *else* works. The condition is tested. If the condition tests true, then the code statements immediately following the `if` statement, stopping prior to the `else` clause, are executed. If the condition tests false, then the code statements immediately following the *else* clause, stopping prior to the *End-if* clause, are executed. Only one set of statements is executed, either the true condition statements or the false condition statements. Refer to the following pseudocode for logic using *else* in an *if* statement:

If condition then

> *Do activity if condition is true*

Else

> *Do activity if condition is false*

End-if

Here's an example to help understand this concept. The Blue Skydiving Company sells sky diving gear and rides. The management wants to determine if they earned a profit or incurred a loss this quarter.

Figure 6-2 shows the pseudocode that has been developed to evaluate the company's profitability. First the pseudocode determines the Sales and Costs amounts. Next, the Net difference is calculated. Then, a decision must be made. If the difference between Sales and Costs is greater than zero, then the company earned a profit and the profit amount is displayed. If the difference between Sales and Costs is not greater than zero, then the company incurred a loss and the amount of the loss is displayed. A third possibility is that the Sales and Costs could be the same, resulting in a zero difference.

6

```
Get Sales

Get Costs

Net=Sales-Costs

If Net>0 then

        Display "Profit of:"Net

Else

        Display "Loss of:"Net

End-if
```

Figure 6-2   Profitability pseudocode for the Blue Skydiving Company

UNDERSTANDING if STATEMENTS

You can implement decision theory in the shell similarly to how you do it using pseudocode. One of the statements the shell uses to make decisions is if. Understanding the syntax of if will help you to write it correctly in a script. If you misspell any word in the syntax, the script generates a syntax error and your script does not successfully execute. The syntax of the if statement is as follows:

```
if list
then
        statement1
        statement2
        ...
        statementN
fi
```

The if, then, and fi clauses are required. First, the commands in the *list* execute. (Refer to Chapter Three for a review of lists.) Then the *list* terminates with an exit status. The exit status is what is tested, not the commands in the *list*. If the exit status is zero, the command statements, *statement1* through *statementN*, following the then clause, but prior to the fi clause, are executed. If the exit status is nonzero, then the command statements are not executed. Processing continues with subsequent statements in the script. The clause fi, which is "if" spelled backwards, terminates the if statement.

An alternate way for writing the shell's if statement is using else to execute statements if the exit status of *list* is nonzero. The else clause is optional but is needed when you want to process commands when a false condition is reached. Using the `else` clause in an `if` statement takes the following form:

```
if list
then
        statements
else
        statements
fi
```

Notice the indention of statements within the `if` statement. Although indenting statements is not required, it makes the code more readable in case the script needs to be modified later. Generally, you indent the statements following `then` as shown in the various examples in the section.

To help you understand what this means, let's look at Figure 6–3 as an example. Sven's Fruit Stand is asking each customer what his or her favorite fruit is. If the customer's favorite fruit is the same as Sven's, then the customer receives free groceries for the day. Figure 6–3, shows a detailed explanation of the script.

Remember that in shell programming, an exit status of zero is true and an exit status of one is false.

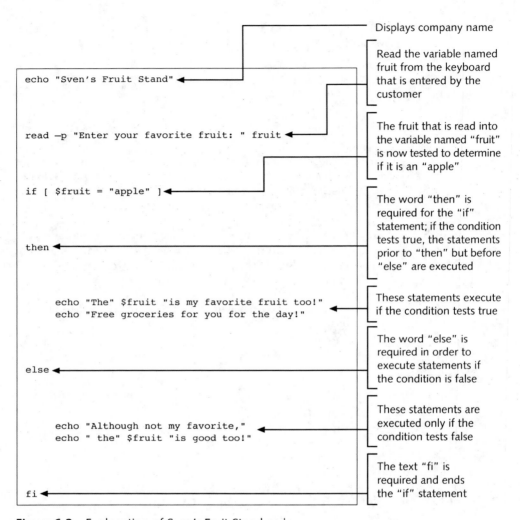

Displays company name

Read the variable named fruit from the keyboard that is entered by the customer

The fruit that is read into the variable named "fruit" is now tested to determine if it is an "apple"

The word "then" is required for the "if" statement; if the condition tests true, the statements prior to "then" but before "else" are executed

These statements execute if the condition tests true

The word "else" is required in order to execute statements if the condition is false

These statements are executed only if the condition tests false

The text "fi" is required and ends the "if" statement

```
echo "Sven's Fruit Stand"

read -p "Enter your favorite fruit: " fruit

if [ $fruit = "apple" ]

then

        echo "The" $fruit "is my favorite fruit too!"
        echo "Free groceries for you for the day!"

else

        echo "Although not my favorite,"
        echo " the" $fruit "is good too!"

fi
```

Figure 6-3   Explanation of Sven's Fruit Stand code

Next you will create a script that tests whether the mv command successfully moved a file by using the if statement to test the exit condition of the list command.

To create a script that tests the exist status of a command:

1. Log in to the Linux system as a user, and then open a Terminal emulation window.

2. Create a script named **MoveTest** in the **$HOME/bin** directory.

3. Insert the following lines of code to create an `if` statement that checks to see if the `mv` command moved the specified file:

```
#!/bin/bash
if mv bike1.txt bike2.txt
then
        echo "Move completed successfully — file moved.
        Status " $?
else
        echo "Move completed unsuccessfully — file not
        moved. Status " $?
fi
```

4. Save the script, quit the editor, and then make the script executable.

5. Create a file named **bike1.txt**. Make sure you save the file, and then quit the editor.

6. Execute the script. The bike1.txt file is moved. You know this because of the message echoed to the screen. See Figure 6-4.

7. Execute the script again. See Figure 6-4. A message indicating the file has not been moved is displayed. This is because the file, bike1.txt no longer exists. It was moved in the previous step.

8. Close your window, and then log out.

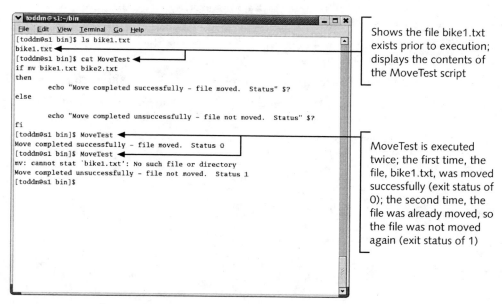

Figure 6-4 The MoveTest script and resulting output

Using Conditional Expressions in an `if` Statement

You can use conditional expressions as well as commands in an `if` statement. Using conditional expressions allows you to compare numbers, make string comparisons, and perform command substitutions. The conditional expression takes the following general form:

```
[[ conditional expression ]]
```

This is where the `conditional expression` tests for values being equal, greater than, less than, or not equal. (Refer to Chapter 3 and the `man` pages for additional conditional expressions.)

 There is a space before and after each pair of square brackets, `[[` and `]]`. If you do not put a space before and after each pair, you receive an error when executing a script that uses these.

Next you will create a few scripts that utilize the `if` statement and that perform various tests. The scripts will be explained prior to creating and running them. You can then use these samples as guides to help you create additional scripts later.

The first script tests two positional parameters and displays a message only if the first number is larger than the second. The goal of this activity is to help you understand how to implement the `if` statement to perform comparisons of numbers.

To create a script that uses the `if` statement to compare positional parameters used as numbers:

1. Log in to the Linux system as a user, and then open a Terminal emulation window.

2. Create a script named **NumberGreater** in the `$HOME/bin` directory.

3. Insert the following lines of code to create an `if` statement that utilizes a conditional expression to compare two positional parameters:

```
#!/bin/bash
if [[   $1 -gt   $2   ]]
then
        echo $1 " is greater than " $2
else
        echo $1 " is less than " $2
fi
```

4. Save the script, and then quit the editor.

5. Make the script executable, and then execute the script using **4** as the first parameter and **3** as the second parameter. See Figure 6-5. A message displays indicating that the first parameter, 4, is greater then the second parameter, 3.

6. Execute the script again. This time use **6** as the first parameter and **9** as the second parameter. See Figure 6-5. Compare the differences in output of this step with Step 4. A message indicates the first parameter, 6, is less than the second parameter, 9. This is different from the previous run because there are different values being compared.

7. Do not log out.

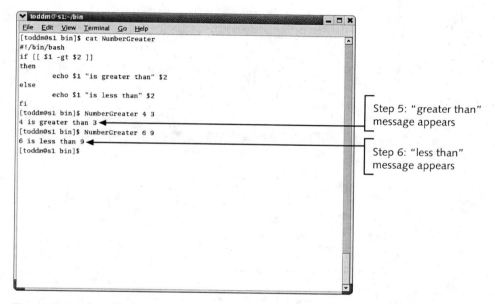

Step 5: "greater than" message appears

Step 6: "less than" message appears

Figure 6-5   The NumberGreater script and resulting output

Next you will create a script that tests a declared variable named "Color" that is read into the script using the **read** statement. The script will display a message if the value is equal to the literal string "red." The goal of this exercise is to help you understand how to implement the **if** statement to perform string comparisons. The practical use of this script is to test whether or not a value entered is equal to a string of letters.

To create a script that uses the if statement to determine if a value read from the keyboard is equal to a literal string:

1. Create a script named **ColorRed** in the **$HOME/bin** directory.

2. Insert the following lines of code. Notice that you are using the **read** statement instead of positional parameters.

```
#!/bin/bash
declare Color
read -p "Enter color: " Color
```

```
if [[    $Color = "red"    ]]
then
        echo "The color is red"
else
        echo "The color is not red - it is " $Color
fi
```

3. Save the script, and then quit the editor.

4. Make the script executable, and then execute it. Type **red** when prompted to enter a color. See Figure 6-6. A message indicating that the color is red appears.

5. Execute the script again. Type **blue** when prompted to enter color. See Figure 6-6. The message "The color is not red — it is blue" is displayed.

6. Do not log out.

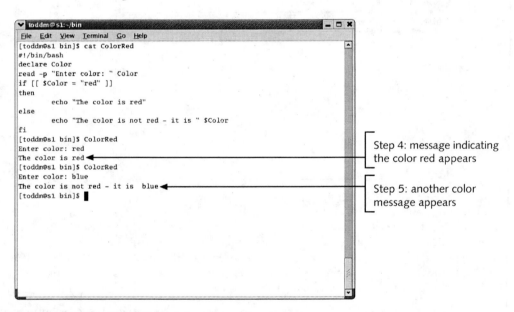

Figure 6-6   The ColorRed script and resulting output

In this third script you will use command substitution to determine if the current directory is equal to a specific directory. The goal of this exercise is to help you understand how to implement the `if` statement using command substitution. One practical application for this script might be to determine if a user's current directory is a directory they should not be in.

To create a script that uses the if statement to determine if the current directory is a specific one:

1. Create a script named **IsDirTmp** in the $HOME/bin directory.

2. Insert the following lines of code to display a message based upon your current directory. If your current directory is /tmp, you are instructed to change to your home directory. Otherwise, your current directory is displayed. Note the command dir1=`pwd` uses command substitution. This is discussed in Chapter 4. Also, the variable dir1 contains the output of the pwd command. So, if the present working directory is /tmp, then dir1 literally equals /tmp.

```
#!/bin/bash
dir1=`pwd` # The variable dir1 contains the output of the
 pwd command.
if [[   $dir1 = "/tmp"   ]]
then
      echo "Your current directory is /tmp"
      echo "Change to $HOME immediately"
else
      echo "Your current directory is " $dir1
fi
```

3. Save the script, quit the editor, and then make the script executable.

4. If you are not in the $HOME/bin directory change to it, and then execute the script. See Figure 6-7. A message displaying your current directory appears.

5. Change to the **/tmp** directory, and then execute the script. See Figure 6-7. A message appears indicating your current directory is /tmp and that you need to change out of the /tmp directory. If you compare this step to the previous step, you see a difference in the messages displayed. In the previous step, because you are in your home directory, you are not told to change directory locations.

6. Close the window, and then log out.

You should now be able to adapt the concepts presented in these scripts to other scripts you may write in the future.

 You can place the entire if statement on a single line. However, you must use a semicolon to separate each element of the statement. The syntax is if *list*; then *statements*; fi. One line is considered to be if *list*, the next is then *statements*, and the last one is fi. To execute the ColorGreen script on a single command line, you enter if [[$Color = "green"]]; then echo "The color is green"; fi.

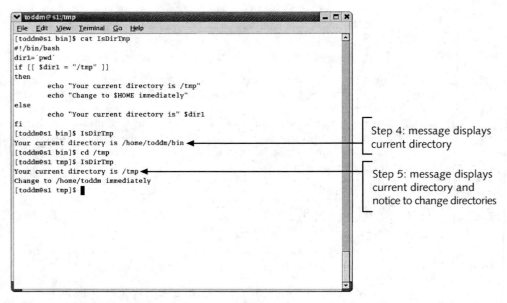

Figure 6-7   The IsDirTmp script and resulting output

Conditional Processing Using Single Square Brackets

Instead of using double square brackets for conditional processing, you can use single square brackets, [and], or the **test** command. Because there is no set standard in the Linux operating system and often several ways to accomplish the same thing, script programmers and System Administrators write in a style with which they are most comfortable. However, you need to beware of these alternatives because the system scripts in the etc/rc.d/init.d directory use them.

Figure 6-8 demonstrates the use of double and single square brackets and the **test** command. The script contains the same logic implemented three different ways to give you an idea how to use [ ] and **test** as alternatives. The results are the same provided you input the same data. Another alternative is to write three different scripts to do the same as this one script. You can see from the script that you could adapt this code to a script that inquires of a user whether he or she wants to continue or not. This type of prompting logic is useful in menu structures, which will be covered in Chapter 9.

Figure 6-8   The YesNo script and its resulting output

> The single square brackets are actually a link to the test command. So, using the single square brackets and the test command are the same. They exist for compatibility with other shells and versions of the operating system. Because single square brackets are built into the shell and remain in memory, their use is more efficient because the shell does not have to locate them on disk. However, what to use is the preference of the script programmer.

USING LOGICAL OPERATORS

You can implement the *AND*, *OR*, and *NOT* pseudocode logical operators in the shell. These logical operators allow you to test multiple commands and conditional expressions, as well as allow you to make decisions based upon multiple criteria. The result of using these operators is a more powerful and flexible logic in your scripts.

Let's look at the *AND* operator first. The shell uses **&&**, two ampersand symbols, for the *AND* operator. It takes the following form in the shell, given two conditions:

```
if [[ condition1 && condition2 ]]
then
        statements
else
        statements
fi
```

This is where each condition, *condition1* and *condition2*, is an exit status from executed commands. The results of each condition must return an exit status of zero, for true, in order for the statements following **then** to execute. If either condition results in an exit status of one, for false, then the *statements* following **else** execute.

Next, let's look at the *OR* operator. The shell uses | |, two vertical bars, for the *OR* operator. It takes the following form in the shell with two conditions:

```
if [[ condition1 || condition2 ]]
then
        statements
else
        statements
fi
```

In the case of | |, only one of the conditions must have an exit status of zero in order for the statements following **then** to execute. The statements following **else** only execute if *both* conditions return an exit status of one.

Lastly, consider the *NOT* operator. The shell uses !, a single exclamation point, as the *NOT* operator. It takes the following form in the shell:

```
if [[ ! condition ]]
then
            statements
else
            statements
fi
```

Here is how this logical operator works. An exit status is returned from the command, as a *condition*. This *condition* is then negated. That is, an exit status of zero becomes a one and an exit status of one becomes zero. Thus, the ! operator negates the *condition*. It is the negated *condition* that gets evaluated; other than that, it works the same as the previous operators. If the negated *condition* has an exit status of zero, the statements following **then** execute. If the negated *condition* has an exit status of one, the statements following **else** execute.

 The logical && operator is more restrictive than the logical | | operator because both conditions must return an exit status of zero.

Look at the following sample business scenario that creates scripts that use these conditions. The Have Fun Hotel and Resort Software Company writes application software for beach and mountain lodges. The company management would like to give the technical support personnel who are hourly employees (**Status = "H"**) and who work the third shift (`Shift=3`) an annual bonus of $500. Before you can write this script, you need to turn this problem into pseudocode. Here is the logic:

Bonus=500

Read Status

Read Shift

If Status="H" AND Shift=3

Then

    Display "Your bonus is "

Else

    Display "You are only eligible for a bonus if you are hourly working shift 3"

End-if

Next you will create the resulting script.

To create a script that uses the && operator:

1. Log in to the Linux system as a user, and then open a Terminal emulation window.

2. Create a script named **ShiftBonus** in the `$HOME/bin` directory.

3. Insert the following lines of code to initialize the bonus variable, read data from the keyboard, and then display results of the data based on an `if` statement that makes use of the **&&** operator. Figure 6-9 displays the contents of the ShiftBonus script.

```
Bonus=500
read -p "Enter Status: " Status
read -p "Enter Shift: " Shift
if [ $Status = "H" ] && [ $Shift = 3 ]
then
    echo "Your bonus for working shift $Shift is"
    '$'$Bonus"."
else
    echo "You are only entitled to a bonus if you are
        hourly and work shift 3."
fi
```

4. Save the script, quit the editor, and then make the script executable.

5. Execute the script, and then type **H** when prompted for Status and type **2** when prompted for Shift. See Figure 6-10. A message indicating you do not receive a bonus appears.

6. Execute the script again, and then type **H** when prompted for Status and **3** when prompted for Shift. See Figure 6-10. A message indicating you do receive a bonus appears.

7. Execute the script a third time, and then type **S** (for Salaried) when prompted for Status and **3** when prompted for Shift. See Figure 6-10. A message indicating you do not receive a bonus appears.

8. Do not log out.

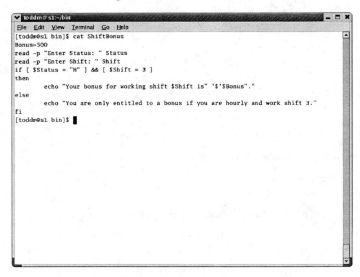

Figure 6-9   Contents of the ShiftBonus script

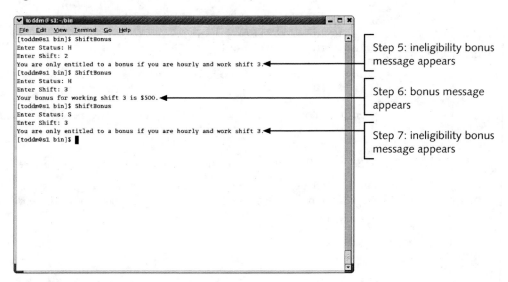

Figure 6-10   Output of the ShiftBonus script

If you use the || operator in the ShiftBonus script instead of the &&, the logic would provide for a bonus if either the Status equaled "H" or the Shift equaled 3. Only one of the conditions needs to be true in order for the true condition statements to execute. Using the correct logical operator is important. Otherwise, you can experience logic problems. Even when the script is syntactically correct, the logic you use to set up your script can be incorrect.

In this next example, the management at the Have Fun Hotel and Resort Software Company has decided to reward the technical support personnel in the call center based upon the amount of calls they take and the amount of calls they close. Calls Handled is the amount of calls a support person takes. Calls Closed is the amount of calls that are completed to customer satisfaction. Here is the partial logic:

If Calls Handled > 150 OR Calls Closed > 50

Then

> *Display "You are entitled to a bonus"*

Else

> *Display "You are only entitled to a bonus if the calls handled exceeds 150 or calls closed exceeds 50"*

End-if

Next you will create the script for the Have Fun Hotel and Resort Software Company using the logical *OR* operator.

To create a script that uses the || operator:

1. Create a script named **Calls** in the $HOME/bin directory.

2. Insert the following lines of code to read data from the keyboard and create an if statement that makes use of the || operator:

```
read -p "Enter the calls handled: " CallsHandled
read -p "Enter the calls closed: " CallsClosed
if [[ $CallsHandled -gt 150 || $CallsClosed -gt 50 ]]
then
        echo "You are entitled to a bonus."
else
        echo "You are only entitled to a bonus if the calls
            handled exceeds 150 or calls closed exceeds 50."
fi
```

3. Save the script, quit the editor, and then make the script executable.

4. Execute the script, and then type **159** when prompted for calls handled and **40** when prompted for calls closed. See Figure 6-11. A message indicating you are entitled to a bonus appears.

5. Execute the script again, and then type **120** when prompted for calls handled and **76** when prompted for calls closed. See Figure 6-11. A message indicating you are entitled to a bonus appears.

6. Run the script a third time, and then type **76** when prompted for calls handled and **44** when prompted for calls closed. See Figure 6-11. A message indicating you are only entitled to a bonus when you exceed 150 calls handled or 50 calls closed appears.

7. Do not log out.

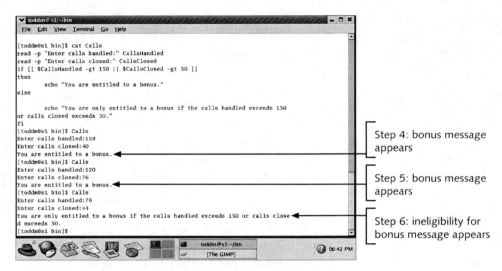

Figure 6-11   The Calls script and resulting output

In the Calls script, consider what the result would be if one of the conditions were left off or the **&&** operator were used instead of the || operator. The script would be syntactically correct. However, it would logically be incorrect because it would not follow the desires of the management. In the case of the input for Steps 4 through 6, only one employee would be eligible for the bonus, not two.

In this final example for the Have Fun Hotel and Resort Software Company, the management wants a script created that indicates whether personnel with 25 years of service can retire. Here is the partial logic using the *NOT* logical operator.

If Years of Service is NOT less than 25

Then

> *Display "You can retire now."*

Else

> *Display "You will need 25 years to retire."*

End-if

Next you will create the script using the logical *NOT* operator.

To create a script that uses the ! operator:

1. Create a script named **Retire** in the `$HOME/bin` directory.

2. Insert the following lines of code to read data from the keyboard and create an `if` statement that makes use of the ! operator:

```
read -p "Years of Service: " Years
if [[ ! $Years -lt 25 ]]
then
        echo "You can retire now."
else
        echo "You will need 25 years to retire."
fi
```

3. Save the script, quit the editor, and then make the script executable.

4. Execute the script, and then type **32** when prompted for Years of Service. See Figure 6-12. A message indicating you can retire now appears.

5. Execute the script again, and then type **21** when prompted for Years of Service. See Figure 6-12. A message indicating you need 25 years to retire appears.

6. Close your window, and then log out.

Note that if you left off the ! operator, the code would indicate that that you could retire *only* if you had been there less than 25 years. Of course, this would be incorrect based upon the requirements of the scenario.

Although you created the Retire script using the ! operator, you could have written it without using this operator. You could modify the script as follows:

```
read -p "Years of Service: " Years
if [[ $Years -ge 25 ]]
then
        echo "You can retire now."
else
        echo "You will need 25 years to retire."
fi
```

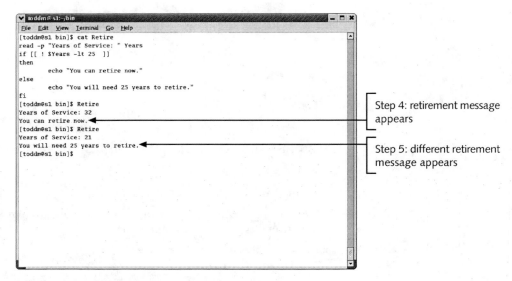

Step 4: retirement message appears

Step 5: different retirement message appears

Figure 6-12 The Retire script and resulting output

Notice the main difference between the two versions is that they are opposite in terms of logic.

Now that you've looked at some sample scripts using the `if` statement and logical operators, review Table 6-2 for a summary of the conditions used in this section. You read this table by looking at the evaluation of the conditions in the Condition 1 and Condition 2 columns. Next, look to the right under the heading for the operation you are using. For example, if Condition 1 is true and Condition 2 is false, then the *AND* operator result would be false, and the *OR* operator result would be true. In the last column, only one condition is tested, which is Condition 1. So, in this case if Condition 1 is true, false is the result of the *NOT* condition operator.

Table 6-2 Logical operators

Condition 1	Condition 2	Condition 1 AND Condition 2 Result (Script uses &&)	Condition 1 OR Condition 2 Result (Script uses | |)	NOT Condition 1 (Script uses !)
True	True	True	True	False
True	False	False	True	False
False	True	False	True	True
False	False	False	False	True

You can have multiple conditions with these logical operators. For example, `if true && true && true; then echo "True"; else echo "False"; fi` displays "True" on the screen. Also, `if true && false && true; then echo "True"; else echo "False"; fi` displays "False" on the screen. However using the `||` operator, `if true || false || true; then echo "True"; else echo "False"; fi` displays "True" on the screen. But, `if false || false || false; then echo "True"; else echo "False"; fi` displays "False" on the screen.

USING THE `elif` CLAUSE IN AN `if` STATEMENT

The `if` statement allows you to use the optional `elif` clause to further test a false condition of an `if` statement. Figure 6-13 shows the placement of the `elif` clause within the `if` statement.

The phrase `elif` stands for "else if." It is part of the `if` statement and cannot be used by itself. In other words, you could not have just the `elif` clause followed by a condition.

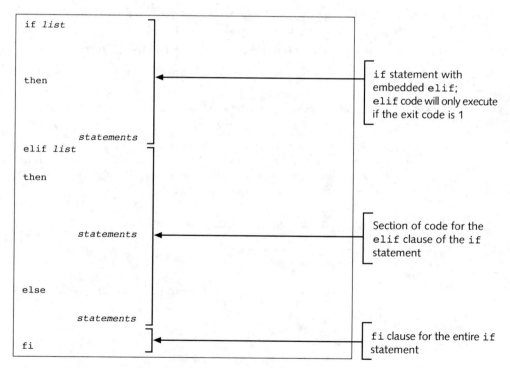

Figure 6-13 Position of the `elif` clause in an `if` statement

Using this form of the if statement, then if *list* must return an exit status of one in order for the elif clause to process. Once control passes to the elif clause, processing occurs as if this were an if statement. The commands that are executed for the elif clause begin with the then clause and end with the last statement prior to fi. Note that there is only one fi clause for the entire if statement.

If the condition for the elif *list* clause returns an exit status of zero, then the then statements within the elif statements are executed. If the condition for the elif *list* clause returns an exit status of one, then the else statements are executed.

 If if *list* returns an exit status of zero, the statements immediately following the first then clause are executed up to the elif clause. Then, processing skips the elif clause altogether and resumes after the fi clause.

To help you understand this, take a look at another business scenario. Rose's Bubblegum and Popcorn Factory is interested in knowing whether they have made a profit, experienced a loss, or broken even with respect to their cash flow. They want a script that reads in sales and costs and calculates their difference. If the difference is zero, they have a breakeven. If the difference is greater than zero, they have a profit; otherwise, they have a loss.

Next you will write the shell script to determine profitability for Rose's Bubblegum and Popcorn Factory, using the elif clause.

To create a script that uses the elif clause in the if statement:

1. Log in to the Linux system as a user, and then open a Terminal emulation window.

2. Create a script named **ProfitLossBreakeven** in the $HOME/bin directory.

3. Insert the following lines of code. The code is structured this way because you have three possible scenarios—profit, a loss, or a breakeven. In this exercise, the breakeven possibility is tested first. This is simply programmer preference. You could test any of the three conditions first. However, you would have to change the existing code.

```
#!/bin/bash
read -p "Enter Sales Amount: " Sales
read -p "Enter Costs: " Costs
((Net=$Sales - $Costs))
if [[ $Net -eq "0" ]]
then
        echo "Profit and Costs are equal — breakeven."
elif [[ $Net -gt "0" ]]
   then
        echo "Profit of: " $Net
   else
        echo "Loss of: " $Net
   fi
```

4. Save the script, and then quit the editor.

5. Make the script executable, and then execute the script inputting **5000** when prompted for Sales Amount and **6500** when prompted for Costs. See Figure 6-14. Because Sales is less than Costs, a loss of –1500 is reflected in a message.

6. Execute the script again. This time input **6500** when prompted for Sales Amount and **6500** when prompted for Costs. See Figure 6-14. Here is the breakeven. Both Sales and Costs are the same resulting in neither a profit nor a loss. Thus, a message indicating a breakeven has occurred is displayed.

7. Execute the script one final time and input **6500** when prompted for Sales Amount and **5000** when prompted for Costs. See Figure 6-14. In this execution, a profit of 1500 is displayed because Sales exceeds Costs by that amount.

8. Close your window, and then log out.

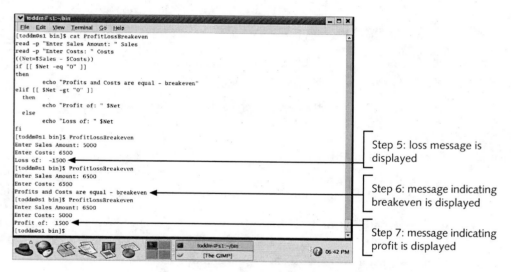

Figure 6-14   The ProfitLossBreakeven script and its resulting output

There are a variety of ways to write a script that yields identical results. Let's look at an alternative to this script, named ProfitLossBreakeven2. In this alternate version, there are two `elif` clauses used—one nested within the other. The way this works is that if the net amount is not equal to zero, for a breakeven, then the first `elif` is tested. If the net amount is zero, the fact that a breakeven exists is displayed and the script terminates.

With the first `elif` clause, if the net amount is greater then zero, you have a profit. The amount of profit is displayed and the script terminates. Only if the net amount is less than zero will the second `elif` be tested. In this case, the amount of the loss is displayed. Because the second `elif` is nested, testing of the second `elif` is conditional; it is only tested if the first `elif` results in false. Look back to Figure 6-14 and you see only one elif clause. Look at Figure 6-15 and you see two elif clauses. If you compare the figures, you see the end result is the same.

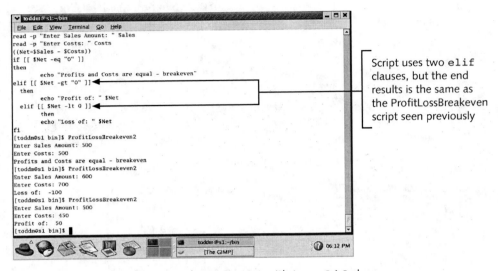

Script uses two elif clauses, but the end results is the same as the ProfitLossBreakeven script seen previously

Figure 6-15   The ProfitLossBreakeven2 script with two elif clauses

NESTING if STATEMENTS

As you are creating more and more complex scripts, you may find that one condition depends on the result of another. Similar to nested elif statements, the shell allows you to nest your if statements, meaning that you can create a complete if...then...fi statement within another if...then...fi statement. With nesting, you can have whole sections of code embedded within other whole sections of code.

Consider the following example. An organization named Lucy's Books and Tapes, Inc. has specific retirement requirements. An employee must have 25 years of service regardless of age, or an employee must have 10 years of service and be at least 60 years of age in order to retire. Figure 6-16 demonstrates this example. The first if is a data validation test. Although not a stated requirement, it makes sense for the employee's age to be less than the number of years. If this were not in the script, then the script would technically allow someone to be 15 years old with 30 years of service. Because it is not possible for the age to be less than the years of service, it needs to be considered as part of the script. Many times, you must go beyond the stated requirements of a program to prevent inaccurate data from getting into the scripts.

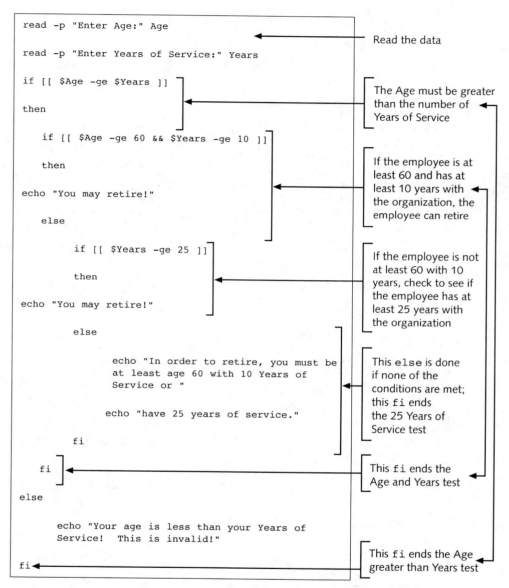

```
read -p "Enter Age:" Age                                          ◄─────────────  Read the data

read -p "Enter Years of Service:" Years

if [[ $Age -ge $Years ]]                                          ┌──  The Age must be greater
                                                                  │    than the number of  ◄──
then                                                              └──  Years of Service

   if [[ $Age -ge 60 && $Years -ge 10 ]]                          ┌──  If the employee is at
                                                                  │    least 60 and has at
   then                                                           │    least 10 years with  ◄──
                                                                  │    the organization, the
echo "You may retire!"                                            └──  employee can retire

   else

       if [[ $Years -ge 25 ]]                                     ┌──  If the employee is not
                                                                  │    at least 60 with 10
       then                                                       │    years, check to see if
                                                                  │    the employee has at
echo "You may retire!"                                            │    least 25 years with
                                                                  └──  the organization

       else

           echo "In order to retire, you must be                  ┌──  This else is done
           at least age 60 with 10 Years of                       │    if none of the
           Service or "                                           │    conditions are met;
                                                                  │    this fi ends
           echo "have 25 years of service."                       │    the 25 Years of
                                                                  └──  Service test

       fi

   fi  ◄─────────                                                 ┌──  This fi ends the  ◄──
                                                                  └──  Age and Years test
else

       echo "Your age is less than your Years of
       Service!  This is invalid!"
                                                                  ┌──  This fi ends the Age  ◄──
fi ◄─────────────────────────────────                            └──  greater than Years test
```

Figure 6-16   Lucy's Books and Tapes, Inc. retirement requirements script

  Data integrity is discussed in greater detail in Chapter 9.

Next you will create the script shown in Figure 6-16.

To create a script that uses the nested `if` statements:

1. Log in to the Linux system as a user, and then open a Terminal emulation window.

2. Create a script named **RetirementStatus** in the **$HOME/bin** directory.

3. Insert the lines of code shown in Figure 6-16 to create a script that uses nested `if` statements.

4. Save the script, and then quit the editor.

5. Make the script executable, execute the script, and then input **50** when prompted for Age and **10** when prompted for Years of Service. See Figure 6-17. A message indicating you have not met the requirements appears.

6. Execute the script again. This time input **62** when prompted for Age and **26** when prompted for Years of Service. See Figure 6-17. A message indicting you have met the requirements appears.

7. Execute the script one last time. Input **15** when prompted for Age and **20** when prompted for Years of Service. See Figure 6-17. A message indicating that your input is invalid appears.

8. Close your window, and then log out.

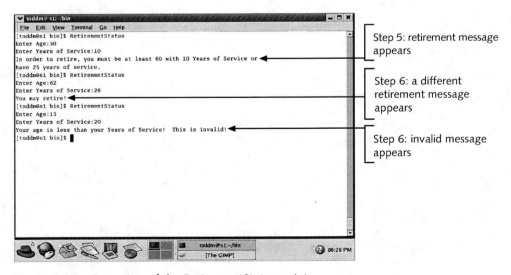

Figure 6-17   Execution of the RetirementStatus script

Let's take a look at a more complex example of a script using nested `if` statements. In this example, Hugh Nguyen Airways needs a script to help with the passenger-booking system. This script will serve as a prototype for the company's main booking system that will be written in another programming language. The company needs a program that determines the price of a fare for a booking. Figure 6-18 demonstrates the logic that the script needs to follow to meet the demands of the passenger-booking system.

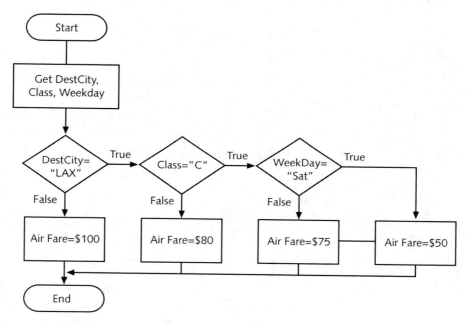

Figure 6-18   Flowchart of the logic for calculating airfare prices

Figure 6-19 shows the actual script that applies the logic shown in the flowchart in Figure 6-18. Notice that the AirFare script shown in Figure 6-19 accepts three variables—DestCity, Class, and WeekDay, and determines the price based upon these inputs. The logic established in Figure 6-18 maintains that if the passenger travels to Los Angeles (city code of "LAX") and is in Coach class (Class "C"), he or she will pay an airfare of $50 for travel on a Saturday and $75 for travel any other day. If the passenger travels to Los Angeles in any other class, he or she pays an airfare of $80. Airfare to any other city is $100.

```
toddm@s1:~/bin                                                    _ □ ×
File  Edit  View  Terminal  Go  Help
[toddm@s1 bin]$ cat AirFare
read -p "Enter Destination City" DestCity
read -p "Enter Class" Class
read -p "Enter Day of Week" WeekDay
if [[ $DestCity -eq "LAX" ]]
then
# Class C is Coach
   if [[ $Class = "C" ]]
       then
          if [[ $WeekDay = "Sat" ]]
          then
               ((AirFare = 50))
          else
               ((AirFare = 75))
          fi

   else
       ((AirFare=80))
   fi
else
   ((AirFare = 100))
fi
echo "Air Fare: "'$'$AirFare
[toddm@s1 bin]$
```

Figure 6-19   Airfare calculation script for Hugh Nguyen Airways

UNDERSTANDING THE case STATEMENT

The case statement is another implementation of the decision structure. You should use the case statement when you have a decision that is based upon multiple inputs such as the feedback received from a user based on several menu options.

 Although there are no set rules, you should consider using the case statement when you have three or more decisions. Again, it is up to the programmer to decide which approach to use.

Generally, using the case statement instead of an if statement is more readable for a programmer when there are several inputs. Logically speaking, the case statement functions similarly as one large if statement.

Pseudologic of the case Statement

Let's first look at the general logic of the case statement:

Case variable-name

> *Case1: Perform activity if contents of Case1 are equal to the contents of variable-name*

> *Case2: Perform activity if contents of Case2 are equal to the contents of variable-name*

> *Case3: Perform activity if contents of Case3 are equal to the contents of variable-name*

Case Else: Perform activity if none of the previous Cases are equal to the contents of the variable-name

End-Case

Here's how the case statement works. The *variable-name* is tested to see if the contents match one of the cases, specified as *Case1*, *Case2*, or *Case3*, then the activity to the right of the match is performed. Once the match occurs, none of the other cases is tested. Processing continues to statements that come after the case statement. You can use a case else clause in the event there are no matches. This clause is useful if a user has not entered a value from a list of choices that have been given.

Syntax for the case Statement

Let's look at the shell's implementation of the case statement:

```
case word   in
        pattern1) statements
                statements
              ;;
        pattern2) statements
            statements
              ;;
        patternN) statements
            statements
              ;;
   esac
```

The case statement, and the in and esac clauses are required. The phrase case *word* in is required. This code phrase is analogous to the verbal phrase "What case is the pattern to match?". The *word* is a variable that matches one of the patterns. For a pattern, you can use characters and numbers. You can also use the pattern-matching symbols, *, for matching all characters; ?, for matching a single character; or [...], for matching a range of characters.

 Most scripts use * as a form of the *case else* pseudocode. It matches anything, and it is generally placed at the end of a case statement for catching cases that do not match any previous pattern.

The right parenthesis symbol,) is required for each *patternN* and separates each individual case from the statements that are to be performed if a match occurs for that case. The ;; symbols are required and are used to terminate each case. The esac clause terminates the entire case statement. Similar to if and fi, esac is "case" spelled backwards.

Next you will create a simple shell script using the `case` statement.

To create a simple script that uses the `case` statement:

1. Log in to the Linux system as a user, and then open a Terminal emulation window.

2. Copy the script named `$HOME/bin/ColorRed` used in an earlier exercise to a new script named `$HOME/bin/ColorRed1`.

3. Modify the script so it contains the following lines of code:

```
read -p "Enter color: " Color
case $Color in
   red) echo "The color is red"
      ;;
   *) echo "The color is not red — it is " $Color
esac
```

4. Save the script, and then quit the editor.

5. Execute the script. Input **red** when prompted for color.

6. Execute the script again. This time input **blue** when prompted for a color.

7. Close your window, and then log out.

Pattern matching and the case Statement

Suppose you want to write a script that asks users to respond to a yes or no question in order for a specific activity to occur. They might input a "Y," "y," or "Yes" for a positive response. You can set up your code to allow several patterns to be matched for one case. To do this, you need to use the vertical bar, |, to separate the patterns that are possible. So, in the ColorRed1 script, you could modify the first pattern statement, `red) echo "The color is red"` with `red|Red|RED) echo "The color is red"` to accept either "red," "Red," or "RED" as valid input. Any one of these three causes "The color is red" to display on the screen. You can think of the | operator as a logical *OR* in this case.

Next you will learn how to use the | operator to match one of several possible values in a variable. You will use the `tr` command to translate the answer into uppercase and test the translated result. Another alternative to attempting to guess the patterns a user may input using the | operator, is to combine the | operator with the `tr` command to translate the user's input into all uppercase letters, and thus limit the number of possible inputs your script needs to anticipate. For example, when translating characters, you won't have to worry about testing multiple combinations of "Yes," "yes," "Y," or "y" for a positive response on the part of the user. Command substitution is used to hold the translated result, and that is what is tested in the `case` statement.

To create a script that uses the | operator for pattern matching in a case **statement:**

1. Log in to the Linux system as a user, and then open a Terminal emulation window.

2. Create a script named **YesNoCase** in the $HOME/bin directory.

3. Insert the following lines of code to accept input from a user, translate the user's input into all uppercase, and create a case statement to display the desired files:

```
read -p "Do you want to see all files? (Y or N)" YesNo
YN=`echo $YesNo | tr [:lower:] [:upper:]`# Turn the
response into uppercase.
case $YN in
      Y|YES)
            echo "Displaying all files..."
            ls -a
            ;;
      N|NO)
            echo "Displaying all files except hidden..."
            ls
            ;;
      *) echo "Invalid response!" ;;
esac
```

4. Save the script, and then quit the editor.

5. Make the script executable, and then execute the script. Input **Y** when prompted. Because "Y" is entered, the ls -a command is executed and displays all files, including hidden files.

6. Execute the script again. Input **y** when prompted. Because "y" is entered, it is translated to an uppercase "Y." Again, the ls -a command is executed and displays all files, including hidden files.

7. Execute the script again. Input **N** when prompted. Because "N" is entered, the ls command is executed and displays all files, except hidden files.

8. Execute the script another time. Input **No** when prompted. Because an "n" is entered, it is translated to an uppercase "N." The ls command again executes and displays all files, excluding hidden files.

9. Execute the script one last time. Input **Ok** when prompted. A message indicating an invalid response was entered is displayed.

10. Close your window, and then log out.

Note in the next to the last statement that the ;; symbols for ending a case are on the same line as the statement. This is acceptable and saves some space in your script.

Command Substitution and Pattern Matching

You can also use the case statement to perform pattern matching on a command's output. You learned about command substitution in Chapter 4. When combining command substitution with pattern matching, you use the `...` or $(...) characters to substitute the command's output in place of the command. Then, you use the case statement to test the result. For example, say the pwd command displays "/tmp" as your current directory. Then the command case `pwd` in literally translates to "case /tmp in." You must then create the cases for the patterns you want to match.

Next you will use the case statement, along with command substitution, to determine if the current directory is /. If it is (/), then the current directory is changed to the user's home directory using the cd $HOME command.

To create a script that incorporates command substitution in a case statement:

1. Log in to the Linux system as a user, and then open a Terminal emulation window.

2. Create a script named **DirRootCase** in the **$HOME/bin** directory.

3. Insert the following lines of code to create a case statement that changes the directory to the user's home directory when the current directory is (/):

```
case `pwd` in
      /) echo "Changing to $HOME"
         cd $HOME # Note: cd or cd ~ would also work.
      ;;
esac
```

4. Save the script, quit the editor, and then make the script executable.

5. Change to root.

6. Execute the script. A message is displayed indicating the current directory is being changed to your home directory.

7. Close your window, and then log out.

Matching Individual Positions

You can create a script that uses pattern-matching techniques to match individual character positions. Figure 6-20 shows a script written for Samuel's Movie Theater that helps determine the price of an admission ticket based upon the age of the movie goer. The owners of the theater want the price of admission to be as follows: if the patron is 12 years of age and younger, the price is $3.00. If the patron is between 13 and 59, the price is $6.00. If the patron is a senior citizen, above age 60, the price is $4.00. The first pattern-matching code, [1-9]|[1][0-2], accounts for the ages 1 through 9 or 10, 11, or 12. The next pattern matching code, [1][3-9]|[2-5][0-9], matches the ages 13 through 19, or 20 through 59. The next pattern matching code, [6-9][0-9], matches the ages 60 through 99.

```
ChildPrice=3

AdultPrice=6

SeniorPrice=4

read -p "Enter your age: " age

case $age in

    [1-9]|[1][0-2]) echo "Price is Child's price of " $ChildPrice ;;

    [1][3-9]|[2-5][0-9]) echo "Price is Adult price of " $AdultPrice ;;

    [6-9][0-9]) echo "Price is Senior price of " $SeniorPrice ;;

    *) echo "Enter a valid selection" ;;

esac
```

6

Figure 6-20   Samuel's Movie Theater admission pricing script using case statements
to create menus

The case statement is an ideal tool to use when you want to create a menu system where a user can enter one of several choices.

In Chapter 7, you will learn how to build a loop around the case statement so the menu processes a selection and then refreshes the screen choices for further selection. This is known as a true menu system.

Next you will combine some of the concepts you've learned so far into a partial menu script. This script is partial in that each selection is processed and then the script terminates. This helps you get familiar with the fundamentals for building a menu system.

To use the case statement to build a partial menu system:

1. Log in to the Linux system as a user, and then open a Terminal emulation window.

2. Create a script named **Choices** in the **$HOME/bin** directory.

3. Insert the following lines of code. These statements create the menu selection numbers for the script. A user will be able to select a number to run a command.

```
echo "1.  The ps command"
echo "2.  The who command"
echo "3.  The ls command"
```

```
echo "4.  View a file using the cat command"
read -p "Enter Selection: " Answer
```

4. Now, insert these lines of code. This creates the first two possible statements to be executed. For example, if the user selects "1," then the ps command executes. If the user selects "2," then the who command executes.

```
case $Answer in
1)  ps  ;;
2)  who  ;;
```

5. Now, insert these lines of code. This creates the third possible set of statements to be executed. For example, if the user selects "3," then the user is prompted to enter "Y" for a long listing. If the user enters a "Y," a long listing is executed. If "N" is entered, then a regular listing is executed.

```
3) read -p "Do you want a long listing? (Y or N) " YesNo
        YN=`echo $YesNo | tr [:lower:] [:upper:]`
        case $YN in
                Y)  ls  -l  ;;
                *)  ls  ;;
        esac ;;
```

6. Now, insert these lines of code. This creates the fourth possible set of statements to be executed. For example, if the user selects "4," then the user is prompted for a filename to enter. If the file exists, then it is displayed. If it does not exist, a message appears indicating that the file does not exist.

```
4)    read -p "Enter file name to view: " FileName
      if [ -a $FileName ]
      then
              cat $FileName | more    # Or more $FileName
      else
              echo "File does not exist!"
      fi  ;;
      *) echo "Enter a valid selection"  ;;
esac
```

7. Save the script, quit the editor, and then make the script executable.

8. Execute the script for choice **1**. A process listing is displayed because the ps command executes.

9. Execute the script for choice **3**. Input **Y** when prompted to answer the question about the long listing. A long listing appears.

10. Execute the script for choice **2**. A listing of users currently logged on is displayed because the who command executes.

11. Execute the script for choice **4** to view an existing file. Type **ColorRed** to display the contents of this file. The ColorRed file is displayed.

12. Close your window, and then, log out.

CHAPTER SUMMARY

❑ A decision is a choice of possible alternatives. Once a choice has been made, the path of the program is set. You can use decision structures to change the flow of a program, thereby creating powerful programming constructs. Flowcharts utilize symbols and arrows to represent program flow. The flowcharting symbol for a decision is the diamond.

❑ One of the shell's decision statements is the `if` statement. It allows you to test a condition, and then perform statements based upon the condition.

❑ The shell uses the `&&` operator for a logical *AND*, a `||` operator for a logical *OR*, and a `!` operator for a logical *NOT*.

❑ The optional `elif` clause allows you to test another condition in the event the `if` condition tests false. When using the `elif` clause, there is only one `if` for each `if...elif` pair.

❑ You can nest `if` statements by placing whole `if` statements within other `if` statements. You should consider nesting `if` statements when you have a condition that depends upon the result of a previous condition.

❑ The shell allows you to use the `case` statement as a substitute for the `if` statement. The best use of the `case` statement is when one variable has several potential values.

REVIEW QUESTIONS

1. The _____ is the flowcharting symbol used for a decision.

   a. diamond

   b. oval

   c. parallelogram

   d. square

2. Which of the following uses symbols to assist you in understanding the flow of a program?

   a. Pseudocode

   b. Flowchart

   c. The `case` statement

   d. The `if` statement

3. Given the following script, which of the subsequent answers is true?

```
#!/bin/bash
((x=1)); ((y=2))
if [ $x -gt $y ]
then
        echo $x $y
```

```
        else
                echo $y $x
        fi
```

a. The use of semicolons is incorrect.

b. The output is 2 1.

c. The output is 1 2.

d. The use of square brackets is incorrect.

4. Given the following script, which of the subsequent answers is true?

```
#!/bin/bash
((x=2)); ((y=(3*$x)/2))
if [ $x -le $y ]
then
        echo $x $y
else
        echo $y $x
fi
```

a. The use of semicolons is incorrect.

b. The output is 3 2.

c. The output is 2 3.

d. The terminating word is misspelled.

5. A _____ is used as a delimiter when an if statement is on a single line.

a. colon

b. comma

c. semicolon

d. question mark

6. When using an if statement, you use the _____ symbol to test that a variable is either "cat," "Cat," or "CAT".

a. &&

b. !

c. –

d. ||

7. You use the _____ symbol to negate a condition in a shell script.

a. &&

b. !

c. –

d. ||

8. You use the _____ symbol as a logical AND condition in a shell script.

   a. &&

   b. !

   c. -

   d. ||

9. Which clause would you use if you wanted to further test a false condition in an if statement?

   a. case

   b. !=

   c. else

   d. elif

10. _____ is the terminating clause for the if statement.

    a. end-if

    b. fi

    c. elif

    d. esac

11. _____ is the terminating clause for the case statement.

    a. end-if

    b. fi

    c. elif

    d. esac

12. Placing a complete if statement within another complete if statement is called _____.

    a. flowcharting

    b. nesting

    c. conditional processing

    d. using a usage clause

13. Given the following script, which of the following is true?

```
#!/bin/bash
((x=5)); ((y=10))
if [[ $x -eq 5 || $y -gt 12 ]
then
        echo "Hello"
else
        echo "Bye"
fi
```

   a. The output displays "Hello."

   b. The output displays "Bye."

   c. There is a square bracket missing.

   d. The `((x=5))` statement contains incorrect syntax.

14. Given the following script, which of the following is true?

```
#!/bin/bash
((x=5)); ((y=10))
if [[ $x -eq 5 || $y -gt 12 ]]
then
        echo "Hello"
else
        echo "Bye"
fi
```

   a. The output displays "Hello."

   b. The output displays "Bye."

   c. There is a square bracket missing.

   d. The `((x=10))` statement contains incorrect syntax.

15. Given the following script, which of the following is true?

```
#!/bin/bash
((x=5)); ((y=10))
if [[ $x -eq 5 && $y -gt 12 ]]
  then
        echo "Hello"
else
        echo "Bye"
fi
```

   a. The output displays "Hello."

   b. The output displays "Bye."

   c. There is a square bracket missing.

   d. The `((x=5))` statement contains incorrect syntax.

16. Given the following script, which of the following is true?

```
#!/bin/bash
((x=5)); ((y=10))
if [[ $x -lt 5 || $y -gt 84 ]
then
        echo "Hello"
else
        echo "Bye"
    if
```

a. The output displays "Hello."

b. The output displays "Bye."

c. There is a square bracket missing.

d. There is no terminating clause.

17. Given three *AND* conditions, what is the end result if one of the conditions is false?

a. The end result is true.

b. The end result is false.

c. You cannot have three *AND* conditions.

d. Statements following the then in an if execute.

18. Given the following script, which of the following is true?

```
#!/bin/bash
((x=5)); ((y=10))
case $x in
        [1-5]) echo $x
        ;;
        echo $y
        ;;
esac
```

a. The output displays 5.

b. The output displays 10.

c. There is a square bracket missing.

d. There is no terminating clause.

19. Given the following script, which of the following is true?

```
#!/bin/bash
((x=5)); ((y=10))
if [[ $x -eq 4 ]]
then
        if [[ $y -ge 10 ]]
        then echo $x $y
        else echo $y $x
else echo "Hi"
fi
```

a. The output displays 5 10.

b. The output displays 10 5.

c. The output displays "Hi."

d. There is no terminating clause.

20. Given the following script, which of the following is true?

```
#!/bin/bash
((x=4)); ((y=10))
if [[ $x -eq 4 ]]
then
        if [[ $y -ge 10 ]]
        then echo $x $y
        else echo $y $x
else echo "Hi"
fi
```

a. The output displays 4 10.

b. The output displays 10 4.

c. The output displays "Howdy."

d. There is no terminating clause.

HANDS-ON PROJECTS

Project 6-1

In this project, you will create a shell script that tests whether a file has been removed with the rm command. You will test for the exit status of a command's execution and use a decision structure to determine if the command successfully executed or not. If the exit status of the rm command equals zero, then the file has been removed. If the exit status of the rm command equals one, then the file has either been removed or never existed. Remember to turn on debugging with set -xv if you need to troubleshoot the script. Turn it off with set +xv when through debugging the script.

1. Log in to the Linux system as a user, and then open a Terminal emulation window.

2. Create a shell script named **Project6-1** in your **$HOME/bin** directory.

3. Insert the following lines of code:

```
touch FileIsHere.txt
rm FileIsHere.txt
FileHereStatus=$?
if [[ $FileHereStatus -eq 0 ]]
then
        echo "File successfully removed"
else
        echo "File not present"
fi
rm FileNotHere.txt
FileNotHereStatus=$?
if [[ $FileNotHereStatus -eq 0 ]]
```

```
then
        echo "File successfully removed"
else
        echo "File not present"
fi
```

4. Save the script, and then quit the editor.

5. Make the script executable, and then execute the script.

6. Record the results.

7. Close your window, and then log out.

Project 6-2

6

In this project, you will create a shell script that uses the `case` statement to implement a usage clause (refer to Chapter 5 for more on usage clauses). The script requires only three positional parameters. An appropriate message is displayed if an incorrect number of parameters are entered.

1. Log in to the Linux system as a user, and then open a Terminal emulation window.

2. Create a shell script named **Project6-2** in your **$HOME/bin** directory, translate the following pseudocode into actual lines of code, and then enter the appropriate code into the Project6-2 script:

Case number-of-positional-parameters

> *0: Display a message indicating how to run the script and indicate to the user that no positional parameters were entered.*

> *1 or 2: Display a message indicating how to run the script and display the number of positional parameters entered.*

> *3: Display the three positional parameters.*

> *Case Else: Display an error indicating that too many positional parameters were entered.*

End-Case

3. Save the script, and then quit the editor.

4. Make the script executable, and then execute the script with no parameters.

5. Record the result.

6. Execute the script again with one parameter, execute it again with three parameters, and then execute it once more with five parameters.

7. Record the results.

8. Close your window, and then log out.

Project 6-3

In this project, you will implement the `elif` clause. A nonprofit organization, named Helping Hands for All, has hired several contract programmers to work with their permanent programming staff. They want to give the employees, who are hourly (status of "H") or salaried (status of "S"), a $500 bonus. The programmers with contractor status (status of "C") will not receive a bonus. Any other status is invalid.

1. Log in to the Linux system as a user, and then open a Terminal emulation window.

2. Create a shell script named **Project6-3** in your `$HOME/bin` directory.

3. Insert the following lines of code:

```
read -p "Enter Status: " Status
if [[ $Status = "S" || $Status = "H" ]]
then
        ((Bonus=500))
          echo "You get a bonus of" '$'$Bonus
elif [[ $Status = "C" ]]
then
        echo "You are a contractor. You need to become
          permanent to receive a bonus."
else
        echo "Invalid status"
fi
```

4. Save the script, and then quit the editor.

5. Make the script executable, and then execute the script four times. Input "S," "H," "C," and "T" respectively, when prompted to enter status.

6. Record the output.

7. Close your window, and then log out.

Project 6-4

In this project, you will convert pseudocode that uses a decision structure into a shell script. The script then will accept three grades, calculate an average, and then display a letter grade based upon the average. You will need to use either the `if` statement or the `case` statement to implement this script.

1. Log in to the Linux system as a user, and then open a Terminal emulation window.

2. Create a shell script named **Project6-4** in your `$HOME/bin` directory.

3. Convert the following pseudocode into code for the script:

Read in three grades from the keyboard

Average the grades

Display the appropriate letter grade for the number grade using this scale:

90 to 100: Display a letter grade of "A"

80 to 89: Display a letter grade of "B"

70 to 79: Display a letter grade of "C"

65 to 69: Display a letter grade of "D"

0 to 64: Display a letter grade of "F"

Insert appropriate comments

4. Save the script, quit the editor, and then make the script executable.

5. Execute the script and then input **100**, **90**, and **100** when prompted for each grade.

6. Record the output.

7. Execute the script again. This time input **99**, **68**, and **70** when prompted for each grade.

8. Record the output.

9. Execute the script one last time. Input **80**, **96**, and **72** when prompted for each grade.

10. Record the output.

11. Close your window, and then log out.

Project 6-5

In this project, you will convert pseudocode into a shell script and implement either an `if` or `case` decision structure that determines the bonus level for a salesperson.

1. Log in to the Linux system as a user, and then open a Terminal emulation window.

2. Create a shell script named **Project6-5** in the `$HOME/bin` directory.

3. Convert the following pseudocode into code for the script:

Read SalesPerson and QuarterlySales from the keyboard

Display an appropriate message regarding the bonus when the QuarterlySales for a SalesPerson falls within these ranges:

Over $1,000,000	*$1,500 Bonus*
$100,000 to $999,999	*$750 Bonus*
Under $99,999	*No Bonus*

4. Save the script, and then quit the editor.

5. Make the script executable, and then execute the script inputting **Mike** when prompted for the salesperson and **67000** when prompted for sales.

6. Execute the script again. Input **Mary** when prompted for the salesperson and **1000000** when prompted for sales.

7. Execute the script one last time. Input **Lisa** when prompted for the salesperson and **250000** when prompted for sales.

8. Record the output.

9. Close your window, and then log out.

Project 6-6

In this project, you will apply conditional processing logic by writing a shell script that uses the `if` statement to accept one positional parameter from the keyboard. If the parameter does not equal a value specified in the script, display an "invalid data" error message.

1. Log in to the Linux system as a user, and then open a Terminal emulation window.

2. Create a shell script named **Project6-6** in your **$HOME/bin** directory, and then translate the program requirements into the appropriate code:

   The script accepts one positional parameter

   The script verifies a positional parameter was entered; if not, a message is displayed

   The positional parameter is saved as StateCode

   If the positional parameter is equal to "GA" or "KY," display a message indicating a valid StateCode was entered

   If the StateCode does not equal one of the previous codes, display an error indicating an invalid StateCode was entered

   Insert appropriate comments

3. Save the script, and then quit the editor.

4. Make the scripts executable, and then execute the scripts using "GA" as the first positional parameter.

5. Record the result.

6. Execute the scripts using "OK" as the first positional parameter.

7. Record the result.

8. Execute the scripts using "KY" as the first positional parameter.

9. Record the result.

10. Close your window, and then log out.

Project 6-7

The goal of this project is to turn a flowchart into a shell script.

1. Log in to the Linux system as a user, and then open a Terminal emulation window.

2. Create a script named **Project6-7** in your **$HOME/bin** directory.

3. Using the flowchart shown in Figure 6-21 as a guide, create the code that fulfills the program logic shown there.

4. Record or print the script.

5. Execute the script inputting **5** as A and **10** as B.

6. Record the result.

7. Execute the script again. Input **5** as A and **4** as B.

8. Record the result.

9. Execute the script one last time. Input **3** as A and **10** as B.

10. Record the result.

11. Close your window, and then log out.

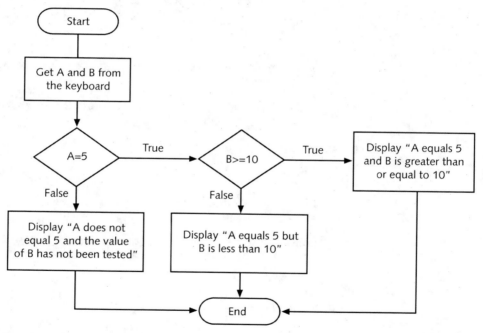

Figure 6-21   Flowchart for Project 6-7

Project 6-8

In this project, you will implement conditional processing and nest `if` statements. The firm named TJ Liu & Associates needs a shell script written. The script needs to accept two values, Status and Years. The status must be either "S," "H," or "C" (for "salary," "hour," and "contract" respectively); otherwise, an error message is displayed. An employee with a status of "H" or "S" and who has been employed for at least two years will receive 50 shares of company stock. A contractor who has been working with TJ Liu & Associates for more than three years will receive a $100 bonus. An appropriate message must be displayed for employees or contractors not meeting the requirements.

1. Log in to the Linux system as a user, and then open a Terminal emulation window.

2. Create a shell script named **Project6-8** in your `$HOME/bin` directory.

3. Insert the following lines of code:

```
read -p "Enter Status " Status
if [[ $Status = "S" || $Status = "H" || $Status = "C" ]]
then
read -p "Enter Years " Years
if [[ $Status = "S" || $Status = "H" ]]
then
        if [[ $Years -ge 2 ]]
        then
                ((NumOfShares=50))
                echo "You get a bonus of" $NumOfShares "shares
                    of company stock"
        else
                echo "You must be here at least 2 years for
                receiving company stock."
        fi
    elif [ $Status = "C" ]
    then
        if [[ $Years -gt 3 ]]
        then
                ((Bonus=100))
                echo "You get a bonus of" '$'$Bonus
        else
                echo "You must be here at least 3 years for
                    receiving company stock."
        fi
    fi
else
        echo "Invalid status"
    fi
```

4. Save the script, and then close the editor.

5. Make the script executable, and then execute the script. Input **H** when prompted for status and **5** when prompted for years.

6. Record the output.

7. Execute the script again. Input **C** when prompted for status and **2** when prompted for years.

8. Record the output.

9. Execute the script again. Input **S** when prompted for status and **15** when prompted for years.

10. Record the output.

11. Execute the script one last time. Input **T** when prompted for status.

12. Record the output.

13. Close your window, and then log out.

CASE PROJECTS

Case 6-1

TMI has asked you to create a script that will allow the user to enter one of several choices from the command line. The only allowed choices are as follows:

1. Copy one file to another. Allow the user to enter a source filename to copy. If the source file exists, read the name of the destination file and copy the file. Display a message indicating success or failure based on the return status.

2. Remove a file if it exists. Display a message indicating success or failure based on the return status.

3. Display only the current day of the week.

4. Display a calendar.

Case 6-2

Wendy Tran-Patel owns Working Out For Fun, Inc., and wants to create a rewards contest for her customers. She hires you to help develop the rewards program as well as implement it. She would like to give three rewards each month. There will be a $25 movie pass, a $50 restaurant gift certificate, and a $100 cash prize. You are required to propose the method of determining the reward, and write a script to meet your proposal. The methods used to determine the reward can be based upon total number of minutes on a treadmill machine, total pounds lifted, or total number of aerobic workout classes attended. You need to determine appropriate levels for each prize. You must create a flowchart or prepare pseudocode for your proposal, and then implement your proposal in a script that displays the reward given.

7

LOOPING STRUCTURES

In this chapter, you will:

♦ Understand loop theory
♦ Understand the `while` statement
♦ Understand the `until` statement
♦ Understand the `for` statement

Although shell scripts statements are executed sequentially, you can change the flow within the script by implementing looping structures. Looping structures allow your scripts to repeatedly execute the same set of statements for different data as long as some specified condition exists. Once the condition no longer exists, processing continues to the statements following the looping structure. In this chapter, you will learn about the shell's implementation of looping structures using the `while`, `until` and `for` commands.

UNDERSTANDING LOOP THEORY

In programming theory, a **loop** is when a condition causes a specific set of programming statements to be repeated. The statements within the loop repeat until another condition occurs which then terminates the loop. The term **iteration**, or **pass**, refers to each completion of the statements within a loop; therefore, if a loop repeats its statements three times, it has completed three iterations, or passes.

The flowchart in Figure 7-1 shows the general form of the basic looping structure. You can see that a set of statements is executed prior to the condition being tested. If the condition tests true, then the program repeats the statements prior to the decision. If the condition tests false, the program does not repeat the steps, and subsequent statements continue to execute as normal.

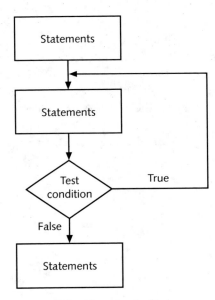

Figure 7-1   Flowchart of a loop

The biggest advantage of using looping structures is that they allow you to enter data without knowing how much data needs to be entered. For example, a bank may need to process thousands of transactions in customer accounts. A program can be created to read all of the records and process them. When there are no more records to read in the file, the loop terminates. Similarly, a teacher may need a program that calculates grades. Because the number of grades the teacher needs to enter may vary, a program can be created using loops to prompt the teacher for each grade. Once all grades are entered, the loop terminates and calculates the grade.

Figure 7-2 shows a more complex example that contains more than one loop. A loop allows code to repeatedly execute until a condition exists. Sally Mingledorf's Ice Cream & Cones, Inc. Main Menu page allows users to access a variety of other submenus. A menu uses looping structures to allow the menu selections to continually appear on the screen. Once users choose other menu items, another loop for the submenu executes allowing users the ability to choose selections on the submenu. When users are finished with the submenu, they can return to the menu on which they started. Here they can go back into the submenu or go into other submenus which are also made of looping structures. It is the loop that facilitates the ability to go back and forth between menus.

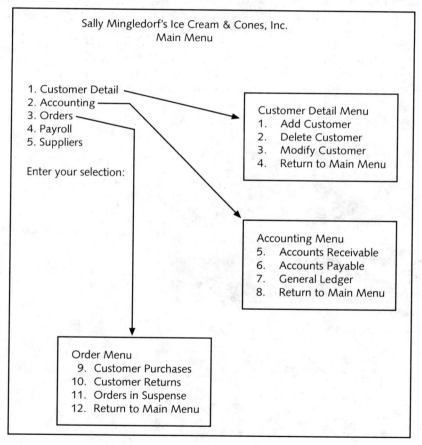

Figure 7-2   Menu system that uses loops

An Infinite Loop

Sometimes the logic of your program can cause the program to go into what is called an infinite loop. An **infinite loop** is a loop that theoretically repeats without end. It does not stop unless you terminate the script's process. You can terminate a script with a `kill` signal.

One disadvantage of a script going into an infinite loop is that it consumes an excessive amount of processing time. You can test this yourself by opening up two windows. In one window, run the **yes** command and in the other run the **top** command. Figure 7-3 and Figure 7-4 show the before and after System Monitor screens for the **yes** command running and consuming all of the CPU time, and then being terminated. Notice the line zigzagging in the "% CPU Usage History" section of the System Monitor window shown in Figure 7-3. Each of the horizontal lines running across the background represents a 20% increment. You can see that utilization started off low because the **yes** command had not been started yet. However, once the command is started, you can see the utilization rise and plateau at the 100% mark. At the time the screenshot was taken, the utilization rose to 101.00%. The act of taking the screenshot is CPU intensive, too. The reason that the utilization exceeds 100% is that this is an average time.

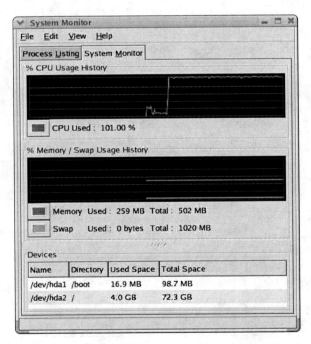

Figure 7-3   An infinite loop consuming CPU utilization

Notice, in Figure 7-4, that the CPU utilization dropped to 11% after the **yes** command is terminated by pressing Ctrl+C.

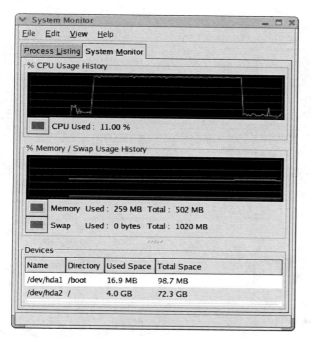

Figure 7-4   Terminating an infinite loop causes CPU utilization to drop

UNDERSTANDING THE while STATEMENT

The theoretical *While* statement tests whether a condition is true or false. If the condition is true, the *While* statement repeats the instructions, following the *Do* clause up to the *End-While* clause. If the condition is false, the loop terminates and program flow continues subsequent statements. The logic of the *While* statement is:

While true-condition

Do

     Perform activity for true-condition

End-While

Figure 7-5 shows a flowchart depicting the *While* statement. The shaded area represents the *While* loop.

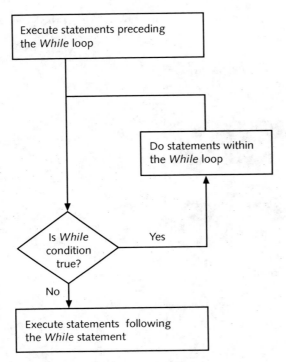

Figure 7-5   Flowchart of the *While* statement

Consider the following business application structured using the pseudocode for the *While* statement. In this example, the *While* loop is used to process multiple records in a file.

Open file

While you have records

Do

      Read record

      Process record

      Write record

End-While

Close file

Notice that first the file containing the records is opened. Then, as long as you have records in the file, they are read and then processed. A record must be read prior to processing it. Processing a record might include performing computations or logic operations on the fields within the record. As long as there are records in the file, they are read and then processed. Once the loop terminates, the file is closed.

The while Statement Syntax

Like the theoretical *While* statement, the shell's while statement also tests for a condition being true or false, and if the condition is true, performs the loop's statements; if false, it bypasses the loop's statements. The while loop in the shell takes the following form:

```
while listA
do
        listB
done
```

The listA statements are a set of commands that is executed and that results in an exit status. If the commands in listA exit with an exit status of zero, then the commands in listB are executed. If the commands in listA exit with a nonzero exit status, the commands in listB are not executed. The statements following done are executed whether or not commands in listB execute.

To prove that the while command performs the do statements as long as the exit status is zero, run this command:

```
while true
do
        echo $?
done
```

The statement true always returns an exit status of zero. It displays the value zero an infinite number of times. You can terminate this statement or any other infinite loop by pressing Ctrl+C.

You can accomplish the same proof by entering this command: while ! false; do echo $?; done. The statement false always returns an exit status of one. However, by placing the negation operator (!) prior to it, the condition is zero. This loop displays the value zero an infinite number of times.

Using the while Statement

You can use the while statement to test for characters. Consider the script shown in Figure 7-6. In this script, a listing of the users who are logged on as well as a listing of current files are displayed. The script user is then prompted as to whether he would like to stop the script once the network information is displayed. If the user enters a "Y," then the script terminates; otherwise, the loop continues. Let's look at this in closer detail.

In the WhileLoopStop script a variable named Stop is initialized to "N." Next, the while statement uses the logical negation operator to determine if the variable is not equal to "Y." The first time through, the variable named Stop is equal to "N", so the while condition tests true. Because it tests true, the do statements are executed—these are the who, ls, and read statements. The user is then prompted by the read statement for an answer. If the user enters anything but a "Y," the while loop continues.

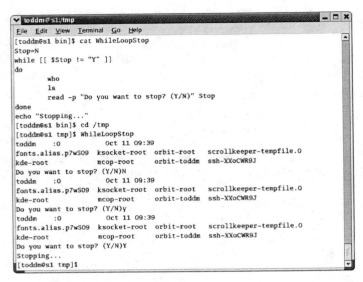

```
toddm@s1:/tmp
File  Edit  View  Terminal  Go  Help
[toddm@s1 bin]$ cat WhileLoopStop
Stop=N
while [[ $Stop != "Y" ]]
do
        who
        ls
        read -p "Do you want to stop? (Y/N)" Stop
done
echo "Stopping..."
[toddm@s1 bin]$ cd /tmp
[toddm@s1 tmp]$ WhileLoopStop
toddm     :0          Oct 11 09:39
fonts.alias.p7wSO9  ksocket-root  orbit-root    scrollkeeper-tempfile.O
kde-root            mcop-root     orbit-toddm   ssh-XXoCWR9J
Do you want to stop? (Y/N)N
toddm     :0          Oct 11 09:39
fonts.alias.p7wSO9  ksocket-root  orbit-root    scrollkeeper-tempfile.O
kde-root            mcop-root     orbit-toddm   ssh-XXoCWR9J
Do you want to stop? (Y/N)y
toddm     :0          Oct 11 09:39
fonts.alias.p7wSO9  ksocket-root  orbit-root    scrollkeeper-tempfile.O
kde-root            mcop-root     orbit-toddm   ssh-XXoCWR9J
Do you want to stop? (Y/N)Y
Stopping...
[toddm@s1 tmp]$
```

Figure 7-6   WhileLoopStop script that tests for characters

It is important to understand how to use the while loop to test for character values because there may be times when you need to do just that. For instance, you may need to loop through code to prompt users to enter certain values, and then test their input. Or, you might need to create a script that repeatedly asks the user to enter a valid password. Next you will create a script that tests a condition. If the condition is true, then the while loop will display a listing of processes using the ps —e | more command, and then prompt the user to continue.

To create a script using while to test character values:

1. Log in to the Linux system as a user, and then open a Terminal emulation window.

2. Create a script named **WhileLoopB** in the **$HOME/bin** directory.

3. Insert the following lines of code to create a loop which shows the processes that are running:

```
Continue=Y
while [[ $Continue = "Y" ]]
do
        ps —e | more    # The "-e" option shows all
        processes.
        read —p "Do you want to continue? (Y)" Con
        Continue=`echo $Con | tr [:lower:] [:upper:]`
           # Convert answer to uppercase and test that.
done
```

4. Save the script, and then quit the editor.

5. Make the script executable, and then execute the script. A listing of all processes is displayed.

6. When prompted, enter "**Y**," and then press **Enter**. Because you answered "Y," a listing of all processes is displayed again. You are prompted again.

7. This time when prompted, enter "**N**," and then press **Enter**. Because you answered "N," the script terminates.

8. Close your window, and then log out.

The while **Statement and Command Exit Status**

You can use the while statement to test the exit status of a command. Why would you want to do this? Testing the exit status of a command in a while statement is useful for determining whether or not a command succeeded or failed. Once you determine the exit status, you can perform iterations based on that knowledge. See the following script:

```
while ! cp fileX.txt fileY.txt
do
        echo "Attempting to copy…"
        sleep 10      # Pause the script for 10 seconds.
done
```

In this example, the while statement attempts to copy a file. If the file is present, it is copied. If the file does not exist, the while statement loops continually until the file gets created. Notice that the negation operator (!) is used. The while statement negates the exit status of the cp fileX.txt fileY.txt command; thus the copy command fails if fileX.txt is nonexistent. This results in a nonzero exit status. The negation operator turns that status to a zero, for true. As long as the while ! cp fileX.txt fileY.txt is true the file is never copied. As part of the while loop, a message is displayed indicating that the script will attempt to copy the file again. The script pauses for 10 seconds so you have time to read the message. The script continues to try to copy the file as long as fileX.txt is not present. Once the file is created, it is copied to fileY.txt and the script terminates. It is possible for the file to be created by a background program or by you using another Terminal emulation window. Figure 7-7 shows the WhileCopy script running.

Notice that there are two windows in Figure 7-7. In the window on the left, you can see the contents of WhileCopy and its execution. You can see that it is attempting to copy the file but cannot do so because it did not exist at the time the script was executed. However, in the terminal window on the right in Figure 7-7, you can see that the file, fileX.txt, is created using the touch command. It is important to understand that the script in the left window was started before fileX.txt was created. Once fileX.txt is created, the script copies fileX.txt to fileY.txt.

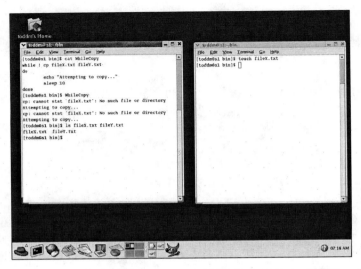

Figure 7-7   The WhileCopy script, its output, and another Terminal emulation window used to create a file

Terminating a Loop

There may be times when you need to terminate a loop before a condition terminates the loop; for instance, if you wanted your loop to terminate prematurely because the script encountered an error within the loop or a user decided to exit a menu that uses a loop. In these cases, you can use the `break` command to end the loop. This command is used within the shell's looping structures and is often accompanied by a variable count. Consider the following code:

```
((count=1))
while true
do
    echo $count
    ((count++))
    if [[ $count -gt 3 ]]
    then
            break
    fi
done
```

In this example, the `while` statement tests for a zero exit status. As you know, the `true` command always returns a zero exit status. You then set a variable count to increment and test if the variable's value is greater than three. Once the variable is greater than three, the `break` command is activated, causing the loop to terminate. Then, control of the script is passed to any statement following the `break` clause.

There may be times when you want to exit just one iteration of the loop instead of terminating the whole loop. In this case, you would use the continue statement.

Nesting while Loops

The shell also allows you to nest while statements to create a loop within a loop. One reason you might consider using a nested while loop is to create a menu that uses the while statement to repeatedly display available options. You could then embed the case statement within the while statement to handle those options. Also, you could set it up so that one of the options has a loop that requires a specific value to be entered and that displays the same prompt if the correct value is not entered. Thus, you end up with the menu loop, and within it, a nested loop that prompts for a certain value.

Figure 7-8 depicts how nested loops fit together, as well as how you structure the syntax for those loops.

7

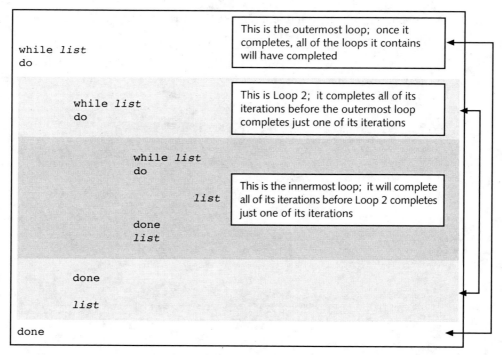

Figure 7-8   Understanding nested loops

In Figure 7-8 there are three loops. The innermost loop's condition is reached before Loop 2's condition is reached. Loop 2's condition is reached before the outermost loop's condition is reached. In other words, each loop completes all of its iterations before the loop surrounding it goes through only one of its iterations.

When nesting loops, if you have just two loops, the one embedded inside the other is called the inner loop. The other is called the outer loop. When you have more than one nested loop, the additional loops are referred to as "Loop *Number*," where *Number* is the number of the loop beginning from the outer loop. For example, if you have three loops, you would have the outer loop, Loop 2 and then the inner loop.

Figure 7-9 shows an example of nesting `while` loops. The WhileNest script contains two loops. On the first pass of the first while loop, called the outer loop, the condition `$x -le 3` is tested. If "x" is less than three, then the second `while` loop, the inner loop, is tested. This is where the condition `$y -le 3` is tested. As long as "y" is less than three, then the variables are displayed using the statement `echo $x $y`. Then, "y" is incremented with the statement `((y++))`. Once "y" reaches three, then "x" is incremented using `((x++))`. At this point, the inner `while` statement has made three complete iterations. Meanwhile, the outer loop has only made one. So, the outer loop makes one iteration, and the inner loop makes iterations until "x" finally reaches three, and the script terminates. The inner `while` loop then displays the values 1, 2, 3 for every one occurrence of "x."

```
toddm@s1:~/bin
File  Edit  View  Terminal  Go  Help
[toddm@s1 bin]$ cat WhileNest
((x=1))
while [[ $x -le 3 ]]
do
        ((y=1))
        while [[ $y -le 3 ]]
        do
                echo $x $y
                ((y++))
        done
        ((x++))
done
[toddm@s1 bin]$ WhileNest
1 1
1 2
1 3
2 1
2 2
2 3
3 1
3 2
3 3
[toddm@s1 bin]$
```

Figure 7-9   A script using nested *while* statements

The result of the WhileNest script's execution displays the "x" variable in the first, or left, column and the "y" variable in the second, or right, column. Notice that the "y" variable changes three times for every one change of the "x" variable. In total, the variables are displayed nine times. In this example, you can multiply the two numbers in each condition, (in this case, three multiplied by three) to determine how many times the inner loop passes through its do statements.

Next you will implement the code in Figure 7-10 to help you understand how to nest while statements. The variables used in this example, "outer" and "inner," are used for incrementing and testing the iterations of the nested loops.

To create a script using nested while statements:

1. Log in to the Linux system as a user, and then open a Terminal emulation window.

2. Create a script named **WhileLoopNest** in the $HOME/bin directory.

3. Insert the following lines of code to use two while statements to implement nested loops:

```
((outer=1))
while [[ $outer -le 3 ]]
do
      ((inner=1))
      while [[ $inner -le 3 ]]
      do
            echo $outer $inner
            ((inner++))
      done
      ((outer++))
done
```

4. Save the script, and then quit the editor.

5. Make the script executable, and then execute the script. Two columns of numbers appear; they are the contents of the variables outer and inner. See Figure 7-10. The first column represents the change of the variable outer within the outside loop. The second column represents the change of the variable inner within the inside loop. Notice that inner changes three times as often as outer because it is incremented in the inner loop.

6. Close your window, and then log out.

7

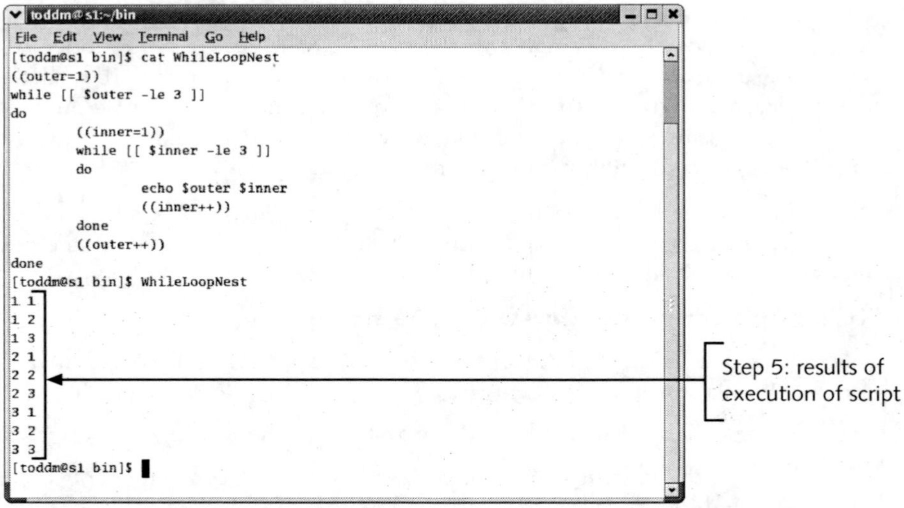

```
[toddm@s1 bin]$ cat WhileLoopNest
((outer=1))
while [[ $outer -le 3 ]]
do
        ((inner=1))
        while [[ $inner -le 3 ]]
        do
                echo $outer $inner
                ((inner++))
        done
        ((outer++))
done
[toddm@s1 bin]$ WhileLoopNest
1 1
1 2
1 3
2 1
2 2
2 3
3 1
3 2
3 3
[toddm@s1 bin]$
```

Step 5: results of execution of script

Figure 7-10   The WhileNestedLoop script and a sample run

UNDERSTANDING THE until STATEMENT

Like the theoretical *While* statement, the *Until* statement also tests whether a condition is true or false. The *Until* statement repeats statements until a condition becomes true. Think of the *Until* statement as the opposite logic of the *While* statement. The logic of the *Until* statement is shown below:

Until false-condition

Do

> *Perform activity for false-condition*

End-Until

Figure 7-11 shows a flowchart displaying the *Until* statement.

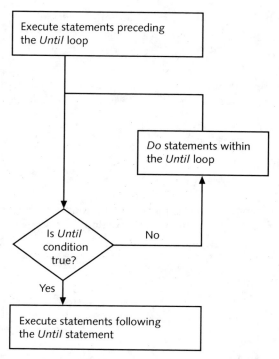

Figure 7-11 Flowchart of the *Until* statement

Recall the pseudocode for the *While* statement used to process records. Now, you will see how to turn the *While* statement into the equivalent *Until* pseudocode. When using the *Until* statement, you need to rephrase the condition. In this case, the condition being tested is, "Are there any more records?" If there are more records, process them. Once there are no more records, terminate the loop, and close the file.

Open file

Until there are no more records

Do

> *Read record*
>
> *Process record*
>
> *Write record*

End-While

Close file

Because the logic of *Until* can be a bit tricky, consider one more section of pseudocode for the *Until* statement to help you get a better idea how it works. Take a look at an example that has happened to you—what to do on a rainy day.

In this example, as long as it is raining, you will stay indoors. Once it stops raining the condition turns false, and the loop terminates. Then, you can do an outside activity, such as washing the car or planting vegetables, in this case. Here is the pseudocode:

Until it stops raining

> *Stay inside*

End-Until

Wash car or plant vegetable garden

Now, here's the rainy day pseudocode for the *Until* statement converted into the *While* statement, so you can compare the two. Notice that the logic of the two statements is just the opposite.

While it is raining

> *Stay inside*

End-While

Wash car or plant vegetable garden

The `until` Statement Syntax

Whereas the `while` statement performs its `do` statements if the exit status of the condition or list is a zero or true, the `until` statement performs its `do` statements if the exit status of the condition or list is nonzero, or false. The `until` statement syntax is:

```
until listA
do
            listB
done
```

 Like the `while` statement, you can also write the `until` statement as a single statement, as in: `until listA; do listB; done.`

The *listA* statements are a set of commands that is executed with an exit status. If the commands in *listA* result in a nonzero exit status, then the commands in *listB* are executed. If the commands in *listA* result in an exit status of zero, the commands in *listB* are not executed. In either case, the program flow continues normally after the done clause.

As you saw with the while statement, you can prove this by running the following command:

```
until ! true
            do echo $?
    done
```

This command displays the value one an infinite number of times. You can terminate this statement by pressing Ctrl+C.

 You can accomplish the same proof by entering this command: until false; do echo $?; done, which also displays the value one an infinite number of times.

Using the until **Statement with Logical Operations**

Recall the script named WhileLoopStop that continually displays the logged-in network users and then prompts to see if the script user would like to continue. Consider how this script might function if you modify it to use the until statement. As long as the user does not enter a "Y," the script loops, displaying the currently logged-in users. Notice that the original code for WhileLoopStop has been slightly modified to show you how this script works using the until statement and that it has been renamed the UntilLoopStop script:

```
Stop=N
until [[ $Stop = "Y" ]]
do
        who ls
        read —p "Do you want to stop? (Y)" Stop
done
echo "Stopping..."
```

Figure 7-12 displays the UntilLoopStop script. You can see that the script continues to display the contents of a directory until the user presses "Y" to stop it.

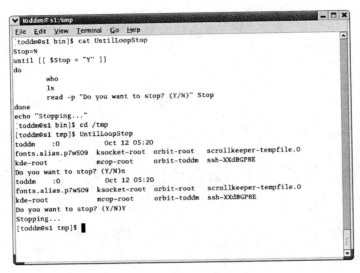

Figure 7-12 The UntilLoopStop script and its output

Consider the following example. Say you work as a shell programmer in the Information Technology Department for Plane Parts, Inc., a manufacturer that produces a generic line of tools used for airplane maintenance. The production manager requires employees to fill out a daily timesheet for the previous day's activities. However, most of the time, employees are days late in filling out the timesheet. She requests your help eliminating the timesheet delay. Next you will write a script to remind employees to complete their timesheets each day. The script runs for the first five minutes of each hour, unless it is terminated. In the script, the variable minute contains the minute derived from the date command using the cut command. As long as the current system's minute is less than five, then the until loop performs an iteration. With each iteration, a message is displayed indicating the user should complete the daily timesheet; a pause of 15 seconds occurs, and then the current minute is derived again. Until the newly determined minute becomes greater than or equal to five, an iteration occurs.

To create a script using the until statement:

1. Log in to the Linux system as a user, and then open a Terminal emulation window.

2. Create a script named **TimeSheet** in the **$HOME/bin** directory.

3. Insert the following lines of code to create a message that asks the employee to complete a daily timesheet and displays the message until five minutes after the hour in which the script is run.

```
declare -i minute
minute=`date +%M`
until [[ $minute -ge 5 ]]
        do
                echo "Complete daily timesheet!"
                sleep 15
                minute=`date +%M`
done
```

4. Save the script, and then quit the editor.

5. Make the script executable, and then execute the script to check that it runs correctly. To implement this script, you would add this to one of the login files discussed in Chapter 3. (*Note*: For this to work properly, your system time must be between 0 and 5 minutes past any given hour.) You can either wait for the time to meet this requirement or, within the script, change "5" to "10" for minutes from your current time so the script will work with the current time on your system. See Figure 7-13. Notice that three messages appear on the screen. As long as the minute is less than or equal to five, the message "Complete daily timesheet!" is displayed. Once the minute exceeds five, the message is no longer displayed.

6. Close your window, and then log out.

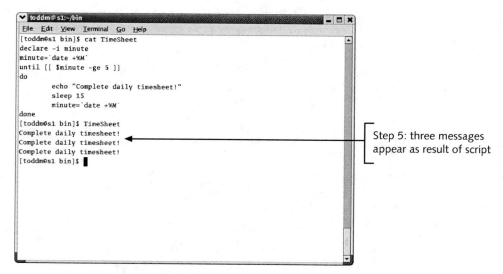

Step 5: three messages appear as result of script

Figure 7-13 The TimeSheet script

Consider one more example. Plane Parts, Inc. wants you to create a script that checks to see if the nightly run for the Accounting program failed. If it did, an error file is automatically created by the program. Also it's important to note that if the nightly run did fail, the application that generated the error will not restart because of the error, and this results in other users being unable to do their work. Next, you will create a script that continually displays a message indicating that an error file exists resulting from an error in the Accounting program. The error file should not be removed before an investigation determines the reason for failure. If the file exists, then an error must have occurred. You can use the until loop to determine if the error file does exist, and if it does, then generate messages indicating just that. Have the loop continue until the file no longer exists. In the until statement, the −e option returns true if the file exists. This condition is negated with the ! operator.

In general, it is not uncommon for files to get processed overnight, and if the program processing the files fails, a System Administrator is usually contacted and an error file is left.

To create a script using the until loop to test the existence of a file:

1. Log in to the Linux system as a user, and then open a Terminal emulation window.

2. Create the **NightlyRunError.txt** file in your **$HOME/bin** directory.

3. Create a script named **UntilFile** in the **$HOME/bin** directory.

4. Insert the following lines of code to display a message indicating that an error file exists and needs to be deleted before the Accounting program can run. Note the code does not remove the script because the programmer or System Administrator needs to investigate the reason for the failure. When the file is ultimately removed, then the loop terminates, and the Accounting program can be restarted.

```
until [ ! -e NightlyRunError.txt ]
do
    echo "The NightlyRunError.txt file exists and
      it needs to be deleted in order to run the
      Accounting program."
    sleep 3
done
echo "Starting Accounting program..."
# The full path to accounting program would go here.
```

5. Save the script, quit the editor, and then make the **UntilFile** script executable.

6. Execute the script. See Figure 7-14. A message appears indicating the file exists and must be removed in order for the Accounting program to run.

7. Open another Terminal emulation window, and then remove the **NightlyRunError.txt** file so you can see what happens when the file is not present.

8. Execute the script again. See Figure 7-14. The message "Starting Accounting program..." appears on the screen because the NightlyRunError.txt file is not present.

9. Close your windows, and then log out.

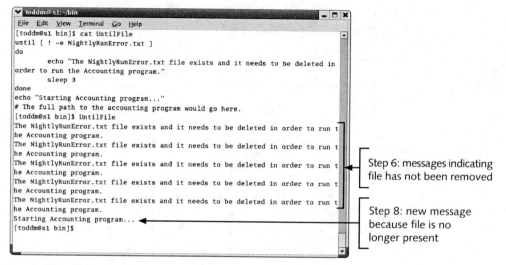

Figure 7-14 The UntilFile script

UNDERSTANDING THE for STATEMENT

The *While* and the *Until* statements are useful when you do not know how much data you have to process. There is another logical looping structure, the *For* statement, that allows you to process a set number of iterations.

Look at the general form of the theoretical *For* statement:

For variable goes from initial-value to ending-value

Do

       Perform activity as long as variable is not equal to the ending-value

       Increment or Decrement value of variable

End-For

The *For* loop begins with a starting value for a *variable*. The starting value is set with *initial-value*. Then, the statements in the loop body are executed. After that, the *variable* is changed; it is either incremented or decremented. The *Do* statements are repeatedly executed until the *variable* reaches the *ending-value*. Figure 7-15 shows a flowchart displaying the *For* statement.

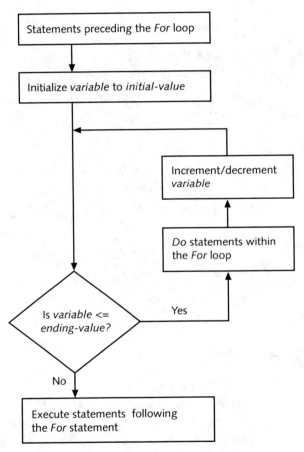

Figure 7-15   Flowchart of the *For* statement

Let's look at an example. In the following pseudocode, the variable "x" starts at one, the contents of "x" are displayed, and then "x" is incremented by one. The loop repeatedly displays the contents of "x" and increments "x" until "x" equals the number five. Here is the pseudocode:

For x in 1 to 5

Do

       Display x

End-For

You can also decrement by following the same logic. In this case, the variable "x" starts at five, displays "x," and then automatically decrements "x" by one until it reaches one. The pseudocode for decrementing a variable is:

For x in 5 to 1

Do

       Display x

End-For

The for **Statement Syntax**

The advantage of the for statement is that it allows you to control the number of iterations a loop performs. Let's say you work for a small radio station, and the on-air meteorologist wants you to take the average of last week's outside temperature. You could use the for statement to loop through seven iterations—one for each day of the week. Or, in another scenario, if you want to find the average of five grades for your Advanced Programming class, then you can use a for statement to complete this task.

There are two variations of the for statement.

- Using for with a word list
- Using for with an arithmetic expression

You can place both forms on a single line, using semicolons, or on separate lines. The syntax of the two variations is covered in the following sections.

Using for **with a Word List**

You use the word list version of the for statement to loop through items in a word list. It is not used for controlling a numeric variable in the word list and incrementing or decrementing it. The arithmetic expression form of the for statement does that. Let's look at an example where the for statement is performed five times:

```
for number in 1 2 3 4 5
do
        echo $number
done
```

With the statement for number in 1 2 3 4 5, the variable named number is assigned to the first item in the list, which is 1. The statement between the do and done clauses is performed for each assignment of the variable. Next, the value of the variable named "number" changes to each item in the list until the last item is reached. Essentially, number is set to 1, then the do statements are executed, then number is set to 2, and the do statements are executed again, and so on until the variable number equals the last item in the list, in this case 5. The do statements are performed for the last item. The numbers are displayed one at a time on one line each.

The variable name is a user-defined name. The items in the word list do not have to be numeric. Next you will create a script that uses characters instead of numbers in the word list.

To create a script using for with a word list:

1. Log in to the Linux system as a user, and then open a Terminal emulation window.

2. Create a script named **WordList** in the $HOME/bin directory.

3. Insert the following lines of code to create a script that makes use of a for loop to insert items, in this case various fruits, in a word list:

```
for fruit in pear banana peach
do
        echo "I need a $fruit from the store."
done
```

4. Save the script, and then quit the editor.

5. Make the script executable, and then execute the script. Three statements appear indicating that a pear, banana, and peach are needed from the store.

6. Close your window, and then log out.

Using Arithmetic Operations

You can also perform arithmetic operations on the words in the word list as long as they are numbers. For example, consider the following lines of code:

```
for var in 2 4 6 8
do
        ((power = $var ** 2))
        echo $var "to the second power is" $power
done
```

In this example, the variable named var is assigned to a number—2, 4, 6, 8, in the word list. In the first iteration, var is set to 2. Then, inside the loop, the variable named power is equal to the value of var, which is 2, to the second power, using **2, in the third line. Then, a message is displayed indicating that 2 to the second power is 4.

This repeats for the values in the word list. The output is four lines and indicates that 2 to the second power is 4, 4 to the second power is 16, 6 to the second power is 36, and finally, 8 to the second power is 64.

Next you will create a loop that will allow you to enter seven daily temperatures and display their average.

To create a script using for **to enter a specific number of temperature values:**

1. Log in to the Linux system as a user, and then open a Terminal emulation window.

2. Create a script named **ForAvg** in the **$HOME/bin** directory.

3. Insert the following lines of code to create the loop that iterates seven times:

```
for num in 1 2 3 4 5 6 7
do
```

4. Insert the following lines of code to read the temperature values, accumulate the value in a variable named TempTotal, and then terminate the loop. The accumulation is done because on the next pass of the loop, the current value of Temp changes to the next temperature reading.

```
    read -p "Enter Daily Temperature for day $num:" Temp
    ((TempTotal = $TempTotal + $Temp))
done
```

5. Insert the following lines of code to calculate and display the average:

```
# After $num reaches 7, average the temperatures and
    display the average.
((AvgTemp = $TempTotal / $num))
echo "Average weekly temperature was:" $AvgTemp
```

6. Save the script, and then quit the editor.

7. Make the script executable, execute the script, and then enter the following seven temperatures when prompted: **100**, **90**, **88**, **102**, **91**, **97**, and **95**. See Figure 7-16. A message is displayed indicating that the average weekly temperature was 94.

8. Close your window, and then log out.

7

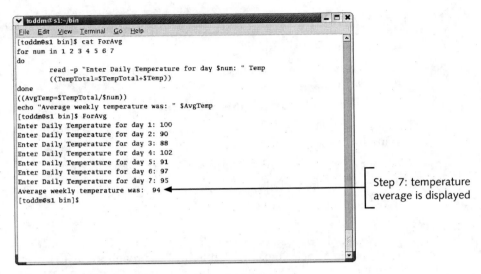

```
[toddm@s1 bin]$ cat ForAvg
for num in 1 2 3 4 5 6 7
do
        read -p "Enter Daily Temperature for day $num: " Temp
        ((TempTotal=$TempTotal+$Temp))
done
((AvgTemp=$TempTotal/$num))
echo "Average weekly temperature was: " $AvgTemp
[toddm@s1 bin]$ ForAvg
Enter Daily Temperature for day 1: 100
Enter Daily Temperature for day 2: 90
Enter Daily Temperature for day 3: 88
Enter Daily Temperature for day 4: 102
Enter Daily Temperature for day 5: 91
Enter Daily Temperature for day 6: 97
Enter Daily Temperature for day 7: 95
Average weekly temperature was:  94
[toddm@s1 bin]$
```

Step 7: temperature average is displayed

Figure 7-16 The ForAvg script and its output

Using `for` with an Arithmetic Expression

Using a `for` loop with an arithmetic expression allows you greater control over the loop by initializing, testing, and changing a numeric value. The `for` loop uses a control variable to determine the number of loop iterations. There are three parts to this type of looping structure. They are:

- Initialize the loop's control variable with *expression1*
- Test a conditional operation with *expression2*
- Change the loop's control variable with *expression3*

Consider the following example:

```
for ((num=1; num<=5; num++))
do
        echo $num
done
```

In this example, *expression1* is num=1, *expression2* is num<=5, and *expression3* is num++. Here is how it works. The variable num is initialized to a starting value in the first expression. Then, the value of num is compared to five. If num is less than or equal to five, as shown in *expression2*, then the command(s) in the do *list* are executed. Finally, the variable is incremented in *expression3*. Then the test starts all over. In this example, the loop continues until the value of the variable num exceeds five. The execution of this script causes the numbers 1 through 5 to appear one after the other on separate lines in one column.

Consider what happens if you modify the ForAvg script by combining the read command with the arithmetic expression form of the of for statement—you create a very flexible script. Here you have the number of days of temperatures to be entered determined by the user. Here is the code for the ForNum script which is based on the ForAvg script:

```
read -p "Enter the number of days: " Days
for ((num=1; num <=$Days; num++))
do
    read -p "Enter Daily Temperature for day $num: " Temp
    ((TempTotal=$TempTotal+$Temp))
done
((AvgTemp=$TempTotal/($Days)))
echo "Average weekly temperature was: " $AvgTemp
```

This script allows the user to enter any number of days for which temperature averages are taken. See Figure 7-17. Here the user enters the numeral 4 for the number of days, and then inputs the temperatures to obtain the average for those days. There is also another run where the user enters temperatures for two days that are also averaged. You could not do this using the logic in the ForAvg script created in the last exercise.

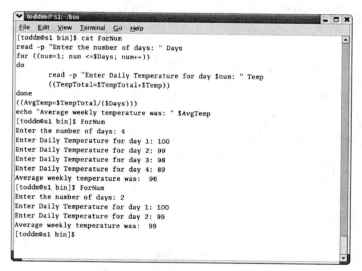

Figure 7-17 The ForNum script and its output

Next you will create a for loop, increment the variable num, and use the mathematical operation for squaring the number.

To create a for loop script using expressions:

1. Log in to the Linux system as a user, and then open a Terminal emulation window.

2. Create a script named **SquareLoop** in the **$HOME/bin** directory.

3. Insert the following lines of code:

```
for ((num=1; num <= 10; num++))
do
        ((squared = $num ** 2))
        echo $squared
done
```

4. Save the script, and then quit the editor.

5. Make the script executable, execute the script, and then record the output. The numbers 1 through 10 are squared and the result is displayed.

6. Close your window, and then log out.

Nesting for Statements

You can also nest **for** statements. Like previous looping structures, you must embed a complete **for** statement within another one. With nested loops, the outer loop starts one iteration, and the inner loop must complete all of its iterations before the outer loop begins another iteration. Let's look at the ForNestA script in Figure 7-18. The variable "i" is the control variable for the outer loop and the variable "j" is the control variable for the inner loop.

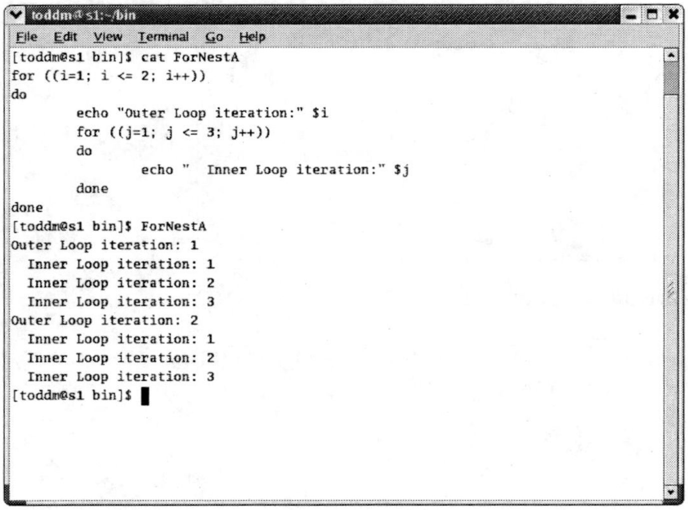

```
[toddm@s1 bin]$ cat ForNestA
for ((i=1; i <= 2; i++))
do
        echo "Outer Loop iteration:" $i
        for ((j=1; j <= 3; j++))
        do
                echo "  Inner Loop iteration:" $j
        done
done
[toddm@s1 bin]$ ForNestA
Outer Loop iteration: 1
  Inner Loop iteration: 1
  Inner Loop iteration: 2
  Inner Loop iteration: 3
Outer Loop iteration: 2
  Inner Loop iteration: 1
  Inner Loop iteration: 2
  Inner Loop iteration: 3
[toddm@s1 bin]$
```

Figure 7-18 The ForNestA script with nested for loops and its output

Notice that even though the outer loop begins first, the inner loop must complete its cycle, in this case three iterations, before the outer loop can begin its second iteration, at which point the inner loop must again complete its cycle of three iterations before the outer loop can begin its final iteration.

Next you will nest three `for` loops. The outermost loop uses variable "i," Loop 2 uses variable "j," and the innermost loop uses variable "k." These are displayed in the innermost loop. Notice that for each iteration of "i," "j" changes from 1 to 2 and "k" changes from 1 to 3 twice.

To create a script that uses nested `for` loops:

1. Log in to the Linux system as a user, and then open a Terminal emulation window.

2. Create a script named **ForNested** in the **$HOME/bin** directory.

3. Insert the following lines of code to create a three-level nested loop. The first two lines are heading lines.

```
echo "i j k"
echo "----"
for ((i=1; i <= 3; i++))
do
        for ((j=1; j <= 2; j++))
        do
                for ((k=1; k <=3; k++))
                do
                        echo $i $j $k
                done
        done
done
```

4. Save the script, and then quit the editor.

5. Make the script executable, and then execute the script. See Figure 7-19. After the two heading lines, the output is 18 rows of numbers three columns deep.

6. Close the window, and then log out.

7

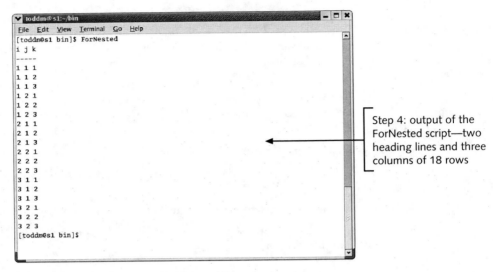

Step 4: output of the ForNested script—two heading lines and three columns of 18 rows

Figure 7-19 The ForNested script and its output

CHAPTER SUMMARY

◻ A loop is a set of statements that are repeated for some purpose until some condition changes. Once the condition is reached, the loop terminates. An iteration occurs each time the statements within the loop are processed. An infinite loop occurs if no condition exists to terminate the loop; this consumes an excessive amount of processing time and should be avoided. The major looping structures in programming theory are *While, Until,* and *For.*

◻ The `while` loop is useful when you don't know the number of iterations. You can use it to test the condition of numeric amounts, characters, and commands. The syntax of the shell's `while` statement tests the exit status of the commands in the *listA* statements. If *listA* returns a zero exit status, then *listB* statements execute. If *listA* returns a nonzero exit status, then *listB* statements are skipped. Statements following the loop structure are executed regardless of the loop's condition. The `while` statement supports nested loops. Nested loops allow you to implement loops within loops.

◻ Like the `while` loop, you use the `until` statement when the number of iterations is unknown. You can test the condition of numeric amounts, characters, and commands. The shell's `until` statement tests the exit status of the commands in *listA*. If *listA* returns an exit status of one, then the *listB* statements execute. If *listA* returns an exit status of zero, then the *listB* statements are skipped. Statements following the loop structure are executed regardless of the loop's condition. The `until` statement supports nested loops.

❐ The shell's **for** statement is used when the number of iterations you want to perform is known. There are two forms of the **for** statement. The word list form is used to loop through any type of item in a word list. These items can be numbers, characters, or commands. The arithmetic expression form is used for incrementing and decrementing numeric values.

REVIEW QUESTIONS

1. Using the _____ statement, the **do** statements are executed for a true condition.

    a. **until**

    b. **break**

    c. **continue**

    d. **while**

2. A(n) _____ occurs when a set of programming statements are repeatedly executed.

    a. iteration

    b. pass

    c. true condition

    d. loop

3. Using the _____ statement, the **do** statements are executed for a false condition.

    a. **until**

    b. **break**

    c. **continue**

    d. **while**

4. A(n) _____ is the action of a loop performing its statements one time.

    a. iteration

    b. pass

    c. false condition

    d. loop

5. The _____ statement is used to terminate a loop.

    a. **until**

    b. **break**

    c. **continue**

    d. **while**

7

6. The _____ statement is used to terminate the loop for one iteration.

   a. `until`

   b. `break`

   c. `continue`

   d. `while`

7. The following statement will execute _____ time(s).

   ```
   for ((num=1 ; num<=5; num++))
   do
           echo $num
   done
   ```

   a. 0

   b. 4

   c. 5

   d. 6

8. The following statement will execute _____ time(s).

   ```
   for ((num=1 ; num<=5; num++))
   done
           echo $num
   do
   ```

   a. 0

   b. 1

   c. 5

   d. 6

9. A(n) _____ loop loops forever until terminated.

   a. iteration

   b. pass

   c. infinite

   d. `continue`

10. The following statement will execute _____ time(s).

   ```
   for ((num=1 ; num<5; num++))
   do
           echo $num
   done
   ```

   a. 0

   b. 4

   c. 5

   d. an infinite number of

11. What is the result of the following statements?

```
for animal in cat dog bear
do
            echo $animal
done
```

   a. The words "cat," "dog," "animal," and "bear" are displayed on the screen.

   b. The word "animal" is displayed on the screen.

   c. The words "cat," "dog," and "bear" are displayed on the screen.

   d. Nothing occurs because the statement has a syntax error.

12. The following statement will execute _____ time(s).

```
((t=0))
while [[ $t=1 ]]
do
            echo "Blue Ocean!"
done
((t++))
```

   a. 0

   b. 1

   c. an infinite number of

   d. 2

13. What is the result of the following statements?

```
((t=0))
while [[ $t -lt 3 ]]
            echo "Taco"
done
```

   a. The text "Taco" is displayed only once.

   b. The text "Taco" is displayed an infinite number of times.

   c. The text "Taco" is displayed three times.

   d. Nothing occurs because the statement has a syntax error.

14. What is the result of the following statements?

```
((g=5))
until [[ $g -lt 1 ]
do
            echo $g; ((g--))
done
```

   a. The numbers 5, 4, 3, 2, 1 are displayed on the screen on separate lines.

   b. The numbers 5, 4, 3, 2 are displayed on the screen on separate lines.

   c. The numbers 4, 3, 2, 1, 0 are displayed on the screen on separate lines.

   d. Nothing occurs because the statement has a syntax error.

15. The following statement displays "Popcorn" _____ times.

```
for ((num1=1 ; num1<=3; num1++))
do
        for ((num2=1; num2<=2; num2++))
        do
                echo "Popcorn"
        done
done
```

   a. 0

   b. 4

   c. 5

   d. 6

16. What is the result of the following statements?

```
((g=6))
until [[ $g -lt1 ]]
do
        echo $g; ((g--))
done
```

   a. The numbers 6, 5, 4, 3, 2, 1 are displayed on the screen on separate lines.

   b. The numbers 5, 4, 3, 2, 1, 0 are displayed on the screen on separate lines.

   c. The numbers 5, 4, 3, 2, 1, 0 are displayed on the screen on separate lines.

   d. Nothing occurs because the statement has a syntax error.

17. What is the result of the following statements?

```
((i=10)); ((j=2))
while [[ $j -lt $i ]]
do
        echo $j; ((j++))
        if [[ $j -gt 5 ]]
        then break
        fi
done
```

   a. The numbers 2, 3, 4, 5, 6 are displayed on the screen on separate lines.

   b. The numbers 2, 3, 4, 5 are displayed on the screen on separate lines.

   c. The numbers 5, 4, 3, 2 are displayed on the screen on separate lines.

   d. The numbers 10, 9, 8, 7, 6, 5, 4, 3, 2, 1 are displayed on the screen on separate lines.

18. Given the following code, what value of the variable named total will be displayed?

```
((total=0))
for ((num1=1 ; num1<=3; num1++))
do
        for ((num2=1; num2<=2; num2++))
        do
                for ((num3=10; num3>=1; num3—))
                do
                        ((total++))
                done
        done
done
echo $total
```

   a. 20

   b. 30

   c. 60

   d. 120

19. What is displayed if the following code is executed?

```
for name in 'pwd'; do echo $name; done
```

   a. name

   b. the present working directory

   c. a syntax error message

   d. nothing

20. What is displayed if the following code is executed?

```
for name in 'echo hi'; do echo $name; done
```

   a. hi

   b. echo hi

   c. a syntax error message

   d. nothing

HANDS-ON PROJECTS

Project 7-1

In this project, you will create a file that contains a list of directories. You will use the for loop structure to control the process. Command substitution is needed to read the contents of the file containing the list of directories. A directory needs to be created for each line in the file.

   1. Log in to the Linux system as a user, and then open a Terminal emulation window.

2. Create a file named **inlist** in the **$HOME/bin** directory. This file will contain the list of directories, on separate lines, that are to be created.

3. Insert the following lines of code:

```
Dir1
Dir2
Dir2/Dir2a1
Dir2/Dir2a2
Dir2/Dir2a2/Dir2b1
Dir2/Dir2a2/Dir2b2
```

4. Create a shell script named **Project7-1** in your **$HOME/bin** directory.

5. Insert the following lines of code:

```
for dirname in `cat inlist`
do
        mkdir $dirname
done
```

6. Save the script, and then quit the editor.

7. Make the script executable, and then execute the script.

8. Record the output.

9. Close your window, and then log out.

Project 7-2

In this project, you will use a looping structure that allows you to determine if a host computer is available. You will use the ping command to accomplish this. If it is available, you will telnet to the host computer.

1. Log in to the Linux system as a user, and then open a Terminal emulation window.

2. Create a shell script named **Project7-2** in the **$HOME/bin** directory.

3. Insert the following lines of code:

```
read -p "Enter IP address or host name to ping " PingName
ping -c 2 $PingName
until [[ $? -eq 0 ]]
do
        sleep 2
        echo "Host not available.  Pinging again..."
        ping -c 3 $PingName
done
echo "The host is available."
echo "Telnetting to the host."
telnet $PingName
```

4. Save the script, and then quit the editor.

5. Make the script executable, and then execute the script, and input an existing host address.

6. Execute the script again. This time use a host that does not exist.

7. Close your window, and then log out.

Project 7-3

In this project, you will create a script that generates a random number using the shell's builtin RANDOM variable. The user will be asked to enter a number between 1 and 10, inclusive. The loop will continue until the user guesses the correct answer. The $RANDOM statement will generate a random number between 0 and 32,767; therefore, a $RANDOM statement within the loop will ensure a random number between 1 and 10, inclusive, is generated by the system.

1. Log in to the Linux system as a user, and then open a Terminal emulation window.

2. Create a shell script named **Project7-3** in the $HOME/bin directory.

3. Insert the following lines of code:

```
read -p "Guess a number between 1 and 10: " guess
rand=$RANDOM
while true
do
if [[ $rand -ge 1 && $rand -le 10 ]]
    then
        if [[ $guess -eq $rand ]]
        then
                echo "Right"
                break
        else
                echo "Try again"
                read -p "Guess a number between 1 and: 10 "
                  guess
                rand=$RANDOM
        fi
    else
        rand=$RANDOM
    fi
done
```

4. Save the script, and then quit the editor.

5. Make the script executable, execute the script, and then enter the same number until you guess the number.

6. Record the number of times it takes you to guess correctly.

7. Close your window, and then log out.

Project 7-4

In this project, you will use the `while` and `until` statements as well as nested loops.

1. Log in to the Linux system as a user, and then open a Terminal emulation window.

2. Create a shell script named **Project7-4** in the **$HOME/bin** directory.

3. Insert the following lines of code:

```
let "x=1"                        # Same as ((x=1))
while [[ $x -le 5 ]]             # Outer loop begins
do
        let "y=4"
        until [[ $y -le 1 ]]     # Inner loop begins
        do
                let y--          # Same as ((y--))
                echo $x $y
                let c++          # Same as ((c++))
        done                     # Inner loop ends
        let x++                  # Same as ((x++))
done                             # Outer loop ends
echo "The number of times looped is: " $c
```

4. Save the script, and then quit the editor.

5. Make the script executable, and then execute the script.

6. Close your window, and then log out.

Project 7-5

In this project, you will create a script that displays "Happy Birthday!" if the current month and day happen to match the system date.

1. Log in to the Linux system as a user, and then open a Terminal emulation window.

2. Create a shell script named **Project7-5** in the **$HOME/bin** directory.

3. Insert the following lines of code:

```
read -p "Enter your three-letter birth month
  (e.g., Feb) ?" BirthMonth
read -p "Enter your two-digit birth day
  (e.g., 07) ?" BirthDay
month=`date | cut +%b`
day=`date | cut +%d`
if [[ $BirthMonth -eq $month && $BirthDay -eq $day ]]
then
        HappyBirthday="Y"
else
        HappyBirthday="N"
fi
```

```
while [[ $HappyBirthday = "Y" ]]
do
        echo "Happy Birthday!"
        sleep 10
done
```

4. Save the script, and then quit the editor.

5. Make the script executable, execute the script, and then input your birth month and birthday.

6. Record the result.

7. Execute the script again. This time input the current day and month.

8. Record the result.

9. How would you terminate the script?

10. Close the window, and then log out.

Project 7-6

In this project, you will rewrite the "Happy Birthday!" script using the **case** statement for the decision and the **until** statement for the looping structure.

1. Log in to the Linux system as a user, and then open a Terminal emulation window.

2. Copy **Project7-5** to **Project7-6** in your **$HOME/bin** directory. (If you did not complete Project 7-5, the code for this script is included in Step 3 of that project.)

3. Write the pseudocode or draw a flowchart for using the **case** statement for the decision and the **until** statement for the loop.

4. Modify **Project7-6** to use the **case** statement and the **until** statement.

5. Record the script.

6. Save the script, quit the editor, make the script executable, execute the script, and input your birth month and birthday when prompted.

7. Record the result.

8. Execute the script again. This time input the current day and month.

9. Record the result.

10. Close your window, and then log out.

Project 7-7

In this project, you will create a script that allows the user to enter a password. The password the user enters will be suppressed with the **-s** option of the **read** statement. If the user fails to input the correct password after three tries, then a message will be displayed indicating that the number of attempts has been exceeded, and the script will terminate.

1. Log in to the Linux system as a user, and then open a Terminal emulation window.

2. Create a shell script named **Project7-7** in the **$HOME/bin** directory.

3. Insert the following lines of code:

```
pw=" "
password="cactus207"# This is the password to compare.
((count=1))
while [[ $pw != $password ]]
do
    ((count++))
    read  -s -p "Enter password: " pw
    echo ""
    if [[ $pw = $password ]]    # Is there a match?
    then
        echo "Correct!"
        break

    fi
    if [[ $count -gt 3 ]] # Limit the number of times to 3.
    then
        echo "Too many attempts!"
        break
    fi
done
```

4. Save the script, quit the editor, and then make the script executable.

5. Execute the script several times using the correct password (cactus207) and incorrect passwords.

6. Close your windows, and then log out.

Project 7-8

In this project, you will create a menu script allowing a user to enter options to run Linux commands.

1. Log in to the Linux system as a user, and then open a Terminal emulation window.

2. Create a shell script, named **Project7-8** in the **$HOME/bin** directory.

3. Insert the following lines of code:

```
YN="Y"
while [[ $YN = "Y" ]]
do
        clear
        echo "  MAIN MENU"
        echo " 1.  Long Listing"
        echo " 2.  Current Users"
        echo " 3.  Process Listing"
        read -p "Enter a valid selection [1-3]" selection
        case $selection in
```

```
     1) ls -l | more ;;
     2) who | more;;
     3) ps | more;;
     *) echo "Enter a valid selection [1-3]" ;;
   esac
   read -p "Continue (Y/N) ?" YesNo
   YN=`echo $YesNo | tr [:lower:] [:upper:]`
done
```

4. Save the script, quit the editor, and then make the script executable.

5. Execute the script, inputting the numbers **1**, **2**, and **3** for the menu options.

6. Record your observations.

7. Close your windows, and then log out.

CASE PROJECTS

Case 7-1

TMI is requesting your services again. You are to create a menu script that allows the user to enter all of the options given in Case 1 in Chapter 6. Be sure to create a flowchart or pseudocode before implementing your script. Make sure you run and test your script.

Case 7-2

You are to create a menu of Linux commands that a user can run. You will need to copy the Project7-8 script and modify it. There will be a fourth menu option that brings up another menu, called the Remote System Menu. Users must enter a password to gain access to this menu. The password should not be displayed on the screen. If an incorrect password is entered, an appropriate message is displayed indicating an invalid password and the user is returned to the MAIN MENU. If the user enters a correct password, then two options are displayed. The first option allows the user to ping to another system. You need to allow for the user to input either an IP address or hostname to ping. For the second option, allow the user to telnet to another system. Provide for the user to input either an IP address or hostname for use with telnet. You will use a looping structure within the Remote System Menu to allow the user to ping or telnet until he or she decides not to continue.

A

GUIDE TO LINUX COMMANDS

This appendix is a quick reference for essential Linux utilities available on most systems. Table A-1 lists the commands alphabetically, including the command name, its purpose, and any useful options. Table A-2 summarizes the vi editor commands. Table A-3 lists the shell script programming-related commands. Table A-4 lists the special characters used by the shell.

Table A-1 Common Linux commands

Command	Purpose	Useful Options and Examples
alias	Creates an alias for a command; created by editing the .bashrc file	alias dir='ls -l'
awk	Invokes a pattern-scanning and processing language operation	-f indicates code is coming from a disk file, not the keyboard; -F specifies the field separator
bc	Runs the arbitrary precision calculator	-l uses the math library; -q executes in quiet mode
cal	Shows the system calendar for a specified year or month	-1 shows a single month; -3 shows three months beginning with the previous month; -j displays the calendar in Julian date format
cat	Concatenates or displays files	-n displays line numbers
cd	Changes directories	cd changes your position within the tree to a specified one. For example, the command cd dirA, changes your position to a directory named dirA. When used by itself, cd changes your position to your home directory.
chmod	Changes security mode of a file or directory (r: read, w: write, x: executable); sets file permissions for specified users (u: user, g: group, o: others, a: all)	chmod a+x sets the execute bit for owner, group, and other
ci	Checks a file into RCS	
clear	Clears the screen	Commonly aliased to cls (see the alias command)
co	Checks a file out of RCS	
cp	Copies files from one directory to another	-i requests confirmation if the target file already exists; -r copies directories to a new directory

Table A-1   Common Linux commands (continued)

Command	Purpose	Useful Options and Examples
cut	Selects and extracts columns or fields from a file	−c specifies the character position; −d specifies the field separator; −f specifies the field position
date	Displays the system date	−u displays Greenwich Mean Time
dialog	Creates menu-based scripts	
diff	Compares and selects differences in two files or directories	diff /dir1 /dir2 compares the file entries in both directories and shows only the missing files for each directory
df	Displays the amount of free space on file systems	
. (dot)	Represents the current directory	Used mostly to specify that something happen in the current directory; for example, cp /dir/file . copies the file to the current directory
.. (dot dot)	Represents the parent directory	Used for referencing the parent directory of the current directory; for example, cd .. changes directory locations up one directory level while cp file2.txt .. copies a file named file2.txt to the parent directory of your current directory
echo	Displays the specified arguments on the output device	echo $VAR, where VAR is the variable name; echoes the data from an environmental variable to standard output
emacs	Starts the emacs editor	
exit or logout	Logs out of your current session	Ctrl+D also logs the user out of a session or a subshell and places the user back in the parent shell
export	Exports a specified list of variables to other shells; makes a variable an environmental variable	−f exports a function
find	Locates files that match a given value	−amin n finds files accessed more recently than n minutes ago; −atime n finds files last accessed n*24 hours ago; −user uname finds files owned by user matching uname
grep	Selects lines or rows that match a specified pattern	−c displays the count of matching lines; −i ignores case; −l lists only filenames that contain the pattern; −L lists only filenames that do not contain the pattern; −n displays line numbers; −v displays line numbers of lines in a file that do not match the specified pattern

Table A-1   Common Linux commands (continued)

Command	Purpose	Useful Options and Examples
groff	Processes embedded text-formatting codes	
gunzip	Uncompresses a file	
gzip	Compresses files	
head	Displays the first few lines of a file	Shows the first 10 lines by default; -n *n* displays the first *n* lines of the specified file
history	Lists all the commands contained in the bash history file	Bash history file is .bash_history by default and resides in the user's home directory; default number of last commands kept in the history file is 500
kill	Ends a process	-9 destructively ends a process; -HUP causes the service or daemon to stop (hang up) and restart, which causes the rereading of its configuration files; this option is often used to make changes to a running service
last	Shows the login history of all users on the system	-a displays the host name from which the user connected; -d shows the corresponding IP address for a remote connection
less	Allows you to scroll long files on the screen where the more command only allows advancing down a file	
let	Stores the results of arithmetic operations in a variable	
ln	Creates symbolic or hard links to files	By default, creates a hard link, which is another name for a particular inode; -s creates a symlink to a file, like a shortcut
lpr	Prints a file	-d prints on a specified printer; -n prints a specified number of copies of the file
ls	Lists a directory's contents, including its files and subdirectories	-a lists hidden files; -l lists files in long format, showing detailed information; -r lists files in reverse alphabetic order, -s shows the size of each file
man	Displays the on line manual for the specified command	-k searches for a specified pattern in the man pages; -t formats the output for printing using ghostscript
mkdir	Makes a new directory	

A

Table A-1   Common Linux commands (continued)

Command	Purpose	Useful Options and Examples
more	Displays a long file one screen at a time	Pressing the spacebar advances a screen at a time; pressing Enter advances one line at a time
mv	Moves or renames files	−f never prompts before overwrite of existing files and directories; −i prompts before overwriting files and directories; −u moves only when the source file is newer than the destination file or when the destination file is missing
passwd	Changes your Linux password	User can only change own password; root user can change others' passwords
paste	Pastes multiple files, column by column	
ping	Tests the status of another TCP/IP host	
pr	Formats a specified file before printing or viewing	−a displays output in columns across the page, one line per column; −d double-spaces the output; −h customizes the header line; −1n sets the number of lines per page
printenv	Prints a list of environmental variables	
printf	Tells the awk program what action to take	
ps	Shows processes on a system	−a shows all running processes; −u shows associated user for process; −x shows background system processes
pwd	Displays your current path	
read	Reads input from the keyboard	−s suppresses text; −p displays text as a prompt
readonly	Reads input that cannot be changed from the keyboard	
rcs	Manages RCS	
rlog	Displays information about an RCS file	
rm	Removes a file	−i requests confirmation before deleting a file; −r deletes a specified directory and its contents
rmdir	Removes a directory	−i requests confirmation before deleting a file; −r deletes a specified directory and its contents

Table A-1   Common Linux commands (continued)

Command	Purpose	Useful Options and Examples
sed	Specifies a stream editor command	-a \ appends text after a line or a script file containing sed commands; -d deletes specified text; -e specifies multiple commands on one line; -n indicates line numbers; -p displays lines; -s substitutes specified text
sort	Sorts and merges multiple files	.+ designates the position that follows an offset (+) as a character position, not a field position; +n sorts the field specified by n; -b ignores leading blank characters; -d sorts in dictionary order; -f indicates that a specified character separates the fields; -m merges files before sorting; -n sorts numbers arithmetically; -o directs the sorted output to a specified file
tail	Displays the last 10 lines of a file by default	-n n displays the last n lines of the specified file
tar	Backs up and restores files to a tar archive	-v indicates the verbose setting which gives additional information; -t takes a table of contents listing; -f filename backs up files to filename; -c indicates to create a tar archive; -x indicates to extract files from a tar archive
tee	Clones output stream to one or more files	
telnet	Opens a TCP/IP connection to a host	
test	Compares values and validates	! logical negation; -a logical AND; -b file existence tests if a file exists and is a block special file (which is a block-oriented device, such as a disk or tape drive); -c tests if a file exists and is a character special file (that is, a character-oriented device, such as a terminal or printer); -d tests if a file exists and is a directory; -e tests if a file exists; -eq equal to; -f tests if a file exists and is a regular file; value1 -ge value2 tests whether value1 is greater than or equal to value2;

Table A-1   Common Linux commands (continued)

Command	Purpose	Useful Options and Examples
		value1 -gt *value2* tests whether *value1* is greater than *value2*; *value1* -le *value2* tests whether *value1* is less than or equal to *value2*; *value1* -lt *value2* tests whether *value1* is less than *value2*; -n tests for a nonzero string length; -ne not equal to; -o logical OR; -r true if a file exists and is readable; -s true if a file exists and its size is greater than zero; *string* tests for a nonzero string length; *string1* = *string2* tests two strings for equality; *string1* != *string2* tests two strings for inequality; -w true if a file exists and is writeable; -x true if a file exists and is executable; -z tests for a zero-length string
top	Displays a list of the most CPU-intensive tasks	-c displays the command that initiated each process; -i ignores any idle processes; -q displays output continually, with no delay between outputs (Use with caution! Try the spacebar for periodic updates); -s causes the top command to run in secure mode, disabling its interactive commands; -s runs top in cumulative mode, which displays the cumulative CPU time used by a process
touch	Changes a file's time and date stamp	-a updates access time only; -c prevents touch from creating a file that does not exist; -m updates the modification time only
tput	Formats screen text	clear clears the screen; cols prints the number of columns on the current terminal; cup moves the screen cursor to a specified row and column; rmso disables boldface output; smso enables boldface output

Table A-1   Common Linux commands (continued)

Command	Purpose	Useful Options and Examples
tr	Translates characters	-d deletes input characters found in *string1* from the output; -s checks for sequences of *string1* repeated consecutive times
trap	Executes a command when a specified signal is received from the operating system	
tty	Displays a terminal pathname	
uniq	Selects unique lines or rows	-d outputs one copy of each line that has a duplicate; -u outputs only the lines of the source file that are not duplicated
yes	Displays a string repeatedly until terminated	
w	Displays users currently on the system	Shows user's originating host, idle time, his or her current command, CPU utilization, and login time
wc	Counts the number of lines, bytes, or words in a file	-c counts the number of bytes or characters; -l counts the number of lines; -w counts the number of words
whatis	Displays a brief description of a command	
whereis	Locates source, binary, and manual	-b only searches for binaries; -m only entries for a specified string or searches for manual entries; -s only searches command for source entries
who	Shows who is currently logged onto a system	-H displays column headings; -i displays session idle times; -q displays a quick list of users

Table A-2   vi editor commands

Command	Purpose
!	Leaves vi temporarily
.	Repeats your most recent change
/	Searches forward for a pattern of characters
D$ or D	Deletes from the cursor to the end of the line
D0	Deletes from the cursor to the start of the line
Dd	Deletes the current line
Dw	Deletes the word above the cursor; if the cursor is in the middle of the word, deletes from the cursor to the end of the line
I	Switches to insert mode
P	Pastes text from the clipboard

Table A-2 vi editor commands (continued)

Command	Purpose
Q	Cancels an editing session
R	Reads text from one file and adds it to another
Set	Turns on line numbering
U	Undoes your most recent change
:w	Saves a file and continues working
:wq	Writes changes to disk and exits vi
:x	Saves changes and exits vi
x	Deletes the character at the cursor location
Yy	Copies (yanks) text to the clipboard
ZZ	Saves changes in command mode and exits vi

Table A-3 Shell script programming-related commands

Commands	Purpose
#	Establishes as a comment
ArrayName[subscript]=value	Sets a value to an array at a specific subscript location; for example, GroceryList[10]=strawberry
ArrayName=(valuea valueb valuec...valueN)	Populates an array with values beginning with subscript 0; for example, GroceryList=(apple pear peach)
${array-name[subscript]}	References an array value when performing an operation on the value; for example, echo ${GroceryList[i]}
${ArrayName[*]}	References all elements within an array; for example, echo ${GroceryList[*]}
${#ArrayName[*]}	Determines the number of elements within an array; for example, echo ${#GroceryList[*]}

case word in
    Pattern1) statements
        ;;
    Pattern2) statements
        ;;
    PatternN) statements
        ;;
esac
	Makes a decision when multiple inputs exist for a variable; for example, case $response in
	1) ls
	    ;;
	2) who
	    ;;
	*) echo 'Invalid response!'
	    ;;
	esac

declare or typeset	Defines variables; -a defines an array; for example, declare -a array5

Table A-3   Shell script programming-related commands (continued)

A

Commands	Purpose
```function function-name ()` `{` ` statements` `}```	Defines a function; for example, ```Function Divide ()` `{` ` Answer=$value1 / $value2` `}``` To call the function from another script or the command line, divide value1 by value2
```if condition` `then` ` statements` `elif` ` statements` `else` ` statements` `fi```	Makes decisions for example ```if [[$x -gt 5]]` `then` ` echo $x` `else` ` echo 10` `fi```
```for variable in value1` `value2 value3...` `do` ` statements` `done```	Performs looping constructs when the number of times to loop is known, for example: ```for tools in hammer wrench saw` `do` ` echo $tools` `done```
```for ((variable=initial value;` `variable operator value;` `increment or decrement value))` `do` ` statements` `done```	Performs looping constructs when the number of times to loop is known; this type of looping construct is particularly suited to traversing an array, for example: ```for ((i=1; i<5; i++))` `do` ` total=a[$i] + $total` `done```
`return n`	Returns a status from a function, for example to return success, return 0
`shift`	Shifts positional parameters, for example to shift four positional parameters, shift 4
```select name in word1 word2 ...` `do` ` list` `done```	Creates a menu-based script, for example: ```select cmd in who pwd date` `do` ` $cmd` `done```
`set`	Turns on debugging with -xv; turns off debugging with +xv

Table A-3   Shell script programming-related commands (continued)

Commands	Purpose
`source filename`	Reads and executes commands from *filename*; this command is typically used to utilize a function library, for example, `source function27`
`unset name`	Unsets a function that has been created or a variable that has been set, for example, `unset variableA`

`until list`
`do`
`   statements`
`done`
	Performs looping constructs using do statements as long as `list` returns a nonzero (false) exit status; for example:
	`while [[ $YN = 'Y' ]]`
	`do`
	`    echo "continuing..."`
	`done`

Table A-4   Special characters

Symbol(s)	Purpose
`>`	Creates a new file by redirecting output
`>>`	Redirects output and appends to a file
`<`	Redirects input
`|`	Pipes output of one command as input into another
`*`	Wildcards all character positions
`?`	Wildcards a single character position
`&`	Runs a job in the background
`[characters]`	Wildcards multiple characters
`;`	Places commands in sequence
`(command)`	Runs a command in a subshell
`{command};`	Executes a command in the current shell
`[Space]`	Separates words
`||`	Executes a command depending upon the failure of another; also used as logical OR
`&&`	Executes a command depending upon the success of another; also used as logical AND
`++`	Increments a variable
`--`	Decrements a variable
`**`	Is used for exponentiation
`*`	Is used for multiplication
`/`	Is used for division

Table A-4   Special characters (continued)

Symbol(s)	Purpose
+	Is used for addition
-	Is used for subtraction
%	Is used for remainder
==	Compares values as equal to one another
!=	Compares values to establish values as not equal to one another
>=	Compares values as greater than or equal to one another
<=	Compares values as less than or equal to one another
>	Compares values to establish a greater than relationship
<	Compares values to establish a less than relationship
\	Protects the character immediately following a symbol
'...'	Protects characters within the single quotes
"..."	Protects all characters except $, ' (single quote), and \
`command`	Substitutes a command
$(command)	Substitutes a command
${variable}	Allows for the mixing of numbers and characters in the shell
${!variable}	Allows for the mixing of numbers and characters in the shell
$$	Expands to the PID of the shell
$?	Expands to the return status of the previously executed foreground command
$#	Expands to the number of positional parameters
$@	Expands to all of the positional parameters
$0 through $9	Expands to the positional parameters passed to a script
2>filename	Redirects standard error to filename
&>filename	Redirects standard output and standard error to filename